Paul Ferris v
raphy of C   ham College
Dylan Thomas. His novel

By the same author

FICTION
A Changed Man
Then We Fall
A Family Affair
The Destroyer
The Dam
Very Personal Problems
The Cure
The Detective
Talk to Me About England
A Distant Country
Children of Dust
The Divining Heart
Infidelity

REPORTING
The City
The Church of England
The Doctors
The Nameless: Abortion in Britain Today
Men and Money: Financial Europe Today
The New Militants: Crisis in the Trade Unions
Gentlemen of Fortune: The World's Investment Bankers
Sex and the British: A Twentieth-Century History

BIOGRAPHY
The House of Northcliffe: The Harmsworths of Fleet Street
Richard Burton
Dylan Thomas: The Collected Letters (ed.)
Sir Huge: The Life of Huw Wheldon
Caitlin: The Life of Caitlin Thomas
Dr Freud: A Life

Dylan Thomas

The Biography

PAUL FERRIS

PHŒNIX

For Marjorie Moreton

A PHOENIX PAPERBACK

First published in Great Britain by Hodder and Stoughton in 1977
The revised edition first published in Great Britain in 1999 by J. M. Dent
This paperback edition published in 2000 by Phoenix,
an imprint of Orion Books Ltd,
Orion House, 5 Upper St Martin's Lane,
London WC2H 9EA

A CIP catalogue record for this book
is available from the British Library.

ISBN 0 75381 083 2

Typeset by Selwood Systems, Midsomer Norton
Printed and bound in Great Britain by
The Guernsey Press Co. Ltd, Guernsey, C.I.

CONTENTS

List of Illustrations — vii

Acknowledgements — ix

Introduction — xiii

1. Names from the Past — 1
2. His Father's Son — 23
3. A Sort of Schoolboy — 38
4. Reporter, Actor, Poet — 62
5. A Case of Cancer — 88
6. London — 119
7. Caitlin — 150
8. Marriage — 169
9. War and 'Fern Hill' — 201
10. A Voice on the Radio — 230
11. Laugharne and America — 255
12. No Money, Few Poems — 289
13. The Knot — 314
14. Running Faster — 334
15. Alcohol and Morphia — 351

Postscript: The Thomas Business — 364

Appendix — 372

Notes — 374

Bibliography — 436

Index — 440

ILLUSTRATIONS

Between pages 136 and 137
Aunt Dosie and the Rev. David Rees
Old folks at home
The family about 1909
Tea on the table[1]
Dylan – angel or demon[1]
Grammar School mile winner[2]
Unscholastic schoolboy[3]
Rhossili beach[4]
Dylan and Pamela[5]
Thomas and Vernon Watkins[6]
Bert Trick
Glyn Jones[7]
Thomas and Fred Janes[8]
Page from Thomas notebook[9]
Picnicking on the beach[10]

Between pages 312 and 313
Croquet at Pennard[6]
Augustus John and Caitlin[3]
Caitlin and baby
Family man[11]
Thomas and Dan Jones[3]
Thomas in Picasso play[12]
High tide at the Boat House[13]
Edith Sitwell;[12] John Davenport;[14] Marged Howard-Stepney[15];
Cyril Connolly[12]
Caitlin at Boat House[16]
Elizabeth Reitell[17]
Thomas and Brinnin[18]
Under Milk Wood worksheet[16]
Signing books[3]

Thomas at film symposium[19]
The survivor: Florence Thomas at the Boat House

Acknowledgements
1 Paul Ferris; 2 British Library Newspaper Library; 3 Jeff
Towns/Dylans Book Store; 4 Kathy de Witt; 5 Lady Avebury;
6 Gwen Watkins; 7 *New Welsh Review* Photo Library; 8 Mary
Janes; 9 National Library of Wales; 10 Gabriel Summers; 11 The
Estate of Nicolette Devas; 12 Hulton Getty Picture Collection;
13 Carmarthenshire County Council; 14 Frank Monaco/Rex
Features Ltd; 15 Mark and Molly Murray Threipland; 16 Harry
Ransom Humanities Research Center; 17 Elizabeth Reitell;
18 University of Delaware; 19 Amos Vogel

ACKNOWLEDGEMENTS

The Trustees for the Copyrights of Dylan Thomas all helped with the original edition of this biography. The three – David Higham, Stuart Thomas and Wynford Vaughan-Thomas – knew Dylan Thomas and understood the problems of trying to write about him; in particular I benefited from the robust cooperation of Stuart Thomas. David Higham, Dylan's literary agent, let me see the office files relating to his client; Dent, his publishers, were similarly helpful. A later trustee, Michael Rush, has been supportive in his turn.

Dylan Thomas's widow, Caitlin, read the book when it was first published, and complained to me that it failed to put sufficient emphasis on 'the booze', which gobbled up their lives, according to her. I was grateful to her when she was alive for various insights and bursts of honesty, mixed up with mischief.

Thomas's daughter, Aeronwy Thomas Ellis, talked to me at length. His son, Llewelyn, has made some sagacious comments. I am grateful to Professors Walford Davies and Ralph Maud, who know Thomas's texts better than anyone else; to Jeff Towns, Meic Stephens, James A. Davies; and Dr Ken Paterson of Glasgow Royal Infirmary.

For interviews, correspondence or other assistance my thanks are also due to the following:

Dannie Abse, Leo Abse, John Ackerman, Jerome Agel, William Alfred, Gladys Laugharne-Allen, Edgar Anstey, Lindsay Avebury.

Mary Ellin Barrett, Lyn Bartlett, Vernon Bartlett, Eric Barton, John Bennett, Roger Bierne, Tom Blackburn, Oswell Blakeston, Thomas E. Blantz, Samuel N. Bogorad, J. McG. Bottkol, John Malcolm Brinnin; British Diabetic Association; Marianne Brock, Cleanth Brooks, D. J. R. Bruckner, Louis J. Budd, Marie Burke, Gray Burr.

Max Chapman, Waldo Clarke, Douglas Cleverdon, Nest Cleverdon, Brenda Cole, Leslie Cole, Mrs B. J. Connors, Gwendolyn

Courtney, Fred Cowley, Mrs Gardner Cox, Raymond Coxon, Armour Craig.

David Daiches, Elizabeth Daniels, Jane Dark, Aneirin Talfan Davies, Mrs Emlyn Davies, J. Davies, Ken Davies, Lorraine Davies, Mary Davies, Gwevril Dawkins, Peter De Vries, Nicolette Devas, Francis Dillon, Armel Diverres, John F. Dowd.

Anne C. Edmonds, J. Griffith-Edwards, Addie Elliott, Mrs Albert Evans, Gwynfor Evans, Reg and Eileen Evans, Will Evans, Joe Everingham, Gavin Ewart.

David Farmer, Ronnie Farr, Mrs Pat Feltenstein, Charles Fisher, Constantine FitzGibbon, Roy Fuller.

David Gardner, David Gascoyne, K. C. Gay, Don Gifford, Brendan Gill, Pamela Glendower, Sir William Glock, Mark Goulden, Malcolm Graham, Ruby Graham, W. Greville-Griffiths, Geoffrey Grigson, Bernard Gutteridge.

Leonard Hamilton, Jack Heliker, Ian Henderson, Nigel Henderson, Wyn Henderson, Bill Henry, Rayner Heppenstall, Barbara Holdridge, Irene Howell, David M. Hughes, Mr and Mrs Eric Hughes, Bruce Hunter, Noel Husbands.

Fred Janes, Mary Janes, Marjorie Jarrett, Graham Curtis Jenkins, Edgar Johnson, C. B. Jones, Evelyn Burman Jones, Francis Jones, Glyn Jones, Kitty Jones, R. M. Jones.

J. R. K. Kantor, P. J. Kavanagh, William Killick, Vera Killick, Evelyn Kirkpatrick, Seymour Klein.

Kevin Lane, James Laughlin, Theodosia Legg, Mervyn Levy, Annie Lewis, E. Glyn Lewis, Mrs Mansell Lewis, Jack Lindsay, Cordelia Locke, Harry Locke, George Long, David Lougée, Roger Lubbock, T. D. Lucy, Elisabeth Lutyens.

Andrew MacAdie, E. F. McInerny, Charles McKelvie, Rollie McKenna, Charles W. Mann, Marianne Mantell, David Markson, Lord Marley, Brigit Marnier, Arthur Calder-Marshall, William H. Matchett, Roland Mathias, Ossie Mayo, Samuel Middlebrook, Raymond Mitchell, Ceridwen Lloyd-Morgan, Frank Morley, Royston Morley, Howard Moss, B. W. Murphy.

Judith Neal, Jack Nener, Geoffrey Nicholson, Gwen Nobbs.

John Ormond, Hettie Owen, Ruth Wynn Owen.

Denys Parsons, Norman Holmes Pearson, Hugh Porteus, Anthony Powell, H. A. Prescott, Cecil Price, John Prichard, Bill Pritchard, Cyril Pritchard, Doris Probert, John Pudney, Marshall Pugh.

Bill Read, Jan Read, George Reavey, Gertrude Reed, David Rees, J. R. Rees, Alastair Reid, Ben Reid, D. V. Rhydderch, Keidrych Rhys, Peggy Richards, Alan Road, Ann E. Robinson, Bill Rogers, Rutherford D. Rogers, Ethel Ross.

Jacob Schwarz, William Scott, Lorraine Scourfield, Harvey Shapiro, Ben Shephard, Rupert Shephard, Rose Slivka, Elizabeth Smith (formerly Reitell), Janet Adam Smith, R. D. Smith, Lady Snow, Stephen Spender, Frances Steloff, Anthony Storr, Ernest A. Strathmann, John Sundell, Lola L. Szladits.

Haydn Taylor, Margaret Taylor, Saundra Taylor, David J. Thomas, Eve Thomas, Kent Thompson, Mark Murray Threipland, Molly Murray Threipland, John Thurgar, William York Tindall, Nell Trick, Ronald Tritton.

Barry Ulanov.

Edward Vasta, Vernon Venable, Peter Viereck, Amos Vogel.

Sybil Walters, Armitage Watkins, Gwen Watkins, Ray B. West, Jr, Antonia White, Emlyn Williams, Emrys Williams, Gordon Williams, J. Morgan Williams, Mary Ann Williams, Oscar Williams, Tudor Williams, W. G. Willis, Dorothy Wilson, Garff B. Wilson, T. R. Wiseman, Ralph Wishart, Basil Wright, David Wright.

Stan Yonge.

For permission to see and make use of material, I am grateful to the Harry Ransom Humanities Research Center of the University of Texas at Austin; the Lockwood Memorial Library, State University of New York, Buffalo; the Houghton Library of Harvard University; the Berg Collection, New York Public Library; the Lilly Library, Indiana University; University of Delaware, Special Collections; University of Victoria, British Columbia; the National Library of Wales; the British Library; the BBC Written Archives Centre; Swansea University College; Swansea Public Library (as it used to be called), and Llanelli Public Library. The University of London Library let me use their facilities for borrowing and reading microfilm. The then head of the *Observer* Research Department, Valerie Ferguson, dealt patiently with some odd inquiries.

The author and publisher are grateful to the Trustees for the Copyrights of the late Dylan Thomas for permission to quote material. Also to Dr Daniel Jones for extracts from unpublished poems written jointly with Dylan Thomas, and to Mrs Gwen Watkins for extracts from 'Notes on Dylan Thomas' by Vernon Watkins.

The following books have also been quoted:
Dylan Thomas – Craft or Sullen Art, ed. Alan Bold (Vision Press, 1990), *Dylan Thomas in America* by John Malcolm Brinnin (Dent, 1956), *Closing Times* by Dan Davin (OUP, 1975), *Two Flamboyant Fathers* by Nicolette Devas (Collins, 1966), *The Magical Dilemma of Victor Neuberg* by Jean Overton Fuller (W. H. Allen, 1965), *Here at the New Yorker* by Brendan Gill (Random House, 1976), *The Party's Over Now. Reminiscences of the Fifties* by John Gruen (Viking Press), *Four Absentees* by Rayner Heppenstall (Barrie & Rockliff), *Augustus John.* Vol. II: *The Years of Experience* by Michael Holroyd (Heinemann, 1975), *Important to Me. Personalia* by Pamela Hansford Johnson (Macmillan, 1974), *The Dragon Has Two Tongues* by Glyn Jones (Dent, 1968), *Meetings with Poets* by Jack Lindsay (Muller, 1968), *A Goldfish Bowl* by Elisabeth Lutyens (Cassell, 1972), *Memoirs of the Forties* by J. Maclaren-Ross (Alan Ross, 1965), *The Days of Dylan Thomas* by Bill Read (Weidenfeld, 1964), *Selected Letters* by Edith Sitwell (Macmillan, 1970), *A Personal History* by A. J. P. Taylor (Coronet, 1984), *Dylan Thomas: The Legend and the Poet*, ed. E. W. Tedlock (Heinemann, 1960), *A Reader's Guide to Dylan Thomas* by William York Tindall (Thames & Hudson, 1962), *Dylan Thomas: 'Dog among the Fairies'* by Henry Treece (Lindsay Drummond, 1949), *Portrait of a Friend* by Gwen Watkins (Gomer Press, 1983).

INTRODUCTION

Poets aren't expected to be model citizens, and Dylan Thomas has been a gift for writers who want to show him in all his wicked glory. Accounts of his bad behaviour are easily authenticated by quotes from the man himself, who liked to make comic capital from tales of wild living that were only half true or not true at all. But behind the public cavortings was a private agony, which is the real subject of biography.

Thomas's life as a poet, the only career that ever occurred to him, was pursued at the expense of others. Apparently unable to manage his affairs, he relied on friends, patrons, wife and the occasional mistress to keep him in business, enjoying middle-class comforts. Being dependent didn't worry him. It was his nature so he made the most of it, exploiting that side of his character in order to reap the benefit. His begging letters were stylish and unashamed.

When young he liked to dwell on himself, the poet, enclosed in a private world of words, which for him had a reality of its own. Thomas was once quoted as saying that 'when I experience anything I experience it as a thing and a word at the same time'. Lines like 'My busy heart who shudders as she talks/Sheds the syllabic blood and drains her words,' written when he was eighteen or nineteen, touch on this obsession.

It is almost as though words, for Thomas, could be a substitute for deeds and their consequences; an excuse, even, for whatever else happened. He revelled in his facility as a writer but it made him uneasy as well. Here he is in 1932, aged eighteen, writing to a contemporary, Percy Smart, from the address in Swansea where he still lived with his parents. He had been to a schoolmaster's funeral, perhaps in his job as a newspaper reporter, and used it to brood on his own mortality ('Will the handkerchiefs flutter, white flags in a green place ...?'). He continued:

The trouble is, you see, that I can go on writing like that all day, turning, in that case, poor old Lulu's funeral into an occasion for precious writing, cynical, idealistic, half-baked prose; make of old Lulu's funeral an opportunity for the higher witticisms of a low mind.

There I go again. Give me pen & paper – the trick's done: a thousand conceits, couched in a hermit's language spoiling the whiteness of the page. In my ivory tower of silence sit I brooding, clad in owls' feathers ... splitting an infinitive with a conoisseur's [sic] care & purpose, dipping, on occasions, into a more exotic ink-bottle & fetching out, at the end of a J. nib, little Wilde words ...

Not that Thomas spent his time (though he spent more of it than is generally thought) behind closed doors. He liked pubs, company and keeping people in stitches, at which he was very good. By managing to be larger than life, he has endeared himself to those who expect a poet to be like that, and irritated others who find him pretentious and juvenile. Either way, Thomas undeniably has become a cult, perhaps because his poetry as well as his life went to extremes in a way that people can recognise and admire. He was an answer to the machine; his poems contain few images from the twentieth century. As for the exotic legend, it was not only encouraged but was originally created by Thomas himself, with its trappings of poverty and wickedness. In the end, the poet who was determined from adolescence to act like a poet, even if it killed him, had the last laugh: he did write boldly, he did make readers and listeners catch their breath. He was taken at his own valuation.

In the original (1977) Introduction to this book, I said I had tried to understand Thomas as a tormented, exaggerated man, often his own worst enemy, in whom others (no doubt I meant myself) could recognise their own experiences, both good and bad. My private reason for wanting to write about him was modest enough: we came from the same place. I was born in a hilltop suburb of Swansea, fifteen years after him and a mile from his house. The fence of the newly built lunatic asylum that 'leers down the valley like a fool' in one of his notebook poems was at the top of the garden, its hooked nails pointing both ways. As a child I remember waking in terror, thinking I had heard the madmen talking in my dreams. I was twelve before I heard of

Dylan Thomas, when I came across his story 'The Peaches' in *Penguin New Writing* for July 1941. But at the Grammar School we soon became Thomas fans and imagined some lingering presence in the place.

There was already half a shelf of Dylan Thomas books when a publisher suggested I write another one, in 1974. Several full-length studies had appeared, although only one had proper access to primary material. This was the official Life, commissioned by the trustees of the Dylan Thomas estate, a three-man band that I came to know all too well before I finished. The three were David Higham, the literary agent, whose firm handled (and still handles) Thomas's work, which provides the trust's income; Stuart Thomas, a sardonic Swansea solicitor, a boyhood acquaintance of the unrelated Dylan, who administered the trust; and Wynford Vaughan-Thomas, the amiable broadcaster, who was there to make up the numbers. All are now dead.

Their first choice as biographer, Ruthven Todd, a Scots poet and old acquaintance of Dylan Thomas, failed to deliver in 1962. Their second choice, Constantine FitzGibbon, an Anglo-American writer who was a chum of Thomas's during the war, initially refused the commission. 'Dylan really did nothing except write poems and be tremendous fun,' he told Higham in September 1962. 'I cannot see a full-length book in it.' Soon after, he changed his mind. With access to Thomas's papers, he wrote a convincing Life that was well reviewed when it appeared in 1965.

Nine years later I hesitated, as FitzGibbon had done, when it came to signing a contract. Time passed while agreements with a British and an American publisher were drawn up. These, together with a promise of £5000 for serial rights in the *Observer* when the book was written, guaranteed me about £13,000, but not all at once, and little more than half of it before I delivered the typescript. I went ahead in mid-1974, keeping the pot boiling with journalism, uncertain what I would find.

Anxious to reassure myself that I was on safe ground with the early Thomas, at least, I began in Swansea and West Wales, talking to women (their memories usually sharper than their husbands') who had known the Thomases; a schoolfriend or two; distant relatives at farms in Carmarthenshire, who drew genealogical trees for me on the back of auction handbills;

sceptical citizens of Laugharne, the little town by the sea where Thomas made his last home, at the Boat House. In Swansea, in a steep street above the docks, Addie Elliott, who went to work for the Thomas family two weeks before Dylan was born in 1914, gave me an inkling of life at Cwmdonkin Drive. We sat over her antiquated cooking range, which had hobs and ovens around an open coal fire, and ate toast while she described the scatty Mrs Thomas, and the aloof, disappointed schoolmaster husband who set the tone of the household and (I came to suspect) of his son's life as well.

So far no writer had taken much interest in all this. Gwevril Dawkins, once a friend of Dylan's sister Nancy, who was eight years older than her brother, remembered Nancy's first husband, an Englishman called Haydn Taylor, then a travelling salesman, who met her when he was based in Swansea in the early 1930s. Nancy was dead; she and Taylor had left Swansea after their marriage in 1933, and it was weeks before I traced him, via a chain that led through a chamber of commerce, a branch of Rotary, a fire brigade, a police station, an orchid nursery and two estate agents. He lived in a large house near Reigate, in Surrey, and I parked my dented VW Beetle next to his Rolls-Royce; the journalism wasn't going all that well.

Taylor had memories of the nervy, quarrelsome Thomases. Even better, he had letters that Nancy, whom he had always addressed as 'Thomas', wrote to him about goings-on at Cwmdonkin Drive. The unhappy family sprang to life. Father grumbled and shouted; Mother steamed open envelopes to read Haydn's letters; Nancy wished she was dead, while Dylan, not averse to stealing any cash he found lying around, exploited his position as the favoured son who had to be given his own way.

None of my researches, in Swansea or anywhere else, had a focus in the shape of an omniscient family or a comprehensive archive. The perils of dealing with living relatives, familiar to biographers, were absent, except for Thomas's widow, Caitlin, and she was a threat of a peculiar kind. His parents were dead. Jack Thomas the schoolmaster preceded his son by less than a year. Florence Thomas died five years after him, in 1958.

In her later years old Mrs Thomas was a dignified figure – not quite matriarchal, but long-suffering and good-humoured. She was the only Thomas I had met earlier, long before I embarked on the biography, having interviewed her for a magazine article about the poet's childhood in 1955, eighteen months after Dylan died, when she was living with a friend in Carmarthen. We sat by an electric fire in a small sitting room. Her husband's books were everywhere, his Browning, his Walter Scott, his Dante. On the wall was the well-known photograph of Dylan and Caitlin posed ironically under a framed 'Prepare to meet thy God'. 'Such a lovely picture!' said Mrs Thomas. To her, Dylan was the wonderful son whose life was beset by ill-health and accidents, which she recounted as if they had happened yesterday. There was no whisper of drink or any impropriety.

In 1974, none of Thomas's three children had a vested interest to preserve; or if they had, they made no attempt to parade their own versions of events. Llewelyn, aged thirty-five and the oldest, was an advertising copywriter with J. Walter Thompson in Sydney. He never spoke publicly about his father, nor has he done so since; we became friends many years later, and he says little in private, either. The youngest child, Colm, of whom I know nothing except by hearsay, was and is similarly reticent; he, too, was in Australia in 1974, working for the Trade Practices Commission. Dylan's daugher, Aeron, then aged thirty-one, was the only one of the three whom I approached, in the London suburb where she lived with her husband. She was prepared to discuss her parents and life at the Boat House in Laugharne, where the family moved in 1949, when she was six; she was ten when her father died. She had the knack of being tactful about the domestic maelstrom she grew up in without sounding defensive.

Caitlin was another matter, the vociferous widow who had published an account of her marriage to Dylan and its aftermath, *Leftover Life to Kill*, and now lived in Italy with her Sicilian partner, Giuseppe Fazio, and the child she had by him when she was forty-nine years old, Francesco. Her cooperation was needed for the positive reason that she had been Mrs Thomas for sixteen years and the negative reason that once we became acquainted she was less likely to sue for libel. She was known to be litigious and the publishers were nervous; so was I, and I wrote her carefully worded, all-cards-on-the-table letters in an attempt to persuade her to meet.

In April 1975 she was in London after Aeron's first child was born, and I took flowers round to the London International

Hotel, ashamed of such a ploy, with another of my letters giving her three good reasons for talking to me. This produced no more than a telephone conversation, where she spoke vaguely of 'the charm boys' who pestered her. Later, when I came to know Caitlin, I realised that my mistake had been to not offer her money. The publishing equivalent of chequebook journalism would have softened her heart, as it did in 1978, when I paid her five hundred pounds for a long interview, and again in 1991, when I came to write her biography, and gave her fifteen per cent of the advance. In the event, in 1975, I pressed on without her. I learned later that even the official biographer had received small assistance, despite the wartime friendship between FitzGibbons and Thomases. She referred to him as 'C. Baboon' and found fault with his inaccuracies (as she found fault with mine), while conceding that she had only herself to blame.

Thankfully, her permission was not needed to quote the large quantity of Thomas's words, published and unpublished, without which the biography could not have been written. To negotiate with Caitlin, or with any agent who was under her thumb, would have been a nightmare. The trust (there is more about it in the Postscript) held the copyrights, having been set up soon after Dylan died to secure a regular income for her and the three children, and accumulate capital for their future. This seems an admirable object, but Caitlin – who in 1953 had agreed to create the trust – spent the next forty years at war with the trustees, accusing in particular the senior trustee, Stuart Thomas, of cruelty, deceit and malpractice, and spending tens of thousands of pounds, mainly on other lawyers, in fruitless attempts to break the trust and ruin Stuart in the process. In between there were cordial intermissions, and at one time her son Llewelyn was married to Stuart's stepdaughter Rhiannon.

Although I could manage without Caitlin, I needed the trust's goodwill. David Higham took the professional view that 'one can't prevent people writing lives', and there was never any problem about buying copyright permission. Of the other trust members, Wynford Vaughan-Thomas offered names and anecdotes, together with the observation that 'everything to do with Dylan Thomas is fantasy. Everything ends in fantasy.' He also told me that Caitlin would be sure to want money, but at that stage I was too naive or priggish to take him seriously. Only

Stuart Thomas, who also handled the trust's day-to-day legal affairs and charged it for his professional services, was discouraging. 'I don't want to be involved in any way, for reasons I can't go into now,' he said, and slammed the phone down.

His reticence, which didn't last, probably arose because he feared that Caitlin would use a new biography as another excuse for harassing him. Years of threats and litigation had made him suspicious. Handling the trust, he once told me, was boring but earned some money. Every so often, boredom was replaced by drama, as Caitlin demanded extra cash to buy a vineyard or a boat, or appointed new lawyers and urged them to police the trust, or got herself written up in newspapers as the poet's penniless widow, left to rot in Italy.

The decaying offices of his firm, D. O. Thomas & Co., were in Walter Road, a tree-lined avenue between the town and the Uplands, where Dylan Thomas was born. Once he relented, I spent profitable days reading papers at a vacant desk, never certain whether the cardboard boxes and brown folders were being produced at random or in response to some hidden perception of what I should or shouldn't see. The orderly archive, indexed and cross-referenced, is what curators of manuscripts aspire to, organised so that researchers can pick their way along signposted routes. Chaos, however, has its advantages. I never knew what to expect from the Stuart Thomas filing system; no one had been there before me.

Item, a typescript statement by Caitlin, undated, complaining that Dylan should have been buried in the old churchyard of St Martin's at Laugharne, not in its modern extension, and expressing a wish to have his body reburied in the garden of the Boat House. Item, a letter from David Higham to Stuart Thomas, 12 December 1953, to say Caitlin had jumped out of a window in Hammersmith for no apparent reason and broken her collarbone.

Item, a statement from Lloyds Bank, Chelsea, 30 November 1953, to say that Dylan Thomas held two accounts at the branch when he died. The No. 1 account contained one shilling and sixpence; the No. 2, eleven shillings and elevenpence. The bank added triumphantly that charges had accrued against the accounts of one pound eleven shillings. Item, correspondence dated 1962 about a proposal to use the Boat House for a TV commercial for Cadbury's Drinking Chocolate. Item, a foolscap

envelope containing photocopies of thirty-four letters from Dylan
to Caitlin.

In a back room smelling of damp was a half-open fibre suitcase
labelled 'United States Lines. Cabin Class'. In it were a mildewed
suit, a once-white 'Wings' shirt and a black 'Ace' comb, last relics
of Dylan's fatal trip to America. 'Been here ever since,' said
Stuart, and we pushed off to the Bristol Channel Yacht Club for
lunch.

In due course I went to America myself. There, on visits in
1950, 1952 and twice in 1953, Thomas lived a caricature of
himself at cocktail parties and on the college campuses where he
read, and became a public figure, something he had never been
in Britain. Thousands of admirers thought they had discovered
what a modern poet with Celtic blood was like. With his willing
participation they helped create the portrait of Thomas as lecherous, drunken clown that has survived to the present, though
most of the witnesses told me a different story. It would have
been necessary to visit America even if Thomas had never been
there, since the University of Texas at Austin had (still has) the
nearest to a central Thomas archive, having outbid its rivals
when letters and other material came on the market. Shut away
in an air-conditioned cubicle at what is now the Harry Ransom
Humanities Research Center, I found a stained worksheet with
grains of sand adhering to the paper; salvaged, I liked to think,
from the shore below the Boat House after Caitlin threw it out
of the window in a temper.

All that is ancient history. The Dylan Thomas legend has matured;
many of those I talked to are dead; a new century relegates his
life to the first half of the previous one. He is not exactly in
fashion but he is not out of it, either; his life and work between
them have ensured him a niche. A dozen or more of the poems
are widely anthologised, and a core of his writing continues to
find a popular audience – poems like 'Fern Hill' and 'Do not go
gentle into that good night' (which is read at many funerals in
America); the reminiscent 'Child's Christmas in Wales'; the 'play
for voices', Under Milk Wood. For a poet who died in 1953, that
is not bad going; his copyright estate turns over a six-figure sum
every year.

'Critical opinion' remains sharply divided. Michael Hulse,

constructing an 'imaginary dialogue' among critics (1990), has one of them comment, 'To suggest that Dylan Thomas, the most florid fabricator of bubbling fustian known to modern verse, has anything at all in common with a Donne or a Milton, a Blake or a Yeats, is plain absurd.' To which another replies that Thomas's poetry triumphantly survives 'in that increasingly diminished sector of the [literary] tradition where the academic and popular readerships are willing to tolerate each other's presence and taste ... Thomas, whether he is altogether understood with the rational mind or not, strikes me as bridging a vital gap ideally.'

In the 1977 Introduction I wrote that I had found far more fresh material about Thomas's life than I could reasonably have expected. That was a trick that can't be repeated on the same scale. Nevertheless, there are many fresh insights. New correspondence has continued to emerge. Among the material used here for the first time is a group of letters written in the early 1930s to Percy Smart, which fill a gap in the record, in the period when Thomas was busy doing nothing scholarly in his last year at Swansea Grammar School, then working on the local newspaper, and finally marking time before his first poems appeared in print. Letters to the American writer Emily Holmes Coleman, with whom he was involved after he met Caitlin Macnamara but before he married her, have been used. So have two new letters to Caitlin, sold after she died in 1994, and, best of all, the first known letter he wrote to her, datable to 17 July 1936, within months of their meeting. According to Sotheby's in London, where the letter was sold to a private collector in 1997, it originally came to light during the Second World War when 'Mr Thomas Topp of Ringwood, Hampshire, requested [news]papers for his wet-fish shop. This letter was among a bundle of waste paper given him for that purpose by the Macnamara family.' Mr Topp was a far-sighted fishmonger.

The Caitlin story can now be told with more authority than I could give it before. One reason is that I came to know her over the years; we met at intervals and corresponded in between, and eventually I wrote her biography (1993). The other is that when I wrote *Dylan Thomas* I wasn't free to say as much as I already knew about her difficult character and the nature of her relationship with her husband. The lawyers were nervous. Even the extensive quotations I planned from the letters that Dylan wrote to her were cut back at the last minute, not because she held the copyright – which was, and is, vested in the Thomas trustees – but because she retained physical ownership of the letters, and might have concocted an argument involving some nebulous right of marital confidentiality. That, at any rate, was the excuse Stuart Thomas gave, anxious not to receive more of her ten-page letters from Rome; there are enough of them in the trust's files as it is, hissing with anger. I was allowed to quote verbatim only from letters that had already appeared elsewhere; the rest had to be paraphrased. That material has now been restored, and new extracts added, to give a fuller portrait of the artist as married man.

More than one reference to Caitlin in the manuscript made the libel lawyer shake his head and issue dire warnings. One of her sisters, Nicolette, had published a book about their childhood, *Two Flamboyant Fathers* (1966). I quoted from it and included her remark that while Caitlin was still a child, 'men were drawn to her as bees to a honey pot'. Bees and honey pots were not permissible. Nicolette had been nervous about her own book, and took out libel insurance in 1966 in case she was sued by her sister. I thought this was a good joke and tried to include it in *Dylan Thomas*, only to have the lawyer object that it might be defamatory because it implied that Caitlin was litigious. I suggested mildly that if she did sue, that would be self-defeating because it would prove how litigious she was, but the lawyer was not impressed, and the joke had to go.

The essential truth about the Dylan–Caitlin relationship, omitted by the 1977 biography, was that his dependent nature left him vulnerable in later years when his wife withdrew her affection and became blatantly promiscuous. Always the stronger partner, she was the fixed point in his life. But he treated her badly, and after suffering his chronic fecklessness and flights from reality (especially his escapes to America and a mistress or two there), she retaliated with anger and contempt that he may have deserved but couldn't endure. In that sense she helped to break him.

Other correspondence, not available for the original edition, includes letters to Edith Sitwell, Pamela Hansford Johnson, Elizabeth Reitell (one of the American mistresses) and Desmond Hawkins, who edited a literary magazine in the 1930s and managed to provoke Thomas into explaining difficult poems. Letters to another editor, Keidrych Rhys, who founded the legendary literary periodical *Wales* in 1937, throw light on Thomas's (highly sceptical) attitudes to political Wales and Welshness.

Various biographies, memoirs and studies have appeared during the last twenty years. One of them, *The Death of Dylan Thomas* (Nashhold and Tremlett, 1997), seeks to explain his decline and fall by a theory that he was an undiagnosed diabetic. I disagree with their conclusions, and address the matter in the narrative. David Gascoyne's journals, published in 1991, contain a vivid passage about Dylan and Caitlin before their marriage. Rupert Shephard's manuscript memoirs describe Caitlin in Ireland, before she married Dylan. Many of the conversations I had when writing Caitlin Thomas's biography have come in useful here, in particular those with her sisters Brigit and Nicolette (who have both died), Jane Dark, David Gardner, Pamela Glendower and Sir William Glock.

In respect of all the interviews that went into this book, I repeat the caution of the 1977 Introduction. The fact that Thomas was notorious from an early age has advantages and disadvantages. People had reason to remember things about him (and to keep his letters); but stories change in the telling, and because he was a chronic liar himself, there is an ample supply of tall tales. I have cross-checked where possible and either weeded out the less probable stories or printed them with reservations.

A Dylan Thomas Centre was opened in Swansea in 1996, and contains the Jeff Towns/Dylans Book Store exhibition. The town itself, now officially a city, has lost much of the atmosphere of the 'old Swansea' that Dylan knew, but when I go there, I still find myself catching an echo of it, and him, in a park or a pub. Or in one of those eternal back streets 'where the small and hardly known and never-to-be-forgotten people of the dirty town had lived and loved and died and, always, lost'.

Paul Ferris
Boughrood, 1999

Chapter One

NAMES FROM THE PAST

The Boat House at Laugharne on the South Wales coast is built into the side of a cliff, and seems a suitable property for a poet. In Dylan Thomas's time the wooden verandah that juts over the rocks and shelly mud of the estuary was patched with tin. These days, repaired and refurbished, it has a bookshop, tearoom and video to bring in the visitors. After Thomas's death his widow went on owning the place and occasionally living in it for years, selling it in 1974 for eight times what it cost in 1949, when Mrs Margaret Taylor, Thomas's most consistent benefactor, obtained it for the family. She rented it to them; they didn't own it in Thomas's lifetime. They owned remarkably little – a minimal amount of cheap furniture, an old bicycle or two, a radio, some books. Poets are not supposed to be breadwinners, as Thomas had already decided when he was a schoolboy. The ravens would feed them – 'soft, white silly ravens', he used to say. The method worked, after a fashion. Dylan Thomas made begging into a cottage industry in the last few years of his life, despite not inconsiderable earnings. Few if any contemporary British poets were as prosperous on paper, although at the same time he managed to be perpetually poor. Drink helped to make the money go, but his poverty was more complicated than that. The Thomases spent money on ordinary, bourgeois things. They had a son at boarding school in England. Thomas belonged to a gentlemen's West End club. He liked a good cigar and went to a private dentist. Taxis were his normal way of moving about London. In Laugharne the Williams family, who ran the local transport (and much else), did a brisk trade in hired cars as the poet came and went. Things in real life were not quite as the legend has them.

At high tide the sea comes up close to the Boat House, and the estuary, a complicated affair of sands and channels where three rivers meet, becomes part of Carmarthen Bay; fishing boats and occasional yachts slide up and down the long forks of water. Fifteen miles away to the south-east is the flat sea-serpent line of Worms Head, a promontory at the tip of Gower, the oblong peninsula that breaks the coast between Carmarthen Bay and industrial Wales to the east. Laugharne has no industry, apart from farming, fishing and Dylan Thomas. In the poet's day and until recent times, busloads of men went to work daily at a Government proving ground for munitions just along the coast, and he would have heard the regular thuds of explosions from his desk. But the juxtaposition of herons on the mudflats and weaponry on the sand dunes didn't appeal to him as material for poems.

Thomas lived in Laugharne for four and a half years before his death in November 1953, writing only six complete poems in that time. Sea birds and sea vistas creep into some of them. His subject was still himself, as it had always been, but in those last years he filled the background with scenes and creatures from nature, celebrating the world but seeing death in the living – 'Now curlew cry me down to kiss the mouths of their dust.' One of his vantage points was the window of his work-hut behind the house, higher up the cliffs. It had once been a bicycle shed. Much of his radio play, *Under Milk Wood*, was written there, too, although it was pressure from the Americans, who wanted it for stage performance first, that made him finish it, not long before he died among them. He was not a happy man by that time. He was drunk less often and less extravagantly in Laugharne than in London and New York, but life plagued him wherever he went. His wife Caitlin said he was rehashing his adolescence, one of her many accurate barbs. He had gout and trouble with income tax. Time slipped through his fingers; he never seemed to get to grips with anything. He must have spent long hours in the shed not doing very much, not always sober, in between the times when he was painfully assembling 'Lament' and 'Poem on his Birthday'. Some of his worksheets that were scooped from floors or out of cupboards after his death, and later sold for good money to American collectors,* are covered with doggerel verses

---

* The bulk of Thomas's manuscripts are at the Harry Ransom Humanities Research Center of the University of Texas at Austin, which has acquired material both piecemeal and in quantity from private collectors. The index of the Thomas

and lists of debts ('Milk £25, Butcher £25, Post Office £67 ...').
There are some self-pitying verses that begin as a letter to
'Dear Marged', a rich Welshwoman who was another of his
benefactors:

> And Money is the dunghill King
> And his royal nark is the dun...

The back of the work-hut opens on to the cliff walk, and
visitors see it before they reach the path leading down to the Boat
House. The door used to have a plaque, later lost or stolen, that
said: 'In this building Dylan Thomas wrote many of his famous
works, seeking inspiration from the panoramic view of the estuary.' There is a grain of truth in the suggestion that a view helped
him to write. Much of Thomas's real work was done on high
ground, looking down on things: usually the sea, usually in
Wales.

The places he lived in during a restless life would make the
bones of a scholarly thesis. He never owned a house or flat: they
were all rented, borrowed or camped in. Before the Boat House,
Thomas and family were in an Oxfordshire village, South Leigh,
for a year and a half. Before that they lived in a damp summerhouse at the end of a garden in Oxford as the guests of A. J. P.
Taylor, the historian, and his wife, Margaret. (It was she who
bought the house in South Leigh, and after it the Boat House).
This post-war period was barren; in three years he wrote only
one poem, during a visit to Italy. He was in the wrong places.
Like many writers he drew energy from a location, even though
he scorned it at times; West Wales, imprinted on him as a child,
was the place that consistently provoked him to write, and his
rude remarks about it were irrelevant to what he felt at a different
level. This is not to say that absence from Wales was the root of
his problems. But it is a fact that nearly all his poems were written
there. The last period in which he wrote intensively over a short
period, faintly echoing the frenzy of his adolescence, was the year
from mid-1944 to mid-1945. He was based in Wales all that
time, with intermittent trips to London. At first he stayed in

collection covers more than six hundred file cards; the material, in boxes and
bound volumes, occupies many shelves. It is referred to throughout as 'Texas'.

another part of Carmarthenshire, at a place called Blaen Cwm ('the end of the valley'), a pair of stone cottages by a stream running down to the River Towy, owned by his mother's family, who can still be found living on the small farms and buried in the big churchyards of the district. Fernhill, the farm where he used to go for summer holidays as a child, was only a mile away, although the aunt who lived there had died years before.

Thomas had been writing poems at Blaen Cwm since he was a teenager, when he thought it was dismally wet and Welsh. ('I can smell the river and hear the beastly little brook that goes gurgle-gurgle past this room,' he wrote to Pamela Hansford Johnson when he was nineteen.) At least one of his early published poems, 'My hero bares his nerves', was written there when he was eighteen. Some authorities think it a poem about masturbation. (Its last line, 'He pulls the chain, the cistern moves', presents difficulties to scholars who might be reluctant to admit they are reading about a lavatory.) Eleven years later, at Blaen Cwm again in 1944, he made the simpler statements of 'Poem in October' –

> It was my thirtieth year to heaven
> Woke to my hearing from harbour and neighbour wood

– and provided anthologists with one of their favourite pieces of straightforward Thomas.

From Blaen Cwm the family moved in the autumn of 1944 to New Quay, on the Cardiganshire coast, and lived in a bungalow on the cliffs, rented from a doctor. This was the site of a shooting incident, when the bungalow with Thomas in it was machine-gunned late one night by a drunken Army officer. Television researchers call there occasionally, when someone is making a programme about Thomas, and look in vain for bullet scars in the walls. The lawn ends abruptly; steps go down to the beach below. The steep-streeted village of New Quay is a mile away across the water, and the broad eye of Cardigan Bay fills the scene, with the Snowdon range of mountains sitting like clouds on the horizon to the north. On the grounds of output, the bungalow deserves a plaque of its own. Among the poems written there were 'The conversation of prayers', 'A Winter's Tale' and 'A Refusal to Mourn the Death, by Fire, of a Child in London'.

In all, that year supplied eleven of the ninety poems in *Collected Poems*. The last of them was 'Fern Hill' (Thomas wrote it as two words), which drew the loudest applause from his American audiences a few years later – a poem about lost childhoods that ended a phase of his life.

Going back in time, the middle years of the war, when Thomas lived mainly in and around London, produced no serious verse at all. Early in the war he wrote eight or nine poems, most of them in Wales, either at Laugharne – not in the Boat House – or at a house on the outskirts of Swansea where his parents were living. The only time in his life when he performed steadily as a poet without having a Welsh view from the window was between his marriage in 1937 and the first year of the war, 1940, when he and his wife spent long periods at her mother's house in the South of England because they could not afford to go elsewhere. Over three years, ten or eleven of the *Collected Poems* were written there. During those years he was busy cannibalising his notebooks of adolescent poems, and several of the ten or eleven owe something to earlier versions.

Most important of all is the period before Thomas left Swansea in 1934, aged twenty, for 'smoky London paved with poems'. It was not a sharp break, since from 1934 until the next turning point, his marriage, he was out of London more than he was in it, as often as not back in Swansea: the gritty seaside town where he felt safe. More than thirty, probably more than forty, of the ninety *Collected Poems* in their final or near-final versions, as well as others that provided skeletons to go back to later, come from this enclosed world of adolescence that was an end in itself; he never wrote like that again.

The house where he lived with his parents is semi-detached, which means there is room to squeeze past one side of it into a square of back garden. A plaque on the front wall, put there by a television company, gives the name and dates, 1914–1953, for pilgrims who trudge up the hill via the lower reaches of the suburb, the Uplands. A tall person standing in the garden can see the humps of the Mumbles Head, enclosing Swansea Bay on the west, and a strip of sea between the chimney-pots of the street below. From bedroom windows at front and back upstairs, there are views of docks, sea and untidy town, and, in one direction, distant trees and commonland where the suburbs dissolve into

Gower. Dylan Thomas's bedroom was small and poorly lit. A hot-water tank rumbled inside a cupboard. Presumably he did some of his writing there, and some of it downstairs in his father's study, a schoolmaster's den full of books; its door has ancient stained glass in it that may have been there since the house was built in 1914, just before Thomas was born.

In some ways the places are immaterial. His poems of adolescence, or of the last bitter days of his maturity, read no better as poems because of a connection with a provincial villa or a cliff in Laugharne. But a place helps to fix a poem in the mind. No. 5, Cwmdonkin Drive, Swansea, with its over-fond mother and disappointed father, seems just the place for a raw-nerved boy like Thomas to incubate his private germs.

In an autobiographical story written after he left Swansea, 'The Fight', Thomas described his 'bedroom by the boiler', and left a clue for the observant. He wrote: 'A poem I had had printed in the "Wales Day by Day" column of the *Western Mail* was pasted on the mirror to make me blush, but the shame of the poem had died. Across the poem I had written, with a stolen quill and in flourishes: "Homer Nods".' Under the title of 'His Requiem', it was his second poem to appear in print (a previous piece was published in the school magazine), and the first to earn money.

The date was January 1927; he was twelve years old, and the *Western Mail*, a Cardiff paper on sale throughout Wales, was a natural target for an ambitious schoolboy. The poem he sent them was the kind that newspapers used to print in more genteel days. It was about a man who died unmourned, except for a linnet he once fed:

> Nobody cared a bit, folks said,
> When the wicked old man at the gate lay dead...

Thomas's delighted parents kept the ten-shilling cheque without cashing it, as a souvenir. Years after Thomas was dead, someone discovered that 'His Requiem' wasn't Thomas's at all: he had copied it from an issue of the *Boy's Own Paper* of four years earlier. It was the poem that was stolen, not the quill. Whatever lesson one draws from that, and from a further attempt at plagiarism a couple of years later in the school magazine, it suggests how badly Dylan Thomas wanted to be a poet, and how uncertain he was of his talent.

The Thomas family was the result of a common enough process, people growing away from a rural background into the life of cities. In Wales, which is a country that the twentieth century did its best to turn into a region of Britain, the process was often more complicated and more painful, because it meant shifting from the Welsh language to English, and exchanging one culture for another. This process was modified, and to some extent reversed, in the last quarter of the century, when an aggressive concept of Wales as both a cultural and political entity established itself to an extent undreamt of in Dylan Thomas's lifetime. But in Victorian Britain, when his forebears were making their way in the world, few regarded the exchange of Welshness for Englishness as betrayal: it was merely commonsense.

Dylan Thomas's father, David John Thomas, was part of this flight from the national past. He came from a rural family, first identifiable in the shape of William and Ann Thomas, who were married and living in Brechfa, in North Carmarthenshire, by the early 1830s. Among their children was Evan. By the 1870s Evan was married (to another Ann), with his home at Johnstown, then a village on the edge of Carmarthen town. Among Evan's children was David John, the father of Dylan, who was born at Johnstown in 1876.

Even for Evan Thomas's generation, the drift to new ways had begun. Evan worked for the Great Western Railway, and was known locally as 'Thomas the Guard'. A job on the railway, for a villager who was steady and reliable enough to find one, was a way of bettering oneself without leaving the district. Anglicised Swansea, thirty miles away down the line, where the red furnace-light shone on the clouds at night, was a different world; people who went there to live didn't come back. Carmarthen was a market town, with a deep hinterland of dairy farms, sheep-walks and smallholdings to the north, south and west. The railway passed through the countryside, Welsh-speaking and chapel-going, without changing it.

Evan Thomas the Guard had a brother, William ('Gwilym' in the Welsh form), who was a clergyman and a poet; he was a figure of some importance, although to have a poet in the family was nothing unusual at that time and place. Poetry was nearer the surface than in a comparable English community. The 'Celtic imagination', a tired phrase but a useful one to describe a streak of temperament with its roots in prehistory, makes much of ghosts, gods, dreams and the natural scene – rocks and forest, birds and horses, the weather and the sea. Is there meaning behind these things? It is the child's question, greeted in silence. But at least the things become more real and more accessible when they are seen through a poet's eye, and are treated accordingly. Words, it seems, are more important than deeds. The Welsh are not men of action. When they are caricatured – as they have been, often enough, by the English and by the Welsh themselves – they appear as over-excited people with sing-song voices who wave their arms about and never stop talking except to burst into a hymn. They have, in the contemptuous phrase of practical men, the gift of the gab. The Welsh have also a lingering reputation for being sly and devious, perhaps because of their earlier status as a conquered people, defeated centuries ago but never absorbed: inbred, suspicious, living on their wits, whiling away the time with private songs and memories behind the stone wall of their language. Altogether an odd collection, with poets on all sides – a farm labourer or a miner or a quarryman, writing verses in fearsome metrical patterns for a knowledgeable audience that expects him to be a craftsman, chiselling away at the language. In the correct idiom, a writer who composes an englyn, a complex verse-form, is said to 'chip' it, as a sculptor chips a stone. What the poet says may be less important than the way he says it.

In Evan Thomas's generation – that is, the generation before D. J. Thomas, who was to be Dylan's father – brother William or Gwilym became a local celebrity. He was born in 1834, and brought up by an aunt and uncle in a strict religious atmosphere in a Carmarthenshire village. In his youth he was a cobbler. He went to the theological college in Carmarthen, then on to Glasgow University, and returned home in 1860 as a Unitarian minister. He also kept a school, and wrote extensively as a radical, advocating social reform. His poetry is said to be mystical rather than religious, though not particularly distinguished. The *Dictionary of Welsh Biography* (which lists about twenty William Thomases, several of them poets) describes him as 'minister, social reformer, writer and schoolmaster', in that order. But he had a 'bardic' name, which is something between a pseudonym and a courtesy title, calling himself Gwilym Marles after a stream, the Marlais, that ran out of the hills near his birthplace. His reputation (and the reason that biographical details survive for him and not for Evan and a third brother) is largely due to his role as an activist on behalf of tenants against landowners. He and his congregation were evicted from their chapel by the local landowner, and he enjoyed brief fame as a preacher–politician, dying at the age of forty-five, in 1879. He was the family's claim to distinction. D. J. Thomas, his nephew, was to give Gwilym's bardic name to Dylan and Dylan's sister, Nancy. Gwilym's life and character sound remote from those of Dylan Thomas. But his presence may have reached through to his great-nephew via D. J. Thomas, who cared deeply about the poet's vocation and was proud of the ancestral bard.

Meanwhile, Gwilym's brother, Evan the Guard, and his wife Ann were bringing up their family. The son who was to be Dylan Thomas's father was born three years before his Uncle Gwilym died. He was one of at least four children, with two brothers and a sister. His forenames, David John, were (and still are) a favourite combination in Wales, which has thousands of David John Thomases. He grew up as 'Jack' Thomas, a poor boy with brains, he used to say later. He was ambitious, though it's not clear for what; he had a clever tongue, took care of his appearance and held a good opinion of himself. His character was aloof and fastidious, and in later years many people called him a snob, though not to his face; his temper was respected. It must have been this backbone of angry dignity that his son grieved to see breaking long after, when he wrote 'Do not go gentle into that good night'. In the draft notes for another poem to his father, the 'Elegy' that he left unfinished, Dylan Thomas wrote: 'His mother said that as a baby he never cried; nor did he, as an old man.'

Whatever feelings of pride he carried in himself, Jack Thomas was unable, as a boy with brains but no money, to avoid doing the inevitable thing for someone of his talents and background. Thomas the Guard was determined his son should be a school-master. He resisted at first, but succumbed in the end, probably by easy stages. For a year, in Carmarthen, he was a pupil–teacher. Welsh was still regarded as no language to use when educating young Victorians of the British Empire, although a movement to reinstate it began in the 1880s. 'Welsh Wales' is still a world that many ambitious boys want to escape from; when D. J. Thomas was a teenager, it was more circumscribed than it is now. He took the natural course, escaping from the language, at least, by going to the University College of Wales at Aberystwyth, and specialising in English, history and education. Given his talents, he might have escaped altogether. He was able to go to Aberystwyth, in 1895, because he won a scholarship; four years later he graduated with a first-class honours degree in English. According to Florence, his wife, he was offered a travelling fellowship. If this was his chance, he missed it. He became a schoolmaster in South Wales, and grew to be an unhappy man. Mrs Thomas, elaborating her tale, said he declined the fellowship because he was 'tired'. She was not always a reliable witness; and the university has no record of offering D. J. Thomas any award. Perhaps she was reflecting some other disappointment when she said that 'he was sorry afterwards, of course'. He was undoubtedly a man with regrets. They put an edge on his tongue. He despised many of his colleagues, resented the fact that important academic appointments in Swansea went to those he considered his inferiors, and left behind the memory of a sardonic provincial schoolmaster who was his own worst enemy. There are stories that he had written poetry (presumably in English) as a young man, even that it was published in local papers; Dylan Thomas once told this to the poet Ruthven Todd, adding that D.J. was bitterly disappointed at its reception. D.J. cultivated the air of a man who deserved better things. Some of those who knew the family were convinced that he graduated from Oxford University; or that, having gone to Oxford, he had to leave because his parents could not afford to keep him there. In these local memories there survives a trace of D.J.'s regrets.

Memories lingered of another matter, closely related. It seems that D. J. Thomas, the young schoolmaster with prospects, was forced to marry in a hurry. Perhaps this is why he was 'sorry afterwards'. Mrs Addie Elliott, who later worked for the family, came from St Thomas, the same working-class district of Swansea as Florence. She said that 'they definitely had to get married. We all knew in St Thomas.' It is generally agreed that Jack and Florence had little in common; when their children were growing up, she could still aggravate him over the tea-table with chatter about clothes or children that he considered foolish, making him lose his temper and leave the room in an uproar, with Florence in tears. But as a young woman she was attractive: small, round-eyed and vivacious, a deacon's daughter who believed in enjoying herself.

Her family name was Williams. They, too, were from Car-marthenshire, where the family was thick on the ground between the villages of Llanybri and Llangain, four or five miles south-west of Carmarthen town. The family is difficult to trace, not least because Williams is such a common name in Wales,* and these particular Williamses had little to distinguish them, unlike the Thomases with their bard, Gwilym Marles. But they were a close-knit family, with (in retrospect) a slightly sinister air of inbred lives spent in primitive places, that was to creep into Dylan Thomas's childhood, perhaps into his life. His obsession with horrors in general no doubt sprang from his obsession with the horrors of the flesh – his own flesh – but they were fed and may have been shaped by the spirits of his maternal ancestors, the 'undeniably mad unpossessed peasantry of the inbred crooked county', as he once called them. Thomas's real subject was to be the tormented landscape of West Wales – haunted, ingrowing, ill-fated – that seeps into some of his prose, and is now and then on the edge of his poems. For this he can thank the Williamses.

Florence's mother, Anna, was a Williams, and so was her father, George. George and Anna were probably first cousins. Intermarriage was a recognised way of keeping farms and money in the family, but at the same time there was always the fear of promoting a strain of insanity. Traces of this fear among the Williamses a century ago can still be heard in conversations, and must have been heard by Dylan Thomas.

George and Anna were both born in or very close to 1840. George was a son of Waunfwlchan, a small farm near the road that runs beside the River Towy from Carmarthen to Llan-stephan; it is just behind the cottages at Blaen Cwm. Anna seems to have come from a larger farm a mile away, Pen-y-Coed. Among

---

* A handful of surnames serves much of the population. Welsh society, more clannish and isolated than England's, made do with Christian names until com-paratively recent times. Eventually John became Jones, William became Williams and so on. After the ubiquitous Jones, the commonest Welsh surnames are probably Thomas and Davies.

close relatives of George and Anna (they may have been her siblings) were two, a man and a woman, with a reputation as heavy drinkers. The best-remembered in the area is Daniel – 'Dr Dan', because he often needed to see a doctor. Dr Dan, a bachelor, once worked in a big store in Swansea or London, or both. He is remembered for chronic chest trouble ('weak chests' were later to be an obsession with Florence), said to have been aggravated by dust produced by 'ripping the calico in the shop'. The skeleton in Dan's cupboard was drink. According to an ancient anecdote, 'The doctor told him to get a bottle of whisky and rub it in his bad leg, but he drank the whisky and rubbed the bottle instead.'

George and Anna were to rear seven children, of whom Florence was the youngest. One of the sons, Bob, was 'not quite the round shilling', as the Welsh say, a mental defective of sorts. There are hints of another child who was mentally unstable, thus confirming the family's fears about inbreeding. The mystery is too distant to unravel. A gravestone at Capel Newydd, in Llanybri, where many of the Williamses are buried, records the death of an eighth child of George and Anna – David George, in 1892, aged eighteen. No one remembers anything about him, though, even in this district of long memories.

George Williams, like Evan Thomas of Johnstown, worked on the railway. But he took the plunge and went to Swansea. It was there, in St Thomas, on the east side of the town, that he and Anna brought up their family in the latter part of the nineteenth century. Their close links with Carmarthenshire remained, and were still strong a generation later when Dylan Thomas was a child. But henceforth they were urban people. Anna is still referred to on farms as 'Auntie Anna, Abertawe' – the Welsh name for Swansea.*

Like most districts of Swansea, St Thomas is built on a hill, in this case Kilvey, though it covers only the lower slopes. The neighbourhood was in general poor. The town was originally on the west bank of the Tawe. Castle, parish church and harbour were there, and so were the first coal and cargo docks. Industry spread to the north of the town, straddling the Tawe up the once-green Swansea Valley. By the last quarter of the nineteenth

---

* 'Abertawe' means 'at the mouth of the Tawe', the river on which the town stands. 'Tawe' is pronounced 'Tow-air', like 'plough-air'.

century, smoke had charred the edges of Kilvey, and rows of terraced houses for workmen were being built there. While middle-class suburban Swansea developed to the west, towards Gower, cheap brick boxes for dockers and tin-plate workers spread to the north and east.

The grandly named Delhi Street, where George Williams lived eventually at No. 29, was a broad avenue leading nowhere, the width of the road making the little houses look all the pokier. But it was the kind of street where front steps were scrubbed and door-knockers polished daily, lived in by families who were on their way up, not down. George rose from porter to inspector. He was made a deacon of Canaan Congregational Church, the usual square stone edifice, around the side of the hill that looks down at the Tawe. The roads peter out at this level. Wind bumps against rock outcrops and low walls chalked with *Jesus loves me*; the district is decaying now, but at the end of the nineteenth century it was part of an industrial heartland.

George and his wife shared in the new prosperity. They gave their children a respectable start. Thomas, the eldest, became a clergyman, but later married a woman with money, and was to be seen driving around in a hansom cab, arousing envy. Ann married a farmer, Jim Jones, from the same part of the countryside as her parents – when they were children, the Williamses used to spend holidays on one or other of the farms, and there were regular comings and goings between St Thomas and Carmarthenshire. Jim was a bad farmer: he drank. He and his wife began married life on a smallholding; moved to a larger property at Pentowin, which looks across the estuary to Laugharne; and came to terms with failure a few miles away at Fernhill, which Ann Jones kept going with willpower and a strong pair of hands. This is the 'Gorsehill' of Dylan Thomas's story 'The Peaches', thinly concealed on the random principle that he used in all his autobiographical fiction; Uncle Jim is there undisguised as Jim Jones, and so is Aunt Annie. She was the Ann of 'After the funeral', one of the comparatively few poems where Thomas rose to the occasion of a subject other than himself.

Polly, the next sister, was a kindly girl who didn't marry. Then there was Theodosia, or 'Dosie', who bore a favourite name in the family (there are still Theodosias on farms in South Carmarthenshire, distantly related). Dosie did well for herself by marrying a clergyman, the Rev. David Rees. She met him when he 'answered a call', in the chapel phrase, and came to be minister at Canaan, where she played the organ. Rees was a desirable husband, a man with presence, a notable preacher, something of a classical scholar: a figure cut from a traditional Welsh pattern, and someone who was sure to be pained in the unlikely event that he should ever have a nephew who drank like a fish and wrote strong poetry. A few years later he answered another call, to the church of Paraclete, in the Mumbles, then a fishing village and now a western suburb of Swansea, where Dylan Thomas went to stay with his aunt and uncle as a child, and saw religion in action, close to. 'I hate you from your dandruff to your corns,' wrote Dylan, and Uncle David was heard to say that the boy should be in a madhouse.

Some of these aunts and uncles from Florence's side of the family, as well as at least one uncle from D.J.'s side, are the figures of Thomas's Christmas reminiscences who dozed and rumbled in the front parlour at Cwmdonkin Drive while young Thomas looked at his toys and the Useful Books that told him everything about the wasp, except why. There were two further brothers in the St Thomas family, John and Bob. Both worked on the docks, which had now spread to the east bank of the river, either as stevedores or coal trimmers. Eventually John seems to have owned a small cargo-handling business and to have built up a modest capital, probably not more than a few thousand pounds, but sufficient in those days to set him apart. His house was in Bay View, better placed than Delhi Street below – 'John was the senior one, he lived higher up the mountain', they recalled in draughty Carmarthenshire farmhouses more than sixty years after his death. Altogether he owned three houses in St Thomas, and according to his daughter – another Theodosia – he once lent a brother two thousand pounds. It was John's money and gifts in kind, going either direct or funnelled via the kind-hearted Polly, that helped sustain his sister Florence's family in Cwmdonkin Drive, on the other, more pretentious, side of town, when they were in one of their financial pickles. John made himself unpopular among the Williamses by marrying a Swansea girl when he was aged about forty. They saw the houses and bank balances fade away, and there was much bad feeling.

When John died a few years later – not long before the First

World War – brother Bob inherited enough to keep him in comfort. He was the simple one, shy and slow-witted, who could be seen shuffling over the bridge from St Thomas with a shopping bag, wearing an overcoat green with age that came down to his ankles. In the end he went to earth in the cottages at Blaen Cwm with his sister Polly to look after him, where he outlived all his brothers and sisters. Relatives at a farm along the lane, Llwyn Gwyn, brought him up to the house during his last illness, and he died there. The family Bible records: 'W. R. Williams (Bob) died September 17, 1962, aged 85.' The day I was there, in 1975, an ancient wooden cradle, heavy with linen, was airing in front of an open coal fire. A daughter was due back from hospital with her new baby during the afternoon. They were going to call it Dylan.

Finally, there was Florence, the youngest child of George and Anna Williams, born in 1882, when her mother was in her early forties. She was nineteen years younger than her eldest sister, Ann. Being the baby of the family, fussed over by grown-up brothers and sisters, may have helped make her sparkle; she was livelier than the others. She attended two schools, and when she first knew D. J. Thomas, was employed as a seamstress at a local drapery store. The date of their meeting isn't known; it may have been only a short time before they were married, at the end of 1903. One Swansea story is that D.J., by this time resigned to schoolmastering, saw her at the fashionable Congregational church in Castle Street, where they were later married. But this sounds like a genteel version, describing what ought to happen to a deacon's daughter, and what did happen to sister Dosie. D.J. was no chapel-goer in later years, though it's conceivable that he behaved differently when he was a young man, and chapel was a social occasion.

Florence's account to Ethel Ross, a younger friend with whom she stayed towards the end of her life, sounds the true one. They met one weekend at a fair in Johnstown, she said, and her new sweetheart asked to see her outside the shop in Swansea on Monday evening. Probably both had been spending the weekend with their respective families, Florence on one of the farms, perhaps Fernhill with sister Ann, and Jack with his parents at Poplar Cottage, where Thomas the Guard brought up his family. In a photograph taken, probably at Poplar Cottage, a few years later, D.J. is still good-looking and youthful. His thinning hair is carefully brushed over the baldness. He is clean-shaven, in contrast to his two brothers, who are heavily moustached, and his father, whose face is barely visible between the patriarchal white beard and tall-crowned hat. They all look content to belong to the old-fashioned world they live in, except D.J.

Jack and Florence were married on 30 December 1903, and the child was born some time the following year. Reputedly it was stillborn or died within a few days; at the time there was no legal obligation to register such births, and no record of it can be traced. They had set up home in Sketty, a village to the west of Swansea that was already turning into a suburb. The small terraced house in Sketty Avenue, near a pond and a junction of muddy roads, would have been as good an address as D.J. could have afforded. Perhaps, too, it was conveniently remote from prying eyes. Children conceived out of wedlock were common enough, certainly in country districts; when she was old and gossipy, Florence used to tell gleeful yarns about (significantly) incest and other goings-on in Carmarthenshire. But her parents could hardly have been indifferent.

For a few years the Thomases stayed in Sketty. There was a dairy farm just behind the house, and the shops of the old village, down the hill, weren't far away. The Grammar School, an undistinguished group of buildings on a hill in the town, was less than two miles distant, not far for a man who enjoyed walking, as D.J. did; and the new electric trams already came part of the way from Swansea. But by the time the next child was born, a girl, in 1906, they had moved into the town itself, to Montpellier Street, close to the Grammar School. The midwife who attended Mrs Thomas said that they left Sketty Avenue because it lacked mains drainage, and Florence feared for the health of another child. The baby was christened Nancy Marles, keeping alive the name of D.J.'s poet–uncle, and promptly lived up to Florence's fears by being 'delicate'. Mrs Thomas fussed endlessly about her children's health, always making them iller than they were. Tuberculosis, still rampant at the start of the twentieth century, though already on the wane, was her bugbear. Her father died two years after her marriage, in 1905, and she used to tell people that he had TB (the death certificate shows pneumonia). Her uneasy regard for the disease was handed on to her son Dylan, who was able to adapt it to his own strange needs, and who fell in readily with her anxieties about wheezy chests, pale cheeks and flushed brows. On the other hand, it is true that Nancy was dead before she was fifty, Dylan before he was forty. The fussy mother may have had something to be fussy about.

Her husband, too, was something of a hypochondriac; perhaps of the kind that fears illness because it can degrade as well as harm. He couldn't bear physical crudities. Later, living in retirement in the cottages at Blaen Cwm, he would go out for the day when the council lorry was due to empty the earth closets at the back. At school, where his tongue was much feared, one of his favourite words of abuse was 'guttersnipe'. He sought perfection in the classroom in a hopeless kind of way, rapping knuckles with a ruler when a boy mispronounced Chaucer, warming to anyone who cared about the language. Stupid boys enraged him, dirty boys revolted him. A boy who was unwise enough to break wind would be told icily to control his bowels. A snigger at a poetic thigh or bosom provoked the full blast of his anger, and the class would be called little swine, unfit to receive the pearls of English literature.

Because he cared about his subject, his standard of teaching was high. He had a reputation for getting boys into Oxford and Cambridge; people still remember that he could predict which poems from the set books would feature in the Central Welsh Board examinations. He loved to read aloud in clear, rich tones, barely flecked with an accent. It was the style on which his son came to base his own sonorous delivery, that way of reading poems and telling funny stories that some found unforgettable, others fraudulent. When a journalist was writing an article about Dylan Thomas in 1948, he sent a draft for the poet's comments. Back came a letter with a page about D.J., the lonely figure who was so important in Thomas's life. In uncharacteristically quiet style, he wrote: 'His reading aloud of Shakespeare in class seemed to me, and to nearly every other boy in the school, very grand indeed; all the boys who were with me at school, who have spoken to me since, agree that it was his reading that made them, for the first time, see that there *was*, after all, *something* in Shakespeare & all this poetry ...' But for most of the time, D.J. seems to have found it an uphill fight to advance the cause of

Virtue and Good Literature, the school motto. The trouble lay in his exacting nature rather than in the school itself, which was probably better than average, in a country where education was taken seriously, and where few boys were sent away to private schools in England. For the doctor and the works manager, as for the shopkeeper and the railway clerk, the Grammar School was the natural place for a son to go.

According to Caitlin, Dylan Thomas's wife, who saw much of her father-in-law over fifteen years, he longed all his life to be the cultivated gentleman as well as the successful man of letters. Perhaps he was fighting against traits in his own nature as well as his provincial surroundings. He had what could have been regarded as weaknesses – sex, possibly, drink, definitely. It is said that he drank to excess when young. He certainly drank enough as a schoolmaster to make people smile. At school there were boys who claimed to be able to tell when he and the classics master, W. S. ('Soapy') Davies, had been to the Mountain Dew for pints of beer in the lunch-hour. 'Soapy' was his only close friend among his colleagues, supposedly because he alone had a good enough degree to win D.J.'s respect. They could be seen drinking in town on Wednesdays, the school half-day. At home, his wife and anyone who happened to be there learned to look out for the red cheeks, the voluble manner and the flashes of temper. He didn't drink dangerously or wildly; just a little too much to go unnoticed by the neighbours.

In 1914, when Nancy was seven, Florence was pregnant again, and the Thomases decided to move to a bigger house. They chose the Uplands, a busy suburb nearer the town centre than Sketty, and already well populated with prospering citizens. It seems to have been more than the Thomases could afford. They were always short of money. When they were first married, D.J. added to his income by teaching Welsh at evening classes, which must have gone against the grain for a man whose daytime colleagues never heard him speak the language. Mrs Thomas used to pay the tradesmen in rotation: the butcher had to wait for the fish-monger, the fishmonger for the grocer. It was the price of keeping up with the bourgeoisie, a game that both the Thomases played, though his reasons were more complicated than hers. Seen from working-class districts on the other side of the town, such places as St Thomas, this was the hypocrisy of the self-important suburbs – which were not as distant in mood or income as they would have been in an English town with a deeper-rooted middle class. It made places like Sketty and the Uplands all the more visible as targets for scorn. 'What is sex?' ran a Swansea gibe at the accents affected by the anglicised suburbs. It was, said the answer, what Sketty people had their coal delivered in.

D.J. must have found the charitable hand-outs from Florence's family painful to receive, always assuming he knew about them. Florence tried to intercept the morning mail so that he wouldn't see bills she had neglected to pay. His salary of four or five hundred pounds a year should have been sufficient, although the beer he drank and the books he accumulated in his study must have eaten into it. But Florence seems not to have been the world's best housekeeper. She was not realistic. Neither was he, for that matter. D.J. withdrew into himself as the marriage progressed. Walled up in his study, marking schoolboy essays or dreaming over Lamb and Coleridge, he didn't want to be bothered with household affairs unless they were forced on his attention. Domestic trivia he found irritating. A colleague remembered him in the staffroom on a Monday morning, complaining that he was worn out after a weekend with his family. 'My God, Williams,' he said, 'these women, they don't half chat.' And if he was unrealistic because he wanted to shut out his failures, his wife was unrealistic in a simpler and less tormented way. She ignored unpleasantness; she was a romancer. The bills could wait. She liked to be happy. At the end of her life, when she had outlived husband, son, daughter and nearly all her brothers and sisters, the eyes would sharpen in the small face at any hint of a disagreeable inference about Dylan. She doggedly deceived herself about his drinking, his marriage and his general roguery – as most mothers do, perhaps, but on a grander scale. When necessary, she did the same for Nancy. She told Ethel Ross, her Swansea friend, that Nancy's first husband was dead, which was how she came to be married a second time. Miss Ross didn't believe her, but said nothing. Next morning Florence said, 'I told you a fib last night. He isn't dead, but I didn't want to say she'd been divorced. I've always told a white lie for Nancy's sake, and do you know, I've almost come to believe it.'

Both the children followed her in this little weakness. Gwevril

Dawkins, a close friend of Nancy, in childhood and after, who remembered her with affection, said that 'like Dylan, she had an amazing imagination. She exaggerated things. Some of the reasons she gave me for leaving her husband were most improbable. I never believed them.' As for Dylan Thomas, his lack of interest in such a boring thing as the truth in everyday affairs is one of the characteristics that made him famous. His embroidered anecdotes and comical letters are one aspect; his evasiveness, duplicity and general dishonesty another. He was a marvellous liar; or, as people who resent the word insist vehemently, 'a romancer'.

The house the Thomases moved to in 1914, that was to be Dylan Thomas's observation post until he was twenty, was brand-new. Cwmdonkin Drive is a steep road, with the Uplands below, and at that time mainly farmland above. Opposite the house, on the same level of the hill, were the uneven grounds of a mansion, later a school, and beyond that again, thick with trees and sunk into a contour of the land, Cwmdonkin Park. The setting is still green and relaxing to the eye. The visitor looks over his shoulder to the smooth metal plate of the bay, bolted to the town. Far away is the north Devonshire coast, on the other side of the Bristol Channel. It remains a genteel address.

The builders were in and out of the house finishing the plastering and doing odd jobs when the Thomases moved in during the early summer. The baby was expected in September, but somebody must have miscalculated. There was time for Florence to engage a living-in maid, a sure sign of pretensions. The war had begun in August and it was not easy to find domestic help. But a friend of Polly in St Thomas had a daughter of eighteen, Addie, who was already 'in service', and she agreed to go to Cwmdonkin Drive at six shillings a week. She was there for a fortnight before the baby arrived, helping with the coal fires, the big coal oven that had to be lighted every day, and eight-year-old Nancy, who inconveniently caught measles. A washerwoman came in on Mondays and worked in the wash-house, a shed in the tiny garden, boiling clothes in the copper for two shillings and sixpence and her meals. The house had more rooms to be kept clean than appears from the outside. Downstairs, a good-sized front room looking out on Cwmdonkin Drive, used mainly for Sundays; a middle room with a separate entrance at the rear, which was D.J.'s study; and a breakfast room and kitchen at the back of the house. Upstairs were four bedrooms: one for the Thomases; one for Nancy; the big one at the front 'for best', in the Welsh way, and thus rarely occupied unless there were visitors; and the tiny boxroom where the maid slept.

The best bedroom was used for the confinement, and the baby was born at about 11 p.m. on 27 October. They had difficulty in finding a name, and it was seven weeks before the birth was registered in the names of Dylan Marlais. 'Marlais' was the river from which D.J.'s uncle took his bardic title, so that both children now had a version of it in their names. 'Dylan' was an obscure figure from the *Mabinogion*, the Welsh medieval prose romances. As a noun the word means 'sea' or 'ocean'. In the *Mabinogion* Dylan makes a brief appearance when Math the son of Mathonwy challenges Arianrhod, who claims to be a virgin, to step over his magic wand. 'A fine boy-child with rich yellow hair' drops from her as she does so. Math son of Mathonwy calls him Dylan, and the child makes for the sea, his natural element.

Presumably this fragment appealed to D.J., who may have known the work in Welsh, or in Lady Charlotte Guest's version of 1849, which he could have bought in the cheap 'Everyman's Library' series from 1906. He was anglicised and yet he was a Welshman. He had opted for English literature, but he remembered the preacher–poet in the family. Was he hoping to bottle up some magic in a name? No doubt he was trying to do better for his son than the 'David John' that his parents had hung around his neck.

Florence, however, raised a practical objection. The orthodox Welsh pronunciation of Dylan is 'Dullan', which has since led to tedious arguments between the Welsh-language purists who want 'Dullan' and Dylan's friends and family who point out that he himself always said 'Dillan'. But this pronunciation, which in the end Thomas had to instruct the Welsh region of the BBC to use when introducing him, came later. D.J., whose Welsh was said to be as impeccable as his English, said 'Dullan'. He must have done, because when he proposed the name (and it was unknown in common use before that), Florence was afraid that people would make fun of the child: 'I didn't know if we were doing right or if they'd be calling him "dull one" before the end.

Anyway, like that we left it.'* So, by the obscure magic that gives famous people appropriate names, he was labelled 'Dylan', where a 'John' or a 'William' would have been adequate.

---

* This account was given to me by Mrs Thomas in 1955. It is only fair to say that she had another version. In an interview with Colin Edwards, recorded at the Boat House in the summer of 1958, she said flatly that the pronunciation was always 'Dillan', not 'Dullan'. But Jean Overton Fuller, who knew Thomas when he was first in London, quoted him on the subject in 1935, when he said that 'in Wales, it's pronounced Dullan', adding that English people called him 'Dillan' in their minds, 'and I think perhaps Dillan sounds more elegant than Dullan.'

Chapter Two

HIS FATHER'S SON

The problem for anyone who wishes to chronicle the first fifteen years of Dylan Thomas's life is that the outward episodes were essentially trivial, of the kind common to many childhoods, while inwardly the odd process of becoming a poet was in progress. To some extent this is true of all his thirty-nine years. What happened on the outside was a certain amount of sitting at desks and writing, and a great deal of fantasising, comical storytelling, horseplay, borrowing and drinking. If Thomas the Clown is worth anatomising he must have connections with Thomas the Poet. But Thomas's disorderly style of living makes good copy by itself. He lived, looked and sounded like the popular idea of a poet, with recognisably poetic poems to show for it; and if there were fears and empty spaces in his life, he concealed them with bizarre language and behaviour.

The interior Thomas is another matter – difficult enough to write about at any point, and especially when he was a child. For a few years at the end of his adolescence it becomes easier. From the age of fifteen until he was past nineteen, a series of notebooks preserve about two hundred poems that reflect much of what he felt and thought; and before the notebooks finished he had begun his densely packed letters to Pamela Hansford Johnson, an autobiography in themselves. But in his earlier years he was merely a child growing up in a town by the sea, about whom things are remembered and inferences can be drawn, at the observer's peril.

He was pretty, he was spoiled, he was the darling of the family. As far as love and attention go, he seems to have lacked nothing. Mrs Thomas used to say stubbornly in later years that she had spoiled both her children, and if she had her time over again, would do the same. It may be that Dylan was especially indulged. There is some evidence that the child who died or who was stillborn in 1904 was a boy. It is plausible to suggest that his mother, brought up against the background of Canaan Chapel and the Carmarthenshire Bible-belt, saw his death as a pun-ishment for her wickedness; and the birth of another son, ten years later, as a sign that she was forgiven. Or she may simply have been a warm and affectionate mother who was instantly seduced by Dylan's angelic features and precocious ways.

All his life Dylan Thomas hankered after the warm beds and mother-love of his childhood. He liked to be looked after, and by the time he was an adult, his skill at extracting attention and sympathy was prodigious (so was his disgust with himself for doing it, sometimes, but this was no deterrent). Many of the anecdotes about his helplessness as an adult concern food and drink, making an obvious connection for psychiatrists who would define Thomas as a child, and then a man, with powerful 'oral traits'. He learned the advantages of demanding to be fed: by his mother, by his wife, by his friends, by the 'silly ravens' with money in their wallets. His mother was still removing the tops of his boiled eggs when he was seventeen. His sister-in-law, Nicolette, having breakfast at the Thomases' ten years after that, was surprised to hear him ask his wife to do it. One of his harmless treats was sugared bread and milk, as given to sleepy children, served in bed by his wife when he was unwell or had a hangover. Nicolette said that Caitlin used to take it to the bedroom and lock him in with it: 'He was perfectly all right. But bread and milk is what his mother used to give him.' It even had to be cut neatly into squares, as Florence did it in Cwmdonkin Drive. Robert Pocock, a BBC friend, found him in bed at Laugh-arne, sitting up with a woollen shawl around his shoulder, stuffing himself with sweets and calling hoarsely to Caitlin for his milky treats.

The safe room with goodies for the little boy cropped up all his life. He would have himself shut up in a room, accompanied by sustenance, to encourage himself to write. Ruthven Todd saw him staying with friends in a London flat in the mid-1930s. At Thomas's request they locked him in a room with two bottles of beer between the times the pubs closed after lunch and opened again in the early evening. A few years later, at his mother-in-law's house in Hampshire, he was working in a locked room with a supply of beer and cigarettes. He is said to have produced a radio script in the same way near the end of his life, secured in the BBC library overnight. These stories about locked rooms for writing in were probably exaggerated by Thomas; the night in the library (as opposed to a few hours there) may have been one of his tales. But the fact that he told them showed the way his mind worked.*

As a child he received much physical affection. Mrs Thomas liked to kiss and cuddle. After her husband's death, when she was an old lady, she was observed in a big feather bed with one of her grandchildren, a 'naked Cupid', and two giggly country girls who slept there to keep her warm; the four of them cosily wrapped up together. Dylan's cot stood in his parents' bedroom at the back of the house, a common enough practice in families of modest means, though it can set a psychiatrist's teeth on edge. When Dylan cried, which he did often, Addie the maid would be sent for; with D.J. barking, 'Put the little bugger through the window,' she would take him into her own warm bed in the boxroom and cuddle him.

In the opinion of some psychiatrists, such experiences – especially with an imaginative child – can arouse sexual fantasies, followed by feelings of guilt and inadequacy. These may produce fears about his body and lead him to lose confidence in his sexual powers, with unfortunate results later in life.† That (runs the general argument) may lie behind a fear-ridden immaturity in Thomas, and his need to prove himself masculine with drink and women. His mother's over-indulgence may have had similar effects, helping to produce a passive child and a passive man. Such speculations don't 'explain' a poet but they may throw incidental light. Dylan Thomas's poems, especially the early ones, certainly contain phrases that suggest a preoccupation with subconscious sexual fears, in particular a fear of having his sex organs mutilated. These phrases revolve around images of tailors and scissors. Such images, it has been suggested, stem from

* It is unwise to believe too many anecdotes about Thomas; equally unwise to believe none at all. Vague stories that he was locked in an hotel room to write a film script have every sign of being apocryphal. But Leigh Aman, later Lord Marley, who was production manager of *Three Weird Sisters* after the war, insisted that Thomas spent three weeks virtually locked up on the top floor of the Royal Court Hotel in London, writing the script. Aman sometimes took him his food and limited amounts of drink.

† An American psychiatrist, B. W. Murphy, has commented at length in *Creation and Destruction: Notes on Dylan Thomas*. This was written without specific knowledge of Thomas's infancy.

Struwwelpeter, the illustrated book of children's stories which includes the sinister tale of 'Little Suck-a-Thumb', a child who is punished by having his thumbs sliced off by a grisly tailor with flying hair and enormous scissors, the 'great, long, red-legged scissor-man'. According to Freud, the stories, written by a Frankfurt doctor, succeed precisely because they touch on childhood complexes. Thomas knew the book when he was small, and refers to it in reminiscences of childhood. Various lines of poems – such as the 'scissors stalking, tailor age' of 'When, like a running grave' – can be cited as evidence of how his earliest fears worked their way into the open via the scissor-man. So can some of the early stories, like 'The Mouse and the Woman', which has 'a child who had cut off his double thumb with scissors'.

Women played a large part in Thomas's writing and conversation, but there is an undercurrent of failure. In several published stories they are pursued and lost. Nowhere in print does Thomas describe or even imply an ordinary, successful act of sex. Either it fails to happen or it is part of a nightmare. In another early story, 'A Prospect of the Sea' (first published in 1937), a boy meets and is sexually terrorised by a gipsy-like girl in a torn cotton frock. She has more than a touch of *Struwwelpeter*: 'The stain on her lips was blood, not berries; and her nails were not broken but sharpened sideways, ten black scissor-blades ready to snip off his tongue.' In real life it is likely that most of his public overtures to women – typically, at cocktail parties in America – were crude, comical lunges with small chance of success. It is said that his penis was of modest size, another cause of uneasiness. As an adolescent he was obsessed with being 'little': a little person, a little poet.

The case can be extended to explain Thomas's fears of failure as a poet. A number of the early notebook poems ask whether he dares to fly, to move away, to break out. The eventual tragedy of Thomas may have been a loss of nerve that stopped him using his powers and left him creatively impotent. This is a large speculation from a slender base of evidence. In any case, if his early experiences, whatever they were, had unfortunate effects, they were also part of a process that helped produce a poet of Thomas's uniquely morbid self-interest. The one was not available without the other. As he once wrote to the poet Henry Treece in another connection, 'My horrible self ... would not be itself did it not possess the faults.'

Whatever the influence Florence Thomas and her family had on her son's future life, it was largely accidental. The same is not true of D.J. A clever, disappointed man, he probably hoped for a son who was a more successful edition of himself, with a double first at Oxford – he badly wanted Dylan to go to university – followed by the gilt-edged career that eluded the father. But had it been no more than that, the bond that existed between the two would hardly have been so strong, and certainly not when Dylan was still an adolescent, making a conventional show of rebellion. Dylan Thomas was critical enough, in his youthful letters, of a narrow provincial background and a chattering mother. His father, though, is never censured. To Pamela Hansford Johnson he wrote of D.J.: '[A] broader-minded man I have never known.' Dylan respected his father, perhaps because from the child's earliest years, D.J. encouraged his natural passion for words; he was an authority on the only subject that Dylan cared about.

Thomas the Schoolmaster can hardly have thought rationally that a poet could be constructed out of his own unrealised hopes, however deep-rooted they may once have been. Nor did he take kindly to Dylan's bohemian way of life when his son became a professional poet. Yet behind the rational man, cold-lipped and overbearing, that D.J.'s colleagues at the Grammar School took him for, can be seen the shadow of an obsession. Dylan Thomas once told Ruthven Todd that his father determined his son should be more successful as a poet than he had been himself. That may be a simplified or romanticised version. But there is a story that D.J. was reading him Shakespeare before he could speak. Addie Elliott, who left the Thomases when Dylan was two years old, remembers D.J. reciting poetry to the baby, some of it his own doggerel. Her name then was Addie Drew. So

> Poor Addie Drew,
> She had the flu,
> Then stayed in bed
> Until she was dead.

Thomas used to say that the first poems he knew were nursery rhymes – which is true for most people. In written answers to a student who caught him in the right mood in 1951 he said that 'what the words stood for, symbolised, or meant, was of very secondary importance; what mattered was the *sound* of them as I heard them for the first time on the lips of the remote and incomprehensible grown-ups who seemed, for some reason, to be living in my world'. Rhetorical as ever, especially when answering questions about so important a matter as how he came to write poetry, Thomas described 'the colours the words cast on my eyes ... and though what the words meant was, in its own way, often deliciously funny enough, so much funnier seemed to me, at that almost forgotten time, the shape and shade and size and noise of the words as they hummed, strummed, jigged and galloped along. That was the time of innocence; words burst upon me, unencumbered by trivial or portentous association; words were their springlike selves, fresh with Eden's dew, as they flew out of the air.'

Thomas added the Bible to his list of things that 'first made me love language and want to work *in* it and *for* it'. He had known its 'great stories' from his early youth; 'the great rhythms had rolled over me from the Welsh pulpits; and I read, for myself, from Job and Ecclesiastes; and the story of the New Testament is part of my life'. D. J. Thomas was agnostic, and the Thomases were not a chapel-going family. But D.J. knew his Bible; Addie used to hear him quoting from it. His mother, who visited them from Johnstown, was a strict chapel-goer. It would have been remarkable if Dylan had not been sent to chapel as a formality. Before he was five he was attending Walter Road Congregational Church, near the Uplands, where, as everywhere else at that age, he was remembered as 'looking like an angel'. Whether many sermons thundered over him from pulpits is less certain. Perhaps Uncle David Rees at Paraclete was his model; he is said to have been a popular preacher who could work up a 'hwyl', or religious fervour. But Thomas's experience of powerful sermons very likely came from the angry evangelists he would have heard on Swansea sands, standing on soapboxes and castigating the lusts of the flesh, when he was a teenager. There are two views about Thomas and religion. One is that he was a 'religious' poet, and his life a movement towards God. The other (which seems to me the only feasible view) is that religion was a stage-prop of his poetry; he used its language and myths, which he learned in childhood, without ever absorbing or caring much about its central beliefs. But in either case, plenty of religion was available to him in childhood, and became seeded in his brain, along with nursery rhymes and folk tales.

Outside his home, the first place that mattered to him may have been Cwmdonkin Park, where he was taken when he was a few days old. This was an isolated place with no entrance or frontage on a main road; although it is surrounded by houses, there are people living within half a mile who have never been inside it. Originally a town reservoir was built there, half a century before; then it was turned into a lake in a hillside park. With its air of faint secretiveness, which it retains, it fits nicely into Thomas's tales of a lost, magical boyhood. Addie Elliott took him there almost daily in the pram to hear pigeons make their hollow noises and see the gulls come looking for bread in windy weather. It seems almost too appropriate, considering Thomas's later fantasies about flying, that the first word he spoke was 'bird', but that is what Mrs Elliott remembered.

In his book of more-or-less autobiographical stories, *Portrait of the Artist as a Young Dog*, Thomas wrote about an early visit to Cwmdonkin in 'Patricia, Edith and Arnold'. Edith is the 'servant girl', a successor to Addie. She takes him with her when she and her friend Patricia go to confront their mutual boyfriend, Arnold. It snows, as it frequently does in Thomas's childhood. Nothing escapes his attention, from the 'brown stains' under Edith's arms to the black hairs that show through a tear in Patricia's stocking. He is aged perhaps five or six, a clever, lovable, naughty child who relishes the thought of how spoilt he is; he seems to have shed some of his innocence already, though this may be only the way the story was written, twenty years afterwards. The park became one of Thomas's reference points, a locked corner of childhood to brood over.

The farm at Fernhill was another place that became fixed in his imagination. About the countryside in general, Thomas always seemed in two minds. He needed to break away from urban life, but he soon tired of rural retreats. It was part of his inability ever to settle anywhere for long. But Fernhill, the green enclave, was not the ordinary countryside. He must have gone there from his earliest years. The farm is on a rise above a wooded valley, shielded from the road by fir trees; on a summer's day the plump little hills nearby are blue and green. The living quarters, slate-roofed, form three sides of a square around a small courtyard, an arrangement that makes the place a trifle more distinguished than its neighbours. It is no longer worked as a farm; electric-power lines crackle in the damp air above the barn and the remains of an orchard. Fernhill is a rare English place-name in the district. In the 1920s, when Ann and Jim Jones scraped a living from it, they kept a few cows, pigs and chickens. The premises were dirty and bedraggled. Ann, eight or nine years older than her husband, did most of the work. She made the butter, then the main product of many Welsh smallholdings. Her husband's character was blackened by distant relatives of Ann: 'a terrible man', they said, lazy and hard-drinking. He was known to visit Swansea to borrow money from Bob Williams, his brother-in-law, to pay the rent.

Dylan Thomas gave much the same picture in another of his *Portrait of the Artist* stories, 'The Peaches'. Uncle Jim sells a piglet when he needs money for the pub, and returns drunk after consorting with loose women in Carmarthen, staggering into the lamp-lit kitchen 'like the devil with a red face and a wet nose and trembling, hairy hands'. He still had two years to live when the book was published in 1940, and can hardly have failed to recognise himself, if anyone sent him a copy. Annie, too, is part of this earthy world, so unlike home life at Cwmdonkin Drive. Thomas presents her as warm and kindly, 'a little, brown-skinned, toothless, hunchbacked woman with a cracked, sing-song voice'. She was more than fifty years older than Dylan. In 'The Peaches' he is a Grammar School boy, aged eleven or more. But the story compresses many summer holidays into one. He made it the first story in the book, and it remained one of the two he liked best, a central memory that went on vibrating. In some disjointed manuscript notes, probably made towards the end of his life, Thomas wrote of Fernhill as 'a place with which I have come to associate all the summer of my chil ... a lovely farm – a lonely farm – and a place with which I have come to associate all the golden – never shone a sun like that old rolling...'

In 'The Peaches', Jim and Annie's son Gwilym (in real life it was Idris) is 'aged nearly twenty, with a thin stick of a body and spade-shaped face'. He was born in 1897, making the year 1917,

and Dylan Thomas three years old. No doubt his first memories
of Idris dated from then. By the time Dylan was old enough for
the Grammar School, Idris was nearer thirty. Was it then, or
earlier, that Thomas, up a tree, saw his cousin, sitting on the
outside lavatory? 'He was reading a book and moving his hands',
a vignette that somehow slipped past the publishers in 1940.

Sex is always hovering in the background of these stories. At
Fernhill it is part of the raw, exciting strangeness of the place.
The run-down family countryside, still living in its past, helped
to feed Thomas's love of the macabre. His childhood dreams
were thick with ghosts and vampires, but he seems to have
taken a perverse pleasure in frightening himself with them. 'The
Peaches' includes a demon with 'wings and hooks, who clung
like a bat to my hair'. When he arrives at the farm with his uncle,
at night, he imagines that 'nothing lived in the hollow house at
the end of the yard but two sticks with faces scooped out of
turnips'. Curiously, in 'The Peaches' Thomas made scarcely any
capital from the fact that, as he knew, the Carmarthen hangman
was supposed to have lived in the house, as recently as the end
of the nineteenth century. There seems to be some truth in the
story, which is still current in the district. But the man, by the
name of Evans, was only an assistant executioner, and hanged
no one himself. In 'The Peaches' Thomas identifies the hangman's
home as a deserted house down the road; probably he wanted to
confuse local readers and stop them recognising Fernhill too
easily.

'The Peaches' was based on a true incident, the visit to the
farm of a well-to-do friend called Jack Williams from Swansea.
Jack's mother, stout and beringed, brings him to stay as a paying
guest, arriving in a Daimler. It is for her benefit that Annie,
making a pathetic attempt to be polite, brings out the tinned
peaches, which, inevitably, Jack's mother declines. Mrs Williams
is the epitome of suburbia, the other pole of Thomas's life. She,
too, is trying to be something that she is not. Thomas painted an
unkind and perhaps inaccurate picture ('she was fitted out like a
mayoress or a ship') that was recognised by the original in
Swansea when the story appeared. She was really Mrs Bassett,
the second wife of a local man of property who at one time was
mayor of the town. The family lived at Rosehill, a large house
not far from Cwmdonkin Drive, higher up the slope, and Mrs

Bassett and Florence Thomas were friendly. Reach-me-down clothes from the Bassett children found their way to Cwmdonkin Drive, another reason for Dylan not to like her. An acquaintance met Mrs Bassett shopping in the Uplands, and the former may-oress told her the dreadful thing that the poet who used to be their neighbour had done to her. 'He must have thought we were dull if we couldn't recognise who it was,' she said, 'but we aren't *that* dull. I shall never forgive him.'

Unfortunately writers are always greedy for material, and Thomas found his bricks and mortar where he could. Mrs Bassett fared badly. Aunt Annie might be pleasantly surprised to find herself in the anthologies as the 'sculptured Ann' who is 'seventy years of stone', in the elegiac 'After the funeral'. That poem was written, in its final form, at a time – not long before he wrote the stories in *Portrait of the Artist* – when Thomas turned briefly towards a cooler, more outward-looking view of life. He was writing compassionately about a real woman in a real place. Seven years after that, when he produced 'Fern Hill', his mood was different again, and the farm was transformed into Eden as regrets and nostalgias gnawed at him. By then aunt and uncle were dead, and Fernhill was left to its owls and nettles. It is a poem without people, occupied only by child, house, countryside and animals.

Dylan must have seen his mother's relatives often, both at Fernhill and during visits to and from the St Thomas clan. His father's family was not so close-knit. One brother, William, lived in London and seems to have been in the drapery business. Another, Arthur, lived a few miles from Swansea at Aberavon, and worked for the Great Western Railway. When Arthur's shift-working allowed, he spent weekends in Cwmdonkin Drive: a dour working man, crossed in love and unmarried, quite unlike his brother Jack. Arthur, too, used to help the family with money from time to time. Dylan grew up amid a threadbare respect-ability. At the age of seven he was sent to a private day school. By this time he was accustomed to having his own way, at least where his mother was concerned. Gwevril Dawkins, who was Nancy's closest friend in Swansea, first knew him at the age of five. She and Nancy used to babysit when the Thomases went out. Dylan, she said, was 'an absolute tartar, an appalling boy. I remember him grabbing for oranges. He never asked.'

Mrs Thomas said it was his health that kept him away from school for so long. She thought he was not strong enough. If it wasn't anaemia it was asthma or a weak chest, unspecific ill-health. The school he finally went to was one of those private establishments that used to cater for ambitious parents in suburbs. Jackie Bassett went there. A lady called Mrs Hole ran it at her house in Mirador Crescent, just around the corner from Cwmdonkin Drive, and charged a few pounds a term. It sounds like Mrs Thomas's choice. Dylan would have been better taught at the local 'elementary' school, as his father must have known. Perhaps he had his own fears, that the twangy local accent would contaminate Dylan's vowels. Mirador was no more than two rooms for general teaching, with music lessons in the drawing room upstairs. There was a uniform: cap, tie and blazer in dark red and navy blue. Mornings began with a hymn and a prayer, and a local parson addressed the children once a term. Summoned to test the children in geography, Mr Hole would arrive red in the face and breathing heavily. Evelyn Burman Jones, who was there as a child with Dylan, said her clearest memories of the place were the piano being thumped, the metronome ticking and Mrs Hole shouting for her husband.

The dame school in Mirador Crescent provides the first glimpse from the outside of Dylan Thomas as the person whom people loved to indulge. The cherubic face on a thin stalk of a body sent him off to a good start. He was teacher's pet, more often than not to be found occupying the lap of Mrs Hole's daughter, who helped with the teaching. 'Who put water in Joyce's galoshes, every morning prompt as prompt?' he asked in one of his radio reminiscences. Evelyn Jones, a friendly witness who later acted with him in amateur theatricals, said he was impregnable at Mrs Hole's. Once he seized the leg of Evelyn's chair and she flew backwards, knocking an aspidistra off a pedestal; Evelyn took the blame. She recalled that 'he always had a pain in his stomach if there was anything he didn't want to do'. Once he fell in the lane behind the school where the children played, and cut his knee on a piece of glass. He ran home saying that Evelyn had pushed him, and Mrs Thomas came down to the school to complain – 'She worshipped Dylan. They were all scared to death of her.'

Fondly, his mother sent him off each morning wrapped in thick jerseys and plenty of underclothes to keep chills and draughts at bay, even in summer; his adolescent letters often mention vests. He was all shimmering curls and mischief – that word used of attractive children, whose instant appeal is already segregating them for life from their lumpish brethren, who are liable to have it called nastiness. He was the joker; you couldn't help laughing. Term ended with a little play. One Christmas, Dylan was supposed to be a colonel, carrying a walking stick and reading a newspaper. He poked a hole in the paper and blew orange peel through it at the audience, then rushed about slashing the air with the stick. They brought the curtain down; Mrs Thomas loved it.

No doubt people choose to remember early incidents that fit in with later legends. One of Dylan's admirers, a little girl called Vera Phillips, had a friend who lived in Mirador Crescent. One day the two girls were in the lane behind the school when they were amazed and delighted to see Dylan doing something rude. 'He was shouting, "Look, I can write *God Save the King*," and peeing all over the wall. My friend and I gazed at this in astonishment. All the other little boys were trying to do it, too.' Years later when both families were living in New Quay, it was Vera's soldier husband who arrived outside the Thomas bungalow with a sub-machine gun and sprayed it with bullets, in a muddled sort of way. 'The lane was always the place to tell your secrets,' wrote Thomas, in his radio talk, 'Reminiscences of Childhood', and 'occasionally now I dream that I am turning out of school into the lane of confidences when I say to the boys of my class, "At last, I have a real secret."

' "What is it? What is it?"

' "I can fly."

'And when they do not believe me, I flap my arms and slowly leave the ground...'

The day he fell and cut his knee, when Evelyn Jones was blamed, he had been pretending to fly by jumping off the wall of the house. The image of flying recurs into adolescence. Where did he want to fly to? In the radio talk he crosses the docks and 'Inkerman Street, Sebastopol Street, and the street where all the women wear men's caps'. He is above St Thomas. But soon he is back over 'the trees of the everlasting park', and finally 'the yellow seashore, and the stone-chasing dogs, and the old men, and the singing sea'. Perhaps, as Kent Thompson said in his unpublished thesis on 'Dylan Thomas in Swansea', the sea that Thomas flies towards in his imagination is at once life and death. The sea was the most powerful of all symbols for Thomas, rarely absent for long from stories or poems.

To anyone who spends his childhood in that part of Swansea, the sea is inescapable. The low-lying town centre and the older working-class districts give only occasional reminders. But the hilly western suburbs and parks look down roads that point to the bay, where the town comes to a halt against six miles of tidal sands, a watery perimeter that takes in parkland, sports ground, houses, pubs, slipways, a promenade and long stretches where there is nothing but a thin layer of dunes and a stony embankment. In Thomas's day the tram-like Mumbles Railway ran the full six miles, and the tail end of a main railway line about three of them.

The foreshore was a natural place to go to throw stones, dam streams, hear hellfire preachers, mooch about in arches under the railway embankment, whistle after girls, and later lie down with them in saucers of the scrubby dunes, while passing trains threw out showers of hot cinders, and the lovers would sometimes see the silhouette of a Peeping Tom rise up slowly above the spiky marram grass. Thomas haunted the seashore. He remembered it with dogs and old men, watching oil tankers and banana boats coming out of the docks, shouting at the sea. He seems never to have gone *in* it, though, there or on the Gower beaches where he went with friends as soon as he was old enough. They remembered him throwing stones at it, or just looking. Caitlin used to say that his hands were delicate and useless, like fins. But he had no interest in swimming.

It was a happy childhood, or Thomas never suggested otherwise, although he did say to Margaret Taylor, 'There's only one thing that's worse than having an unhappy childhood, and that's having a too-happy childhood.' He was absorbed in himself, the child that parents smile at proudly behind his back and call imaginative. But he was unusually intense. In his stories of childhood he sometimes tries to photograph himself at a particular instant. In 'The Peaches', playing Indians with Jackie Bassett alias Williams, 'I felt all my young body like an excited animal ... I was aware of me myself in the exact middle of a living story, and my body was my adventure and my name.' This seems to have become a central part of Thomas's consciousness: what was going on inside his head sometimes was the thought that there he was, wondering what was going on inside his head. At a given moment he was taking part in the drama of himself. Writing to Vernon Watkins at the start of the war he said, 'I go for long bicycle rides, thinking: "Here I am on a bicycle in a war." ' By that time he had learned to laugh at himself for this quirk of narcissism, but he continued to do it, adding a further layer to the joke, which underneath was not a joke, by describing the process for an audience. 'I was walking, one afternoon in August, along a river-bank,' he said in a radio talk, 'thinking the same thoughts that I always think when I walk along a river-bank in August. As I was walking, I was thinking – now it is August and I am walking along a river-bank.'

His poetry was to reflect this obsessive self-awareness by the time he was fifteen. His earliest verse shows few signs of it. The first poems which are presumed to be Thomas's are in manuscript, fair copies in a childish hand. After Dylan's death Mrs Thomas gave them to a friend, Mrs Hettie Owen; apparently she destroyed other juvenilia. Her account of how these early poems came to be written was a fond mother's view of the clever child, happy with pencil and paper: 'He'd come and annoy his sister. She'd say, "Write something, write a poem about an onion or the kitchen sink," and he would. I kept a lot of them for a long time and then I burnt them. But they were clever little things.' She gave the impression that some of this writing was done before he was ten. The poems are precocious. 'La Danseuse'* begins:

> She moved like silence swathed in light,
> Like mist in moonshine clear;
> A music that enarmoured sight
> Yet did elude the ear.

Above 'enarmoured' another hand has written 'enamoured'. In the margin, against the word 'epitome' in the next verse, is: 'ep/i/to/me – 4 syllables'. Presumably this was D.J. at work. In another poem, 'real' and 'steel' are made to rhyme. A marginal

---

* See Appendix.

note says firmly: 'Real is two syllables and cannot rhyme with steel.' In 'Inspirations' there is a hint of subject matter to come. Thomas is writing about the business of writing, looking at poetry as his personal means of coming to terms with the world. This was to be a favourite area, a vein he never tired of working, poems about poetry and himself the poet: more self-awareness.

> The night is full of poetry and desire,
> And eager with unanswerable things;
> O that my beating brain could borrow wings,
> And shake the shackles of the mind's attire.
>
> For then indeed, my songs might near the touch
> More envied than the jewelled crown of kings;
> And I should be a happy heart who sings,
> Nor questions why, no[r] wonders overmuch.

Dylan may have been using a convenient formula that he had found in other people's poetry. But he soon learned to adapt it to his needs.

Chapter Three

A SORT OF SCHOOLBOY

At the age of eleven, Dylan Thomas found his first outlet for verse in the Grammar School magazine. He entered the school in the autumn of 1925, shortly before his eleventh birthday, and went into the 'A' stream, where the middle-class, anglicised boys were usually placed. It is probable that he was a fee-paying entrant, though the cost to his father would have been small. D. J. Thomas was by now resigned to a lifetime of being senior English master. In 1920 he had entertained hopes that the chair of English at the newly established Swansea University College might come his way. It went to a namesake, W. D. Thomas, whose abilities he thought inferior to his own. Colleagues said it soured him. It irked him, too, that a fellow-student at Aberystwyth, T. J. Rees, who began by teaching at a lesser school in Swansea, was now the town's well-liked Director of Education, and earning more than he was. 'My degree is better,' he would say. But even if it was, D.J.'s manner alienated people. When he was ill and away from school, as frequently happened, no one bothered to visit him. He and Florence didn't socialise with other masters and their wives. He could tell a good story with appropriate Welsh mannerisms when the mood took him, but more often he made people uneasy. A teacher who joined the school the year before Dylan, J. Morgan Williams, came upon D.J. unexpectedly one evening in the Bush, a public house in Sketty. He was sitting alone in the corner. He accepted the offer of a fresh pint from his young colleague and sat drinking it in silence. His tallish figure, balding and severe, was often to be seen there about nine o'clock of an evening. Local drinkers called him 'The Professor'.

As master in charge of the school magazine, which was published each term, D.J. had to approve its contents. He can't have been troubled by his son's first effort, a harmless piece of humour about a dog whose

greatest delight is to take a good bite
At a calf that is plump and delicious;
And if I indulge in a bite at a bulge,
Let's hope you won't think me too vicious.

This was printed in December 1925, at the end of Dylan's first term. It was a year before his next effort appeared there, another piece of light verse, and soon after that he sold his first poem to the *Western Mail* in Cardiff. This was the stolen lyric, 'His Requiem'. It appeared in the 'Wales Day by Day' column on 14 January 1927, signed 'D. M. Thomas', and might have been attributed to him for ever if it had not been reprinted in 1971 in a collection entitled *Dylan Thomas: The Poems* edited by his friend, Dr Daniel Jones. The *Sunday Telegraph* printed 'His Requiem', and an observant reader wrote to say that the poem was not Thomas's: it had appeared in the *Boy's Own Paper* for November 1923, above the name of Lillian Gard. Miss Gard was a regular contributor to children's journals at the time. Thomas had not even retitled his version; he made six small changes but otherwise the poems were identical. He would hardly have taken such a risk unless he badly needed to prove – to himself, to his father, to his friends – that he could write acceptable poetry; and unless he was uncertain of his ability to do so.

It raises the question of why he wrote poetry in the first place. In some ways this is as pointless as asking why he had brown eyes and curly hair. He wrote poems because he was born with certain characteristics, among them great verbal ingenuity and a tortured imagination. But students of Thomas, even friendly ones, have nagging doubts concerning the way he set about his craft. There is a feeling that at times he is more interested in proving himself a poet than in getting on with the business of conveying whatever it is that he wants a poem to convey. The desire to display himself to the world as an artist was very real to Thomas. He did it in his life and in his work. His poems are thick with the affectations of poetry. It is hard to avoid a suspicion that one of the forces that drove him was the desire to be a poet: perhaps, to follow in the footsteps his father never took. Given that premise, and the streak of bravado in his nature, it is not difficult to see how he came to steal Gard's little poem. It contains a concrete episode (the unloved old man, mourned by the bird) of a kind that Thomas may have found difficult to incorporate in his own verse, which was vaguer and wordier, if the juvenile manuscripts are any indication. He seized it and ran. Apparently Thomas never disclosed the deception. His most likely confidant would have been Daniel Jones, his closest friend from their Grammar School days. But if Jones knew, he would hardly have included the poem in the collection. It was removed from a subsequent edition and replaced by the verse about the dog.

A month after 'His Requiem', the *Boy's Own Paper* published 'The second best', which was light verse with an attempt at a serious message: remember life's failures. On 28 July the *Western Mail* printed 'If the Gods had but given', signed 'Dylan Morlais', a mis-spelling of 'Marlais'. It is thirty lines long; presumably this time it was Thomas's own work:

> If the Gods had but given me one long day,
> From fresh of the morning to stars at night,
> With never a glance at the clock to say
> The moments are slipping, farewell's in sight...

By now the school magazine had printed a third poem, 'The Watchers', a competent parody or imitation of Sir Henry Newbolt's patriotic verse; and by 1928, when he was thirteen, Thomas's poems were appearing there regularly, as they did throughout the rest of his time at the school. Some, the least successful, were 'serious', some were 'humorous'. By 1930 he was writing poems of a different kind altogether. But for the moment these stayed in exercise books that he kept in his bedroom.

As a student, Thomas is said to have been ludicrously bad at every subject except English. The accounts may have been exaggerated to suit the legend. His father was anxious for him to go to university, and the man who was a martinet at school can't have put aside his sternness when it came to his own son. Eventually they agreed to differ with a remarkable absence of bitterness. But D.J. was still capable of being angry and disappointed at his son's exam performances when he was in the upper part of the school. It is unlikely that in his first two or three years at the Grammar School, Dylan was as undisciplined and contemptuous of the curriculum as he became in the end. As

an adult he was often unhappy in the presence of clever academics. He rejected a formal education, probably with misgivings
at first, and with traces of regret afterwards. Later he wrote of
'the kind of mock self-deprecating writers who always boast that
they were boobs at school; that their place in the form was always
black-marked bottom ... Neither particularly subtle or honest, I
must say I was awful. Whether this was because of stupidity or
arrogance, I am still not asking myself.' His real education, he
added, consisted of 'the liberty to read whatever I cared to'
among his father's books.

His progress towards schoolboy anarchy was not impeded as
it might have been at a stricter school. The headmaster, Trevor
Owen, was a big, genial man with a booming voice and a mild
speech defect that boys would imitate, just below hearing level.
The school was permissive for those days, even lax. Owen was
popular with the staff and the four hundred or so pupils. He
rarely used the cane, and is said to have gone out of his way not
to embarrass boys with sarcasm, unlike D. J. Thomas, whose
tongue was always ready to inflict punishment. He is remembered
standing at the door as the boys pour in, shouting 'Take your
time!' and being swept aside. In one version of a school anecdote,
he catches Dylan Thomas sneaking off the premises. 'Where are
you going?' he asks. Thomas says he is taking a few hours off.
'Well, I hope you get caught,' replies Owen. In another version,
the head catches him hiding in a bush in the 'Lower', a grassy
sub-playground below the school.

Headmaster: 'What are you doing?'

Thomas: 'Playing truant, sir.'

Headmaster: 'Well, don't let your father catch you.'

Thomas was protected by being his father's son. J. Morgan
Williams said that 'Dylan took advantage of the fact that his
father was a master. No question.' Williams taught him Latin in
his first year, in Form 3A. At the beginning of a lesson he would
say, 'Hands up the boys who haven't done their homework.' On
one occasion he found that 'Dylan hadn't put his hand up and
he hadn't done his homework either. So I gave him a clip.' He
mentioned it to another master, who said, 'Look out, you'll have
Jack after you.' It was months before D.J. referred to it, and then
he said he wished others had done the same. But it remained a
situation that Dylan could exploit, as he exploited his mother's

anxiety about his health. 'I cut my knee with a penknife,' he wrote in 'The Peaches', 'and put the blood on my handkerchief and said it had come out of my ears so that I could pretend I was ill and frighten my mother.' Mrs Thomas was always ready to be frightened. She told Ethel Ross in 1954, 'Dylan used to get asthma very badly as a little boy. If one of the masters spoke sharply to him at the Grammar School he'd come home gasping in the middle of it. So they knew that if they checked him he'd be home for a week with a bad attack. In the end no one checked him and he got away with everything ... As a child he would collapse while he played with his toys. Often I'd find him lying on the rug. He suffered from acute anaemia...'

Gwevril Dawkins, who knew the family well, said that had he been anyone else, the school would have expelled him. The trouble was not only his work or lack of it. There was a rumour of thieving. As far as Nancy was concerned it was more than a rumour. Later, when her girl friends came to the house to tea, she warned them not to leave their handbags upstairs with their coats because they were not safe from her brother. A pound note once vanished from a girl's purse. It didn't seem much of a crime to Dylan: nothing involving property ever did. 'I stole from my mother's bag; I stole from Gwyneth's bag,' he wrote in 'The Peaches', carefully listing the thefts along with the other peccadilloes, drinking his urine to see what it tasted like and looking through the keyhole with Dan Jones while the Joneses' maid took a bath.

From now on there is no shortage of stories reporting minor larceny and miscellaneous wickedness. Like many anecdotes about the famous, they can be used for laughing at or being scandalised by, depending on one's degree of sympathy with the subject. In the Uplands he is seen in Mrs Ferguson's sweet shop, waiting till she goes into the back room to get the lemonade, then plunging his hands into the box of wine gums – 'He was a bugger for wine gums,' said a friend. He could be found filing farthings to use as sixpenny bits in cigarette slot machines – 'I wouldn't say he was alone in this, but let's say he had a better supply of filed farthings than anyone else.'* He impressed his

---

* The same friend, Raymond Mitchell, said that Dylan also made money for the gang by writing 'cheap love stories' for the *Happy Mag*. Nothing signed by

neighbourhood gang by collecting for Dr Barnardo's with a box that was then broken open and the money taken for trips to the Uplands cinema, the local fleapit, where he lounged in the broken plush seats, puffing cigarettes and sometimes cigars. A school friend wrote later that 'the parents of the rest of us regarded him as a bad boy'. He was acquiring a reputation.

His bad language was noticeable, even by other boys. People who saw Cwmdonkin Drive from the inside said they knew where he got it from – his father, who swore and shouted when he lost his temper, usually as a result of something Florence said or did. He used to make fun of her less-than-perfect 'Swansea Welsh', so she didn't speak it in his presence. In later years she recalled it without apparent bitterness; she survived worse wounds than that. Mrs Dawkins remembered her as 'the hen-pecked wife of an intellectual. We'd all be sitting having tea, quite happily, but if she made some remark he considered intellectually puerile, he'd start shouting and yelling and swearing. He used to be extremely rude to Mrs Thomas, and as a result, Dylan became rude to her, and then to Nancy, and Nancy's friends.'

But Dylan continued to win people over with his charm. He could be almost excessively polite when he chose; he said such funny things; he looked so nice. Despite his frail appearance, he enjoyed normal out-of-door recreations. He played cricket, a game to which he remained loyal. Cwmdonkin Park was always there for his games, organised and otherwise. In 'Return Journey', Thomas's radio script about Swansea, it is the empty park in the snow, where the park-keeper remembers the boy who used to 'climb the reservoir railings and pelt the old swans. Run like a billygoat over the grass you should keep off of.' It was another of Thomas's vanished lands. In real Swansea the park-keeper was 'old Smalley', a council employee called Smallcombe. He is the keeper of the poem 'The hunchback in the park', with his stick for picking up leaves. Dylan took pleasure in raising his blood pressure. Once, enraged by some horseplay, the keeper flung the spiked stick and drew blood from Dylan's ankle. Old men remembered Smallcombe, shouting through the trees.

Thomas took part in the Grammar School sports. In his first

Thomas seems to have appeared there between 1926 and 1930, the most likely period. Lillian Gard ('His Requiem') was a contributor.

summer term, in June 1926, he won the one-mile race for under-fifteens. Because of his size he was given a handicap of a hundred yards. Local newspapers reported the event, and Thomas is said to have carried a cutting in his wallet all his life. One report headlined him as 'Smallest Competitor'. In a newspaper photograph he is thin-shouldered with skinny arms. His face is gentle and large-eyed: the child who has to prove himself against bigger boys. He ran successfully in school races and the cross-country for years.

He was always prone to do violence to himself. His nose was broken at an early age when he fell over or through the banisters at a neighbour's house while jeering at a small friend; it was never the same again. He fell over a high wall and knocked himself out, while being chased from an orchard with a gang of boys. Not long after his Sports Day victory he collided with a van while bicycling to a regatta at the Mumbles. His right wrist was broken, foreshadowing a lifetime of fractures; what Caitlin called his 'chicken bones' were always cracking. Mrs Thomas was terrified; she told neighbours that she feared for his life. Soon he was back on form, having oranges and lemonade smuggled into the hospital by other boys. (One day a concealed bottle burst under the bedclothes and cut his leg.) But, sure enough, the bones took a long time to knit, and he was there for almost a month.

Occasionally there were camping holidays in Gower. Thomas's account of camping at Rhossili, at the end of the peninsula, in the story 'Extraordinary Little Cough', is true in most of its details, down to a party of older girls in a tent near by, and the records of *No, No, Nanette* that the boys played on a clockwork gramophone. Even Brazell and Skully, the school bullies, who appear and steal the girls, were real. ('We hear great things of Brazel [*sic*] and his goal-kicking,' reported the school magazine.) Thomas is in the story as himself, but George Hooping, known as Little Cough, also has traces of his character. To prove he can do it, Little Cough runs the miles of Rhossili sands before collapsing by the camp fire – 'And when I stared round at George again he was lying on his back fast asleep in the deep grass and his hair was touching the flames.' John Bennett, who was one of the campers on those green cliffs, said that Dylan ran the length of the beach more than once. Each morning began with a walk to the post office to see if anyone's mother had sent him a postal order. Once they had only porridge left to eat all day. 'But it never rained,' said Bennett.

Dylan Thomas was never short of friends, but those he made in Swansea stayed in a special category all his life. The first and most important of these was Dr Daniel Jenkyn Jones. A professional composer who remained in Swansea (he was a doctor of music), Daniel Jones rather than Dylan Thomas was generally thought to be the boy with the shining future. He wrote poetry as well as music, and played the piano and other instruments. His family was more broadly cultural than Thomas's; but the real importance of their meeting, which is described in the *Portrait* story 'The Fight', was that it provided Thomas with a clever, arrogant friend who could be audience, critic and collaborator. Jones was the elder by two years. Their inaugural fight took place in the 'Lower' playground, and for the next eight or nine years they were in and out of one another's houses. The Jones family lived a mile away, in Sketty, in a more comfortably bourgeois house called Warmley. There, and less frequently in Cwmdonkin Drive, they wrote joint poems and plays, organised joke concerts, played with words and generally egged one another on to be cleverer or funnier or noisier or bolder. On their first evening at Warmley, according to 'The Fight', Thomas read poems from an exercise book while Jones, bespectacled, 'like a boy aged a hundred', listened in silence. 'Nobody had ever listened like that before ... The future spread out beyond the window, over Singleton Park crowded with lovers messing about, and into smoky London paved with poems.' Their friendship had something magical about it for Thomas, perhaps for Jones as well. It also had practical significance. The private self that Thomas was to explore in his mature poetry was territory to be entered alone, but the process of acquiring skills and trying out ideas might have been less effective and less entertaining without Jones's companionship.

For their poetry collaborations they invented a lunatic name for themselves, Walter Bram; 'bram' is Welsh for 'fart'. Many of the Bram notebooks and sheets, some of them the blank sides of gramophone price lists, have found their way to the University of Texas. One of them has a date, 27 December 1929; Thomas was then fifteen. Jones wrote that these poems, of which about two hundred survive, were 'serious play' and sometimes 'very,

very beautiful; very'.* He wrote the odd-numbered lines, Thomas the even lines. Jones has quoted from one poem:

> They had come from the place high on the coral hills
> Where the light from the white sea fills the soil with ascending
> grace.
> And the sound of their power makes motion as steep as the sky,
> And the fruits of the great ground lie like leaves from a vertical
> flower.
> They had come from the place; they had come and gone again
> In a season of delicate rain, in a smooth ascension of grace.

The Texas collection has many more poems, some of them no more than jingles, others achieving their effect by violent juxtaposition. Jones writes: 'Little body: long tail: animal of Heaven: frail comet!' Thomas supplies: 'I love naked women.' Some of Thomas's lines, in particular, have touches of surrealism, as if the images came unprocessed from his subconscious. One poem, with Thomas writing lines 2 and 4, reads:

> A coin burns my hand, and the street is dark:
> You are propped at every bending lamp, like flimsy dolls, dreaming,
> with rotten lips,
> A robe coiled, rent and heaving:
> I am dreaming, with thoughts like shining fish in a silver sea: and
> you, with lips and skin that will wither, and pass.

John Bennett, the Rhossili camper, who was more friendly with Jones than with Thomas, remembered the big upper-floor drawing room at Warmley, with 'violins, violas, cellos and a beautiful piano. Sometimes I would scrape a violin, and Dylan would place one across his knees and draw the bow across the strings, producing sounds utterly beyond bearing, whereupon

* According to Jones, introducing his edition of *The Poems*, some of the collaborations have 'created a trap into which many students of his work, including commentators and bibliographers, have fallen'. This was hardly surprising when Dr Jones (who was himself caught out by the unfortunate 'His Requiem' in *The Poems*) remained close-lipped. Three or four of the poems printed above the initials 'D.M.T.' in the Grammar School magazines were apparently jointly written.

Danny would seize a cello, and play in a higher register, which seemed to be the criterion of excellence, as far as we were concerned.' To Bennett, 'Dylan did not appear remarkable to me for his poetry, but rather for his long-distance running. Dr Jones seemed to be (and indeed in my opinion was) a giant, intellectually, whereas Dylan seemed to be a somewhat feckless but very likeable person.' Jones had stature; Dylan was inclined to be a clown, a joker. Once Mrs Jones left some fresh figs in the room. As Thomas bit into the flesh-coloured fruit he said, 'God, it's like chewing a girl's cunt.' There were people in Swansea to whom a remark like that conjured up the 'real' Thomas they knew when young; Thomas the Poet made them frown, as if it was something that happened behind their backs, when they weren't looking.

In Warmley, Thomas was at home. He seems to have found much satisfaction in the fantasy world that he and Jones created. One of their elaborate jokes when they were teenagers was the 'Warmley Broadcasting Company', using loudspeakers to transmit programmes from one room to another. They invented grotesque characters and episodes. A manuscript in Thomas's hand begins: 'WBC (Warmley Broadcasting Company). Founded in November 1932 by Daniel Hautboy Jones and Dylan Moreorless Thomas, acting upon the suggestions of Tom (Tiptoes) Warner, advisory mechanician.' (Warner, another friend who became a schoolteacher, was friendly with them both.) Thomas was eighteen, already a serious and accomplished poet, though it is doubtful if anyone knew it, except perhaps Daniel Jones.

On this unique occasion [says the script] the *Very Rev. Percy*, patron and president of the WBC, has consented to play his most recent pianoforte composition, 'Buzzards at Dinner', which was written on the aged minister's last seal-hunting expedition. It is interesting to note that the piece was written with a piece of blubber on a block of ice. Unfortunately the ice melted beneath the rays of the midnight sun, and tonight, ladies & gentlemen, he is therefore forced to play another of his recent compositions, 'Badgers Beneath My Vest'. This piece was written by the Rev. Percy when he was in the Zoological Gardens, Old Kentucky. He scribbled the music with an old hat on the back of a passing walrus. The walrus then ran away and, owing to his great age, the rev. gentleman was unable to catch him. 'Badgers

Beneath My Vest' is therefore lost to posterity. The aged gentleman will therefore play 'Salute to Admiral Beatty' . . .

Thomas and Jones, looking over Swansea from suburban windows, surveyed their future and mapped out their lives. How much their friendship, their fantasies and Swansea itself meant to Thomas is spelt out in a sad, sentimental letter he wrote to Jones from Ireland later still, in August 1935. It begins with the injunction that it should be read 'either late at night or when at least *half* tipsy', and says it is 'the first long letter I've ever written to you'. Thomas, whose book of *18 Poems* was already making his name, was writing the letter in memoriam for the 'WARM-DANDYLANLEY-WORLD' as he calls it, with its puns and jokes and fancies. By now both were living in London – Jones had settled in Harrow. The past was fading; Thomas couldn't bear to see it go. There is no 'Dear Dan':

I'm not much good at writing letters. I can't strike the, if I may coin a phrase, happy medium between trying to be funny, not trying to be funny, and trying not to be funny. I can't write as I talk – thank God I can't talk as I write, either – and I get highflown and flyblown and highblown and flyfalutin if I try very consciously not to be self-conscious. Take me as I come – sounds like Onan – and remember the dear dead days that had to have a gallon or two of nonsense (often awfully good nonsense) ... I never can believe that the Warmley days are over – ('just a song at twilight when the lights Marlowe and the Flecker Beddoes Bailey Donne and Poe') – that there should be no more twittering, no more nose-on-window-pressing and howling at the streets, no more walks with vampire cries, and standing over the world, no more hold-a-writing-table for the longest, and wrong adjectives; I can't believe that Percy, who droppeth gently, can have dropped out of the world, that the 'Badger Beneath My Vest' and 'Homage to Admiral Beatty' are a song and a boat of the past; that Miguel-y-Bradshaw, Waldo Carpet, Xmas Pulpit, Paul America, Winter Vaux, Tonenbach, and Bram, all that miscellaneous colony of geniuses, our little men, can have died on us; that the one-legged grandmother – remember the panama-hat-shaped birds, from the Suez Canal, who pecked at her atlas-bone – doesn't still take photographs of Birmingham; that the queer, Swansea world, a world, thank Christ that was self-sufficient, can't stand on its bow legs in a smoky city full of snobs and quacks. I'm surer of nothing than that that world, Percy's world in Warmley, was, and still is, the only one that has any claims to permanence; I mean that this long, out-of-doored world isn't much good really, that it's only the setting, is only supposed to be the setting, for a world of your own – in our cases, a world of our own – from which we can interpret nearly everything that's worth. And the only world worth is the world of our own that has its independent people, people like Percy, so much, much more real than your father or my mother ... places and things and qualities and standards, and symbols much bigger than the exterior solidities, all of its own. Didn't we work better, weren't poems and music better, weren't we happier in being unhappy, out of that world, than in – not even out of – this unlocal, uncentral world where the pubs are bad and the people are sly and the only places to go are the places to go to? I think it is the same with you, though it's so long since I've seen you, dry months, too, that you may be, though you couldn't be, all different, all older, in your cat's lights more learned, even Harrowed to some sort of contentment, never regretting for one moment the almost-going of Percy's celestial circle. No, that couldn't be; that world *does* remain, in spite of London, the Academy, and a tuppenny, half-highbrow success. I never thought that localities meant so much, nor the genius of places, nor anything like that. I thought that the soul went round like a Gladstone bag, never caring a damn for any particular station-rack or hotel-cloakroom; that gestures and genius made the same gestures in Cockett and Cockfosters; didn't we look at our geniuses and say, 'We're taking you somewhere else to live, but we won't part.' I placed my hand upon my heart and said that we would never part; I wonder what I would have said had I placed it on my head. So on and on; like an unborn child in the city I want to get born and go to the outskirts. Here in Ireland I'm further away than ever from the permanent world, the one real world in a house or a room, very much peopled, with the exterior, wrong world – wrong because it's never understood out of the interior world – looking in through the windows. This sort of nostalgia isn't escapist by any means, you know that; just as the only politics for a conscientious artist – that's you and me – must be left-wing under a right-wing government, communist *under* capitalism, so the only world for that WARMDANDYLANLEY-MAN must be the WARMDANDYLANLEY-WORLD under the world-of-the-others. How could it be escapism? It's the only contact there is between yourself and yourselves, what's social in you and what isn't – though, God knows, I could shake Bram's intangible hand as seriously as the hand of Dean Inge, and with far greater sense of reality. Even surrealism, which seemed to have hopes and promise, preaches the decay of reality and the importance, and eventual dominance, (I don't like those words however much I try to look on them coldly), of unreality, as though the two could be put in two boxes: isn't Percy flesh, bone, and blood, isn't Evangeline Booth a shadow, isn't Percy a shadow, isn't Evangeline flesh, bone, & blood, isn't Percy flesh-bone-& blood-shadow, isn't Evangeline flesh-bone-and-blood-shadow, isn't Percy-Evangeline flesh bone and blood? – and so on and on. I'm not going to read this letter over afterwards to see what it reads like; let it go on, that's all; you don't mind the dashes and the hyphens and the bits of dogma and the brackets and the bits of dog-eaten self-consciousness and the sentimentality because I'm writing by candlelight all alone in a cottage facing the Atlantic. From the WARMDANDYLANLEY-WORLD I'd no more think of writing this letter than of using words like 'Proust' and 'flounce' and 'akimbo' and 'schedule' and 'urge' when talking in that W-W; I wouldn't have or need to; this is only covering old ground in words and phrases and thoughts and idioms that are all part of that world; it's only because, now, here in this terribly out-of-the-way and lonely place, I feel the need for that world, the necessity for its going on, and the fear that it might be dying to you, that I'm trying to resurrect my bit of it, and make you realise again what you realise already; the importance of that world because it's the only one, the importance of us, too, and the fact that our poems and music won't and can't be anything without it. Soon I'm going out for a walk in the dark by myself; that'll make me happy as hell; I'll think of the almost-but-never-going-gone, and remember the cries of the Bulgarian scouts as I hear that damned sea rolling, and remember the first world ... as I stand under an absurdly high hill – much too high, our world has its hills just the proper, the *nice* length (I'm arching my index-finger & thumb and joining them tastefully) – and shout to it, 'Go on, you big shit, WARMDANDYLANLEY-WORLD has a hill twice as beautiful and with a ribbon and bell on it, & a piece of boiled string on the top, if the WARMDANDYLANLEY-MAN wants it like that' ... We must, when our affairs are settled, when music and poetry are arranged so that we can still live, love and drink beer, go back to Uplands or Sketty and found there, for good and for all, a permanent colony; living there until we are old gentlemen, with occasional visits to London and Paris, we shall lead the lives of small-town anti-society, and entertain any of the other members of the WARMDANDYLANLEY-WORLD who happen to visit the town ... So Jones and Thomas, that well known firm of family provisioners, shall not move out of their town. So be it.

Jones had an overbearing nature that must have complemented Thomas's softer, more devious character; Thomas was never in any doubt about the traits that made his friend a difficult man to get on with. In a letter he wrote from the same cottage in Ireland to another correspondent, Thomas dwelt on Dan Jones's cleverness and erudition, adding that 'He's a prig, a snob, & a boor, but I like him.'

This letter, and the account of his friendship with Jones, has gone ahead of the story, through and beyond Thomas's adolescence in Swansea. These were the most important years of his life. During them he completed his education, such as it was, left school, worked on a newspaper, learned to drink, had (perhaps) his first sexual encounters; and wrote several hundred poems that survive, and probably several hundred more that do not. From the age of thirteen or fourteen there is an increasing amount of verse to look at. At first they are school-magazine poems. Thomas tried a variety of styles.

> Her garden blooms with iris, and it seems
> The moons are white flames, like the moons in dreams

he wrote in December 1928, no doubt in imitation of the Imagists who were fashionable at the time. In general his poems were straightforward, although the magazine editor once challenged a line. This was in 'Idylls of Unforgetfulness' (February 1929), which began:

> To have seen countries which were glorious,
> Immutable and finely dun like secret suns;
> To have known them in their blue-hued valiance,
> Felt their serenity of ripple-woven loveliness...

The editor, E. F. McInerny, said he found the second line incomprehensible. Thomas obligingly offered to change it to 'Immutable and ardurously consecrated'. This seems no clearer, but was accepted and appeared in print. Thomas was capable of writing simple but accomplished lyrics. Daniel Jones has printed six poems from manuscripts in his possession, all dated 1929. This is 'The Elm':

> They are all goddesses;
> Nodding like flowers,
> They are further and more delicate
> Than the years that dwindle;
> They are deeper in darkness
> Than the hours.
>
> Celestial,
> Slenderly lethal things,
> Beautifully little like clouds:
> Leaf driftwood that has blown.

'The Elm' is an improvement on most of his magazine verse at the time. It may be that the editors (although he was one himself by the end of 1929) had idiosyncratic ideas of what constituted a poem. His desire to please was perhaps the reason behind a second attempt at plagiarism, in 1929. McInerny received a short poem from Thomas. He found it suitable for the magazine, but his co-editor, H. M. V. Thomas, thought it sounded familiar. It was traced to Arthur Mee's *Children's Encyclopaedia*, Volume 8, page 5669, where it is one of the 'Thousand Poems of All Times and All Countries'. The author was an American with a Welsh name, Thomas S. Jones. It is called 'Sometimes':

> Across the fields of yesterday
> He sometimes comes to me,
> A little lad just back from play,
> The lad I used to be.
>
> And yet he smiles so wistfully
> Once he has crept within;
> I wonder if he hopes to see
> The man I might have been?

Once again, it seems not to have been worth the trouble for someone who could do so much better himself. D. J. Thomas was told, and McInerny reported him as saying, 'After this, everything he writes is suspect.' McInerny said nothing to Dylan, and as far as he was concerned the matter was forgotten. At the time he assumed it to be plagiarism; Thomas didn't protest his innocence. Later McInerny thought charitably that it might have been an example of 'unconscious recall', an opinion he changed again when he heard of the *Western Mail* episode. He concluded that Dylan was 'in an anti-social, devil-may-care mood, like a secret agent fingering a false and superfluous moustache'. It could have been one of Thomas's pointless untruths, another attempt to cover his tracks: a habit that amounted to a compulsion. He wrote in 'The Fight': 'If I lost my cap and found it in my bedroom, and my mother asked me where I had found it, I would say, "In the attic," or, "Under the hall stand." It was exciting to have to keep wary all the time in case I contradicted myself ...' Or it could have been that other compulsion, to prove himself at all costs; in which case every little helped.

From 1930, the prime source of early Thomas is a series of four so-called notebooks – in fact they are students' exercise books – which begins in April that year, and covers, though not entirely, the next four years. They are owned by the State University of New York at Buffalo, which bought them for a few pounds one day when Thomas was more than usually hard up. At least one notebook, and probably several others, no longer exist, or are being kept well concealed by their owners. At the start of the '1930 Notebook', Thomas has written 'Mainly free verse poems'. The first poem in it is dated 27 April. It is called 'Osiris, Come to Isis', and uses Egyptian mythology to make some shaky pronouncements about love. A number of his poems that spring take love as their subject, including one that makes the familiar poetic plea for something more than sex – 'Your breasts and thighs and navel are not enough,' writes Thomas, implying that he is acquainted with such things.

He was fifteen years old, and apparently doomed to spend still more time at school. Some of these awkward, fumbling poems have a sharp sense of the uncertain boy standing still, not knowing which way to go. Can he dare to act, to move, to fly? It is the problem of what to do with his life and what to do with his poetry; each is bound up with the other. When he took this uncertainty as the subject for a poem, the writing became noticeably terse. In a poem that begins, 'No, pigeon, I'm too wise' (8 August 1930) he wrote that 'I'm not secure enough/To tell what note I could reach if I tried' and concluded:

> I'm all for ground,
> To touch what's to be touched,
> To imitate myself mechanically,
> Doing my little tricks of speech again
> With all my usual care.
> No bird for me:
> He flies too high.

Thomas seemed to be looking for a directness, a boldness, in his attitude. 'I want reality to hold within my palm,' he declared, in a poem whose first line hints at the violence that was soon to break into his writing, 'I know this vicious minute's hour' (November 1930). He was torn between the alternatives of going and staying. 'I go or die,' he concluded, none too confidently.

Anyone reading the poems at the time might have assumed that young Thomas was striking a pose when he wrote like this. Perhaps he was, to some extent. Like most adolescents he was preoccupied with girls, death, and what, if anything, 'life' meant. He had a streak of timidity that made him afraid to fail and anxious to prove he could succeed. He also knew about the attitudes that writers in general and poets in particular take to life's problems. In his father's study he had read 'indiscriminately, and with my eyes hanging out'. He once listed the models for his early writing: 'Sir Thomas Browne, de Quincey, Henry Newbolt, the Ballads, Blake, Baroness Orczy, Marlowe, Chums, the Imagists, the Bible, Poe, Keats, Lawrence, Anon., and Shakespeare.' When he wrote about 'Your sweet inducive thighs/And raven hair', or presented himself as the unhappy lover watching a dancer –

> I, poor romantic, held her heel
> Upon the island of my palm

– he was borrowing other people's language. When it came to questioning the purpose of his life and his poems, he would have found innumerable examples in his father's books. No doubt he had poetry on the brain. The previous year he contributed a thoughtful survey of modern verse to the school magazine which dwelt on the unsettling effects of the First World War, still only a decade away – 'No poet can find sure ground; he is hunting for it, with the whole earth perturbed and unsettled about him.' Aged fifteen, he was learning the literary ropes.

But it was more than that. The poet of that first notebook – it ends in December 1930, not long after Thomas's sixteenth birthday – was carried away by his convictions. If he took up a poetic posture it was not because he was following other poets – or if he was, the pose was becoming the reality. At the end of the last poem in the notebook, 9 December 1930, he was once more questioning his function as a poet, but at the same time asserting his talent:

> Purpose is gone;
> I try to hold, but can't,
> Compress, inflate, grow old,
> With all the tackle of my certain magic
> Stone hard to lift.

The feeling that he had a vocation was probably both cause and effect of his failure at school. The more he thought about himself as a poet, the less attention he paid to work; the worse his prospects of passing examinations, the more attractive the prospects of being a poet. The year before, 1929, at the end of the summer term, he had sat the Central Welsh Board examination for a school-leaving certificate, with disastrous results. The normal course for a bright boy would have been to pass his 'CWB' in the correct mix of subjects to satisfy university entrance requirements, then to move up to the sixth form for two years or longer, until he was old enough for university. Dylan failed altogether, allegedly floundering in every subject except English language (no records survive of pupils who didn't reach the minimum standard for a school certificate). Gwevril Dawkins was at Cwmdonkin Drive the day Dylan sat the history paper. For some of the other papers he had stayed only long enough in the examination room to know that all was lost. This time he lasted the course, and told his father that he had written twenty-two foolscap sheets. D.J. was anxious to learn what his son had had to say about Tudor England, which was in that year's syllabus. Dylan replied that he had written twenty-two pages about the French Revolution. 'D.J. was hopping mad,' said Mrs Dawkins. 'He was hitting the roof, calling Dylan a dolt and a donkey, asking what the hell he knew about the French Revolution. "I don't know anything," said Dylan. "I wrote about why it shouldn't have happened." '

It is possible that he attempted the CWB the following summer, 1930. Whether he did, or not, he languished at school for a further year, but it seems unlikely that D.J. gave up without a fight. Dylan probably found his health a useful defence. Mrs Thomas once spoke of a 'rather bad haemorrhage' when Dylan was fifteen, implying a chest haemorrhage. On another occasion she recalled that 'Dylan had a breakdown when he was sitting his CWB at sixteen, and we had to send him down to a farm at Cardigan'. If she remembered the age correctly, this would put the breakdown in 1931.*

Outwardly he was leading an aimless life. For his last year, 1930–31, he moved into the Lower Sixth. Charles Fisher, a friend, remembered him that year 'in the prefects' room, where he would sit before a coal fire boring holes in the floor with a poker'. His mood may be echoed in the story 'Just Like Little Dogs', where he stands under a railway arch opening on to Swansea sands, and two brothers talk to him about their sexual affairs. They wear working-class caps and have the air of the unemployed. All three have nothing better to do than stand 'looking at the miles of sands, long and dirty in the early dark'. Thomas, a 'lonely night-walker and a steady stander-at-corners', tells them he is there because 'I've got nothing to do when I'm in and I don't want to go to bed'. At the end of the story he runs home; a sentence deleted from the original manuscript read, 'A clock struck one. There'd be hell to pay now', which seems to confirm that he is still a schoolboy.

---

* Mrs Thomas insisted (wrongly) in later years that Dylan was a year younger than everyone assumed – that he was born in October 1915, not 1914. She said that he added a year 'because he wanted to seem older'.

In a letter of December 1930, written from that prefects' room to his friend Percy Smart, he is the world-weary young man, aged sixteen. Smart, two years older, had left the school to work in a bank in London. He and Thomas were joint editors of the magazine until July 1930; thereafter Thomas did the job alone until he left school. The first of Thomas's letters to survive (except for a verse letter to his sister), it acknowledges a piece that Smart has sent him – 'I am not altogether sorry you refrained from writing on the joys and sorrows of early banking life' – then slips comfortably into cynicism.

We all have our troubles (!), and very few of us want to increase them. Even that third-former, who is running along the corridor now, has probably an inherent cancer, or a mind full of lechery. The child grows from the cradle, soaked in a morbidity and restlessness he cannot understand, does a little painful loving, fails to make money, builds his life on sand, and is struck down before he can accomplish anything. Is it worth me lifting up my pen to write? Is anything worth anything? It is in moments like this that I emphatically reply 'no'. Very striking and all that. I can hear you in your suburban lodgings laughing at my theatrical gestures. [?Every] in the room look up because I am laughing at them, too. 'What's the latest story?' they ask me. I tell them.

The notebooks show a different face, darker and more consequential. They give little support, though, to the legend of Thomas the inspired boy-poet, pumping out words in a frenzy. They are not easy poems. They are often difficult to follow, sometimes incomprehensible. But the difficulties arise because they are so intensely worked out. Writing verse seemed to be a hard discipline for Thomas. He was the would-be poet in search of a subject. When he found it momentarily, the language changed: the lines hardened, the words acquired an edge. That subject was himself, the secret Thomas that only Thomas knew about. A continuity that would last all his life was already established.

> Classic, erotic, and obscene,
> Dead and alive,
> In sleep and out of sleep,

> Tracking my sensibilities,
> Gratifying my sensualities...

The next poem (the one of 9 December 1930) began

> How shall the animal
> Whose way I trace
> Into the dark recesses,
> Be durable
> Under such weight as bows me down...

Eight years later this became the germ of a published poem, 'How shall my animal', the first notebook poem directly linked to successful publication. Soon there were other forerunners. Notebook 2, which begins in December 1930, again headed 'Mainly free verse poems', has 'Today, this hour I breathe' as its second entry, dated 18 December. Later this was to be revised, thickened and made more difficult to follow as 'Today, this insect, and the world I breathe'. The original version made at least one direct and characteristically sceptical statement:

> I have divided
> Sense into sight and trust.
> The certain is a fable.

And in 'The spire cranes' (27 January 1931), Thomas looks at the poet's situation, in a version that resembles the form in which it was eventually printed in 1938.

In some of the poems, Thomas began to use the harsher words and images that were typical of his mature verse. In the more softly romantic pieces it was still 'my golden bird the sun' or 'the rainbow's shy embrace'. But as his days as a schoolboy-poet came to an end, there was an occasional flurry of biological words: *grains*, *blood*, *seed*, *sucking*, *dust*, *wax*, *cancer*, *egg*. The effect was not sustained; on the whole they were the fragmentary poems of an adolescent trying to come to terms with his world. In a poem copied into the notebook on 6 April 1931, he snarled at love in four of its lines whose style was edging towards the 'authentic' Thomas:

Where love is there's a crust of joy
To hide what drags its belly from the egg,
And, on the ground, gyrates as easily
As though the sun were spinning up through it.

For the moment, nothing happened to these poems. They were fair copies, obviously transcribed from whatever sheets once held the original drafts, although heavily corrected in places. Once they were written they stayed in the exercise books, except for two short pieces, dated December 1930, which were printed in the school magazine the following year as 'Two Images'. One is the poem that contains the phrase 'my golden bird the sun'; against them in the margin of the exercise book, Thomas has written 'Ugh' and 'Ogh' to show what he thought of them later. The style of poetry he began to write in was not suitable for the school magazine, or for any other journal that he might have been bold enough to approach. London and its literary magazines must have seemed a long way off. He might have been a boy writing verses in the middle of the desert. Culture, in those days, was metropolitan, and regional Britain was not a fashionable breeding ground for writers and painters. He was working in the dark. In the summer of 1931, and for a year or so after, he was planning to produce a magazine called 'Prose & Verse' as a vehicle for young authors, especially himself. Percy Smart and another friend, a clerk with literary ambitions called Trevor Hughes, were drawn into the scheme, which depended on guaranteed subscriptions. Thomas managed to touch the Grammar School's new headmaster, J. Grey Morgans, for ten shillings. Nothing came of it.

Most of his writing must have been done in Cwmdonkin Drive, either in D.J.'s study or in the 'bedroom by the boiler', as he implies in the *Portrait* stories. Two years later he was telling Pamela Hansford Johnson that he wrote at the rate of two lines an hour. The first notebooks show an average of a poem a week, but companion sets of rhymed poems may have been accumulating in other notebooks. Five such poems are quoted in 'The Fight'.* For Thomas, writing poetry was a major activity,

---

* These poems sound as if they were written when Thomas was fifteen or sixteen, rather than several years earlier, as 'The Fight' implies. They appear

the most important thing he did. The notebooks show a neurotic energy accumulating; it is like a storm building up. But apart from his friendship with Jones, and possibly with one or two others, the real poems remained a private activity. In the school magazine (of which he was now sole editor) he appeared as the author of amusing verse and a de la Mare-like ghost story, as Hon. Sec. of the Debating Society ('The first subject chosen was "That the modern youth is decadent". D. M. Thomas took the affirmative') and co-founder of a Reading Circle for drama. As for his education, even a father who believed that study was the road to happiness must have realised by 1931 that Dylan was not teachable. He would leave school in the summer term. University was out of the question.

In the early summer, the note of urgent self-exploration is heard page after page. He is less plaintive, more resolute. On 1 June, in the second poem copied and perhaps written on that date, he found his tongue, and sustained the mood throughout. The subject was himself, the poet. He slid easily into a powerful sexual image of orgasm and its aftermath, of living and dying. The poem was not interested in white necks and raven hair. It was concerned exclusively with his own sexuality, his own nervous system:

> High on a hill,
> Straddle and soak,
> Out of the way of the eyes of men,
> Out of the way,
> Straddle her wrinkled knees
> Until the day's broken –
> Christ, let me write from the heart,
> War on the heart –
> Puff till the adder is,
> Breathe till the snake is home,
> Inch on the old thigh
> Till the bird has burst his shell,
> And the carnal stem that stood
> Blowing with the blood's ebb,

nowhere else. When Thomas wrote 'The Fight', about 1939, he presumably copied them from a notebook that is now lost.

> Is fallen down
> To the ground.

A few days later he was trying out what reads like a piece of automatic writing, a surrealist babble of words. But he continued, more or less, in the same single-minded direction. On 28 July he warned his non-existent readers that

> I shall turn the strongest stomach up
> With filth I gather
> From the thousand minds, all lust and wind,
> Like a beachcomber in the time of light.

But by that time he had shut his desk and handed in his books. The summer issue of the school magazine – the last that Thomas edited, though he was still writing for it as late as 1934 – contained his essay on 'The Sincerest Form of Flattery (A Literary Course)', parodying fashionable genres.

> The patriotic poem is still as popular as ever:
> A Flag! ah yes, a flag,
> Perchance a faded rag upon a stick...

The magazine says that term ended on 31 July 1931. Thomas was no longer there. He had gone to work on the local newspaper.

Chapter Four

REPORTER, ACTOR, POET

It is doubtful whether Dylan Thomas saw himself as an ace reporter, or as any kind of reporter at all. Although the journalist's trade had raffish characteristics that appealed to him, he showed no great interest in being an orthodox member of the reporters' room at the *South Wales Daily Post*, the Swansea evening newspaper (its title changed to *Evening Post* while he was there). But he can hardly have been as nonchalant as some of the accounts suggest; as in the case of the Grammar School, the legend has been at work, making him bold and comical too early. He was one of a small editorial staff. The *Post* could not afford specialist and feature writers, and reporters were expected to do a little of everything. Thomas was no exception; he was merely the latest recruit from the Grammar School, where the newspaper often found its young reporters and sub-editors. It is likely that the editor, an urbane local character called J. D. Williams, knew D. J. Thomas, and that it was his father who arranged the job, not Dylan. Mrs Thomas used to say that 'Daddy thought it would be a good opening for him'. Each morning she sent him off to work in a clean shirt and well-creased trousers.

At first he was not on the editorial staff. He began in the 'readers' room' of the printing department as a copy-holder, one of the juniors who (in the days before computer technology) read reporters' copy aloud in a droning voice, while their seniors, the 'correctors of the press', checked and amended the proofs. Thomas was too slow; a reader he worked for said he was 'inclined to dramatise everything'. After a couple of months he moved on to the reporters' room, and his brief career as a journalist began.* For a while he took shorthand lessons, to no

* Thomas apparently did some writing for the paper before he was officially a reporter. He probably wrote the account of an interview with Nellie Wallace, the music-hall star, which appeared in the *Daily Post* of 15 July 1931. Wynford Vaughan-Thomas remembered visiting Miss Wallace in her dressing room at the

purpose. From his own accounts, in the radio 'Return Journey', and a story called 'Old Garbo', he did the usual chores of a junior reporter, the 'calls' to hospital and fire station in search of news, the visits to the mortuary, the reports of concerts and chapel bazaars. An older colleague who sub-edited his copy said it was 'appalling, with many lacunae'. Funny stories of how he reported events that never took place, or failed to report events that did, are unlikely to have been funny at the time, assuming they ever happened. Even when he was established as a 'character', licensed to be as unreliable as he chose, Thomas would sometimes kick against his reputation. 'My selfish carelessness and unpunctuality I do not try to excuse as poet's properties,' he wrote to Henry Treece in 1938. 'They are a bugbear & a humbug.' If that was the truth, then his shortcomings as a reporter must have bothered him. One story which seems to be true is that he missed the death of the matron of Swansea Hospital, in February 1932. His mother said that 'somebody rang up the *Post* to ask why her death wasn't in the paper. He should have gone to the hospital to find out if there was any news. But he didn't go there that day.' In written reminiscences, Thomas smiled at his innocence as a reporter but said nothing about incompetence. In 'Old Garbo' the worst thing anyone accuses him of is 'platitudinous verbosity' in his report of an oratorio.

He wrote a series of five articles about 'The Poets of Swansea', an historical survey, for the *Herald of Wales*, the weekly companion-paper of the *Post*. He lingered on one tragi-comic figure, Llewelyn Prichard, a nineteenth-century actor, poet and hack writer with a wax nose who drank too much and died in obscurity in Swansea when his bed caught fire. The headline was 'A Figure Lost in Lies and Legends', and the article began: 'No one can deny that the most attractive figures in literature are always those around whom a world of lies and legends has been woven, those half mythical artists whose real characters become cloaked for ever under a veil of the bizarre.' The parallel was obvious. Thomas was already identifying himself with the likes of Prichard, cutting himself off from the local 'literary life', such as it was: 'Out of all the spinsters and thin-lipped amateurs spinning their little

Swansea Empire with his friend Dylan, who had 'just become a reporter on the local newspaper'.

webs of sound, the versifiers, linking cliché to cliché with metrical perfection, the bards and the old gentlemen; out of all the poetical products of a small town, Prichard stands out flaming and aloof against the horizon. He failed to be great, but he failed with genius.' That, if necessary, was the way Thomas intended to fail.

In a sixth article Thomas devoted himself to a living poet, a Swansea schoolmaster called Howard Harris, describing him cruelly as 'a small poet with large ambition'. Later J. D. Williams (who edited both newspapers) said that the whole series had given him 'dreadful pangs', and that it had been 'heartbreaking to give the right of way to an irreverent youth'. Thomas had to watch his step. Sent to review a chapel rendering of Longfellow's *Hiawatha* set to music, his copy damned poet, composer and performers; Williams was consulted and the sub-editors watered it down to make it fit to print. Thomas submitted a short story to the *Herald of Wales*. It ended with a head in a gas stove, hardly the thing for a weekly paper that kept reality for the news columns and liked to brighten up people's weekends with weddings and gossip. A gas stove would never have done – 'Laughingly we agreed that it would not,' wrote Williams.

The eighteen months or less that Thomas spent on the newspaper (the dates are not certain) taught him nothing he needed to know about writing but a great deal he wanted to know about growing up. At sixteen he could still look almost girlish. His thin body was crowned with curls; his eyes bulged, soft and melancholy. The dreamer with the haunted features was one of his poses in early photographs; the world-wise young sinner was to be another. With fellow reporters he developed a half-serious imitation of the American newshound, hat pulled down over his eyes and a cigarette that stayed in the mouth once it was lit; the dangling cigarette was a habit he kept all his life.

Acquaintances of the time retain bizarre images of Thomas the Poet-and-Reporter. Gwendolyn Courtney (then Gwendolyn Bevan) was the girlfriend of another *Post* reporter, Cliff Williams. One winter's afternoon Cliff and Gwendolyn set off for Parkmill, a Gower village. Dylan, uninvited, went along too – he had seen them meet in Swansea, and walked behind them to the bus. Mrs Courtney remembered his lips, 'yellow with over-smoking'. They had a beer in the Gower Inn and walked towards the sea, Dylan still in attendance. He was morose, because, he said, a manuscript had been rejected. The day was cold and blustery. When they reached the ruins of Pennard Castle, Thomas 'stood on the rampart, if you can call it a rampart, waving his trilby and shouting, "They are rejecting me now but the day will come when the name Dylan Thomas will be echoed from shore to shore. Only I won't be alive to hear it." ' Mrs Courtney thought it a ridiculous performance.

Manly drinking was another habit to be learned. The story of 'Old Garbo' concerns a drunken Saturday night out with Mr Farr, a senior reporter, followed by a remorseful Sunday afternoon in Cwmdonkin Park ('An article called "Our Lord Was a Flower-lover" moved me to tears of bewilderment and contrition'), followed by bravado in the office on Monday. Freddie Farr, who came to Swansea from another part of Wales in 1925, was a tough and skilful court reporter who also covered boxing. He was in his middle forties. In 'Old Garbo' he is a great shorthand-writer, heavy smoker, drinker of bitter beer, a humorist and a dandy gone to seed. His son said he was accurately described; he died soon after Thomas left the newspaper, despite the line near the end of 'Old Garbo', 'When I showed this story a long time later to Mr Farr...'

If Llewelyn Prichard fitted Thomas's stereotype of a poet, Freddie Farr fitted his ideas about a man of the world. Farr is a man who can hold his drink. Their pub crawl begins in a respect-able bar, 'The Three Lamps', which was much used by pro-fessional men before wartime air raids destroyed it. Thomas half wishes his father could see him now – 'He could not fail to see that I was a boy no longer, nor fail to be angry at the angle of my fag and my hat and the threat of the clutched tankard.' Soon they move on to poorer pubs towards the docks. Thomas is determined to keep up. He drinks rum and makes himself sick. But he has seen a slice of life. He observes (from a safe distance) a back-street tragedy, or black comedy, involving a mother, a daughter and her stillborn baby. More important, he has stood at the elbow of 'Half Hook' Farr, a man among men. He has served an apprenticeship of some kind.

Drink was to be important. Perhaps it began as a game. Long before lager was heard of, South Wales was a beer-drinking region where a strenuous night in male company was part of the popular culture. A youth who wanted to prove his manliness, especially if he was slightly built and inwardly timid, found a well-worn remedy in sinking pints in squalid circumstances; being sick was part of the initiation. Eventually the game became more serious. The raconteur with the bellyful of beer still makes a convenient disguise for someone who is uncertain of himself, who has trouble establishing his true identity. There are ample indications that Thomas was an unsure, divided man. Drink would have been useful here. There are further possibilities. In 1932, aged seventeen, Thomas was beginning to rebel against provincialism; like others before him, it was not until he left the place that he missed it. He was outgrowing his suburban home, the nondescript town, its little poets. Getting drunk was a blow against his elders, an obvious gesture by the artist as a young dog. It was more than that, it was Sin. Beer, rather than spirits, was traditionally the drink that sent men to ruin in South Wales; it was the reeking public bar and the twelve pints of flat, soapy beer on pay-night that the chapels inveighed against. Thomas liked to spell out his sinning in obvious ways. After beer the next wickedness was women, where he was soon to try his hand. His autobiographical stories make symbols of sinful pleasure out of actresses and dancers, once good for a delicious shudder in nonconformist Wales. His first recorded confession of sex, aged nineteen, which was very likely invented for the benefit of Pamela Hansford Johnson, was about three days of alleged love-making with a Swansea girl who had been an amateur dancer. And Caitlin Macnamara, the girl he eventually fell in love with and married, had been a professional dancer. It is hard to avoid the conclusion that he wanted to feel wicked. Johnson was to observe him when they came out of pubs in Chelsea. He might have had no more than a pint of beer, but if he saw someone he knew, he pretended to be drunk. He had no difficulty in becoming genuinely drunk. The smaller the body-weight the greater the effect of alcohol. But when he grew plump he was still susceptible. Alfred Janes the painter, who said that 'Dan Jones could drink me under the bed', added that 'I could drink Dylan under the table'.

Perhaps Thomas drank from the start for the pleasure of being rescued afterwards. It is said that some rebellious adolescents reveal their true motives by their habit of being incontinent when drunk: they behave like babies so that they can be looked after.

Thomas in his cups certainly wet and soiled himself more than once. In one instance, when he was twenty-three, an older woman who mothered him had to clean him up after a drinking bout that ended in collapse. Perhaps there was an inherited tendency to drink. His father was a heavy drinker; his mother's family, the Williamses, were susceptible.

The drunken poet, or the ex-schoolboy posing as one, wrote a letter to Percy Smart in his newspaper days that could have been composed to make him sound wild and artistic, and perhaps was. This enigmatic document covers three pages of lined paper, with a fragmentary poem on a fourth, and has many deletions and alterations, some illegible. It is undated, headed with the Cwmdonkin Drive address, and has 'READ THIS FIRST' written at the top. The salutation, 'Dear Trevor' (presumably Trevor Hughes, the other 'Prose & Verse' collaborator) has been crossed out and replaced by 'Percy' scrawled in thick pencil.

There was a time, so far away it is little higher than the grass, but gray not apple-green as grass is, high hopes had high words, and the things in the twenty-four hour dream, heartaches, irrelevancies, knowing for a moment nothing's worth knowing, the self-consciousness, the pain, & the ribs of fire across the eyes, these were not counted. So little, they could be drowned under the high hopes. Now, if the high hopes have dwindled, & the words drifted away, these things have all the words I know. Call a dog when in a groove, dogs no wish, or hope, of [?moving]. Such weary thought, so crabbed its written, theres no truth in it you might say, there's no sense you can find, but who cares for you know I don't, and my head is burning, & my hands, their pencil silly-writing, drip damp from wrist to finger. Nerves, so the dentist says, are all on edge. The drill is lifted & [?moved] to the sebaceous belly of the all-flaming Christ it were over, put by, all by, the white sheets & then the white sheet, put out the light, & then it does not matter, I am so comfortable, whether the light is put out or not. Look what the stream of consciousness has done for me. I have no Joyce; I must write so mad whether I like it or not. This is what comes out of the brain, though I prune the weeds. If these not weeds, these weak words, help, God help, the buds (tra la) that in the spring do sit & [?simper] high upon a plant's high lap.

For the 1000th time this morning the sub-editors' door has swung to with a noise like the falling of the walls of jericho. Soon, though friend may say sooner, I shall lie upon the floor & gibber; I shall swing upon the chandeliers & yap; I shall bark like a dog, show my discoloured teeth, crying out 'Muzzle me for the sake of Magdalena & the Eaten Heart, muzzle me, muzzle me.' For the 1000th time this morning the telephone bell rings. Is this Mr – ? No, this is Joan of Arc. Can't you hear me sizzling. Is this Mr ...? No he is away at the moment, sprinkling [*illegible*] over his grandmother, who is a staunch Tory. For the 100th time I hear the noise of the engines, I hear the voices of men I loathe & distrust, I feel them breathe upon my cheek, I am called here, I am called there, there is an accident in Landore, there is a marriage in Killay, there is a newly dug grave in garden & Mother has bought me a razor blade, a razor blade, to cut my throat so early.

For the 1000th time I say to myself 'I am dying.' Once I say to myself 'I am dead,' & 1000 times again, 'Tonight, I shall be Queen of The May. Wake me early, preferably before the buds are in full voice.'

The strain is telling on me. I lift my tumbler of neat acid. Your face, Edith, looks remarkably beautiful through its glass. I smile, but you are looking somewhere else. At the boxer perhaps, though I luv more than he does. For I have written a poem about you, which, though not beautiful, is highly coloured, & liberally tinted with the conventional exotic dyes. Never to lose her, that is the high hope, Percy. Now she is Mother, now she is Soldier, now penny [?paper], now Betty, now Music, now Poems, now Maisie, now Music & Poems & Painting, now Maisie (subtle these names are) now Tumbler, now Tumbler, now Edith, now Tumbler, now Tumbler ... and that chronologically is as far as I've got ... but always feminine, so must not lose her, Grip her waist. Hold her tight. Kiss her, read her, drink her. Dylan.

The fourth page has 'EXCUSE DRAFT OF POME' written alongside ten lines of verse that can be disentangled from the crossings-out.

> War would be kind; this peace
> Lies sveltly on the knitter's head,
> Fit for old men & geese
> Or rather Rodericks on their knees

Praying for woman or for cheese,
Is shabby, dull, & lie-a-bed,
I would lie wounded, burst, or dead
Rather than breathe such peace,
Be maggot-ridden by armistices
Illnesses & vilenesses

Whatever Thomas was about, he sent the outburst to his friend. Its mood belongs to the back-bedroom by the boiler rather than the reporters' room at the *Post*, and he probably wrote it at home after an evening out. Is there a hint of 'Fern Hill', fourteen years into the future, in 'apple-green as grass is'? The hand that he dwells on, 'drip damp from wrist to finger', will be just as self-important in his story 'The Orchards', only a few years away, where he fingers 'the pencil tower, the half-moon of his thumbnail rising and setting behind the leaden spire'.

A sober 'after note' that seems to belong here was written on reporters' copy-paper cut from sheets of *Daily Post* stationery, and presumably was sent to Smart at the same time. This is the other face of young Thomas; there was always a lower-middle-class boy from the suburbs alongside the aspiring Welsh Joyce. All his life he could turn away from drunken behaviour. Shortly before Thomas died, the writer John Morgan interviewed him at length in a Swansea pub. For hours Thomas sipped beer and talked quietly; there were no excesses.

I look at the pieces of paper I wrote on last night, and think Christ! Have I written that? Is that rubbish mine? Was I drunk, or mad? Now, thank God, I am sober, sane (What a disquieting thought it is – that last night's was my real mood, & this but a superimposed sanity, a false cleanness of mind forced upon me by the wind & the English – or rather the Welsh – morning.)

Another thing strikes me. Once you said, sententiously but truly, 'How different people are inside and outside. No one would think you were a modern poet.' No, they wouldn't, would they? If you & I went – mind, I only suggest it – into an hotel-bar, which would the barmaid think the most capable of churning out unrhymed, unrhythmical, rubbish? You, yes, you. I have a weak jaw & a loose mouth, & very wide eyes & a hat at a daft angle. I am ordinary. You, outsize in intellects, are extraordinary. Yet you have more common-sense & sanity in your big toe than I've in my whole head. Odd, very odd.

As far as the *Post* was concerned, Thomas seems to have been regarded as mildly eccentric but no more. The chief reporter, a lay preacher and teetotaller called Job ('Solomon' in 'Old Garbo'), claimed later that Thomas escaped his memory altogether. The paper had other talented young men who wanted to be writers. Charles Fisher, who became a close friend of Thomas, was thought too promising to remain a reporter. Thomas was part of a widening circle of ambitious friends linked by the newspaper or amateur dramatics or simply because they lived on the same side of the town. Alfred Janes, whose parents kept a greengrocer's shop, was already at art school in London, but came back to Swansea often. He met Thomas through Daniel Jones. A lean, meticulous man who was always loyal to him, he was later the butt of amiable Thomas jokes about his painstaking still-lifes ('One Egg, June 1936 – June 1940'). Janes was something of a father-figure. Mervyn Levy, another painter who was to make his reputation in London, had already left the town, but sometimes reappeared to join the fluctuating circle of coffee drinkers in the Kardomah Café or pub crawlers in the Mumbles. They were part of a Swansea network that lasted throughout Thomas's life, people he could trust and relax with. In general they don't remember him behaving badly, no doubt partly from loyalty but also because with them he was not under pressure, and so less likely to be eccentric. Wynford Vaughan-Thomas, who became the broadcaster and writer, was another member of the network; he was six years older than Thomas, and had already come down from Oxford with a degree. Jones was at the local university reading English. He was somewhat apart from the group. To Levy, he seemed 'a bit high and mighty, the great man. He didn't join our badinage and filthy jokes. But Dylan didn't come to us for help, he went to Dan. His relationship with Dan was a very serious one.' Thomas's other important Swansea friendship was to be with Vernon Watkins. When Thomas was on the *Post*, Watkins was working in a bank, as he did all his life. But he and Thomas had not yet met or begun their bemused exploration of one another's poetry.

While Thomas was being a reporter of a kind, he was dabbling in another trade that was to be more profitable in the long run. He became a member of the Little Theatre, an amateur group that staged several plays and revues each year. At the Grammar School he had acted in a couple of plays. He joined the Little Theatre soon after reviewing one of its productions for the newspaper, and in February 1932 appeared in Noël Coward's *Hay Fever* as Simon, described by a local reviewer as 'an artist with an explosive temper and untidy habits'. He seems to have flung himself into parts and achieved his effects by over-acting. 'The more fantastic the part,' said Malcolm Graham, later a professional actor, 'the better Dylan was.' For the next two or three years he appeared regularly in Little Theatre plays. His voice was already strong; soon it would thicken and begin to acquire the boom that made him as famous as his poetry. Strangely, he never refers to the amateur acting days in his copious reminiscences about Swansea; it is the one thing he leaves out. An actor in so many things he did, he preferred not to remember himself as one.

His appearance on the street was becoming more flamboyant. He was busy escaping from his mother's well-laundered linen. In 'Return Journey' he is now 'a bombastic adolescent provincial bohemian with a thick-knotted artist's tie made out of his sister's scarf, she never knew where it had gone, and a cricket-shirt dyed bottle-green'. He fancied himself in a green pork-pie hat with a feather. D. J. Thomas was always careful of his appearance: he shaved when he was ill, wouldn't dream of going down to breakfast in a shirt without a collar, and kept his hat on whenever he could to cover his baldness. Dylan had his less orthodox brand of vanity. He may have come to look like an unmade bed, as his wife once remarked, but he was never indifferent to his appearance.

His sister Nancy was a fellow member of the Little Theatre. They appeared together on the stage. Her life-story, one feels, should be important to her brother's, but it doesn't appear so. In his reminiscences Thomas wrote her out of the script, more or less. He did the same with his parents, but there are many references to them elsewhere, in letters and reports of conversations. Nancy is a blank space. When Dylan was seventeen, she was twenty-five, and still living at home; she had been there, doing nothing in particular, since she left the High School, the girls' equivalent of the Grammar School, seven or eight years before. Her chief interests seem to have been men friends, of whom she had many, and the theatre, which presented itself briefly as a possible career. She was an attractive, loquacious young woman, with the Thomas facility for mixing up fact and fiction. Her friend Gwevril Dawkins said that 'a lot of the time she burbled absolute rubbish, but she could keep a roomful of people in stitches'. On the stage she is said to have out-acted her brother, and according to Mrs Dawkins there was once talk of her going to London and joining a theatrical company. But a doctor advised against it: her health was delicate, like Dylan's, and her girlhood had been full of septic knees and attacks of asthma. So she remained in Swansea, which is probably what she would have done in any case, and spent much of her time at the Mumbles, where the Little Theatre had its headquarters. Once, helping to sew costumes, she pricked her finger and let out a stream of coarse language; the wardrobe mistress was shocked to hear such words from a girl whose family was so respectable.

By 1932, no doubt to her father's relief, she looked like settling down. Her friend was an English commercial traveller based in Swansea, Haydn Taylor. He was another of the Little Theatre set. He drove a two-seater car, earned £300 a year and planned to earn a great deal more in the near future, and saw the Thomases with a quizzical outsider's eye. 'It wasn't a naturally happy family,' he said forty years later. 'There was something unreal about it, primarily because D.J. and Florence had nothing in common. She worshipped him, waited on him hand and foot, but it wasn't a *natural* family. They never went away for holidays together.' According to Taylor, Nancy – whom he always called 'Thomas' – was afraid of her father and his sarcastic tongue. 'It was always a problem for Thomas to get money out of him if she wanted to go somewhere. He never had a bean. He used to say, "I am without money. I do not mean I don't have much money. I mean that I am *without money*." He said it in very measured tones. It was a funny family.' Taylor left the town in September 1932. An unsigned paragraph in the *Evening Post* said that 'Swansea is to lose one of its keenest dramatic exponents and followers in Mr Haydn Taylor ... who leaves this week for London, where he will take up an important business appointment'. It was written by Dylan Thomas, being nice to his future brother-in-law. By the standards of Dylan and his friends, Haydn

Taylor was affluent. He was usually good for a small loan; sometimes for a quick theft. When he returned to Swansea for weekends over the next few months – he and Nancy were married the following May – Taylor stayed in Cwmdonkin Drive. He learned not to leave his wallet in the bedroom if he went to take a bath.

Nancy wrote regularly to Haydn Taylor after he had left the town, and her letters give another kind of insight into life at Cwmdonkin Drive. They don't sound as if she is embroidering the facts. She was unnerved by constant rows, which were usually about money and drink, those Thomas bugbears. As Taylor says, it was a funny family. Nancy had much affection for her father ('I have realised how terribly worried Daddy is & how sad he is,' she wrote to Taylor in an earlier letter, of 1930), but he was enclosed in too many skins. Her mother's habit of steaming open Taylor's letters suggests the close, watchful atmosphere inside those drably wallpapered rooms. This was Nancy writing to her fiancé (they announced their engagement at Christmas 1932) on 16 January 1933:

> Mother is in hellish mood because I've had letters from Mrs Bevan & Mrs Ted & have showed her neither – 'You never show me your letters as other girls do to their parents. Don't think I haven't noticed sealing wax on Haydn's letters. It's quite the rudest thing I ever heard of, you must have suggested to Haydn that I'd open them, etc. I noticed that there was no sealing wax on the letter to Aunty Polly, etc.' Your letter to Blaencwm must have been read by Mother – damn ... Yesterday Mother said, 'Your wedding – remember Daddy won't have any money & any sort of a fuss will kill him. If you expect any sort of special fuss or clothes you ought to be ashamed of yourself ...'

Letters in the previous months suggest hard times at home. Perhaps the atmosphere provoked Thomas as a writer, providing something to escape from, into the parallel world of poetry. Nancy's only escape was going to be marriage. D.J. may have been afraid that his daughter's love affair would come to nothing, and keep her financially dependent on him. Dylan's career as a reporter was not flourishing. Nancy wrote to Haydn on 25 September 1932:

This morning I went to town with Gwevril, returned home for lunch
at 1.30. Mother & I dined in peace – at about 2.45 Pop enters –
then the fun began. A very usual Saturday scene – Mother raving
and in tears – I tiniest bit frightened rush upstairs dress & go out in
the rain. It pours down & the wind howls ... Question, what could
I do? Nothing, I hadn't as usual, any money. I walk to Brynmill &
on into the town, get grit in both eyes ... By teatime Pop is little
better. I have to sit with them all the evening – a cheerful prospect.
Then I think of tomorrow – all a long Sunday sitting with the
family – a family who are nervy & quarrelsome.

Then last night was Friday night – & that's the day on which
Dylan gets paid – he arrived home at 12.15 (midnight). Then there
was much row – nowadays, of course, I come in for Pop's nightly
nay hourly grumbles ... Thursday night – for the first time in years –
Daddy had a night out, arrived home 11.15 & smelt & looked
awful ... (*Postscript, Sunday morning*) When I came to bed last
night I wrote four pages to you, telling you of how Dylan arrived
home past midnight, very drunk, & of all the horrible things that
happened. This morning I tore the letter up ...

On 7 October 1932:

This evening Phyllis Bevan and Winnie King arrived. I made coffee
for them in the kitchen, Father standing over me saying, 'This sort
of thing must stop, I will not have you making food for half Swansea.
If they want to eat tell them to go home. Who pays for this food I'd
like to know? You must put an end to this bloody rot – if you don't
tell your friends I shall.' ... It's now eleven thirty. Dylan has just
come in: another row, Oh God! ... Do seal my letters carefully &
put lots of wax – yesterday the wax was off – but it was sealed very
firm. Do you seal it like that – or did someone open it & seal it back
with gum? ...

(?) 23 October 1932:

At present I'm eating alone in the dining room. Mother grumbled
at me & I asked her to shut up. Daddy heard & threw a book at
me, hit me & behaved in a back street way. Finally after using
language that I couldn't repeat – it was filthy – said, 'Who are you?
Nobody cares what happens to you, it's a pity you're alive. All

you & your beautiful brother do is to take my money from me.' To be classed with Dylan is ghastly; I now eat alone, it's better. I honestly do wish I were dead ... Last night Dylan said one day he'd strangle me...

16 December 1932:

This lunch hour [Father] arrived home – I'd cooked a special pie & I thought he'd feel cheerful because school was over. He grumbled & grumbled & raved & swore. I like a silly gump said 'Now, Daddy' – which completely put the lid on it. 'Who the bloody hell did I think I was, etc. etc. Dictating to him, was I? He'd screw my bloody head off, etc.' Result was I had to fly upstairs for safety. I have packed my small bag & told them I'm leaving. Pop said, 'No such luck, you'll come cringing back, I know' ...

4 January 1933:

Another thing has gone ... I left 2s 6d in my small black bag that I'd taken to the Gower Inn. On Monday the 2s 6d had gone. Mother & Daddy blamed me, said I must always carry my purse with me...

10 January 1933:

Yesterday Eluned, Sadie & Eira came to tea. This morning Eira arrived & said that when she returned a £1 note was missing. No one was here but Dylan so he *must* have taken it ... Tomorrow I have to go out to Eira's & take a £1 from Pop, one that he can ill afford. Dylan denies the charge & has not been home since early morn...

13 January 1933:

Dylan has just risen (11.30) & is in the most foul temper – rushing & raving like a tormented thing. He stays in bed most mornings & then gets up & writes. In the evening he visits Danny. *Unless* he gets any sum of money – then he goes and drinks. What will become of him Heaven knows. Last night I put a shilling in my evening bag; on arriving at the cloakroom – discovered it missing ... I must stop;

ink is wanted by raving brother ... Mother has just been in & given me a bloody row over the ink question. 'Dylan has got up to work & now no ink, etc. Not fair for the child, etc.' ...

By this time, the child had lost his job on the *Evening Post*, adding further to his father's worries (and accounting, no doubt, for the raids on handbags). One of his last signed articles as a reporter was a dutiful piece about Uncle David Rees, who was retiring from Paraclete Chapel. Under the headline, 'End of a Great Ministry,' he told *Herald of Wales* readers that 'Mumbles, and indeed the whole of Gower, will lose one of its best-known and best-loved inhabitants'.* Comic stories were told of the last straw that broke the editor's back. Mrs Thomas said that 'we saw the only thing to do was to take him from there'. Dim memories survived of the reporters' room being told on a Saturday that Thomas would not be in on Monday. This was late in 1932, probably in December (in her 16 December letter to Haydn Taylor, Nancy says that one of her father's latest problems is 'Dylan home'). But Dylan continued to write for the paper. What finally ended his career may have been an article that the *Evening Post* published on 7 January 1933. In it he mentioned a recent autobiography, Nina Hamnett's *Laughing Torso*. Miss Hamnett was a bohemian figure, once a talented painter who had spent many years in Paris, and was now enlightening the young in London with her stories of famous friends and lovers; Thomas was to meet her in the Fitzroy pub. Under the heading 'Genius and Madness Akin in World of Art', he trotted out a theme that he found attractive, but unwisely referred to Miss Hamnett as 'author of the banned book *Laughing Torso*'. A week later the paper carried an apology, obviously dictated by lawyers, for having suggested the book was banned – 'We are informed by Miss Hamnett it enjoys a very wide circulation'. The *Evening Post* was by now part of the Northcliffe Group, controlled from London, and the apology must have been arranged by head office. Percy Smart was told a different story, that he had been offered a five-year contract with the *Post* 'because I could – & many of

---

* A notebook poem dated the following August is about 'The Reverend Crap, a pious fraud'. Above it, Thomas has added 'Rev. David Rees'.

the staff couldn't – string a grammatical sentence together in quite reasonable time.'

Early in 1933, then, Thomas was a poet and writer living on his wits and his pen. His parents would have been dismayed to realise that apart from one period of three or four years in the 1940s, this state of affairs was to last for the rest of his life. Nor does it seem to have occurred to Thomas as a fully-formed intention. His letters over the next year or two talked about finding a job, before he subsided into the life of artistic poverty for which he had long been preparing himself, consciously or unconsciously. For the moment he had a home and an indulgent mother, and it was possible to have the poems without the poverty. It was under these comparatively tranquil conditions that his talents presently flared up, producing more poems in a brief period than ever before, or after.

When he first went to work for the newspaper, his output seems to have suffered. If he was copying and dating poems for the exercise books soon after they were written, he wrote only two between December 1931 and March 1932. This was when his 'Poets of Swansea' articles were appearing. Unfortunately there is a break in the sequence of notebooks later in the year. No. 2 (the '1930 – 1932 Notebook') ends with a poem dated 1 July 1932, and No. 3 is headed 'This Book started 1 February 1933'. No easy line of progress can be identified in the poetry Thomas was writing, either before the missing notebook or immediately after it. The poems swerve from one style to another, striking a rhetorical attitude one day, speaking almost conversationally the next. The 'biological' language of nerves and eggs makes fleeting appearances. His themes are unremarkable for a boy of seventeen and eighteen: the fact of death, the mystery of life, the contradictions of love. A few poems reiterate his uneasiness about girls. 'Love's a descension of the drawers,' he says in one poem and in another talks of 'sawdust beneath the skirts'. Life is often empty and senseless. Man grows up only to suffer. An early version of 'The hunchback in the park' is dated 9 May 1932; according to Daniel Jones it was about a real hunchback who 'seemed to have nowhere else to go' and could be seen in Cwmdonkin. Another of his themes is madness. In one poem (25 June 1932) Thomas is the tormented adolescent who can't sleep and who thinks he is going mad. A psychiatric hospital (lunatic asylum, in those days) with a raw red tower which was then being built above Sketty is an ominous presence in this poem, where it 'leers down the valley like a fool'. It was still doing useful symbolic service a year later, when he wrote to Trevor Hughes to say 'We have a new asylum. It leers down the valley like a fool, or like a snail with the two turrets of its water tower two snails' horns.' Madness was frightening but it was also exciting. No doubt Thomas was genuinely concerned about madness, but this did not prevent him taking pleasure in his fears as well. Going insane was a risk that poets took, like dying of consumption.

Trevor Hughes was an appropriate person to write to about such matters. He was a railway clerk, ten years older than Thomas – most of Thomas's early friends were older – who had sent him a short story in June 1931, after an optimistic paragraph in the *Post* announced the projected 'Prose and Verse'. The two were soon friendly. Hughes lived with his widowed mother, who was an invalid. His brother had died of tuberculosis. In Thomas's story 'Who Do You Wish Was With Us?' he is Raymond Price, happy at first to be walking in Gower, until he begins to dwell on sick rooms and death. While Thomas was still working for the newspaper, Hughes and his mother moved to London.

In an undated letter of late 1932 or early 1933 he wrote approvingly of Hughes's

solidity & perception of detail, sense of values, if you like, an at-the-root indestructibility of matter, which I haven't got. All I may, eventually, do is to

Astound the salons & the cliques
Of half-wits, publicists & freaks.

I was cut out for little else. The majority of literature is the outcome of ill men, and, though you might not know it, I am always very ill.

Did he mean that the poet's perception is feverish and disoriented? Or did he see himself as romantically ill, knowing he was sure to strike a chord with his melancholy friend? Hughes, like Smart, was given true confessions about his writing. In February 1933 Thomas was telling him:

Give me a sheet of paper & I can't help filling it in. The result – more often than not – is good & bad, serious & comic, sincere & insincere, lucid or nonsensical by the turns of my whirligig mentality, started from the wrong end, a mentality that ran before it walked, & perhaps will never walk, that wanted to fly before it had the right even to think of wings.

As time went on, Thomas began to concentrate his energies. In the notebook poems he is trying to confront himself. The high-powered whimsy of the Warmley games has no counterpart there. The poems proceed like paragraphs of a single secret letter. They grind forward earnestly. Every so often the effort produces its reward for Thomas in the shape of a deeper, richer note. It is there briefly in 'Written for a personal epitaph', dated 17 October 1931:

> I am man's reply to every question,
> His aim and destination.

It is there again in the summer of 1932, this time more sustained. The poem is 'Out of the sighs', and it was the first to be taken from a notebook and published (in 1936) virtually unchanged. In it, Thomas rides above his uncertainties and finds comfort, of a sort, in accepting things as they are:

> Out of the sighs a little comes,
> But not of grief for I have vanquished that
> Before the agony. The spirit grows,
> Forgets, and cries.
> A little comes, is tasted and found good...

The poem is entered in two parts, or was originally written as two poems with more than three weeks between them. The poem's sombre conclusion is not entirely clear. But it has undeniable authority:

> Were this enough – bone, blood, and sinew,
> The twisted brain, the fair formed loin,
> Groping for matter under the dog's plate –
> Man should be cured of distemper.

> For all there is to give I offer:
> Crumbs, barn, and halter.

With that bleak promise on 1 July 1932, the second notebook comes to an end, except for Thomas's scribbled line, 'This has taken a hell of a time'. The break in the series occurs here. When we see him at work again, in Notebook 3, it is the following February, and he is as busy as ever. One of the subjects he found was Ann Jones, the aunt at Fernhill. That February she was dying of cancer in Carmarthen Infirmary. Thomas wrote to Trevor Hughes, minutely inspecting his reactions, and wondering why he was 'utterly unmoved' apart from 'the pleasant death-reek at my negroid nostrils'. A telegram had summoned his mother to her deathbed. Thomas sat at home savouring the drama:

> Many summer weeks I spent happily with the cancered aunt on her insanitary farm. She loved me quite inordinately, gave me sweets & money, though she could little afford it, petted, patted, & spoiled me. She writes – is it, I wonder, a past tense yet – regularly. Her postscripts are endearing. She still loves – or loved – me, though I don't know why. And now she is dying, or dead, & you will pardon the theatrical writing. Allow me my moments of drama.

Was he callous or nasty? he asked Hughes. Should he weep and feel pity? The letter shrugged its shoulders:

> There must be something lacking in me. I don't feel worried, or hardly ever, about other people. It's self, self, all the time. I'm rarely interested in other people's emotions, except those of my pasteboard characters. I prefer (this is one of the thousand contradictory devils speaking) style to life, my own reactions to emotions rather than the emotions themselves.

Ann Jones died on 8 February, aged seventy. The same day Thomas wrote a first version of 'Was there a time', and informed himself that 'Time has put its maggots on my track'. Ann was buried at Llanybri, a few miles from Fernhill. Thomas, who was presumably a mourner, then wrote 'After the funeral'. Unlike the famous later version, this was not a sad celebration of her death but merely a comment on the pointlessness of dying and the hypocrisy of the mourners. Thomas may have been wrapped up in himself, but at least he was trying to be honest about it.

So far he had made no progress towards finding a publisher for his poems or for the stories that he was also writing. Whatever he thought privately about his ability as a poet, he lacked confidence in the practical nature of the product. Nor had a single distinctive style merged. With hindsight it is easy enough to see flashes of it, but in 1933 Thomas was merely a working writer making some interesting experiments.

In the circumstances he was lucky to meet a new face from outside his circle who could offer kindly criticism and knowledgeable advice. The new friend was not a schoolmaster or a journalist, but, improbably enough, a grocer and former income-tax clerk of strong left-wing views who dabbled in literature, called Bert Trick. Again it was an older man. No doubt Thomas, with his powerful instinct for finding friends to lean on, knew what he was after when he called at the shop one evening with poems in his pocket. It stood on the corner of two residential avenues at the lower end of the Uplands, facing a park, Brynmill. Trick was about to put up the shutters. Thomas bought some cigarettes and said he had read a poem by Trick in a local newspaper. Invited into the living room behind the shop, he soon produced his own poems, and was asked to read them. From childhood Thomas liked to read his work aloud; to listen was to be his friend. Trick listened and said the right things. He was a hard-bitten little man in his mid-thirties, almost twice Thomas's age, who began life as an engineering apprentice in a neighbouring town, and was now active in the local Labour Party. His family had helped him buy the shop a few years earlier. Disgusted with capitalism and fascism, he looked hopefully to socialism to build a better and more spiritual future, where good literature would find its place as naturally as social benefits. Thomas seized on all this, and for a while was a muddled disciple of Trick, who regarded him fondly as a brilliant but erratic younger brother. Dylan, he said, was 'politically illiterate' to begin with, and 'found the jargon of left-wing politics quite incomprehensible'. Trick tried to educate him, without great success. The times were right for anger about social conditions. Unemployment was especially high in Wales. Swansea had ten thousand on the register, of a total population of 170,000, and more than two thousand families on the Means Test. But the workless factories and coal mines were not very noticeable in middle-class Uplands. The dole queues were on the other side of town. Bert Trick did his best to bring them closer for Thomas.

His own poetry, which he wrote in his spare time, was likely to have Marx and Jesus in it: he was an agnostic somewhere on the fringes of belief who liked to argue about religion, far into the night. Thomas was enthusiastic about socialism because it meant rebelling against established values. He would debate injustice and decadent Western society for hours. But with minor exceptions, the poems he was writing seem impervious to political ideas. London was full of politically committed poets with a sense of social responsibility, many of whom felt guilty because their families were members of the governing class that was alleged to be doing the damage. Thomas went no further than some references in notebook poems to despair and a sense of horror engendered by the First World War. 'The Western man has lost one lung,' he wrote on 16 February, echoing a thought that Trick put in a poem of his own about 'lungs chewed by poison gas'. In published poems the mood seems to be part of Thomas's inner landscape, rather than prompted by the political wasteland of Europe between the wars; though James A. Davies and others who discern a Thomas with political sensitivities disagree. The one poem with a positive political content that Thomas published was 'The hand that signed the paper felled a city', which could have been inspired by Hitler – in power in Germany since earlier that year – but has a flavour of far-off tyrants, perhaps from the Bible. It is dated 17 August 1933, and inscribed 'To A.E.T.', Trick's initials, in the notebook.

Their friendship was literary as well as political. Trick was introduced to word-play; the grocer's house in Glanbrydan Avenue became a plebeian version of Dan Jones's Warmley, the centre of an informal group of friends who met there to talk and play games. Trick (who died in 1968) told Kent Thompson that they used to juxtapose unlikely words and experiment with vowel changes. 'Too many cooks spoil the broth' became 'Too many cocks spoil the breath', a typical Thomas joke. He never tired of taking words to pieces, as if they were bits of machinery, to see how the letters worked. Trick noted (wrongly) that when it came to his poems, 'Dylan was concerned with the words, and the meaning could look after itself.' If they moved on to the interpretation of his poems, Trick claimed, Thomas would say, 'Your meaning is as good as mine.'

He was at home with the Tricks. Bert's wife, Nell, had an infant daughter, Pamela. One night, just before sleep, Pamela asked, 'What colour is glory?' Thomas pounced on the phrase and fitted it into a poem, later transferring it to another, 'My world is pyramid', where the question survives, obscurely. He was often at the house, bringing the small ration of beer that was all he could afford, concealed in a dandelion-and-burdock bottle of brown glass, having uproarious jokes with Trick. Nell was pregnant. When the child, a boy, was born, Dylan was her first visitor. He and Bert decided a good name for it would be Kerith, presumably from George Moore's book *The Brook Kerith*, but Nell was suspicious. She thought it was one of their silly words or an anagram for something rude, and had to be convinced otherwise before she would agree to it.

Early in 1933, Thomas sent two of his poems to London. One went to the BBC, which had announced a poetry competition at the end of the previous year, with a closing date of 28 February. It was called 'The Romantic Isle'. This was his first attempt to have a serious poem published outside Wales. The other was a first version of 'And death shall have no dominion', later one of his best-known poems. Trick claimed that it was he who persuaded Thomas, with difficulty, to send it to a magazine, the *New English Weekly*. More than that, it was apparently thanks to Trick that it was written in the first place.

The background to the poem was Thomas's need to find a 'philosophy'. Like most adolescents he wanted a system to believe in. The notebook poems show him painfully aware of life's contrasts. He often used the image of 'black' versus 'white', and 'black' threatened to get the better of him. Thomas had a peculiarly morbid streak. A poem dated 1 February 1933, in which he contrasts day with night, is stocked with typical ingredients: maggots on dead flesh, a vulture, a 'redcheeked vampire at the neck', a skeleton, a ghost, an eaten corpse. In another poem, two months later, he declared that 'I have been frightened of the dark for years', and dredged up more night scenes, where

                              a skeleton
                   Sits back and smiles, a tiny corpse
                   Turns to the roof a hideous grimace,
                   Or mice play with an ivory tooth.

Could the 'tiny corpse' have been his mother's first child, the
baby that died? Thomas knew there had been another child.
Whatever its origin, the key to the poem was where he declared
that

                   Unless I learn the night I shall go mad.
                   It is night's terrors I must learn to love ...

No doubt dreams played an important part in the writing of
poems all his life, and certainly during adolescence. His correspondence with Hansford Johnson reports dreams and nightmares. If the letters are to be believed, often he slept badly and
lay awake for hours. Perhaps the strangeness of his early poems
owes something to the words and images that rise up in the mind
in those hallucinatory periods between sleep and waking.

   Horrors were undeniable; Thomas had to learn to live with
them. His need to reconcile living flesh with dead flesh was a
permanent obsession that reached down to the roots of his nature.
He was aware of his body with a glandular mixture of pleasure
and fear, as his poems were soon to demonstrate. But when he
was with Trick, he could see the problem of black versus white
in Trick's more pedestrian terms. He could write about 'exsoldiers
with horrors for a face' and 'the living dead left over from the
war', and consider the merits of saving the world with a faith of
some kind, perhaps Christian. The notebook poem ends: 'Believe,
believe and be saved, we cry, who have no faith.' It sounds as if
he was being influenced by Trick, the agnostic with the old-
fashioned socialist's interest in Christian values.

   One day that spring, Trick suggested they each write a poem
about 'immortality'. Trick's contribution, which was published
in a local newspaper the following year, spoke of the soul going
up like a bird to 'a living God', and had the refrain, 'For death is
not the end!' Thomas wrote 'And death shall have no dominion',
dated 'April' in the notebook. Persuaded by Trick, he sent it to
A. R. Orage, the editor of *New English Weekly*, who published

it the following month. An expert piece of rhetoric that booms like an organ, it sounds more an act of defiance than a declaration of faith: as if Thomas was willing himself to be optimistic because it was the only way of preserving his sanity. He nearly decided against republishing it in book form. Perhaps it was part of a lifelong effort to look on the bright side that finally came to nothing.

But for the moment he was making progress. Instead of the asylum leering down the valley like a fool, he changed the image in an April poem to make the moon peer down the valley like a saint. On 22 April he wrote a poem that spelt out his new state of mind. For the last five years, he said, he had found 'no hope of harmony', no way of 'bridging white and black' –

> and now this year
> Has found a cure.
> New music, from new and loud, sounds on the air.

On 18 May, 'And death shall have no dominion' appeared in print. Trick recalled Thomas's disgust when he found that Orage didn't pay for contributions. 'It won't buy me any Woodbines,' he said. But he was now a published poet. Presently he was told that 'The Romantic Isle' was one of thirty poems chosen for broadcasting by the BBC competition judges, Walter de la Mare and Edward Marsh. Eleven thousand offerings had arrived at Broadcasting House, most of them, announced the BBC, with an 'astonishing absence of any understanding of the business of writing poetry'. Thomas's was read in the National Programme, late in the evening, at the end of June. The poem has not survived but the title suggests one of his blander pieces.

Thomas was still uncertain what style to adopt in his verse. His next published poem, in July, had an improbable origin, an open-air performance of *Electra* in the garden of Mrs Bertie Perkins, a well-to-do resident of Sketty Green. Pigeons cooed above, harp and drums played accompanying music by Daniel Jones, and 'Soapy' Davies, classics master at the Grammar School, was annoyed to see his ex-pupil, the wastrel Thomas, mooning about under the trees, not paying attention to Sophocles. He is said to have been suitably repentant a week later when the *Herald of Wales* published Thomas's 'Greek Play

in a Garden'. It was well wrought without being particularly
Thomas-like. Far more ambitious poems were being added to
the current notebook at the rate of two or three a week. But no
single style predominated. Thomas's old doubts about himself
both as person and poet recurred in 'Ears in the turrets hear' (17
July) where he was undecided again, wondering what the world
had to offer. The poem (later published almost unchanged) had
characteristic images – he saw himself as an island with 'a thin
sea of flesh' and 'a bone coast' – but its tone was quiet, even self-
pitying.

It was not until the poems he began to write late in the summer,
which peered morbidly into his adolescent anatomy, that the
density and violence of the 'real' Thomas began to take over. The
end of August 1933 marked a turning point. Up to that date,
when he was still only eighteen, Thomas had written, mainly
since he left the *Evening Post*, twelve of his ninety *Collected
Poems* in a form close to their final version. (He had written a
further eleven of his final output that were to be more substantially revised or entirely rewritten before they appeared in
print.) The twelve poems are straightforward; most can be understood at a first reading; there is little scope for critics to contradict
one another about the meaning. Had Thomas been satisfied with
this style, in poems like 'Ears in the turrets hear' and even the
haunting 'Why east wind chills', the literary establishment would
have greeted him with interest but hardly such excitement as
they were to show. This group was to be the backbone of the
second book he published, in 1936, *Twenty-five Poems*, which
disappointed some critics because it lacked the intense self-
absorption of its 1934 predecessor, *18 Poems*. They wondered
which way young Thomas was going. In fact, he had already
gone. The violently introspective poems that went into the first
book were mostly written after August 1933, that is, later than
the 'straightforward' group that went into the second. It was
these later poems, pumped out in the year from September 1933,
that were quickly assembled for *18 Poems* and made him
famous.

This is an over-simplified version of what was happening.
Thomas was producing poems, not material for theses. There are
no precise categories. The break between styles was not absolute –
he wrote some straightforward, non-anatomical poems after the

end of August. But a shift is apparent. After much hesitation he settled for a particular style, probably without realising it at first. The act was part of the process of resolving his uncertainties. It went with the change of mood that had enabled him to subdue his nightmares, or at least to accept that black and white must coexist. A knot of nervous energy waited to be released. He had often felt sorry for himself, the poet who hung back, afraid to risk failure by trying too hard. 'No bird for me:/He flies too high', he wrote in 1930. In July 1933, 'Ears in the turrets hear' was equally apprehensive; its original title for publication was 'Dare I?'. Now he was to answer his questions and resolve his doubts with a surge of energy.

Chapter Five

A CASE OF CANCER

There are obvious dangers in looking too enthusiastically for connections between Thomas's poetry and his everyday life in the crucial closing months of 1933. The interplay between the nature he was born with and the surroundings he was born into may have done its work when he was a child. In that case his talent was ticking away like a piece of sealed clockwork, unconnected with events at Cwmdonkin Drive or anywhere else. But it is possible that the mechanism could be, and was, modified by events.

In August he went to London for what was probably his first visit, and furthered his career, so he hoped, by meeting some editors. Two of Thomas's friends (Trevor Hughes and the writer George Reavey) have said they met him in London in 1932, but no other evidence of such a visit has come to light. In 1933 he stayed at least some of the time with his sister and her husband, Haydn Taylor. They had married by special licence (because neither was living in the parish) in a Gower village at the end of May, and had gone to live in a houseboat on the Thames near Chertsey, on the south-west edge of London. This made a good jumping-off point for Thomas. During his visit he is said to have seen Orage of *New English Weekly* and Sir Richard Rees, who edited the monthly *Adelphi* from a flat near Albert Bridge; next month Rees published a poem by Thomas, 'No Man Believes'. It seems to have been a quiet visit; either there were no London anecdotes of the fiery boy worth telling, or, if there were, no one was yet collecting them. There is one story, but it concerns something that almost certainly never happened. Thomas is supposed to have stolen his sister's engagement ring from the houseboat. Fiction abounds in Thomas's life, and makes the business of biography even more hazardous than usual. He lied for fun or profit, and so did his sister. It was she who told the story to Gwevril Dawkins, when Mrs Dawkins (then unmarried) stayed on the houseboat in the summer of 1933. Nancy described to her what had happened the previous weekend. The Taylors had been to a party on the Saturday evening. They were late returning, but about half past five on Sunday morning they were awakened by the sound of someone leaving the boat. Haydn Taylor's loose change had gone from the chest of drawers. So had Nancy's engagement ring, a square-cut emerald set in diamonds, valued (according to Nancy) at eight hundred pounds, say twenty-five thousand pounds at end-of-century values: an unlikely tale. Taylor drove to Reading, where trains for Swansea call, caught up with Thomas, who had hitch-hiked there, and took back the ring. Mrs Dawkins believed the story for forty years. But Haydn Taylor said it was a fabrication. He could not have afforded a ring costing more than twenty or thirty pounds. It was never stolen. There was no dawn departure. The obvious conclusion is that Nancy invented the story to impress her friend with her brother's awfulness.

At home again, Thomas sent poems to Geoffrey Grigson for the magazine *New Verse* that he had started in January that year. *New Verse* had a tiny circulation, never much more than a thousand copies. But Grigson, then in his late twenties, soon made it influential. A parson's son from Cornwall, he was a clever man, a poet himself, who soon knew his way around literary London, and was to flourish as an editor with a sharp tongue and a sharper pen. The well-connected Cyril Connolly, another writer and editor, called him, 'one of the shrewdest operators on the kerb-market of contemporary letters'. Thomas picked him out as a target and accompanied his poems with a country boy's apologia: '... I have developed, intellectually at least, in the smug darkness of a provincial town, and have only on rare occasions shown any of my work to any critics, generally uninterested or incompetent ... Grinding out poetry, whether good or bad, in such an atmosphere as surrounds me, is depressing and disheartening.' For the moment, Wales had a sharply diminishing appeal. The last poem in Notebook 3, dated 16 August, is the jingle about 'The Reverend Crap'.

Grigson sent the poems back. Thomas was luckier in another direction. In April the *Sunday Referee* had announced a feature called 'The Poets' Corner' and invited contributions ('We care nothing who holds the stylus'), with predictable results. Poems poured in. The newspaper was edited by Mark Goulden, later a successful publisher, who was trying to interest a level of readership between the heavier Sunday journals, the *Observer* and *Sunday Times*, and the sex-and-crime papers farther down the market. Goulden commissioned writers like Bernard Shaw and Compton Mackenzie; it was a time when 'good writing' was still an adequate weapon for a circulation war. In charge of the Poets' Corner was a literary journalist called Victor Neuburg. Neuburg, then in middle age, was a highly strung bisexual of peculiar habits who for years was under the spell, literally, of Aleister Crowley, the deranged magician. Together, according to Crowley, they materialised spirits and practised assorted magic. Neuburg had parted from the magician (and been ritually cursed, which gave him a nervous breakdown) twenty years before he joined the *Sunday Referee*.

At the end of July 1933, Daniel Jones comes briefly into the story. He was at a literary gathering in the cottage at Steyning, in Sussex, where Neuburg spent much of his time. So was a young London woman whose poetry had already been published in the *Referee*, Pamela Hansford Johnson. Jones was not impressed with his afternoon under the Downs, but he talked about it to Thomas, who presently sent a poem to Neuburg. It began, 'That sanity be kept I sit at open windows', and had a strong flavour of T. S. Eliot. Neuburg printed it on 3 September, describing it as 'perhaps the best modernist poem that as yet I've received'.

But by the time the poem appeared, Thomas had other things to think about. On or about 27 August, his father had visited a dentist in the Uplands. The dentist noticed an ulcer on the floor of his mouth, below the tongue, and suggested he see a doctor. D.J. was always careful of his health. His wife said that in his teaching career, there was only a single term in which he was never absent through illness. This time it was not hypochondria or a cold. He saw his family doctor, who called in a specialist, who diagnosed cancer. He was fifty-seven years old, and Haydn Taylor, who hurried to Swansea with Nancy, was given a gloomy prognosis. His chances of being alive in five years were small. The Taylors took him by car to London, where he was admitted to University College Hospital on 10 September. Next morning a painful week of treatment with radium needles began.

Over the following months he made a number of journeys between Swansea and London. In October he was treated with radium again, this time for more than two weeks. For a while his voice was affected. Haydn Taylor, collecting him from hospital to return him to Swansea, found his temper unchanged. The car was late arriving and D.J. was furious. They stopped at a pub for him to have a Guinness. By early in 1934 the malignant ulcer was fading, and near-by glands were seen to be unaffected. D.J. was lucky, a good advertisement for early diagnosis. But it was another year or so before the family could breathe again. Dylan, who regarded cancer with special awe, and used the word often in his early poems, wrung the last drop of agony from the situation. He told Trevor Hughes (January 1934) that his father had been 'operated upon for cancer of the throat', and this is the version of the illness that most people remember. (Knowing that D.J. lived for nearly twenty years more, and how Dylan loved to dramatise, sceptical friends of the family have gone to the other extreme and concluded that D.J. didn't have cancer at all.)

What effect, if any, did his father's illness have on Dylan Thomas's poetry? One or two direct references can be traced. A poem in Notebook 4 (the final poetry notebook, begun on 23 August) with the date 12 September, two days after his father entered hospital, has the opening line, 'Take the needles and the knives'. On 17 October, the day his father was readmitted to hospital, the poem later published as 'From love's first fever to her plague' has the line, 'The root of tongues ends in a spent out cancer'. But these are only curiosities. More significant is the fact that the first complete, full-blooded 'anatomical' poem is also the first poem to follow the news of his father's cancer, if, as is almost certain, the illness had been diagnosed by 6 September, the date in the notebook. The poem is 'Before I knocked', where he sees himself as (among other things) an unborn child:

> My throat knew thirst before the structure
> Of skin and vein around the well
> Where words and water make a mixture
> Unfailing till the blood runs foul;
> My heart knew love, my belly hunger;
> I smelt the maggot in my stool.

As Ralph Maud, who edited the poetry notebooks, commented, 'The stage is set for Thomas's distinctive organic imagery.' His concern with death, his morbid self-awareness, had been in the background for a long time. He had (for the moment) come to terms with his neurotic fears, if the evidence of the notebooks is to be believed. Now came the knowledge that his father had cancer and was likely to die. Thus, while he had become more sure of himself as a poet, his father's illness gave his imagination something near and frightening to bite on. It was not a distant episode like the cancered aunt on her insanitary farm; a contemporary remembers Thomas as deeply upset in the autumn of 1933. The effect on his writing can only be guessed at. But the dates of poems and illness connect. After 6 September, poems of the new kind begin to appear regularly in the notebooks, among them 'My hero bares his nerves' (17 September). On 12 October he composed, or copied out, 'The force that through the green fuse drives the flower'. Recognising a good thing when he wrote it, Thomas sent it to Victor Neuburg, who printed it on 29 October. Poets' Corner was typographically cramped that weekend, and the text, which told perceptive readers that here was something beyond the usual run of *Referee* verse, was unceremoniously split in the middle and continued in the next column. The poem had no doubt of its own importance; apart from puns, there are no jokes in Thomas's early poems, and very few in later ones. Thomas identifies himself with natural phenomena – flowers, rocks, water, wind – as he was to do elsewhere. (Disguises were part of his basic repertoire. He might be the landscape or the weather; he could be the foetus or the egg; he took on the role of The Poet or Man or Christ, separately or at the same time.) Neuburg described it as 'cosmic in outlook'; he was the first to use such language about Dylan Thomas. This did not stop Thomas being contemptuous of Neuburg and his coterie.

'The force that through the green fuse' was one of the early poems that Dylan Thomas still liked, when he came to look back on them. But he preferred not to look back at all. His early poems haunted him. He spoke later of their 'vehement beat-pounding black and green rhythms like those of a very young policeman exploding', and said he had forgotten why he wrote them, no doubt because they represented an achievement in a short space of time that was never repeated. Five days after 'The force

that through the green fuse' (and ten days before his nineteenth
birthday) he completed 'From love's first fever to her plague',
where he is the embryo, the child, the poet:

> I learnt the verbs of will and had my secret;
> The code of night tapped on my tongue.

November produced three more of the *Collected Poems*, all in
his 'cosmic' style, including the mysterious 'Light breaks where
no sun shines' that did more than any other single poem to
draw attention to Thomas when the BBC's journal, the *Listener*,
published it the following spring. Everything was packed tight in
these poems. 'I like things that are difficult to write and difficult
to understand,' he wrote to Charles Fisher a year or so later.
'... I like contradicting my images, saying two things at once
in one word, four in two words and one in six.' Poetry, added
Thomas in one of his infrequent bursts of explanation, should
be 'as orgiastic and organic as copulation ... Poetry is a medium,
not a stigmata on paper. Man should be twotooled, and a poet's
middle leg is his pencil.'

The early poems steam with sexual energy. Their death
symbols, the maggots and ghosts, are entwined with sex images –
the 'rainy hammer' of his father's penis against the womb, or the
boy who masturbates, 'rehearsing heat upon a raw-edged nerve'.
The act of masturbation is implicit in several poems, reflecting
Thomas's sexual experience at the time. The style in which he
was writing may have been contrived for maximum effect, but
there is no doubt that he is describing what he feels, what he *is*.
He is trying to encompass (in powerful 'poetic' language as
befitted his vocation) what it meant to be this particular man or
boy at the age of nineteen.

It is not at all certain that he had slept with a girl at the time
of his nineteenth birthday, in October 1933. At that time and
place, to be a male virgin at nineteen would have been unexceptional (as it still was a generation later). Conditions were not
conducive; girls were apprehensive; there was nowhere to go.
Mervyn Levy, a few months older than Thomas, discussed sex
with him when they were sub-adolescents, and they shared a
book with reproductions of nude paintings. 'We were bred in the
masturbatory era,' said Levy, 'and I think Dylan carried it with

him all his life.' Aged eleven or twelve, they spied on the Levys' maid and saw her washing her breasts in a handbasin.* Levy was sexually precocious, but he didn't sleep with a girl until he went to London, aged seventeen. On the other hand, Thomas used to claim that he was sexually experienced at fifteen. In the last weeks of his life, when *Time* magazine was having him shadowed by a private detective in New York, he was heard to say he first had sexual relations at that age. No doubt he could have been heard to say it in various places over the years. 'I should be ashamed,' he said in a lecture, 'had not shame been lost to me in the back of a lorry in, I think, nineteen hundred and thirty.'

If his claim was true, and he had sexual intercourse at a tender age, it was presumably with a girl he picked up from outside his circle. The traditional place to find a willing girl of one's own age was on the 'prom', the path along a stretch of seafront, beside the railway and the dunes. All-girl and all-boy groups would march from end to end on summer evenings, past the pallid war memorial in the middle, colliding with one another and occasionally, very occasionally, pairing off. One of Thomas's Swansea friends told Kent Thompson of an incident with a girl they took into the sand dunes. They sat on either side and attempted to fondle her, without much success. Their ages are not given. It is said that Thomas went to the Strand, then a slum district near the docks, to look for girls, presumably prostitutes. This is the area that Thomas the Reporter visits in his pub crawl with Freddie Farr in 'Old Garbo'.

In the last of his *Portrait of the Artist* stories, 'One Warm Saturday', Thomas describes an encounter with a girl in roughly this category, except that she is supposed to combine sex with romantic love. Thomas sees himself as a clumsy but dogged lone wolf, in search of excitement on a summer evening. The story, like others in *Portrait*, is full of details that those who know the town can recognise. Probably it reflects an amalgam of incidents, as in 'The Peaches'. Aged perhaps eighteen or nineteen, he first sees the girl in a little park by the seafront, reading a novel. She is sitting 'opposite the white-tiled urinal', no doubt an intentional detail; she is 'innocent' and demurely dressed, but at the same

* In 'The Peaches' Thomas wrote, 'I looked with Dan Jones through the keyhole while his maid had a bath.' Perhaps there was a lot of it going on.

time 'her smile confessed her body bare and spotless and willing and warm under the cotton'. Later he sees her with friends in a pub. She is called Lou and is instantly attracted to him. Eventually he accompanies the party to a tenement block beyond the docks, for what he and the girl expect to be a night together. The story is heavy with sexual frustration. When he first sees the girl, and is afraid to speak to her, Thomas thinks, 'She could drive my guilt out; she could smooth away my shame.' When he sees her again in the pub, he is tempted to go home to dream about her – 'But only a sick boy with tossed blood would run from his proper love into a dream, lie down in a bedroom that was full of his shames, and sob against the feathery, fat breast and face of the damp pillow. He remembered his age and poems, and would not move.' In other words he resists the temptation to do as he usually does, and enjoy himself with masturbatory fantasies in his bedroom. But as the story progresses, his attempt to be grown-up comes to nothing. He leaves her in the tenement – to find a lavatory – and loses his way in the decaying block. There is no night of love. He ends as he began, by himself, on a patch of waste ground with the remains of houses, where people had 'lived and loved and died and, always, lost'. This is Thomas's compassion operating through his own sense of loss and defeat. Perhaps he did meet a Lou in Swansea, and have more success with her; certainly he took her to bed in various shapes and sizes later on. But the theme of sexual failure is apparent.

Thomas's reputation in Swansea was for amusing and occasionally outrageous behaviour; not for chasing girls. Nell Trick had no memory of seeing or hearing about a girlfriend. Evelyn Jones was one of the Little Theatre group. She acted with Thomas, drank in pubs and went for walks with him. She said he made no sexual advances to her or to anyone else as far as she knew. He used to say naughty things and make the girls blush; they loved it. 'He'd say, "Let's go roistering and rude bathing," but when we got to Langland Bay he never took his socks off.' They appeared together in Congreve's *The Way of the World* in January 1934, Evelyn wearing a low-cut dress. Thomas delighted in referring to her as 'Tess of the two big villes'. She played Mincing. He kept enticing her, in her bosomy dress, into the pub that adjoined the theatre. 'He'd say, "Come on Mincing, let's mince off." I could never not go. I used to die of embarrassment, but I liked it so much.' He was a joker, a card. On the Little Theatre programmes he wrote 'C.B.' against the names of girls who were supposed to be sexually unwilling. 'C.B.' stood for 'chastity belt'. On Evelyn's twenty-first birthday Thomas sent her a letter from London to be read at her dance. It went something like –

> Sorry I cannot pavane at the tavern.
> I'm off to galliard with a Spaniard.
> Here's a toast from me to thee:
> A pox upon your chastity.

With the verse came an 'outrageous drawing' of Evelyn in a chastity belt which was being unfastened by a man labelled 'Pox'.

Thomas's first serious girlfriend was almost certainly Pamela Hansford Johnson, later a novelist and the wife of a novelist, Lord (C. P.) Snow. In 1933, Pamela lived with her widowed mother in south London, not far from Clapham Junction. Her recollection was that when Thomas's Eliot-flavoured poem, 'That sanity be kept', appeared in the *Referee* at the start of September, she wrote to say she admired it – presumably she had already heard about him from Daniel Jones when they met at Steyning. This began a short but intense correspondence and a love affair; all her letters to him have vanished, but about twenty-five of his survive. As though a door has suddenly blown open, Dylan Thomas is revealed in action. The mix of confession and artifice that ran through most of his important letters achieves a harmony in the case of Johnson that could never be repeated; he was the boy looking over the edge of his future, testing his powers, spelling out his uncertainties, at once artful and innocent.

The full correspondence totals more than fifty thousand words, and has to be read entire to do it justice. About half the surviving letters were written before they met, in February 1934. Thomas presents himself as an unhealthy little poet with a sense of humour, struggling to write in unhelpful surroundings. The word 'little' occurs time and again. He watches his little vest blowing on the line on washday and sees his little body in the armchair. 'I'm an odd little person ... a thin, curly little person, smoking too many cigarettes, with a crooked lung, and writing his vague verses in the back room of a provincial villa ... little with no health at all ... I hardly weigh anything at all ... I look about fourteen, and I have a large, round nose; nature gave it to me, but fate, and a weak banister, broke it ... lonely little person ... nice little soul ... little Welsh ear ... little feet ... little poet.' In fact (as he said in one letter) his height was about five feet six inches and he weighed eight stone ten; he was not big, certainly, but the extreme littleness, the feeling of frailty, seem to have been largely in his mind. He made a virtue of it. Perhaps to be small (or to be a mouse or a pig, both affectionate epithets he gave himself in letters to others) was to be safe and baby-like again.

Associated with his size was his health. 'Cough! cough! cough!' he writes, 'my death is marching on.' He made jokes about it. Behind the jokes is a real melancholy, but behind that again there may be a further layer of jokiness, and so on, layer by layer, making it impossible to be sure when the 'real' Dylan is reached, if ever. 'A misanthropic doctor, who apparently did not like the way I did my eyebrows, has given me four years to live,' he wrote in early November. 'May I borrow that foul expression of yours – it isn't yours really – and whisper Sez You into his ear.' A few days later he implies he has consumption. He writes: 'Four years, my sweet. 1340 days & nights. And thank you for the optimistic remarks. I don't believe it either, but then it would be very odd if I did. You should hear me cough, though.' He adds that 'your belief in my power to write' is one of the things that make him deny what the doctor said. But all this has been deflated in advance by a side-heading in the letter: *Pathos*.

Johnson became worried. When they met, and there was talk of them getting married, she begged him to see another doctor. He promised, and later told her he had done as she asked. 'But it was a lie,' said Lady Snow. She came to see his tuberculosis as something he wanted, not something he had. He found the disease romantically appealing. When Thomas was first in London, the writer Rayner Heppenstall was told that Thomas's lungs would kill him within months unless he lived quietly. Thomas lived noisily and thrived. It is doubtful if any doctor delivered a four-year warning, or whether he suffered from anything worse than a tendency to be 'weak-chested' and asthmatic, aggravated by a large intake of cigarette smoke from the age of eleven. A gargantuan smoker's cough was one of his trademarks. Towards the end of his life he suffered from breathlessness. But the post-mortem found no trace of scars from old tuberculosis. There is a parallel with his liver, another organ that was unkindly treated. Thomas liked to say that he had cirrhosis of the liver, a later version of the story that he had TB. Again, although the post-mortem showed that his liver was fatty and in bad shape, it reported no cirrhosis. Thomas was a man in search of ailments to suit the poet's personality.

If his health was a bad joke in his letters to Johnson, so was his situation. 'Swansea is a dingy hell, and my mother is a vulgar humbug,' he wrote. After a bus journey to Carmarthenshire, to stay at the Blaen Cwm cottages, he described what he had seen in the small towns they passed through, the women 'all breast and bottom', the colliers 'diseased in mind and body as only the Welsh can be ... It's impossible for me to tell you how much I want to get out of it all, out of narrowness and dirtiness, out of the eternal ugliness of the Welsh people, and all that belongs to them, out of the pettiness of a mother I don't care for and the giggling batch of relatives.' Thomas's view of Wales was always equivocal. Later on he was nostalgic for the neighbourhoods of his youth, but towards Welshness in any 'political' sense he showed indifference, even contempt.

The Blaen Cwm letter was written late in October 1933, when his father's cancer was still causing maximum distress. He makes only one or two direct references to D.J. Under the heading, 'My life. A Touching Autobiography In One Paragraph', in a letter written soon after 'The force that through the green fuse' was published, he told Pamela, 'I first saw the light of day in a Glamorgan villa, and, amid the terrors of the Welsh accent and the smoke of the tinplate stacks,* grew up to be a sweet baby, a precocious child, a rebellious boy, and a morbid youth. My father was a schoolmaster: a broader-minded man I have never known.' Early in 1934 he was describing how his father had spent 'the last three months ... undergoing treatment for cancer of the throat. He is home now, partially cured and exceedingly des-pondent. His time limit is even shorter than mine (!). Ours is a nice 'ouse. There is one unintelligent dog, too, with the highly original name of Spot.'

Fantasy is ingrained in the letters, modifying and shaping his experiences for Pamela. In a letter just before Christmas 1933 he

---

* The Uplands is comfortably distant from smoking chimneys.

felt 'like a dead man exulting in the company of his beetles, incarnadining the monstrous earth – words, words, words – with the blood of the worms (yes, worms again, my dear) that he breaks – as a housemaid crushes a flea – between the tips of his nails. Sometimes I am very nice, but today I'm awful; I'm caught in my complexes, and they're giving me immense, if unholy, joy.' They are often very 'literary' letters, apparently heartfelt but carefully contrived. At least some (he told Pamela) were first written as notes, then copied out later. Perhaps they are most revealing when they deal, as they often do, with his poetry. Thomas was then writing about something, probably the only thing, of absolute importance to him. 'I do not want to express only what other people have felt,' he wrote. 'I want to rip something away and show what they have never seen.'

He admonished Pamela for not being sufficiently personal in her poetry, as he was: 'Everything comes out of yourself, and darkness, despite what you say, has infinitely more possibilities than day.' Reproving her for calling his poetry ugly – she jibbed at his worms and cancers, until she grew accustomed to them – he pointed out that it was 'nothing but the strong stressing of the physical', with its images drawn from

> my solid and fluid world of flesh and blood . . . The greatest description I know of our own 'earthiness' is to be found in John Donne's Devotions, where he describes man as earth of the earth, his body earth, his hair a wild shrub growing out of the land. All thoughts and actions emanate from the body. Therefore the description of a thought or action – however abstruse it may be – can be beaten home by bringing it onto a physical level. Every idea, intuitive or intellectual, can be imaged and translated in terms of the body, its flesh, skin, blood, sinews, veins, glands, organs, cells, or senses.

> Through my small, bonebound island I have learnt all I know, experienced all, and sensed all.

He liked to think he was in control of his material: the idea that the poems erupted from unconscious levels upset him. Sir Richard Rees of the *Adelphi* wrote to ask for more poems. Thomas sent them off, only to be told by the puzzled editor that they had 'an insubstantiality, a dreamlike quality' that reminded him of automatic writing. In that case, Thomas wrote to Pamela,

'I am nothing but a literary oddity, a little freak of nature whose madness runs into print rather than into ravings and illusions ... But he is wrong, I swear it. My facility, as he calls it, is, in reality, tremendously hard work. I write at the speed of two lines an hour. I have written hundreds of poems, & each one has taken me a great many painful, brain-racking & sweaty hours.'

His letters were pessimistic about his future as a poet. This is hardly surprising. He was writing unfashionable poems in a provincial town. No one in London (or in Wales for that matter) was clamouring for them, apart from Victor Neuburg, 'the Vicky Bird', and Thomas regarded him with disdain from the start. Pamela had been chosen (before she and Dylan began to correspond) to begin what the *Referee* saw as a long line of prize poets, whose first book of verse would be sponsored by the newspaper. Neuburg had gushingly called her 'one of the few exquisite word-artists of our day'. Thomas did his best to criticise her poems without being too cruel; in any case she soon realised that poetry was not her vocation. But his own success was just as limited. The low-powered *Referee* was still his best hope, and by the beginning of February 1934, even the *Referee* had printed only three poems.

Thomas's situation at home had grown more precarious since his father's illness, although at the hospital in January 1934 there was no sign of malignancy, and even the patient admitted he was feeling better. He began to teach again; according to a colleague, no one from the school had visited him while he was ill. A mellowing is said to have been noticeable soon after; his sarcasm was not so sharp; he was a changed man. Dylan was under pressure to find work and earn money. His writer's day, as described to Pamela, was not encouraging for anxious parents: breakfast in bed at a quarter to ten, a leisurely morning with newspapers and books, a lunchtime pint at the Uplands Hotel, an afternoon of reading, writing or walking in Gower, an evening of pubs or Little Theatre, and finally more writing. 'Not a very British day,' as he remarked.

He was now drinking steadily, or at least he gave that impression. At the Little Theatre he went too far one night and was removed from a major part at the last minute. The play, their February production, was *Martine* by Jean-Jacques Bernard. Ethel Ross, a member of the company, said it was because he

went for a drink during the dress rehearsal, after a final warning
from the producer. Malcolm Graham, who took over the part
(of a journalist) from Thomas, said it was because he arrived at
the rehearsal speechless with drink. Either way, there was a scene.

A week after this fiasco he went to London for his first meeting
with Johnson and to look for work. They had already spoken on
the telephone, arranging the visit. 'Such a rich fruity old port
wine of a voice,' she wrote in her diary. When he arrived from
Paddington Station she found him 'charming, very young-
looking, with a most enchanting voice'. A scrap of cigarette paper
was stuck to his lower lip. His sweater was large, his trousers
were baggy, and under his pork-pie hat was what Lady Snow
recalled as 'the most beautiful curling hair, parted in the middle,
the colour in those days – when he washed it – of dark gold'. But
the bulging eyes and sonorous voice were what captured her, as
they captured others. Her mother was enchanted, too. This was
just as well for the young lovers. Life at the Johnsons' in Wands-
worth (and in Chelsea, where they moved later in 1934) was
well regulated. Mrs Johnson would not have been amused by
coarseness. Pamela – short and pretty, with an Oriental look
about her eyes – worked in a bank. Her father had been a colonial
civil servant. When she turned from poems to novels, at which
she was much better, she wrote a book for which Dylan suggested
the risky title of *This Bed Thy Centre*, and she was temporarily
ostracised by her father's side of the family when it was published
in 1935. During the ten days of Thomas's visit they went for
walks, talked late, saw an O'Casey play, wrote alternate-line
poems in the Jones-and-Thomas manner, and drank a little beer
from the local off-licence. Thomas had arrived with a quarter-
bottle of brandy, but this was one of his gestures to the reputation
he was groping for. There was no hard drinking as far as Pamela
was concerned, although he wasn't under her eye all the time.
Any host of Thomas's in London was rarely certain what else
their guest was up to. Some of the time he probably spent at the
houseboat with Nancy and Haydn.

Before he returned to Swansea, he told Pamela that he had
sold some poems and stories, but had failed to find a job that
suited him. She saw him off on the train, depressed to see him
go. Three days later he wrote to say he was in love with her. At
the end of March he was back again to spend Easter, and now

he was 'my love Dylan'. He was a gentle and on the whole a well-behaved bohemian. One day before breakfast he was on his way out to buy cigarettes, wearing pyjamas, dressing gown and a black felt hat. Pamela's aunt told him to come back at once; he obeyed meekly. She persuaded him to go with her to the near-by store of Arding and Hobbs to have a portrait photograph taken. He wore a tie and faced the camera with a solemn expression, looking quite unlike the winking boy with a fag in his mouth. Pamela hoped to change him. 'Dylan tight, little devil,' the diary says once, indulgently.

'You are my only friend,' Thomas wrote on 15 April 1934, when he was back in Swansea. 'I say quite seriously that I have never really spoken to any other human being.' He dreamt of the two of them together – in front of the fire reading Beddoes, or living on a Mediterranean island. In the same letter he looked out on Cwmdonkin Drive (on a Sunday morning) at 'the rehearsed gestures, the correct smiles, the grey cells revolving around nothing under the godly bowlers. I see the unborn children struggling up the hill in their mothers, beating on the jailing slab of the womb, little realising what a snugger prison they wish to leap into ...' But he could now talk about himself in a matter-of-fact way:

> I've often wondered – I thought of asking you, but am always so vastly happy with you that I don't like introducing morbid & egotistic subjects – whether you think me as conceited a little young man as I often think you must do. I'm not, really; profoundly the other way ... I'd hate you to think that I was all self-contented, self-centred, self-satisfied in regard to – well, only one little thing, the things I write. Because I'm not. And I'm not half as brave, dogmatic & collected in the company of Literary persons as I might have led you to believe.

His affairs seemed to be prospering. The *Referee* had printed more poems, 'A process in the weather of the heart' and 'Where once the waters of your face', both within a week of being written. The *Adelphi* had published a poem written the previous summer, 'The Woman Speaks', which brought an admiring letter from another young Welsh writer, Glyn Jones; confused by the title and the unfamiliar name 'Dylan', Jones was uncertain at first if the poet was man or woman. Most important of all, on 14 March 1934 the *Listener* had published 'Light breaks where no sun shines', with its portentous opening lines,

> Light breaks where no sun shines;
> Where no sea runs, the waters of the heart
> Push in their tides...

Few critics have agreed what the poem means. Glyn Jones, who became a friend and admirer of Thomas, thought that it 'probably expresses something pretty trite and commonplace, in prose terms, about the foetus and the pre-natal state', adding that the actual machinery of the verse is so filled with energy that it arouses the same feeling in the reader as a 'great and intelligible poem'. Other critics have tried to be more specific. Does the light that breaks 'behind the eyes' indicate the moment of conception, or the start of man's consciousness? Is the poem about the universe seen through the human anatomy? Or the cycle of life and death? All these explanations have been proposed at one time or another. One critic even thought the poem was about sexual intercourse. Sex undeniably enters into it. Certain phrases gave offence to sensitive *Listener* readers. In the second stanza 'A candle in the thighs/Warms youth and seed and burns the seeds of age' was clear enough. According to Dylan, writing to Pamela about it, a 'host' of letters came from 'smut-hounds', and consequently 'the BBC have banned my poetry'. This was an exaggeration. The advertising department of the *Listener* was worried that advertisers might be offended, but the BBC management supported the editor. Later in the year the magazine published another Thomas poem, 'Especially when the October wind'.

One result of 'Light breaks' was that three important figures in literary London wrote to him: T. S. Eliot, who was then editing the *Criterion*, Stephen Spender, and Geoffrey Grigson, who now became interested in the poet he had rejected the year before. The following month, April, Grigson's *New Verse* printed its first Thomas poem, the newly written 'Our eunuch dreams', which uses images from the cinema ('love on a reel') to explore the unreality of modern society. This poem caught the eye of Edith Sitwell, who didn't like it and used it as a stick to beat *New Verse* with. Sitwell, already an imposing figure, was soon to change her mind and praise Thomas as the new comet in the sky. But in a book published later in 1934, she called the poem 'an appalling affair', saying little and doing it badly. Sitwell's real reason may have been loyalty to her brother Sacheverell, who had been lambasted in *New Verse*. Thomas was becoming involved in the games that critics play.

Towards the end of April the *Referee* chose him as its second prize poet to have a collection of verse sponsored by the paper.* Compared with a year before, his prospects as a poet were much improved. But he sounded nervy and unhappy that spring. 'Monday was a dead day,' he wrote to Johnson on 15 April, 'the hole in space you talk of, such a deep, damp hole as I must have fallen into when I last left you.' The threatening hole, the emptiness that swallows up life, later occurred more than once in his writing. Much of his uneasiness concerned money, which he lacked, and London, where he hoped to live. Writing to Glyn Jones in mid-March he spoke of moving to London, 'possibly to starve', circumstances having made it necessary that he go 'out into the bleak and inhospitable world with my erotic manuscripts thrown over my shoulder in a sack'. The implication, here and elsewhere, is that his father's health was the reason. A letter to Glyn Jones in the summer said D.J. was about to retire, which meant that Thomas had to 'face the bitter world alone'. But it was another two years before D.J. left the Grammar School. It is as though Thomas was slowly building up the energy he needed to escape from Swansea. Part of the problem was doubtless Johnson. Whatever plans he had for her, she undoubtedly had plans for him. If he married her he would have to provide for her. He wrote to her on 2 May 1934 to say that he must earn money. He was trying to write a novel, which, he said, might be more profitable than poetry; but he was not optimistic. 'So what's the alternative? Six months ago I'd have suggested the docks or the oven with the greatest equanimity. But now I've got to live. It's when I'm with other people more than when I'm by myself

---

* Mark Goulden said that before he agreed to Thomas having the prize he insisted he visit London to be interviewed at the *Referee* office, because, he told Neuburg, 'I think we are the victims of a con-trick. Someone has done a brilliant job of sticking together bits of poems.' He met Thomas and was satisfied he was genuine. Later he lost interest in him 'because he became a disreputable person'.

that I realise how much I want you and how very far away you are from me.' Thomas was trying to be practical about their future, but it didn't seem to suit him. The letter continued, 'I'm willing to work. I do work, but in an almost anti-mercenary direction. Which is no good at all for you or me. Something has to be done, but Christ knows what it is.' He talked vaguely about becoming an actor with 'a bad repertory company in Coventry, or some place like that', or going to Russia with 'a Welsh Communist organisation'. But he knew what would happen: 'I sink back into a usual lethargy and continue to write of my uncommercial maggots.'

This was not the tone of his earlier letters, before they met. Then, he was writing that 'There is no necessity for the artist to do anything. There is no necessity. He is a law unto himself, and his greatness or smallness rises or falls by that.' However grandiose and ill-tuned to the times he lived in, this was Thomas's true philosophy. Now that he thought himself in love with Pamela, 'nice, round Pamela', a personable, middle-class girl who wrote girlish things in her diary, he found himself thinking about practical bourgeois matters like getting a job. All his life part of him hankered for stability and an 'ordinary life'; when his wife Caitlin lost her temper she used to laugh at him for being bourgeois at heart, a charge that no one could level at her.

On 9 May he began a long, neurotic letter. 'I am ill,' he said, 'ill as hell. I have had a headache for a fortnight, and haven't slept for longer than that. I've lost all hope of ever going to sleep again. I lie in the dark and think. I think of God and Death and Triangles. I think of you a lot. But neither You nor the Triangles can make me sleep. I've drugged myself up to the eyelids.' He reported trouble with writing: 'The old fertile days are gone, and now a poem is the hardest and most thankless act of creation.'

Between September 1933 and April 1934 Thomas had written thirteen of the poems that he was beginning to assemble for his *Referee* book, eventually to be called *18 Poems*. In April alone he wrote three, including 'I see the boys of summer' and 'If I were tickled by the rub of love'. The latter, with its declamatory final line, 'Man be my metaphor', concludes the fourth and final notebook on 30 April; after that it is no longer possible to date poems accurately. In the remaining eight months of 1934, he probably wrote sixteen that were published in *18 Poems* and elsewhere; his output remained high. But a new kind of obscurity had set in.

It is difficult to generalise. But after April 1934, and for some years to come, Thomas seems to be working against the grain of his material, producing verse that was often impenetrable to the ordinary reader. His work in this period lacks some quality of instant recognition that makes the poems written in the winter and spring of 1933–4 acceptable even when their full meaning isn't clear. Thomas's favourite explanation for his obscurity (as he explained in a letter to Henry Treece in 1938) was that he tried to pack so much into a small space: 'Much of the obscurity is due to rigorous compression; the last thing [my poems] do is to flow; they are much rather hewn.' It may be that he regarded obscurity as fashionable; his letters suggest it is inevitable for a contemporary writer. A complementary explanation has been put forward by Glyn Jones: 'I sometimes think Dylan did not speak out more clearly, and concealed the meaning of his poems, because he was conscious of some intellectual inadequacy in them.' Arguably, then, Thomas's natural tendency to write in private parables combined with an anxiety to appear intel-lectually respectable, an ambition that his father must have encouraged from an early age. It was only gradually, in the 1940s, that he began to work a new vein of clarity, though obscurity dogged him to the end.

His letter to Pamela of 9 May continued:

I have written a poem since my last letter, but it is so entirely obscure that I dare not let it out even unto the eyes of such a kind and commiserating world as yours. I am getting more obscure day by day. It gives me now a *physical* pain to write poetry ... I shall never be understood. I think I shall send no more poetry away, but write stories alone. All day yesterday I was working, as hard as a navvy, on six lines of a poem. I finished them, but had, in the labour of them, picked and cleaned them so much that nothing but their barbaric sounds remained. Or if I did write a line 'My dead upon the orbit of a rose,' I saw that 'dead' did not mean 'dead', 'orbit' not 'orbit' & 'rose' most certainly not 'rose'. Even 'upon' was a syllable too many, lengthened for the inhibited reason of rhythm. My lines, *all* my lines, are of the tenth intensity. They are not the words that express what I want to express; they are the only words

I can find that come near to expressing a half. And that's no good. I'm a freak user of words, not a poet. That's really the truth. No self-pity there.

Thomas began this letter on Wednesday, 9 May. He was still writing it on Sunday, 13 May, after (he said) an incident on Saturday night in 'the deserted smokeroom of a seaside pub', where three 'repulsive looking young men' cornered him and made him hand over cigarettes and money. His mood on Sunday was as black as ever. Neuburg, writing about him in that morning's *Referee*, had called him an experimentalist. This led Thomas to remark, 'I found myself wondering who this sadnamed poet was, & whether he had any separate existence from the sadder person, of the night before, bullied out of his lawful cigarettes by three strongmen & falling back, in the event of his comic cowardice, on to a stony pile of words.' He went on:

Anyway, I'm not an experimentalist & never will be. I write in the only way I can write, & my warped, crabbed and cabinned stuff is not the result of theorising but of pure incapability to express my needless tortuities in any other way. Vicky's article was nonsense. If you see him, tell him I am not modest, not experimental, do not write of the Present, and have very little command of rhythm ... Tell him, too, that I don't know anything about life-rhythm. Tell him I write of worms and corruption, because I like worms and corruption. Tell him I believe in the fundamental wickedness and worthlessness of man, & in the rot of life. Tell him I am all for cancers. And tell him, too, that I loathe poetry. I'd prefer to be an anatomist or the keeper of a morgue any day. Tell him I live exclusively on toenails and tumours. I sleep in a coffin too, and a wormy shroud is my summer suit ...

A week later it was Whitsun, and he was in Laugharne with his new friend, Glyn Jones, who had a car, and whose ancestors, like Thomas's, were buried at Llanybri, not far from Fernhill. Jones, who had been having his poems published for two or three years, was yet another older friend, aged twenty-eight; he was a schoolteacher in Cardiff, and had no ambition to be a sinner. Thomas described him to Pamela, with the suspicion of a sneer, as 'a nice, handsome young man with no vices'. Glyn Jones thought it was Thomas's first visit to Laugharne for years, perhaps the first visit he ever paid to the place, which has the River Taf between it and the Fernhill area. They crossed it in the rowing-boat ferry, perhaps on Whit Monday, 21 May, and had tea at Brown's Hotel, already owned by the ubiquitous Williams family.

In the gloomy parish church, Dylan fantasised about Black Masses and satanic rectors; he said he could feel evil 'oozing out of the walls'. His Whitsun letter to Pamela, written (probably) on the same day, has a feverish quality, as

> the eye of truth, tired of romancing, turns back with a material squint on my self, and marks the torture in my too-bony hand and the electric livingness in the bodies of the goldfish I carry in the lining of my hat ... I am tortured today by every doubt and misgiving that an hereditarily twisted imagination, an hereditary thirst and a commercial quenching, a craving for a body not my own, a chequered education and too much egocentric poetry, and a wild, wet day in a tided town, are capable of conjuring up out of their helly deeps.

Thomas repeats the phrase, 'helly deeps', and launches into a tormented passage about words:

> There is torture in words, torture in their linking & spelling, in the snail of their course ... In the beginning was a word I can't spell, not a reversed Dog, or a physical light, but a word as long as Glastonbury and as short as pith. Nor does it lisp like the last word, break wind like Balzac through a calligraphied window, but speaks out sharp & everlastingly with the intonations of death and doom on the magnificent syllables. I wonder whether I love your word, the word of your hair ... the word of your voice. The word of your flesh, & the word of your presence.

In this strange passage, reminiscent of his previous musings about the poem where 'dead' didn't mean dead and 'rose' didn't mean rose, Thomas was close to his great obsession. Words had a disturbing quality for him. In the poem 'Especially when the October wind' (date unknown, but of early Swansea vintage) he seemed to enter a dream-like or nightmare-like state, shut inside 'a tower of words'. An everyday scene – park, children, trees, birds – and the words to describe it were somehow fused together, 'as though' (says one critic) 'there were no gaps between language and reality'. In an earlier, unpublished version of the poem, Thomas made words sound like a punishment. 'Chained by syllables at hand and foot', he sought to escape into an ordinary way of life, and 'be no words' prisoner'. Was he striking a pose or expressing a true dilemma? Glyn Jones said that one of his favourite quotations was the Biblical 'In the beginning was the word'. That day in Laugharne, Jones happened to use the word 'huddled'. Thomas kept repeating it, 'savouring it', wrote Jones, 'as though it were as outlandish as Chimborazo or Cotopaxi and not an ordinary English vocable in common use'. Once, in America, Thomas told Alastair Reid that 'when I experience anything I experience it as a thing and a word at the same time, both equally amazing'. Failure to see that an image is only an image, not the reality, may have been, for Thomas, not a failure at all, but a positive capacity that was at the root of his perception. The state of mind in which a person cannot tell the difference between saying that 'Jane is a rose' and 'Jane is like a rose' is familiar to psychiatrists. Mescaline and other substances can induce it. In one experiment, 'with loss of insight into the difference between analogy and the literally meant, the responses assumed psychotic-like forms'. These are dangerous waters for a biography; no doubt the poet and the madman may both have heightened or distorted perceptions. It is enough to say that Thomas's view of his own body, and thus the poems that made him famous, may have been influenced by the fact that he wrote in a state of mind where words and objects became, for the moment, essentially the same.

Thomas liked to say that his poems began with words, not ideas. He was telling Johnson in 1934 that every writer worked either 'out of words' or 'in the direction of them', and he continued to say it all his life in letters, talks and book reviews. He was convinced that poetry should begin (as he put it to Charles Fisher) 'with the substance of words'. This was, for Thomas, a statement of the obvious. Reviewing Clare's poems in 1935, he complained that 'Clare worked towards them, not out of them, describing and cataloguing the objects that met his eyes. In the beginning was the object, not the word. He could not realise, and consequently his expression suffered, that the word is the object.' The idea obsessed Thomas. He rammed it home like a slogan, not arguing or elaborating the point, but stating it as a profound revelation, which for him it was, of the mystery of language.

Perhaps words were preferable to the reality of the things themselves. The physical world was always capable of giving him the horrors. They were there when he imagined goldfish squirming on his scalp. Wriggling things and small creatures, especially mice, both fascinated and repelled him. Nicolette Devas said he used to invent 'tortures'. He imagined what it would be like to eat a sandwich of honey and mouse. Worst of all was to be 'naked in a bath of white mice'. A sandwich of dried eyes was another of his fancies. Thomas, of course, made it enjoyable as well as horrific; once again there are the successive layers, the nightmare that becomes the material for the story, which genuinely frightens him, producing more sensations that he can enjoy talking about afterwards. Oswell Blakeston, a writer he met in London, said that 'Dylan's face would light up and he'd say, "How *often* have you thought of cancerous meat?" ' Or he would talk elaborate nonsense about how he poured boiling water on decaying meat, and the meat screamed. A severed lip with a moustache, lying on the pavement, first occurred in a *Portrait* story, and reappeared in anecdotes. Geoffrey Grigson remembered drawings (now destroyed) that Thomas made in his early twenties – 'people having their throats cut, bad dreams, a "world-devouring ghost creature" biting out genitals – Dylan was always inventing such creatures'. Glyn Jones remembered 'women with milk coming from them, a half-wit running through a wood – they struck me forcibly because they so obviously came out of the same imagination as his early stories'. The stories that Thomas began to write in Swansea, and produced for several years, continued to draw on this vein of shudders experienced with relish. Heads burst open, someone drinks a cup of semen and bird's blood, intestines dribble from a rabbit, madmen howl, a doctor grafts a cat's head on to a chicken. With a few exceptions, the stories manage to be both tedious and unpleasant, but they were important to Thomas at the time, and they show his morbid imagination at work without the constraints of verse.

The final horror may have been his body. Without a feeling that he was caught in the machinery of his own flesh and blood, presumably the anatomical poems would not have been written. His body was a trap. One notebook poem talks of 'man ... like a mole within his fleshy prison'; another of 'the jailing skin'. A friend in later life recalled him after a three-day drinking bout, scratching at his hands and saying, 'To be able to tear off my flesh, to get rid of this awful, horrifying skin we have, to get at the bone and then to get rid of that! What a wonderful thing!' When he became a public performer, he would stand at the lectern, rotund and grinning, and speak, as though of someone else, about 'that creature whose sad-sack body encircles me and whose fat head wakes up on my pillow every morning'. And the phrase he used to Pamela that damp Whitsun afternoon at Laugharne, 'a craving for a body not my own', hints at his fears.

His neurotic state in 1934 reached its climax with an undated letter, probably written a week after Whitsun, where he confessed or pretended that he had spent three days and four nights of drink and sex at a bungalow in Gower with 'a lank red-mouthed girl with a reputation like a hell', and asked Pamela to forgive him. The letter was written in a loose scrawl, unlike his usual rounded script, and headed 'Sunday morning in Bed'. He was 'absolutely at the point of breaking in little bits'. The confession was brief and lurid. He had left Laugharne to stay at the bungalow with

a friend of mine in the waster days of the reporter's office. On Wednesday evening [...] his fiancée came down. She was tall & thin and dark with a loose red mouth & a harsh sort of laugh. Later we all went out & got drunk. She tried to make love to me all the way home. I told her to shut up because she was drunk   When we got back she still tried to make love to me wildly like an idiot in front of [...]. She went to bed and [...] and I drank some more and then very modernly he decided to go & sleep with her. But as soon as he got in bed with her she screamed & ran into mine

I slept with her that night & for the next three nights   We were terribly drunk day & night   Now I can see all sorts of things. I think I've got them.

Oh darling, it hurts me to tell you this but I've got to tell you because I always want to tell you the truth about me. And I never want to share It's you & me or nobody, you & me & nobody. But

I've been a bloody fool & I'm going to bed for a week   I'm just
on the borders of DTs darling

This is Thomas the Sinner in full voice. He was to use drink
as a reason for breaking with Pamela later in the year, implying
that he was in its grip. Here he is both lecher and drunkard. The
story sounds too good to be true. It fits Thomas's stereotype
of wicked behaviour. The name Thomas gives in the letter is
uncommon, and a woman of that name, who knew him at the
time, later lived in Swansea. She agreed that the description fitted
her, but insisted that the bungalow story, or any story about a
sexual relationship between her and Thomas, was nonsense. All
one can be sure about is that she had been an attractive young
woman who did some amateur dancing. That would have been
enough to put her in a sinful category as far as Thomas was
concerned. If he wanted to tell a tall story involving sex, perhaps
half hoping to put an end to his relationship with Pamela, the
dancer with red lips was a useful ingredient for a fantasy.

Pamela replied to say it was all over, but Dylan begged for
another chance, and on 6 June she was writing to forgive her
'darling'. On 7 June he was telling a tale again to Trevor Hughes,
the Swansea friend who was already living in London:

Here I am getting older and no wiser, and have lately become
entangled with an erotic girl with whom I indulge in unrepeatable
displays of carnality. In *your* tight-tided little island, does the hank
of bone and the curled slit play its hot, customary part? . . .

Thomas adds that in marriage, perhaps, 'lies your salvation and
mine, though I doubt whether I, personally, could remain sober
and faithful for more than a week on end ... write soon to me,
before I see you on my next visit to London, which will be in the
next week or two'. He arrived a week later for a reconciliation
with Johnson, and she and Hughes agreed to form a 'watch
committee' to keep an eye on his drinking. This was an optimistic
gesture. The summer of 1934 was the eleventh hour for any well-
meaning friend who was anxious to turn Thomas into a sober
citizen, ready to obey the rules that society unkindly lays down
for poets as well as for clerks.

Under Bert Trick's tutelage he was still grappling with problems of the day, writing letters to the *Swansea and West Wales Guardian* (a short-lived weekly paper with radical leanings) advocating communism, compulsory sterilisation and free clinics for psychoanalysis. One of his letters ('A Plea for Intellectual Revolution') indulged in some high-powered name-dropping. He had met Stephen Spender during a London visit earlier in the year. Thomas, briefly dabbling in political commitment, wrote that

> once I walked with Spender along a desolate London street, late one rainy afternoon. 'The streets of London – after the revolution', he said, and pointed to the empty shops, the bare stones, and the grey mist over them. And London, to us, was like a city of the dead. We imagined the silence and the distant noise of guns. There would be stillness and greyness, and blood in the streets. On a hill of bones we imagined the last financier counting his pennies before they shot him down ... *

In July, Sir Oswald Mosley, who led the British Union of Fascists, visited Swansea to address a rally at the Plaza cinema. 'I have just left the Socialist Party, and offered my services to the communists,' Thomas wrote to Johnson. 'I *was* in time for Mosley's meeting, and was thrown down the stairs.' There is no evidence that he ever belonged to a political party, and he was not thrown down the stairs. The meeting ended with the usual scuffles; according to Trick, he and Thomas 'scuttled out like a brace of frightened rabbits'. But already the dominant stories were more eccentric than that. They were about a comic figure, a little out of control even at this early stage, balanced unsteadily between his poems, which were closely controlled, and the rest of his life, which was becoming unconfined, as he considered a poet's ought to be, and tinged with scandal and farce. Thomas was successfully manufacturing a character for the world to be entertained by, part-poet and part-clown; the two went together.

---

* Spender said that he had asked to meet Thomas after reading his poems. He took the poet William Plomer with him. They found Thomas painfully shy, and 'we talked above his head, I suppose'. He didn't recall talking about the revolution; only walking in St James's Park and laughing at a statue.

Not everyone thought him amusing, but shrieks of laughter
followed him around. At the Mermaid, a popular hotel in the
Mumbles, he ran about on all fours barking like a dog and
scampered out to find a lamp-post. 'We thought he was going to
piddle over it,' said Ruby Graham, a Swansea friend, 'but he said
he was a dog with rabies and bit it instead, and to the end of his
days he had a chip out of a front tooth.' Evelyn Jones remembered
a night they put on a play in Gower, when Dylan later led some
of the cast up Cefn Bryn, a long ridge of commonland, for some
ludicrous pretence of invoking spirits at a prehistoric monument,
Arthur's Stone. It was a joke but it managed to be frightening as
well. 'He said he had things – juice from the wortleberry, slime
from a snail. I nearly passed out with fright.'

Pamela still had hopes of a normal courtship; perhaps Dylan
had, too, in some corner of his mind. He was in London again
for a month from the middle of August, and she was alternately
in ecstasy and despair. One Sunday he went to tea with Geoffrey
Grigson and didn't return till ten past one in the morning. 'Think
we shall have to call things off,' says the diary. In a letter to
Grigson, written from Pamela's chaste address, probably on this
visit, he says that 'my world of good, dying fathers and bad,
female poets is proving affectionately unstable'. He was trying
to borrow money from Grigson. He began to have rows with
Pamela. In mid-September he accompanied her and her mother
to Swansea, where the visitors stayed at the Mermaid, and saw
the Thomases every day. It rained and rained. Pamela had hys-
terics and went to a doctor. Soon she was back in London. That
October, in the last of his long, intimate letters to her, Thomas
says, in passing, 'I've always wondered why you won't come to
bed with me.'

At last he was making serious plans to move to London. By
the end of 1934 he would be a poet with a book to his name.
New Verse had taken four of his poems since the spring, he was
reviewing for the *Adelphi*, and publishing short stories like 'The
Enemies', where instead of the dark world of his own body he
looked outward to the darkness of a landscape, the 'Jarvis Valley',
and (as in other early stories) put his misshapen characters into
a witch's Carmarthenshire. In October he was one of the writers
whose answers to a questionnaire appeared in *New Verse*, declaring that his poetry was 'the record of my individual struggle from

darkness towards some measure of light'; that craftsmanship was what mattered, not inspiration; that he had been influenced by Freud ('whatever is hidden should be made naked'); and that he supported any revolutionary body that believed in fair shares for all. Thomas was on the edge of a reputation, although no doubt he was less sure of himself than his confident answers to Grigson's questionnaire suggest. Glyn Jones noted Thomas's anxiety, when he was still in Swansea, that another poet like himself might be at work in a provincial town: he needed to feel himself unchallenged, and since he had few worries about published writers, it was an unknown competitor that he feared. To Glyn Jones, who went on to make his own reputation but remained in Wales, Thomas was a curious phenomenon, with his fierce determination to be The Poet. He found it unhealthy. He was more used to the traditional Welsh view of a poet as someone who is part of his community, a man with a useful trade, not a man with a mission. In Glyn Jones's eyes, had Thomas taken a less romantic view of his function, he might have been happier and lived longer. Whether he would have written such striking poetry is another matter.

At Jones's suggestion they went to Aberystwyth one Saturday in his Austin 7 motor-car to see Caradoc Evans, the writer, whose novels and stories about Wales so offended his fellow countrymen earlier in the century. They had tea with the great man, then went to drink by themselves in the cold little sea-town. They stayed the night in an hotel, and while Thomas lay on his bed smoking and absent-mindedly burning holes in the sheet, Jones told him the story of Dr William Price, the Welsh eccentric who called his illegitimate son Jesus Christ and burned his body on a hill when the child died. This bizarre episode was just right for Thomas, who turned it into a still more bizarre story called 'The Burning Baby'.

But Wales was incidental. Thomas had no intention of being regarded as a provincial poet, and there was no substitute for living in London. It was only later that the question of Thomas as a specifically 'Welsh' poet arose; and when it did arise, he decried it. In 1938, for example, in a letter to Henry Treece, he said that 'the Welsh-ness of my poetry' was 'often being mentioned in reviews and criticisms, and I've never understood it'. In 1952, in a letter to Stephen Spender, thanking him for his review

of *Collected Poems*,* he wrote, 'Oh, & I forgot, I'm not influenced by Welsh bardic poetry. I can't read Welsh.'

Both his remarks need qualifying. First, there is the obvious
sense in which Thomas seems to be, if not Welsh, at least non-
English. Many of his poems have the rich, dark melancholy
and the flamboyant imagery that go with the 'Celtic' character,
whatever that may be. The temperature of the language is above
normal by English standards. The poems are songs about mysteries without solutions, gravely set out for his audience by the
Poet, a man with a recognised function. Second, there is the
narrower sense in which Thomas's poems may have been technically influenced by Welsh-language verse. Many critics have
dismissed the matter. The classic devices are alien to English
poetry. *Cynghanedd*, the best-known, is a complex and obliga-
tory system of alliteration and internal rhyme within each line.
Some readers claim to find echoes of it in Thomas. Welsh-
speaking critics are sceptical. One theory is that Thomas was
influenced via Gerard Manley Hopkins, who taught himself
Welsh and imported some features of Welsh prosody into his
verse. When Treece wrote to Thomas to point out Hopkins's
influence, Thomas wrote back to deny it.

What can be demonstrated is that Thomas wrote a number
of poems within strict patterns of rhyme and metre. This is
characteristic of classic Welsh verse, although Thomas was
usually following rules that he invented for the purpose of a
particular poem, not traditional rules laid down for poets in
general. He liked technical virtuosity for its own sake. In 'I, in
my intricate image' (1935), seventy-two of the one hundred and
eight line-endings are variants on the sounds of the letter 'L'.
Vernon Watkins failed to notice it when he first heard Thomas
read the poem. Another friend who was a poet, Louis MacNeice,
had to have the rhyme-scheme of 'Prologue' (1952) explained to
him: the first line rhymes with the last (the 102nd), and so on,
working from both ends towards the middle of the poem, where
'farms' meet 'arms' in lines 51 and 52. Thomas wrote to his
publisher, 'Why I acrosticked myself like this, don't ask me.' But

---

* Spender wrote, 'His poetry is not so much influenced by, as soaked in,
childhood experiences of the Bible, and doubtless, also, Welsh bardic poetry.'

he was also heard to say,* 'It may be a waste of time for the reader, but not for the poet.'

The oddest piece of evidence is the draft of a letter that Thomas wrote to an editor in 1934, enclosing three poems, one of them 'I dreamed my genesis'. The rhythmic basis of the poem, as critics have pointed out, is the number of syllables in each line, not the pattern of stresses, which is more usual in English. Syllable-counting is a standard feature of traditional Welsh verse, and Thomas subsequently used it in many poems. Was there any connection? According to Thomas's 1934 letter, there was. He wrote that 'I dreamed my genesis' was 'more or less based on Welsh rhythms, & may seem rhythmically a bit strange at first'. Thomas may have had his tongue in his cheek, hoping to bamboozle an editor who wouldn't recognise a Welsh rhythm if he saw one. But it suggests that he was not quite as innocent about bardic techniques as he pretended.

The move to London was scheduled for November 1934. The plan was for Thomas to share a room with Fred Janes. He told Pamela they would be arriving with 'typewriters, easels, bedclothes, brassières for lady models, & plum cakes for Nelson's lions'; they didn't want to pay more than fifteen shillings a week, and he wondered if she happened to have a spare mattress, a chair and a table. Before he left he gave Swansea something to remember him by, with an address to a local literary society, the John O'London's. As he described it to Pamela, he lectured to an audience of thirty-five, most of them women, about sex and the revolution. 'At the beginning there was a frozen & horrified silence, but eventually I induced a few titters, &, at last, real, undeniable interest. A glassy look came into the eyes of the spinsters. I put in several wisecracks & ended with "Let Copulation Thrive".' He answered questions. How could a woman defend her honour in a communist society? Tin drawers, said Thomas. Did he believe in contraception? The day they legalised

---

* By Aneirin Talfan Davies, a Welsh BBC producer, who commissioned several of Thomas's radio talks. Davies suggested that 'Dylan's whole attitude is that of the medieval bards. They gave themselves tasks. He said he knew nothing about Welsh bardic poetry, but I often talked to him about it. You have to be wary of Dylan – he was always laying false trails. Is there a communal memory that a man taps? He may have been able to pick things out of the atmosphere, like a magician.'

birth control and abortion would go down in history as a French Letter day, he said. Or so he told Pamela, adding that 'The more I see of Wales the more I think it's a land entirely peopled by perverts. I don't exclude myself, who obtain a high & soulful pleasure from telling women, old enough to be my mother, why they dream of two-headed warthogs in a field of semen.'

A letter Thomas wrote to Trick the following year, and Trick's own account of the evening, confirm that it was not all fantasy. On their way to the meeting they stopped at a pub, and on coming out, stumbled into some roadworks. Trick's boots were festooned with mud, which added to the hilarity when they reached the meeting place, a carpeted room above an iron-monger's. Thomas sat at a card table, clutching a silver-knobbed walking stick and the notes that Trick had been trying to persuade him to water down. The subject seems to have been pornography and the nineteenth-century novel. When Thomas looked back on it from his bedsitter in London a few months later, he told Trick that 'I still think of that evening with a faint glow of "something attempted obscenely, something dung", and remember your muddly boots with pride'. He had turned his back on the tiresome reality of Wales, parochialism, middle-class values and the bedroom by the boiler. Or so he hoped.

Chapter Six

LONDON

Thomas's first address in London, the room he shared with Fred Janes, was at 5 Redcliffe Street, near the Brompton Cemetery and just south of Earls Court: a place in bedsitter-land. Here they lived (he told Trick in a letter) amid poems, butter, eggs, mashed potatoes and Janes's canvases. Janes was an artist but a clean-living one, and Dylan's parents trusted him to keep an eye on their son. He was physically fit; he practised with dumb-bells and could do things with his stomach muscles while Thomas watched in amazement. It was Janes who boiled up nourishing soup and kept the squalor in check. The room was unfurnished apart from two camp beds, a table from Pamela's mother, an oven like a biscuit tin which stood on the gas ring, and one chair that Janes appropriated as an easel. Mr and Mrs Thomas worried about their boy. Florence sent him a pound a week, and on at least one occasion they came to London and visited Redcliffe Street. Dylan's books were neatly arranged on the mantelpiece above the coal fire. D.J. sat on a camp bed because there was nowhere else; it collapsed under him. 'But I think the boys had a very happy time,' Florence used to say.

The district was a seedier adjunct to Chelsea. 'This is the quarter of the pseudo-artists,' Thomas wrote to Trick, 'of the beards, the naughty expressions of an entirely outmoded period of artistic importance, and of the most boring Bohemian parties I have ever thought possible.' In his role of young socialist, Thomas struck a note of austerity with the serious-minded Trick. No doubt he saw through the pretensions of pseudo-artists. But from the start he found the raffish and bohemian irresistible, just as he found the academic a waste of time. 'Naughty', his word for other people's self-conscious goings-on, was really the word for his own way of doing things. While Fred Janes worked slowly at his still-lifes – 'his apples carved in oil', Thomas said later, 'his sulphurously glowing lemons, his infernal kippers' – his room-mate was seeing how far he could go in shocking people, now that he was beyond the immediate grip of Swansea. Mervyn Levy occupied another room in the house. One of their favourite outings was to Friday-night hops at the Royal College of Art, where Levy was studying. They would have a beer or two, buy a half-bottle of port and take it into the college, where they gulped it down in the lavatory and then charged on to the dance floor, drunk and pretending to be drunker. 'We used to fall down on the floor screaming about mice and worms and magpies and things,' said Levy. 'It's incredible now. We especially wanted to affront members of Christian associations. We used to get dragged away and put on couches. I don't know why we thought this was wicked, except that we both had an acute sense of literature and literary figures – Wilde and Dowson, gutters and drink. We used to like to think we were in the gutter.' In quiet Chelsea streets, a London version of the Uplands, they climbed lamp-posts and shouted at passers-by.

Soon they all went round the corner to a house in Coleherne Road, where a landlady called Miss Mackenzie kept the wireless on loud and sang snatches of opera in the small hours. Thomas was there irregularly, sleeping on a mattress, or in a bed if somebody was away, attired for the night in assorted clothing, never pyjamas. Levy used to sing him to sleep with a song learned from his father called 'I am the Bandolero'. Thomas loved a line that went, 'For I am waiting and watching, an outlaw defiant', and would ask for it over and over again. In the morning, still in bed, he breakfasted on beer, cake and apples, in between coughing, smoking and fanciful conversations. Just suppose, Mervy, he would say, if everything was covered in oil, we'd be living in an oilyverse – nobody would be able to stand up, the pope would be His Oiliness, and instead of Christmas we'd have Oilmas. Or he and Levy would discuss how many mice were needed to pull a train from Glasgow to Euston. 'We could be involved for hours or even days on things like that,' said Levy. 'They became very real, they dominated our whole existence for a time.'

In appearance Thomas was still the cherub with the broken tooth. Levy recalled a black hat and a vast check overcoat. William Scott, another painter who lived at Coleherne Road, found him opulent, even sporty, in a thick tweed coat and a good suit. A third painter who saw him there, Will Evans, said that 'he seemed to be all overcoat – you were never aware of his body'. His mother kept an eye on his clothes from two hundred miles away. Haydn Taylor, his brother-in-law, once had a letter from Cwmdonkin Drive to ask if he could locate Dylan because Florence was afraid he didn't have enough socks. Thomas's clothes came and went; often they were other people's. He borrowed a pair of Will Evans's trousers and eventually returned them with the ends of the legs worn to shreds because they were too long for him. It was no use complaining; Dylan only pouted or giggled. He was heard giggling, one day, that he had just messed his trousers and left them in a laundry in the Fulham Road.

Thomas was the naughty boy from the provinces. It was how he depicted himself in the novel he began to write during the war and never finished, *Adventures in the Skin Trade*, a poor successor to the *Portrait of the Artist* stories, and the only piece of fiction that carries on in London where the other leaves off in Swansea. Samuel Bennet begins by smashing the best china and scribbling in his father's school books. His mother brushes his collar and makes sure he has plenty of vests. The story is funny enough before he reaches Paddington. But it runs out of steam as Samuel moves into an unreal London of picaresque adventures involving drink and women. Thomas abandoned the story, and it became a semi-derelict property on which he raised money more than once without ever having the will to complete it. London as a subject didn't stir his imagination; or if it did, it resulted in a vivid life at the time, not vivid prose about it afterwards.

Meanwhile *18 Poems* was published in December 1934, a month or so after he went to London. The *Referee* had decided to sponsor the book the previous April. But Thomas was not a commercial proposition; the newspaper had difficulty finding a publisher to share the risk, and for most of 1934, while Thomas was planning to leave Swansea, the poems languished. This left him free to keep changing his mind about which poems he wanted to include. He had hundreds to choose from, the contents of his notebooks, but the selection was made from the much smaller number of 'anatomical' poems (thirty or forty are known) written after August 1933. Writing to Johnson from Swansea in (probably) October 1934, after he had told Neuburg that he wanted his poems returned, he said they were a 'poor lot, on the whole, with many thin lines, many oafish sentiments, several pieces of twopenny Christ, several unintentional comicalities, & much highfalutin nonsense expressed in a soft, a truly soft language. I've got to get nearer to the bones of words, & to a Matthew Arnold's hell with the convention of meaning & sense...'

While the *Referee* dithered, the poems were being considered by a proper publisher, Faber & Faber, where T. S. Eliot was a director and had charge of a distinguished poetry list which included Auden, Spender and Ezra Pound. Because 'Light breaks' had prompted Eliot to write when it appeared in the *Listener*, Thomas tried the eighteen poems on Faber. But Eliot dithered, too. His secretary wrote to Thomas on 1 November to say that he 'hopes that you will not make any decision about the publication of your poems before hearing from him'. By this time it was too late. Neuburg had found someone who would help bring out the book: David Archer, an unbusinesslike character, once described in Wodehousian terms as 'a left-wing Bertie Wooster,' who ran the Parton Bookshop off Red Lion Square in Holborn and encouraged young rebels with the help of a private income. Archer agreed to publish Thomas, and supplied twenty pounds against the *Referee*'s guarantee of thirty, which together was sufficient to pay for a tiny edition of two hundred and fifty copies; Thomas grumbled later that no publishing contract was drawn up, and because of 'my ignorance & Archer's vagueness', all he got was four or five pounds, paid in 'small irregular sums'. Eliot, who could have secured Dylan Thomas for the Faber list, came to regret that he had been 'so fussy', saying that 'one ought to have accepted the inferior with the first-rate'.

The slim volume, with the joint imprint of 'Sunday Referee & Parton Bookshop', contained a note by Neuburg to say that it was 'unaccompanied by either portrait or preface, at the author's request'. It was published about 18 December, and Thomas arrived back in Swansea to spend Christmas in Cwmdonkin Drive, taking with him a pile of presentation copies. He marched into the Kardomah Café and distributed signed copies to his friends.

The literary and social scene that received *18 Poems* has been described by Henry Treece:

Auden's first poems had been published four years ago, Spender's had been published one year ago. Surrealism was not to be explained by David Gascoyne, nor *Murder in the Cathedral* published for another year ... The Sitwells were still written of as 'Eccentrics'; T. S. Eliot was, according to the *Listener*, 'A Major Critic and a Minor Poet'. And any anthology one picked up would concentrate mainly on W. H. Davies, Harold Monro, Ralph Hodgson, Chesterton, Squire, and Blunden: with lots of Brooke and a little Owen ... Generally, music-lovers still held up their hands in horror at the mention of Stravinsky; young men wore plus-fours for all outdoor occasions and girls wore Russian boots: Cab Calloway was the dance-band star; and all aircraft were expected to be biplanes; D. H. Lawrence wasn't to publish *Pornography and So On* for two years: readers of Freud still felt rather daring.

According to some accounts, *18 Poems* was ignored by the critics. It is true that reviews were slow in starting. In December, the only attention Thomas received was a comradely interview in the *Referee*. He was quoted as saying, 'Most writers today move about in gangs. They haven't the strength to stand and fight as individuals. But even as "gangsters" their machine guns are full, not of bullets, but of dried peas.' Thomas spoke of a happy childhood and a father who encouraged him to write. He added that life wasn't always easy for a poet determined to live by his work; that there were times when 'I'd give much to be a bank clerk in a safe job'; and that 'no poet ever understood everything he wrote himself'. On 1 January the *Morning Post*, where Grigson worked, reviewed him prominently under the heading, 'A New Poet'. The anonymous reviewer, probably Grigson, found fault with a monotony of rhythm and language, adding that 'a psychologist would observe Mr Thomas's constant use of images and epithets which are secretory or glandular'. But in general he was impressed by 'close, constricted, dark poems, individual but not private'. Later in January the *Swansea and West Wales Guardian* carried an anonymous notice, probably by Bert Trick, which observed that although the poems were not political, 'one knows instinctively his politics are correct'. In February a well-known critic, Desmond Hawkins, wrote enthusiastically in the weekly *Time and Tide*, 'This is not merely a book of unusual promise; it is more probably the sort of bomb that bursts not more than once in three years.' The *Listener* followed by observing that 'the essential principle of his poetry is delight, but the delight is bound to disgust in a very close and tenacious way'; it found affinities with Webster and Donne, and concluded that 'this is one of the most remarkable volumes of poetry that have appeared during the last few years'. *Spectator, New Verse* and *Times Literary Supplement* all published favourable reviews in the spring. It was more than enough to launch a poet.

Meanwhile Thomas was doing more drinking than writing. Still declaring intermittently that he was in love with Pamela, he now announced that drink had come between them. 'Dylan over for evening,' she wrote in her diary on a Saturday early in January 1935. 'Says he loves me but can't resist Comrade Bottle.' A month earlier she had heard him boasting of his 'rather revolting Bloomsbury fun and games'. Rayner Heppenstall, another arrival from the provinces, who was two or three years older than Thomas, met him at the end of 1934, and they had various drunken outings that winter. Thomas's constitution seemed well able to stand the strain; and it was Heppenstall who was locked up for the night, after a drunk and disorderly outing. His circle of acquaintances grew quickly – literary journalists, poets, art students, advertising copywriters. He circulated in Soho, a more amiable place then, and in the contiguous district to the north of Oxford Street, 'Fitzrovia', from the Fitzroy public house. There he met Nina Hamnett and other minor celebrities. He began to brush against major figures; he was soon telling Trick that he had met Henry Moore and Wyndham Lewis, which may or may not have been true. His behaviour depended on his audience. Anthony Powell, an unbohemian young man who was beginning to make a name for himself as a novelist, met Thomas on several occasions. He recalled later that he was 'good company, amusing, intelligent, perfectly at his ease, drank no more and no less than the rest, was neither embarrassed nor showed off'.

Writing to Trick in February 1935 Thomas said that he and Wynford Vaughan-Thomas intended to 'have a peep, in our country cousin way, at the Literary Great in the Cafe Royal'. He gave a low-key version of London life:

Some rude reviews of mine you'll see in the Feb Adelphi, and also a review of my own book (what a thrill of pride overcame me when I put those long wished for words on paper) by Rayner Heppenstall who is a nice little Yorkshireman with an aptitude, even an obsession, for singing Yorkshire songs about the Seven Immoral Joys of the Holy Mary – at least he sings them when he's drunk, and drunk he was when I first met him.

Celebrities I meet often and too often, they being a lousy set on the whole, or off it. Herbert Read, Grigson, Cameron, the Muirs, and Heppenstall are the best. Racketeering abounds, and the only racket a comparatively honest person such as myself can belong to is that of the squash racket; squash 'em right, and left, that's the motter.

Thomas went on to castigate left-wing intellectuals: an explicit statement that he was to echo in many later asides and gibes at politically committed poets:

Since I've been in London I've come into contact on a number of occasions with intellectual communism and communists, with A. L. Morton, editor of the Daily Worker, Cockburn, proprietor, with a youthful notoriety, Esmond Romilly, editor of the schoolboys' communist monthly, Out of Bounds, and with all the pseudo-revolutionaries such as John Lehmann, John Pudney etc. And I dislike all of them. Not so much as persons; most of them, I'm sure, would be quite kind to dumb animals; but *as* revolutionaries and as communists, for, born in fairly wealthy middle-class or upper middle class homes, educated at expensive prep schools, public schools, and universities, they have no idea at all of what they priggishly call 'the class struggle' and no contact at all with either any of the real motives or the real protagonists of that class struggle. They are bogus from skull to navel; finding no subjects for their escapist poetry, they pin on a vague sense of propagating the immediate necessity of a social conscience rather than the clear sense of expressing their own un, pro, or anti social consciousnesses. The individual in the mass and the mass in the individual can be made poetically important only when the status and the position of both mass and individual are considered by that part of the consciousness which is outside both. I shall never, I hope, be mixed up in any political ramifications of literary, or pseudo literary London; honest writing does *not* mix with it; you can't be true to party *and* poetry; one must suffer, and, historically, poetry is the social and the economic creed that endures.

Early in March, Thomas was back in Swansea, telling Glyn Jones that 'the trials of life have proved too much for me'; the bolthole was always there. To Pamela Hansford Johnson he wrote offering to help edit the typescript of a second novel she was writing; their affair was nearly over, although as late as the end of 1935 he could stir himself to send perfunctory endearments, 'my mole, my badger, my little blood-brown Eve'. When she received the March letter, Johnson wrote in her diary, 'I wish he hadn't written.' He said he was sorry for 'all the silly and careless things I've done'. Apology, usually in the opening sentence, was to characterise Thomas's letters; he was forever disarming criticism in his first breath by saying how sorry he was. In Swansea he recuperated. His father was back at school. Bert Trick was at the shop, the remnants of the old gang still met at the Kardomah. It was one thing to scorn Wales as an abstraction, but another to break with the particular bits of Wales that solaced him. A poem written in the notebook two years earlier was published in the *Herald of Wales* in June 1935. The adolescent boy walks in Cwmdonkin Park:

> Who are his friends? The wind is his friend,
> The glow-worm lights his darkness, and
> The snail tells of coming rain.

As a poet, he was established in the capital of poetry by this time. But he still took the trouble to disinter a notebook poem for the local paper – possibly to make half a guinea, more likely out of nostalgia.

It was on one of these 1935 visits to the town that he met Vernon Watkins. Watkins, a stubborn Christian without guile in everyday life, was a strange friend for Thomas, an athlete, a scholar and an intellectual; he was eight years older. He first read *18 Poems* in a Swansea bookshop, not intending to buy it; he was absorbed in his own writing, and apart from Yeats he had no time for contemporary poets. He paid his three and sixpence reluctantly. Then he bumped into David Rees, the retired minister of Paraclete, whom he had known as a child, and obtained

Thomas's address. They met soon after in Pennard, the village on the cliffs in Gower where Watkins lived with his parents. Soon they were close friends, reading their work aloud to one another and discussing technicalities, line by line. This was something that Thomas did rarely, if ever, with anyone else, once he was established as a poet. Even with Watkins, he may not have been always as enthusiastic as he appeared. Caitlin said she remembered him saying what a bore it was that he had to go and discuss poetry with Vernon.

Oddly it was Watkins – unpublished for years after their meeting – who was touchy about criticism, and who took less kindly to suggestions. Thomas may not have cared for Watkins's poetry; Spender, who once heard him on the subject, thought so. But there is no doubt that Thomas liked him as a friend and respected him as a poet and critic. Many small details of Thomas poems are due to Watkins, usually single words or phrases like 'cloud-sopped hands' in 'After the funeral'. Watkins was a bulwark of some kind ('the one happy person I know', Thomas wrote to him), a charitable, humorous man who teased out a quieter Thomas. He was at the opposite pole to the sodden evenings in London. There may have been an additional reason for their affinity: the gentle, even-tempered Watkins had had a severe breakdown a few years before, and been temporarily insane. Madness was a subject that fascinated Thomas. Whispers about the inbred Williamses and their fears of lunacy would have reached him since childhood. He referred often to insanity in early letters and poems, and in stories like 'The Mouse and the Woman', where the figure of the madman is probably Thomas himself. His clowning could be violent, which is what some people found so entertaining, and others scandalous. Once, with Antonia White the novelist, he went into his all-fours routine. White was recovering from a psychotic breakdown; it was assumed that Thomas was trying to see if he could unhinge her again.

Watkins had been ill in 1927. The son of a Swansea bank manager, he was educated at a public school, Repton, went to Cambridge, and left abruptly because he wanted to be a poet. His father refused to support him, he was pressed into becoming a bank clerk, and while lodging in Cardiff, withdrawn and unhappy, became manic and stormed about the house, declaring that he had conquered time and could control his destiny. A motor-cycle crashed outside and the rider was killed; Watkins thought he had willed it to happen. Next day, a Sunday, he took a train to Repton, attended chapel, then burst into the headmaster's study (it was Dr Fisher, later the Archbishop of Canterbury) and attacked him, shouting that Fisher was a destroyer of youth. Committed to a clinic, he kept the patients awake at night by reciting Blake, and attempted to jump from windows to see if angels would bear him up. He recovered slowly and came to view what had happened as a religious experience: he had been dragged back from the abyss. The bank let him return for his father's sake, and he was transferred to Swansea, where he worked in a small branch for the rest of his life.

There is no way of telling whether Thomas knew about the madness; Vernon Watkins's widow, Gwen, thought that probably they did discuss it, 'in poetic terms, at least'. He intrigued Thomas; they intrigued one another. Gwen Watkins regarded Dylan Thomas as the most important person in her husband's life. Watkins would hear no ill of him, insisting that he was a religious poet in the broad sense of the word, if not a religious man; he read many of his friend's poems as religious statements. Mrs Watkins saw Thomas with a colder eye than her husband: 'I always felt the seeds of destruction were there, that he couldn't grow up.' But 'Vernon thought the drink and the unreliability were only incidental, that he'd go on to be an old man writing poetry, like Yeats.' He grieved deeply when Thomas died, and wrote many elegies.

In March 1935 they had time to begin their friendship before Thomas went to stay at a cottage in Cheshire with a young historian, A. J. P. Taylor, and his Welsh wife, Margaret, who was interested in the arts. Taylor loathed him. At the cottage, he recalled in his autobiography, Thomas sat in the window writing poems, crossing out words and substituting others 'in the manner of a *Times* crossword puzzle'. Asked why he did it, Thomas is supposed to have 'answered with a cruel giggle, "He, he, it makes things more difficult for the readers".' Either Taylor was having his leg pulled or he invented the story; Mrs Taylor's expensive obsession with the poet later on gave him reason to be malicious. The machinery of 'looking after Dylan' was creaking into motion. Thomas met Taylor through a poet and advertising copywriter,

Norman Cameron – the 'Cameron' of the letter to Trick quoted earlier – who in turn was a friend of Geoffrey Grigson. The idea that Dylan Thomas needed to be fussed over and saved from drink, women, late nights and bronchitis – that he must be mothered and kept in one piece – seems to have blossomed during his first months in London. Cameron apparently regarded Thomas with a mixture of distaste and affection. Like Grigson, he had a moralistic streak and felt it his duty to do something for the young provincial, nine years his junior. Cameron's own eating, drinking and womanising were well organised. He lived just off King Street, Hammersmith. When his guests got drunk and stayed the night, they were given lime-juice at bedtime to guard against hangovers. Grigson described him as 'both worldly and very upright'. As well as being a good poet, he earned a comfortable living writing advertisements for J. Walter Thompson. Thomas called him 'Norman the Nagger'.

Cameron and Grigson were at the upper end of Thomas's London life. Grigson, later disenchanted with Thomas and his poetry, was at first an active patron, publishing his poems in *New Verse* ('a malignant egg', Grigson called it) and sending him thrillers to review for the *Morning Post*. The scruffy young Welshman and his fantasies made amusing company, in limited doses. 'Night custard', an imaginary product that was both magical and obscene, had a long conversational life. But to Grigson, at least in retrospect, he cut a poor figure beside poets like Spender and Cameron, 'better educated and highly sophisticated'. Intrigued at first, Grigson came to regard him as two-faced and intellectually bogus, with an equally unattractive private life. He found the drunken Thomas hard to take. No doubt Grigson saw him at his worst, showing off and determined to live down his background. It was Caitlin who later wrote of Thomas's puritanical streak, which she assumed he inherited from his father, the unhappiest man she ever met. What Grigson saw was the other side of the coin – 'He was such a physically, sexually unattractive little runt that Norman Cameron and I always wondered how he managed to get any girl to sleep with him. I remember when he came to stay with us in Hampstead in a filthy and squalid condition. My wife got his clothes off and got him into the bath, then found he was covered in a pink rash. We were worried – we had a child in the house – so we put him in a cab and took him to a doctor by the British Museum, who told us it was all right, he didn't have VD.' Grigson, as he relates in his autobiography, had been through one or two inelegant encounters of his own when he was younger. Perhaps Thomas reminded him uncomfortably of things he had outgrown.

One of Thomas's nicknames at the time was 'Ditch'. Somebody else called him 'The Ugly Suckling'. Grigson settled for 'The Changeling' – 'without human affection, left by the underworld under a foxglove'. Others, too, noticed an absence of warmth or intimacy in Thomas. It is one of the contradictions that is difficult to resolve. To some he was the boon companion, raising their spirits, making their day. To others his ultimate self-centredness was chilling. There is a story, ten or so years later in date, of Thomas in a bar, telling an anecdote about a visit to the barber, and being interrupted by one of his audience who had been called to the telephone. Lamentably, said the man, his wife had just had a stillborn child, the third they had lost. Thomas said, 'Well, lamentably, you're a stillborn little couple, aren't you?' and went on with his monologue.*

One or two of Thomas's relationships in his early days in London are said to have been homosexual. His references to homosexuals in letters to Johnson were contemptuous; they were 'sodom-hipped young men', 'willing-buttocked, celluloid-trousered degenerates'. But according to Oswell Blakeston and the painter Max Chapman, Thomas dabbled in gay behaviour. Such stories, circulating in private, have been decried by others who were friends of Thomas at the time. Neither Blakeston nor Chapman made extensive claims. According to Blakeston, who said Thomas stayed with him in Wimbledon on an early visit to London, 'He looked like a beautiful grubby angel in those days. Maybe the whole thing was an act to please one. That would have been much more likely. But he was in bed with me.' According to Chapman, 'My own experience is really based on one boozy evening, the first, when affectionate expression went beyond

---

* Richard Burton, who was one of the audience at the bar, told the story when he reviewed FitzGibbon's biography. He added, 'I was nineteen at the time and I remember feeling immensely superior to ordinary human feelings and immensely cruel.'

accepted bounds and physical contacts of a kind were recip-
rocated. All we ever did was feel under the table and do some
kissing, french-kissing. You wouldn't say he was a queer, but he
wasn't averse to being affectionate to his own sex if he found
them in some way interesting.' Chapman suggested that Thomas
at twenty was 'more just generally warm and sexual than disposed
one way or another. In fact, that technically his ratio of hetero
to homo, if any, could not be less than 80/20 – which would thus
make him accountable as "normal".' Ruthven Todd annotated
his copy of Thomas's *Selected Letters* (1966), against a passage
about homosexuality, 'Dylan once decided to try buggery with
O.B., but when O. reached for the vaseline it was too much.'
This sounds suspiciously like one of Thomas's comic narratives.

Thomas sent some odd letters to Blakeston, perpetuating a
fantasy that he was a Rat and Blakeston a Mouse. Probably in
March 1936 he wrote, 'I haven't seen you for so long, not since
we spent an evening in not going to the Queen's Hall, and not
since I left you, outside the Café Rat, very rudely for a sillie. I'm
coming back, travelling under the seat all the way, nibbling brown
paper, at the beginning of next month. Will you meet me? And
this time I'll promise not to be bad; I'll powder my snout and not
run after hen-rats.'

The trite conclusion, possibly the true one, is that Thomas was
anxious for experience, and set about acquiring it indiscriminately, but never letting things get entirely out of hand: what
he desired was the effect on others. This is what happened with
drink. His behaviour in London in 1935 had his friends rallying
round. Arriving in the city in April after staying with the Taylors
in Cheshire, he was soon the worse for wear. It is never clear
exactly what happened on these occasions, except that he made
himself very drunk, and an object of sympathy. One of his new
acquaintances about this time was Cyril Connolly, a rising young
literary figure. A copy of *18 Poems* inscribed to him by Thomas
was dated May 1935. Connolly entertained writers and painters
at his flat in Chelsea. He gave a dinner party to help launch
Thomas – disastrous, according to Connolly, who recalled a
'slight hush' when the guest of honour, asked what he would like
to drink, replied, 'Anything that goes down my throat.' The
anecdote tells one more about Chelsea dinner parties in 1935
than about Thomas, the young provincial. In Connolly's account,

Among the other guests were Desmond MacCarthy and Evelyn Waugh. Evelyn fled as soon as he could because, he said, Dylan was exactly like himself at that age when he came up to Oxford, and he couldn't bear to be reminded of it. I remember another awkward moment when Desmond was talking about Swinburne's novel *Lesbia Brandon*, and explained that it was about flagellation. Dylan's round-eyed childish face, with its innocent, slightly plastered gaze above the broken tooth, fixed on him and made him feel he had gone too far. 'Did you say "flagellation"?' asked Dylan, in his rusty cackle. Desmond drew on the exquisite tact which had enchanted the literary world ... and reverted to the schoolboy language which cuts through age and class – 'Yes, he liked swishing.' There was a long, even more embarrassing silence. 'Did you say swishing? Jesus Christ.'

Grigson and Cameron decided it was time to separate Thomas from Comrade Bottle again. Grigson took him to Ireland for a summer holiday, to a makeshift studio (converted and then abandoned by an American artist, Rockwell Kent) in Donegal, facing the Atlantic. It had been a donkey shed, and belonged to a farm near by, which supplied the food. Here they spent a couple of weeks together. They fished in the lakes, listened to the farmer's tall tales, ate his wife's wholesome food, and frightened one another by standing under the mountains at dusk, shouting 'We are the dead' for the echoes to repeat. Away from London, Thomas was more agreeable than Grigson had known him: 'My nicest recollections of Dylan are in Ireland. He loved footling about there, by the lakes above the farm. Or on the edge of the sea, looking at the gannets.'

Left alone to continue his holiday when Grigson returned to his newspaper, Thomas worked on stories and poems, probably some of the difficult pieces that were to go into his next book. A long letter to Bert Trick said he was 'ten miles from the nearest human being (with the exception of the deaf farmer who gives me food), and in spite of the sea and the lakes and my papers and my books and my cigarettes (though they're damned hard to get and I've few left of them) and my increasing obsession with the things under the skin, I'm lonely as Christ sometimes and can't even speak to my Father on an ethereal wave-length.' The usual fancies were there to provide thrills and shivers. In the letter to Daniel Jones dated 14 August, quoted from in Chapter 3, Thomas wrote:

> ... it was so late when I came back that I padlocked out the wild Irish night, looked through the window and saw Count Antigarlic, a strange Hungarian gentleman who has been scraping an acquaintance (take that literally) with me lately, coming down the hill in a cloak lined with spiders, and, suddenly very frightened, I hurried to bed. This is written in the cold of the next morning, the Count is nowhere to be seen, and it is only the thin mouth-print of blood on the window pane, and the dry mouse on the sill, that brings the night back. It's hard to pick up the night threads; they lead, quite impossibly, into the socket of a one-eyed woman, the rectums of crucified sparrows, the tunnels of coloured badgers reading morbid literature in the dark, and very small bulls, the size of thimbles, mooing in a clavichord ...

Thomas saw himself and his fantasies, not Ireland. 'I find I can't see a landscape,' he told Trick,

> scenery is just scenery to me ... little He wotted when he made the trees & the flowers how one of his Welsh chosen would pass them by, not even knowing that they were there. My own eyes, I know, squint inwards; when, and if, I look at the exterior world I see nothing or me; I should like very much to say that I see *everything* through the inner eye, but all I see is darkness, naked and not very nice.

Thomas looked at himself with a degree of self-pity, unsure of where he stood. He described his homesickness for the Uplands, his father's study ('writing by my gas fire, opposite the tall, Greek nudes'), and the Sunday-night talks with Trick –

> sitting by the fire until we've set the whole world straight, and the whole Welsh world is dark. But I wouldn't be at home if I were at

home.* Everywhere I find myself seems to be nothing but a resting place between places that become resting places themselves. This is an essential state of being, an abstraction as concrete as a horsefly that's always worrying the back of your neck, plaguing and bothering before it draws blood. I'm at home when the blood's spilt, but only until the pricked vein heals up again, and my water and sugar turn red again, and the body and the brain, all the centres of movement, must shift or die. It may be a primary loneliness that makes me out-of-home. It my be this or that; & this and that is enough for to-day. Poor Dylan, poor him, poor me.

When the time came for Thomas to leave Donegal, he walked away and caught the bus without paying for his food and lodging. There was a row when Grigson and Cameron heard; they had to pay the farmer. This was probably the start of his estrangement from Grigson, who came to dislike (and perhaps envy) Thomas over the next year. His poems, too, ceased to interest Grigson. 'My taste changed,' he said. *New Verse* was a magazine of rigorous standards that carried more prestige than any other regular outlet for English poetry in the 1930s. When it ceased to publish Thomas, he found no immediate substitute. In all, *New Verse* published nine of his poems, the last three in December 1935.†

Work on poems for a new collection occupied Thomas for much of 1935 and 1936. Despite the warm reception for *18 Poems*, he had difficulty in finding a publisher who would take the obscure along with the straightforward. Archer's Parton Street bookshop again played a part. A son of Lascelles Abercrombie, the poet, worked there. Abercrombie was friendly with Richard Church of the firm of Dent, and sent him a copy of *18 Poems*

---

* Thomas seems to be echoing a phrase from the journal of John Clare, the Northampton poet who went mad, when he had escaped from the asylum and was looking in vain for his childhood sweetheart – 'so here I am, homeless at home and half gratified to feel that I can be happy anywhere'. He had reviewed Clare's poems for the *Adelphi* in June.

† The three were all simple poems, at least two of them written early, 'I have longed to move away', 'The hand that signed the paper' and 'Should lanterns shine'. Even these were too much for Grigson a year later. Reviewing Thomas's *Twenty-five Poems* – which included the three – for *Poetry* (Chicago) in November 1936, he said that 'twenty-four twenty-fifths of them are psychopathological nonsense put down with a remarkable ineptitude in technique'.

and some unpublished material. Church, then in his early forties, was a poet and novelist of a traditional kind; he had been a civil servant before he entered publishing. He was both impressed and alarmed by Thomas's poetry (and by Thomas, who embarrassed him by borrowing half a crown at their first meeting). He found the sexual images unwholesome, but he was a sufficiently good judge of talent to want to publish Thomas if only he could be persuaded to concentrate on poems that people, or Church, could understand. A dignified difference of opinion began between them and lasted for years, with Thomas calling Church a cold fish and worse behind his back, but remaining polite to his face, while Church, and Dent in general, kept hoping that Thomas would begin to write less alarming poetry. They also took care not to publish stories (there were several later on) that they thought indecent.

The first selection of poems for a book went off to Church early in October 1935 from Swansea, where Thomas had returned from Ireland via London. They included the first six parts, as much as he had written at the time, of the sequence of sonnets beginning 'Altarwise by owl-light', where images of birth, sex and death are so packed and squashed together that the poems, or poem, have been having their contents variously explained ever since. It took Church nearly two months to reply. He apparently regarded some of the poems, and especially the unfinished group of six, as surrealistic, a view guaranteed to upset Thomas. The idea that he was letting strange images fly straight out of his unconscious on to the page didn't appeal to him. But Church pressed home his criticisms. Surrealism in poetry was abhorrent and anti-social, and 'dissociated symbolism is a private eccentricity'. He asked for more poems like 'Ears in the turrets hear' and 'The hand that signed the paper'.

Thomas resisted. Although he was willing to say on other occasions that 'the meaning can look after itself', he regarded the assembling of a poem as a conscious act. It may not have been as conscious as he liked to think, but that was his philosophy and his intention. He replied politely but firmly on 9 December to say that Church had got it wrong. He was not influenced by 'such a "pernicious" experiment as surrealism', nor, as Church had alleged, was he 'caught up in the delirium of intellectual fashion of the moment'. He went on, 'I think I do know what some of the main faults of my writing are: immature violence, rhythmic monotony, frequent muddleheadedness, and a very much overweighted imagery that leads too often to incoherence. But every line *is* meant to be understood; the reader *is* meant to understand every poem by thinking and feeling about it, not by sucking it in through his pores, or whatever he is meant to do with surrealist writing.' Finally he told Church that he had plenty of 'simple' poems, though he thought them nothing like as good as the ones Church disliked.

In the next two months, until early February 1936, Thomas revised four or five more of the simple poems dating from early 1933. At the same time, he was adding to the other kind, both by writing new poems and by revising old ones. Vernon Watkins helped make the selection. He tried to persuade Thomas to leave out two newly written poems, 'Now' and 'How soon the servant sun'. He thought that 'their obscurity really amounted to mean-inglessness, at least for me, which was not true of any of the other poems', and warned Thomas what the reviewers might say. 'Give them a bone,' said Thomas, and included the manuscripts. Watkins was more successful in doing the opposite, persuading Thomas to use a poem that he wasn't happy with, 'And death shall have no dominion'. There was no shortage of poems to choose from. More than half the contents of *Twenty-five Poems* was based on notebook material. There are other notebook poems, never published in Thomas's lifetime, which would have done as well as some that were, if he had chosen to print them.

Few if any of *Twenty-five Poems* were written or revised in London. Thomas was in Swansea for his twenty-first birthday on 27 October. He wrote to his sister and brother-in-law to acknowledge their present of money:

Thank you both very much. It is nice to be remembered, especially at such an important, if I may coin a phrase, cross-road in life's journey.

The family lawyers, Paff Grabpole and Paff, have just departed: there's been a little bother, you know, over the transferring of the estate. Later on this evening I'm going down to the Marlais Head to give a formal address to the tenants. They're to present me, I believe, with a platinum walking-stick, complete with bell. Lord

(LEFT) Aunt Dosie – Theodosia, Dylan Thomas's aunt – and her husband, the Rev. David Rees. He said, 'The boy should be in a madhouse.'

(BELOW) The old folks at home: Dylan's paternal grandparents – 'Evan Thomas the Guard', the railwayman, and his wife Anne outside their cottage at Johnstown, Carmarthen.

The family about 1909, a few years before Dylan was born. His sister Nancy is the baby. Her parents, D.J. (Jack) Thomas, the young schoolmaster, and Florence, are on the right. Evan and Anne are with Nancy, their grandchild. Extreme left is D.J.'s brother Arthur ('Uncle A. from Aberavon'). Next to him may be another brother, Tom, and his wife.

Tea on the table at 5 Cwmdonkin Drive, Dylan Thomas's childhood home in Swansea. A later photograph, probably from the early 1930s, before he moved away.

Dylan – little angel or little demon – poses in a Swansea photographer's studio with his adoring mother (right), big sister Nancy and a friend of the family.

Grammar School Mile Winner.

D. M. Thomas (Mansel), who won the mile race for boys under 15 years of age, at the Swansea Gramm School sports. He is only 12 years of age.

(ABOVE) This may have been the 'yellowed newspaper clipping' that Thomas took from his wallet and showed John Malcolm Brinnin in America years later. The *Cambria Daily Leader* (23 June 1926) got his age wrong: he was eleven. (LEFT) The unscholastic schoolboy, in striped grammar school tie; (BELOW) Rhossili beach, on the Gower peninsula. Dylan and friends camped on the cliffs nearby in his story 'Extraordinary Little Cough'.

Dylan, never keen on splashing about in water, makes an exception for Pamela Hansford Johnson at Caswell Bay, near Swansea, Friday 21 September 1934. He said he was in love with her. But Comrade Bottle intervened.

Dylan Thomas, aged about twenty-two, and Vernon Watkins, aged about thirty. Watkins remarked, 'Two of Wales's greatest poets. Don't we look soppy?'

Bert Trick, the socialist grocer (LEFT) who briefly influenced the adolescent Thomas. 'And death shall have no dominion' was written in friendly competition with him. The writer Glyn Jones (RIGHT) knew Thomas from 1933 but kept his distance. (BELOW) With Alfred Janes, the Swansea painter, about 1935, sunbathing at the boarding house in Coleherne Road, Earls Court, London – 'the quarter of the pseudo-artists', he told Trick.

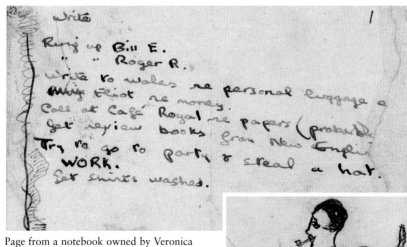

Write

Ring up Bill E.
"   "   Roger R.
Write to Wales re personal luggage a
Write Eliot re money.
Call at Café Royal re papers (probably
Get review books from New Englis
Try to go to party & steal a hat.
WORK.
Get shirts washed.

Page from a notebook owned by Veronica Sibthorp, briefly Thomas's lover in Cornwall, summer 1936. 'Bill E.' may be William Empson. 'Roger R.' is Roger Roughton, literary journalist. The androgynous figure, a self-caricature, has been added here from a different page of the notebook.

Dylan and Caitlin, married in 1937, picnic on a Dorset beach with Caitlin's mother, Yvonne Macnamara, in whose house near the New Forest they lived for months at a time in the late 1930s.

Hunt-Ball has given me a glass tube for holding tiny flannel shirts. Lady Utterly has presented me with a wooden leg.

Thanks again for the present. I bought a grey hat and a book of ballads. I also have a tweed suit covered in coloured spots, a new mackintosh, new shoes, a book, new trousers, a pullover, & no hope for the future.

There's no news. I'm working moderately hard and Dad has a very painful throat.

I'm coming to town for three days in the first week of November, and am already preparing my small jar of red paint.

The tenants are clamouring. I must go.

The November trip took place, but for most of the remainder of the year he was in Swansea. He was there all through January 1936. For the moment he had reverted to being the provincial who made trips to London. If one reason was the need to get on with his poetry, another may have been his health. He may have had gonorrhoea. This is another cloudy episode, if it is an episode at all. His infection has been attributed, on uncertain evidence, to a girl he met at the Surrealist Exhibition in June 1936.* He certainly boasted in London that he had caught 'a dose of clap'. Gonorrhoea was not unusual among his acquaintances; at least one close friend of Thomas in London said he was infected by a woman around this time. But the woman denied she ever slept with Thomas, and the friend didn't think it likely.

The only suggestion in writing that he had gonorrhoea is in a letter to Geoffrey Grigson, sent from Cwmdonkin Drive. Undated, it may belong to the latter part of 1935. Thomas refers in it to the thriller reviews he wrote for the *Morning Post*, but there were nearly thirty of them, published between April 1935 and September 1936.

I'm an old twicer, aren't I? Here I lie, lily-faced between the sheets,

* FitzGibbon's account of the 1936 incident seems to confuse two possible candidates for the honour. One was the girl at the exhibition; FitzGibbon avoids giving her name. He adds that she had been 'involved in a notorious sex scandal', which suggests that she is someone else altogether, another of the rumoured candidates: a girl whose name was mentioned in a tragi-comic trial of the early 1930s. Further confusion arises because FitzGibbon dates his account of Thomas's gonorrhoea by a letter written to Thomas's wife-to-be, Caitlin. But he places the letter a year too early, in 1936 instead of 1937.

looking like Shelley and the Three Little Pigs rolled into one, very pretty in my white pyjamas with a droshki cough. Thanks so much for your letter, dear Doctor, and I'm so glad the *Morning Post* has taken me back without a scolding. I promised to explain to you what happened and why after I left you in London, but now I try to I can't. I drank the night custard of the gods, but they must have been the wrong gods, and I woke up every morning feeling like hell in somebody else's bedsitting room with concealed washbasin. This morning I have battled with a venomous doctor who wanted me to go places with him and do things, but, old Terry, I won by a short lung. I have to stay indoors for six or eight weeks, during which time I feel sure I'll be able to work hard and well. So do send me thrillers, and I promise the most satisfactory reviews. But, for the love of the great grey cunt of the world, don't tell the details of my present indisposition to anyone but Norman the Nagger: they might ruin my lecherous chances. No, I shan't begin dying yet. I've lived a bit quicker than lots of people, so I *can* begin five years under the scheduled time. But that gives me nearly ten years, and ... that embryo you told me about is going to produce many strange and good things...

If his sickness was venereal, his parents are unlikely to have known of it. Mrs Thomas was busy mothering him and turning a blind eye. Her condensed version of events for the two or three years after 1934 was that Dylan went to London to share a flat with reliable Fred Janes; had a 'breakdown'; and returned to Cwmdonkin Drive, where he remained until he married. Nothing was too much trouble. When Dylan stayed up late, writing a last-minute book review that he took to the station to catch the overnight mail-train to London, his mother stayed up late as well, making him cups of coffee.

Early in 1936, Thomas was off to London again for another round of city life. Before he left, he heard from a new friend in high places, Edith Sitwell. As Grigson faded out, Sitwell became Thomas's chief advocate. The fact that Thomas was willing to be flattered and approved of by her may have been a significant reason for Grigson's disenchantment with him. Her letter to Thomas in January 1936 foreshadowed an article that was to appear in the next month's *London Mercury*, belatedly reviewing *18 Poems* and a single poem, 'A grief ago', written the previous year and published in a small magazine. This poem had made Sitwell look again; she changed her mind about Thomas. D.J. was visibly impressed when her letter came. Mrs Thomas hurried to tell her cronies. On 17 January Thomas was replying in his best-behaved manner on pages torn from an exercise book. The 'starch-itch-trash' poem, which Thomas now disparaged for her benefit, was 'Our eunuch dreams', the one Sitwell had attacked in her book two years earlier.

I wouldn't be able to thank you enough for your letter, so I won't try, but I loved it and appreciated it, and I'll owe you a lot always for your encouragement. No, of course, I don't care a damn for an audience, or for 'success', but it *is* exciting – I suppose it's the only external reward – to have things liked for the reasons one writes them, to be believed in by someone one believes in who's right outside the nasty schools and the clever things one (me) doesn't want to understand, like surrealism and Cambridge quarterlies and Communism and the Pope of Rome. And yes God does permit everything, and health's only a little thing, and to the devil anyway with 'personal troubles' which *are* the devil – (mine are only the indescribably mean naggings of having absolutely no money at all, for I live on my few poems and stories and you know what that means, and a few rowdy habits, and the very insignificant melancholies of 'things not coming right' etc, and really nothing very much more). I'm a very happy sort of bird, and I don't care much.

How I would like you to be able to do something about those new poems of mine, because there are quite enough to make a small book and I would like to have nothing more to do with Richard Church. I've a contract for poems with Dent's, but if Church dislikes my surrealist imitations so strongly that he'll be willing to break the contract – and I think he does hate them and will be willing – could I let you know then and would you help me? It *is* kind of you to suggest wanting to help them be published.

I don't think I should have mentioned that I was eighteen when I wrote that Welsh-starch-itch-trash poem; it sounded like an excuse, but it wasn't because I'm twentyone and the same excuse would apply to every line I write. I know, though, that you didn't take it as an excuse – and anyway why should I talk about that silly poem? Why, by the way, Miss Sitwell, are people of my age – and I would say that when I know that age doesn't matter a bit in poetry, (does

it?) – so terribly frightened, in their talk and letters, of being solemn
and earnest for one moment? I know I am...

From then on he could do no wrong as poet or man in Sitwell's
eyes. Soon she was advising him to take a regular job, and he
was agreeing that it was the most sensible suggestion in the
world, except that he had no qualifications. This was true enough.
But work, in any case, would have pinned him down, would
have made him crystallise something that he preferred to keep
fluid.

In London before the middle of February, he had another brief
spell of city life, in and out of pubs, sleeping wherever there was
a spare bed or couch, before stumbling away again, back to the
west. Any attempt to chronicle these London trips in detail or
even with coherence is impossible. They are one long anecdote
in the collective memory of those who knew him then. Rayner
Heppenstall, who claimed he had a wonderful memory, reported
that on the morning of 12 February 1936, while proceeding in
the direction of Charlotte Street to find a pub, Thomas coughed,
spat, regarded the spittle and said, 'Blood, boy! That's the stuff!'
Such police-court detail is rare. John Pudney, the poet, remembered walking in Richmond Park with Thomas who was apparently in rude health but insisted there was something wrong with
his eyes. They had to call at a chemist's to buy medication. 'I've
got death in me,' Thomas kept repeating. But when it happened,
give or take a couple of years, Pudney couldn't recall.

Episodes in pubs are the most difficult, for obvious reasons. It
is hard to distinguish between one year and another; occasionally
between decades. The stories have blurred edges; it is part of
their essence that they should not be tied to anything so pedestrian
as a date. It is not as if very much happened, except that beer
was drunk and stories were told. Margaret Taylor said that
Thomas was always 'awfully like a Welshman up for the Cup'.
Many found him the funniest man they had ever heard. He
provided instant entertainment. Heppenstall remembered scato-
logical limericks from 1934 or 1935 that Thomas would recite
to saloon-bar audiences who liked that sort of thing. One of
them (unpunctuated, because Heppenstall never saw it written
down) went:

There was an old bugger called God
Who put a young virgin in pod
  This amazing behaviour
  Produced Christ our saviour
Who died on a cross poor old sod.*

When Thomas was in the mood he was a relentless performer. Nigel Henderson said that 'Dylan was a Pied Piper. The word used to go round that he was in town and the call was to let it all hang out. I remember one occasion we put on a pansy act in Leicester Square, when there was some rugger celebration going on. We decided to go and take the mickey. We put a couple of enormous chrysanthemums in our buttonholes, and in we minced, into the pub where they all were. Of course they razzed us, and the more they razzed, the more we minced.' Henderson, later a painter, was an ex-public schoolboy, trying to write poetry and determined to shed his public-school background. The first time he met Thomas he was introduced to the night-custard fantasy. At first he was puzzled; soon he was laughing hysterically like everyone else. He showed Thomas his poems, and Thomas, who had (or said he had) little respect even for his famous contemporaries, looked at them for a while and said, 'Ah. Fucked-out Yeats.' Henderson was susceptible to Thomas but not too susceptible to notice the appetite for an audience. 'There were always new waves of people coming in, and Dylan seemed to have this quite sickening need to charm and enchant them. He had to win them to his side.' Glyn Jones, who went to stay with Thomas in London, had been seduced by his warmth from the start – 'he appeared at will to be able to lap his friends in a gay and loving atmosphere' – and by such tricks as his gift for mimicry, when he imitated Welshy art students in Swansea discussing one another – "e's not 'alf a good shader, aye.' Jones found him sensitive to every shift of mood in a companion. But Thomas's knack of changing his opinions to suit whatever group he was with made him uneasy.

John Pudney, another friend with reservations, found him too

* Heppenstall added, 'I always want to alter the last three words to "the poor sod" because of the "old" in the first line, but the words are strictly as I heard them from Dylan.'

anxious to perform. 'Meeting Dylan in a pub, he could get to be rather boring. He'd offer to bite the caps off bottles of beer with his teeth, if he could have the beer. Or he'd say, "Let's be dogs." That used to be one of his great things – he'd go behind the counter, biting people. Then he'd say, "Let's go somewhere else," and he'd want to do the same thing there. The need for an audience, that was the boring part.' The dog-on-all-fours act was also performed at Cambridge University. Thomas was there to read poems to a literary group. This was presumably the occasion that the late Professor E. M. W. Tillyard described in 1962. Tillyard was taken to an undergraduate's rooms. 'Luckily there were other people there, for meeting Thomas brought no reward. He was in the feeble, maudlin state of intoxication and spent his time crawling under the table and round the furniture, making vague animal noises. He was entirely good-natured and was kept happy by an occasional stroke of the head or pat on the back.'* This foreshadowed many encounters with academic figures; they didn't bring out the best in Thomas, who (especially in America) felt an uneasy need to amuse or insult.

One common observation by friends is that he was different and on the whole nicer if he was in a small group, preferably not in London. He did not have to try so hard. But it was the trying that produced most of what there was to notice; perhaps in his poetry as well as in his saloon-bar performances. Tom Blackburn, poet, then a schoolteacher, knew him in the 1930s and after, but never to talk to away from a crowd. What he saw was a man who 'liked to be the centre of a group, to be a precipitate for laughter'. Blackburn was present when Thomas and the painter Francis Bacon were introduced. The meeting produced no exchange of brilliance. 'It was a deadly failure. They both wanted to do the same thing: talk.'

On the whole, people don't seem to have had much chance to see Thomas plain. It was not his intention that they should. He spun clouds of fantasy and deceit, making a virtue of a preference for concealment. He kept reality at arm's length with his comic monologues about the ludicrous things that happened to a funny

---

* The same occasion was described more favourably by an undergraduate, quoted by Gwen Watkins, who described Thomas's 'wild, brilliant, anarchic comments on the contemporary literary scene'.

little Welshman called Thomas who was a surrogate for somebody else, whose voice was different. Looking back at people's reminiscences of Thomas the Raconteur in action, it is possible to catch a more sinister note behind the laughter. Howard Moss of the *New Yorker*, an American friend in the 1950s, wrote that 'often, in Thomas's conversation, one could hear a tune rather different from what the words implied, orchestrating them somewhere off in the distance'. 'His reality was his poetry,' said John Pudney. 'His unreality was his way of life.' Even his poems, where he sought to make direct statements of the truth, had to be enormously contrived, the intricate mechanisms packed tight inside their shell. Writing letters or talking in bars, he described fantastic or bizarre happenings which ballooned out of trivial events, or no events at all. Glyn Jones 'once heard him describe to a ring of middle-class English bohemians the daily stripping and bathing of Welsh miners before the kitchen fire', which Thomas turned into 'a sort of unbridled sexual rout'. It is unlikely that he had ever seen a miner bathe, however innocently. But it made a good story. One monologue (which started life some years later) concerned a railway journey in wartime, when three American soldiers were in the same compartment. He had a packet of sandwiches, and a crossword puzzle to pass the time. While he ate the sandwiches he did the puzzle. Presently the pencil became blunt, and he sharpened it with a razor blade he had brought for the purpose. Then he cut himself. All the time the soldiers were watching. He tried to go on eating but he bled into his sandwich. Nobody said anything. Desperately, he put the razor blade into the bloodstained sandwich and threw it out of the window. Cordelia Locke – with her actor-husband, a post-war friend of the Thomas family – heard the story in an Oxfordshire village. It must be the same story that G. S. Fraser heard in another version, in a bar near Broadcasting House, 'about a wartime railway journey in the blackout, in a carriage crammed with large, grim, silent Canadian soldiers, and about Dylan's embarrassment in opening in front of them an untidy brown paper parcel full of sandwiches, finding that the sandwiches almost choked him under the Canadians' steady stares, and fumbling hopelessly to parcel the sandwiches up again. He made this stretch half an hour, getting funnier all the time.'

There were people in London who believed he was summoned

to Buckingham Palace to read his poetry to the royal family, accompanied by his wife. He gave the Queen a piece of his mind, after which the amazing Dylan, retreating backwards from the presence, skidded on the carpet and shot out of the chamber on his bottom. There were people who believed that Dylan was introduced to the Queen and tried to stub out a cigarette on her hand (royalty always goaded him to an extreme verbal response among friends). The woman who told the first royal story also said that she personally was in the bar of the Wheatsheaf one night when Thomas, standing at the counter with a crowd of people, opened his trousers and offered his penis to a girl, who screamed. Did she actually see it? No, but she knew what was happening. Arguably it matters little whether he did it or not. But it would be useful to know, with the Thomas Legend, where fantasy (both his and others') ends, the better to understand what reality meant to him.

A few years before Thomas died, Glyn Jones, who saw him only rarely by now, went to Laugharne to discuss a BBC radio programme (which was never made) in a series on 'How I Write'. From the work-shed above the Boat House they could see the farmhouse across the estuary where Jones's grandfather was born. Ah, said Thomas, and that farm next to it is Pentowin, where *my* grandfather was born. It was not, as Jones heard later from old Mrs Thomas; the only family connection with Pentowin was that Annie and Jim had farmed it before they went to Fernhill. Jones saw the remark as 'another of those charming and rather childlike attempts of his at saying what would please and be of interest, and create a bond between himself and his listener'. In any case, Thomas may have thought it was true. The borderline between fact and fiction may have been blurred inside his head as well as outside it.

In the spring of 1936, Thomas's London friends thought it was time they sent him off, yet again, for a holiday in the country. Thomas (according to Oswell Blakeston) was showing signs of stress; he insisted that a bus conductor said to him, 'It's a two-penny fare, but for you, Rat, it's sixpence.' Blakeston introduced him to an unshockable woman called Wyn Henderson over dinner in a Soho restaurant, an occasion master-minded by Norman Cameron, who knew that Mrs Henderson had a cottage in Cornwall, near Land's End. Mrs Henderson, handsome and auburn-haired, in her late thirties, was the mother of Nigel Henderson; she had had three children before she was twenty-one. She was at various times a writer, a typographer and a publisher, and she knew all about the vagaries and bad habits of artists, whose company she craved. In March 1936 she wrote to Thomas, who was back in Wales again, inviting him to the cottage. He replied – 'a scrubby Welshman with a three-weeks-accumulated hangover and a heart full of love and nerves full of alcohol' – to say that 'it sounds just what I want it to be, and I can write poems, and stories about vampire sextons deflowering their daughters with very tiny scythes, and draw rude little pictures of three-balled clergymen, and go [to] pubs and walks with you. It's all too lovely to be good; and I'd enjoy it so much.' Soon they were catching the train from Paddington. Thomas stayed with Mrs Henderson for a couple of months, first at Porthcurno, then at a house she moved to in Mousehole, a few miles away. She used to hear him working in another room, reciting poems aloud. Her brief was to look after him, so she would try to stop him slipping out for too many drinks. Once when she went to collect him from a pub he boasted that he had drunk forty pints. Farm workers helped her get him home – 'raving all the time about vampires,' said Mrs Henderson, 'telling me to be sure to shut the windows.' Thomas was incontinent on this occasion. She brought soap and water, 'washed him like a baby', and left him in clean pyjamas. His relationship with her, she said, was 'very much son to mother', but that didn't stop them ending up in bed. She found him a straightforward lover who liked to be mothered. He was inhibited and slightly furtive. 'One thought of him always as a *little* man,' she used to say, adding that 'the more women who responded to him, the more secure he felt'. Henderson noted 'a curious sense of unreality about Dylan's personality. He was always building it up and reassembling it – almost as if he didn't believe in himself, not as a complete person.'

Thomas found her overwhelming. In a letter to Norman Cameron's wife Elfriede, written from Porthcurno, which is a few miles from Land's End, on 25 April, he said what he really felt about her and the place they were in:

I wish I hadn't come here; this is a little London, even though the

Out-of-Doors is lovely and there's lots of Nature about. I don't like the big, natural spaces between houses much, but Cornwall's a nice, nice county as the exterior world goes, and Mousehole is the best village. I want to live there (Mousehole), not with our Wyn but cosy and cheaply with something dumb and lovely of my own choice, with a woman who hasn't been psycho-analysed or rodgered by celebrities. Wyn at her best's at her booziest, when she sings her simple song about the Sparrow:

> There was a bloody sparrow
> Flew up a bloody spout,
> Came a bloody thunderstorm
> And blew the bugger out.

I think that's awfully good; I say it about twice a day and laugh and laugh; but perhaps it's not so funny.

In Cornwall he was probably working on the final poems for the new book. Before leaving Swansea he had written to Richard Church with a polite ultimatum: either Dent published the 'not-so-simples' alongside the 'simples', or Thomas would take his poems elsewhere. Stories about 'vampire sextons', too, were being written around this time. The fantasies that Thomas produced in the mid-1930s were his nearest approach to surrealism, full of nightmarish scenes, hallucinations and dream-episodes. Also in April he wrote to Vernon Watkins to say that he was halfway through a story and had almost finished a poem. As in many of his letters over the next ten years, he seemed to be going out of his way to make his life sound a muddle. Watkins heard more faint praise for Cornwall: a suburban hill, with houses called the Elms and Rookery Nook, was more to his taste: 'I'm not a country man,' said Thomas. He deprecated his behaviour in London ('Life No. 13: promiscuity, booze, coloured shirts, too much talk, too little work'). In Cornwall, his work stopped him being unhappy. But (he went on)

here again I'm not free; perhaps, as you said once, I should stop writing altogether for some time; now I'm almost afraid of all the once-necessary artifices and obscurities, and can't, for the life or the death of me, get any real liberation, any diffusion or dilution or anything, into the churning bulk of the words; I seem, more than ever, to be tightly packing away everything I have and know into a mad-doctor's bag, and then locking it up: all you can see is the bag, all you can know is that it's full to the clasp, all you have to trust is that the invisible and intangible things packed away are – if they *could* only be seen and touched – worth quite a lot ... I don't fear – we talked about it, do you remember – any sudden cessation or drying-up, any coming to the end, any (sentimentally speaking) putting out of the fires; what I do fear is an ingrowing, the impulse growing like a toenail into the artifice ...

What Thomas feared was real enough. His adolescent burst of energy was fading into the past. By the spring or early summer of 1936 – that is, when he was still only twenty-one – he had written about half the *Collected Poems* in their final or near-final versions, and drafted early versions of another ten or so. Writing became a slower process; the words had to be dragged out. 'The impulse growing into the artifice' was a problem without an easy solution; perhaps without a solution at all. But there was some short-term consolation. Church wrote to him at Porthcurno at the end of April, 'Still I cannot understand the meaning of the poems, but in this matter I have decided to put myself aside and let you and the public face each other. I am accordingly taking steps to have the book set up in type.' The original title was to be 'Poems in Sequence'. Thomas wouldn't have this. Writing to Church at the start of July, he said he wanted it to be 'just the number of poems there are in the book' – he didn't know how many there were, 'as I've sent the poems in batches and in such a muddly way'. The final batch had been sent nine days earlier. Counting the ten-part sonnet sequence 'Altarwise by owl-light' as one poem, there were twenty-five of them. Preparations went ahead for an edition of seven hundred copies.

By now he had left Cornwall, and was once more to-ing and fro-ing between London and Swansea. From Wales he travelled up to the Surrealist Exhibition in June, where strange exhibits and stranger people were to be seen at the New Burlington Galleries. Salvador Dali gave an inaudible lecture from inside a diver's suit, and nearly suffocated when the helmet jammed. The girl who is said, unreliably, to have given Thomas gonorrhoea was there. He read poems, with others, at an evening session to accompany the exhibition; 'I haven't discovered why,' he said in a letter to Church. T. S. Eliot had accepted a story, 'The Orchards', sent to him from Cornwall, for the *Criterion*, and it appeared there in July 1936. The two had met that spring. 'I've never seen him human,' Thomas wrote to Desmond Hawkins, 'only in his office telling me "And what is more, surrealism is a dead horse".' They also drank in a pub and had lunch. Vernon Watkins, not one of the boozy pals who laughed behind Eliot's back and called him 'the Pope', was told that Eliot was 'charming, a great man, I think, utterly unaffected'; Thomas said they talked mainly about rheumatism.

Seven or eight poems from the forthcoming book appeared in magazines during the summer, and the book itself was published on 10 September 1936. The reviews were generally favourable, but with one exception they were not as enthusiastic as they had been for *18 Poems*. The *Times Literary Supplement*, reviewing him the week after publication, was perturbed by his obscurity, and picked on one of the poems that Vernon Watkins had found meaningless, 'How soon the servant sun'. (Thomas's old editor in Swansea, J. D. Williams, picked on the other, 'Now', in a kindly but baffled notice in the *Herald of Wales*.) Desmond Hawkins, this time writing in the *Spectator*, praised Thomas's talent but found difficulty with syntax and imagery: 'On the whole he has been less successful than before in subduing his material to a communicable form.' The *New Statesman*, which managed to ignore *18 Poems* when it was published in 1934, now reviewed it (a reprint of 250 copies had been issued earlier in 1936) along with *Twenty-five Poems*, and announced that it preferred the first book – 'the record of a volcanic adolescence' – to the second, with its sharp contrast between the simpler, more ordinary pieces and the 'eerie bombast' of the rest. The review ended by observing that Thomas, a 'really original poet', was 'for the moment, perhaps, wondering which way to turn'. This was probably true. Thomas's remark to Watkins that he couldn't 'get any real liberation, any diffusion or dilution or anything, into the churning bulk of the words' was a shrewd assessment of his situation. For the first time since he was a schoolboy, he almost stopped producing poetry. After *Twenty-five Poems* he seems to have written little verse in 1936. In 1937 he produced one new poem and one notebook revision. It was not until 1938 that he was again writing with any degree of fluency.

For the moment, in 1936, the most important thing that happened to his poetry was that Edith Sitwell reviewed *Twenty-five Poems* for the *Sunday Times*. This was not a literary magazine or a weekend review, but a middle-class newspaper with a comparatively large number of readers, some of whom bought books. Sitwell's name would impress people who might never have read her poetry (and would certainly not have read her eulogy of Thomas in the small-circulation *London Mercury*). Her review on 15 November was packed with phrases to delight a publisher – 'The work of this very young man (he is twenty-two years of age) is on a huge scale, both in theme and structurally ... here, alone among the poets of the younger generation ... nothing short of magnificent ... I could not name one poet of this, the youngest generation, who shows so great a promise, and even so great an achievement.' She had some reservations about 'the intense concentration of each phrase', but these were immediately softened by her remark that even when the poems were difficult, their images had 'a poignant and moving beauty'. The day the review appeared, Alfred Janes remembered going down to Pennard on the bus with Thomas to visit Vernon Watkins; the Swansea gang were still together.

No doubt as a result of Edith Sitwell's enthusiasm, *Twenty-five Poems* was reprinted the following month; the total number of copies in print was then probably 1500. This compared favourably with most poets of the day. Dylan Thomas was finding a wider public. But it was still a tiny one by commercial standards, and there was no money to be made. It has been said that *Twenty-five Poems* reprinted three times. So it did; but the second reprint was not until 1939, the third and last not until 1944. That printing was finally exhausted in 1950. From start to finish the book earned just fifty-eight pounds for Thomas, or a little over four pounds a year. A poet who was determined to make his living as a poet, with only a bare minimum of book-reviewing as a sideline, was not going to live very well. But Thomas, in 1936, was still determined.

Chapter Seven

CAITLIN

Early in 1936, Dylan Thomas met the woman he was to marry, Caitlin Macnamara; she was almost certainly the 'something dumb and lovely' that he had in mind when he wrote to Elfriede Cameron from Porthcurno. Caitlin, in reality a brooding, fiery creature, Irish with a dash of French, was more self-centred even than Dylan. Afraid of no one, she was waiting for a man who would be worthy of her. She had trouble in her blood.

The Macnamaras had been Protestant landowners in Co. Clare, living at Ennistymon House, a Georgian mansion on a hill outside a market town. Her paternal grandfather inherited an estate worth ten thousand pounds a year, an enormous sum in the nineteenth century. Her father, Francis, born 1884, would have inherited the estate in time. A tall, flamboyant man who 'carried himself like a conqueror', and was more interested in the arts than in estate management, he married Yvonne Majolier, who had a French father and an Irish mother, and lived in London on an allowance. She produced a son and three daughters, the last of them Caitlin, who was born in a house by the Thames at Hammersmith in December 1913.

If anyone asked Francis his profession he said 'Poet'; he published only one book, *Marionettes*, in 1909, but had an invincible belief in his talents. He also liked to hobnob with writers and painters, and thought it the duty of an artist to be free of domestic preoccupations. One of his friends was Augustus John, who stayed with the Macnamaras and painted in Co. Clare, and in passing slept with Francis's wife, Yvonne. This gave rise to persistent gossip over the years that Caitlin was his daughter. The story has no roots within the family and is almost certainly make-believe.

Three or four years after Caitlin's birth, Francis left his family for what he hoped was a new life as a writer and lover of women. He never prospered. Nor did the Macnamara lands in Co. Clare, which slipped away as the south of Ireland began to break loose from the United Kingdom after the First World War. Yvonne survived and led her own life. Her French father helped with money. She and the children stayed with friends in the south of England; for a while they found shelter with Augustus John's household. Eventually they settled in a former pub at Blashford, on the edge of the New Forest, and it was there that Caitlin was brought up.

Money was short at Blashford; tradesmen banged the door and thrust their bills at anyone who was unwise enough to answer. Mrs Macnamara looked down her nose at commerce. Paying bills promptly was not the way of gentlefolk; she thought it 'common', a word she used with feeling. An American author seeking information from her in 1963 was unwise enough to use the word 'colleen' in writing about Caitlin. 'Please do not use the word colleen,' replied Mrs Macnamara. 'It is common and means a girl from the bogs.' While Francis, always hovering in the background, continued to pontificate about love and the artist, Yvonne quietly conducted a long lesbian affair with a painter, Nora Summers, who was married to a rich man and lived near by. Nora was a photographer as well, and liked to take nude pictures of the pre-pubescent Caitlin. By the standards of Cwmdonkin Drive, these were unspeakable goings-on. The Macnamara children grew up with relaxed ideas about art and artists, not least because the Augustus Johns became neighbours when they moved to Fryern Court, a house a few miles away, in 1927.

Caitlin, by far the boldest of the three daughters – the others were Nicolette and Brigit – was a remarkable accident of styles, uninhibited and delectable. Nicolette – who, as Nicolette Devas, wrote a book about their childhood – said that at the age of eleven Caitlin was 'already precocious and physically attractive to men', and a year later was 'a honey pot for men and boys'. Like Dylan Thomas, Caitlin made early use of her looks. Nicolette described her, aged twelve, with

Francis's bright blue eyes, thick mass of curly gold hair, her vitality and her wit that later on was to become no less than brutally cruel. As a child she was a sentimental, cuddly, chocolate-box beauty, a hard centre to Brigit's soft, sweet cream. Though determined, she was no more wild than any spirited girl with not enough to do. At this time there was no indication of the underlying savagery in her character.

Caitlin did as she pleased. She liked to lead her sisters on desperate pony rides, revelling (in retrospect) in her animal sensations. Once, when the three of them were walking on a near-by estate, a gamekeeper cornered them in a fork between rivers. Nicolette was terrified. But Caitlin 'whipped down her knickers, pulled up her skirt and waded across the stream with the water waist high'. Her sisters followed; the keeper was left on the other bank, staring.

As she grew up, the family joke, not entirely a joke, was that nothing less than a duke would do for her. She thrived on emotional scenes and 'always seemed to get away with murder'. Educated, briefly, at a boarding school in Bournemouth, as a teenager she fell in love with Augustus John's second son, Caspar, who was eleven years older, and already an officer in the Royal Navy. In her own account, she put on make-up and a pretty nightie and climbed into his bed when he was on leave at Fryern Court. Nothing happened, or perhaps he threw her out; either way she was left feeling wounded, so wounded that when she was an old woman and Caspar John was an Admiral of the Fleet, she still felt embittered. His legs had been amputated as a result of vascular problems; Caitlin said, and insisted she meant, that this was God's punishment for hurting her.

Augustus John himself painted her, nude and clothed, and seduced her, as he did her sister Brigit, and many of his models. In later years Caitlin represented this as a random attack by a disgusting billy-goat of a man, although in fact they slept together intermittently for years. In 1930, when Caitlin was sixteen, she and one of John's daughters, Vivien, ran away to London to become dancers. They were allowed to go to dancing school, but the only work Caitlin ever found was a spell in the chorus line at an unidentified theatre, and occasional engagements in cabaret and pantomime. London didn't meet her expectations. Just as Dylan Thomas retreated to Swansea, Caitlin went to Macnamara country in Co. Clare for refreshment. Passing through Dublin once, she met an eccentric dancing teacher, Vera Gribben, who taught eurhythmics, the 'expressive' dancing of the Isadora Duncan school, and was deeply influenced. She learned to swirl with dramatic gestures to recordings of classical music; solitary dancing became an important part of her life. As she wrote, dancing by herself gave her more ecstasy than an orgasm. In the early 1930s she and Mrs Gribben danced for small audiences in Dublin and Paris. At Fryern Court they performed in the open air, at night, under the trees; muffled laughter came unkindly out of the dark from spectators who didn't care for eurhythmics. Another venue was the Group Theatre, founded in London in 1932. When they danced there, T. S. Eliot was in the audience; he was seen staring at his shoes.

Much of her time Caitlin was probably in Ireland. In Paris she lived with a painter whose name she couldn't remember in old age. Early in 1936 she seems to have returned to London, and soon after, probably in April, she met Dylan Thomas in a pub, the Wheatsheaf in Rathbone Place, north of Oxford Street. Augustus John, with whom she was still sleeping, may have introduced them; or he may have told her about this curious young Welshman who hung out in bars with artists. Caitlin said they slept together the same night.

All this happened not long before Thomas went off on his recuperative trip to Cornwall. Caitlin at the time was close enough to the 'dumb and lovely' description: not at home in rowdy pubs (though she was no stranger to drink even then), not full of gossip and opinion. Full-cheeked and clear-eyed, she still had the face of a schoolgirl. When Thomas was back in London in the summer, she crept into more letters. On 15 July 1936 he wrote from Swansea to John Johnson, a literary journalist in London, 'I should have had a proper lunch with you, not a few bolted drinks with Betty Boop.' Betty Boop was a cutie in a film cartoon, first seen in 1915; Johnson said that this was what Dylan then called Caitlin.

On the same day, 15 July, Thomas went to Laugharne in pursuit of her. She had gone there with her old lover, Augustus John, to stay with the author Richard Hughes (whose novel *A High Wind in Jamaica* had made him famous a few years earlier). Thomas had invited himself there for the day, and got his friend Fred Janes the artist to drive him to Laugharne, using an art exhibition in Pembrokeshire as an excuse for their being in west Wales. After an involved expedition and the breakdown of Fred's car, Dylan and Caitlin ended up during the return journey to

Laugharne in the back of Augustus's powerful motor, kissing and cuddling while Augustus glared at them in the mirror. An argument outside a pub in Carmarthen ended in a scuffle. According to the legend, John punched him and drove off with Caitlin, back to Richard Hughes's. Painter and poet had fought over her; Hughes said she looked 'like a cat that's been fed on cream'. But Thomas may have spent the night at Laugharne, conceivably with Caitlin, and been there the next day.

Whatever happened, the Laugharne outing marked the real start of the affair. On the Friday, 17 July, Thomas was back in Cwmdonkin Drive, writing to say 'I love you Caitlin. I love you more than anybody in the world.' The letter*, probably the first he ever sent her, has echoes of the gothic fancies he liked to inflict on Pamela. But the resemblance ends there.

> I dreamed all sorts of funny dreams in my big respectable feather bed – which is much much better than a battlement bed full of spiders [Hughes's house was next to a ruined castle] – dreams with you in them all the time, and terrible ticking clocks, and vampires, and ladies with long arms putting out the light ... I love you for millions and millions of things, clocks and vampires and dirty nails and squiggly paintings and lovely hair and being dizzy and falling dreams...

She can teach him, he says, to walk in the air; he can teach her 'to make nice noises on the piano without any music', and they will have a bed in a bar and live on other people's money.

> I don't know what I love you means, except that I do. [*four words are deleted*] (I crossed that out. It was, 'In 21 messy years,' but I don't know what I was going to say). Write to me soon, very very soon, and tell me you really meant the things you said about you loving me too; if you don't I shall cut my throat or go to the pictures...

Presumably she wrote, but none of her letters to Dylan has survived, except for one in 1953 that he didn't receive because

---

* Previously unpublished. The owner, Andrew MacAdie, has given permission for these extracts to appear.

he was dead. A couple of weeks later, around the time of the August bank holiday, which fell on 3 August in 1936, they were together in London. He told Desmond Hawkins that he had stayed 'in Chelsea with my Ireland'. Writing on 21 August, he complained about his 'hellish lack of money' and how he dreamt of 'possessing it in great milky wads [five-pound notes were white] to spend on flashy clothes and cunt and gramophone records and white wine and doctors and white wine again', and the 'very vague young Irish woman whom I love in a grand, real way but will have to lose because of money money money money'. Proving his point, he was back with his parents again at Cwmdonkin Drive. He may have been the rebellious young poet in love, but home comforts and a roof over his head were prerequisites for producing the poetry.

The next known letter to Caitlin also came from Cwmdonkin Drive: a postcard headed 'Sunday', which must have been 18 October 1936, the day before the date-stamp on the card.

Darling, thank you for your long lovely letter and the handkerchief which isn't a handkerchief at all but my very very favourite scarf which I wear all the time – and for the photograph. I like you when you climb,* but I'm awfully prejudiced, I like you when you do anything, (and that's quite separate from loving you altogether). This squiggle is only to tell you that I've almost finished a letter for you and a nice story, but that I won't be able to send them off until tomorrow: I have an ill father who's horribly fond of talking about death, so I sit and read to him. I love you, it's almost too wonderful (to me) to say; but I want to say it and I want to say it and I am saying it – ; I love you; and we'll always keep each other alive. We can never do nothing at all now but that both of us know all about it. You can do anything & be anything, so long as it's with me. This, as you might gather Miss Macnamara is from Dylan – & God, he must be with you soon

XXXXXXXXXXXXXXXXXXXXXXXXXXXXXXXX

Soon afterwards, probably in late November or early December, Caitlin was in London's Royal Free Hospital, being treated for

---

* Nicolette Devas had a photograph of Caitlin in a tree at Blashford, dated 1936. The Macnamara girls were all tree-climbers.

gonorrhoea; caught, she said later, from a stranger at a party, not from Dylan. Many of his letters, including those to Pamela and most that he wrote to Caitlin in later years, had complicated agendas. But this is just a love letter.

Nice, lovely, faraway Caitlin my darling,

Are you better, and please God you aren't too miserable in the horrible hospital? Tell me everything, when you'll be out again, where you'll be at Christmas, and that you think of me and love me. And when you're in the world again, we'll both be useful if you like, trot round, do things, compromise with the They people, find a place with a bath and no bugs in Bloomsbury, and be happy there. It's that – the *thought* of the few, simple things we want and the *knowledge* that we're going to get them in spite of you know Who and His spites and tempers – that keeps us living I think. It keeps *me* living. I don't want you for a day (though I'd sell my toes to see you now my dear, only for a minute, to kiss you once, and make a funny face at you): a day is the length of a gnat's life: I want you for the lifetime of a big, mad animal, like an elephant. I've been indoors all this week, with a wicked cold, coughing and snivelling, too full of phlegm and aspirins to write to a girl in hospital, because my letter would be sad and despairing, & even the ink would carry sadness & influenza. Should I make you sad, darling, when you're in bed with rice pudding in Marlborough Ward? I want so very much to look at you again; I love you; you're weeks older now; is your hair grey? have you put your hair up, and do you look like a real adult person, not at all anymore beautiful and barmy like the proper daughters of God? You mustn't look too grown-up because you'd look older than me; and you'll never, I'll never let you, grow wise, and I'll never, you shall never let me, grow wise, and we'll always be young and unwise together. There is, I suppose, in the eyes of the They, a sort of sweet madness about you and me, a sort of mad bewilderment and astonishment oblivious to the Nasties and the Meanies; you're the only person, of course you're the only person from here to Aldebaran and back, with whom I'm free entirely; and I think it's because you're as innocent as me. Oh I know we're not saints or virgins or lunatics; we know all the lust and lavatory jokes, and most of the dirty people; we can catch buses and count our change and cross the roads and talk real sentences. But our innocence goes awfully deep, and our discreditable secret is

that we don't know anything at all, and our horrid *inner* secret is
that we don't care that we don't. I've just read an Irish book called
Rory and Bran, and it's a bad charming book: innocent Rory falls
in love with innocent Oriana, and, though they're both whimsy and
talk about the secret of the language of the hills and though Rory
worships the moon and Oriana glides about in her garden listening
to the legendary birds, they're not as mad as we are, nor as innocent.
I love you so much I'll never be able to tell you; I'm frightened to
tell you. I can always feel your heart. Dance tunes are always right:
I love you body and soul: – and I suppose body means that I want
to touch you & be in bed with you, & I suppose soul means that I
can hear you & see you & love you in every single, single thing in
the whole world asleep or awake.

Dylan X

I wanted this to be a letter full of news, but there isn't any yet. It's
just a letter full of what I think about you and me. You're not empty,
empty still now, are you? Have you got love to send me?

Thomas liked or needed to stress their innocence: they were
not to be corrupted by the world's dirty devices. For the moment,
they went on with their separate lives. Caitlin went to Ireland in
December, shortly after her twenty-third birthday, telling a
painter friend, Rupert Shephard, that she was madly in love with
someone. She travelled out to the west and stayed at Ennistymon
for four months with her father, Francis. Still hoping for better
things, he had furnished the decaying family mansion and turned
it into the Falls Hotel, where she made herself useful in the bar,
painted in watercolours and wrote poems with gleams of talent.
Perhaps she was there to convalesce after her illness. Francis,
lavishly hospitable, was losing money on the venture, maliciously
observed by Caitlin, who noted his ineffectual bombast and
decided in later years that he had passed the trait to her; his lost
promise haunted her then, as she came to see similar patterns of
bravado and frustration in her own life.

Rupert Shephard, who joined her at Ennistymon over Easter
1937, painted her there but was kept at a distance. He wrote
later, 'Her life was largely a physical one of day and late-night
dancing & drinking, alternating with long periods of sleep. She
was as usual restless; she quarrelled with Francis much of the

time & ignored her job as barmaid ... I had no ruthless streak in my character to cope with her arrogance; her kiss was hard and so unlike the loving, gentle ones that I got from Irish girls, and I was unprepared to be the full-time drinking companion she required.' In the 1990s, there were still one or two elderly men in that part of Co. Clare who claimed to have been her lovers there long ago; when, exactly, they couldn't remember.

By Easter, Caitlin was ready to return to Britain. Dylan meanwhile had continued to float between London and Wales. Not much work was in progress. He hoped to find a book publisher who would bring out a collection of the dreamlike short stories (some of them written three or four years earlier) which he had been selling to literary magazines for trifling sums. Royston Morley was co-editor of the short-lived *Janus*, which printed 'The Horse's Ha' (a Welsh rural nightmare that begins, 'He saw the plague enter the village on a white horse') in 1936. As a rule the magazine paid nothing. When Thomas insisted, Morley bought him a cheap meal at Bertorelli's and handed over half a guinea. Thomas reviewed books spasmodically, but the income from that was tiny.

Writing them could earn proper money. Thomas acquired an agent, David Higham, and in February 1937 was trying to interest him in a Welsh travelogue, an idea that dated from the previous year, when he thought of combining a journey from North Wales to South with some autobiography. His inspiration was J. B. Priestley's *English Journey* (1934) and the poet Edwin Muir's *Scottish Journey* (1935). On his travels he would stay with famous Welshmen such as Caradoc Evans and Richard Hughes, and bring them into the narrative. Augustus John had even promised to do a painting, which the publishers could use as a frontispiece (books still had such things). As a piece of good-class hack work, Thomas could probably have polished it off in a few months. But his heart wasn't in that kind of writing. It was not how he saw himself.

While he waited for Caitlin that winter, he was seeing an American writer who lived in London, Emily Holmes Coleman. Friends thought they might get married. Coleman's autobiographical (and only) novel *The Shutter of Snow*, published 1930, is about a woman who has a psychotic episode after the birth of her child, and spends two months in a lunatic asylum, thinking she is Christ. Feminists later admired it as the portrait of a victim. In the 1930s the book made her a minor literary celebrity, and Thomas would have seen her at pubs like the Wheatsheaf and the Fitzroy. One of the attractions for him may have been the madness. Also she was fourteen years his senior, thirty-six to his twenty-two, another older woman in the Wyn Henderson mould. Perhaps he wanted to get his teeth into one more literary intellectual before settling down with something dumb and lovely.

On 28/29 January 1937 he was writing to her from Cwmdonkin Drive, giving a fanciful account of his train journey back from London ('the ticket-collector abused himself over his punching-machine and the driver buggered the fireman on the footplate'). The letter began, 'darling Emily dear, dear Emily darling, Emily Emily dear Emily', and was full of literary touches that deadened the intimacy. 'I think of you so much,' he wrote. She was 'always tall and death-mouthed and big-eyed and no-voiced, with a collegiate ribbon or a phallic hat. I think of us in pubs and clubs and cinemas and beds. I think I love you.' Much of the letter was gossip and slander about mutual friends, especially Norman Cameron and Antonia White. Then he came to Caitlin.

> I don't really know about Caitlin. I don't know how tough my Caitlin is, how powerful her vagueness is, whether the sweet oblivion in which she moves about is proof against the little tiny hurts that can eat through a mountain while the big hurts just batter against it. I know she hasn't got much feeling about *physical* pain: she once wanted to boil a lobster but hadn't got a saucepan big enough, so she found a small saucepan and boiled the thing bit by bit while it screamed like a frog or a baby and drove us howling out. I know she's done away with most of the natural sense of surprise; nothing, I think, can shock her except squeamishness; and she can blush like a naked schoolgirl too. Of course I shall sleep with her; she's bound up with me, just as you are; one day I shall marry her very much – (no money, quite drunk, no future, no faithfulness) – and that'll be a funny thing.

The suggestion that he hadn't yet slept with Caitlin may have been meant to placate Emily: Thomas ended the letter by saying what a 'lucky little man' he was 'to love you & have you loving me', and spoke of seeing her again in March, when they could do 'everything in the world (though I know what we'll do, of course: just go to pubs and bed').

He was writing to her again on Easter Monday, 29 March, from Swansea; in the less extravagant manner that he could use when he felt like it, presumably encouraged by the kind of person Coleman was.

> I have made some new old friends; I am, if you read Dickens, Dylan Veneering.* The only democratic conception of human equality is that all men are tragic and comic: we die; we have noses. We are not united by our drabness and smallness, but by our heroisms; the common things are wonderful; the drab things are those that are not common ... It's only among poor failures that I find the people I like best.

Caitlin was still in Ireland, at the Falls Hotel. The Easter letter to Emily contained fewer endearments; perhaps Caitlin had written to say she was returning (she had recently 'knitted me a sweater out of raw brown sheeps' wool,' he told Emily, 'and I look like a London shepherd in 1890'). The letter refers obliquely to his Welsh travelogue – 'on Thursday I'm going to North Wales with a haversack and a flapped cap' – and the following week, on Tuesday 6 April, he sent a telegram to her in Chelsea at 7.30 in the evening that said, 'LETTER ARRIVING I'M IN GODS KNOWS WHERE ON ADJECTIVAL JOURNEY ALL LOVE DYLAN'. It was handed in at Machynlleth, a little market town in north-west Wales. But the project soon faded away, although Thomas seems to have persuaded a publisher to advance him thirty pounds.

Caitlin returned with Rupert Shephard on the Irish ferry from Dun Laoghaire to Holyhead in North Wales, probably in the first week of April. (According to Bert Trick, Thomas told him, before he left on his abortive journey, that he meant to start from Holyhead. Was Caitlin his real reason for being in North Wales?) Soon after, on 13 April, David Gascoyne bumped into Dylan and Caitlin at Piccadilly Circus. Gascoyne was a poet and champion

---

* Mr Veneering, a social upstart in *Our Mutual Friend*.

of surrealism, two years younger than Thomas; they had met through Victor Neuburg. He kept a journal.

> Walked with them as far as Villiers Street, where they were going to a cinema to see *The Golem*.* (On the way, in Leicester Square, Dylan got a lump of dust in his eye and we had to take him to a chemist to have an eyebath. Really rather repulsive as he sat there with his inflamed eye and ugly nose, his face thrown back, the boracic dripping between his corduroyed knees; but one did not feel repulsed, all the same). He apparently intends to marry Caitlin M. in a few days' time. She is small – florid in miniature, with an incipient Roman nose – blonde, *almost* fluffy, wearing a brick-red coat and skirt. My first impression was of a hard innocence, obtuse, hermetic, with a concealed but very precise knowledge of how to deal with anyone she might want to deal with. (This may be all wrong; I have never pretended to be a good judge of character, and am often very unfair to people on first impressions).
>
> Until quite recently, Dylan has been living with Emily Coleman who was 'in love' with him. Yesterday or the day before, he confronted her with Caitlin M., whom he announced his intention of marrying almost at once.

Gascoyne's assessment of Caitlin was shrewd; he was aware of the machinery behind the innocence. Thomas was not, or chose not to be. But for the moment there was no marriage.

On 21 April Thomas was to make his first radio broadcast, a short programme titled 'Life and the Modern Poet' from the BBC's Swansea studio. He had told Coleman about it in his Easter Monday letter ('I'm reading some poems: Auden's Ballad, John Short's Carol, one of my own'). When the day came, Thomas was in the wrong place. A contract (for four guineas) was sent to him at his parents' home in good time. On 21 April, however, he was in London. A train would have taken him to Swansea in a few hours, but he left it too late. John Pudney, who now

---

* The 1936 remake of a German film about a clay monster brought to life, forerunner of the *Frankenstein* movies. Thomas was a keen cinemagoer. In 1935 he recommended to Bert Trick that he see 'Morgenrot, the German Nazi propaganda film about submarine warfare, The Forbidden Territory, a sort of Boys' Own Paper version of an anti-Soviet message, The Thin Man ... the best American film I think I've seen, and any of the new Walt Disneys.'

worked for the BBC, rescued him by arranging that he make the broadcast from London. It went out successfully, though the harassed studio assistant forgot to take Thomas's script before he left the building. The BBC was never sure whose poems Thomas had read, or whether he had permission to read them; plaintive requests followed him around for months.

Caitlin was evidently with him on the morning of the broadcast, but later in the day he 'lost' her, and they had another spell apart. Their courtship was fitful; perhaps Emily was being tenacious. An undated letter from a London address* said:

Caitlin Caitlin my love I love you, I can't tell you how much, I miss you until it hurts me terribly. Can you come up to London before I go to Wales again, because I think I shall have to be in Wales a long time, a couple of months almost; I've been in a nursing home with bronchitis and laryngitis or something, no voice at all, no will, all weakness and croaking and spitting and feeling hot and then feeling cold, and I'm about now but quavery and convalescent and I must see you. I haven't seen or written to you or let you know I'm alive – which, at the moment, and remembering neurasthenically my days of almost-death, I don't think I was – since Wednesday, the 21st of April, when I lost you in the morning, found money, and shouted on the wireless. Darling, you mustn't have been angry with me for not writing my love, my love which can't ever move but is growing always; you must not have disbelieved, for one little split hair of the day or night, that day and night I think of you, love you, remember everything all the time, and know forever that we'll be together again – & Christ knows where – because it must be like that. But I don't want to write words words words to you: I must see you and hear you; it's hell writing to you now: it's lifting you up, (though I'm sure I'm not strong enough), and thinking you are really my flesh-&-blood Caitlin whom I love more than anyone has loved anyone else, & then finding a wooden Caitlin like a doll or a long thin Caitlin like a fountain pen or a mummy Caitlin made before the bible, very old and blowable-away. I want you. When you're

* 56 Gt Ormond Street, W1. This was the home of a woman called Veronica Sibthorp with whom Thomas had a brief affair in Cornwall, where she and her husband had a cottage, when he was there with Wyn Henderson. In later years Mrs Sibthorp used to tell people that Thomas had wanted to marry her. She was another 'older woman', but only by six years.

away from me, it's absolutely a physical removal, insupportable &
irreparable: no, not irreparable: if I lost a hand when you weren't
with me, when you came back it would grow again, stronger &
longer than ever. That's my cock words again, though all it means
is true as heaven: that it's nonsense me living without you, you
without me: the world is unbalanced unless, in the very centre of it,
we little muts stand together all the time in a hairy, golden, more-
or-less unintelligible haze of daftness. And that's more words, but I
love and love you. Only love, and true love. Caitlin Caitlin this is
unbearable. Will you forgive me again – for being ill and too willy-
minded & weak and full of useless (no God, not useless) love for
you, love that couldn't bear writing even if it could, to write &
say, I'm dying perhaps, come & see me quickly, now, with some
gooseberries and kisses for me. I'm not dying now, much. If you're
where I'm writing to – please everything you are – can you telephone
here? And come up? & be with me somewhere, if only for an only
I don't know how long? Please, Caitlin my dear.

XXXXXX

Caitlin

Dylan X Caitlin

Dylan

I have to be abstemious.

By this time, 'Wales' no longer meant Cwmdonkin Drive. D.J.
had retired from schoolteaching the previous Christmas at the
age of sixty. His health was uncertain. Grammar School colleagues made him a presentation and expected a speech. Instead
he read them Charles Lamb's essay on 'The Schoolmaster'. There
was a vague feeling that he was laughing at them. He wrote to
his son-in-law, Haydn Taylor, on 18 December 1936, 'I left the
Grammar School today: had a small cheque from the staff; a few
books & many cheers from the boys; a letter of appreciation of
my 36 years' service from the Education Committee – and that's
that.' Three months later, March 1937, the Thomases left the
Uplands; D.J. sold sacks of unwanted books to a dealer, and took
Florence to live in Bishopston, a Gower village on the edge of
Swansea, at the head of a wooded valley running down to the

sea. His childhood home gone, Dylan edged towards a home of his own.

Whatever tensions may have existed between Caitlin and Dylan were resolved by the summer. When it came to getting married, there was no question of doing it in secret. Thomas, as usual groping for his respectable origins when an important decision had to be taken, wrote to tell his parents what was intended. He and Caitlin were in Cornwall, staying by themselves at the Sibthorp cottage at Lamorna Cove, not far from Mousehole. The first page was headed 'Important Letter'.

Dear Mother & Dad,

There's no doubt whatever that I've been a careless, callous, and quite unreasonable person as regards letting you know about myself since I left you at the beginning of April, and, as usual, I've no excuse, and you know me well enough to realise that if I did genuinely have one I wouldn't be long in explaining and elaborating it. Since I last wrote, and that was much too long ago, I've been working hard, but not too productively, have secured a little, but not extravagantly much, money on advance for the Welsh master-piece [the travel book], and have – I'm not sure how much of a shock this might be to you – during the last three days moved on to Cornwall for a little – I can't actually call it a holiday – change of sorts and of weather and of companions. I intend, things which I want to explain permitting, to stay here until the end of June, and then return home for a while – to see mother and you – before continuing the rest of this daft & postponed journey of mine. I'm staying here with Caitlin Macnamara (whose writing on the envelope mother'll probably recognise) in a cottage lent to me by a man called Sibthorp; the address isn't really Mousehole, but, as the postal system here is so bad, I've been told that a Mousehole address is far easier & quicker to write to. The cottage is in Lamorna Cove, a beautiful little place full of good fishermen and indifferent visitors. I suppose that I'm piling on the shocks and surprises in this very late letter, but I must tell you too that Caitlin and I are going to be married next week by special licence (I think that's what they call it) in the Penzance registry office. This isn't thought of – I've told mother about it many times – speedily or sillily; we've been meaning to for a long time, & think we should carry it out at once. Everything will be entirely quiet & undemonstrative, two of the villagers here will be witnesses, and neither of us, of course, has a penny apart from the three pounds which we have carefully hidden in order to pay for the licence. We'll stay on here until the end of the month, then for a time Caitlin will go home to Hampshire & I'll come back to Wales until I can make just exactly enough money to keep us going until I make just exactly enough money again. It may, & possibly does, sound a rash and mad scheme, but it satisfies us and it's all we ask for. I do hope it won't hurt you; though I know I'm a thoughtless letter-writer & (this sounds like a novelette, doesn't it?) a pretty worthless son. I want you to know now & forever that I think about you every day and night, deeply & sincerely, and that I have tried to keep myself, (& have succeeded) straight & reasonable during the time I've been away from you: a time that seems years, so much has happened. I'm completely happy at the moment, well-fed, well-washed, & well looked-after. It's a superb place – the haunt, unfortunately, of aged R.A.s and presidents of West Country Poets' Rambling Clubs – and a delightful cottage, and weather full of sun and breeze, and I'm so glad mother's being well again, & I send her all my love. Do you mind, but I've got to ask you to do a few things for me, simple things and, to me, very necessary ones: could you send on some clothes, my green suit, a shirt or two, one of the pairs of shoes I've left, & those dark gym-shoes. I've had to buy an extra pair of flannel trousers, but I'm still a little short of clean and changeable things. Is it too much to ask, on top of all I ask you – & on top of what so rudely I rarely acknowledge? I would be so grateful, & I mean that with all my heart. I'll write again tomorrow, because then I'll know the exact Penzance date. I'm terribly terribly without money, so can't phone or get up to Penzance to find out: Rayner Heppenstall, who's staying with his wife a few miles away, is going to lend me a few shillings tomorrow, & I can then see to the few essential things.

Please write to me quickly; I would appreciate, so very much, you sending clothes & letters; and I'll try to be much more explicit & less (I should imagine) sensationally full of Dylan-life-altering news when I write tomorrow.

All my love, apologies, & hopes,
Dylan. X

D.J. was appalled at the news. According to Florence in later years, he sent twenty pounds. In the end he gave his blessing as well, but reluctantly, and not until he had done what he could – it wasn't much – to stop the 'mad scheme' of the 'young irresponsibles'. He turned to Haydn Taylor, a man of affairs, for advice; in letters and phone calls they discussed what could be done. According to Nicolette Devas, Taylor telephoned Caitlin's mother in Hampshire, and suggested that Dylan might not make an ideal son-in-law. Taylor certainly offered to go to the Cornish cottage, but D.J. concluded that it would do no good. In two letters to his son-in-law – these, and the one mentioned above, are among his few surviving letters – the old schoolmaster stuck to his principles but despaired of Dylan. On 15 June he wrote to Taylor.

> I said all I had to say in my letter to him, & I put things as wisely & strongly as I could. What else to do I don't know; but perhaps you can think of some way to prevent what is a disaster. The idea, if it were not so serious, would be comic. The whole thing, to any normally-minded person, is grotesque & farcical – but the farcical comedy is tragic...

His own marriage and his own disappointments of thirty years earlier came to mind –

> I'm sure both Nancy & yourself must feel very upset over the insane idea of Dylan's marrying in his desperate financial straits. Marriage, too, as I pointed out to him, would still further damn his potential success as a writer or poet...

On 25 June, D.J. was writing again to Taylor, reporting that two letters and a parcel to Dylan had gone unanswered:

> We don't know therefore whether he is still in Cornwall, or whether the mad marriage has taken place. So far as I can see, there is nothing we can do to 'forbid the banns'. All we know, vaguely, of 'the lady in the case' is that she is of age (approximately of Dylan's age); that she is the niece of Augustus John; that her father & mother live apart...

D.J.'s world of books provided no solutions. In Cornwall, meanwhile, Dylan and Caitlin were still not married, probably because they didn't have the three pounds for a licence. Thomas had heard that his brother-in-law was taking an interest in his welfare, and on 20 June he wrote to him to fend him off politely and borrow a pound or two. The letter is clumsily written; Taylor inhibited him. It was addressed to Nancy and Haydn, and posted without a stamp.

I heard from my late London address that you had been ringing up during the last week to try to get hold of me, and that you'd heard – from father, I suppose – of my plans for a pleasant and eccentric marriage. The people in the London address told me that they had carefully been evasive in their replies to your questions about my whereabouts as they didn't know whether or not I wished them, for whatever strange reasons I might have had, to be broadcast. Father may have told you my Cornwall address, but, in case he didn't, here it is. It's a borrowed cottage with a jungle garden and three lavatories, and is only a few miles from where I stayed last year. But I don't imagine that that's of any interest. I lead a most mysterious life, on the surface; actually, it is the almost inevitable life of any penniless drifter with a liking for odd places and odder people, very few regrets about anything and no responsibilities. You mightn't agree with 'no responsibilities' considering that I'm so very nearly married, but Caitlin is – whether that's a fortunate thing or not in the opinion of others – sufficiently like myself to care little or nothing for proprietary interests and *absolutely* nothing for the responsibilities of husbandly provision. It will not yet, of course, be possible for us to live together all the time, & we'll go away whenever we feel like it or – & this will be, until the days of our comparative prosperity, which still would mean a genuine but never-yet wretched poverty, more frequent – whenever it is, from the point of view of money or/and accommodation, essential. (I'm sorry about these tortuous phrases but I've just been reviewing, with unction, cunning & entire literary dishonesty, a book on Social Credit & the Economic War.) Incidentally, I'd like to explain about my not returning home the day after Nancy and I met at Paddington Station: the lent pound note I gave back to the original lenders, my own expected cheque did not arrive for several days, & by that time I was again in debt for almost the complete worth of the cheque. It was unfortunate in some ways, but good in others, as, had I not been in London when I shd officially have been working at home, this lovely three-lavatoried cottage would never have been mine for the summer, Caitlin & I would not have come to a decision so quickly, and (perhaps, but I think it unlikely, bloody unlikely) another social catastrophe would have been averted. So much for that. I'm sending this letter of explanation to your Laleham cottage, as I haven't had any news about your moving. I hope it reaches you. As a gesture, Christian, gentlemanly, ladylike, sisterly, in-law-brotherly, friendly, & (in face of your obvious distrust of what could be, & has, by father, been called 'this lunatic course of action') congratulatorily from a married couple of some years' standing to two younger persons about to embark on the voyage of legal matrimony, would you like to slip me a couple of quid? I'm afraid the last few words are a sorry come-down after the grandiloquence of my previous circumlocution, but I do, actually, want to buy a hell of a lot of things almost at once, &, though father's been desperately kind & sent me five pounds last week with sort of resigned wishes for my happiness, I'm still really short of the bare amount I need...

Early in July Thomas persuaded his literary agent, David Higham, to raise a few pounds from Dent, the publishers; he didn't say what it was for. Wyn Henderson paid for the marriage licence. She and Max Chapman were running a guest-house at Mousehole called the Lobster Pot, and it was from there that Dylan and Caitlin were married on 11 July 1937, a Sunday. 'My wife is Irish and French,' Thomas wrote later to Desmond Hawkins, 'she is two months younger than I am, has seas of golden hair, two blue eyes, two brown arms, two dancing legs, is untidy and vague and un-reclamatory. I am lost in love and poverty and my work is shocking.' For the record, she was ten months older.

Chapter Eight

MARRIAGE

The honeymoon began at the Lobster Pot, where Wyn Henderson got things off to a good start by suggesting the three of them go to bed together. Caitlin claimed she was agreeable. Dylan is said (by Caitlin) to have been shocked, and Mrs Henderson retreated. From Mousehole the Thomases moved a few miles to Newlyn, just outside Penzance, where Max Chapman had a studio. Oswell Blakeston was amused when Chapman and Caitlin wandered off during a pub crawl and Thomas had a fit of jealousy. There was more jealousy when Augustus John arrived to take them for a trip in his car. Thomas refused to sit at the back, and jammed himself in front with John and Caitlin. No doubt he resented the painter's proprietorial air towards his model and ex-mistress. A letter that John wrote her, some time in the month before the marriage, said that he wanted to complete a 'pink picture' of her – probably the painting that shows her in a multi-coloured summer dress – adding that he hoped she hadn't caught any more diseases from Dylan or anyone else, and advising her to keep her pleasures clean, 'also your quim my little seraph'.

All along the coast were minor writers and painters from London, enjoying the summer. Rayner Heppenstall was there with his wife. As they walked back from a local inn one night, with the moon on the English Channel, 'the splendour of the spectacle infuriated Dylan, who made savage remarks about picture-postcards and visual clichés'. There was the usual drinking. One sunny morning Thomas and friends were in a field above Newlyn, sampling a 'champagne wine tonic' sold by a local herbalist. Thomas talked and talked, then stopped abruptly. 'Somebody's boring me,' he said. 'I think it's me.'

Pamela Hansford Johnson, who had married the previous year, wrote to congratulate him, and received a mainly comic reply about his improvidence. He was full of worries and happiness lazing away all the writeable days, writing an occasional bad love poem of the sort that begins, 'It was not love until you came,' drinking scaly beer in the pubs near the Fish Market, counting Caitlin's change – if any, fighting with primus-stoves, spending the rent. Caitlin can only cook one thing, and that is Irish bread which requires a very special type of oven, unobtainable in England; she drinks a lot though, so we eat in the morning as we're too unsteady in the evening to open the tins.

Johnson had asked what they wanted for a present. Thomas suggested a pound.

Edith Sitwell sent them money, and was given a more sober version of life in Penzance. No drunkenness or bad behaviour was chortled over; instead there was a picture of respectable poverty. 'With smells from the fishmarket in front of us and dust from the coal-yard below us and flies from the dump behind us, we might as well live in the street.' Knowing that she expected writers to find jobs and earn livings, Thomas obliged with a maritime fantasy. For ten days, he said, he had been 'in and out on the Newlyn fishing-boats, making a little money', and had 'hardly been on shore at all during the daytime'. Rough seas and a twelve-foot boat were conjured up. So was a plan to sail to Swansea, working their way round to North Devon and across the Bristol Channel in fishing vessels. He remained on her list of nice young men.

Having nowhere to live, they moved on to Swansea (by train) later in the summer, to stay with his parents; then to Hampshire, to stay with Mrs Macnamara. They were there through the winter and most of the spring of 1938. 'This is a very lovely place,' he wrote to Watkins late in October 1937. 'Caitlin & I ride into the New Forest every day, into Bluebell Wood or onto Cuckoo Hill. There's no one else about; Caitlin's mother is away; we are quiet and small and cigarette-stained and very young.' He liked to see them as two terrible children, said Caitlin. When her sister Nicolette stayed there she would see them going off on the bus for a lunchtime beer in Ringwood and returning an hour later with paper bags of dolly mixtures and liquorice allsorts, and bottles of fizzy children's drinks, all of them things that Thomas loved. In the afternoon they disappeared to bed with the sweets and pop; their voices could be heard reading to one another.

Some days they went to the coast and collected shells to use as counters in card games.

Caitlin, by all accounts, was good for him sexually. Below the surface he was uneasy with women; probably she could comfort him as mother and mistress in ways he found agreeable or even essential. She was buxom then, and he was still skinny; she claimed to have carried him across streams under one arm. Her vigour was what he liked. Her husband's strength, as far as Caitlin was concerned, lay in his talent, his nature, his 'gift'. He was the poet her father had never been. Later on she grew sardonic about his appearance, his short stature, his finlike hands, the seedy clothes. In 1946, when they were in Ireland together, she found excuses for not visiting her old haunts in Co. Clare because she didn't want former friends and lovers (who would not be impressed by Thomas's literary reputation) to see the unhandsome little man she had married.

Early in their marriage she could be quiet in company, sipping a beer or a lemonade, lost in a dream; marriage, wrote Nicolette, 'quelled Caitlin's early wildness and soothed her scratchy grudge against the world'. But she never ceased to catch the eye, with her bright-coloured skirts and the high colour in her cheeks. Sometimes she looked birdlike – a bird of prey or paradise, depending on her mood. Nigel Henderson met her in London and found her 'like the figurehead of a ship, a fantastic poet's girl, a sort of corn-goddess'.

There was certainly sexual jealousy on Thomas's part. He expressed it in a poem he was writing at about the time of their marriage, originally published, in 1938, as 'Poem (for Caitlin)', although the language he uses is fairly impenetrable. This is not because Thomas made it so in order to disguise the meaning; rather, that his poetry at the time was choked with images. Its first line (which was later used as the title), 'I make this in a warring absence', evidently refers to an episode when Caitlin had metaphorically sailed away, forgetting 'her pride in mast and fountain', by which he means their sexual life together.

Thomas explained the poem in letters to two correspondents, one of them Desmond Hawkins, who (in 1939) wanted to know what it all meant before he reviewed a book that contained it. Thomas said he was examining the conflicting character of the woman 'in whose absence, and in the fear of whose future unfaithful absences, I jealously made the poem'. The 'emotional question' provoked by her absence was how to confront the opposites in her nature – good and bad, black and white, kind and cruel – so as to 'decide for myself whether I fight, lie down and hope, forgive or kill'. At this point what he was telling Hawkins became as obscure as the poem itself. 'The question,' wrote Thomas, 'is naturally answered by the questions in the images and the images in the questions.' If this means anything, it is presumably that the poem is an end in itself, a statement of how he felt, not an indication of how he was going to act. He was facing up to Caitlin's promiscuity in a poem but meant to do nothing about it. 'Yet this I make in a forgiving presence' is the last line of the poem.

There is no third-party evidence of Caitlin's infidelity (or of his) in their early marriage. But she admitted it. After the first edition of this book, she wrote to me to say that the best things Dylan left her were his children, whose looks and character reminded her of who their father was. Only a miracle had saved them from being somebody else's. God had seen to it.

Their first child, Llewelyn, was born at the end of January 1939 and so was conceived in the spring of 1938, less than a year after their marriage. She repeated, long afterwards, that she meant exactly what she had written.* There had been plenty of flirting, she said, and sometimes it ended up in bed. When Llewelyn was born, she was relieved to see his bulging eyes and turned-up nose, a little Dylan.

At the time, infidelity was less of a problem than poverty. Thomas's income was tiny. Determined to live like a poet, he still hankered for a regular income. From Blashford he wrote to Watkins in March 1938:

... I have been in London, in penury, and in doubt: In London, because money lives and breeds there; in penury, because it doesn't; and in doubt as to whether I should continue as an outlaw or take my fate for a walk in the straight and bowler-treed paths. The conceit of outlaws is a wonderful thing; they think they can join the

---

* But one was never sure of anything Caitlin Thomas said. She could be painfully truthful, about herself and about others. She could also be mischievous, hoping to outrage or confuse.

ranks of regularly-conducted society whenever they like. You hear young artists talk glibly about, 'God, I've a good mind to chuck this perilous, unsatisfactory, moniless business of art and go into the City & make money.' But who wants them in the City? If you are a money-&-success-maker, you make it in whatever you do. And young artists are always annoyed and indignant if they hear a City-man say, 'God, I've a good mind to chuck this safe, monotonous business of money-making & go into the wilderness and make poems.'

Many of Thomas's friends regarded him as a natural bohemian, indifferent to everything but his art. It is true that he knew how to arrange his affairs so that writing poems took priority. In the spring of 1938, while they were still at Blashford, he was suddenly at work again, rewriting four notebook poems, one of them 'After the funeral', which re-emerged as a clear statement that broke away (though only temporarily) from the cloudy, awkward style that had overtaken him. But however dedicated an artist he tried to be, and indeed often succeeded in being, his background clung to him. 'I am as domestic as a slipper,' he once observed to Margaret Taylor. Gwen Watkins heard him say, 'All we want is the little semi-detached with the little regular income.' Perhaps his tongue was in his cheek. But perceptive friends noted a nervous devotion to some version of life as it was lived in Cwmdonkin Drive. Caitlin, not her husband, was the real bohemian, because she was indifferent to what people thought. 'Dylan had the proper Welsh background,' said Vera, the Swansea woman who knew him from childhood. 'The fact that he was continually misbehaving was a cross to him. He wanted people to think well of him. He was brought up like me, worrying "what will the neighbours think?" Whereas Caitlin didn't care a bugger what anyone thought. She was an aristocrat, and that was that.' Caitlin noted his taste for warm slippers and a dish of things to nibble, pickled onions or sardines, while he listened to cricket on the radio.

At intervals throughout his life, it seemed to worry Thomas that he was unemployed in the sense of having no regular work. John Pudney thought he detected it in the 1930s. William Empson (who, like most poets, earned his money by teaching) wrote that Thomas told him 'how frightening it was always to have nothing to do next day: sometimes, he said, "I buy a Mars Bar, and I think tomorrow I will eat that, so then I can go to sleep because I have a plan." I did not much like this highly polished bit of tear-jerking, but there is little doubt that unemployment would have driven me to drink too.' Writing to Charles Fisher in March 1938, Thomas spoke of getting a job with the BBC. Later in the year he broadcast again, in a poetry reading from Manchester,* after he had demanded his rail fare in advance. He had the wrong sort of attitude to be a BBC employee.

From Blashford, the Thomases moved to Wales in the late spring of 1938. They went to a cottage in Laugharne, that large village with an ancient charter which insists on its rights as a town. A mildly eccentric place, its raffish air may have appealed to Thomas as much as its watery panoramas. Little or no Welsh was spoken there, although it was only a few miles from Fernhill and the family farms, where Welsh was the everyday tongue. The town was off the beaten track, a clannish and inbred community with a reputation for fighting with fists and knives. The Williams family owned and operated Brown's Hotel, the local buses, the local taxis and the diesel generators that made the electricity. When there was street-fighting or a brawl on a Saturday night, Ebi Williams would throw the switches and put Laugharne in darkness. Here, for the first time, the Thomases had a home of their own. It was a poor community between the wars, and rents were cheap. The cottage they took was small and damp, on the hill running out of the bottom end of Laugharne, opposite the ruined castle – 'four rooms like stained boxes in a workman's and fisherman's row, with a garden leading down to mud and sea'. It was called Eros. There was no bathroom. Neighbours peeked through the curtains to catch glimpses of young Mrs Thomas in a flowing purple housecoat, or watch her husband, who was thought to be a writer of some kind, trotting down the hill to fetch water from the public tap, dressed in pyjamas and an overcoat. He was chubbier now; his body was filling out.

After a couple of months they moved to Sea View, a narrow important-looking house, pink-washed and taller than its neighbours, which they rented from the Williamses. The three storeys

---

* 'The Modern Muse', 18 October 1938. Others taking part included Auden, Spender and Louis MacNeice.

piled three pairs of rooms side by side, like a child's idea of what a house should be. Here they lived with little money and begged or borrowed furniture, in that easy-going solitude that writers crave but are apt to grow restless with, as time goes by and nothing happens except writing. At Sea View, temporarily, the mixture was right, or it would have been, given an income of a few pounds a week. Thomas was back again in a small room in Wales, working steadily. To Henry Treece he described himself as 'small, argumentative, good-tempered, lazy, fumbling, boozy as possible, "lower-middle-class" in attitude and reaction, a dirty tongue, a silly young man'. Friends came to stay, and Caitlin took them for tiring walks across the mud-flats or over the top of Sir John's Hill. She had been pregnant since the spring. The family doctor, David Hughes, examined her in their double bed, which, he said, was the only piece of proper furniture in the room. Tea chests did service as tables; one held paperbacks, another was Dylan's desk. In the evenings Caitlin made stews or boiled fresh cockles, and the floors underfoot crackled with shells. The Williamses' electricity hadn't reached Sea View, and candles stuck in empty beer bottles lit the guests to bed. Augustus John stayed there. Treece, who admired Thomas and had decided to write a book about his poetry, came armed with questions to which Thomas gave quirky answers, or no answers at all. Vernon Watkins came down from Gower, bringing small gifts of food or money. He arrived once with a bag of soft plums, which he handed to Caitlin. Dylan, stretched on the sofa, said 'Ca-at. Can I have a plum?' She insisted he come and get it. He kept on wheedling – 'Ca-at?' In the end she bombarded him with every plum in the bag and went off to the kitchen. Dylan picked one from his lap and said, 'Right, now we can get on with our poems.' According to Watkins, the time at Sea View was the happiest of Thomas's life.*

Quarrels with Caitlin evaporated quickly. She was quick-tempered yet oddly complaisant, providing, quite often, the

---

* Watkins was then unmarried. Gwen Watkins, whom he married six years later, said that on an earlier visit to Laugharne, when the Thomases were living in the cottage, Dylan mischievously arranged that Vernon should sleep in their bed, 'to see what would happen. There was an element of cold freakishness on his part.' Nothing did happen. Watkins thought innocently that they had only one bed. He remembered hearing Dylan cursing in the night, and Caitlin giggling.

domestic virtues that he looked for. Drinking buddies from the big city would scarcely have recognised him. John Davenport, writer and critic, was invited to Laugharne. He found that 'Dylan on his native heath was a different being from the extravagant buffoon I had met five years before in London'. In London everything was different. There, Caitlin was the poet's girl. In Laugharne she was expected to keep the house moderately clean and have meals on the table. A woman's place was at the sink or in the bed; it was how people saw things in Cwmdonkin Drive. Elisabeth Lutyens, the composer, noticed the trait in Thomas when she stayed in Laugharne ten or twelve years later. In London, where they were both working for radio after the war, they were colleagues and friends, and 'Dylan took me utterly seriously as a fellow-professional'. In Laugharne she was merely another woman around the house; Thomas infuriated her with a 'cocky, masculine, women-in-their-place attitude', and by grumbling jealously when she and Caitlin went walking or bathing together. If Caitlin herself was more accommodating than might have been expected, perhaps it was because she had been brought up in circles where the artist was licensed to lord it over the lucky females. Her father Francis once declared that a woman was a blank slate for a man to scribble on. But as time went by she grew less acquiescent.

For Thomas, Wales was a place and a frame of mind he settled into because it was convenient. He had the artist's instinct for self-preservation. Caitlin noted that the groove he worked in was narrow but his feelings about the place his forbears came from was not, since he never really left it. His attitudes were ready-made, his poems already matured inside him. What gave his work its intensity, she thought, was this snail's-eye view of his world.

Not long after his marriage, when they were with Caitlin's mother at Blashford, he wrote to a Welsh friend, Keidrych Rhys, to say, 'I want to be in Wales, but it offers me nothing at all; I'd take any job in Wales, because I like living there best.' But a 'political' Wales was alien to him. Like most of the Welsh in the 1930s (and many of them still), who saw the nationalist dream as a delusion, Thomas had no time for secessionists.

The true divide in Wales has always been between those who speak Welsh, and claim that 'Welshness' belongs to them, and those who don't, and resent the exclusivity of the others. Rhys, a London journalist and poet of Thomas's age, who came from Carmarthenshire, was hostile to the Welsh-speaking literati who dismissed 'Anglo-Welsh' writing as somehow impure (declaring, as one of them did, that the Welsh writer should regard Wales as 'the place of his milieu and his audience', the alternative being to 'seek his fortune in the midst of a cosmopolitan confusion of poetasters and minors and literary racketeers'*). Rhys founded the magazine *Wales* in 1937, with Thomas looking over his shoulder, and it became a vehicle for Anglo-Welsh writing; stories and poems by Thomas appeared frequently. While the magazine was still being planned, Thomas wrote to Rhys to suggest it should not be 'stridently Welsh in tone or approach – that is that Welsh politics, for example, should not enter into it'. His preferred title was *Welsh Writers*. This would have given hostages to the Welsh-speaking establishment, and Rhys may have thought that *Wales* was safer.

In 1938, much of Thomas's work consisted of stories, though not stories of the kind he had been writing since adolescence. Those, the fantasies and nightmares, were supposed to have been collected and published as a book by now. George Reavey was meant to be arranging it through the Europa Press, but the printers were afraid of being prosecuted for obscenity. Thomas tried to pinpoint the offensive sentences. 'The only story I can think of which might cause a few people a small and really unnecessary alarm,' he wrote to Reavey on 16 June, 'is The Prologue To An Adventure; this I could cut out from the book, and substitute a story about my grandfather who was a very clean old man.' On 24 August he was telling John Davenport:

I write pathetically to George [Reavey], but he just won't answer. Publication, he has condescended to tell me on a postcard, of the stories as they stand would lead to imprisonment. What he will not tell me is the particular words, phrases, passages to which objection is taken; these my scruples will allow me to alter without hesitation; but how do I know, without being told, what words etc. the dunder

* W. T. (Pennar) Davies (1911–1996), poet, clergyman and scholar, in the Cardiff *Western Mail*, August 1939.

printers and lawyers think objectionable: piss, breast, bottom, Love?

The list finally arrived. (One of the troublesome phrases occurred in a story about clergymen, 'The Holy Six': 'The holy life was a constant erection to these six gentlemen.') But the book never appeared. The following year the stories were still giving trouble, this time when a new book of prose and poems, *The Map of Love*, was being discussed with Dent. Richard Church refused to print some of them, in particular the one that Thomas regarded as the best, 'A Prospect of the Sea', because it had 'unwarrantable moments of sensuality'.* One naughtiness did evade the censors, in 'The Orchards', the story he first sold to T. S. Eliot, an extravagant piece about a poet called Marlais. Thomas invented a few innocent place names, LlanAsia and Aberbabel, and one that could be read backwards, Llareggub. He seems to have tried spelling most names backwards as a matter of course, to see what he could make of them. T. S. Eliot, he once remarked, was nearly 'toilets', and Llanmadog, a village in Gower, was nearly 'God man all'. Nobody noticed 'Llareggub' at the publishers. Thomas liked the joke so much that he used it again for *Under Milk Wood* (by which time the publishers had woken up, and after his death insisted on spelling it Llaregyb).

In the stories that he was writing in 1938 and 1939, later published as *Portrait of the Artist as a Young Dog*, Thomas abandoned extravagance and turned to autobiography in the shape of fiction. The original suggestion came from Church, who in 1936 proposed 'a tale of the world where your early years have been spent'. The story about the 'clean old man', 'A Visit to Grandpa's', seems to have been the first, written before he left Blashford. It is the least factual of the group, and probably the least successful.† 'One Warm Saturday', ostensibly about sex but

* The story had already appeared in the magazine *Life and Letters Today* in 1937. When Dent finally published it as the title story of a Thomas collection in 1955, two years after his death, a reference to masturbation, 'the death from playing with yourself', was still regarded as too daring, and was omitted.

† The story has been taken as an account of D.J.'s father, Thomas the Guard. According to Florence it was about Thomas the Guard's father – D.J.'s grandfather, William – who lived with his son and daughter-in-law at Poplar Cottage in Johnstown until he died, long before Dylan was born. D.J. told Dylan about him as a child.

really about loneliness, was written at Sea View in the summer of 1938. So was the Fernhill story, 'The Peaches', 'a long story about my true childhood'. He called them 'illuminated reporting'. He also called them 'mostly pot-boilers'. But they read like a true record, free from hesitations. Of the ten stories, two are about Carmarthenshire, two are set in Gower, and the remainder in Swansea. All were written by the end of 1939. A manuscript version of 'Patricia, Edith and Arnold', one of the last to be completed, lists the stories already written and adds some new ideas: 'An out-of-doors story; another Dan story; a Trevor Hughes story; a little boy watching a man hang himself.' Of these, only the Hughes story, 'Who Do You Wish Was With Us?', was ever written.* The war interfered, or perhaps the vein was exhausted. Thomas's 'dead youth in the vanished High Street nights' was a subject he returned to often enough in radio reminiscences, but (apart from 'Return Journey') they lacked the energy of the stories. As with *18 Poems*, the mood was not sustained; another door had closed.

Thomas's mood in 1938 seems to have been confident enough. Aged twenty-three, he was already a candidate for a critical study. Henry Treece was an earnest young poet, later a leader of the so-called 'New Apocalyptic' movement. When he wrote to Thomas at Blashford, Thomas replied to say he was flattered and would be glad to help. Treece had also been in touch with Richard Church, who thought that such a study was premature. Thomas agreed, up to a point. He wrote to Treece to say that 'two small books of verse have never, to my knowledge, produced, in their writer's lifetime, a book of explanation and assessment by another writer, nor has such an adequately small reputation as mine needed an analysis of it to make it bigger. But this is not to say that I personally consider it inadvisable ...' He dealt briskly with the unenthusiastic Church: 'A cliché-riddled humbug and pie-fingering hack, a man who has said to me, when I told him I was starving, that a genuine artist scorns monetary gain.'

In the letters that followed, Thomas told Treece a lot about

---

* The list is headed with another of Thomas's backward-reading jokes, 'Llaberos & Muberab in Llareggub', perhaps an alternative title for *Portrait*. Thomas told Vernon Watkins that he thought *Portrait of the Artist as a Young Dog* a 'flippant' title, and used it only for 'moneymaking reasons'.

himself and his poetry, though the information began to dry up after they had their not very successful meeting in the summer. (A few years later Thomas was describing him as 'a loud and brawling hypocrite'.) Writing from Blashford, Thomas spelt out his solution to the poet's problem of living on air: 'I have achieved poverty with distinction, but never poverty with dignity; the best I can manage is dignity with poverty, and I would sooner smarm like a fart-licking spaniel than starve in a world of fat bones.' In June came more descriptions of poverty from the fisherman's cottage – they hadn't yet moved to Sea View – where they were facing a weekend without cigarettes, bread or stamp for the letter: 'We wait for shillings which we have no right to expect. Bitter, cruel Laugharne; my pipe is full of buttends from the grate, my table crowded with the dead ends of poems, my head full of nonsense. The sun is shining on the mud, my wife is out cockling ... a little girl has called with buns, I say "No buns", though all my everlasting soul shouts for them ...' Treece obliged by sending buns and other small gifts. He was anxious to penetrate Thomas's mysteries and lay him out for critical inspection, and Thomas was forthcoming. Treece learned that most of the 'straight poems' in *Twenty-five Poems* were written before *18 Poems*; it seems to be more than Watkins was ever told. He was given an account of how Thomas wrote poetry, which has become the most widely quoted of Thomas's self-analyses. It described a process that began with an image based on the emotions, which then bred conflicting images within an intellectual framework, until finally the contradictions were resolved in 'that momentary peace which is a poem'.

In other letters Thomas insisted that his poems be taken literally. This advice, not always easy to follow, was directed at, among others, Edith Sitwell, whose explanation of certain lines, he said, missed their literal meaning. Another remark to Treece that has been extensively quoted was Thomas's assertion that 'I hold a beast, an angel, and a madman in me, and my inquiry is as to their working, and my problem is their subjugation and victory, downthrow & upheaval, and my effort is their self-expression'. But Thomas was equally good at rhetoric and anti-rhetoric. A year later he was writing to Treece, begging him to 'cut out that remark of mine about "I have a beast & an angel in me" or whatever it was; it makes me sick, drives me away from drink, recalls too much the worst of the fat and curly boy I know too well ...' As he grew older he became less inclined to make any serious comment on himself as a writer.

In the Treece letters he frequently expressed himself on contemporary poets. He was rude about most of them:

Today the Brotherhood of Man – love thy neighbour and, if possible, covet his arse – seems a disappointing school-society, and I cannot accept Auden as head-prefect. I think MacNeice is thin and conventionally-minded, lacking imagination, and not sound in the ear; flop Day Lewis; and Spender, Rupert Brooke of the depression, condemns his slight, lyrical, nostalgic talent to a clumsy and rhetorical death ...

Some of his best friends were poets, but in general he seems not to have liked them for their poetry. 'Putting little trust in most of the poetry being written today,' he told Treece, 'I put a great deal in mine.' Thomas had an endless supply of invective for fellow writers. 'No,' he wrote to Keidrych Rhys, 'I don't blame the world that doesn't give them (and Saunders Lewis)* money.' He went on:

I think poets are treated well enough; no-one beats them with a little whip; they can walk safely in the streets. The only trouble is that a bad poet is treated as well as a good one. I think Spender should be kicked in his headquarters once a week, regularly & officially. And Day-Lewis should be hissed in public, and have his balls beaten with a toffee hammer. After all, it's a comic thing to be a poet; we should be treated with more flippancy. I want money not as a poet, but as a hungry & thirsty man; a poet doesn't want meat & drink, only paper. God help those who have no bowels, only consonants & vowels. What would happen if there was a poet's strike? I'd love to stand on picket-duty in [George] Barker's scribbling-room, and cosh him for every half-rhyme. 'Unless we're paid three pounds ten a week, we won't write another bloody poem.' That'll set the dogs barking. We'd come to an agreement with the critics: fifty per cent of every article about us. Hear Mr Leavis cackle! There goes Day-Lewis, ratting to the London Mercury! Apes

* Saunders Lewis, 1893–1985, prominent Welsh writer and nationalist.

on strike! Down tools in Bloomsbury! (a bankrupt Grigson offers 25%).

Nor could he stomach being part of a group or movement; he was himself, someone apart. When Pennar Davies tried to inveigle him into a society of Welsh authors, he wrote polite replies but made his position clear: 'I don't think it does any harm to the artist to be lonely *as* an artist. (Let's all "get together", if we must, and go to the pictures.) If he feels personally unimportant, it may be that he is. Will an artistic milieu make his writing any better? I doubt it.'

As for his own writing, in 1938 he produced little but prose between the spring, in Blashford, and the autumn, when he was still in Laugharne. Then he wrote five poems, quite quickly, two of them based on notebook versions, the others newly conceived. 'A saint about to fall' was Caitlin's child, due to be born in the New Year. He was writing the poem in September, when Germany invaded Czechoslovakia and there was talk of war. 'Remember,' he told Watkins, 'this is a poem written to a child about to be born ... & telling it what a world it will see, what horrors & hells ... It's an optimistic, taking-everything, poem. The two most important words are "Cry Joy".' His verse continued to be difficult, almost wilfully so, with the one exception, that autumn, of a short, disturbing poem written for his birthday at the end of October, 'Twenty-four years'. After the complicated images of the other poems the message arrived like a telegram: life means death.

His shortage of money was chronic. He was borrowing from anyone who would lend, receiving food and other hospitality from the Richard Hugheses, and running up debts in Laugharne. The BBC, as he had already realised, was a possible way of earning without having to make himself into a writing hack. He could be a reading hack instead. He had a shrewd idea of his powers; in a 1939 letter, written before he had a reputation as a reader of poetry, he talks of his 'breathless boom boom boom'. Reading – it must have seemed to Thomas – would not interfere with his real work. In October he was writing to the BBC in Cardiff, suggesting a radio anthology of Welsh poets, old and new, to include contemporaries 'who are now making what is really a renaissance in Welsh writing'. The producer he wrote to replied that he was looking for 'long dramatic poems in verse'. This didn't appeal to Thomas. 'I take such a long time writing anything,' he said, '& the result, dramatically, is too often like a man shouting under the sea ... It sounds full of dramatic possibilities, if only I was.'

He was unable or unwilling to deny himself those long stretches of time when he had to do nothing but work at a poem, or lie fallow between poems. The Thomas legend has exaggerated the extent of his poetic labours. It has made him seem an artist of abnormal dedication who habitually spent hours or days on a single line. It is true that (like many other poets) he was a craftsman who sometimes built up his poems slowly; this was especially true towards the end of his life. But most of his successful poems were written comparatively quickly. This is so of *18 Poems*, and of the 'Fern Hill' and 'Winter's Tale' group at the end of the war on which a great part of his popular reputation rests. In 1938 the revised version of 'After the funeral' was probably produced in less than a month; the second half, he told Watkins, 'came in a rush'. No doubt he produced poems at the rate that was natural for him, no faster and no slower. It was natural for him to let months or even years go by without producing one at all. Probably it was equally natural for him to sit in his work-room, ostensibly writing but in fact regarding the birds or calculating how much he owed the butcher and what cheques were due from editors; fragments of worksheets indicate as much; it is how most writers behave, after all. Thomas was different only in that he adopted the theatrical posture of a poet entitled by his vocation to work things out in his own time. Whether this was an indulgence or a necessary safeguard – whether it enabled him to write what he did, or interfered with a more practical and productive approach – it is impossible to say. It was simply his nature to regard himself as a special case; and to persuade others to agree.

Re-publication in America of poems and stories already published in Britain was an obvious way of earning money without extra work. Early in 1938 he was in touch with the young James Laughlin who had founded his own publishing house, New Directions. America was always a promised land for Thomas; it spelt one thing, money. He began by trying to mortgage his royalties on books to be published in America, as well as on books not yet written, in return for immediate cash. Laughlin sent him a few pounds, and made plans to bring out a first collection of Thomas's work in a small edition the following year.* New Directions – and Dent in London – often came in for abuse behind their backs from Thomas, but they were both loyal publishers who made little or no profit from him until the end of his life; although as it happened, they were laying up treasures for themselves. The same was true of Thomas's long-suffering literary agent, David Higham, whose ten per cents were trifling sums for many years.

Patronage seemed another good idea in 1938. An institution called the Royal Literary Fund had been known to make grants to deserving authors. Thomas roped in supporters, among them T. S. Eliot and Edith Sitwell, and presented himself as a good cause, without success. In trouble with local creditors, he wrote to John Davenport from Laugharne on 14 October:

No grant was made me. My literary claims 'were found not strong enough for the purposes of this society'. Who *do* they give their money to? I'm an excellent and most disturbing case. Must you be a Georgian writer of belle-lettres, suffering in Surrey? Must you be in the evening of your days, with nothing to look forward to but nostalgia, borrowed copies of new books about Wilde, and inclusion in any Gawsworth anthology of the unburied dead? Or is the Royal Fund available only for successful writers having a bad year? Only *recommended* this year by the Medium Book Society! Poor chap, send him a large cheque and a luncheon invitation from a publisher's nark; let Miss Du Maurier knit him a smoking-coat, & don't forget the special, indelible inkstains. But I'm furious. And after Miss Sitwell wrote two pages to the secretary, too. You don't know, do you, any rich person I can try now? I'll dedicate my next poems to him, & write a special sponger's song. Can't I live even on the immoral earnings of my poems? No, but there must be someone, somewhere in England, who'd like to do a poet a good turn, someone who wouldn't miss just enough money to ensure me peace & comfort for a month or two to get on with the work I'm in the

---

* *The World I Breathe*, published in December 1939 in an edition of seven hundred copies. In the five years it was in print, it earned Thomas forty-five pounds.

middle of now & which I so much want to finish. All my hopes were in that Royal set-up, & now we'll have to abscond from here, as from everywhere else I've ever lived in, leaving, this time, a house full of furniture we had the devil of a lot of cringing trouble to obtain. Thirty bloody pounds would settle everything. If you know any rich chap fond of a jingle who knows his Peters & Quennells, do let me know at once. Otherwise it'll be traipsing again, no stability at all, no hope, and certainly no work. Try to think of some sap, some saint. There's no reason why I should bother you like this, but here I can't get in touch with anybody with more money than a betty with no cunt or more generosity than a fucked weazel.

They had planned to go back to Hampshire in the winter, in any case, 'to stay a little bit before our saint or monster', and they were there by the end of November – 'halfstarving, worrying, and escaping from things', he told Higham, urging him to raise fifty pounds, or anything, on a projected collection of poems and stories for Dent. A few days before Christmas he was writing to Watkins:

... I've just come back from three dark days in London, city of the restless dead. It really is an insane city, & filled me with terror. Every pavement drills through your soles to your scalp, and out pops a lamp-post covered with hair. I'm not going to London again for years; its intelligentsia is so hurried in the head that nothing stays there; its glamour smells of goat; there's no difference between good and bad ... Last year at this time Caitlin and I were doing an act in a garret. This time we're just as poor, or poorer, but the ravens – soft, white, silly ravens – will feed us.

At least three new poems were written at Blashford, including one that gave hostile readers, among them the critic James Agate in the *Daily Express*, an excuse for poking fun at what they regarded as nonsense verse. Originally called 'January 1939', the poem began:

Because the pleasure-bird whistles after the hot wires,
Shall the blind horse sing sweeter?

Like many Thomas phrases, it has the ring of a nursery rhyme.

It refers to the practice of blinding song-birds to improve their singing. Perhaps Thomas is supposed to be the blind horse. According to Watkins, the poem originated in a dream about a blind horse which began to sing. A man in Thomas's dream said, 'He sings better now.' It was intended as a poem or prayer for the New Year. Desmond Hawkins was told that it showed the poet looking back on the old year and refusing, blindly, to learn from it. The work was hardly nonsense, but it was undeniably difficult.

Presently, resolutions forgotten, Thomas was in the insane city again, meeting Lawrence Durrell and Henry Miller. Once again it was 'shabby saloons' and 'nightmare London'. A few weeks later Caitlin was in hospital at Poole, having her baby. It was a boy, born on 30 January 1939; they gave it one Welsh name, Llewelyn, and one French, Edouard. Thereafter events seemed to be repeating themselves – a few more poems, a few more debts, a few more attempts to raise money. He wrote to Bert Trick to tell him about the baby, a letter tinged with nostalgia for Swansea, and 'long virulent Sundays with you and scrapbooks and straw-berry jelly at the end ... We're all moving away and every single decisive action happens in a blaze of disappointment.' Neither Dylan nor Caitlin wanted to stay at Blashford, but they still owed thirty pounds in Laugharne. In May, however, they were back at Sea View. The pattern seemingly could go on for years or a lifetime. Could Higham raise money from Dent against books to be written in future? Could patrons help? An ingenious notion occurred to Thomas: if a dozen people could be persuaded to send him five shillings a week, he would have a regular income. This idea occupied him, on and off, for months. He called it 'Thomas Flotation Limited', and talked about making people 'Thomas-minded', but it was not a joke. 'I've got to get twelve chaps,' he told John Davenport. Davenport – a generous man, who had written film scripts in Hollywood, and had a wife with money – sent him names and a cheque. Thomas perked up at once. 'No dank debtors' walls obscure us,' he wrote. 'The fawning tradesmen doff their horns. I'll draft a letter for the five bob fund & let you have it, it's grand to have your assistance. A witty letter, do you think? I'll write very soon. Or a straight-from-the-shldr? ...' Davenport became chief organiser. The potential patrons included Edith Sitwell, Augustus John, Norman

Cameron, the rich Lord Tredegar (Augustus John knew him) and the rich Peggy Guggenheim (Thomas was once introduced to her). Occasionally his letters to Davenport sound cross at people's tardiness in agreeing to help a poet in need. 'Surely there must [be] – if people can't be bothered with sending 5/-[five shillings] a week – some very simple method of them sending it to me monthly?' he wrote.

The scheme came to nothing. Thomas hinted to Davenport that it was his fault. But by this time it was September 1939 and the war with Germany had started at last. From Thomas's point of view, this was bad news directed personally at Dylan Thomas and family. The war was other people's concern. That was not the consensus view of the British Left, but Thomas was not adopting a political attitude. He was sulkily wishing the war would go away. In the last week of August he told Watkins he was 'messing about in the sun and pub', overcome with 'horror & terror & lassitude' as the news grew worse. To his father he wrote (thanking him for the gift of a dictionary) to say that it was 'terrible to have built, out of nothing, a complete happiness – from no money, no possessions, no material hopes – & a way of living, & then to see the immediate possibility of its being exploded & ruined through no fault of one's own'. To others he was indignant about events in Europe. 'I think a squirrel stumbling at least of equal importance as Hitler's invasions,' he wrote to Treece in July 1938; and a year later, 'What are you doing for your country? I'm letting mine rot.' A few weeks after war was declared he was telling Bert Trick,

My little body (though it's little no longer, I'm like a walrus) I don't intend to waste for the mysterious ends of others; and if there's any profiteering to be done, I, in my fashion, wish to be in on it ... I can't raise up any feeling about this War at all and the demon Hitlerism can go up its own bottom: I refuse to help it with a bayonet. To talk about keeping Hitlerism out of this sink of democracy by censorship and conscription, mystery-mongering, umbrella-worship, atrocity-circulation, & the (thank God mostly unsuccessful *so far*) fostering of hate against a bewildered, buggered people, is only to encourage the rebellious pacifism of anti-social softies like myself ...

He tried to persuade fellow writers to send him contributions for an article to be called 'Objection to War'. As he pointed out to D. S. Savage, this would be to the advantage of writers who intended (as Thomas did, at the time) to register as conscientious objectors. But he got little response. To Kenneth Patchen, an American poet, he wrote an immensely long letter in November 1939, complaining about his situation. Thomas, in his 'rotting room', without a fire to keep him warm, sounded cross and middle-aged, not a man of twenty-five. A new figure, the clown with a grievance, was being created. The letter was headed '12th week of the war to end war to save my democramatic Aunty Titty'.

With neither faith nor hope, and despising the charity I seek, I'm working quickly and mostly badly on a book of stories [the *Young Dog* collection] so that I may work slowly on poems, and, at the same time, whining, with my tongue in their cheeks, to a few old-fashioned humbugs for enough money to live better than they do. I'm not angry because the large public does not support me; I give the large public very little, probably nothing, and there is every reason against them supporting me. As a public entertainer who entertains very few, I cannot grumble – or, rather, I can grumble but only for the pleasure of grumbling – and must either change my entertainment, take up some other occupation or be angrily content (which I am) with my present one ... When I lived in London a few years ago, in the bedsitting-room with the scribbled card on the door, cultivating a number of voices and obtaining at considerable cost the clap and the itch, first at the bottleparty and last to go, paying for the rent and the kippers on the gasfire with a pound a week from my parents, determined to get there, not knowing where 'there' was but having a very good idea, covering with crabs and cracks and wild dirt, with eccentricities I had long possessed but had never, until that moment, been frightened enough to expose and expand, my confusion at the shockingly liberated behaviour of other young men and women two stages further, from the provinces into another conventional life, than myself, enviously scorning the well-poised manner of the intelligent well-to-do, racing against time as though time were another young writer with a suburban home address, but always, in myself, naturally and fortunately thick-skinned and stubborn, I decided never to forget the importance of money and to devote all my spare time to gathering it from other than literary sources, and never to live below the imagined standard I had set myself, and always to live within those luxuries I enjoyably deceive myself into thinking I was born to enjoy. Although I have never forgotten the importance, the rest of my monetary decisions have come to little. Sometimes, indeed, I think I am living far *above* the standard I imagine myself to have been born to deserve; but that soon grows into an unworthy thought, and the wind again, blowing from penniless places, is thick with rich cigar smoke ... Angrily satisfied with the shape of things as they should not be, a man used to riches but born poor, I continue to think of money as it moves about beautifully beyond my reach, money that burns and multiplies and smells of hot food...

And to call me an escapist is no insult. As far as a country at war goes, I'm hermetic. I want, among other things, to go on working, and I know I can work only in peace; I can't do a Brooke in a trench; mud shells shit and glory will make me swear & vomit, not write. So I want to be where there still is peace, peace at least from the propagating of hate, the enforcements of military discipline, the extraordinarily rapid growth of dictatorship all around me, and the immediate prospect of a noble death ha ha or ignoble detention ho ho as an antisocial shirker and – worse still – unrepentant individualist.

The immediate effect of the war had been to jeopardise his earnings. A Welsh Region broadcast scheduled for 6 September, a discussion with Keidrych Rhys about 'Modern Welsh Poets'*, was cancelled; the BBC paid part of the fee and asked for their rail ticket back. Two weeks earlier Thomas's third book, *The Map of Love*, had been published. It contained seven stories, all fanciful and some surrealist, and sixteen poems. They included 'After the funeral' and 'Twenty-four years'. But in general these poems of the 'middle period' (as it turned out to be) are less

---

* The discussion, which was to have been scripted in advance, worried the BBC. 'We *must* have this man's script before he appears in the studios,' wrote an official in disapproving blue pencil. The fears were well grounded. When the producer, Watkin Jones, raised objections to the script, Thomas wrote to Rhys, 'It's worth agreeing with their piddling suggestions in order to get across what we really want to. I may myself, later & with, probably, the disgust of Mr Jones, change one of my selected poems; but that can be left until the rehearsal.'

rewarding than those Thomas wrote earlier and later. The book was respectfully and sometimes warmly reviewed, with a few dissenters. Cyril Connolly – who presently founded the magazine *Horizon*, published Thomas regularly, and praised him energetically – found *The Map of Love* poems 'difficult and baffling ... The technique remains, the inspiration gone. His being a purely Celtic writer makes his forgeries difficult to detect, but I think one can say that many of his images are nonsense, and that his hit-or-miss method is unsatisfactory, while his writing is inflated and faked.' This review, in the *New Statesman*, was one of the harshest that Thomas ever received. But Connolly, like Edith Sitwell, changed his mind.

The war was presumably the reason the book flopped as it did. Dent printed three thousand sets of sheets, and bound one thousand. Four months after publication, a colleague of David Higham wrote to say that sales were two hundred and eighty copies. 'Pretty discouraging, eh?' he added. Commercially this was worse than *Twenty-five Poems* three years earlier. Thomas had been paid seventy pounds in advances on *The Map of Love* but when it finally went out of print in 1950, his royalty earnings were still below that figure. His fourth book did little or no better. This was the collection of stories, *Portrait of the Artist as a Young Dog*, his record of the background to the poems. An edition of 1500 copies was published in April 1940.* *Time and Tide* saw it as 'a superb evocation of boyhood and adolescence'. The *Times Literary Supplement*'s reviewer found that 'the atmosphere of schoolboy smut and practical jokes and poetry is evoked with lingering accuracy but with nothing more'. Under other circumstances it might have sold well, but the times buried it.

In the early months of the war, Thomas was seeking work in a reserved occupation where he wouldn't have to do military service. He had abandoned the idea of going before a conscientious objectors' tribunal after sampling one as a spectator at the Shire Hall in Carmarthen with Keidrych Rhys. Vernon Watkins told the story at second-hand: 'As each objector came forward he was asked on what grounds he objected to military service, and in each case a mean little voice answered, "'ligious".

---

* In America, Laughlin's New Directions published an edition of a thousand copies in September 1940.

Each was then asked what he was prepared to do, and each answered, in an even meaner little voice, "Nothing".' It was hardly practical, let alone decent, for Thomas to make a stand on religious grounds. A political excuse sometimes worked, and he clutched briefly at this straw. He wrote to a prominent Welsh nationalist, Gwynfor Evans, who was secretary of the Welsh Pacifists; this had twelve thousand members and was opposed to military conscription. Evans replied sharply and negatively to this 'unheroic' approach.

How Thomas eventually avoided military service has not been satisfactorily explained. His mother said he was unfit because of 'punctured lungs'. Vernon Watkins said it was 'scarred lungs'. Neither condition agrees with the 1953 post-mortem. He seems to have been examined at least twice. On 6 May 1940, writing to Stephen Spender from his parents' house in Bishopston, he said, 'I went, by the way, to have another army medical examination, this time in Wales, & was found to be Grade III, which will keep me out of all the main army nastinesses and perhaps out of the army altogether.'* This implies a previous examination in England. It was possible to appear voluntarily before a military board in London, in advance of the compulsory medical interview. This may be what Thomas did, hoping to impress the examiners with his unsuitability. In a letter of 22 June to Laurence Pollinger at the David Higham agency he said that 'I'm not in the army – yet. I took Higham's advice & went before the military board who found me 3. Whatever that will come to mean.' Higham was unable to remember what he advised. Perhaps Thomas was failed because of his recurrent asthma; or even on psychological grounds. Conceivably things were rigged in Wales by a friendly doctor. Nicolette Devas heard such a rumour.

All this time Dylan and Caitlin were shifting from place to

---

* A week later he wrote to Spender again to say he now understood Grade III men would be called up, probably for non-combatant work. Dr Oscar Williams, chairman of the medical tribunal in Llanelli during the war, was certain that Thomas was never examined there (as several accounts say he was). Margaret Taylor heard a story that Thomas appeared for his examination in front of a doctor who had heard him read poetry the night before. 'Oh Mr Thomas, it can't be you!' said the doctor. Tudor Williams of Laugharne said Dylan was known as a 'conchie' (i.e. 'conscientious objector') early in the war, and was given 'a good hiding' one night by a soldier home on leave.

place – Swansea for Christmas 1939, then Blashford for a few months, then back to Laugharne, then back to his parents in May 1940 with another pile of debts left behind. Watkins had been helping with money. They were buying a bed on hire purchase at seven shillings a month, and needed a pound to stop it being taken away for non-payment. Watkins sent the money. He was forever providing little life-savers. 'TA for the great pound,' Thomas wrote on another occasion. 'I heard it singing in the envelope.' The latest flight from Laugharne was more serious than usual. Thomas appealed to Spender, telling him that books, clothes, beds, china and chairs had all been left behind at Sea View and would be sold up unless he paid his debts. This time he needed seventy pounds. Spender organised a superior whip-round – Henry Moore and Herbert Read were among the contributors – and Thomas, back in Laugharne, wrote to say that 'life's quite different now, and I'm beginning to work like a small, very slow horse'. But the relief was only a postponement. Neither Dylan nor Caitlin was any good at managing money, and there was always Brown's Hotel or a fish-frail of bottled beer to take care of any surplus cash. Drink continued to play an important part in his life. When it threatened to deprive them of furniture and clothing, Caitlin rebelled and there were rows. Fond of drink, she wasn't keen on the pub life that went with it. She wrote of hours of boredom in pubs while Dylan was living up to his reputation. He was not yet an alcoholic; perhaps was never one, in the full sense of the word, although drink was woven into his life. In any case, in 1940 the disasters were still in the future.

That summer he and Caitlin stayed with John Davenport and his wife Clement at their house in the town of Marshfield, Gloucestershire. This handsome building in the main street, The Malting House, was one of Davenport's last gestures to the gracious life before his money ran out. For a while, in the early part of the war, he held open house for musicians and writers. Lennox Berkeley the composer was here, and William Glock, then a music critic. Antonia White went there after she saw Davenport at an exhibition in London, and he told her she must come and join in the fun. The house hummed with music and jokes, not to mention jealousies. Mrs Davenport was having an affair with Glock. She would sit with her husband while he played one of the grand pianos loudly in the music room, turning the pages and humouring him. Sometimes he lost his temper and threw things. He was a short, broad, clever man, inclined to be a bully when drunk, good at mimicry and general fooling about. There was a fair amount of that. Antonia White heard screams coming from upstairs. Caitlin had insisted it was time for Dylan to take a bath, and was busy with soap and water, covering the ceiling with blobs of foam.

Thomas and Davenport spent much of their time writing a novel called *The Death of the King's Canary*, a not very funny satire on writers and painters of the time.* In 1938 Thomas had thought of writing it with Charles Fisher, when he saw it as a detective story with 'inevitable Chinaman, secret passages etc', parodying the genre. The new, less promising version parodied a group of cultural figures, attending a grotesque house party. Augustus John made a brief appearance as Hercules Jones. No doubt Yvonne Bacon was meant to be Nina Hamnett. Perhaps it had echoes of life at The Malting House. The verse parodies were the best. Among them was one of Spender ('Christopher Garvin'), 'The Parachutist', apparently written by Thomas. Cyril Connolly had it set up in type for *Horizon* but never used it. He printed another of Thomas's *Canary* parodies, 'Request to Leda: Homage to William Empson', in 1942.

In the evenings they drank the remains of Davenport's pre-war cellar and tried ineffectively to keep the black-out curtains drawn. The Battle of Britain was being fought over Southern England. Europe had fallen, the air raids were under way. His mother wrote to tell him about the first raids on Swansea. At Marshfield, a hundred miles from London, they heard war-planes from time to time. Thomas wrote to Watkins, 'Are you frightened these nights? When I wake up out of burning birdman dreams – they were frying aviators one night in a huge frying pan: it sounds whimsical now, it was appalling then – and hear the sound of bombs & gunfire only a little way away, I'm so relieved I could

---

* It was eventually published in 1976, following hints that it had been 'rediscovered'. But it had been in the hands of Thomas's copyright trustees all along, and an extract appeared in book form in 1971. In general it is not clear who wrote what. A note from Davenport, at Texas, says: 'I wrote Chapter 1 and most of the parodies. Dylan did the one on Empson (Dudley) and some are collaborated on. From Chapter 1 on the book is almost exactly 50–50. Dylan finally took the manuscript away and typed it himself.'

laugh or cry.' What frightened him, he said, was the thought of German troops marching silently up the street. Invasion seemed imminent that September, and Thomas had nightmares about it. He wrote a harsh, oblique poem about invasion, 'Deaths and Entrances', the first of a small group about the war. Cyril Connolly, liking it more than he liked *The Map of Love*, took it for *Horizon*.

'The summer talked itself away,' said Thomas later. But something awkward happened: Caitlin began flirting with William Glock, the guest who was already involved with Clement Davenport, and decided to have a little fling of her own. Glock, later Sir William, the BBC's Controller of Music, was a good-looking man. Caitlin decided she was in love with him, and they arranged an assignation at a Cardiff hotel. In order to give herself a cover story, she went first to Swansea to see Dylan's parents, then on to Laugharne. There she sold furniture, blankets and crockery in a pub, to have money for dresses and underclothes, and look pretty for her lover.

The adventure wasn't a success. Glock, unnerved by the occasion or by Caitlin, was unable to perform. According to her own version in old age, she herself was habitually unrelaxed when it came to love-making, requiring men to get on with the job in an uncomplicated way. In Cardiff, they stared at the ceiling; then returned separately to Marshfield, where later they were able to try again, this time, said Glock, successfully. But Dylan found out about Cardiff. A letter from his mother, probably written with intent, referred to Caitlin's movements and gave the game away. During the subsequent row he threw a fork at her; she used to laugh at the idea of being threatened by a *fork*. For a while he refused to sleep with her. Then life went on as before. A short poem by Thomas, 'On a Wedding Anniversary' – supposedly written for 11 July 1940, but not published until the following year – may have echoes of the infidelity, with its gloomy mood ('This ragged anniversary') and air-raid metaphors.

The Thomases left Marshfield in a hurry; Dylan apologised to Davenport the following January, writing that 'I was very muddled and unhappy, and didn't feel a bit like having any contact at all – until the muddles were straightened in my head'. Very likely this referred to the Glock episode.

In December he was in London briefly, squeezing money from

the BBC for a script, meeting friends, travelling back to Wales on a slow train and (he said) being asked for his identity card by Army officers because he was wearing a black hat and they thought he was a spy. He and Caitlin were back in Bishopston with his parents, squashed into little rooms. He had been writing more letters to literary persons, seeking help. Alec Waugh suggested he should write more stories and fewer letters, a joke that annoyed Thomas, who wrote crossly to Davenport, 'When I want advice from Alec Waugh, I'll go to his brother.' He wrote to Davenport on 8 January 1941, 'Today the pipes burst, and Caitlin, in a man's hat, has been running all day with a mop from w.c. to flooded parlour, while I've been sitting down trying to write a poem about a man who fished with a woman for bait and caught a horrible collection.' This was the 'Ballad of the Long-legged Bait', completed in April 1941 and published in *Horizon* three months later. Connolly thought it too long (at 216 lines, it was the longest poem Thomas ever wrote), and he had it set in small type to save paper, which was rationed. Thomas was upset; according to Connolly, 'he refused to come in and correct his proofs, so that there were some appalling misprints – I remember "Jew" for "due" was one of them – for which I got all the blame.'

Thomas did hack work when he could. At Marshfield he had written two short scripts for the BBC's South American Service, one of them about Christopher Columbus. Next he was commissioned to write a programme about Czech heroes. 'Could I have a script to do without battles, d'you think?' he wrote to the producer when he sent in his draft. 'Or perhaps with only 20 or 30?' Besides earning a few guineas, BBC scripts were a means of showing that he was a writer, doing essential war work. He had escaped the Army but he was still liable to be directed into civilian employment. He corresponded hopefully with the BBC, writing on 6 May 1941 that 'what you said in your letter, and what you said you could say to the Ministry of Labour if necessary, will, I hope, do the trick: that is, keep me for a while longer out of the factories'. To Clement Davenport he had written from Bishopston the previous month:

... I'm awfully busy with a long poem, and I've just borrowed this typewriter to type out the never-ending Canary, God moult it, and

I'm helping about the house, shuffling and breaking, and I think that unless I'm careful and lucky the boys of the Government will get me making munitions. I wish I could get a real job and avoid that. Clocking in, turning a screw, winding a wheel, doing something to a cog, lunching in the canteen, every cartridge case means one less Jerry, bless all the sergeants the short and the tall bless 'em all blast 'em all, evenings in the factory rest centre, snooker and cocoa, then bugs in digs and then clocking in and turning and winding and hammering to help to kill another stranger, deary me I'd rather be a poet anyday and live on guile and beer...

This self-contained philosophy kept him afloat. The war machine left him alone. Perhaps the nearest the war came to him was earlier that winter, in February, when the Swansea town centre and parts of the working-class suburbs were destroyed in three nights of air raids. Bert Trick bumped into Dylan and Caitlin on the corner of a ruined shopping street on the morning immediately after the third and worst raid. The weather was cold; the future unpromising. It was the last time Trick was to see Thomas. He wrote, 'The air was acrid with smoke, and the hoses of the firemen snaked among the blackened entrails of what had once been Swansea Market. As we parted, Dylan said with tears in his eyes, "Our Swansea is dead".'

After these air raids, Thomas's parents began to make plans to leave Bishopston for the family cottages in Blaen Cwm, where it would be safer and cheaper. Florence's sister Theodosia and her husband, the Rev. David Rees, had been living there, but they were dead. In the other cottage were the unmarried brother and sister from St Thomas, Bob, the recluse, and Polly, the chatterbox. D.J. was dismayed at the prospect of having his wife's relatives on the doorstep, but he was getting old and he had no option. 'Oh Gawd, here's that bitch again,' he would say when he heard Polly's voice approaching; unfortunately she was very fond of him. He told Ken and Hettie Owen, family friends from Port Talbot, that he was starved for intelligent conversation. 'There's nothing here but cows and clots,' he said. His son's visits were increasingly important; they did *The Times* crossword together. He still tried to maintain his standards, with a clean shirt every day and an upright walk. His contempt for people who spoke shoddy English or shoddy Welsh persisted. The conductor of the bus from Carmarthen to Llangain, shouting 'Stoppo!' to the driver, made him frown. On fine days he walked to Llanstephan – where his grandfather was determined to go to be buried in 'A Visit to Grandpa's' – for a quiet pint in the shadow of the castle, away from the women.

Dylan and Caitlin returned to Laugharne, to stay at the Hugheses' house alongside the ruined castle. Richard Hughes was away at the war. 'I have the romantic, dirty summerhouse looking over the marsh to write in,' Dylan told Watkins, 'and Caitlin an almost empty, huge room to dance in. Also, we have lots of records now, and we hear, quite often, another word than "ration".' To bring in some money he had decided to sell his first-edition novels, and, more important, the old exercise books full of poems. In the letter to Clement Davenport quoted above he wrote:

> In the pink bedroom we slept in and stored apples in and knocked about [at Marshfield], you'll find unless they've moved, a number of, I think, red small exercisebooks full of my old poems and stories. Would it be a lot of trouble for you to send them to me? I mean, will you? I've got a chance of selling all my mss, for about the price of two large Player's after the next budget, and it's easier, and more honest too, to send the real mss rather than to copy out the copies in different coloured inks and with elaborate and ostentatiously inspired corrections...

FitzGibbon notes that when Thomas sold the exercise books he was almost the same age as Keats when he died, twenty-six. Certainly he must have been aware of a break. He felt himself being separated from his past, whether it was long Sundays with strawberry jelly at the Tricks', or Swansea before the fires. Nostalgia came easily all his life; at seventeen he was already contemplating his vanished past, remarking (in a poem in one of the exercise books now up for sale) on 'how much was happy while it lasted'; he had the Welsh weakness for backward glances. The sale was made to the Lockwood Library of the State University of New York at Buffalo via a London dealer, Bertram Rota. As well as the four poetry notebooks, Thomas sold a prose notebook and the worksheets of 'Long-legged Bait'. Rota was paid $140. Whatever Thomas received, it was less than that.

The last poem to be quarried from the notebook was 'The hunchback in the park', originally written on 9 May 1932, when Thomas was on the *Evening Post*. When he revised it, on 16 July 1941, the Thomases were still at Laugharne Castle, still apparently penniless. 'Jesus, I loathe my poverty,' he wrote to Charles Fisher the day before. Watkins, who would soon be serving with the RAF, continued to send half-crowns and five shillings. 'See if you can squeeze another drop from your borrowed-to-death body,' wrote Thomas. 'I'm not going to tell you how grateful I am and have always been; or how vile I feel when I ask you again. Really vile. Weazels take off their hats as I stink by. No, I am sorry. I have no right. I hope I am spoiling nothing. It is just that I am useless, & have nowhere to turn.'

His publishers were reluctant to keep advancing him money for books that were either not written or failed to cover their costs. In August 1940 Laurence Pollinger, at the Higham agency, was reporting that Dent had paid a total of two hundred and twenty-six pounds under various contracts, and were refusing to pay any more; the Welsh travel book and a book of verse (perhaps an anthology) were still outstanding. Thomas then tried to oblige by writing a book that would carry on where *Portrait of the Artist* left off. This was *Adventures in the Skin Trade*, first mentioned in a letter to Watkins from Marshfield. By May 1941 Thomas was writing from Laugharne Castle, 'My prosebook's going well, but I dislike it. It's the only really dashed-off piece of work I remember doing. I've done 10,000 words already. It's indecent and trivial, sometimes funny, sometimes mawkish, and always badly written which I do not mind so much.' Soon after, 'My novel blathers on. It's a mixture of Oliver Twist, Little Dorrit, Kafka, Beachcomber, and good old 3-adjectives-a-penny belly-churning Thomas, the Rimbaud of Cwmdonkin Drive.' His heart wasn't in the tale of his provincial hero, Samuel Bennet, once he had moved him from 'his parents' six-room house' to London. Dent were willing to pay twenty-five pounds for a sight of the first ten thousand words. But when they saw it they didn't like it.

'This material is not good enough', John Hadfield wrote to Laurence Pollinger in July, 'and we would like you to put this fact plainly before the author. It seems to us that Dylan Thomas has reached a crucial point in his literary career. He made a flying start, and there has been no lack of recognition of his uncommon talent ... In our view, however, he has not maintained the position which he gained by his early work. We have been very disappointed. Not a single [publisher's] reader has more to say in its favour than that it contains a number of flashes of the essential Dylan Thomas together with some music-hall laughs. At the best it is a fragment of frolicksome dirt.' Hadfield quoted phrases from the readers' reports – 'more coprolitic than ever ... his vivid but perverse and mudlarkish quality is original but it is running amuck with emphasis on the muck ... unless he pulls himself together he is going to fizzle out as an author most ignominiously'. The letter added, 'Let me make it quite clear we still retain a great interest in Thomas, and these objections to his new manuscript are not governed by prejudice against his unconventionality or experiments – indeed these are among the reasons why we have had faith in his future. It seems to us that he is now slipping into a state of literary irresponsibility ... Our urgent recommendation is that he should scrap this material and pull himself together for a much more carefully thought out and deliberately written job of work.'

A few decades later the dirt seemed non-existent. But the publishers, like Thomas himself, saw through the book. Watkins was staying with him when the letter arrived. He reported that Thomas was indignant but amused. Rejection, however, meant there would be no more money from his publishers. Thomas lost heart or interest soon after, and the book remained unfinished, although ultimately it was profitable to all concerned. The war, or poverty, or some growing seed of unease, or a combination of them all, was reducing his capacity to write. The only poem he wrote that summer, apart from the revision of 'The hunchback in the park', seems to have been his second 'war' poem, a sonnet, 'Among those Killed in the Dawn Raid was a Man Aged a Hundred', where he took a detached and (for him) light-hearted view of the incident. Published in August in *Life and Letters*, it was the last poem he was to complete for a year or two. At the end of August he and Caitlin were in 'stinking, friendless London', having left Llewelyn with his grandmother at Blashford. Caitlin said in old age that she felt agonies of guilt, but was unable to deny herself the pleasures of London. She wasn't prepared to be the virtuous woman who stayed at home.

As usual they had no money; presumably the need to earn some is what drove Thomas to London. He wrote to Watkins, 'We've been having an awful time, and I have felt like killing myself ... I am still looking for a film job, & have been offered several scripts to do "in the near future", which might mean weeks. In the meantime, we sit in our bedroom and think with hate of the people who can go to restaurants ... We are prisoners now in a live melodrama.'

Script-writing turned out to be the answer. Documentary film-making for Government and industry, much of it plain propaganda, was thriving. He was offered full-time work by Donald Taylor, who ran a company called Strand Films. This removed any possibility of being drafted into uncongenial work. Thomas accepted, and went on the payroll at ten pounds a week. For the first time since he left the *Evening Post* he had an adequate income. But for the moment he was out of the poetry business.

Chapter Nine

WAR AND 'FERN HILL'

Between 1942 and 1945, Dylan Thomas worked on at least ten documentary films, writing scripts by himself or in collaboration, and in one or two cases acting as director. Strand had a good reputation, and his work there was well thought of. Donald Taylor took pains to point out later that Thomas was 'a technician' and 'just one of the boys'. He said he offered Thomas a job because he felt sorry for him, after hearing that he was starving and ill. But Ivan Moffat, an American writer working for Strand, who introduced Taylor to Thomas, said that 'even if I'd wanted to go to such an extreme to get Dylan a job, the robust effrontery of Dylan's pub-style must immediately have dispelled any illusions Donald may have had'. There was no question of the company carrying Thomas out of charity. Nor did he act the wild poet. When he was in London, and not working on location, he kept normal office hours, or as normal as anyone else in the film industry. Moffat said it was a lackadaisical office, with much sitting about and playing cards. Thomas was always scribbling on scraps of paper. Once Moffat did an imitation of him talking. Thomas 'took an envelope, scribbled on the back and handed it to me:

> What a pity there's nothing in Moffat
> For Moffat to imitate
> Nothing for Moffat to scoff at
> In all that juvenile spate.'

Another co-writer, Julian Maclaren-Ross, who joined Strand in August 1943, met him for the first time in the lift. Thomas wore a green pork-pie hat and a soiled raincoat, which he removed to reveal 'a very respectable dark blue suit and a white shirt with a bow tie and celluloid collar, too tight round the neck and giving the effect of someone strapped in the stocks. In these clothes he might have been a young provincial tradesman or perhaps a farmer up in London for the day on business.' His more usual office uniform was a brown check tweed jacket and grey flannels. According to Maclaren-Ross his daytime drinking was moderate, perhaps a pint of bitter at midday in the back bar of the Café Royal, the rear entrance of which was close to the Strand offices in Soho. The day they met they went drinking after work, and next morning, when they were in the office feeling seedy, Maclaren-Ross suggested they keep a bottle of whisky there to guard against future hangovers. Thomas replied, 'Whisky? *In the office?*' and 'seemed absolutely appalled'. Like most Thomas anecdotes it is suggestive, not definitive; it was the response that appealed to Thomas at the time.

Donald Taylor wanted to produce feature films for the commercial cinema. His favourite idea was a film about Burke and Hare, the Scottish body-snatchers, and after the war he commissioned Thomas to write a script based on his story-line, 'The Doctor and the Devils', which was published as a book but had to wait another forty years before it became a film, in 1986. In 1943, Maclaren-Ross and Thomas spent much time discussing a horror film they wanted to write. There was even talk of filming *Adventures in the Skin Trade*, which came to nothing, like most ideas in the film business. As for the documentaries, they ranged from prosaic to fanciful. 'New Towns for Old' was about town planning after the war. 'Balloon Site 568' besought women to join the anti-aircraft balloon service.* A more ambitious project was 'These Are the Men', a twelve-minute film using clips from the Leni Reifenstahl picture 'Triumph of the Will', which recorded the Nazi Party Rally at Nuremberg in 1934. Thomas's commentary superimposed his words on film of Hitler, Goebbels and the rest addressing the rally. For Hitler he wrote:

I grew into a discontented and neurotic child.

---

* Moffat directed this film, which was made at Cardington, a Women's Auxiliary Air Force base. He recalled that 'the lady commandant, a senior W.A.A.F. officer, was on a raised platform reviewing perhaps two hundred uniformed W.A.A.F.s as they marched past. Dylan and I were both on the platform with her, improbable as that may seem now, and seemed then. Dylan turned to her in the course of this and said, "You have the most superb body, ma'am," and as she cast a look of reproof at him, added, "of women".'

My lungs were bad. My mother spoilt me and secured my exemption
from military service. Consider my triumphant path to power.
(*The crowd roars.*)
I took up art.
I gave up art because I was incompetent.
I became a bricklayer's labourer...

Some projects fell by the wayside. A film about the Home Guard,
for which, said Maclaren-Ross, they envisaged a village 'stuffed
full of eccentrics' (perhaps an early forerunner of Llareggub in
Under Milk Wood) was cancelled by the Ministry of Information
before the script was completed. 'Is Your Ernie Really Necessary?'
(a parody of the wartime slogan 'Is your journey really necessary?') used light-hearted optical effects to make its points about
travel. It was filmed but never released. There were problems
over a film about Wales, 'Green Mountain, Black Mountain',
for which Thomas wrote a lyrical script:

Morning is breaking over Wales at war. Not the long and faraway
wild war of the mountain Welshman and English kings, but the
terrible near war of England and Wales and her brothers and sisters
all over the earth...

Parts of the script had an Auden-like ring. Thomas could parody
most poets when he chose. But here he was using the style for its
effectiveness, not as a joke:

Remember the procession of the old-young men
From dole queue to corner and back again,
From the pinched, packed street to the peak of slag
In the bite of the winters with shovel and bag,
With a drooping fag and a turned up collar,
Stamping for the cold at the ill lit corner
Dragging through the squalor with their hearts like lead
Staring at the hunger and the shut pit-head
Nothing in their pockets, nothing home to eat.
Lagging from the slag heap to the pinched, packed street.
Remember the procession of the old-young men.
It shall never happen again.

The film was made for the British Council, to be shown to overseas audiences. But the Council disliked the references to un-employment, among other things, and the film was offered to the Ministry of Information. Protocol laid down that it should go to the MOI's Welsh office. For months nothing was heard. Then word came from Cardiff that the words were thought to be unsuitable. Dylan Thomas was not a *real* Welshman – he lived in London – so perhaps a certain Welsh professor might be approached to write a new script? London brushed aside the objections, and the film was issued with the commentary intact.

The most ambitious project that Thomas worked on was a fifty-minute film for the MOI about wartime Britain, 'Our Country'. This had John Eldridge as the director, and music by William Alwyn. The film was much discussed at the time, although the high-flown commentary was not to everyone's taste:

Outside the kitchens and music
the laughing the loving the midnight talking the resting the sleeping
in all the blind houses
outside
the searchlighted night is at war with another darkness
and men who were late at harvest stand cold and calm and armed
on hilltops under the punishing rush of planes . . .

Perhaps Thomas's scripts were facile, but perhaps this was the quality that was needed. The work suited him. He was a poet, going through a period of uncertainty about his own writing, who had transplanted himself to a job that required facility with language but little else. He became a small part of a large propaganda machine that kept up morale and encouraged a family feeling among the British while the business of total war went ahead. He may even have welcomed an excuse not to have to write poetry for a while. Caitlin apparently regarded his film-writing as dishonest. She accused Donald Taylor of corrupting her husband. She told Jack Lindsay, the writer, how he had ripped up poems and thrown the pieces in the bin. Lindsay assumed that Caitlin had rescued them. 'It's the last thing I'd do,' she said. 'Dylan's corrupt. Corrupt right through and through. It's not for me to save him from himself. If he can't do it himself, let him rot.'* Lindsay wrote that 'against my will Caitlin by the force of contempt and suffering in her voice had convinced me that he was charlatan as well as marvellous boy, unscrupulous entre-preneur as well as dedicated poet'.

Thomas's film work meant periods of separation, and this may have helped turn Caitlin against Dylan as script-writer. Later in the war, presumably when he knew more about the technicalities of film, he wrote scripts without attending the office regularly, and lived mainly in the Home Counties or in Wales. But at first he was based in London; and Caitlin was not always there. Their domestic arrangements were as ill-organised as ever. At one time they lived in Hammersmith Terrace, a few doors from the house where Caitlin was born, in a studio owned by Sir Alan Herbert, whose daughter Crystal was then married to John Pudney; the Thomases had arrived on the doorstep, asking for shelter. They were often in Wales. For much of the summer of 1942, Caitlin was in the remote village of Talsarn, in Cardiganshire, in the valley of the River Aeron a few miles from the sea. This had been Thomas-country in the previous century; the little River Marlais was just to the south. Caitlin stayed there with Vera, who knew Dylan as a child in the Uplands. Vera was friendly with the Thomases in wartime London. She met and married a young Commando captain, William Killick; Thomas was best man. Then her husband was posted overseas and was away for years. Some of Vera's family had moved to Talsarn to escape the bombs, and she and Caitlin stayed there. Thomas came from time to time. 'I have been here for over a week with Caitlin, with milk and mild and cheese and eggs,' he wrote to a friend in London, T. W. Earp, on 30 August 1942, 'and I feel fit as a fiddle only bigger; I watch the sun from a cool room and know that there are trees being trees outside and that I do not have to admire them; the country's the one place you haven't got to go out in, thank Pan.' Caitlin was pregnant again by the end of the summer. The child, a girl, was born the following March in a London

---

* Ripping up manuscripts for dramatic effect was one of the games the Thomases played. Elisabeth Lutyens stayed with them at Laugharne in 1951 when Caitlin tore up a long poem, then remorsefully collected the pieces, while Dylan 'slyly remarked to me, with a chuckle, that he had dozens of copies'.

hospital and christened Aeron, after the river.* (She was also called 'Aeronwy'.)

Their home was a broken-down studio in Chelsea, in Manresa Road, one large room with a kitchen behind a curtain. The roof leaked, and Aeron's cradle had an umbrella over it. A reek of cats came from the next-door studio. A piece of dirty carpet on the floor served as an eiderdown for the bed in cold weather. But the Thomases made it a congenial place with books and a gramophone. FitzGibbon, who went there as a friend, recalled 'a rich smell of stew, and the rich sound of Dylan's voice talking or reading poems, and beer in bottles and music'. Without Caitlin to keep it in order it must have been less inviting. She was in Laugharne, staying with Frances, Richard Hughes's wife, when Dylan wrote from Manresa Road to 'My Own Caitlin, my dear darling', heading the letter '*Monday*, in misery in our leaking studio, among vermin and falling plaster & unwashed plates'.

> It's never been so useless and lonely away from you as it is this time; there is nothing to live for without you, except for your return or when I can [come] down to Laugharne which must, somehow, be this week because I love you far more than ever and I will not exist without your love and loveliness, darling, so please write and tell me you miss me, too, and love me, and think of us being, soon, together for ever again. By the time you get this, you'll also have got, I hope, *a bit more money* which I will wire either tonight or tomorrow morning. I could not send any more on Friday as there were so many things to pay; & some rent, too.
>
> There is *nothing* to do without you; so terribly terribly sad to come back to our empty barn, lie all night in our big bed, listening to the rain & our mice and the creaks & leaks and the warnings; so sad I could die if I hadn't got to see you again & live with you always & always, when I woke up without you, think of you hundreds of miles away with Aeronwy Lil at your breasts that I want to kiss because I love you, my Cat. I hope to God I can come down for 2 or 3 days at the end of the week...

As in the letters he was to write from America in the 1950s,

---

* Aeron was always told she had been conceived on the bank of the River Aeron.

Thomas was anxious to stress the emptiness of his life without her. A tone of pleading and apology began to emerge. Another undated letter of the same period was written from a pub called the King's Arms in Hertfordshire, near Elstree and its film studios. 'Darling: Darling: Caitlin my dear dear Cat', it began:

It's awful to write to you because, even though I love writing to you, it brings you so near me I could almost touch you and I know at the same time that I *cannot* touch you, you are so far away in cold, unkind Ringwood and I am in stale Barnet in a roadhouse pub with nothing but your absence and your distance, to keep my heart company.

I think of you always all the time. I kiss my uncharitable pillow for you in the nasty nights. I can see you with our little Mongolian monkey at your breast; I can see you in that unfond house listening with loathing to the News; I can see you in bed, more lovely than anything that has ever been at all. I love you. I love Llewelyn & Aeronwy, but you above all and forever until the sun stops and even after that.

And I cannot come down this weekend. I have to work all day Sunday. I am working, for the first time since I sold my immortal soul, very very hard, doing three months' work in a week. I hate film studios. I hate film workers. I hate films. There is nothing but glibly naive insincerity in this huge tinroofed box of tricks. I do not care a bugger about the Problems of Wartime Transport. All I know is that you are my wife, my lover, my joy, my Caitlin.

Oh Cat darling I miss you too much to bear.

Come Back on Wednesday. I'll send you another inarticulately loving letter tomorrow, with some money. You should have it by Saturday morning. No, it's better that I wire the money so that you can have it for the weekend. Even though I dislike Blashford very much, I envy it because all my love is there with my children and with you.

Come back on Wednesday. *Please*.

I haven't been in London at all as I have to start working unlikelily early in the morning & carry on until six o'clock.

I love you more, even, than when I said I loved you only a few seconds ago... I am writing on the back of a script by Mr. J. B. Priestley. But that doesn't spoil what I have to say to you. I have to say to you that I love you in life & after death, and that even though

I drink I am good. I am not drinking much. I am too lonely even for that.

Write.

Give my love to the pigmy baby & kiss Llewelyn on the forehead for me.

Touch your own body for me, very gently. On the breast & the belly. My Caitlin.

Your Dylan X

Probably unknown to Caitlin, he was seeing other women in London. Pamela Glendower, a drinking friend of them both, said that Thomas slept with her when his wife was in St Mary Abbott's Hospital, giving birth to Aeronwy. She was apprehensive of what Caitlin might do if she found out. Infidelity was not something that Dylan's wife was likely to overlook, and when, in the 1950s, she had clear evidence of his unfaithfulness, she was enraged. Her attitude, put plainly years later, was that her adultery was not the same as his. *She* was allowed to do it because it meant nothing. Going to bed with a man was a casual act, like a man's going to bed with a whore. A nice body was, as she put it, nice, and that was the end of it. After all, she said, she was the dancer with the marvellous body. Dylan had the brains. So she was entitled to be mad with rage when he betrayed her. Who can tell if she talked like that because she meant it, or because it suited her to be outrageous?

Keidrych Rhys saw Thomas with a girl in the Swiss pub, in Soho, one evening. Thomas was mocking her, drinking beer from a man's shoe. Then he left to go home with her, on a bus. Rhys was on the bus, too. Caitlin and Vera boarded it, and saw Thomas with the girl. There was a scene, the girl vanished and Thomas went home with his wife. The extent of his infidelities may have been exaggerated. Maclaren-Ross remarked that 'he would talk bawdily about sex in general but never about any woman in particular'; though Jack Lindsay found differently, when Thomas spoke of a film producer's mistress that he claimed to have slept with. She wore leg irons. Thomas told Lindsay, 'Last week when I lay between her legs, I got a shock as the iron scraped against me. I'd forgotten it.' As in his written stories, the sexual encounter is given a twist; there is some impediment, a deformed limb or gonorrhoea or simply a failure to make love to the loved one.

One apparent affair during the war turns out not to have been an affair at all, in the sexual sense, though not for want of trying. Ruth Wynn Owen, a young Welsh woman whose family came from Anglesey, was an actress in a touring company that was at Bradford in 1942. Thomas was there to make a documentary about the theatre in wartime. The unit wanted to film a rehearsal with smoking chimneys in the background. She saw 'this little man' standing in the wings as she came off the stage, and as the filming progressed, they got to know one another. He told her: 'Now that I've found you, don't go and die.' She noticed how small his hands and feet were. Soon after, he was writing to her from Strand Films, 'a ringing, clinging office with repressed women all around punishing typewriters, and queers in striped suits talking about "cinema" and, just at this very moment, a man with a bloodhound's voice and his cheeks, I'm sure, full of Mars Bars, rehearsing out loud a radio talk on "India and the Documentary Movement". I wish I were on the Halifax moor talking to you, not to dishonest men with hangovers.'

They met, and failed to meet, in London. At the end of August, Thomas wrote from Talsarn, where he was staying with Caitlin, about a missed appointment at the stage door:

I think I must have willed my lateness and weakness, willed it because, simply, I was ashamed of my hysterical excitement of the wet-eyed and over-protesting night before. I remembered losing my head in Piccadilly, which left very little for my heart had gone two months ago, gone into your by-me-unkissed breast. And you'll have to forgive now, along with my tears, protestations, and denials, my almost archly over-writing writing in this late, loving letter. I can be natural – my behaviour, then, in the black streets was as natural as my too-much drink and my giddiness at seeing you again allowed me – but perhaps my nature itself is over-written and complicate me out of this, you Ruth in a well. Was there something a little clinical in your attitude, or was it my windy head that blew your words about and got me dancing with love and temper among the bloody buses? ...

Ruth was married. She fell in love with Thomas but refused to become his mistress. She found him gentle and vulnerable, inclined to boast in order to prove himself. He talked to her about his childhood. Perhaps he thought he was in love with her. But his letters are uneasy. He gave her the manuscript of a poem, and wrote her one further letter, in September 1943, from Carmarthenshire, sending her 'with all my heart, my love'. He remained very much married to his wife.

Yet London was still the pleasure-city. Thomas's reputation as a raconteur, a clown, a dog, a good man for a night out, had widened since the 1930s. He was still a long way from being famous, but his work for films and radio was enlarging the already long list of acquaintances who knew him and his funny ways rather better than they knew his poetry. Thomas anecdotes flourished. A streak of violence ran through many of them. He was said to have sliced off his drinking companions' ties with a razor blade. In the Café Royal he was said to have cut the lead of a dachshund, which scampered out into Regent Street and was lost. There were stories of thieving. He took shirts when he stayed with people. Caitlin's old admirer, Rupert Shephard, the painter, and his first wife Lorna loaned Thomas their flat earlier in the war; they returned to find many things missing, including a fur coat, a gramophone and the silver. Cloths and polish left lying around suggested he had cleaned the silver before taking it to the pawnbroker. The story circulated widely. In one improved-upon version, Thomas was in the act of polishing the silver when the owners returned. 'How kind, you shouldn't have bothered,' they said. What really happened was that Thomas wrote them a devious letter from Blashford implying that if anything had been stolen, it was because 'someone' kept leaving the front door open. When Mrs Shephard threatened him with the police, Thomas sent a telegram saying, 'Call off hounds, will restore everything.' Eventually the Shephards retrieved most of their goods.

To others he was simply the good companion. He had developed his gift of absorbing those around him – those who were willing, that is – into a private world of jokes and fantasies. Vera, Captain Killick's wife, said simply, 'I had more fun with Dylan, and with Catty too, than with anybody else, before or since.' Elisabeth Lutyens thought him 'the funniest man in the world'. Her husband once asked her in amazement how she could have spent five hours in a pub with Thomas and cronies – 'But to me it wasn't five hours drinking in a pub, it was five hours of incredibly funny conversation.' He was not merely a passive entertainer, a trigger for laughter. He had the knack of drawing emotionally close to people. Ivan Moffat saw an 'extra-ordinary ability, if you had a worry, to take it over completely and make it belong to himself for a while ... rather like a glass-blower taking a piece of hot glass, he would magnify it, produce it on an enormous, almost ludicrous scale, make it into a kind of nightmare, make it entirely his own for a while. When he handed it back to you, it was laughable. He'd made it grotesque...'

These were remarkable gifts; but they exacted a price, or perhaps were gifts only by virtue of a darker side that com-plemented them. John Davenport, who knew him better than almost anyone except one or two Swansea friends, said the ultimate tragedy of Thomas was that he lost his lyrical gift and was left with nothing but a public personality, which he despised. 'When you think of the cloudbursts of laughter,' said Davenport, 'the sheer, roaring, gorgeous seventeenth-century din of laughter which went on whenever he was around, it's difficult to believe that inside was the misery.' It was not until after the war that Thomas's doubts and fears got the better of him. But already he was moving in that direction. Hugh Porteus, a drinking com-panion of the thirties, met him in a pub and was 'horrified by Dylan's grossness ... he seemed stunned'. The American William Saroyan met him on a 'dreary day' in February 1944, with two other writers. Thomas 'seemed to be swollen by sleeplessness, nervousness, boredom, bad eating and general poor health'. He also seemed to need a bath and a change of clothing. His con-versation was a monologue, 'wild, funny and grim all at once', about 'the war, the weather, art, poetry, other writers involved in the same work he was supposed to be doing ... the whole thing seemed to be some kind of rhapsodic throw-away poem'. It was the middle of the morning; all they were drinking was tea. Saroyan wondered why Thomas was knocking himself out and felt 'a little guilty, as if I were urging him on, for he was moving swiftly, towards exhaustion and collapse'.

There is little point in arguing that Thomas was 'really' someone different: to a large extent he has to remain what people took him to be. But a recollection of Gwen Watkins is pertinent. She didn't get on with Thomas, who postured and exploited her husband too much for her liking. But once we did make momentary contact. I reminded him of the time, many years before, when Vernon's mother was asking a group of young men what quality they would look for first in a wife. I said I had been surprised to hear that Dylan most valued seriousness. 'Why were you surprised?' he said, turning to me quickly. 'To be serious is the most important thing there is.' I told him I wasn't surprised by the proposition itself, but because he himself seemed so often to be – as Kierkegaard would say – precisely not serious. 'I am, though,' he said. 'You couldn't write my kind of poem – you couldn't write good poems *at all* – unless you were fundamentally a serious person.' And then a hanger-on touched his shoulder, and 'instant Dylan' was turned on again.

Thomas's usual behaviour was liable to be ruthless, upsetting to those who saw no reason to tolerate his anarchic approach, which made normality crumble away. It is likely that he redoubled his efforts when he felt himself meeting this kind of resistance, and piled on the misbehaviour. Nicolette, Caitlin's sister, had married into a strong-minded bourgeois family, the Devases. During the war they lived in a house in Markham Square, just off the King's Road in Chelsea. The Thomases descended when least expected, requesting food, shelter and money for the taxi they always arrived in. Nicolette's husband called them 'the Visigoths from Wales'. They would arrive at dawn, like refugees, hammering the door, their possessions in a laundry basket. The Devases could never decide whether it was chance or cunning that brought them in the middle of the night, when it was impossible to turn them away. Thomas responded to the atmosphere by urinating against the living-room wall; at another relative-by-marriage's house, he defecated on the floor.

Drunkenness was habitual, but his destructive drinking seemed to come in spasms. He told Ivan Moffat that he drank to correct the imbalance between the disorder outside and the order within himself; he was drunk when he said it. Some people never saw him drunk at all, or not in a way they regarded as exceptional. He would sit in a pub with a friend and make a glass or two of beer last for hours. This was true to the end of his life, and is one reason it is difficult to tell if he was a dependent alcoholic. The hard-drinking poet was so much a part of the picture of himself that he had sought to project since adolescence, that when and if he crossed into alcoholism, the borderline was heavily obscured. Most of the evidence consists of the subjective observations of other drinkers. Jack Lindsay, a careful observer, noted three versions of Thomas during the war: sober and well-mannered; half-drunk and overflowing with humour, the boon companion; and fully drunk, gross and provoking, when he 'rapidly grew his piggish mask, heavy-lipped and snouted, with big white hands floundering, his big brown eyes growing more protuberant'. His drink was still mainly beer, but it is not true that he began to take spirits only in America. In two letters at the end of the war, five years before he went to America, he vowed to give up anything stronger than beer.* By 1944 or 1945, his drinking was more pronounced. It is said that ten to fifteen years of hard drinking are needed to produce changes in body organs that go with chronic alcoholism. The post-mortem on Thomas showed such changes, in particular dilated veins in the lower part of his throat, and fatty infiltration of liver and kidneys. They are not proof of alcoholism, but they are consistent with it, and they may have been in the making since the early 1940s. There is no definitive version. Margaret Taylor, who saw him drunk and sober often enough, insisted that he was not an alcoholic: 'he drank very heavily, but that is quite different'. She thought he was more fond of his food than the true alcoholic – it was an eccentric mixture, ice-cream and nuts and sweets and shellfish, but it gave him reasonable nourishment. 'Call him a drunk,' said Mrs Taylor, 'but not an alcoholic.' Caitlin, asked on television in 1975 what effect drink had on her husband, replied that it ruined him, and but for the booze he would now have been a splendid old man. Caitlin was speaking as a former alcoholic who came to find drink a good excuse for her former excesses as well as his. It wasn't even as though he really liked the stuff, she said (which may have been true): it was the drinker's life and habits that appealed to him.

As the war moved towards its final stages, Thomas began to detach himself from London. For a while, early in 1944, Caitlin

---

* To Donald Taylor, 28 October 1944: 'Have a drink for me, only make it beer, as a new resolution, now a fortnight, nearly, old, has banned all other drinks – for a long time, I trust & believe.' To David Tennant who owned the Gargoyle Club, 28 August 1945: '... beer only, for me, for weeks, for health ...' Both letters were written from Wales.

lived in a cottage at Bosham, on the Sussex coast, and Thomas
was briefly a commuter. The invasion of Europe was pending;
the countryside was full of soldiers. Then they moved west of
London and stayed with Donald Taylor near Beaconsfield, in the
cocktail belt, where (Thomas told Watkins) 'the well-off people
were dry and thin and grieved over their petrolless motor-cars
and played bridge like ferrets'. He rarely saw his surroundings
as anything but comically disagreeable. Soon they were in Wales
again, 'with my mother and father in Llangain, near Llanstephan
where everyone goes into the pubs sideways, & the dogs piss
only on back-doors, and there are more unwanted babies shoved
up the chimneys than there are used french letters in the offertory
boxes. It's a mean place but near Laugharne where we will go
next week.' It was July. The cottage at Blaen Cwm was cramped
but safe. The first of the German flying bombs, the pilotless
weapon that drove more than a million people out of London,
had arrived the previous month. Already there were rumours of
the still more alarming rockets (which began to fall out of clear
skies in September). Since Taylor raised no objection, Thomas
decided he could write his scripts from afar. They failed to find
rooms in Laugharne. Then in August they heard of a summer
bungalow just outside the small Cardiganshire town of New
Quay, thirty miles away to the north, where the coast begins the
long indentation of Cardigan Bay. It was not as well served by
buses and trains as South Carmarthenshire. But cheap accommodation was scarce, and after visiting it with Thomas's parents,
they took it at a rent of a pound a week, and moved there at the
beginning of September.

Thomas was now writing poems again. It was as though he
had disconnected himself from his recent past. One poem had
been written – or completed – in the early part of the year,
probably while he was still living in England. This was the
thundering, exclamatory 'Ceremony After a Fire Raid', where a
wartime death was again the subject. The casualty was a newborn
child; Thomas was using familiar ingredients. But he seemed to
be affirming life in a way he hadn't done before, raising his voice
at the end with

> Glory glory glory
> The sundering ultimate kingdom of genesis' thunder.

The poem is laced with Biblical and ecclesiastical references –

> I know the legend
> Of Adam and Eve is never for a second
> Silent in my service
> Over the dead infants...

Whether Thomas was using these ingredients, and the entire poem, to make a 'religious' statement, or whether the religious symbols and associations were there because of the convenient emotional charge they contain, is open to argument.

In Wales he worked on another war-inspired poem, 'Holy Spring', and the long 'Vision and Prayer'. Written in stanzas of diamond and hourglass shapes, this has been cited as evidence of a crucial shift towards a Christian position. Perhaps it was a sign of the way Thomas would have liked to go, one of several poems (beginning with 'And death shall have no dominion') that groped for a solution he could believe in, but never arrived at.

A few days before the Thomases left Blaen Cwm for Majoda, he sent Watkins the ubiquitous 'Poem in October' –

> It was my thirtieth year to heaven
> Woke to my hearing from harbour and neighbour wood...

Thomas had been writing poems at Blaen Cwm since adolescence, if not childhood. It was an appropriate place for him to produce a new style, simple and nostalgic, looking back to childhood and innocence. According to Watkins, 'Poem in October' had been 'contemplated' since 1941, when Thomas told him the first line would be 'It was my twenty-seventh year to heaven'. It was sent to Watkins nearly two months before Thomas's thirtieth birthday. He called it 'a Laugharne poem: the first place poem I've written'. Technically it was complex, each stanza written to a strict pattern of syllable-counting in the traditional Welsh manner, with persistent vowel-rhymes within the lines. The effort seemed to have gone into the metrics, not the images, which yielded their meaning at once. Some of the language was almost trite for a poet so determined to be original. Having been criticised often enough for being too obscure, he was now criticised (though infrequently) for being too obvious. Geoffrey Grigson detected in the

poem 'a stale sentimentalism of language – "beckon", "set foot",
"set forth", "pale rain", "tall tales", "marvel", "twice told",
"summer noon", "heart's truth", always the inferior choice'.

Grigson's view may not be the general one. But regardless of
whether the plainer language betokens 'stale sentimentalism', it
was not there by accident. Something had happened to Thomas.
He was making direct statements, perhaps because he was more
sure of himself as a poet, perhaps because he was consciously
trying to rid himself of obscurity. There is another possibility. He
may simply have been frightened. The war, his drinking and an
uncertain future may have made it necessary for him to find firm
anchorages to steady himself with. God – some sort of God –
and childhood might serve. He needed safe places. The poems (it
can be argued) were more direct because they were written out
of pressing need, and not, as so often before, out of a desire to
write arresting poetry. Watkins noted the change when he wrote
about the abandoned *Adventures in the Skin Trade*. 'The pressure
of the anarchy of war itself,' said Watkins, 'and the vision of
distorted London took the place of his half-fictional vision and
compelled his imagination forward to the "Ceremony After a
Fire Raid", and to the beautiful poems evoking childhood, "It
Was My Thirtieth Year to Heaven" [i.e. "Poem in October"] and
"Fern Hill". He could still go back to peace, but from there he
could no longer go forward.'

The bungalow at New Quay was called 'Majoda', from the
names of the landlord's children, Marjorie, John and David. 'I
may alter the name to Catllewdylaer,' said Thomas. From the
town it was a mile along the coast road and a few hundred yards
down a lane. One set of windows looked west over the sea.
Thomas wrote a letter in verse to T. W. Earp:

> I sit at the open window, observing
> The salty scene and my Playered gob curving
> Down to the wild, umbrella'd and french lettered
> Beach, hearing rise slimy from the Welsh lechered
> Caves the cries of the parchs and their flocks. I
> Hear their laughter sly as gonococci...

The itch to write, to play with words even when there was
nothing much to say, still consumed him; it filled the time between

the 'real' poems. No doubt the one was necessary to the other. Earp, who made his living as an art critic, was on the receiving end of several sets of these private verses during the war, often dense with puns. 'When next shall we stumble to the stutter of our lewis-gun carols?' begins a poem of 1943, playing on the author Lewis Carroll and the Army's Lewis gun. Thomas's verbal ingenuity was carried to lengths that made it a weakness as well as a talent, as he himself recognised when he was eighteen, writing to Percy Smart about his 'thousand conceits ... spoiling the whiteness of the page'.

At Majoda the Thomases settled down to a quiet winter. The nearest building was another bungalow along the cliff; Vera the Commando's wife lived in it with her baby daughter. Majoda was built mainly of wood and asbestos sheets. Because it was not intended for regular occupation, living conditions were primitive. Lighting was by bottled gas and there were paraffin stoves for cooking and heating. Water came from a rain tank or a tap on the main road. Beer came from the Black Lion in New Quay. Sometimes Thomas brought a nest of flagons back in the baby's pram. Word got around that a poet lived on the cliffs. The landlord–doctor and his wife found Thomas charming, except that he tried to avoid paying the pound a week. They concluded that he heard their car coming and hid in the outside lavatory. Someone else heard about the Thomases, a cousin out of Dylan's past. She was a daughter of the John Williams who made money on Swansea docks. Another of the family Theodosias, she had married and gone to live in New Quay. Relatives warned her to say nothing in case he wanted to borrow money. So when Theodosia saw Dylan and Caitlin in the town, she kept herself to herself.

The bungalow was 'no place to work in when there's a bawling child there, too,' Thomas wrote to Donald Taylor: 'the rooms are tiny, the walls bumpaper thin, & a friend arrived with another baby with a voice like Caruso's. Now, however, I have just taken a room in a nearby house: a very quiet room where I know I can work till I bleed.' Taylor had wound up Strand but he was still in the film business, making documentaries and hoping to make features. One of his projects that Thomas worked on at Majoda was a film script from *Twenty Years A-Growing*, the book by Maurice O'Sullivan about the Blasket Islands, off the Irish coast.

Nothing came of it. The Burke and Hare script was still being discussed, and Taylor seems to have raised some money on it in the autumn.

Thomas also raised a modest sum at about the same time, for an illustrated book about the streets of London for which he was to provide the text. The idea came from a firm of publishers, Peter Lunn, after he had written the captions for some photographs of London in the magazine *Lilliput* that summer. He was to be paid a hundred and fifty pounds, fifty of them more or less straight away. This was sufficient bait. Thomas turned out a three-page synopsis, headed 'A Book of Streets. Words and Pictures about Streets. Streets in London'. Its theme was to be

> Not the great thoroughfares, described, written, painted a thousand times, but the side streets, the back streets, the smaller worlds of life and death...
>
> And the streets of the suburbs, the smug-faced trim treed streets. And the suburban shopping street...
>
> And the dockside streets: the warehouse streets: the unexpected streets where one might feel a hundred miles from water and then, suddenly turning a corner, would see a great ship's funnel over a warehouse or a crane swinging and the voices of the sea...
>
> The life of streets is the life of people. And after the desolation, come:
>
> The streets one would like to see in the future. This section which is really a discussion of townplanning schemes as they exist now in this country, would make the book have, I think, a positive, and a creative end.

Apart from the gesture to 'townplanning', the streets sound more like those of Swansea than of London. In any case, the synopsis was all the publishers ever saw.

At the end of September 1944, Thomas was in London on film business. He was also to be best man at Vernon Watkins's wedding. Watkins, now a sergeant in RAF Intelligence, was to be married at the church of St Bartholomew the Great in the City on 2 October. Thomas failed to arrive on time, or at all. (One of his calls on 2 October was on Messrs Peter Lunn to collect the first ten pounds of his 'Book of Streets' money.) According to Gwen Watkins, 'Vernon was furious. He said, "Right, that's the end. The only possible excuse is that he's paralysed from the neck down, or dead."' The excuse, when it came, was longer and weaker; but as usual, Watkins forgave him. It had taken nearly a month for Thomas to write. He enclosed a grimy letter, well-creased, explaining that he had written it on the train back to Wales, after missing the wedding, and then had forgotten to post it. Headed 'ON NOT TURNING UP TO BE BEST MAN AT THE WEDDING OF ONE'S BEST FRIEND', it explained that he had forgotten the name of the church, and 'never arrived, in black overcoat & shiny suit, rose-lapelled, breathing cachous & great good will'. The letter is scrawled in pencil and has many alter-ations. It pays the usual attention to style. Thomas wrote that he was jammed in the corridor of the train among soldiers 'commando-trained to the last bayonet lunge'; then crossed out the end of the sentence and substituted 'lunge of the bayonet'. Gwen Watkins found anomalies in the letter which suggested it was not written until later. She decided it was a fake; that Thomas 'took immense trouble to soil and crease it so that it should look as though it had lain in his overcoat pocket for weeks', and that the reason for his non-appearance at the wedding was simply that he couldn't face a formal occasion. Two months later, she and Vernon met Thomas in London, at the Café Royal. He arrived hot and morose from Waterloo Station, where he had been seeing Caitlin off to Hampshire. He had put her luggage, which included her handbag and ticket, on the wrong train, which promptly left. There had been a scene. Gwen Watkins expected him to sound apologetic about the wedding, but he didn't refer to it. Then, in February 1945, he wrote Watkins a letter that came to light only in 1972.* Mrs Watkins believed that this was the real apology. Thomas was being sorry for himself again, to a friend he knew would listen. But there is a feeling of events pressing down on him. His spelling in the manuscript is worse than usual; he sounds tired or drunk, or both.

I was very glad to hear and see from you; it's been a long and complicated time since we disappointingly met, and I'm happy and

* Gwen Watkins found it at the bottom of an RAF kitbag. Vernon Watkins had died in 1967.

relieved to think that the offence, (for my lost, preoccupied manner must really have been that) I gave when we did meet in that gabbling drink-grey crush, the worst of the town, has, if never to be forgotten utterly, lost some disfavour (I have just been writing at length to Llewelyn, on the occasion of a fall from a tree and a split tongue, and the effort of not talking to a boy of six has made me adopt the claptrap periods of a leader-writer under gas.) I have found, increasingly as time goes on, or around, or backwards, or stays quite still as the brain races, the heart absorbs and expels, and the arteries harden, that the problems of physical life, of social contact, of daily posture and armour, of the choice between dissipations, of the abhorred needs enforced by a reluctance to 'miss anything', that old fear of death, are as insoluble to me as those of the spirit. In few and fewer poems I can despair and, at rare moments, exult with the big last, but the first force me every moment to make quick decisions and thus to plunge me into little hells and rubbishes at which I rebel with a kind of truculent acceptance. The ordinary moments of walking up village streets, opening doors or letters, speaking good-days to friends or strangers, looking out of windows, making tele-phone calls, are so inexplicably (to me) dangerous that I am trem-bling all over before I get out of bed in the mornings to meet them. Waking to remember an appointment at X that coming evening is to see, before X, galleries of menacing commonplaces, chambers of errors of the day's conventions, pits of platitudes and customary gestures, all beckoning, spurning; and through, over & out of these I must somehow move before the appointment, the appointment that has now become a shining grail in a dentist's surgery, an almost impossible consummation of illegal pleasure to be achieved in a room like a big gut in a subterranean concentration-camp. And especially, of course, in London. I wish that I could have met Gwen 'properly', and glad that she wanted to; I was 'myself' in the sense that I was no one else, but I was broken on a wheel of streets and faces; equally well, I may be just as broken in the peace – what peace? – of the country, hysterical in my composure, hyena-ish in my vegetabledom...

Life was a torment: that seems true, and real, enough.

During the early part of 1945 Thomas was probably busier with new poems than at any time since his youth in Swansea. This was not because everyday anxieties left him alone; on the contrary. The publishers who had been promised the 'Book of Streets' material – in the unlikely time of a few months – had to be placated. Thomas wrote from Majoda on 3 January:

> ... I'm afraid I have nothing of consecutive [*sic*] value to send you by the suggested near-date of January 6th, owing more to domestic troubles beyond my control – my wife has influenza and I am trying to combine the duties of housekeeper and children-minder along with my own work – than to the difficulty, however pleasurable, of the job itself. I suggest that we move the date forward one month: to the end of the first week of February. The plan for the book that I had started work upon I've decided to scrap, as a much better plan came to my mind ... Roughly, my plan is this: to call the book *Twelve Hours in The Streets* and to take the life of the streets from twelve noon to twelve midnight ... the whole might well be an imaginative, picaresque perhaps, cross-section of the life of the English streets for a whole modern day...

This eventually was to be the formula for *Under Milk Wood*. A postscript to the letter promised that he would work on 'nothing else for the next month'. But early in February he was writing to explain that Fate or Nature had intervened again:

> ... I came up to London last month, with the intention of seeing you ... but, almost as soon as I was up, I got caught with this annoying trouble [it was gastric flu] & was forced to travel back, through snow, in an ice-bound train...

This tale of woe kept Messrs Peter Lunn quiet for a while.*

Film work, too, continued at Majoda. Early in March, two of Taylor's staff, John Eldridge and a woman assistant, went down from London to discuss a documentary. It happened that Vera's husband, the Commando captain, was home on leave. He had been dropped behind the German lines in Greece in 1943 and

---

* The publishers (later called John Westhouse Ltd) pursued Thomas with a writ in 1946, but were unable to track him down after he left Majoda. Finally a diligent process-server who had studied his *Radio Times* went to Broadcasting House late one evening in January 1947 and served the writ as Thomas left the studio after reading 'A Visit to Grandpa's'. Soon the solicitors reported to the publisher that 'we have since received a cheque ... for the full amount due'.

had served there for more than a year, training guerrillas in the mountains and helping in sabotage work. When he arrived at New Quay he found his wife on annoyingly close terms with the Thomases. She was short of money and he thought he knew where it had gone. Vera saw it differently. 'Dylan and Catty never sponged off me,' she said. 'We *shared*.' This wasn't good enough for the captain. On a Tuesday evening his wife went with the baby to her mother in another town. The captain went into New Quay and started drinking. He saw Thomas and his friends, and they cut him dead, or he thought they did. Not surprisingly, this upset him. He had spent a year living in caves with a gun in his hand. Now the clever people were laughing among themselves, showing no respect for a fighting man. Thomas, in fact, picked quarrels with more than one serviceman during the war. He had a brawl with Caitlin's brother John, who was also a Commando, and who talked about strangling Germans. This time the trouble started between the captain and Eldridge's assistant, a Jew, who thought he made an anti-semitic remark. He slapped her, she scratched him, and Thomas (who claimed to have been drinking only cider) put up his fists. The captain was a big, powerful man. There was some indeterminate scuffling before they were separated. It seemed to be the end of the incident. But the captain was drunk and unhappy. Back in the empty bungalow he decided to 'put the wind up those buggers'. Like many front-line soldiers, he kept his weapons with him. At ten-thirty he staggered out with a sub-machine gun and a hand grenade, and advanced on Majoda. Dylan, Caitlin and three friends were sitting around the coal fire; Aeronwy and a friend's baby were asleep in a bedroom. Suddenly they found themselves being machine-gunned. The captain meant to fire over the bungalow, but in the dark, and his condition, he mistook the elevation. He loosed off a dozen rounds, at least five of which passed through the asbestos walls of the living room. A moment later he burst into Majoda, waving gun and grenade. He wore dark glasses and there was blood on his face. Told there were babies in the house, he emptied the magazine into the ceiling and shouted, 'You're nothing but a lot of egoists.' They persuaded him to hand over the machine gun. The captain said that he then 'produced the hand-grenade, with no intention of taking out the pin, to see their reactions. They were all quite petrified except Thomas, I'll say that. He was the coolest of the lot.' Eventually Captain Killick went away, the police were called, and he was later charged with attempted murder. At Lampeter Assizes he said he did it to frighten them. The judge told the jury there was no evidence to sustain the charge, and the fighting man was set free.*

Three weeks after the shooting, Thomas wrote to tell Watkins about it, adding that his previous letter 'told of my daily terrors, my everyday traps & pits etc. I'm sure you thought I was exaggerating. At debts' and death's door I now stand with a revolving stomach ...' The letter noted another anxiety: 'My Father is awfully ill these days, with heart disease and uncharted pains, and the world that was once the colour of tar to him is now a darker place.' With the letter came four poems: 'This side of the truth', 'The conversation of prayers', 'A Refusal to Mourn the Death, by Fire, of a Child in London' and 'A Winter's Tale'. All, presumably, had been written during the previous months, ready for a new collection to be called *Deaths and Entrances* that Dent intended to publish in 1945. They were to become well-known additions to the small group of Thomas's poems that identifies him for most of his readers. 'A Winter's Tale' was a fairy-tale narrative of death and rebirth. The meaning of 'The conversation of prayers' may have been on the lines of 'God works in a mysterious way'; or the poem may have been a secular comment on how arbitrary life is. 'This side of the truth' was a piece of disenchanted, almost despairing advice for his infant son about the moral indifference of the 'unminding skies'. 'A Refusal to Mourn the Death' was a striking trumpet-blast from Thomas the Poet (hostile critics have seen it as pretentious) with an equivocal last line, 'After the first death, there is no other'. Read in conjunction with the other poems in the group, and taking account of the mood that his letters to Watkins reveal, it seems likely that Thomas was declaring that death was final; he was affirming the

---

* Thomas told the court that after firing the shots, Killick had laid down his gun.

'We suggested he should go home but he refused to do so without his gun, and raising his hand with the grenade declared, "If you do not give me my gun I will throw the grenade and we will all go up together." '

Mr Justice Singleton: 'What did you do?'

Thomas: 'I gave him his gun.'

present, not the future. Or perhaps the line reflects his own uncertainties: he didn't know what to think.

Nothing about the letters that Thomas was writing suggests he was achieving any harmony with his surroundings, physical or otherwise. On the contrary, now that the war was coming to an end, and he was going to be free, like everyone else, to reorganise his life, he wanted to leave Britain altogether and go to America. His thoughts had turned to it before now. In 1939 he was writing to Kenneth Patchen, 'I want to get out of the war: to America best of all but nobody, possibly quite rightly, will help me to.' Early in 1945, with the end of the war in Europe in sight, America began to take on the outline of a fine place to escape to. A letter to his US publisher, James Laughlin, about a planned volume of *Selected Writings*, said he would 'like to come over to the States after the war for a few months. Any chance of getting a job to keep me while over there? Reading, talking?' He told Oscar Williams, the American poet and anthologist, with whom he had been in touch since 1942, that he would 'love a little ladleful from the gravy pots over there'. Williams, who greatly admired Thomas's poems, was already selling them to magazines, acting as an unofficial literary agent.* But Thomas had his eye on more substantial earnings. He wrote, 'The war, they say, is all over bar the dying; and, when it is, I want to come over to America. How could I earn a living? I can read aloud, through sonorous asthma, with pomp; I can lecture on The Trend of Y, or X at the Crossroads, or Z: Whither? with an assurance whose shiftiness can be seen only from the front row...'

On 30 July he crystallised something of what he felt about his surroundings in a long letter to Williams. The Thomases had left Majoda because the owner wanted it for the summer; they were back at Blaen Cwm – 'in a breeding-box in a cabbage valley, in a parlour with a preserved sheepdog, where mothballs fly at night, not moths, where the Bible opens itself at Revelations; and is there money still for tea?' Thomas feels a fond loathing for the place, an attitude he refined towards West Wales in the last years

---

* 'Poem in October' was published in the British *Horizon* and the American *Poetry* in the same month, February 1945. 'A Winter's Tale' and 'A Refusal to Mourn' were both published in America, respectively in *Poetry* (July 1945) and *New Republic* (14 May 1945), before they appeared in Britain.

of his life. There is another of his obsessive references to condoms;
and in 'establishing my geography' he fantasises on the theme of
his family origins.

The rainy robins tic tac at the pane. Over the hill, the hoarse noise
of a train carrying holes to Hugh's Castle. Near, a grey gulled
estuary, and sheepshanks, corpses of cats, cowteeth, bottles of ether,
jellyfish, frenchletters, indecipherable messages in jars (the secret of
the Marie Celeste, the Number of the Beast, the name of Cain's
wife, pyramid riddles, Tibetan acrostics, next year's newspapers) on
the foreshore. I'm trying to establish my geography. Up the hill-
lane behind this house too full of Thomases, a cottage row of
the undeniably mad unpossessed peasantry of the inbred crooked
county, my cousins, uncles, aunts, the woman with the gooseberry
birthmark who lies with dogs, the farm labourer who told me that
the stream that runs by his cottage side is Jordan water and who
can deny him, the lay preacher who believes that the war was begun
only to sell newspapers which are the devil's sermon-sheets, the man
who, when his pony could work no longer because of old age,
hanged it on an apple-tree to save a bullet, the woman who cries
out 'Cancer!' as you pass her open door.

This kind of thing was part of Thomas's routine, the bizarre
commentary written mainly to amuse. But behind it is something
else, the hold that this particular countryside had on his imagination. He doesn't like it but he has not outgrown it; he will keep
coming back to it, filling it with crooked scenes and twisted
people – 'I had some beer with a man who said he was shot in
the groin in the last war, and who, unable to have a woman ever
since, blames it on the dirty Jews ... He told me the best way to
boil lobsters, which was detailed and painful. I told him Norman
Douglas's recipe for raping a dog ... He told me how he had
once made a child of six dead drunk. It began to rain again, great
wrathful drops. We parted enemies...'

Thomas's vegetable background, as Caitlin called it, gave him
the setting he needed to work in. It was in his blood. But in a
curious way, he never came to terms with it. He needed it and
hated it. Perhaps it was a trap in which he felt himself caught;
and he hated to be trapped. So he continually compromised and
kept moving, always coming back but always going away again.

Thus, in 1945, when a year in Wales, for all its trials, had enabled him to write poems, which was the thing he cared about most, he badly wanted to escape. America was the child's land of promise. It was a long way off, glittering with goodies. He could go there and stop worrying. Money would be different in America. So he bombarded Williams with ideas. Could he work for *Time* magazine? At Harvard University? Thomas doesn't sound over-pleased at Attlee's Labour Government, which had come to power four days earlier. He could sail within three months, he says, with his wife and children – 'We would all come together because I do not want to return to this country for a long time. The rain has stopped, thank Jesus. Have the socialists-in-power-now stopped it? An incometax form flops through the window, the letterbox is choked with dockleaves. Let's get out, let's get out.'

Thomas was in London intermittently in the summer, working on films and looking for somewhere to live before they went to America. He wrote to Caitlin from a flat in London belonging to the writer Mervyn Peake, another lament for their separation. She was staying at the Blaen Cwm cottage with her parents-in-law.

My dear My Caitlin darling more times than ever before to me, I love you. And this time has seemed the very longest since we haven't been together all the time, since I've had to leave you alone, or with parents, for weeks & ten-days and eternities: – the *very* longest; I have never missed you more nor loved you more, and every long night without you has been sleepless and fear-filled, and I've cried to be with you. I've said to you, all these hours away, Oh be around the next corner, Caitlin my own, climb up the stairs of the next bus I'm in, be waiting, somewhere, somewhere very near, for me. But I knew you were in a hutch in a field, so far away, with two neurotics & a baby and a dog, bound to Daddy-likes-his-dinner and eternal afternoon walks. I do, I do, I do think of you all the time. And I love you. I've been having an awful time, too, looking for a house, a flat, a room, a hole in the wall...

And I've no extra money. No house, as yet, no money, as yet. But good chances of money, at least, from the BBC. But *that's* not much good if we can't live in, or near, London to do it. It's acting in plays, especially verse plays for the Empire Service: & they pay well.

So I'm not much good to you, coming home, (not home), but I hope, oh God I hope, you'll say you *are* & kiss me. I want you holding on to me, & me on to you. I love you I love I love you dear sweet Cat, dear mine.

Think that I think of you.

Feel that we know each other forever.

Know that I love you.

Tomorrow I'll see you, poor & a bit dirty but oh so glad.

X

& to Aeron   Dylan

So far the BBC had been only a minor source of income. Thomas was developing the radio reminiscence as entertainment, but this meant taking pains over a script. It was not particularly easy money. Probably his film work as writer and narrator first led him to think seriously of radio scripts, and at the end of 1942 he wrote a fifteen-minute talk, 'Reminiscences of Childhood', for the Welsh BBC, which was broadcast the following February. Towards the end of 1944, when he was living at Majoda, he wrote a radio piece called 'Quite Early One Morning', which gave a fanciful account of a town whose features are those of New Quay. It reads like a sketch for *Under Milk Wood*. (That play is about Laugharne, if it is about anywhere in particular; but Thomas's fanciful West Wales was really one place made up of all the fragments, melted down in his mind.) 'Quite Early One Morning' was recorded in Wales, and the producer, Aneirin Talfan Davies, offered it to London for the national network. But London was not impressed by the 'breathless poetic voice', and the item was heard only in Wales. BBC headquarters had its doubts about Celtic poets. The Welsh Children's Hour producer Lorraine Davies wrote to Thomas in July 1945, to suggest a talk called 'Memories of Christmas'. He thought it 'a perfectly good title to hang something on', and wrote it by the autumn, probably at Blaen Cwm. The Children's Hour Director in London (Derek McCulloch, the once famous 'Uncle Mac') liked the talk but couldn't bring himself to let the 'notoriously tricky' Thomas broadcast it live, which was Children's Hour practice then. They had to pretend to Thomas, who is hardly likely to have cared anyway, that technical reasons made it necessary to record in advance. Years later he enlarged the talk for an American magazine, and in this form, as 'A Child's Christmas in Wales', made a record of it which became his most popular prose work in America.

'Memories of Christmas' is heavily nostalgic. That summer, the same mood, working on a different level, produced what is probably his most famous poem, 'Fern Hill'. It is first mentioned in a letter to Dent on 18 September 1945, when he was returning the proofs of *Deaths and Entrances*. Thomas had been dilatory over the proofs, which were originally sent to him at the end of May; the book had to be put back to 1946. The letter of 18 September shows that Thomas had been busy at Blaen Cwm. 'Unluckily for a death', a 'marriage' poem dating from 1939, had been rewritten. Another poem (unidentified in the letter) was deleted from the proofs, and a newly written one, the rhetorical 'In my craft or sullen art', substituted. And an extra poem was added:

> I am enclosing a further poem, '*Fern Hill*', not so far included in the book, which I very much *want* included as it is an *essential* part of the feeling & meaning of the book as a whole. As so much re-setting etc. will have to be done anyway, I do most earnestly hope that '*Fern Hill*' can be included in the book. I myself would be very unsatisfied were it omitted. (I realise, naturally, that it should have been sent along in the first place with the others, but it was not at that time completed...)

The publishers added the poem at the end of the book. It is not clear how long he had been working on it. John Malcolm Brinnin, the American writer, said that when he visited Laugharne in 1951, Thomas showed him 'more than two hundred separate and distinct versions of the poem'. Presumably Brinnin meant there were two hundred worksheets, not an abnormal number for Thomas. The poem may have been begun at New Quay, then finished at Blaen Cwm, where the farm of Fernhill was only a mile or so away. It is nostalgic for lost beginnings. It is also a doomed poem: the poet will wake to death and 'the farm forever fled from the childless land'. It is tempting to see the machine-gunning at Majoda as an incident, both ludicrous and ugly, that drove Thomas back into himself, to levels of memory that produced the poem. Probably, though, he was responding to a more general unhappiness. He lacked certainties and he wrote accordingly. Some critics have treated it sternly, calling it sentimental or even dishonest. Others have been content to praise its singular melancholy. Thomas's mood when he wrote it is one that people can recognise without hesitation. It was a long backward glance, cunningly assembled. But it was not a poem that led anywhere, unless it was to more of the same, and Thomas did not attempt to repeat the formula. 'Fern Hill' ended an intensely creative year, the last of its kind he was to enjoy.

Chapter Ten

A VOICE ON THE RADIO

Five years passed between the time Dylan Thomas first thought seriously of America as a refuge, in 1945, and the time he finally arrived there, a man on the run. On the face of it they should have been good years. His book *Deaths and Entrances* consolidated his reputation, his voice became familiar on radio, he earned enough money to live comfortably, and Margaret Taylor made sure that he and his family were housed in Wales, by the sea. None of this had much effect on the course of his affairs, which grew steadily more confused.

About the end of September 1945, Thomas and his wife moved from Wales to London. They seem to have stayed where they could, with various friends, for the winter. America receded as Thomas came up against the problems of obtaining a visa, convincing the US authorities that he was being invited by responsible people, and raising the money for the tickets. In February or March 1946 he was in St Stephen's Hospital, in London, for four days, with 'alcoholic gastritis'. He wrote to Watkins on 27 April, 'I had a little time in hospital but I'm out again now and fit as an old potato.' In general Thomas avoided doctors. Jack Lindsay was told by a doctor's wife that about 1945 Thomas visited a hospital, 'described himself as a poet, and asked to be cured of drinking obsessions'. A psychiatrist there 'treated him as something of a joke and bantered him about being a poet; he had never heard of Dylan and was mildly irritated by a patient portentously announcing himself in such terms. Dylan didn't take the raillery at all well and failed to turn up for the appointment that was made.' There is a story that he was treated at St Mary's for alcoholism about 1950. He also visited hospitals when he broke one or other of his arms. Caitlin said sarcastically that he was never himself unless he was ill, and if there was any chance of his being well he would contrive to crack one of his 'chicken bones' and enjoy having his arm in a sling.

After the St Stephen's episode, Thomas and family drifted out of London to the home of the A. J. P. Taylors at Oxford. For the rest of his life, Thomas was to live either free or cheaply in accommodation provided by Mrs Taylor, his staunchest patron. The original arrangement in 1946 was that the Thomases lived in a summerhouse a hundred yards from the Taylors' residence, Holywell Ford. It was a small damp building on the bank of the River Cherwell, overshadowed by poplars. A. J. P. Taylor, who was even less enthusiastic about the Thomases as time went on, was still an academic historian, yet to make a popular reputation. He was a lecturer at Magdalen College, and Holywell Ford was a college property. The high wall of the Magdalen deer park ran alongside. For a year Taylor had a poet at the bottom of his garden. Caitlin would bring Aeron into the house to bath her, and the child slept there with the Taylors' two daughters. In the one-room summerhouse, conditions were not ideal. Water gurgled under the trees and the chime of Oxford bells came across the meadows, but mud, draughts, insects and general squalor prevailed. Jack Lindsay called there once, when Thomas was out. Caitlin had her sleeves rolled up, 'a lovely slattern', and Aeron was crying. A calf's-head on a dish dominated the room. 'It's beginning to stink,' said Caitlin. 'I suppose I ought to throw it away, but Dylan would be annoyed.' Thomas wrote to Watkins on 27 April, 'I want to write a poem of my own again, but it's hard here with peace and no room, spring outside the window and the gascooker behind the back, sleep, food, loud wireless, broom and brush all in one kiosk, stunted bathing-hut or square milkbottle.'

Later Mrs Taylor provided him with a small caravan to work in. Margaret Taylor was interested in all the arts. She studied music as a girl, wrote poetry and later became a painter. Her mother was Irish, her father an inspector of mines from South Wales. Because she had a little money of her own, she was able to help Thomas, who took it gladly, wrote long critiques of her poems, sometimes laughed at her behind her back, as he laughed at so many of his friends, but spelt out his thanks in many letters, as well he might. Her relationship with the Thomases inevitably caused rows, in her family and in theirs (the Taylors were later divorced). At times Mrs Taylor had a possessive attitude towards Dylan that Caitlin resented. But without her, the Thomases would have found living even more difficult than it was already.

Deaths and Entrances was published in February 1946, and widely praised. If his reputation had suffered since his first two books it was now re-established, not least because of the poems he had written between the summers of 1944 and 1945. James A. Davies has called it 'powerful, troubled, uneasy, and probably Thomas's finest achievement'. Three thousand copies of the book were printed. A month later, Dent ordered a reprint of the same number, and bound the surplus sheets they had been storing of the three unprofitable books they had already published – *Twenty-five Poems, Map of Love* and *Portrait of the Artist*. In America, New Directions brought out *Selected Writings* with work from all his books, including most of the *Deaths and Entrances* poems. A new book was planned by Dent made up of published stories and the reminiscences. Thomas wanted to call it 'Top Hat and Gasworks' or 'Bob's My Uncle'. But the collection failed to mature, like other of his post-war projects.

A more reliable income was promised by radio, which helped to fill the gap left when documentary work for Donald Taylor ended in 1945 – Thomas was officially a freelance again from 6 October that year. The BBC offered the best single market in the country to writers and performers. The war and social change had gone some way towards democratising it. Two domestic channels were then in operation, the Home Service (with regional variations) and the Light Programme, as well as extensive overseas services. By the end of 1945, Thomas was a regular reader in a programme beamed to the Far East, 'Book of Verse'. John Arlott, writer and cricket commentator, then a talks producer, handled dozens of these readings – 'he would stand, feet apart and head thrown back, a dead cigarette frequently adhering wispily to his lower lip, curls a little tousled and eyes half-closed, barely reading the poetry by eye, but rather understanding his way through it, one arm beating out a sympathetic double rhythm as he read'. Radio suddenly discovered Thomas. He was useful should a younger-generation poet be needed for a discussion. He appeared with the poet James Stephens on the Light Programme, declaring that 'poetry, to a poet, is the most rewarding work in the world. A good poem is a contribution to reality.' He appeared with Edward Shanks, an elderly poet who didn't care much for his verse, in the North American Service. Shanks said he had shown a book of Thomas's to a friend, who called it a disaster to English poetry. Thomas retorted, 'You've rather stolen my introductory thunder – not that it was very thunderous – because I too was asking a friend whether he knew you, Shanks, and he said, "Well, of course I know his verse. Is he still alive?" '

Readings and discussions were a painless way of earning up to fifteen or twenty pounds a time. Occasionally Thomas wrote scripts, which earned more. For 'The Londoner', a thirty-minute documentary, he was paid fifty pounds for writing and taking part. An account of a day in the life of a working-class street in London, it carried intimations of *Milk Wood*: 'It is summer night now in Montrose Street. And the street is sleeping ...' Laurence Gilliam, the BBC's Head of Features, urged Thomas to write more like it. A documentary about a holiday outing to Margate was recorded for a New York radio station (they swapped it for a documentary about Coney Island). A particular advantage of working for radio was that in addition to a fee, Thomas was paid travelling expenses and a small 'subsistence allowance' if he had to spend a night away from home. This meant he could commute from Oxford to London several times a month at the BBC's expense. Caitlin was not pleased when an afternoon's trip to a studio to spend twenty minutes reading poems developed into a drinking holiday that went on for days. When he wanted to placate her, he would take back an attempt at a peace offering; Elisabeth Lutyens saw him setting off for Oxford with a battered music-case containing two cans of soup. Sometimes he added insult to injury by arriving in a hired car that had brought him from London, a rich man's way of travelling sixty miles.

In the autumn of 1946 the BBC launched its high-culture radio channel, the 'Third Programme', which opened up a new market. Thomas was promptly in demand as an actor and speaker, appearing (as 'Second Brother') in Milton's 'Comus', the first drama production. He read Blake and Edith Sitwell, and talked about Walter de la Mare. He played Aristophanes in a 'panorama of Aristophanic comedy' written by Louis MacNeice, who was on the BBC's staff as a writer-producer. In November 1946 he took the part of Private Dai Evans in a radio version of David Jones's strange romance or allegory, *In Parenthesis*; a minor member of the cast (he played 'A Bombing Officer') was a young Welshman doing his conscript service in the RAF, Aircraftsman

Second Class Richard Burton.* Most of the Third Programme producers who used Thomas worked for Features, a department whose role was never clearly defined except by the programmes they made.

Laurence Gilliam was a burly, cheerful man who had started out in concert parties and somehow found his way into broadcasting. He was not a bureaucrat; nor were his producers. Unless they were in a studio, they were as likely to be found in one of the pubs or clubs near Broadcasting House as in their offices. This suited Thomas; he found himself working among congenial people who behaved more like journalists than academics. They knew about poetry and paid him for reading it, but on the whole they didn't want to have long discussions about it.

Roy Campbell, the poet, was on the BBC staff, and handled many of his Third Programme readings. Campbell found him 'the best all-round reader of verse that I ever produced', but noted that he was more effective with 'wild and woolly poets', where he could use his voice – 'it was with Blake and Manley Hopkins that Dylan became almost Superman' – and that he had difficulty with 'correct' poets like Pope and Dryden. Once (but only once, according to Campbell) Thomas arrived drunk for a live reading on the Third Programme. Campbell found him 'snoring in front of the mike with only twenty seconds left'. He slurred his first title, 'Song for Saint Sheshilia's Day'. Later in the programme he began to wave his arms, and indicated that he didn't know how to pronounce 'Religio Laici'. Campbell said he 'had about three shots at it, bungled it, gave it up'. Next day Campbell was sent for by the Third Programme Controller, George Barnes. Thomas promised to behave himself in future; the incident was passed over.

---

* Burton wrote of this play, 'I worked with [Thomas] a few times or several, and once for instance a director said to him, we were rehearsing a radio play at the time, Dylan will you take the words Mam! Mam! and scream them for me; you understand that you are dying in No Man's Land, and when you hear the Royal Welch sing, I will give you a cue light and then scream for me woodjew there's a good chap ... and the green light flickered and Dylan, short, bandy, prime, obese and famous among the bars screamed as I have never heard, but sometimes imagined a scream, and we were all appalled, our pencils silent above the crossword puzzles, and invisible centuries-gone atavistic hair rose on our backs.' According to Burton, he screamed without taking the cigarette out of his mouth.

But Thomas was never entirely acceptable to the BBC management. A Third Programme memorandum of 1951, dealing with the fees paid to Thomas, said that he was not to be regarded as in the 'celebrity class', along with Eliot, Auden, C. Day Lewis and E. M. Forster. Nor would the BBC ever employ Thomas in a staff job. He had hopes of this more than once. Margaret Taylor went to see a crony, a senior person at Broadcasting House, but he shook his head and said the problem was drink. Having lunch with Gilliam, Thomas drafted his perfect contract with the BBC: ten pounds a week for Caitlin and a monthly trip to London for a 'piss-up'. Once, in 1950, Thomas called on the Controller of the Third Programme, seeking regular employment for a year or two. But Gilliam, who would have had to do the employing, was unwilling to take the chance.

In August 1946 Dylan and Caitlin went to Ireland with friends, Bill and Helen McAlpine, for a holiday. This must have been the trip when Caitlin was ashamed to take him to Ennistymon. Thomas was also supposed to be writing about Puck Fair, held annually in Kerry, for the magazine *Picture Post*, which advanced him money for the trip; but he never did. He wrote to Margaret Taylor from Blaen Cwm, where he and Caitlin broke their journey back to Oxford:

> We had breathless days in Ireland: four in Dublin – oh the steaks, the chickens, chocolate, cream, peaty porter, endless blarney of politics never later than 1922 – & the rest in Kerry, all wild sea and hills and Irish-reeling in kitchens. And a day on the Blasket: a very calm day, they said: the wind blew me about like a tissue-paper man, and dashed us against the donkeys ... I can't tell you how much we're looking forward to being [in Oxford] again. We love it; and can never thank you both enough for having let us descend on you, you being so kind every way.

The summerhouse was still supposed to be a temporary resting place on the way to America. James Laughlin was in London in the autumn, promising to look out for a suitable house. Thomas wrote on 24 November, reminding him. He made conditions: he wanted to write 'poems, stories, scripts', but not until he was in America, with his family, installed in a house in the hills, fairly near New York City, where he could earn his living by broadcasting. Also he needed money for the passage. Once there, 'All I write in America is yours for America (and I want, and mean to, write a lot), but until that is settled I have no intention of writing anything at all.' This was not a very practical ultimatum. No one was prepared to foot the bill for the uncertain rewards of shipping the Thomases to New York. Others were positively anxious to stop them going. Edith Sitwell thought that if he must go, it should be to lecture; eventually she decided it would be a disaster if he went at all. She tried hard to dissuade him. 'I was aghast when I heard he was going there,' she wrote to John Lehmann on 11 December 1946. 'I've tried *everything* – imploring, owl-like prognostications of disaster – saying that Caitlin will have a rotten time because she isn't rich. *Nothing* sways him. And his hostess at Oxford, Mrs Taylor, the wife of a don, says it is like measles – you have to have it and get over it – I mean this mania to go to America.' Edith Sitwell was worried about his drinking, but even more about the prospect of a penniless Thomas in America. She was pulling strings in literary circles to have him awarded a Society of Authors scholarship, if he must go. Alternatively he might be persuaded to try Switzerland instead. In the end he was given the money, a hundred and fifty pounds, and recommended to try Italy. Italy was a natural haven for the English man of letters in need of peace and culture; but not necessarily for Thomas, who once wrote to Lawrence Durrell that 'England is the very place for a fluent and fiery writer. The highest hymns of the sun are written in the dark ... If I went to the sun I'd just sit in the sun.'

Perhaps in 1947 things seemed different. A bitter winter and fuel shortages disrupted Britain (even the Third Programme was suspended). In the middle of the cold spell in February, Thomas was in Swansea, gathering material for a radio feature in an occasional series called 'Return Journey'. One of Gilliam's producers, R. D. Smith, was with him. People were often surprised to find Thomas doing anything as straightforward as making notes. But he could be unexpectedly normal when it came to work. He walked about the chilly Mumbles, writing down the names of boats drawn up above the seaweed. He carried a notebook with floppy covers, rather like the ones he used for his early poems. In it he wrote the names of streets in Townhill and

Mayhill, burnt out in the wartime air raids – 'Emlyn Road badly hit. Teilo Crescent was wiped out.' He observed 'the hill which because of the houses you couldn't see before'. Nothing had been rebuilt in Swansea, the town centre was still gaunt and ruined, clocks showed the hour the bombs stopped them. The script Thomas wrote contained long lists of shops that had stood there before the war. A Swansea friend who heard the broadcast in June (it was recorded before Thomas went abroad) asked him how he could possibly have remembered them. 'Easy,' said Thomas. 'I wrote to the Borough Estate Agent.' In the script, Thomas uncovers his youth in Swansea, layer by layer; the reminiscence, at once nostalgic and comic, is more skilful than in anything he wrote except the *Portrait* stories. In the recording of the original production, his narration is relaxed, without the exaggerated booming. Mrs Ferguson, who kept the sweet shop in the Uplands where he used to raid the wine-gums, heard her name in the programme, and wrote to say, 'Fancy remembering the gob-stoppers.' Mrs Hole of Mirador school was listening. 'I think I must be getting old,' she wrote to Thomas, 'but I don't like children very much these days.'

The Thomases went to Italy in April, taking both their children, Caitlin's sister Brigit, and Brigit's small son. 'I hope to write poems, after a year's stop,' Thomas wrote to Charles Fisher. He succeeded, but in the face of difficulties; most of the time he was in his usual state of amused belligerence about his surroundings, which might as well have been Carmarthenshire, except that it didn't rain. He began by losing their luggage at the Italian frontier – they were travelling by train – and having to track it down in Milan, which he described to his parents, inevitably, as 'a giant, nightmare city'. But he was always careful not to upset his parents. When the party came to rest in the village of San Michele di Pagana, outside Rapallo, on the Italian Riviera, he wrote to them about the sea and sky and the 'excellent food, superlatively cooked . . . dinner being some form of very good spaghetti in a rich sauce, followed by white meat, artichokes, spinach, & potatoes, followed by bread & cheese (all kinds of cheese; my favourite gorgonzola), followed by apples or oranges or figs, & then coffee. Red wine always with the meal.' They were there a month, Thomas dubious about being able to do any writing. 'There is no escape in a small hotel from the too many children,' he told Margaret Taylor.

Thomas saw it as a wife's duty to protect her husband from brawling infants. His daughter Aeronwy recalled that he avoided eating with his children whenever possible: 'He hated the noise and presumably wished to avoid having to shout at us' – which he never did, in any case.

Leaving the children with Brigit in Rapallo, he and Caitlin took an all-night bus to Rome. They stayed for five days, during which the British Council gave them a party, and they 'wandered round', he told his parents, 'rather than go on vast exhausting tours of inexhaustible galleries & churches'. It was, he said, 'very lovely strolling about Rome in the bright bright sun'. But it was Caitlin's kind of country, not Thomas's. A few days later they visited Florence, where they were introduced to young poets and bumped into Stephen Spender. Thomas told his parents he had recently read George Eliot's *Romola* (which is set in fifteenth-century Florence), 'and could follow the city, almost, from my memories of that': a bookish detail that would have pleased the old schoolmaster.

Presently the party left Rapallo and moved to a villa outside Florence. It had a swimming pool and a terrace for sunbathing; there was a pine wood and a vineyard; Thomas hated it. On one of their expeditions to Florence he and Caitlin must have quarrelled; as a result he wrote her a lugubrious letter from a café. Till the end of her life, Catlin kept five of his letters and notes in her handbag, long after the rest had been sold. Among them was the letter from the Florentine café, begging her to forgive him.* It makes painful reading. He sounds abject, dependent on her good will; unquestionably the weaker of the two. That was how she came to see their relationship. It was he who needed her, not the other way round. His handwriting is crammed into small sheets torn from a pocket diary, headed 'CASH ACCOUNT – APRIL 1947', and then the succeeding months, May, June, July.

Caitlin my dear, dear, dear: I am writing this useless letter to you at

---

* The other four were: a short undated letter written from the Savage Club; a letter from New York, 7 May 1953; a birthday letter where the initials that begin each line spell 'CAITLIN THOMAS; a three-line note saying he loves her.

a table in the Giubbe Rosse where, after I saw you go away in a tram, I went, sadder than anybody on the whole earth, to sit and wait. I can only say that I love you more than ever before; which means, I love you for ever & for ever, with all my heart & soul, but this time as a man who has lost you. I will love you. I do love you. You are the most beautiful woman who has ever lived. Every morning when I wake with you, it is like waking with the sun. Now if I am never to wake with you again, I shall die but that does not matter because all that matters is that I love you always, for ever, my own – though you are gone from me – my own true love.

I am sorry for all the bad I have done to you and all the unhappiness I have made for you. I am grateful to you for the miraculous love you once, a million years ago, gave me, and will never now, give me again. I have lost you because I am bad.

I said that waking with you was, all those million years ago, like waking with the sun. That isn't the kind of literary lie you hate. I mean, like the sun which gives life and makes things grow on the earth. I love you, since I was born. I know you in the dark. I can see you in the empty street. You are with me when you are gone away. And when you are with me really, when I can see you you [*sic*] with the eyes of my body, and touch your body with my rotten hands, and can hear you speak, I am so happy that I cannot write any words, in this useless letter, to tell you how happy, how blessed for a moment, and how proud and honoured for ever. I am the [*four lines and his signature are crossed out*] sore on your arm, which I made, your unhappiness & your pain. What I crossed out with my pen was too shameful. I want to keep a little dignity, not because I like it, but because, perhaps, you like me to have a little dignity. Or, you did like me to have that. I love you. That is all there is. There is shame, and disgrace, and grief, and despair, but there is only love about which I know nothing except that what I feel for you must be love because, to me, it is religion, and faith, and the world. I love you, Caitlin. I think you are holy. Perhaps that is why I am bad to you. I love you. I am holding you now, and you are beautiful.
Dylan   10 o'clock, alone, in this place.

Many years later Caitlin showed me an unpublished manuscript, where a passage gloated over Dylan – miserable at being abroad – because Italy had reversed their roles. He was suffering; she was having a wonderful time. I said, 'Poor Dylan,' and Caitlin said, 'Poor *me*.' It was true that domestic drudgery and her husband's fecklessness had worn her down. In a wartime letter to Brigit she saw herself trapped by her womanhood. Profoundly self-centred, she could never reconcile the reality of her life with the dream of some special destiny that awaited her, to which she was entitled. After ten years of marriage she was tired of living in a man's shadow, and wanted redress. In Italy men kept eyeing her, the wine was cheap and the dream came a little nearer. She loved it.

At the villa Thomas worked on a poem, 'the slowest in the world', while the heat shimmered outside. 'I can smell the sun,' he wrote to Margaret Taylor. Compared with cold cottages and borrowed flats, they were living in luxury. But Thomas remained restless and uncomfortable. He wrote to John Davenport at the end of May, 'A few days ago I climbed a tree, forgetting my shape and weight, and hung this shabby barrel from a branch by my white padded mitts: they were torn neatly up the middles. Also, very slowly, I am trying to write a poem, moping over it, every afternoon in the peasant's cottage: our little spankers make so much noise I cannot work anywhere near them. God grenade them.' As the summer advanced, his letters complained increasingly of heat, insects and screaming children. By July he was telling T. W. Earp, in verse,

> In a shuttered room I roast
> Like a pumpkin in a serra
> And the sun like buttered toast
> Drips upon the classic terra,

adding, in prose, that he was 'awfully sick of it'.

His social life didn't help. Florence was too close; people insisted on coming to talk about culture. 'Today we have visitors from Florence,' he wrote to Margaret Taylor on 20 June: 'a brood of translators & their wives, & one American professor. I can hear them gaggling. I haven't gone out yet. Or perhaps it is frogs and cicadas, one with an American accent.' On 11 July, his tenth wedding anniversary, he wrote to her:

My social life: damp litterateurs pedal from Florence; neighbouring labouring men come in to dance; we walk, with Guido the gardener, or Eddo the tractor-driver, or others with shining hair and blue cheeks, to village cantinas. The nearest café, at Mosciano, is no café but a wine-counter in a packed, tiny, fly-black general shop. Sometimes, an Australian professor comes from Florence to shout Dinkum and Good-oh in the garden. A Harvard professor of Romance languages came with rimless spectacles and no lips, and was nasty...

Sometimes he went into Florence to spend an evening in the cafés. Intellectuals gathered round. Thomas gazed into space or fell asleep. Once, visited at the villa by an Italian writer, he is reliably reported to have hidden in the wardrobe. Most of his letters show his thoughts firmly fixed on Britain. His father was chronically ill, and he wrote to Blaen Cwm regularly. He listened to radio programmes from London, among them cricket-match commentaries by his friend John Arlott. At first the problem of where to live when they returned hung over him. America seemed to have been forgotten. But everything depended on Margaret Taylor. 'I do hope that you can help us to find a house in or near Oxford, so that we can see each other again,' he had written to her from Rapallo, cunningly, in April. 'I want so much to come back to Oxford. Oh, anywhere a house. I am lost without one. I am domestic as a slipper, I want somewhere of my own, I'm old enough now, I want a house to shout, sleep, and work in. Please help; though I deserve nothing.' Mrs Taylor busied herself driving around Oxfordshire and neighbouring counties, and by the end of May she had found a house, in the small village of South Leigh. It was a grandly named cottage, The Manor House, which she bought (with her husband's money), repaired and offered to the Thomases for a pound a week. 'How wonderful you are,' he wrote. 'Thank you with all my heart, from the depth of my teapot, from the marrow of my slippers warm before the fire, for finding a house for us ... all I want's a new body and an alchemist's primer. Will you come often, very often? I am so happy and glad about it.' Mrs Taylor worked hard on their behalf. She organised furniture for the house. She promised to help with Llewelyn's education and spoke to the headmaster of Magdalen College School. In return Thomas wrote her long amiable letters, and told her about the progress of his poem, 'In Country Sleep'. On 11 July he wrote:

My poem, of 100 lines, is finished, but needs a few days' work on it, especially on one verse. Then I'll send you a copy. The manuscript is thousands & thousands of foolscap pages scattered all over the place but mostly in the boiler fire. What I'll have to send you will be a fair copy. I think it's a good poem. But it has taken so long, nearly three months, to write, that it may be stilted. I hope not. I want, as soon as the last revision is made, to write, quickly, some short poems. I can't think of anything else; which isn't, of course, true. I mean, when I think, I think of the poems I want to write; not of their shape but of the feeling of them, and of a few words.

Thomas said later that 'In Country Sleep' was to be part of a larger work called 'In Country Heaven'. Two further poems ('In the White Giant's Thigh' and 'Over Sir John's hill') were supposed to be part of the sequence, but when Thomas introduced all three on the Third Programme in September 1950, he had no idea where or how they would fit into the whole. 'In Country Sleep' is usually thought to be addressed to a child, presumably Aeron. It is written without complicated imagery, but it is not an easy poem to understand. The critic William York Tindall told Thomas he thought it was about 'how it feels to be a father'. Thomas is said to have wept at this remark – 'but whether from vexation, beer or sentimental agreement I could not tell'. The poet is reassuring someone and warning her at the same time. She is threatened by an unidentified figure, the Thief, generally assumed to be Time or Death. Thomas told a woman who admired the poem that it was not addressed to a child at all, but to his wife, and that the Thief was jealousy. A third explanation was given in New York to a reporter. Thomas said, 'Alcohol is the thief today. But tomorrow he could be fame or success or exaggerated introspection or self-analysis. The thief is anything that robs you of your faith, of your reason for being.'

The idea that faith is being threatened runs through the poem. The year before he died he told an American student that it was started 'in cold blood', and that he 'never thought it would work'. Having been sent to Italy, Thomas may have felt he had to return with something to show for his visit. Certainly the trip achieved its aim of persuading him to write a poem again. But it was a complicated way of doing it. Nor did 'In Country Sleep' lead to the 'short poems' he mentioned to Margaret Taylor, or to any poems at all, that year or the next; another lengthy silence fell.

From Florence the Thomas party moved to the island of Elba, recommended to them by an editor in Florence. Funds had been running low, but Thomas managed to touch an Italian journalist for a hundred and seventy-nine pounds, rather more than the original grant from the Society of Authors was worth. It was July and very hot. They stayed in a little town, Rio Marina, with a population of iron-ore miners and fishermen, and settled down to bathing and roasting in the sun. The heat 'comes round corners at you like an animal with windmill arms', Thomas wrote to Mrs Taylor. 'As I enter my bedroom, it stuns, thuds, throttles, spins me round by my soaking hair, lays me flat as a mat and bat-blind on my boiled and steaming bed. We keep oozing from the ice-cream counters to the chemist's. Cold beer is bottled God.' Caitlin found a diversion in the hotel proprietor, Giovanni. Manly, soft-spoken and unlettered, he suited her perfectly, and they probably had a brief liaison. (A year after Dylan's death she returned to Elba and carried on where she left off.)

They returned to London in the middle of August, where Thomas broke his arm trying to climb in through a friend's window, stayed briefly in Wales, and so arrived at South Leigh and a roof of their own. The battered caravan was brought from Oxford and put in their unkempt garden for Thomas to work in. It was an unkempt and ancient village, in deep countryside, with no view to speak of, no local gentry, and little traffic. A few trains a day puffed along a branch railway line to the market town of Witney, five or ten minutes to the west, and Oxford, half an hour to the east. The Thomases fitted into this rustic scene. Dylan and Caitlin became local characters. They swerved about the village on muddy bicycles and played shove-ha'penny in the local pub. Limping down the lane, they were only mildly surprised to be told that she was wearing two left-foot wellingtons while he had two rights. Empty beer bottles accumulated on the path outside the house.

Sometimes Thomas went by himself to Witney on market day and came back with a bag of shopping in the afternoon. Caitlin and the children would stand at the level crossing as the train came in, waving. She intrigued the village. One minute she was sweeping about in garish clothes, the next she was slaving like a peasant, with a sack tied about her middle, heaving buckets of coke from the outhouse while her husband sat around apparently doing nothing. The Manor House had no hot water on tap, and heavy black kettles had to be boiled for an antiquated hip-bath; it was said that she bathed him, in front of the fire. To villagers his role was uncertain, except that he was a writer, and could be heard on the wireless from time to time. Once, according to Thomas, a doctor in the neighbourhood invited them to a cocktail party and introduced him to guests as Wynford Vaughan-Thomas, the famous BBC war correspondent, not having heard of Dylan Thomas, the less famous poet.

He continued to spread himself thin in broadcasting, always ready to use his voice. He read the part of Satan in eight episodes of *Paradise Lost* on the Third Programme (apparently as a last-minute substitute for Paul Scofield), and a potted version of W. H. Davies's *Autobiography of a Super-tramp* on fifteen consecutive Sundays for the Home Service. He introduced an edition of a long-running programme, 'Country Magazine', from the Fleece Inn at Witney, and spoke the awkwardly scripted lines that passed for jolly conversation in radio in those days. Only here and there did it sound like his style – 'I like living by the sea so much that here I am, living bang in the middle of England.' But it was worth eighteen guineas plus fifteen shillings for a taxi.

He was no village drunk. South Leigh, like Wales, was a place to escape to. When he returned from exhausting visits to London, Caitlin put him to bed with bread and milk. Occasionally there were incidents at pubs. He suspected youths from a travelling fair of being too familiar with Caitlin in the bar. Outside, in the empty car park, he confronted them, shaking but belligerent, till Caitlin arrived. She gave them a push and they drifted away. As a couple, they had acquired the married persons' quality of unsentimental closeness. Cordelia Locke watched Dylan try to roll a cigarette – it looked, she said, like a burst sausage. He produced a cigarette-rolling machine, chuckling and coughing, remarking, 'I use this and pretend . . .' Mrs Locke missed the rest of the sentence. She asked Caitlin what he had said. Caitlin shook her head. 'Haven't heard a bloody word for years,' she said contentedly. Mrs Locke had known Caitlin in London when they were both teenagers. She and Harry Locke, an actor and comedian, became the Thomases' closest friends at South Leigh. She was another of those who found them incomparable – 'Just to be with them was like having a double whisky.' They were exhilarating and disturbing. Mrs Locke claimed to know of a marriage that broke up because the Thomases unwittingly dragged its emotions to the surface: 'They didn't *do* anything but they had this effect on people. They were destructive in a way.' They aroused people's passions; often their admiration. A village woman who helped with cleaning and child-minding invited Caitlin to tea. Caitlin forgot and arrived a day late. The food was still ready, slightly curled at the edges. The hostess beamed. 'Ah,' she said, 'you beautiful yooman, you.' Years later Mrs Locke looked back on the Thomases at South Leigh like figures in a dream: Dylan strutting up and down the kitchen, a little pompously, declaiming a poem: Caitlin reading by an oil lamp, her features proud and haunted: Christmas decorations left hanging, months after.

Work to earn money was no problem at South Leigh, or it should not have been. Radio provided a small, reasonably steady income; films earned substantially more. Thomas's wartime work for Donald Taylor had led, as he had hoped, to better things. The Burke and Hare script, 'The Doctor and the Devils', was commissioned. by Taylor himself. At some stage he sold the project to the Rank Organisation, where it languished. A letter from Taylor to David Higham on 2 November 1947 said that 'the film is unlikely to be produced before 1949 because of the general decision in the Rank Organisation to avoid horror and murder subjects'. But Thomas appears to have been paid three hundred and sixty-five pounds, in twelve instalments during 1947 and 1948, for his work on the script. (Later he earned more money when the script was published as a book.)

The British feature-film industry was healthy for a few years after the war. In order to conserve foreign exchange, the Government imposed a quota system which restricted the number of American films that could be shown. British studios churned out home products. Thomas was introduced to a company called British National, and collaborated on scripts for two pot-boilers, *Three Weird Sisters* and *No Room at the Inn*. Then Sydney Box of Gainsborough heard of him and signed him up to write three scripts in 1948. For these he was probably paid the best part of two thousand pounds, though none of the films was ever made. *Rebecca's Daughters*, based on material already owned by the studio, was about nineteenth-century attacks by farmers on tollgates in the Welsh countryside. *The Beach of Falesá* was Robert Louis Stevenson's short story, set in the South Seas, and would have been a costly production. The third film, *Me and My Bike*, was to be based on an original idea, which may have been Thomas's; it was seen as a 'film operetta'. A man was to ride a succession of bicycles, ancient and modern, through his life, and finally pedal into heaven to be greeted by a chorus of bicycle bells. The script was not written but Thomas's treatment has been published. For a year or so Thomas was a familiar figure at Gainsborough. He made irregular appearances at the studios in West London to attend script conferences, wearing a shiny blue suit and persuading colleagues to adjourn to the Shepherd's Bush Hotel at an early stage. Otherwise he sent his scripts in instalments, written in longhand, usually late, from South Leigh. There is the usual story that he had to be locked in an hotel bedroom (this time with a bottle of whisky) over a weekend to make him finish a script.

As a writer he was highly regarded by other writers at the studio. The management was less enthusiastic. His gift was for dialogue; when he had to construct a story, he was in difficulties. His idea of a plot was a straight line moving forward in time, as in *Under Milk Wood*. He might have enjoyed a career collaborating with other writers. But the Government quota was removed, the British film industry contracted, and after 1948 he was involved only in a half-hearted Gainsborough project to make a film of *Vanity Fair* with Margaret Lockwood.

His earnings during this period were those of a highly successful freelance writer. By 1948, Higham had introduced him to an accountant who handled his income tax affairs. Thomas's tax year ran from October (the month in which he had become self-employed after the war) to September. In 1947–8 his total earnings, as reported to the Inland Revenue, were £2,482, against which he claimed £612 for business expenses. By the time this figure was established it was the end of 1949, and Thomas, having made no provision for tax, had to find several hundred pounds out of his current earnings, which were much reduced, as well as put money aside for the following year's demand. This simple backlog of tax was the source of all the financial troubles that followed. They could have been overcome in a year or two, once his American tours began. Higham took pains to deduct money from his British earnings for a 'tax fund', while leaving the family sufficient to live on. But Thomas seemed unable to help himself.

Even when he was earning the money, in 1947–8, before income tax overtook him, he appeared to be no better off than usual. He wrote to David Higham from South Leigh on 7 October 1947:

> I've done it again. With a little money behind me, I've settled in a nice new house, bought a few things for it, behaved a little extravagantly, – and now, yesterday morning, comes a letter from the bank saying that, not only am I not as well off as I imagined but that I am overdrawn and, unless something happens immediately, several cheques, made out to local tradesmen, will be returned. If they are returned, it will ruin us for ever in this village. Quite literally. It's enormously important, in a narrow tiny community like this, to keep frightfully well in with everyone, especially trades-men, farmers, publicans, etc. And unless you can pay in for me, at once, a cheque from Dent, we will forever be *out* with the tradesmen, farmers, publicans, etc. to all of whom I have given cheques...

Doctors' bills for the children were burdensome. So were the expenses, later in the winter, of having his parents stay with them when Mrs Thomas had an accident. Yet the BBC was still paying regular rail fares to London. The house itself was costing them barely sixty pounds a year in rent and rates, if Margaret Taylor had been paid regularly, which she was not. Any attempt to discover where a person's money has gone is liable to be frus-trating, let alone if it is Dylan Thomas's money. His friends used to wonder where it all went. There is a story that one Christmas he set off with two hundred pounds in cash to buy presents and food, and spent it in a day. Puzzled friends tried to follow his progress, shop by shop, to see where it had gone, but failed to solve the mystery. Dylan and Caitlin, staying with his parents at Bishopston, are said to have been given five pounds by Florence Thomas to buy essential clothes. They spent the day in Swansea and returned at night, penniless, with their purchases: one bras-sière. True or (probably) exaggerated, the stories suggest the

Thomas tendency. Far from being an artist hounded by tax
collectors, he was, rather, an artist for whom borrowing vor-
aciously confirmed his status as an outlaw. A psychiatrist might
say that by ridding himself of money as fast as he made it,
Thomas was asserting his role as a dependant, a man who must
be looked after. Perhaps he was asserting his right to be the poet
who couldn't be bothered with such trivialities. Either way he
drove himself deeper into muddle and unhappiness; for in the act
of spending the money like a poet, he was worrying like a man
with a mortgage.

Borrowing was second nature, but now the amounts grew
larger. In 1950 the journalist who had loaned him the money in
Italy was still trying to get it back. If he met someone who looked
as if he could afford it, Thomas was likely to ask for a loan or a
subsidy – it made little difference what it was called, since it was
never likely to be returned – as a matter of course. Mervyn Levy
said that 'Dylan had a fair idea of his value as a person people
wanted to have around': in other words, he would sometimes
put a price on his company. Levy, a civilian lecturer with the
Army after the war ended, had a sergeant in his class, a wealthy
young man who wanted to meet Thomas. Told of this, Thomas
asked Levy, 'Will he lend me a hundred pounds?' Levy thought
it likely, and a meeting in a pub was arranged. Thomas asked for
the money towards the end of the evening; he left with a cheque.
On another occasion, Levy took him to dinner at the home of a
psychiatrist in Cardiff. The doctor's wife greeted them and said
her husband would be there soon. Thomas, grubby and down-
at-heel, asked if he might go upstairs to wash. When he reappeared he was wearing the psychiatrist's suit, shirt, tie and socks.
Levy said that no one referred to the incident all evening. Later
the psychiatrist told Levy that what had really offended him was
to find Thomas's filthy clothes stuffed under the bed. But if
people were willing to be treated like that, Thomas had little
compunction.

He was as indifferent as ever to work that didn't interest him;
perhaps more indifferent. Before he went to Italy he told his
parents enthusiastically that he was to write 'a full-length grand
opera for William Walton'. First he was to write a synopsis. He
saw it as 'a very modern tragic opera', set in a dockside slum.
According to Michael Ayrton, the painter, who was a friend of

Walton, Thomas's eventual contribution consisted of a postcard on which was written:

> With a sound like thunder-claps
> The little mouse comes out, perhaps.

Walton went elsewhere for his libretto.

Thomas managed to ruffle one or two radio producers. In January 1947 he was telling a woman in the department that made programmes for schools that he was 'very keen to try to put poetry over to these rather "hostile" children: – or is that too harsh a word?' He was scheduled to make the broadcast in June, but they found he had gone to Italy without telling them. 'I feel that we cannot pander to his artistic temperament any further, and must give him up as a bad job,' said an irritable memorandum. Thomas had never had so many irons in the fire. At the end of 1947 he was concerned with a string of projects, apart from radio and the British National scripts. Dent planned a collection of 'Poems, 1934–47' for the following spring; it was to include 'two new long poems'. The short story collection was still in prospect. He wanted to write a radio play about Laugharne. He was trying to raise money to finish *Adventures in the Skin Trade*, insisting to Higham that it was not merely a 'fragment of comic romantic taradiddle without a real structure & purpose', and asking him to show the manuscript to Graham Greene (who had connections with Eyre and Spottiswoode) and to say that 'there is a *strict* plot behind the book, that it is all planned out, and that, if he feels any interest in it, I should like very much to discuss the *rest* of the book with him'.

Domestic problems arose. His mother broke her leg; she was sixty-five. While she was in hospital at Carmarthen, Nancy went to Blaen Cwm to look after her father. Nancy's first marriage had ended in divorce, and she was living in Devon with her second husband, Gordon Summersby, a colourful ex-colonel who ran a trawler from Brixham and sold seafood to local hotels. Thomas, visiting Blaen Cwm in the middle of the crisis, early in 1948, wrote to Caitlin that it was 'snowbound, dead, dull, damned; there's hockey-voiced Nancy being jolly over pans and primuses in the kitchen, and my father trembling and moaning all over the place, crying out sharply when the dog barks – Nancy's dog –

weeping, despairing.' There had been quarrels with Caitlin before
Dylan left for Wales. The letter has the familiar note of apology
for bad behaviour.

I don't understand how I can behave to you senselessly, foully,
brutally, as though you were not the most beautiful person on the
earth and the one I love forever. The train hourly took me further &
further away from you and from the only thing I want in the world.
The train was icy, and hours late. I waited hours, in Carmarthen
Station in the early snowing morning, for a car to take me to Misery
Cottage. All the time, without stopping, I thought of you, and of
my foulness to you, and of how I have lost you. Oh Cat Cat please,
my dear, don't let me lose you. Let me come back to you. Come
back to me. I can't live without you. There's nothing left then. I
can't ask you to forgive me, but I can say that I will never again be
a senseless, horrible, dulled beast like that. I love you.

The Blaen Cwm problem was worse still when Mrs Thomas
left hospital. Someone had to look after the old couple, or at
least be near at hand. Nancy and her husband couldn't cope;
Dylan and Caitlin had to. He rented Cordelia Locke's cottage,
which was temporarily empty, and his parents stayed there first,
then at The Manor House. Nancy and husband helped with
money, but in any case it meant more work for Caitlin. Her
husband was busy with Gainsborough film scripts and BBC
readings. He was not busy with poems, which may be why the
projected 'Poems, 1934–47' was abandoned. Domestic life gave
him excuses for avoiding serious work. An undated letter to
Caitlin, temporarily away from South Leigh, reported misery at
home. His father was obsessed with 'saucepans and operations'.
Mrs Taylor's visits were not restful. But Thomas liked to exag-
gerate his troubles, the better to hide behind them. When John
Davenport, now in difficulties, wrote to ask for help, Thomas
replied on 26 August to say he was sorry, in detail – Llewelyn
needed clothes for school next term, his parents made demands,
'Caitlin wants a pressure-cooker & a nightgown', he would have
to hire a suit to read at the Edinburgh Festival, he had broken a
tooth and must visit the dentist. As though to clinch the matter,
'At the bottom of the garden, a man, at 3/- an hour, is digging a
new shitpit & will dig on, he says, until he reaches water. By that

time I shall owe him this house, which is not mine.'

Thomas's letters were carefully adjusted to the recipient. He wrote humbly to his parents, lovingly to Caitlin, and with a determination to be clever at all costs to clever friends like Davenport. The less clever his letters, the more informative they are likely to be. He wrote, on 25 May 1948, to a journalist acquaintance, C. Gordon Glover, who had sent him the draft of an article about himself that was to appear in a magazine called *Band Wagon*. The article was of no great significance. Thomas wanted to get it right but he didn't feel the need to mock himself and life in general. This was Thomas taking a straightforward view of Thomas:

Thanks for 'A Poet In A Pub'. The titles you boys think up!

Just a few points.

I am 33, not 31.

I don't think I used, of my father, the words 'the finest Shakespeare reader of his day' . . .*

I would not be surprised – you are quite right – if people said I was a sort of modern Villon. But my lack of surprise would be caused *not* by the fact that I think I resemble, in any way in the world, a sort of modern Villon, but because I am used to listening to balls. I am about as much a modern Villon – I cannot, incidentally, read French – as I am a modern Joanna Southcott, Raleigh, Artemus Ward or Luther.

I wasn't at Mrs Hole's kindergarten with either Dan Jones or Fred Janes (n, not m), whom I met later.

Do you think the extract, about 'Break break break', from my autobiographical sketches† is confused by mixing it up with words not in the extract? Or not? I don't, myself, think that a reader would know that this extract came from my book; or, alternatively, I think that the reader would think the whole thing, including your interpolations, came from my book. It's very tiny, anyway, & doesn't really matter. Just a little point, sir.

It is true to say that I often cover perhaps a hundred sheets of paper in the construction of one poem. But what I said was, that I often covered more than a hundred sheets of paper with drafts,

* This is the passage already quoted on page 17.

† 'The Fight', in *Portrait of the Artist*.

revisions, rewritings, ravings, doodlings, & intensely concentrated work to construct a single verse. Nor is this anything to be proud, or ashamed, of; I do not think any better of a verse because it takes weeks, and quires, to complete it. It is just that I work extremely slowly, painfully, in seclusion.

It was Aeronwy who was born in a blitz – as though it mattered! – not Llewelyn, who anticipated the war by more than six months.

Do, please, for old crimes' sake, cut out my spontaneous, and quite unbelieved-in, disparagement of village cricket. It was something I said for something to say. I'd be *awfully* pleased to see *all* references to cricket omitted. Let's leave cricket to Jack Squire; I have no ambition to join his jolly Georgian squirearchy.*

Finally, as a 'Profile', your admirable article should, I think, have taken, however parenthetically, other aspects of this impermanent, oscillating, rag-bag character into consideration: aspects, I admit, of which you, with great good luck, could have little first-hand knowledge: my basic melancholy; sullen glooms and black studies; atrocious temper; protracted vegetable comas; silences and disappearances; terror of death, heights, strokes, mice; shyness and gaucheness; pompous, platitudinary, repetitive periods of bottom-raking boredom and boorishness; soulburn, heartdoubt, headspin; my all-embracing ignorance; my still only half squashed and forgotten bourgeois petty values; all my excruciating whimsicality; all my sloth; all my eye!

I enclose the article, with many thanks. What a fellow I sound! Thank God I don't have to meet myself socially, listen to myself, or, except when reluctantly shaving, see that red, blubbery circle mounted on ballooning body, that down-at-soul hick, hack, hock-loving hake which now inscribes itself, Yours ever.

Most of the time he was at South Leigh, Thomas was hankering after Wales. If Margaret Taylor could buy them a house in Oxfordshire, there was no reason why she couldn't do the same in Carmarthenshire. Wales could be seen as a practical move. It was the place where he wrote his poems; it turned an emotional key. He wrote to Frances Hughes, 'Here [in South Leigh], I am too near London; I undertake all sorts of little jobs, broadcasting

* Sir John (J. C.) Squire (1884–1958), poet, whose circle came to be derided as 'the Squirearchy'.

etc., which hinder my own work. In Laugharne if I could live there, I would work half the year on my film-scripts, and half on my own poems and stories: cutting out all time-wasting broadcasts, articles, useless London visits.' He caricatured himself in a radio talk: not a very good talk, rehashing old memories, but laying out his nostalgia for inspection: 'Lost and blown about in London town, a barrel-shaped leaf, am I still the same, I said to myself, as that safe and sound loller at the corners of Wales who, to my memory, was happy as a sandman?'

He could still be rude about Wales, in the conventional expatriate manner, if he thought the audience required it. Speaking to Scottish writers in Edinburgh in 'Tributes to Hugh MacDiarmid' (the occasion for which he needed the new suit) he said, 'I am a Welshman who does not live in his own country, mainly because he still wants to eat and drink, be rigged and roofed, and no Welsh writer can hunt his bread and butter in Wales unless he pulls his forelock to the *Western Mail*, Bethesdas on Sunday, and enters public houses by the back door, and reads Caradoc Evans only when alone, and by candlelight.' That didn't stop him wanting to go back there. Laugharne, he decided, was the place, that idiosyncratic corner of Thomas country. He wrote to a friend at the magazine *Picture Post* offering an article about the town, which he planned to visit at Easter 1948: 'I really do know it intimately, love it beyond all places in Wales, and have longed for years to write something about it. (A radio play I am writing has Laugharne, though not by name, as its setting.)'

During the summer the Thomases went there to see a house called Gosport. This was a comfortable place, standing alone, a short way up the hill from the cottage, Eros, where they had lived before the war. At the end of the garden the ground fell away sharply to the estuary. In the garden stood an old summerhouse; a local story said a tunnel connected it with the Castle. Thomas decided he would use it to write in. The only difficulty was that the occupants of Gosport, the Misses Laugharne-Allen, had no intention of selling. It was suggested to them that if they did not, posterity might have something to say. Telegrams arrived from Margaret Taylor, offering four thousand pounds on the nail. But the sisters wouldn't budge. Later in the year Mrs Taylor negotiated unsuccessfully for Richard Hughes's house, attached to the Castle. Thomas remained in the middle of England, not writing poems. He wrote to Vernon Watkins on 23 November, 'Nothing happens to me. I go to London and bluster, come back and sigh, do a little script-writing, look at an unfinished poem, go out on my bicycle in the fog, go to London & bluster.' The following month a lorry knocked him off his bicycle, breaking an arm again and cracking some ribs. It was another unprofitable winter, relieved, at the end of it, by a few days in Prague, where he flew as a guest of the Czech Government for the inauguration of the Czechoslovak Writers' Union. He seems to have been invited because he knew the Czech cultural attaché in London; perhaps they thought he was a communist at heart.

At last, in the spring of 1949, a suitable house at Laugharne came on the market. The Boat House stood under a sea-cliff, away from the town itself. Mrs Taylor paid three thousand pounds for it. By April or May the Thomases were living there. 'You have given me a life,' Thomas wrote to his patron. 'And now I am going to live it.'

Chapter Eleven

LAUGHARNE AND AMERICA

The Thomases arrived at the Boat House in the spring of 1949. Caitlin was six or seven months pregnant when they moved. Florence and D.J. had returned to Laugharne already, to a house in the main street called Pelican, which Dylan rented for them. From now on they could be visited and looked after in their own home. And for the first time, Dylan, Caitlin and their children were secure in a house in Wales that was theirs for the foreseeable future. But she was less enthusiastic than her husband. The Boat House itself was a few minutes from the main street, along an overgrown lane called Cliff Walk, which ran above the shoreline of rocks and mud. From the lane a path slanted back under the wooded cliff to the house, just above the water. In the lane itself, and overlooking the roof of the Boat House, was the old bicycle shed, with a steeper set of steps coming up from below. The setting was agreeable. Across the River Taf were the chequered fields around Pentowin. Beyond Laugharne in the other direction was the low ridge of Sir John's hill. Between the two, to the south-east, Laugharne's River Taf and two other rivers, the Towy and Gwendraeth, met in tidal flats and sandbanks where fishing boats were beached at low water, black specks on the backs of yellow whales. Water dominated the house. When the estuary filled at high tide, it mirrored broken light on to the walls and ceilings. Spring tides flooded the garden, the 'harbour'.

The shape of the coast shielded Laugharne from the worst of the south-westerly winds, but nothing kept out the drizzles and sea-mists, when the foghorn of a lightship groaned and thumped all day in the Bristol Channel. The Boat House was well placed to get more than its share of damp. It made the woodwork spongy and stained the ceilings; a verandah or balcony that ran around two sides of the house had to have its floor strengthened with squares of tin. There were six small rooms and a kitchen, confusingly organised in three storeys, with the main entrance, and the balcony, on the middle level. Until Margaret Taylor paid to have mains water brought over the cliff, the Thomases had to use a well outside the house. Rats scuttled in the outside lavatory and sometimes in the house. But Caitlin made the place snug, with coal fires in open grates. Most of the furniture was cheap and nondescript, with rugs for the floors. On the walls were family photographs, coloured postcards and pages ripped from magazines.

For writing in, Thomas used the shed. Branches scraped the walls, ivy grew through the cracks. A fig tree partially hid the view. It could be damp and draughty, but it was peaceful, and it had the additional advantage for Thomas that he could slip away unnoticed into Laugharne. Once, Elisabeth Lutyens, staying at the Boat House, called at the Pelican to see his parents, and found him there, surreptitiously reading a thriller. His working hours, as usual, were in the afternoon. In the morning he did nothing much. He always called on his parents, and he and D.J. would sit by themselves, doing a crossword. Caitlin recalled long absences in the kitchen of Brown's Hotel, putting money on horses, listening to gossip and drinking slow pints of beer, before coming back to a late lunch of fatty food, eaten apart from any children who happened to be there; followed by an afternoon of scribbling and talking to himself in the shed until seven o'clock sharp. It is said that Thomas never drank while he wrote. But he was sometimes seen going up the steps to the hut with a bottle of brown ale.

He wrote a poem immediately, to celebrate his return. This was 'Over Sir John's hill', which (Thomas said) was intended to fit somewhere into the 'In Country Heaven' design. It is the most topographical of his poems, firmly framed in the view from the hut. Thomas used the scene – and especially a heron at the water's edge, the songbirds, and the hawk that will strike them – to write about mortality. The heron mourns as dusk falls; so does the poet, appearing, somewhat self-consciously, as 'I young Aesop fabling to the near night'. Birds had featured in Thomas's poems from the beginning; the heron seems to have taken on a special significance. When Caitlin's child was born, a boy, they gave him an Irish name, Colm,* and a Welsh name, Garan, which means

* Thomas sometimes wrote it as 'Colum', the way it was pronounced.

heron. Florence Thomas said that when they went through Dylan's clothes after his death, they found pieces of bread in the pockets: he used to lean out of his hut and throw crumbs down to the birds. She liked to pretend that the herons, a common sight in the estuary, came looking for him afterwards.

'Over Sir John's hill' was cunningly filled with assonance, alliteration, onomatopoeia and every poet's trick he could think of. Watkins found it 'perhaps the most perfect poem he wrote'. With its elaborate elegiac statements, drawing heavily on natural surroundings, it is related to 'Fern Hill' and 'Poem in October', written when he last lived in Wales. But a feeling of divine or fateful judgement runs through the poem. God is invoked, but death is coming. Thomas had spoken often of dying young, as poets in fiction were supposed to do, even specifically of dying before he reached forty. Death frightened him but perhaps it also appealed to him as a solution. Caitlin wrote that he wasn't too keen on living. Around this time, Thomas described a dream to Leo Abse, the politician. It was soon after his return from Prague; perhaps when he was already at work on 'Sir John's hill'. A man goes from cave to cave inside a mountain, penetrating deeper into the earth. Finally he reaches a cave where a skeleton is hanging, and falls to his death. The skeleton is himself. As Abse remembered, 'The way he told it, it was a death dream – as if he was being pulled to his death, deeper and deeper into the mountain.'*

Before 'Over Sir John's hill' was finished, Thomas received the invitation he had been seeking since 1945: he was asked to go to America by someone who was willing to pay him. The offer came from John Malcolm Brinnin, who had just been made director of the Poetry Center at the Young Men's and Young Women's Hebrew Association in New York. Brinnin (1916–98) was a poet with a taste for celebrities. Two years younger than Thomas, he became a patron overnight. He had no interest in small-scale events. 'I didn't,' he said, 'want to be a director of a thing with fifty people in the audience.' He admired Thomas's work and

---

* The dream echoes another described by Thomas, years before – see Note to p. 104. There is a further complication. Dannie Abse, the poet, has said that Thomas's 1949 dream, as described to him at second hand by his brother Leo, involved Biblical scenes, and ended, not with death, but with the Garden of Eden and a man and woman hand in hand.

knew of him by hearsay, and as soon as he was appointed, he sent off an invitation to read at the Center; from the start he had a vested interest in a sensational tour. The fee was five hundred dollars plus the air fare, and Brinnin said he would sponsor his guest to give readings for college audiences all over America. The letter took some time to reach Thomas and he didn't reply until 28 May, when he accepted warmly, adding that he would like to spend about three months in America, early the following year. From then on it was only a question of arranging the details.

Thomas's feelings were simple, as they always had been where America was concerned. The trip would make money. When he returned to Laugharne, he would be able to spend an unencumbered year writing. With American money, he told James Laughlin, 'I won't, at once, have to chase again the hack-jobs by which, dear Christ, I live, have at once to set into motion again the insignificant, wheezy little machines that sausage out crumbs and coppers for me, scriptlings, radio whinnies.' In the meantime, the hack-jobs predominated. These were causing him, and everyone else, painful problems. Before returning to Laugharne he had contracted with the BBC to make a Third Programme script of William Wycherley's play *The Plain Dealer*, to include a part for himself; altogether worth a hundred guineas. Part of the fee was paid but the script failed to arrive; telegrams to the Boat House went unanswered. Then Thomas wrote at the end of May to say he had been ill – 'so perfectly bloody that I just groaned at all my obligations & put my head under the blankets'. The letter was written the same day as his letter to Brinnin, in which he said he had had influenza. But when he recovered, no script was forthcoming, then or ever. Still more bothersome was the *Peer Gynt* episode. The BBC television service, moving slowly towards a national network after the war, was experimenting with classical drama. Thomas, who had never seen television at the time, was approached as early as October 1947 to see if he was interested in adapting Euripides' *The Trojan Women*. The project fell through, but a year later he was invited to try his hand at Ibsen's *Peer Gynt*. This was to be a major production in the spring of 1949. Auden is said to have been approached first, and to have refused. Thomas, laid up with a broken arm over Christmas after his bicycle accident, wrote that *Peer Gynt* was 'a great & favourite play' that he 'really would *love*' to adapt, if only they would wait longer. The BBC postponed production to the autumn of 1949, and suggested a fee of two hundred and fifty guineas, by far the largest sum Thomas had been offered for anything except a film script. He cabled his agent telling him to accept and claim immediate payment of half the fee.

This was the state of affairs when the Thomases moved to the Boat House. The television producer whose job it was to prise the script from Thomas was Royston Morley. In the 1930s, Morley was the little-magazine editor who paid Thomas for a story with half a guinea and dinner at Bertorelli's. Now he had a sterner task. No script arrived on 1 July, the promised date. Perhaps Thomas had been writing 'Over Sir John's hill' instead. Pressed to deliver, he wrote angrily to his agent to say that less than half the literal translation he was to work from had arrived. In any case, he said, he was not being paid enough: Louis MacNeice had been given a year on full pay, plus a special fee, to produce a script of Goethe's *Faust*. The BBC, which had been threatening to ask for its money back, retreated. He was given until the autumn, then until the start of 1950, and so on until the BBC abandoned hope about 1953. The half fee was never returned. The *Plain Dealer* and *Peer Gynt* episodes, together with lesser incidents, made the BBC permanently suspicious of Thomas. Eventually they refused to pay anything for a script until they had it in their hands. Later this had an effect on the play that Thomas wanted to write, and in the end succeeded in writing, about Laugharne. In 1949 the embryonic *Under Milk Wood* was still largely unwritten, an uncertain project somewhere between poetry and hack-job. It figured on the optimistic lists of work in hand that his agent drew up; and as an 'awful' and 'wretched' script in Thomas's letters to friends.

Colm was born on 24 July. On 30 July, following a trip to London, Thomas wrote frantically to Davenport:

Arrived back, rather bruised, to find the financial situation here far worse than even I, in my tearful jags of the last week, cd have imagined. They've stopped sending coal, & will, any moment, stop sending milk: essential things in a baby-packed, freezing house. I'm summonsed for rates. No more meat. I cannot write a cheque, of course, so that we are – for the first time for years – literally without one shilling. Four cheques have been returned from the Savage,* but without savage comment. And my father is dangerously ill with pneumonia; and I've had some sort of breakdown. Christ!

So if you ever do come across anyone ... with a single fiver to spare, it would make a difference. Or suggest anyone to whom I could write ... I shall be forced to go to America, God help me, my breakdown, & my guts, but it's *now*, at *once*, *temporarily*, the nine quid for milk, the ten for coal, six for builder, eight for summons, without mentioning cigarettes for Cat, sweets for Aeron etc. If you do see anyone interested, *please*, old boy. For any amount. To be paid after America ... I'm on the *rim* ...

He may have been piling on the agony for Davenport's benefit. On 5 August he was writing calmly to Margaret Taylor, thanking her for a small loan and promising to repay 'my now almost national debt to you' in the near future – writing, he said, 'in the heaven of my hut. Wild day, big seas for Laugharne, & the boats of the Williamses lurching exactly like Williamses.' Yet the clamour of debts and worries grew. The logical solution was to press on with work that would earn money. But work stagnated. He made a few broadcasts, including a discussion from Swansea in October with four Welsh friends: Vernon Watkins, Alfred Janes, Daniel Jones and John Prichard. The BBC's post-war studio in the town was housed a few doors from the building that had once been the Uplands cinema. 'Though Swansea bore me,' said Thomas, 'and though indeed I have bored Swansea in my time, I do not now live in it. I am by nature a globe-trotter. I live in the next county.'

Nor was he writing much poetry. Nothing emerged from the garden hut. 'My table's heaped with odd lines, single words, nothing completed,' he wrote to Laughlin. He was working on a poem late in 1949, 'In the White Giant's Thigh', which dwelt disturbingly on love and the failure of love, through a sheaf of images about barren women in a fecund, rural past. Perhaps they are barren because they are dead. He told Watkins that the

---

* Thomas was elected to membership of this gentlemen's club in March 1949, on John Davenport's proposal. Previously, and improbably, he was a member from January 1947 of the solidly bourgeois National Liberal Club. Thomas used to make himself feel better about such an eccentric choice by calling it the National Lavatory.

opening line, 'Through throats where many rivers meet, the curlews cry,' took him three weeks to write. The poem was not completed for almost a year. In the winter of 1949, Thomas struggled unhappily. On the reverse of a worksheet of lines in mid-poem is the draft of a letter dated 24 November to a wealthy American woman, Marguerite Caetani. As 'Princess Caetani' (or Madame di Sermoneta) she edited a magazine in Rome, *Botteghe Oscure*. Thomas had met her in London on a recent visit, and persuaded her to advance him a hundred pounds against a story he was to write for her. In the draft letter he promised the story by 1 March 'if I am not, before then, stoned to death by writs'. By the time the final version was sent, the phrase was changed to read, 'if I am not, before then, popped into the cooler, peeled, pipped and sliced'. The letter was carefully put together. Thomas was trying to wear a brave smile for her benefit, while hinting at his poverty and problems. 'I do not, now, read any of my poems with much pleasure,' he wrote in the draft, 'because they tell me I should be writing other poems *now*.' He dawdled over letters: words for the sake of words. He thanked another correspondent for 'your extremely kind and helpful letter', then deleted 'kind and' finally settled for 'your extremely nice and helpful letter'. Further down the page he apologised for the delay in writing: 'Procrastination is, like alcohol to Ben Jonson, an element in which I live.' He changed 'alcohol' to 'drink', then refined the sentence to 'Procrastination is an element in which I live.' But he was only writing to Brinnin about the American arrangements. Presumably he slaved over letters because it was more acceptable than slaving over poems.

Was he disturbed because he could not write poems, or was he not writing poems because he was disturbed? It is unlikely that Thomas himself would have known the answer. He muddled along. 'Things are appalling here,' he wrote to Davenport on 13 October. 'I owe a quarter's rent on my mother's house, Llewelyn's school fees (for last term), much to each tradesman. Yesterday I broke a tooth on a Minto. There are rats in the lavatory, tittering while you shit, and the official rat man comes every day to give them tidbits before the kill. Unfortunately for my peace of mind, the rat man has only one arm.'

He had been writing funny letters with exaggerated accounts of disasters for so long that they had become literary exercises, not to be taken seriously. One of his well-known disaster-letters, apologising to the Swansea branch of the British Medical Association for failing to speak at their annual dinner, must have taken almost as much energy to compose as he would have expended on the original function. Thomas was due there on 20 October, on his way back from a trip to London. By now he was beginning to speak regularly, for a fee, to clubs and societies. In his BMA letter, written months later, the excuse boiled down to a car accident: a friend with a fast car drove him from London, they hit a telegraph pole near Bristol, where they spent the night, and next day, which was 20 October, friend and car had vanished, together with Thomas's suit and speech. The real journey seems to have taken longer and been more confused. But fantasy streams through all these stories of Thomas, whoever tells them. The friend with the fast car was the rich young man from whom, as a sergeant in the Army with literary inclinations, Thomas had borrowed a hundred pounds. This time Thomas and other friends hoped to take a larger sum from him to finance a new literary magazine.* Rich friend, Thomas and Bernard Gutteridge, a poet and advertising man, left London with champagne and cold chicken in the boot. Thomas kept insisting he must have a clean shirt for the Swansea doctors. They called at Oxford to see another friend, Dan Davin, and stayed overnight. Thomas read them poems by Hardy that he was planning to use in America. Davin, who kept a diary, said that at the end of one poem 'he burst into tears, too moved to go on'. Davin quoted from his diary for the following day: 'Dylan is very emotional but like a good Welshman also very suspicious. Thus when he has expressed himself very warmly, in fact exposed himself, he will suddenly react violently towards a self-sneering cynicism. It imparts a curious rhythm to his talk.' Later that day Thomas was seen looking out of the window, complaining that the Davins' small daughter had just composed the Thomas-like lines 'I eat the wind And I drink the rain'. Eventually the party drove on to the west. Gutteridge thought they struck another vehicle a glancing blow,

---

* The magazine, *Circus* ('The pocket review of our time'), ran for two issues, in April and May 1950, just long enough to print a whimsical piece by Thomas in two parts, 'How To Be a Poet', which included a cruel parody of Richard Church. John Davenport was the editor.

and there was trouble with the police. So far it had taken them two days to travel a hundred miles. They stayed the night at Bristol, where Mervyn Levy now lived. Thomas, lying drunk and exhausted in an hotel room, asked Levy to sing him to sleep, as he did in their Earls Court days. Levy sang 'I am the Bandolero'. When he reached the line, 'For I am waiting and watching, an outlaw defiant', Thomas said, 'Oh, sing that bit again, Mervy, I'll go to sleep in a minute.' In Swansea, the doctors waited in vain.

His American plans crystallised slowly. Brinnin would act as his agent, for a percentage of the fees. Thomas asked him to help organise the official papers. 'I dare say my London literary agent can help a bit,' he wrote, 'but he's a stiff sod and frightens the life out of me: I believe he is always waiting for an Enormous Novel, which he won't get.' This was an ungenerous way to talk about Higham. Thomas's manner could be harsh and whining now: 'I wish I could sell my body to rich widows,' he wrote to Laughlin; 'but it is fat now and trembles a little. I'm sick of being so damned & utterly broke, it spoils things ... I'm cold, it's raining on the sea, the herons are going home, the cormorants have packed up, I must go and play darts in the cheerless bar ...' He had decided that Caitlin shouldn't go with him to America: 'It would be difficult, expensive, and, I think, bad for her,' he told Margaret Taylor. In the same letter (dated 28 November and headed 'City of Dreadful Night') he described the latest mishap: 'On Saturday night I fell down again and cracked some ribs, how many and how badly I won't know till I'm Xrayed tomorrow ... Also I have gout in my toe, phlegm on my lungs, misery in my head ...' He joked about whether his accident was really an excuse not to work on his 'wretched script' for radio; 'I had decided, quite sternly, to finish it this week – I cd do it in ten days, anyway – but conveniently, and nastily, fell down. Week after week I have put it off, pulling out a poem instead once I got into the littered, great hut ... I may, after all, break my neck as a final procrastination.'

In December, Glyn Jones was to interview him for a radio programme about 'How I Write'. Jones paid a preliminary visit to the Boat House in October, and had the usual shock of the old friend who had not seen him for years: 'His teeth, which he tried to conceal in smiling, were not good, his nose had become enormous, his face bloated and pale. He looked comical, and lovely, and terrible.' They discussed what Thomas would say in the broadcast. But when the time came, a few days before Christmas, the producer in Cardiff received a telegram from Caitlin to say that Dylan was still suffering with his ribs.

And then it was the end of 1949, and he was writing frantically to Davenport, 'You know when I was up last, at the end of my visit, I said "To hell with America, to hell with my visa," and lurched home. Well, now it's quite obvious I have to go to America, so my visa's vital. The plane ticket ... has just been sent to me.' Thus he kept up a shadowy pretence among friends that he was going against his will. He knew that a long programme of engagements at colleges and universities, arranged at his request, awaited him. He visited a 'posh dentist' in London, so he told Caitlin. They were both in London for a farewell party before he flew away on 20 February 1950, to see what America had to offer.

During the hundred days of his first visit, Thomas succeeded in living his own private, eccentric life without paying much attention to the country he was in. He wrote nothing about it, except for a not very funny radio talk, which was full of the broad jokes he had used on his American audiences. One of his favourites spoke of earnest crew-cut students, 'each with at least thirty-six terribly white teeth'. Sometimes he made it forty-two teeth, or described the students as 'brash, antiseptic, ardent'. But he wasn't much interested in students, or their professors, or their institutions. Even the physical geography of America was beyond him. More than one of his hosts felt he might have been on the moon, for all he knew. One place was much like another, except for San Francisco, which he liked, and New York, which is where most of his friends were. He went along with events. People bought him tickets and wrote instructions in his diary; they steered him west towards Ohio and south towards Arizona, and on the whole he arrived on time and performed as arranged. As a poet, he was quite reliable.

His chief guide and adviser was John Brinnin. Thomas seems genuinely to have liked him. Brinnin met him at Idlewild, as New York's airport was then called, and drove him into Manhattan in the cold early morning. For the next few days, Thomas went sightseeing, attended parties and drank in many bars. New York seemed to egg him on. He was asked to leave the Beekman Tower Hotel where he was staying, apparently for drunkenness. At one party, after he had made vague overtures to Katherine Anne Porter, the author, then aged fifty-nine, he suddenly seized her and lifted her up to the ceiling. People were not generally amused at these antics. At a party given by the critic Marshall W. Stearns, Thomas was asked what the 'Ballad of the Long-legged Bait' was about, and replied crisply, 'It's a description of a gigantic fuck'. New York cocktail parties in those days are said to have been more shockable than London's, but even if they were, Thomas gave them more to be shocked at. There is no record of him going out of his way to disconcert Edith Sitwell or Cyril Connolly; in America he acted sometimes as if he wanted to shock everyone. His mood was a more complicated version of the urge to display a poet's credentials that seized him when he first left Wales in 1934. Liberated, he was also nervous. London was supposed to be an escape from Cwmdonkin Drive. America was supposed to be an escape from everything. Such attempts were sure to fail because Thomas could never sever his connections. But the spectacle was bound to be both painful and entertaining.

His first engagement in America was a reading at the Poetry Center, two days after he arrived. He was nervous and vomiting beforehand. The Young Men's and Young Women's Hebrew Association was housed in a gaunt building. 'Remember thy Creator in the days of thy youth' was chiselled in stone at the entrance. An audience of a thousand waited in the Kaufmann Auditorium. Brinnin, a dapper man, introduced their guest by saying that he came 'out of the druidical mists of Wales'. So Thomas was licensed to behave not only as a poet, but as a mysterious figure from a far country.* On that first occasion he read Yeats, Hardy, Auden and other contemporary British poets, and ended with some of his own work. He was loudly applauded. His rich voice overcame any problems of meaning. People frequently said that Thomas's way of reading made them understand

---

* Speaking to an audience on home ground, at Llanelli, in 1952, Thomas said that outside Wales 'one is given a foreign licence to *be* a Welshman, and the odder one is the more typical is it thought to *be* of the character and behaviour of those brutal and benighted songbirds who cluster together, hymning on hilltops, in the woad and llanwigwams...'

poems for the first time; but it may be that under the influence of his voice, the literal meaning of a poem became irrelevant. Some women found the voice aphrodisiac.

To his parents Thomas wrote the kind of letters they expected to receive. 'My old duffle-coat was very helpful,' he said, describing the February cold. He had been 'gawping, like the country cousin I am, at this titanic dream world, soaring Babylon, everything monstrously rich and strange'. Caitlin, too, received a filtered version of events. There had been some parties, where the guests were 'all furiously polite & hospitable', and he had been sightseeing. Even this made him afraid of upsetting her.

And now it must look to you, my Cat, as though I am enjoying myself here. I'm not. It's nightmare, night & day; there never was such a place; I would never get used to the speed, the noise, the utter indifference of the crowds, the frightening politeness of the intellectuals, and, most of all, these huge phallic towers, up & up & up, hundreds of floors, into the impossible sky. I feel so terrified of this place, I hardly dare to leave my hotelroom – luxurious – until Brinnin or someone calls for me. Everybody uses the telephone all the time: it is like breathing: it is now nine o'clock in the morning, & I've had six calls: all from people whose names I did not catch to invite me to a little poity at an address I had no idea of. And most of all most of all most of all, though, God, there's no need to say this to you who understand everything, I want to be with you. If we could be here together, everything would be allright. *Never* again would I come here, or to any far place, without you; but especially never to here...

Soon he was out of New York, beginning his cross-country travels. After a second reading at the Poetry Center, he and Brinnin left the city over the weekend, driving to Westport, in Connecticut, where his host then lived. Among Brinnin's neighbours in the wooded suburbs of Westport were the novelist Peter de Vries and his wife Katinka. Brinnin and Thomas called there on Sunday evening, where, said de Vries, 'Dylan described the plot of a film he had seen, and then declaimed some *Lear*. He rather talked us into the ground. He made some remark to Katinka about talking a lot of bullshit, which she didn't contradict.' De Vries felt sympathetic and friendly towards this strange man coming in out of the night (later he wrote a novel, *Reuben, Reuben*, with Thomas as the poet). But the Thomas legend was not constructed out of such ordinary occasions. The next evening was more satisfactory from this point of view. Brinnin took Thomas to visit other friends in the neighbourhood, Stanley Edgar Hyman, who was a critic, and his wife, Shirley Jackson, who wrote novels. Brinnin, in his book *Dylan Thomas in America*, gave a low-key account of the occasion: 'We stayed too late and drank too much and the evening ended gracelessly, with some of us out in the snow, and some of us silent before a dead television set.' Brendan Gill of the *New Yorker* improved upon this. According to Gill, writing in 1975, a drunken Thomas asked a drunken Shirley Jackson if she would sleep with him, while a drunken Stanley Edgar Hyman was watching television. 'Hearing no negative in response to his question, Thomas made a pass at Shirley, who leapt to her feet and lumbered past Stanley, with Thomas in close pursuit. She mounted the front stairs, ran along the hall, stumbled down the back stairs, and again lumbered past Stanley. Shirley and Thomas made the circuit three or four times before Stanley, irritated at having his view of the ball game repeatedly interrupted by the gross beasts jogging past him, reached out and grabbed Thomas by the belt of his trousers, causing him to fall to the floor, while the winded Shirley mounted the stairs for the last time.'

Brinnin said the account was inaccurate, and in conversation added details that did not appear in his own book. In this unexpurgated version, Thomas and Shirley Jackson went outside, after dark, and were 'fooling about' in the snow. There was no pursuit. Brinnin, too, went outside, because he wanted to be sick; he had drunk too much. He heard 'squeals of girlish laughter, his or hers, and then I came back into the house'. The other two were outside for only a short while. On the way home, Thomas pretended to Brinnin that the cold night air had been too much for desire.

The next few weeks produced the definitive version of the legend as Thomas plunged into his reading tour. His first stop after Westport was Yale University, along the coast at New Haven. He read there on the afternoon of 28 February and was entertained to dinner at Mory's, Yale's private dining club. His host was Norman Holmes Pearson, a critic and scholar, who invited half a dozen colleagues, all professors. As recalled by Brinnin, who was at the dinner, the professors formed 'a brooding druidic circle apparently awaiting an oracle'. After an uncomfortable meal, Thomas 'moved to break the spell', and told dirty stories, which quickly broke up the party. Norman Pearson said that on the contrary, they were not old men who took offence (most of them were in their forties) but hosts who were trying to cope with a difficult guest. According to Pearson, it was Thomas who set the tone with his own uneasiness. 'When I met Dylan before the dinner,' he said, 'I thought he was extraordinarily tense. Then, and again during the dinner, he spent a good deal of time explaining how he could have gone to university, to Cambridge. There was a feeling – this may have been snobbishness on our part – that he was not at ease because he wasn't a university man.' He talked obscenely about the royal family. 'He became very truculent,' said Pearson. 'I can believe it became as unhappy for him as for the group.'

From New Haven and Yale he moved north-east to Boston and Harvard, where he gave a public reading on 1 March and recorded poems for the university's Lamont Library on the morning of 2 March. Then he was to leave for Mount Holyoke, the oldest women's college in the USA, a hundred miles away at South Hadley, in the middle of Massachusetts. Brinnin had written it all down in a diary for him: 'Someone will drive you to South Hadley – you should leave Cambridge no later than noon. Your contact at Mt Holyoke is Anna J. Mill – they are planning a dinner for you before the reading which is at eight o'clock. You will stay at Mt Holyoke overnight.' Brinnin returned to Westport. At Boston, Thomas was in the charge of Brinnin's friends, one of whom, Gray Burr, was to take him to South Hadley. A telegram saying they had left Boston was sent at three thirty in the afternoon. But Thomas insisted on stopping at bars and playing with pinball machines. By the time they arrived at Mt Holyoke, dinner had come and gone, and the audience was restless.

He walked unsteadily from the car, shivering and smelling of beer, asking for a lavatory. One of his hosts, Joseph McG. Bottkol of the English Department, hurriedly took him down to a men's room and filled a basin with hot water. His hands were numb and blue. When he was ready, he was taken to the hall. The reception committee was bracing itself for disaster. His speech was slurred. A teacher from a neighbouring college, Ben Reid, whose wife was at Holyoke, expected 'a painful kind of farce'. The audience waited expectantly. Thomas reached the platform and clutched the lectern. There was an absurd moment when he tried to fill a glass with water from a pitcher that someone had forgotten to fill. Thomas held it up to the light, puzzled. As he stood swaying at the lectern, a few of the girls giggled. Thomas held up his hand. 'That's right,' he said. 'Laugh at an old ham.'

After this unpromising introduction he read, as everyone agreed, 'like an angel'. Bottkol said that 'I hadn't heard anything like it before or since, and I've heard in person almost every major poet of this century except Yeats. We had a whole procession of poets at Holyoke over the years, British and American, and there's been no one like him.' Reid said that 'it seemed a sort of miracle that it could come out of a man in his condition'. On such occasions Thomas may have pretended to be drunker than he was. But there is no doubt that for many of his readings he was far from sober. In some of the recordings, his opening remarks give him away. One was made at the University of California at Los Angeles, later in the tour. Thomas begins: 'Oh, blimey (*thump*). That's the sort of thing that happens to me straigh' away. (*Laughter and pause; he seems to have knocked his water bottle over.*) Is this microphone working? It's always one of my dreads that I talk into a microphone that doesn't work. And here I am, mouthing away, and not a bloody soul can hear me (*laughter*). It's one of those Kafka dreams that occurs to everybody. You can hear? Or shall I shout? You can't hear? I KNEW. I knew it would happen, it was bound to happen one day ...' The voice is thick-tongued. But once he is reading the poetry, he seems to take hold of himself, or the poems take hold of him, and his voice thumps away with customary precision. Drink may even have improved his performance. One of his audience at Mt Holyoke, Marianne Brock, another member of the English Department, said she heard him read three years later at a neighbouring college, when he appeared sober, and his performance was not as impressive.

It was late in the evening when he was helped off the platform at Mt Holyoke. According to Brinnin, there followed a reception – it was the only incident he described at the college – where Thomas was inflamed by the bare flesh of young women. The legend-making machine seems to have been at work again. The general outline of an outrageous Thomas, whose behaviour was promptly reported by letter and telephone to other colleges, is accurate enough. But Brinnin, who was himself anxious to discount the more extravagant portraits of Thomas as a perpetually drunken lecher, here seems to be adding his own mite to the legend. Brinnin described the reception as 'one of those occasions at which a whole harem of college girls in blue jeans and Bermuda shorts sprawl on the floor about the feet of the visiting celebrity. Within this budding grove, Dylan was bewildered, shocked by the proximity of so much bare flesh carelessly displayed, and incautious in some of his remarks. The elder ladies of the faculty, distressed and fidgety, hurried in the name of decency to bring the evening to a respectable conclusion. As I later learned, they lost no time in sending out warning signals...'

Soon after Brinnin's book appeared, in 1956, the Holyoke story was challenged in a University of Vermont magazine. An article quoted 'the wife of a faculty member here' who was a student at Mt Holyoke in 1950, and in the audience for Thomas's visit – 'she says that one was required to wear a skirt for dinner and for any after-dinner engagement, that "Bermuda shorts" were not yet in existence, and that when Thomas appeared – an hour and a half late – very few women (as against "a harem") were there, and those that were were soberly dressed. Whose imagination conjured up that "proximity of so much bare flesh carelessly displayed", and who was it that was "bewildered, shocked" by the fantasy?' Brinnin said that 'I simply put that story together from what Dylan and Gray Burr told me.' Burr's recollections were hazy. Other survivors of the occasion said twenty-five years later that there was no 'bare flesh'. What probably happened, throughout the tour, was that noisy ovations from young audiences, and especially the young women in them, put ideas in Thomas's head that he turned into comic fantasies and passed on to Brinnin, who wrote them down as fact.

Bottkol remembered no reception at which students were present. Thomas went straight to a party; it was there, and mainly with older women, that he was 'outrageous, but not offensive'. Bottkol kept a diary. He wrote in it, 'Dylan Thomas here to read. Hour and a half late. Tight as an owl and the most powerful reader I've ever heard. A ludicrous party afterwards – the poet using very plain language, and making drunken love to all the lady professors of whatever age.' After the party, Bottkol said in 1975, 'I came home and did something I've never done before or since: I sat down and laughed for twenty minutes.' Marianne Brock remembered Thomas at the party 'doing a kind of total recall of female attributes. There was myself and a couple of even more dried-out old maids there, and he began on these physical attributes, starting at the feet and working systematically up to your head. We were just enchanted – it was such a delicious scene. There was no feeling that he was out of hand. But we were getting a little worried because he had a guest room in one of the student halls, and we wondered if it was wise to send him off in case he got loose among the students. But there was no problem. He fell flat on his face over the coffee table and passed out till morning.' Bottkol said he sang 'obscene little ditties', and made a remark about wanting to put his hands in a warm bosom. He also attempted to pinch a few of the ladies. That seems to have been the far edge of his lechery. After he crashed into the table, he was taken off to his lodgings and passed an uneventful night.

In the morning he was back at Bottkol's house by ten o'clock, accompanied by Peter Viereck, a poet and historian on the staff of the neighbouring Amherst College, where Thomas had his next engagement. He asked for a beer. 'He was sweet – even a little pathetic,' recalled Bottkol. 'He hadn't the vaguest idea where he was geographically. He might have been in New Orleans for all he knew.' Snow was still on the ground. The small town of Holyoke – red brick, white wood, trees waiting for the spring – was as quiet as a village in West Wales, but prettier. Soon Thomas was on his way to Amherst, fifteen miles away. The college here was for men only, and exclusive. Thomas was drunk when he arrived at his hotel during the afternoon, and insisted he must have a beer. The hotel bar wasn't open, so one of his hosts, Armour Craig, took him to a drugstore. 'The High School kids started to come in after school, and he began to make observations about bosoms and so on in a fairly loud voice. I was scared – I thought someone would call the cops. I finally got him back to the inn and he promised he would have a nap.' His hosts had arranged an early dinner. 'He had obviously found the bar at the hotel,' said Craig. 'What was disconcerting over dinner was that his conversation wasn't sequential. He would be closed in on himself, nodding. Then he'd emerge and say something irrelevant.'

Before the reading, when Thomas was backstage, he 'suddenly sunk his head in his hands and said, "I can't go on. I miss my wife, I miss my children. I'm sure they're all dead." It was a very startling moment of hysteria.' A minute later he let himself be persuaded to walk on to the platform, where he read with customary vigour. At the party afterwards he went through his usual verbal performance with the women, and some time after midnight was persuaded to recite 'The force that through the green fuse'. He delivered it with his eyes tight shut. 'He was very drunk,' said Craig. 'It was as if he was squeezing it out of himself.'

From Amherst, Thomas returned to New York for the weekend of 4 and 5 March. Over the following weeks Brinnin had arranged engagements in Philadelphia, New York City and State, Washington DC and the Mid-West, followed by a long tour across the country. It is likely that Thomas found the readings less onerous than the threat of academic interrogation afterwards. American literary audiences had a tradition of making demands on their speakers. In 1950, British writing was more highly regarded in the USA than it would be later in the century. A British poet could expect to be taken seriously by professionals who regarded literature as something too serious for clowning. This was not helpful to Thomas's way of doing things. Many poets are reluctant to 'explain' what their poems mean. Thomas was reluctant to talk about poetry at all. Caitlin said he had a horror of discussing such matters as psychology, literary criticism and, especially, poetry. In America his first line of defence was to say as little as possible about his own poems when he introduced them. Mt Holyoke was promised (in a last-minute cable from Brinnin) 'his own poems and selections from other British poets with commentary', but the commentary didn't materialise.

His introductory remarks, as he developed them during his visits, were sprinkled with mild jokes and scraps of autobiography. The manner was self-deprecating. 'I am,' he would say, 'the pig that roots for unconsidered troofles in the reeky wood of his past.' His poems were 'little lyrical cripples', and he had forgotten the original impulse that produced his early work. Such material saw service in many versions, not only for lectures in Britain and America, but for BBC talks. The style was becoming a parody. 'My early days!' he would tell an American audience –

> I've written so much, and talked so much, on the wireless-air and into thin air, of my dull but cramful childhood and my youth in the turbulent doldrums, that they have become to me like the childhood and youth of somebody quite else. What engulfing of young bolsters by tears in love, what salt, raw baying to the sliced dockside moon, to the inhabited stars and the whole wing-gonging Welsh sing-songing world, have I ephemerally commemorated in plush tattles and patches of near-verse prose and prose nearly verse but worse. Who, in the parks and summers, the gutters and seas, of my dead dogdays strutted and foamed and was always a wet wild and gaudily wordy whelp? Not me, O Lord. It was some other, whose hiccupping heartbeats, even, I have forgotten . . .

Thomas's readings often contained fewer of his own poems than audiences would have liked. This, too, may have been defensive. The most-read were probably 'Fern Hill', 'A Refusal to Mourn', 'This side of the truth', 'And death shall have no dominion', 'In my craft' and 'Poem in October'. Those who knew the poems well or carried a text with them noted many small variants. Apart from his own work, Thomas's basic repertoire consisted of poems by modern British writers from Hardy on.* He made his own anthology in longhand, he told Margaret Taylor, and 'never read the *same* selection at more than one place . . . I used to have all the poems on my lectern, & select from them, as I went on, according to the "feel" of the audience'. What comments he made were usually brief and descriptive. Introducing some Hardy – whose poems, perhaps, pleased him most to read aloud – he said:

Modern readers of poetry are often put off Thomas Hardy I think

---

* Thomas's list of poets, as given to Taylor, was: Hardy, Binyon, Edward Thomas, W. H. Davies, Wilfred Owen, Edwin Muir, Robert Graves, Andrew Young, Eliot, Auden, David Gascoyne, George Barker, Alun Lewis, W. R. Rodgers, Vernon Watkins, Yeats, de la Mare, Louis MacNeice, Edith Sitwell, Alex Comfort, D. H. Lawrence, John Betjeman and James Stephens.

by the sheer bulk of his collected works. And the small print, too. I like all his poems. I'm completely unselective about him. I think the worst thing that's going to happen to Hardy is when someone selects his work enthusiastically. I think the best thing is to read the whole damned lot. All of them. The crabbed, gnarled – I'm reading from something I've written down – the crabbed, gnarled, knotty poems, in which he seems to use language as an arthritic wrestler might grapple with a recalcitrant tree...

Thomas's voice, conversational when he was speaking off the cuff, acquired its boom as soon as he began to read from his notes. He was a good impromptu speaker in front of a large audience, and as he gained confidence he found the knack, as he told Mrs Taylor, of gauging its mood. Reading at the Poetry Center on a later visit, he provoked (as far as one can judge from the tape) only hilarity when he introduced William Plomer's poem 'The Flying Bum' – 'I should explain,' he said, 'that "bum" to an Englishman does not mean what it means to an American. "Bum" means "fanny", and "fanny" does not mean to an American what it means to an Englishman (*laughter*), though geographically it's quite close' (*renewed laughter*). As Thomas gleefully told his audiences on occasion, 'I am no grey and tepid don, smelling of water-biscuits.' But having established himself during a reading as a rumbustious plain-man's poet, he had to escape before he was cross-examined on his role. 'You won't ask me any questions afterwards, will you?' he would say. 'I don't mind answering a bit, only I can't.' Then he would poke fun at earnest questions that probably existed only in his head: 'Are the young English intellectuals *really* psychological?' or 'Is it absolutely essential to be homosexual to write love poems to women?'

In a letter to Mrs Taylor, written during the summer, he said he had always tried to talk to students after a reading, either in their common-room or at a party, and to answer their questions informally. This may have been wishful thinking; at the time of the letter he badly wanted an academic sinecure in the USA. He rarely traded serious questions and answers with students. Now and then a student newspaper sent a reporter to interview him. At Bryn Mawr, the women's college in Pennsylvania, the *College News* for 15 March printed an interview headed 'Subjective

Welshman Wants to Write of Happiness'. Thomas had been there the previous week, his first engagement since Amherst. The reporter found it difficult to talk to him – 'unhappily and uncomfortably seated at the other end of the couch ... His hair was dark and lustrelessly curly; his mouth small, full and deeply coloured, like a little crumpled plum ... I had been told that he was not well; his eyes, with their hidden appeal for me to be brief, showed the effort he was making to suppress his discomfort.' She thought him kind but sad.

Her first question was whether he considered a university education important to a poet. He replied, 'I wouldn't know. I never had one myself.' Should a young poet consciously imitate 'the proven great'? Thomas said he had read enormously when he was young. Was a fixed code of beliefs necessary? One's beliefs should be fluid, not dogmatic. Did he write for the eye or the ear? For the ear, said Thomas. The reporter asked him what he had been doing before he came to America. 'Well,' said Thomas, 'for the last six months I've done absolutely nothing. All I did was sit and look at the sea all day – observe it – see if it was still there.' (This response, suitably embellished, became a stock-in-trade. Two years later he was telling a representative of the Dartmouth College magazine, 'I just sit on my bottom by my house in Wales and unscientifically birdwatch, that is, I let the birds watch me. My house is right by the sea. In fact we can spit from my window into the sea, which we often do.') The last question at Bryn Mawr was about Thomas's 'future poetic plans'. He replied, 'I want to write poems of happiness. Not just poems about the little happinesses one experiences in everyday life with other human beings, but the general state of universal happiness which people could attain – if they weren't so barmy, and insane, and stupid.' Alongside the report, a bulb-nosed Thomas stares blankly at the college camera, his bow tie askew like a propeller beginning to turn.

Thomas was now earning steadily. The fees varied. Bryn Mawr paid him a hundred and fifty dollars, which seems to have been about the average for a reading. His outgoings were for rail and plane tickets, and an hotel room whenever he was in New York City. Elsewhere he was fed and accommodated by his hosts. But Brinnin soon noted that once Thomas touched money, it melted away. Whatever the reason for his lifelong flight from solvency, he was now able to indulge it on a bigger scale. Small amounts went to Caitlin. His letters record fifteen pounds on 5 April, another fifteen pounds on 7 April, and fifty dollars on 18 April. Larger amounts turned into rounds of drinks that went down other people's throats; although most of the heavy spending was probably nearer the end of the visit, when he spent several weeks in New York.

Thomas's major cross-country tour began on 14 March, when he flew to Ithaca, in New York State, for a reading at Cornell University. He was to be away from New York City for five weeks. Brinnin saw him off with tickets and instructions. At Ithaca he was met at the airport by David Daiches, who was then teaching at Cornell. Daiches found him asleep on the plane; there had been parties in New York, and Thomas said his hotel room was too hot to sleep in. He carried a jar of insomnia tablets; a doctor had prescribed them, and he had been taking them for his hangover. Daiches put him to bed for an hour or two, then took him for a bracing walk around the campus. It was a cold, sparkling day. They paused on a bridge across a gorge, discussing the merits of retiring to one's native village to write. At one point, recalled Daiches, 'he talked with utter conviction of the fact that he was finished as a poet. I can't swear he said he would die young – that may be hindsight. But he certainly talked about running out of steam.' This contrasts uneasily with his remark to the Bryn Mawr reporter a week earlier about 'poems of happiness'. As they walked through the university grounds, they passed a drinking fountain. Thomas crammed some pills into his mouth and swallowed them. 'I was starting to feel queasy,' he explained.

Daiches was so alarmed that he wrote to Brinnin the next day, to say that at this rate, Thomas was going to kill himself. He expected the worst at the poetry reading. Thomas slept through the dinner party that Daiches had arranged to precede the performance, and arrived at the hall with the usual unsteadiness and look of disarray. In an attempt to prepare the audience for disaster, Daiches gave an apologetic introduction – 'I thought I was being rather adroit. I said Britain was still suffering from post-war austerity, and that in a hospitable place like America, it was possible to kill a man with kindness. And then he made an absolute fool of me by giving a marvellous performance.'

At the Daiches' house afterwards, Thomas was amusing and well behaved. Mrs Daiches had been unable to go to the reading, so he offered to recite her favourite poem; she chose 'Poem in October'. 'There was no coyness or false modesty,' said Daiches. 'He was very quiet and gentle. The only thing that upset him was being asked for explications of his poems.'

The party ended well before midnight. Brinnin had written in the diary: 'Someone *must* drive you from Ithaca to Syracuse in time to get the twelve-thirty a.m. train to Gambier, Ohio.' Daiches put him aboard and saw him safely in his sleeping berth. Thomas had forgotten the name of the man who was to meet him at Gambier, three hundred miles to the south-west, and he had only a vague idea of where he was going to spend the next five weeks. 'Westward into the night,' he said. 'I feel frightened. I don't think I shall ever come back.' But Daiches suspected that he was only scaring himself with melodramas of the West.

From Kenyon College, where he had his Ohio appointment, he wrote to Caitlin that 'I never seem to sleep in a bed any more, only on planes & trains. I'm hardly living; I'm just a voice on wheels. And the damndest thing is that quite likely I may arrive home with hardly any money at all, both the United States *and* Great Britain taxing my earnings – my earnings for us, Colum, Aeron, Llewelyn, for our house that makes me cry to think of, for the water, the heron, old sad empty Brown's . . .' Even finding more paper and a pencil sharpener was beyond him, if what he wrote is to be believed; he was 'too scared to go out and find somebody to ask'. The letter groaned to an end:

Found a razorblade to sharpen my pencil, but no more paper. Out on the grounds – they call it the campus – of this College the undergraduates, looking more like bad actors out of an American co-ed film, are strolling, running, baseballing, in every variety of fancy-dress. Someone in the building is playing jazz on an out-of-date piano: the saddest sound. In a few minutes now I go out for cocktails with the President. I do not want to have cocktails with any President. I want to be home. I want you. I want you with my heart and my body because I love you. Perhaps, perhaps, perhaps, the door may suddenly open & in you will come: like the sun. But I do not think it likely. I love you, my pet.

Next day he was in Chicago, writing from the Quadrangle Club, desperate because he hadn't heard from her.

> Cat: my cat: If only you would write to me: My love, oh Cat. This is not, as it seems from the address above, a dive, joint, saloon, etc, but the honourable & dignified headquarters of the dons of the University of Chicago. I love you. That is all I know. But all I know, too, is that I am writing into space: the kind of dreadful, unknown space I am just going to enter. I am going to Iowa, Illinois, Idaho, Indindiana, but these, though mis-spelt, *are* on the map. You are not. Have you forgotten me? I am the man you used to say you loved. I used to sleep in your arms – do you remember? But you never write. You are perhaps mindless of me. I am not of you. I love you. There isn't a moment of any hideous day when I do not say to myself, 'It will be alright. I shall go home. Caitlin loves me. I love Caitlin.' But perhaps you have forgotten. If you have forgotten, or lost your affection for me, please, my Cat, let me know. I Love You.
>   Dylan
>
> The address is still Brinnin. He forwards all mail to my lost addresses. I love you.

The itinerary was not quite as exhausting as Thomas implied. After his reading at the University of Chicago on 16 March, he was at Notre Dame University, in Indiana, on 17 March; at the University of Illinois, Urbana, on 20 March, a Monday; and at the State University of Iowa, Iowa City, on 21 March. In all, this made seventeen performances in twenty-nine days. But he now had thirteen clear days without an engagement. He spent them at Iowa City, where his host, Ray B. West Jr, who was on the university staff, was at first disconcerted to find his house-guest would be there so long. Brinnin had written to suggest that West might find a local dentist who would make some emergency repairs. His teeth worried Thomas, probably because they damaged his appearance. Neither the Iowa dental school nor West's own dentist was willing to do anything in the time available. Thomas spent most of his days with West and his friends, in houses or bars, drinking beer, telling tall stories and doing little that was outrageous or even unusual.

West's long account of the visit (published in the *San Francisco Fault* in 1972) is the best single report of Thomas as a normal human being in America. He began with the usual successful reading, having already told West that he disliked the atmosphere of universities and couldn't stand the 'bloody nitpicking' of academics. He excluded his hosts, among them the poet Robert Lowell, from this category. After the reading they took him to meet students at the local Writers' Workshop, where a woman asked him how she could earn a living if she wanted to write poetry. Thomas gave one of his ready-made answers, 'Go on the street,' and soon there were shrieks of laughter from his corner of the room. Nothing seems to have happened beyond lewd remarks. That night, when Mrs West, a plump blonde, asked Thomas if there was anything else he wanted before he retired to bed, he said, 'Yes, a nice plump blonde.' This, too, was a mechanical joke. One of his first questions to Howard Moss, the writer who became a friend in New York, was, 'Do you know a short blonde girl?'

At a later session in the Writers' Workshop building, Thomas took over one of Robert Lowell's classes, and read more verse. West (like Roy Campbell at the BBC) noted that 'he was not uniformly good with all poems. He read them all the same, round-bodied, fluent, intense.' Among his choices was John Crowe Ransom's *Captain Carpenter*, a 'satiric ballad, written in mock-heroic style, so there is a temptation to give it a full, straightforward reading. I had heard Ransom read the poem, and he had stressed the irony by giving it a quiet, dry reading.' When they returned home, West played a recording of Ransom reading the ballad. Thomas listened for a few stanzas, then exclaimed, 'Sweet Jesus! The man doesn't know how to read his own poem.' This weakness of Thomas's for the full-blooded reading, no matter what the content, may have been why apparently he disliked to hear his poems read by women. Once, in a letter to a radio producer, who had asked for suggestions about readers, he replied, 'Emphatically no woman. I can't, offhand, think of one poem of mine that needs a woman's voice; any poem, indeed, that wouldn't positively be better off for not having a woman's voice.' Perhaps, too – knowing Thomas's old-fashioned views on the place of women – he felt they were unsuitable for the serious business of reading his poems.

His health, observed in Iowa in detail by West, appears unsatisfactory, though perhaps caused by nothing worse than a general reluctance to look after himself. He coughed and retched every morning, and claimed to be taking tablets prescribed for the morning sickness of his previous host's pregnant wife. (In Oxford a year or two earlier, Dan Davin heard the pre-breakfast coughing – he said it was like a child drawing attention to its health.) Stronger American drinks must have had some effect. Hospitable measures of spirits were larger than in Britain. Thomas was an unfastidious drinker. Big chilled gins and vermouth, so cold that the strength wasn't at first apparent, were gulped down between anecdotes. In Chicago there was trouble with drink, and the word had been passed on to offer him only beer. West reported Lowell as saying that Thomas should be allowed to drink what he liked and liven up Iowa City. But for most of the visit he seems to have been happy with beer. On the two occasions he drank hard liquor, there was some mild trouble. The first time, West left him at a bar called Joe's Place in the morning. Thomas disappeared for the rest of the day, missed a dinner engagement, and arrived late in the evening, very drunk. He said a woman had taken him home and read him her bad poetry for hours while she kept refilling his glass with Scotch. The second time was a party where the hostess refused to serve only beer. Thomas, drinking martinis, fell into conversation with a doctor's wife, who tried to tell him what was wrong with the National Health Service in Britain. He called her a so-and-so bitch.

Nothing worse seems to have happened. Thomas's thirteen days in Iowa City provide little for the legend. West noticed that Thomas didn't use foul language in front of women, and was careful what he said when children were in the room. He told West's children about his own sons and daughter. 'To me,' wrote West, 'he told a different story.' He loved his daughter, he said, but his newborn son he 'detested', because he was jealous of him. Thomas's anecdotes were in his accustomed style. He said Caitlin was a ballet dancer, described a snowball fight with Russian generals in Austria (perhaps some fantasy that he spun out of his week in Czechoslovakia) and recalled how his first landlady in London gave him eggs for breakfast, which he dropped uneaten into a drawer until it was full, when he left. West was even taken to Swansea sands for 'the poignant story of an early sexual experience with a younger girl and a boy-friend of Dylan's, set on the seashore'.

The visit ended with Thomas being driven to the airport for the plane to San Francisco. He wore the faded brown tweed suit with baggy trousers that he had arrived in, and carried a blue duffle bag. West said it reminded him of the last scene of a Charlie Chaplin film.

Thomas was on the West Coast for rather less than three weeks from 4 April, and in that time gave seven readings; he also went briefly to Canada. By now he had heard from Caitlin. He wrote to her aboard a train going from San Francisco to Vancouver:

> thank you (I love you) for your beautiful beautiful beautiful letter and (my love) for the love you sent. Please forgive, Cat dear, the nasty little note I sent about your not-writing: it was only because I was so worried and so deeply in love with you.

Declaring that San Francisco was 'the best city on earth', he said he was trying to arrange to go there again in the spring of 1951, when he would – might – become, for six months, a professor in the English department of the university.

> You will love it here. I am madly unhappy but I love it here. I am desperate for you but I *know* that we can, together, come here. I love you. I love you. I love you. I am glad you are stiff & staid. I am rather overwrought but am so much in love with you that it does not matter. I spent last evening with Varda, the Greek painter, who remembers you when you were fifteen. I wish I did. A long letter tomorrow. O my heart, my golden heart, how I miss you ...

In Vancouver on Good Friday, 7 April, he thanked her again for writing – 'Your faraway voice is saying, now, at my ear, the words you said in your last letter, and thank you, dear, for the love you said and sent ... Over this continent I take your love inside me, your love goes with me up in the aeroplaned air, into all the hotel bedrooms where momentarily I open my bag – half full, as ever, of dirty shirts – and lay down my head & do not sleep until dawn because I can hear your heart beat inside me ...'

He didn't think much of Vancouver, finding it 'more British than Cheltenham'. Everyone was 'pious and patriotic, apart from a few people in the university & my old friend Malcolm Lowry – do you remember Under the Volcano – who lives in a hut in the mountains & who came down to see me last night'. It seemed that only San Francisco would do. Thomas was energised by it: as if his rhetoric was somehow going to save his marriage. One possible professorship became two definite offers. California beckoned.

The wonderful sunlight there, the hills, the great bridges, the Pacific at your shoes. Beautiful Chinatown. Every race in the world. The sardine fleets sailing out. The little cable-cars whizzing down the city hills. The lobsters, clams, & crabs. Oh, Cat, what food for you. Every kind of seafood there is. And all the people are open and friendly. And next year we both come to live there, you & me & Colum & maybe Aeron. This is sure. I am offered a job in two universities. When I return to San Francisco next week, after Los Angeles, for another two readings, I shall know definitely which of the jobs to take. The pay will be enough to keep us comfortably, though no more. Everyone connected with the Universities is hard-up. But that doesn't matter. Seafood is cheap. Chinese food is cheaper, & lovely. Californian wine is good. The iced bock beer is good. What more? And the city is built on hills; it dances in the sun for nine months of the year; & the Pacific Ocean never runs dry.

Last week I went to Big Sur, a mountainous region by the sea, and stayed the night with Henry Miller. Tell Ivy that; she who hid his books in the oven. He lives about 6,000 feet up in the hills, over the blinding blue Pacific, in a hut of his own making. He has married a pretty young Polish girl, & they have two small children. He is gentle and mellow and gay.

I love you, Caitlin.

You asked me about the shops. I only know that the shops in the big cities, in New York, Chicago, San Francisco, are full of everything you have ever heard of and also full of everything one has never heard of or seen. The foodshops knock you down. All the women are smart, as in magazines – I mean, the women in the main streets; behind, lie the eternal poor, beaten, robbed, humiliated, spat upon, done to death – and slick & groomed. But they are not as beautiful as you. And when you & me are in San Francisco, you will be smarter & slicker than them, and the sea & sun will make you jump over the roofs & the trees, & you will never be tired again. Oh, my lovely dear, how I love you. I love you for ever & ever. I see you every moment of the day & night. I see you in our little house, tending the pomegranate of your eye. I love you. Kiss Colum, kiss Aeron & Llewelyn. ... Do not despair. Do not be too tired. Be always good to me. I shall one day be in your arms, my own, however shy we shall be. Be good to me, as I am always to you. I love you. Think of us together in the San Franciscan sun, which we shall be. I love you. I want you. Oh, darling, when I was with you all the time, how did I ever shout at you? I love you. Think of me.

Your Dylan

I enclose a cheque for £15.
I will write from Hollywood in three days.
I will send some more money.
I love you.

In mid-April Thomas was in Los Angeles and met celebrities. Ivan Moffat, his wartime colleague at Strand Films, lived in Hollywood. When Thomas asked if he could meet a movie star, Moffat obliged by introducing him to Shelley Winters in a restaurant. The writer Christopher Isherwood, another of Thomas's hosts in California, was also there. The story comes in several versions. In Moffat's, probably the most reliable, Thomas pointed at her breasts and said, 'Are they really real?' She told him he could touch if he didn't believe, and 'very tentatively, with the index finger, he touched – hardly touched. It seemed to him substantiation enough.' Brinnin, reporting what Thomas must have told him, said the poet was rebuffed 'in language which was as direct as a stevedore's'. Shelley Winters in her memoirs (1990) had Thomas sterilising his finger in champagne and, by permission, delicately brushing each breast, 'leaving a streak in my pancake body makeup', after which 'a look of supreme ecstasy came over the Welsh elf's face', and he said, 'Oh, God, Nirvana.' Whether the elf was making fun of her or himself isn't clear; probably both.

After Winters he met Charlie Chaplin. Various people claimed to have arranged it. Moffat said that Thomas and Chaplin were 'roughly the same size, and both possessed this extremely fluid, rag-doll-like, quick emotion, striding about the enormous drawing room together, talking and chattering'. According to Brinnin, when Thomas said that no one in Laugharne would believe where he was, Chaplin sent a cable to Caitlin; that was apparently true. In the Winters version, Thomas charmed Marilyn Monroe over a drunken dinner, before Winters took him on to Chaplin's, where the evening's guests included Greta Garbo, Thomas Mann and Marlene Dietrich. Thomas, hopelessly plastered, made a fool of himself and was upbraided by Chaplin: 'Even great poetry cannot excuse such rude, drunken behaviour.' Before he left he was seen urinating on a plant in the Chaplin porch.

Moffat agreed there was an 'incident' but declined to give details. He noted that Thomas's drinking was more threatening than in London during the war. 'In California he drank much more and it affected him in even greater proportion than before, if that is an indice of alcoholism. There was a rougher, more insensitive side to his behaviour, a disregard of other people's feelings.' He had let himself go in some way.

In San Francisco he stayed at the house of Ruth Witt-Diamant, who taught English and ran a poetry centre at San Francisco State College, and made a number of friends. Writing to Mrs Witt-Diamant from Laugharne a year and a half later, he said he often thought of them all,

and, of course, of you who made my ranting holiday ridiculously happy, who showed me the exhibitionist floodlit seals and the pansied Pacific baths and the starry city and Miller's mountain, and gave me polar beer and artichokes, and laughed with me and at me till I felt more at home than at home where it's only at [sic], and made me want more than anything to lurch back to the beautiful West where men are sometimes men and the bars are always exultantly open and the wind and sea and people are right and raffish and tins of fruit juice breed in the ice box...

He did return to San Francisco, in 1952, and took Caitlin with him. But it was not for long, and the teaching jobs in California failed to materialise. He might have been given the appointment at the University of California at Berkeley if his drinker's reputation had not stood in the way. His behaviour on campuses, though, seems to have been no worse on the West coast than it was on the East. He lost his books and notes before a reading at Pomona College, Claremont, and he kept muttering 'My God, I can't do this' as he was escorted to the stage. There was confusion over dates. At Berkeley he read without incident; but he failed to appear at a party in his honour organised by the English Department. Either then or soon after, the Department of Speech at Berkeley was considering whether to offer him an appointment to teach courses in the 'oral interpretation of literature'. A departmental committee decided without dissent that Thomas should be invited. But the Dean of the College of Letters and Science ('A conservative gentleman of the old school', according to a member of the committee) overruled the decision, on the grounds that Thomas's drinking made him unstable and a danger to students.

By 24 April he was back in New York. He was based there for the remaining five weeks of his stay, although one of the weeks was spent in a gruelling circuit that took him to New England, Michigan and Indiana. Among his short trips from New York was one to Vassar, the women's college at Poughkeepsie, where he read on the evening of 9 May. The nervous lady from the English Department who introduced him said that Mr Thomas was playing third fiddle to Eliot and Auden, both of whom they had failed to attract to Vassar. Thomas was visibly upset at this. A radiator wheezed throughout. The audience was disappointed that he had so little to say about his poems. A few days later an editorial article in the college newspaper deplored the way Thomas had been received, adding: 'It is a pity that we who are taught appreciation of the immortal of literature cannot appreciate greatness when it is in front of us.' After his Vassar reading, Thomas stayed with a staff member at the college, Vernon Venable. He and his hosts sat up half the night, talking and drinking. When he finally retired, Venable sat on the bed while Thomas launched into a drunken account of his unhappiness. According to Venable it went on for hours – 'just misery, misery, which seemed to me so pervasive that it had no source except a psychological source. That is, the man was deeply neurotic.' Venable was unable to remember details, except that part of the monologue was concerned with his love for Caitlin.

In effect, said Venable, he was declaring that life was a nightmare and he couldn't stand it. Thomas, with his knack of exposing other people's emotions with his own, had a traumatic effect on Venable – 'I had had literary aspirations up to that point, but I remember thinking when he finally got through talking and I went to bed, if I were asked whether all the poetry in the world is worth that amount of suffering, that if I could press a button I'd extirpate the poetry if I could extirpate the suffering.'

In the morning Venable said goodbye to his guest, then discovered to his annoyance that Thomas had stolen his best white shirt. Friends pointed out that this put him in the select company of hosts who had been honoured to have their shirts stolen by Thomas. But Venable felt he had been cheated, not by the theft itself, but by the fact that it came only a few hours after Thomas had opened his heart. Thomas, just by being Thomas, left these minor disturbances, little quaking spots, in places he visited, where they passed into local memory, like a natural cataclysm that happened years before.

A couple of performances in New York City, at the Poetry Center again and at Barnard College, completed his engagements for the tour. He sold an essay, 'A Child's Memories of Christmas in Wales', to *Harper's Bazaar* for three hundred dollars.* Otherwise there was little for him to do in the way of work until he returned. In the meantime he was to be found in bars and at parties. John Gruen was at a party given by Oscar Williams and his wife Gene Derwood, the poet. Williams, who had been placing Thomas's material in America since 1945, seems to have been a kindly, fussy man, sometimes laughed at behind his back. Thomas is said to have tried in vain to avoid his attentions in New York. At the party, wrote Gruen, Thomas slept, then talked about Laugharne. He had his own supply of beer, four quarts. His monologue, 'magical' at first, became 'slurred and finally incomprehensible'. A woman asked him to read from a book of his poems that she had brought with her. He fell on his knees and put his head under her skirt. Eventually he took hold of the book.

---

* It consisted of two pieces edited into one by Thomas, his 1945 BBC talk, 'Memories of Christmas', and an article he wrote for *Picture Post* in 1947, 'Conversation about Christmas'. This quick carpentry created one of his most popular works.

Gene Derwood, meanwhile, was sitting at an easel, trying to paint him. Oscar Williams was handing round paper plates laden with a supper of mashed potato. Thomas turned the book upside down and gave a reading of 'loud mooselike bellows and non-sense syllables ... All the while he was gesturing madly, like a Roman emperor in the throes of an epileptic seizure.' Gruen said it lasted ten minutes, before Thomas collapsed into a chair, mumbling – 'an unreachable, exhausted man on the brink of another long alcoholic sleep'.

Behind his drunken foolery in America, Thomas had real liaisons. He told Brinnin of three women he was involved with. One was a 'boyish poet', unnamed by Brinnin in *Dylan Thomas in America*, who is long dead. Another, 'Doris', was heavily disguised in Brinnin's account, but recognised herself. When Brinnin's book appeared she telephoned him and said, 'How could you *conceivably* think I had gone to bed with that man?' Brinnin was uncertain whether or not to believe her. The third was a New York journalist, clever and attractive; Brinnin and FitzGibbon called her 'Sarah'; her real name was Pearl. Her telephone number seems to have been the last addition to Thomas's American engagements diary, and it's likely that their affair was not under way until late in the trip. He spoke in a letter of a 'liquid, libidinous fortnight' in New York before he went home, but didn't elaborate, as he did at length when making stories out of high jinks on the campuses. (He had been spouting verse, he told Margaret Taylor, to 'thousands of young pieces whose minds, at least, were virgin territory'). Pearl was serious business, and they would meet again, in Britain, when Thomas confided in Brinnin that he was in love with both her and his wife, and didn't know what to do; Brinnin added that this was his first experience of 'seeing Dylan wrestling with a problem rather than seeking out means to circumvent it'. In May, in New York, when the problem was in the making, Laugharne and his marriage could be kept at arm's length.

Because Thomas didn't want to fly back, and there were dif-ficulties in booking a sea passage, he was unable to return to Britain until 1 June. That, at any rate, was the explanation Caitlin was given. His letter telling her this, on 7 May, begged to be reassured that his 'dear golden Caitlin' still loved him. 'Pray God you have not forgotten me ... Pray God you are always good to me, as I to you. Pray God you love me still. I need you. I want you. Oh *dear dear* Cat! Oh my angel.'

Behind these general concerns was a particular anxiety. Halfway through the letter he suddenly clarifies it. He thinks of her 'waking up alone in our beautiful bedroom – please Christ, my love, it *is* always alone – waiting for me, for nothing, for something ... Wait for me a little longer, my own true love.' He sounds lost; devious, perhaps, but undeniably miserable as well. 'I am lonely as the grave ... I want to kiss your breasts ... Who is in our house now? ... I kiss your heart.'

Caitlin certainly found lovers among local men towards the end of the marriage. She liked to say that she was only getting her own back on Dylan; although when he wrote to her on 7 May 1950, before she knew anything about his misdeeds in America, he evidently had reason to fear hers in Laugharne. In general Caitlin saw her behaviour, however outrageous, as mere self-preservation. She never ceased to complain about poverty and the sunless weather. Laugharne debilitated her with its rain and mist coming in from the sea. In letter after letter to Helen McAlpine in London, who became her closest friend, she said how much she hated the climate, making it sound a personal affront to a woman who deserved better. Caitlin saw the place as a grave, and resented what marriage to a 'romantic poet' had brought her to.

At the same time she knew and could name her own weaknesses: vanity, greed, lust. She did her own share of philandering, and when she did she was better equipped than Thomas to face the consequences. She was hard and he was soft; it was a question of character.

His last entry in the engagements diary was made on Thursday, 1 June, scrawled across the page in a shaky hand: 'Sail home'. It was time to go back to wife, children, herons and, hopefully, poems.

Chapter Twelve

NO MONEY, FEW POEMS

Dylan Thomas's mother once said that her son had told her, 'Wouldn't it be nice, our Mummy, if I didn't have a home to keep, so that I could keep this money and go and do my love poems!' But whenever he came back from America, said Mrs Thomas, he was greeted with bills. This was a mother's version of events. Although Thomas's 1950 visit to America earned more than he (or anyone else) expected when the original plans were made, little of the money found its way back to Laugharne. When, later on, he was assessed for British income tax on his earnings (no US tax seems to have been imposed), he had nothing left to pay it with. His income from the tour was $7,680, or £2,800. He paid tax on a smaller amount than this because substantial business expenses were allowed, but the final demand must have run into hundreds of pounds. Where to turn for this money was to be part of the nightmare of the next few years.

Perhaps a few hundred dollars had been posted to Caitlin while Thomas was in America. The only large sum she received came secretly from Brinnin, who hid eight hundred dollars in a handbag that he sent with Dylan as a present. This was nearly three hundred pounds. But it melted away like the rest. As for money in the bank that would enable Thomas to write in peace, the scheme had fallen to the ground. If this was bad news for Thomas, it must have been bitter news for his wife, who had stayed at home in Laugharne, hoping for the best, only to find the familiar state of crisis resumed.

On 18 June, soon after his return, Thomas wrote to Margaret Taylor about his prospects (as he imagined they were) of a university job in America. He also hoped she could help with the British equivalent of a post as 'poet in residence'. And in the short term he simply needed money:

You wanted to know some of the details of my – sweet words –

financial embarrassments, so that your ravens may help. Altho' I left Cat £10 a week – not in one sum, but to be delivered by the Bank – & also sent her several cheques from the States, the extravagant woman managed to chalk up, at the Chemist's [where they bought drink], a bill for £150. Also, I owe Llewelyn's school fees for this term, & Stanier *must* be paid the £50. And I owe Ebie for *many* taxis & for the Pelican. Say another £50. Altogether, £250. And I can raise, immediately, only £50 which I cannot send Stanier as we must manage to live here. I am starting to write some USA articles for Vogue, etc, but this will take a little time. Oh, ravens, come quick, come quick. Is there any hope? And desperately soon? . . .

The articles for *Vogue* were not written. Nor was a radio script about his visit to America that the BBC wanted. So desperate was Thomas that in August, on one of his trips to London, he called on the Controller of the Third Programme, Harman Grisewood, to ask for full-time employment in broadcasting for a year or two. Grisewood thought he might help with coverage of the Festival of Britain the following year. But after discussions with Laurence Gilliam, they decided there was no job for him. He continued to make occasional broadcasts as actor or reader, leaving Caitlin in Laugharne while he travelled to London for the usual days of drinking.

Caitlin's role was changing as time went on. She was hardening into the discontented wife, left behind with the bills while her husband went off to make money, which never came up to expectations. Thomas knew all about her unhappiness, as his letters from America make clear, with their mixture of love and apprehension. In one letter he had thanked her for her 'heartbreaking poem'. In another, he sympathised with her task as daughter-in-law, 'wailed at by old ill Thomases'. But he did nothing about it. Perhaps it was now she began to feel cheated. She must have guessed already that America had not been as he described it. Interviewed on television in 1975, she recalled that in his letters from America, Dylan avoided telling her what a fuss they were making of him. Instead he concentrated on fantasies of the money he was going to earn and the warm climates they would go and live in.

Laugharne's air of mouldering eccentricity didn't help. Dylan, being an unusual man, fitted in better than Caitlin, who was only an unusual woman. Women were expected to know their place in Laugharne. The small-town parochialism angered her. Thomas himself could scorn the place when the mood took him. 'This arsehole of the universe,' he wrote to American friends in July 1950, 'this hymnal blob, this pretty, sick, fond sad Wales.' But it was home for Thomas in a sense it could never be for her. After his death she wrote contemptuously about its mean location and hypocritical inhabitants. She thought, perhaps correctly, that they would have liked to hang her upside down in the square and tar and feather her. But then, to her they were only trash, with, as she put it, their little motor-cars and three-piece suites of furniture. 'They loved him,' said Margaret Taylor, 'but they never loved her.' To the inhabitants of Laugharne she was preposterous, the handsome interloper, swimming in their sea, having ear-splitting rows with her husband under their noses, dancing and laughing and drinking when she felt like it; having men in the house. She belonged to an aristocratic breed of Celt, and Laugh-arne disapproved. To the end, though, she recognised that the local rhythms were what suited her husband. Once a week they went into Carmarthen, shopped in the market, and sometimes went to a cinema, where fleas hopped in the dusty upholstery. Mrs Taylor, who bought a holiday cottage in Laugharne, saw their life as having 'almost a Thomas Hardy rhythm'. Thomas nagged his wife to dress 'properly', which meant inconspicuously, for Carmarthen market. He would have liked her to wear a hat as well as gloves and stockings, she wrote; but he realised that a hat was going too far.

Their rows were a permanent feature of life together. Caitlin told Mrs Taylor that once she didn't speak to him for a month. John Davenport, who observed matters at close range, found the domestic Dylan 'mild and even conventionally henpecked by his wife'. But when they were drunk, they fought and clawed at one another, with Caitlin taking the lead in violence. She described fearful drunken fights in which she was usually the aggressor, after which they would pass out on the bed and (she implied) wake up and make love. One Monday morning she went to see Dr David Hughes with a haematoma 'the size of a Victoria plum' above her eye. She asked him to 'get rid of this bloody thing for me', and insisted it was the result of falling on rocks. 'Tell me the truth first,' he said, and she said, 'Dylan kicked me when I was on the floor.'

Her fury over other women, in particular American women, caused some of the rows. Since her flexible code allowed her to sleep with men she fancied, she was free to rage against any lapses on his part. It was the physical act with anyone else, she said, that she couldn't bear. She had a burning desire not to be betrayed, seeing Dylan as her personal property – this weak-willed man who depended on her.

Her own infidelity might have been expected to cause rows as well, but she said that he learned to look the other way. They all saw her as a wicked woman in Laugharne, she told me in 1978, one day when she felt in an honest mood. Her behaviour, she said, had an element of revenge against Dylan, although she didn't deny she was that way inclined when it came to casual sex. Dylan had a fair idea of what was going on. Ivy Williams, the landlady of Brown's Hotel, was his confidante, said Caitlin, and she whispered it all in his ear. But Dylan didn't want to know, and blinded himself to it. He did bring up the subject with her once or twice, she said, and made a few feeble protests. They were tentative, half-hearted: like the fork he threw at her once, like the hints he concealed in his poems.

The names of various men, a labourer here, a sailor there, were still mentioned in Laugharne long afterwards. Howard Dark, a travelling draper who lived in the town, had a longer relationship than some. After his death his wife Jane, who knew all about Howard's affairs, recalled having supper at the Boat House and asking Caitlin about her taste in men. 'Tall and athletic,' said Caitlin. Dylan grinned at Howard, a short man with a moustache, and said, 'Describes us exactly, doesn't it?'

Caitlin liked to put all the blame on drink – alcohol had ruined her as well, but it was Dylan who led the way. Even the lechery wasn't really lechery. It was just the booze, she wrote to me once, that made them what they were not. In old age, drink and sex behind her, she fostered this delusion.

Caitlin had other resentments during the marriage. She hated to see her husband, the poet she had married for his gift (perhaps because her blustering father lacked it), spend his time reading verse instead of writing it. It pleased her to think she had taken him when he was a nobody: as if it was she who had uncovered his talent. As time went on she thought he was letting flattery and indolence subvert his purpose. But another part of her resented his life as an artist, seeing it as a comment on her failure to be anything more than the poet's wife. She certainly hankered after a creative life of her own, writing poetry in secret, still dancing when she could; an increasingly sad figure. As she said, she always danced, even (and in the end, only) when she was drunk.

Gwen Watkins saw them in the summer of 1950, not long after Thomas returned; they went to spend a day with her and Vernon at Pennard, at their house on the cliffs. Dan Jones and Fred Janes were there as well. It was the last visit Thomas made to the Watkinses' house. By this time Dylan and Vernon saw one another infrequently. Vernon's admiration and loyalty were undiminished. But according to Gwen Watkins, 'Dylan had less use for Vernon. You may think this unkind, but after Vernon married, Dylan concluded that he didn't have the money.' Gwen Watkins, never fond of Thomas, liked him even less that day. He boasted of what an uproarious time he had had in America, 'showing off like a small boy'. He claimed to have taken drugs for the first time; no details were given. They sat on the lawn, by the glare of the sea, eating potato crisps, and Caitlin said the only foods he could still taste were vinegar and HP sauce. He had drunk too much whisky and his taste buds had perished. They bickered about his taste buds and whether they were dead or just sleeping.

Soon they had something worse to quarrel over, worse even than money and suspicions about America. At the end of August, John Brinnin came to London at the start of a European holiday. A few days later Thomas's New York lover, Pearl, arrived. Brinnin found Thomas 'a new man' since New York: 'His clothes were new and well-matched, his shoes glinted with a high shine, his face was serene and ruddy and he was smoking a cigar.' They spent a few days in one another's company, visiting clubs and pubs, eating at Wheeler's restaurant, going to a Marx Brothers film and a revue (Thomas slept and snored on both occasions), until Pearl appeared on 4 September. All three went for an outing on the river to Greenwich – this was the occasion when Thomas told Brinnin that he loved both Pearl and his wife – and then the lovers left London for a brief holiday in Brighton. Thomas seems not to have taken precautions to keep his mistress concealed. Rayner Heppenstall met them in the Stag, a pub much used by

Features staff at the BBC, on a Saturday morning. She was 'dark, with a fringe, strongly built, not small, a bit ... arty in her clothes and manner, intelligent and full of suspicion'. In the afternoon Thomas and friend were at a wedding. They were in and out of places in London where Thomas was well known: the Café Royal, the Salisbury. Soon afterwards she left for France, but continued to write to Thomas at the Savage Club. By this time Margaret Taylor had got to hear of the affair, and made it her business to tell Caitlin, hurrying to Laugharne with the news. Of all people, Maggs Taylor – with her florid devotion to Thomas, her interfering nature and the power that came from being official patroness – was the last messenger whom Caitlin would have chosen. Taylor may have intercepted letters at the Savage and taken them to Laugharne. Caitlin certainly read Pearl's endearments, her 'sugar' as she called it. Later she found more letters in a suitcase.

Desperate to convince his wife that Pearl wasn't a lover, Thomas tried to portray her as a hanger-on; he even likened her to the egregious Mrs Taylor. Caitlin knew this was nonsense, and a wound opened up in their marriage that was never healed. Her letters to Helen McAlpine were full of bitterness, which extended itself to a moral rage on behalf of women in general: downtrodden and, what was worse, resigned. They should rebel; one should begin a crusade to make them. Months later she told Helen McAlpine that but for her youngest child Colm, whom she couldn't bear to think of being left on his own, she might not be there at all; though whether this meant separation or self-destruction isn't clear.

Meanwhile Thomas's one serious extra-marital affair had petered out. An undated letter to Davenport written from Laugharne described himself 'here in my *horribly* cosy little nest, surrounded by my detestable books, wearing my odious, warm slippers, observing the gay, reptilian play of my abominable brood, basking in the vituperation of my golden, loathing wife'. 'I remember the Thames and old Pearl,' he wrote to Brinnin, 'I haven't heard from her since she went away.'

Thomas worked on two poems in 1950. He completed 'In the White Giant's Thigh', presumably after he returned from America, and read it on the Third Programme (along with 'Over

Sir John's hill' and 'In Country Sleep') on 25 September, soon after Pearl's visit. He began or continued 'In Country Heaven', which was intended to be the title poem, or opening sequence, of the group to which the three other poems mentioned above were to belong. In it, God regards his creation with pity and tears. As Thomas described the sequence in the 25 September broadcast, it was to culminate in 'praise of what is and what could be on this lump in the skies. It is a poem about happiness.' But 'In Country Heaven' was never finished, and the concept (like happiness) remained wishful thinking.

Also in 1950 he seems to have made a serious start on his radio play about Laugharne. This now had the working title of 'The Town [sometimes 'The Village'] that was Mad'. The BBC producer assigned to the project, Douglas Cleverdon, specialised in literary programmes. It was he who had cast Thomas as Satan in *Paradise Lost* and as the soldier who screamed in *In Parenthesis*. He was also in charge of the poetry programme on 25 September. A month later he was writing to say that the Third had 'agreed to take "The Town that was Mad" (or whatever title you prefer)'. But so far they were approving only an idea, not a script.

The play was to show a town peopled by free-living eccentrics, who are declared insane by the conformists of the outside world. The citizens (led by their spokesman, Captain Cat) insist that the issue be tried in court. But when they hear the prosecution's description of the sane world, they decide to stay as they are, cordoned off. Thomas quoted sections of it to Vernon Watkins and Daniel Jones at a cricket match in Swansea in the summer of 1950. In one scene, where a mad townsman or villager confessed to lusts of the flesh, a massed male choir (representing the jury) was to chant 'Ach-y-fi!' (a Welsh expression of disgust) at each revelation. This dramatic structure was later abandoned because Thomas was unable to sustain it; as in the feature-film scripts, plots were his weakness. In 1950 he was still trying. A letter from Cleverdon on 5 December urged him to finish 'The Village that was Mad', now that he was 'free from the distractions of this beastly cold metropolis', so that it could be scheduled for broadcasting in the middle of 1951. An undated note from Thomas to Cleverdon, sent from the Savage Club, enclosed the first thirty-nine pages of the manuscript of 'The Town that was

Mad', and said he was 'very enthusiastic to finish the thing. And quickly.'

But the script slid down Thomas's list of priorities. Early in 1951 he set off on another trip, this time to Iran. The Anglo-Iranian Oil Company (later British Petroleum) had commissioned him to write a film about the benefits that British oilmen were bringing to a poor country. Paternalism was still abroad; Iranian nationalism was only just emerging. His fee was probably two hundred and fifty pounds, plus expenses. A company called Green Park was to make the film. The producer, Ralph ('Bunny') Keene, was an acquaintance of Thomas. They flew out on 8 January. Presently Thomas was writing to Caitlin. His despair was louder than ever, presumably reflecting the Pearl fiasco:

All these strange, lost days I love you, and I am lost indeed without you my dear wife. This is so much further than America, and letters will take so much longer to travel to you and yours to me if you will ever write to me again oh *darling* Cat. And if you do not write to me, and if you do not love me any more, I cannot go on, I cannot go on sleeplessly thinking, 'Caitlin my Cattleanchor, my dear, does not love me, o God let me die.' I can't live without you; I can't go travelling with this long, wan Bunny through this fearful, strange world unless I am sure that at the end we will be together as we are meant to be together, close & alone except for our cuckoo whom I miss very very very much, more than I could dream of. But you: I miss you more than I would miss my life although you *are* my life. I can see now, in this grand over-hot Oil-Company Guest House where we are staying, your smiling and your anger, your coldness with me, your once-love for me, your golden hair & blue eyes and our wedding ring from a cracker, I can see you coming to bed, I can feel your coldness turning, in my arms, to warmth and love, I can hear you so beautiful with Cuckoo Colm Colum Column, I can hear you saying, 'I love you', 'I hate you', 'Go away', 'Come close' to me all the blessed days of our life. Caitlin beloved, unless you write to say that we will be together again, I shall die. I love you I love you, day, night, waking, sinking into some kind of sleep. This letter may take a week to reach you, or it may take three days; however long or short a time, oh darling darling write to me. There will be nothing but pains & nightmares & howlings in my head and endless endless nights & forsaken days until you say, 'I am waiting. I love you . . .'

The letter moved on to financial matters. Green Park was to pay her ten pounds a week for the five weeks he was away ('I know it goes terribly quickly') and a cheque was on its way from Marguerite Caetani, no doubt in response to an SOS. Further letters begged for her love. One referred to a letter he had received from her: 'Your letter, as it was meant to, made me want to die. I did not think that, after reading it so many times till I knew every pain by heart, I could go on with these days and nights ... But the bloody animal always does go on ...' If she didn't meet him on his return to London, he would phone their friends the McAlpines. 'If there is no message there from you, I shall know that everything is over.' Determined to engage her pity, he added that he would soon be climbing into bed in his shirt and thinking of her.

Thomas found time to write at least once to Pearl, poking fun at the oilmen and their works. His letters to Caitlin, too, were critical of the 'horrible oilmen', and dwelt on the country's poverty.* After his return in February, either the script was never written or, if it was, the film was never made. He had barely left the country when the Iranians nationalised their oil industry. 'My job was to help pour water on troubled oil,' he wrote to Oscar Williams. In April he provided a few minutes of material for a BBC radio documentary called 'Persian Oil'. This said a good deal about poverty but nothing unkind about the Anglo-Iranian Oil Company.† The script, highly evocative, shows how smoothly he could turn out a piece of superior hack-work when he felt like it – 'On the blue, boiled water the dhows sail out of the Bible ... The vast tribes move, with the heat of the sun, from their winter grounds to the high green places ... Engineers curse

---

* A theory put forward by David Callard, a writer, in 1998 suggested that the film project was a cover for espionage, which is as feasible or unfeasible as any speculation about spying, and that Thomas was in the pay of British Intelligence, which is ridiculous. Callard described a conversation, at an arts festival in 1980, with a poet who told him that in the 1950s he heard an elderly ex-spy, unnamed, say when drunk, 'Just look at that drunken fool, Dylan Thomas. We got to him in the end'. That half-baked gossip, together with a few facts mutated from this book, constitute the 'evidence'.

† A BBC producer who proposed a more elaborate, Third Programme, script about Iran by Thomas was told by a senior colleague that 'I understand the Anglo-Iranian Oil Company has some kind of hold over what Dylan might say'. No doubt the company had paid for exclusive rights to Thomas's material.

their dehydrated ale in the income-classed clubs. The rich are rich. Oil's oily. The poor are waiting.' In London, Caitlin stayed with the McAlpines while she awaited his return: not forgiving her husband, but with no intention of leaving, either. She even passed the time with a poet, David Wright, imagining herself in love with him, making him a sandwich packed with garlic when he told her he was having dinner with a girlfriend, and drifting towards a sexual affair that failed to happen. When they arranged a rendezvous that might have ended in bed, Wright said she 'had the good sense not to turn up'. The Thomases went back to Laugharne; guerrilla warfare continued.

That spring, Thomas activated himself to write a ribald poem, 'Lament', where the poet looks back on his sexual life from his deathbed. It has a chorus line that Thomas thundered out in his readings – 'Sighed the old ram rod, dying of women' (and, in succeeding stanzas, of bitches, welcome, downfall and strangers). A draft version is headed 'The Miner's Lament'. Writing to Marguerite Caetani on 20 March, when it was 'nearly finished', he described it as 'coarse and violent'. It is not difficult to detect in it Thomas's current frustrations with life. One critic sees it as an attempt by Thomas to examine in an 'honest and coherent' fashion his 'inner experience' – those fears of castration and impotence that may have been buried like landmines in his earlier poems.

Another, entirely different poem followed. 'Do not go gentle into that good night' was addressed to his father, now in chronic ill-health, chiefly through heart trouble. It was written as a villanelle, rare in English verse, where two rhymes only are used in five three-lined stanzas, concluding with a quatrain. Thomas used this strict form to contain an exhortation to his father, a plea for him to die with anger, not humility. He sent it to Marguerite Caetani, for her to use in *Botteghe Oscure*, on 28 May, with a postscript to say that 'the only person I can't show [it] to is, of course, my father, who doesn't know he's dying'. Into it one can read Thomas's concern for the proud man with only 'frail deeds' to offer, whose word is still crucial to his son –

> And you, my father, there on the sad height,
> Curse, bless, me now with your fierce tears, I pray.

As in 'Lament', Thomas was writing plainly on a subject, in this case his father and their complex relationship, that had concerned him deeply all his life. Both these poems were written at a time of domestic unhappiness. There were quarrels with Caitlin; debts were accumulating. Yet he succeeded in writing, quite quickly, two poems that in their different ways were, for him, unusually blunt. Perhaps they were an act of boldness, an attempt, conscious or otherwise, to confront the demons and break out of whatever despair enclosed him. If so, the attempt was at least a partial success. Unfortunately it was not to be repeated.

There are two parallel strands to follow for the rest of 1951: first, what others observed of Thomas, or what he told them in his letters; second, the progress or otherwise of Thomas the Poet, shut away in his work-hut.

Outwardly he was a successful writer and broadcaster with a swashbuckling reputation. To the group of students and staff members at Swansea University College whose guest speaker he was at the end of April, he was the local boy of whom equivocal tales were told; neither was at ease with the other. His hosts were the English Society. It was no great occasion. The meeting was held in the basement table-tennis room of the Students' Union building, an old house near the Uplands. An acquaintance on the university college staff thought how unimpressive he looked as he sat through the chairman's introduction: 'His navy blue suit and jersey, full belly and balding crown made one think of a decayed seaman of the type found in small fishing villages.' Fifty or sixty people were present, not all of them from the college. It was Thomas's first appearance before an audience in his home town since his naughty lecture to the John O'London gathering seventeen years before. He began with one of his well-used openings, 'I can't manage a proper talk. I might just manage an improper one.' His remark explaining why he didn't plan to be formal, that 'I would read a lecture if I hadn't written it in invisible ink on toilet paper which I left out in the sun', was not enthusiastically received. The talk was one of his comic variants on the theme of lecturing in America, and led into the usual poetry reading. Kingsley Amis, then a young lecturer at the college – it was another three years before his novel *Lucky Jim* appeared – described the evening in a magazine article in 1957.

'Although obviously without all charlatanry,' wrote Amis, 'he did here and there sound or behave like a charlatan.'

The evening had begun at the Uplands Hotel with some unpromising exchanges. Thomas, who was drinking but not drunk, announced in his 'clear, slow, slightly haughty, cut-glass Welsh voice' that 'I've just come back from Persia, where I've been pouring water on troubled oil'. Amis, already developing a Lucky-Jim style of dialogue, made 'what was in those days my stock retort to the prepared epigram' by remarking, 'I say, I must go and write that down.' Thomas 'looked round the circle, grinning. "I have," he said.' A local acquaintance, not at the college, seems to have irritated the group by his attentions to Thomas, both before the lecture and after, when a crowd returned to the pub. Geoffrey Nicholson remembered Thomas being goaded with questions designed to make a fool of him. 'It's no good treating me as an Aunt Sally,' he said, 'because you'll get back as good as you give. I'm a fool anyway.' Amis concluded that their guest wasn't to blame for the way the evening petered out. The local acquaintance monopolised him, the students drifted away to the other end of the bar, and he was heard to complain that he had been abandoned. The mistake, Amis concluded, was to have made him an object of awe and suspicion. Given a degree of sympathy, 'I think we should have seen that his attitude was the product of nothing more self-aware or self-regarding than shyness.'*

His performance for the English Society earned him a few pounds. There were many such engagements. He earned and spent, or borrowed and spent, like a man in a dream. There is no evidence that his capacity to earn money was destroyed by drink. Nor was his talent for borrowing diminished; on the contrary, he now had a range of patrons, from Margaret Taylor to Princess Caetani and Marged Howard-Stepney, a wealthy Welsh woman whose story comes later. More conventional patrons were still called upon from time to time. On 28 May 1951, he wrote to T. S. Eliot:

---

* Kingsley Amis re-entered the Thomas story thirty-five years later as a trustee of the dead poet's estate, from 1986 until Amis's death in 1995. His dislike of Thomas, as man and poet, was well known. But he was a friend of the senior trustee, Stuart Thomas.

Very many thanks indeed for your letter & your cheque. It was extremely kind of you, and the cheque helped to ease my difficulties here. I was, as you know, very nervous in writing to you at all to ask your help; and especially since your recent reputation for wealth. It was in spite of this, that I managed to write my begging letter. I was, anyway, writing to the best poet I know, and not to a supposedly monied man. Thank you, again, most sincerely.

On the same day he was writing, 'tremblingly & very much in earnest', to Laurence Gilliam at the BBC, concerning a possible programme about the Festival of Britain. It was essential to have 'ADVANCE, IMMEDIATE ... I owe every tradesman in town ...' Gilliam reminded him that the rule said: No script, no money. So the feverish dance continued. It was not as though Thomas rose above everyday trivialities, scorning money as trash and pursuing his real work. His real work, as often as not, was to earn money to enable him to do more of the same work. Anxiety peers out of his letters. Caitlin said that debts kept him awake at night. When he was younger, they sometimes had to live on air. But why were his circumstances still so bad, so often? They suggest a helplessness, an eroding of confidence. Was he letting his affairs drift into chaos because it reflected the chaos in himself?

By the spring of 1951, Thomas was already planning another escape to America. 'I would very much like (I'd adore it) to be imported to the States next year,' he wrote to Brinnin in April, adding that this time he wanted to take Caitlin with him. In July, Brinnin and his friend Bill Read were in Europe, and spent a weekend with the Thomases in Laugharne. Caitlin soon cross-questioned Brinnin about Pearl, and was not pleased at his reticence. There was a disastrous outing (in a Williams-driven car) to Pembrokeshire, marked by high emotional tension. According to Billy Williams, Thomas paid for everything, which angered Caitlin still more. At the end of the day she announced, 'America is out!' Next evening she and Dylan had a fight in the dining room. After he had fled, she harangued the Americans for an hour about her husband's failings, how American flattery went to his head, how foul women pursued him while she was left to rot with three screaming children and no money. If Caitlin was thinking about her own unhappy state, she may have thought about her husband's as well. America, she said once, brought out his weaknesses. Lacking discipline, he was soft and lovable, 'a piece of bread' in the Italian idiom. Whereas a man should have a ruthless streak in him – lacking that, she said, he was eaten alive by the Americans.

No final decision was taken about America that summer. It was among the schemes that revolved hopefully. There was a chance of film scripts from Donald Taylor. Thomas hoped to collaborate with Ted Kavanagh, the comedy scriptwriter who wrote the once-famous ITMA shows for wartime radio. This fell through. Another scheme, that matured slowly and disagreeably through the year, was to move back to London temporarily. Thomas kept threatening or promising it. 'I'm having to sell up my house as soon as I can & move to London, which I hate,' he wrote to Oscar Williams on 28 May – untruthfully, since the house was not his to sell. Doubtless Caitlin was determined to change the system whereby she was left in Laugharne while her husband, now a certified adulterer, disappeared from sight for days on end. An undated letter to her from London, perhaps written about this time, talks hopelessly of finding no job (he was meeting Ted Kavanagh again that evening) and having no money. He has fallen downstairs, cutting his head and blacking his eye. A dark yellow rain is falling: London is terrible, and (he adds quickly) he knows that Laugharne is too. The tone of the letter is sad and placatory.

In the plans for a return to London, Margaret Taylor was a prime mover. She thought that if Thomas could find sufficient bread-and-butter work in London, he would not need to return to America. This hope proved vain. Caitlin withdrew her opposition when she was persuaded, or persuaded herself, to go with her husband on his second grand tour.* Nevertheless during the summer Mrs Taylor bought a house in London, in Camden Town. The address was Delancey Street; it was a worn-out district, near railway yards. The Thomases were to occupy a basement flat. But they didn't move there immediately.

Before he leaves for London, there is the matter of Thomas and

---

* Caitlin was pregnant in the autumn of 1951. She wanted to have the child, but she wanted to go to America more. An expensive Harley Street abortion was paid for by Marged Howard-Stepney.

his poetry that summer and autumn. During this period he wrote or completed a single poem, 'Poem on his Birthday'. Thomas took his birthdays seriously; at least two earlier poems, 'Twenty-four years' and 'Poem in October', were similarly inspired. The particular significance of 'Poem on his Birthday' is that with it Thomas effectively signed off his career as a poet. Only the verse 'Prologue' to his *Collected Poems* came after, and the unfinished 'Elegy'. Thomas, in 1951, can be seen as making one last attempt to find his way. In terms of output he wrote more verse than at any time since 1945; 'Poem on his Birthday' was preceded by 'Lament' and 'Do not go gentle'. But whereas in the first two poems he struck out vigorously, casting a cold eye on man's (and Thomas's, and Thomas's father's) predicament, in the third poem he was waiting for death, passively hoping for the best, counting his blessings on trembling fingers. In July, when he was working on the poem, he told John Brinnin in the work-hut at Laugharne (as he had told others in America) that from now on he was determined to write only 'happy' poems. At about the same time, he gave Bill Read a manuscript summary of what 'Poem on his Birthday' was to be about. The poet, it said,

celebrates, and spurns, his thirty-fifth birthday* ... Birds and fishes move under and around him on their dying ways, & he, a craftsman in words, toils towards his own wounds which are waiting in ambush for him ... Now exactly half of his three score and ten years is gone ... he looks back at his times: his loves, his hates, all he has seen, and sees the logical progress of death in every thing he has seen & done. His death lurks for him, and for all, in the next lunatic war, and still singing, still praising the radiant earth, still loving, though remotely, the animal creation also gladly pursuing their inevitable & grievous ends, he goes towards his. Why should he praise God, and the beauty of the world as he moves to horrible death? He does not like the deep zero dark and the nearer he gets to it, *the louder he sings, the higher the salmon leaps, the shriller the birds carol.*

* In the summer of 1951, Thomas was approaching his thirty-seventh birthday. His thirty-fifth birthday was in 1949. There is evidence that the poem was substantially written in 1951, though it may have been conceived and worked on earlier.

The poem as finally written ended on a different note. In the synopsis, Thomas saw himself singing the world's praises in a despairing attempt to hide the approach of death. In the poem he subdued the note of despair, declaring that

> ... the closer I move
> To death, one man through his sundered hulks,
> The louder the sun blooms
> And the tusked, ramshackling sea exults;
> And every wave of the way
> And gale I tackle, the whole world then,
> With more triumphant faith
> Than ever was since the world was said,
> Spins its morning of praise ...

This was the message that Thomas would have liked to present. But in the context of his life and work in 1951 and thereafter, it has an air of forced optimism.

Many worksheets of 'Poem on his Birthday' survive: Thomas had realised by now that such material was valuable to collectors, and he was careful to keep the scribbled-on pages.* Some of the phrases suggest his mood. 'Yet, though I cry with tumbledown tongue,/Count my blessings aloud' says the published poem, at the point where it leads into the final section. Among the lines that Thomas experimented with, before he arrived at 'Yet, though I cry with tumbledown tongue', were:

> 'And then, before the downpouring rain'
> 'And then before the sea rage breaks and bucks'
> 'Let me then before the blazing night'
> 'And then before the tornado break'.

One worksheet has a drawing of a lighthouse on an island. The tower and the rays are blacked-in. Above it he has written:

---

* The critic David Holbrook, studying reproductions of four of these sheets, noticed numbers – '223', '161', '424' – alongside lists of synonyms, and realised that they referred to groups in Roget's *Thesaurus*. This businesslike approach dismayed Holbrook, who thought it was not at all the way to set about writing a poem.

'Darkhouse'. Occasionally lists of tradesmen's bills are mixed up with trial lines and words. Alongside 'sea-flecked mouth' is 'Ebi=£150 P.O.=£67.'

Further evidence from the work-hut can be found in manuscripts of doggerel verse. These must have survived by accident. They were not worksheets of serious poems that could be sold to American collectors in his lifetime, but anguished scribblings, left as litter, which found their way out of Laugharne when Thomas was dead. A notebook* containing manuscript workings of 'Poem on his Birthday' (with more Roget group numbers) and notes for the Laugharne radio play suddenly breaks into

> How can I write a poem to a human
> Being when every bloody line I write
> Is only about my loving one woman?

Presumably he meant Caitlin: the 'bloody' has been crossed out. There is one rambling, incomprehensible fragment that begins

> When the promiscuous male drunkards with the floating kidney
> And the sexy, overbrimmed tankards
> Were put to timely death...

In another fragment Thomas wrote, obscurely but bitterly:

> I do not admire them, the little thankyous:
> Crying, cringing, abominable hyenas
> Ashamed even of their own acknowledgment,
> Who whine outside the ashbins
> For another titbit.
> They should be put in a sack and drowned,
> Yelps, cringes, and all,
> In a sea of self pity.
> Why do you mingily snarl outside my window,
> Despicable rodents?
> Is it for me you are the self-appointed accusers?

---

* Inside the front cover someone, probably Caitlin, has written in pencil: '1 June 1949. Caitlin.' Under it Thomas has written in ink: 'Laugharne. October 1951. Dylan.'

Down with you, sulphurous ones,
My own degretation [*sic*] is enough,
Having screeched for crumbs. From the table it [illegible]
I do not need the eternal damned apologies of the hairy thankyous.
I prefer sleek, sick animals
Like Disgust:
They are always well fed.

Finally there is a poem in the form of a letter to 'Dear Marged'.
Marged Howard-Stepney came from a wealthy Anglo-Welsh
family, the Stepneys, who claimed descent from the Royal Tudors.
Marged's mother, Catherine Stepney, inherited estates in Carmarthenshire from her father, a baronet. Catherine married
another baronet, Sir Stafford Howard, and when he died she
changed her name from Lady Howard to Lady Howard-Stepney.
Marged, her only daughter, was born in 1913 at the family
mansion in the town of Llanelli; loyal citizens subscribed to buy
her a silver cradle, and called her 'Marged fach', little Marged.
In 1951 she was thirty-eight, a year older than Thomas. Her two
marriages had ended in divorce. She was excitable and energetic,
an ice-skater and tennis-player when younger, now inclined
towards eccentric friendships with the needy, who took full
advantage of her generosity. Her son described her as 'not so
much genuinely interested in the arts as a saviour of lost souls'.
Marged was said to suffer from 'nervous troubles'; one of her
problems was drink. She was a cousin of Frances, Richard
Hughes's wife, and this may have been how she came to meet
Thomas. By 1951 she was giving him money, to the dismay of
her advisers. Thomas's letter to her (written on the back of a
'Poem on his Birthday' worksheet) begins in prose –

> My dear Marged, You told me, once, upon a time, to call on you
> when I was beaten down, and you would try to pick me up. Maybe
> I should not have remembered

– then becomes verse –

> You told me, once, to call on you
> When I was beaten down . . .

A longer version, heavily corrected and smudged, reads

> Dear Marged,
> Once upon a time you told me,
> I remember in my bones,
> That when the bad world had rolled me
> Over on the scalding stones,
> Shameless, lost, as the day I came
> I should with my beggar's cup
> Howl down the wind and call your name
> And you, you would raise me up.
> The same very same time I told you,
>
> And swore by my heart & head,
> That I would forever hold you
> To the lovely words you said;
> I never thought so soon I'd lie
> Lonely in the whining dust;
> My one wish is to love and die,
> But life is all mustn't & must.
>
> I mustn't love, & I must die
> But only when I am told,
> And Fear sits in the mansioned sky
> And the winged Conventions scold,
> And Money is the dunghill King
> And his royal nark is the dun;
> And dunned to death I write this jingling thing
> Dunned to death in the dear sun.
> This jingling thing

Thomas was in a familiar knot. He needed money but evidently loathed himself for going to such lengths to obtain it. His income through his literary agents in 1951 was only a few hundred pounds. The Inland Revenue was collecting its tax on the good year of 1948–9, when he earned £1600, and would soon be demanding a share of the American takings. His plight would have been still worse but for Oscar Williams, the American anthologist, who was acting as his unofficial agent in the United States (officially it was the Ann Watkins agency). Williams made some judicious sales, and passed money to Thomas without taking a percentage. In 1951 he sent at least $725 (about £260) to the Boat House, for 'In the White Giant's Thigh', the article on 'How to be a poet', some anthology rights, and, his best sale for a poem, 'Poem on his Birthday'. Thomas sent this soon after he completed it, probably early in October 1951, with an undated letter in which he told Williams that

> I've spent months writing this poem, and hope you can squeeze out a real huge cheque from some moneyed illerate – it's me that's illerate, I mean illiterate – bastard for it. Months and months, and I think it's the best I've done. As always, I need money in a *terrible* hurry. Particularly urgently now, as next week we move to London, to stay in lodgings at the beginning & then to move into a house. I have gout, strained back, bronchitis, fits, and a sense of disaster, otherwise very ill. My love, and Caitlin's, to you & Gene whom we'll be seeing a lot (I hope) of in February. Please, old crazy friend, get me a lot of dough bloody, bloody *quick*. And thank you a great lot for the fifty dollars.

By the end of October, the editor of *Atlantic*, Edward Weeks, was telling Williams he was 'captivated' by the poem. He was willing to pay $200 for it. (The *Atlantic* normally paid a dollar a line for long poems; this one had 108 lines.) To pay more, said Weeks, would not be fair to Frost, Eliot and Auden.

Meanwhile Delancey Street loomed ahead. They were still at the Boat House on 10 October, when Thomas wrote to his San Francisco friend, Ruth Witt-Diamant:

> ... How could I not have written, when every week of the piggish year I mean to with all my heart, that poor bloody muscle? Oh, easy, easy. The son of a sloth and a turnip, either I hang by my whiskery toes, thinking of nothing and lust, or sit bigheaded in the wet earth, thinking of turnip poems; and time snails by; and San Francisco's six thousand lamenting miles away; and Wales is dead from the eisteddfodau up; and day after day I grow lazier and fatter and sadder and older and deafer and duller; grey grizzles in my dry hairmat; gout snarls in my big toe; my children grow large and rude; I renounce my Art to make money and then make no money; I fall in love with undesirable, unloving, squat, taloned, moist unlovely

women and out again like a trout; I quarrel with Caitlin and make
it up in floods of salt self-pity; I fall downstairs; I frighten myself in
the night, my own plump banshee; I celebrate other people's birthdays with falsely bonhomous abandon; I daydream of Chile, a place
I never want to visit; I write poems and hide them before I can read
them; and next week I shall be thirty-seven horrors old.* Does that,
in any way, explain, dear Ruth, why I haven't written? Of course it
doesn't. I've no excuse, but *please* try to forgive me ... At the end
of January, Caitlin and I are going to New York, financed by
the Poetry Center, Columbia, and the Museum of Modern Art in
collaboration, and I should hate it if I didn't, somehow, manage to
get to California and (if you could bear it) stay with you for a
week ...

His woes seemed endless. The fall downstairs had happened
one Saturday night. 'I fell like a barrel,' he wrote to Mrs Taylor.
'I was in bed, then, for days, with a rumpled back, and gout
came too, grinding gout, and went to bed in my toe, and a
Summons arrived to pay a firm of plumbers for the work they
did, last December, in extricating, from the W.C. pipes of a
London flat we were living in, a bottle of Hammerton's Stout
thrown down by Colm.'

That autumn Dylan and Caitlin had a spectacular row. Elisabeth Lutyens, who stayed there immediately afterwards, said it
was about a man, M., a middle-class friend of them both whom
Dylan suspected of sleeping with Caitlin; so perhaps he was not
always complaisant. Later, when she was widowed, Caitlin told
a lover that Dylan once caught her in bed with M. At the time
Lutyens believed it was merely Dylan being suspicious.
Although she was fond of Dylan as a drinking companion
(in 1951 she had a drink problem of her own), Lutyens' real
sympathies were with his wife. She was impressed with Caitlin
at home – walking and swimming, still dancing alone to the
gramophone, and writing poems which she showed to Lutyens.
Evidently they didn't interest Thomas. He expected her to 'forgo

* Either he was anticipating the date or the letter was written later than 10
October; Thomas's birthday was on 27 October.

all independence or life of her own, staying at home as wife and mother'. His only contribution to domestic life while Lutyens was there was to 'put an onion in the oven and eat it with his grubby little hands'.

Lutyens was not alone in siding with Caitlin. Vera Killick thought that she was 'always justified in what she complained of. As a husband he was quite hopeless. His method of retaliation was to go out and get drunk, and leave her with the children.' Gwen Watkins, who was not particularly fond of either of them, had no doubt that he made her life intolerable – 'I thought mine was hard enough. I suppose the poet's wife has never had a bed of roses to lie on.'

When Lutyens arrived at the Boat House, Thomas wasn't there. He had left after the quarrel, telephoning the same night to say, 'This is the last time you will hear my voice.' But it was a reverse-charge call, and Caitlin knew he had only gone to Swansea. She thought he was hinting at suicide, as he did from time to time: nicking himself with a razor blade on one occasion, claiming to have drunk a bottle of Jeyes Fluid on another. A day or two later Lutyens went with her to reclaim him, not looking forward to the occasion, which turned out to be even less enjoyable than she expected. There were tearful scenes – 'Dylan was on his knees, snivelling. They were both crying. They were having a whale of a time.' It took so long that they missed the last train back to Carmarthen, and Lutyens, the only one with money, reluctantly hired a car. They had to keep stopping because Thomas had drunk so much beer; each time, he pretended to run away in the dark and had to be retrieved.

At home, Thomas retired to bed for several days to recover from the crisis. The Boat House larder was bare. It was difficult being a guest under these circumstances, so Lutyens loaned him ten pounds, which she never saw again. Presently he was telephoning Marguerite Caetani in Rome, trying to raise money on work in progress. Lutyens marvelled at such goings-on. But Thomas was practising the art or craft of survival. He extracted a hundred pounds from the Princess for an unfinished version of his radio play, telling her, as he told everyone, that he had to have the money in order to pay bills in order to leave Laugharne in order to start again, yet again, in London. Finally Thomas had to defuse the Caitlin episode by making it part of his never-ending comic narrative, which was his way of dealing with reality. He wrote to Margaret Taylor:

I quarrelled and fought with Caitlin over something now forgotten but which I remember in every detail, and huffed out of the house to Swansea where I stayed with a barrister who uses brandy like salt or sauce, pouring it over everything, meat, potatoes, porridge, and even boiled egg. And Caitlin & Lizzie Lutyens came & reclaimed me, and, though I am writing this in the upper room of the Pelican, (for my shed keys are lost once more, for I think the sixth time) I can hear Lizzie hissing and gushing and drooling & bubbling ... all the way from her bed in the Boat House where she lies all day monologuing herself to death. Lizzie came into the Pelican yesterday afternoon, raving drunk, and gave my father a heart attack. Today, he is still shaking. Caitlin's black eye has just faded; a boy fell from a tree where he was picking conkers, quite near your Grist house, and his shoulderblade broke & pierced his lung, and at the post-mortem in Carmarthen Infirmary they found he had been eating stamps; a white owl breathes on a branch right outside Phil the Cross's bedroom window, like a hundred people making love, and inflamed Phil so much he ran, for the first time in years, to his wife's bed and set about her so fiercely he nearly died of a fit of silicotic coughing and couldn't go to work next day; a printed form has just come that tells me I shall be prosecuted herewith unless I send in my National Insurance book fully stamped for 1950; Ivy's front teeth fell out one evening while she was playing skittles, and yesterday she told me she had been blind in one eye for twenty years; Colm's scalded chest is better, but he still has nightmares; there is little other news.

Late autumn saw the Thomases in residence in Camden Town. 'Your letter just forwarded from Laugharne to our new London house or horror on bus and nightlorry route and opposite railway bridge and shunting station,' Thomas wrote to Brinnin at the start of December, making arrangements for the new American trip. 'No herons here.' They had arrived chaotically after dark: Dylan, Caitlin, Aeronwy, Colm and the woman who cleaned and 'did' for Caitlin in Laugharne, Dolly Long, accompanied by her own child. (Llewelyn was not with them: by now he was at boarding school.) The children ran about screaming. Caitlin set up her portable papier-mâché bath to wash the baby. Dolly sat in a corner looking scared, and Thomas disappeared to the pub. Nothing was any better; some things were definitely worse. Margaret Taylor, whose idea it was to have poet and family close at hand where she could enjoy their company, became a regular visitor. As soon as Thomas heard her voice saying 'Now, duckies!' he would try and escape, locking himself in the lavatory with a book. One evening in a pub she heard them laughing about her, thinking she wasn't there. They turned round to see her weeping.

Thomas wrote little or nothing. He took part in a quiz show on the BBC Light Programme (' "Say the Word" – half an hour of fun, and a game with words') and said he was anxious to do more. He was reading on the Third; preparing for America; making lists of the stories and poems he would write this year, next year, some time. Among titles listed in the 'Poem on his Birthday' notebook are 'Poem to Caitlin', 'Poem to Colm', 'Continuation of White Giant' and 'Where Have the Old Words Got Me'. Elsewhere in the notebook, three titles of stories – 'The Album', 'Floe's Tusks' and 'The Visiting Celebrity' – are bracketed together, and against them is written: 'for the *New Yorker*'. There are further notes for one of these: 'Story begins with S. Bennet, young remittance poet, writing poem, in London bedsitting room, about Love & the Sea. He goes out, meets Flo, falls in love, finds she has false teeth, goes home, continues his poem & writes down *Floe's tusks*.' Samuel Bennet was the hero of *Adventures in the Skin Trade*; Thomas was going back seventeen years for his material.

A single sheet of manuscript, probably of this date, has the synopsis of a story, 'Such Things Do Happen'. It sounds like an echo of the *Portrait* stories – 'Henry and Fred. Fred the eggeron, the stooge, Henry the real potential writer. Provincial 18–20. Begin with John O'London's literary meeting.' It had traces of 'Where Tawe Flows' and 'One Warm Saturday'. There was to be a girl called Lorelle de Valois. Was she a reincarnation of Lola de Kenway in 'Old Garbo'? Lola was one of the chorus girls at the Swansea Empire for a week – 'Until I died, of a wasting, painless disease, and spoke my prepared last words, they would always walk with me, recalling me to my dead youth in the vanished High Street nights . . . ' But the world of *Portrait* stories,

(LEFT) Croquet on the cliffside lawn at Pennard, Gower, when Dylan and Caitlin were visiting Vernon Watkins.

(BELOW LEFT) An older Caitlin with Augustus John, who painted and seduced her when she was young; Thomas put his jealousy in a poem.

(BELOW RIGHT) Caitlin with her first child, Llewelyn Edouard, born 30 January 1939.

(LEFT) Family man.
With Llewelyn and
Caitlin, early in the
war.
(BELOW) Bosom pal.
With Dan Jones, the
Swansea composer, and
Jones's son,
another Dylan.

(ABOVE) Thomas
appeared in a one-
night performance
of a play by Picasso,
*Desire Caught by the
Tail*, in February 1950.
He was in London on
the way to America for
his first poetry-reading
tour.
(BELOW) High
tide outside the
Boat House at
Laugharne, the
place he left behind.
The Thomases lived
there from 1949 until
his death four years
later.

Some friends (CLOCKWISE, FROM TOP LEFT). Edith Sitwell detested Dylan Thomas's poetry at first but later decided he was a genius. John Davenport, critic and drinking companion. Marged Howard-Stepney, an affluent Welshwoman who ignored advice not to give the Thomases money. Cyril Connolly, one-time editor of the magazine *Horizon*, another admirer who began by scorning Thomas.

(LEFT) Caitlin outside the Boat House in the early 1950s. Dylan's absences in London and America, while she was left behind with children and debts, angered her, and she retaliated with her own infidelities.

(BELOW) Elizabeth Reitell, who helped stage *Under Milk Wood* in America, became one of Dylan's lovers.

(BELOW LEFT) With John Malcolm Brinnin, who ran a New York poetry centre, and first invited him to the United States.

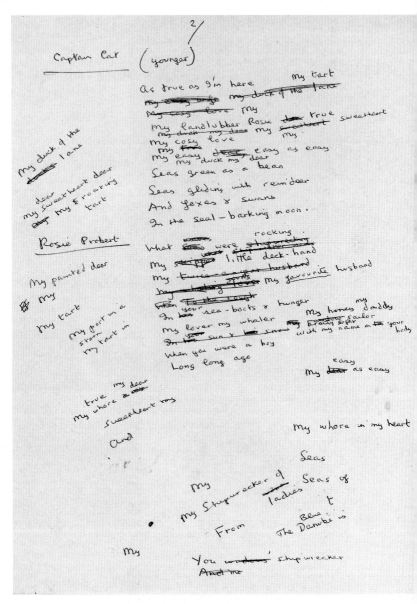

One of the hundreds of draft pages that accumulated as Thomas worked on *Under Milk Wood* at the Boat House and in America. The scene is near the end of the play, where Captain Cat dreams of his youth and talks to the dead Rosie Probert.

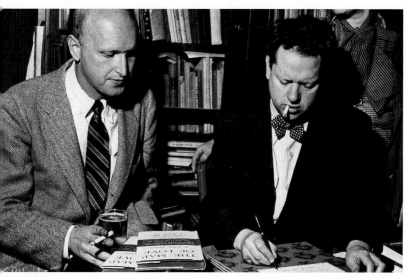

(ABOVE) Signing books in New York, John Brinnin in attendance. (BELOW) Thomas and Arthur Miller (next to him) were among the panel of guests at a symposium on 'Poetry and the Film', New York, 28 October 1953, the day after Thomas's 39th birthday. It was his last-but-one public appearance. Twelve days later he was dead.

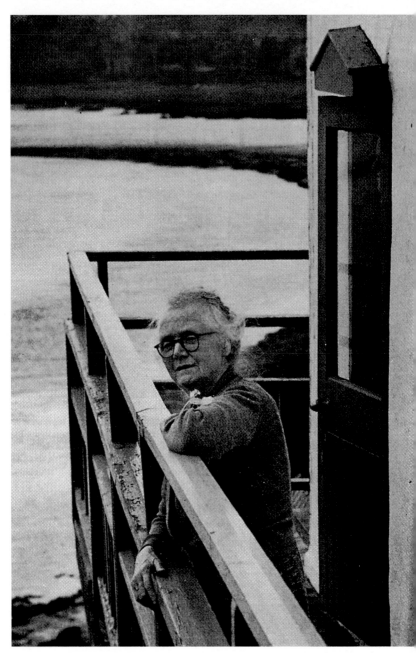

The survivor: Florence Thomas at the Boat House. Husband,
daughter Nancy and son Dylan all died within a year.

as Thomas himself had realised years before, was inaccessible. 'Such Things Do Happen', like 'Floe's Tusks', 'Poem to Caitlin' and 'Poem to Colm', was never written.

Chapter Thirteen

THE KNOT

Dylan and Caitlin arrived in America by sea on 20 January 1952 and left it by the same route on 16 May. They had ten days' holiday at the start, and a second holiday in the middle of the trip, which was marred by a shortage of cash because they were temporarily out of touch with Brinnin, the paymaster. The visit was tinged with farce; perhaps tragedy. Having crippled himself by earning and spending so much in 1950, Thomas went through the performance again, this time with Caitlin to double the rate at which money vanished. Before leaving Britain he had asked Brinnin if he knew anyone who would put them up, free, in New York, because 'the money I earn we want for The Sights, not for board'. No doubt he was determined to give Caitlin a good time, and she was determined to have one.

She added a page or two of her own to the legend, usually by being determined to get the better of her husband. They had spectacular rows in public. He enjoyed the adulation, especially the adulation of girl students, too much for Caitlin's peace of mind. She said she hated to see girls wetting their pants, screaming as if he was a pop star. She knew he was an exceptional reader of verse, but he lacked the austerity that could have let her accept his performances with good grace. A student at Sarah Lawrence College, in New York State, asked her where she would like to sit to hear the reading. 'Sit?' she said. 'I can't tell you how many times I've heard those poems. Isn't there a bar?' She resented the whole enterprise. Capable, as she thought, of putting on a gracious-lady act, she was damned if she was going to do it when all eyes were on Dylan: who, she said, was just as displeased on the rare occasions when she was the centre of attention. So, full of rancour, she went out of her way to antagonise. As Thomas went on stage for a reading, Brinnin heard her say, 'Just remember, they're all dirt.'

They made a fine pair. Thomas was talking to an historian

friend of Brinnin when Caitlin interrupted to ask sweetly, 'Are they all stuffed shirts like yourself?' Nelson Algren, the novelist, met them at a party given in Chicago by Ellen Borden Stevenson, wife of Adlai Stevenson. When he wrote to thank his hostess, he said he liked the Thomases at first, until he began to feel sorry for them. 'I'm neither poet enough nor lush enough to appreciate him fully,' said Algren. 'You have to feel a certain desperation about everything either to write like that or to drink like that ... I really marvelled at your tolerance of our friend, when he put on his small-boy-got-to-have-his-way-or-he'll-bust act. I just don't own that sort of patience myself.'

With Caitlin at his elbow, Thomas had to negotiate even more hazards than usual. In Boston and Cambridge they were guests of honour at a party given on 9 March by the *Advocate*, Harvard's literary magazine. According to Brinnin, they left soon after Caitlin asked the company, 'Is there no man in America worthy of me?' According to Professor William Alfred, who was also there, they left because Thomas detected an attempt to provoke him sexually. Alfred said that a mischievous undergraduate 'hired a model from New York, though I think she was probably innocent. Mrs Thomas was sitting at the end of the sofa, talking to a group of undergraduates. I thought she was talking Welsh, but she had been drinking. Thomas was introduced to this model, a beautiful blonde girl, and sized up the situation immediately. Maybe somebody had warned him. He got Mrs Thomas, and they went straight out.'

As with Thomas, there was more than one side to Caitlin, and she made some straightforward friendships with Americans who penetrated the carapace. She had a soft spot for Oscar Williams and his wife Gene. 'Oscar the outrageous', as she called him, pestered her to show him the poems that he knew she wrote in secret. She liked Rollie McKenna, the photographer. But her closest friend in America was Rose Slivka, in New York. Mrs Slivka, then a sculptor's wife, had met Thomas on his first visit. He made his routine proposition, and she fended him off without difficulty. When Mrs Slivka met Caitlin, she found her 'funny and cruel and real. She was the artist's wife, and that can be a terrible place to be. People were awful to her, and she fought back. "They all hang off Dylan's pants," she used to say. She was supposed to shut up and show her devotion, but she didn't want to be buried.' Mrs Slivka thought that Caitlin once had 'some sort of vision, and the vision turned to fury'. The Irish fighting drunk, Caitlin's own phrase for herself, was never far below the surface. Half the time in America she and Dylan were in a state of open warfare. Perhaps it was already too late to save Thomas from himself, but there is little sign that she tried, unless she thought that railing at him for having compromised his talents was going to help. Thomas's American literary agent, Mike Watkins, took her out to lunch one day when Dylan was out of town. He asked her about Dylan and his drink problem. 'Oh,' she said, 'that isn't the problem. I am the problem.'

The Slivkas and the Williamses lived in Greenwich Village, that small piece of lower Manhattan where the city is on a less intimidating scale. Thomas had been there often on his first visit. He said it was 'a feebler Soho but with stronger drinks', and stayed there some of the time, at an hotel in Washington Square. In 1952 he and Caitlin, having failed to find free hospitality, settled for an hotel not far from the Village, the Chelsea, which offered cheap apartments with their own kitchenette. The Chelsea, much favoured by indigent writers, was large and faintly dilapidated. It stood on 23rd Street, a broad cross-street rattling with traffic; Caitlin was soon complaining that her movements were largely confined to it. Thomas enjoyed Village bars and company. Here he could meet former London friends who had settled in New York, like Ruthven Todd and Len Lye. His favourite bar, which he made famous by going there so often, was the White Horse Tavern in Hudson Street, run by an elderly German and his wife. Thomas's American friends thought it reminded him of London, but the immediate surroundings may have suggested Swansea. Masts and funnels of ships berthed in the Hudson River stick up at the end of streets, above buildings. Stevedores and seamen drank at the White Horse. The area recalled the Swansea between the business district and the docks as Thomas would have known it: small bars, trees with little earth, and streets of quietly decaying houses, once genteel.

On this second visit, his reputation was growing steadily. At the end of February, New Directions published a small volume containing the six poems he had written since 1946, from 'In Country Sleep' to 'Poem on his Birthday'. The week before it appeared, *Time* sent a reporter from its book department. Mary

Ellin Barrett, to interview him. Her account eventually appeared elsewhere, and is valuable as another of those American attempts to observe Thomas in the literal manner that was considered unnecessary or tasteless in Britain. There was no Boswell in London or Laugharne; there was not even a reporter with a shorthand note. Mrs Barrett caught him at lunchtime, at the Chelsea, with a hangover ('Oh God, you are just in time for the laying out'), declaring he felt too squalid to eat in a fashionable restaurant ('I know a little Spanish restaurant around the corner where we can have a squalid, greasy little omelette'), comparing the maraschino cherry in his cocktail to a nipple. Caitlin and John Brinnin were there, a largely silent audience in Mrs Barrett's account. On the way to a steak house Thomas crept up behind a pigeon-toed old lady and imitated her walk. His lunch consisted of oysters and whisky cocktails; he spoke paranoiacally of the 'waves of hostility' from other tables because they were making a noise. Thomas confessed that he had written only six poems in six years ('It seems as if my faculties for self-criticism have grown more than my talent'), adding that he could write a poem in four or five months, 'If I'm fortunate.' Caitlin observed that she didn't know what he did with his time.

As usual when someone was asking him serious questions, he gave oblique or ridiculous answers. 'I used to write violent dreadful things,' he said. 'Now every time I see one of those unpleasant metaphors popping up, I slap it on the wrist, keep it in its place. I'm getting old. Now I write gently, quietly ...' At this point Caitlin told him to be serious. Asked if his self-criticism might lead him to give up poetry in favour of prose, he replied with a 'lopsided smile' that 'You don't give up poetry. It may give you up, but you don't abandon it. It's always chasing you, relentlessly – a nine-foot goblin with two noses. But when you try to turn around and catch it, *pfffft*! It's gone. I've never seen what a poem really looks like. But I keep trying.' He went on to say that the worst prose was written by ex-poets – 'The best prose is written about what happened, and why, to Tom, Dick and Harry, not about witches and dreams and goblins. Though possibly one might compromise – have a Tom Witch, Dick Dream and Harry Goblin.' While Brinnin consulted railway timetables and confided that he had personally to supervise the poet's movements, Thomas told Mrs Barrett that he was writing a film script of Homer's *Odyssey* and a novel called *Adventures in the Skin Trade* about 'one day in the life of a boy – a horrid little prig'. Then he said the novel was pretence. Caitlin said angrily that the novel existed. Thomas conceded that it did, but said the film script did not. A confusing lunch drew to a close. Thomas was due to give a reading at New York University. 'I suppose there is no escape,' he said.

Among Thomas's other visitors at the Chelsea in February were two young women, college graduates, who had what seemed at the time the fanciful notion that recordings of poetry could be commercially successful. Barbara Holdridge and Marianne Mantell were both aged twenty-two. Holdridge worked for a small publisher, Mantell for a record company. Among their ideas for records were medieval music and Shakespeare; possible backers suppressed their yawns. It occurred to them that a recording of a contemporary poet reading his own verse would add a fresh dimension to the process, not necessarily explaining what he meant, but explaining what he thought he meant. At the end of January they heard that Thomas, newly returned to America, was to read at the Poetry Center. He had caught their attention a few months earlier when *Atlantic* published 'In the White Giant's Thigh' and upset some subscribers, who didn't care for 'butter fat goosegirls, bounced in a gambo bed', even if they understood that 'gambo' was a South Wales colloquialism for a farm-cart. But Holdridge and Mantell thought it a dazzling poem. They went to the Kaufmann Auditorium to hear Thomas. After the performance they tried to see him, but could get no further than a group of frustrated admirers, held back by ushers. They sent in a note to say they had a business proposition, writing 'B' instead of 'Barbara' and 'M' instead of 'Marianne' in case he mistook their intentions.

It was a week before they managed to meet him, for lunch at the Chelsea. Caitlin eyed them suspiciously until she concluded they were not a threat. They spent an hour or two bringing the conversation back to their proposal: five hundred dollars advance against the first thousand records, and a ten per cent royalty thereafter, for the rights to forty-five minutes of his poetry, read by himself. Thomas was easily persuaded. 'As far as Dylan was concerned,' said Mantell, 'we were just two young girls with an idea and some money.' Presently a contract was drawn up

between him and Caedmon, the company they formed; no publisher was willing to back them, so the money came out of their
own pockets. The recording was made on 22 February, the day
after Mary Ellin Barrett interviewed him, Thomas having failed
to keep an earlier date. It was a public holiday, Washington's
Birthday, and there was difficulty in finding texts of the poems,
which he had not brought to the studio. They agreed on 'In the
White Giant's Thigh' and four others.* Thomas said he wanted
to read a story: he suggested 'A Child's Christmas in Wales', and
a copy of *Harper's Bazaar*, where it appeared in 1950, had to be
found. Mantell thought he was drunk when he recorded; she and
Holdridge wondered afterwards if he altogether realised what he
was doing. The record was issued on 2 April, and sold modestly.

As for the backbone of the second visit, another forty or so
poetry readings, the pattern was much as before. Where Thomas
visited a campus on more than one trip to America, local memories confuse the occasions. Perhaps his patter was more accomplished, his style a shade brassier. But events came out of the
same mould. At the University of Vermont (15 February) he
performed in the chapel and said he hoped the walls wouldn't
crumble; next morning his hosts noted that he was taking barbiturates at breakfast. At Skidmore College, New York State (13
March), a senior girl student fell off her chair, drunk; Thomas
appeared sober. At the University of California (15 April) he
answered questions for the university magazine:

Q: Who do you think is writing the best poetry at present?
A: Is it a competition?
Q: Mr Thomas, do the English people read poetry?
A: A small section of them – mostly middle-aged female adolescents –
read, still, a few dead poets – but not I think for the words, but for
the hope and somewhat hairy desire that they may one dark night
meet them. Perhaps they will . . . Does poetry care if it is read by the
English people, might be a question. I do know that persons (not
people, which are political) prefer to read *about* poets rather than
read what those bleeders write . . .

At the University of Utah in Salt Lake City (18 April) he ploughed

* 'Fern Hill', 'Do not go gentle', 'Ballad of the Long-legged Bait' and 'Ceremony After a Fire Raid'.

through a student interrogation led by a noted academic, Professor Brewster Ghiselin, where he seemed to alternate between giving modest answers and laughing at his hosts. 'I know and the birds know I'm only a fat little fool ranting on a cliff,' he said, 'but it seems that I am lots of people.' Olive Ghiselin, the professor's wife, heard Caitlin say at a dinner party that she disliked dogs. Thomas said, 'Of course. They know a bitch when they see one.'

By the end of the four months, Thomas was worn out again. Money had plagued them throughout, as he must have known it would. A note in his engagements book soon after they arrived reminded him to write to 'Marged (re money)'. In Arizona in mid-tour a brief holiday with the painters Max Ernst and Dorothea Tanning was crippled because the Thomases arrived penniless, having somehow exhausted the four hundred dollars that Brinnin had given them to last six days. A postcard to Daniel Jones from Arizona, dated 21 March, said:

> Caitlin & I are buried in the Tuzigoot stone teepee
> on the Other side of this card.
> We were killed in action, Manhattan Island, Spring, 1952,
> in a gallant battle against American generosity.
> An American called Double Rye shot Caitlin to death.
> I was scalped by a Bourbon.
> Posthumous love to you & Irene...

Llewelyn's school fees haunted them wherever they went. Early in the trip, when the school was threatening to send him home unless they were paid, Thomas said he was hoping to squeeze a thousand dollars from a woman of means in Cambridge, Mass. Caitlin was rude to her, and the offer was withdrawn (though whether there was really a thousand dollars, or any dollars, at stake, is another matter). Near the end of the trip, Caitlin's mother sent a telegram to say that Llewelyn had been dismissed from the school. Thomas swore he had sent the money from San Francisco.

There are hints of another discomfort. At Utah, he laughed uneasily at himself as the 'fat little fool' and 'a little fat man come to make a fool of himself'. Was this the old obsession with his 'littleness', his inadequacy? At lunch with Mary Ellin Barrett he had noted the 'waves of hostility'. Permanently on the defensive, he was always vulnerable. Twice there were odd stories of Thomas assailed by strangers. Rose Slivka was in the White Horse when a student approached him and said, 'I want to say to you, Fuck you, Dylan Thomas.' At Sarah Lawrence College he told Alastair Reid that a man had just whispered, 'I'll tell you what, Dylan Thomas, if you hadn't written any poems, nobody would have heard of you.' It is not unusual for famous writers to be accosted. But on both occasions, Thomas seemed unduly affected. 'He kept repeating it,' said Reid. 'It had gone through him like a knife.'

His last engagement of the tour was a 'farewell performance' at the Poetry Center on 15 May. From the platform Brinnin declared that he was the Center's favourite son. He read poems by Yeats and an extract from Sean O'Casey's autobiography, making a slurred attempt at an Irish accent. His voice sounded heavy with fatigue. 'I'm going to read a poem of Gerard Manley Hopkins,' he said, and paused. ' "The Golden Echo and the Leaden Echo".' There was a longer pause. Under his breath, and stumbling slightly over the words, he said, 'Thank God my s-ship goes early.' No one laughed. For once, the old ham wasn't joking.

By 1952, Thomas and his publishers had decided it was time to consolidate his reputation. Nothing substantial had been published in Britain since *Deaths and Entrances* in 1946. Two of the six poems he had written since then, 'Lament' and 'Do not go gentle', had not appeared in any form in Britain; the second, perhaps, was withheld so that Thomas's father, seriously ill with heart trouble, would not see it. All six had appeared in American magazines, in three cases* following earlier publication in the Italian *Botteghe Oscure*. These were more lucrative markets, paying in hundreds of dollars where British magazines would have paid in tens of pounds. Thomas's name was widely known through his radio work. But his standing as a poet was due for reappraisal. The only recent excuse for examining his work had been a critical study by Henry Treece, much of it written before the war, finally published in 1949 with the equivocal title *Dylan*

* 'Over Sir John's hill', 'Lament' and 'Do not go gentle'.

Thomas: 'Dog Among the Fairies'. Treece, lumbered with a study that had spread itself over too many years, was not sure what to think of Thomas's future. But he saw a danger: 'It is certain that he may not persist in his self-exploration without loss to himself by stagnation and artistic atrophy, and it is more than likely that he is aware of this.'

Few journals bothered to review Treece's book, which made little impact. Poetry in general was attracting less attention than in the 1930s, when Auden and Spender were seen as poets of their time. The surge of popular literacy during the war, when paperback poems and short stories flourished, was over. Paper shortages kept the literary journals thin. Nor would the reliable middle-class readership that subscribed to magazines before the war ever be quite the same. A number of the journals that printed and discussed Thomas at the start of his career had ceased publication. There was no *Life and Letters* or *Criterion* or *New English Weekly.*

The vehicle for reintroducing Thomas was to have been 'Collected Poems 1934–1950'. This was delayed, presumably until more poems had been written. By the time of Thomas's second trip to America, Dent were going ahead with production. Thomas was supposed to be providing a Preface. A telegram from Higham, sent care of Brinnin, dangled the promise of a hundred pounds from the publishers as soon as they received it. Nothing had been written when Thomas returned to Britain. The proofs awaited him, and Dent were 'howling' for them; Thomas soon saw them back at Laugharne, pausing only for a party at Margaret Taylor's in Oxford, where he managed to lose a manuscript and an overcoat. The Delancey Street interlude was over. At the Boat House he eventually decided to write his preface in verse, telling Higham that he had 'no interest whatsoever' in supplying a straightforward one in prose. Work on it progressed slowly, with many interruptions to read at literary societies and earn guineas from the BBC. Dent howled in vain, while Thomas painfully assembled his poem, with its rhymes drawing closer together towards the middle.

According to Brinnin, Thomas said the poem began as a letter to him that was never sent. A letter from Thomas to Oscar Williams the following March, when Thomas was hoping his friend would sell the worksheets, said it was 'going to be a piece of doggerel written to someone in the States on my return from there to Wales, but soon grew involved & eventually serious'. The poem praises the natural world; again it is possible to detect a forced note. Critics have pointed out that the second half is addressed exclusively to birds, fish and animals; on the back of a manuscript draft, Thomas drew a large cat looking down at a tiny mouse. He sent proofs of the book and the manuscript of 'Prologue' to E. F. Bozman of Dent on 10 September, saying 'Why I acrosticked myself like this, don't ask me' and hoping that 'it *does* do what it sets out to do: addresses the readers, the "strangers", with a flourish, and fanfare, and makes clear, or tries to make clear, the position of one writer in a world "at poor peace".' Writing to another publisher, Charles Fry, the following February, he called it a 'tangled, sentimental poem'.

While he waited for *Collected Poems* to appear, a matter of two months or so after 'Prologue' was delivered, he tried to finish his radio play. The idea of 'the town that was mad' being put on trial had to be abandoned some time in 1951. John Davenport said he was deeply dissatisfied at this failure. But by giving up the original concept, Thomas freed himself to write the kind of loose-knit script, without a plot, where he could best use his powers as a comic writer. The play was to portray twenty-four hours in the life of a seaside town. He called it 'Llareggub', resurrecting the joke from his early stories. The characters were caricatures, the town they inhabited a fantasy – funny, sad and sentimental. At this level, which was not the level of his poetry, he was better able to keep the anguish out of his writing. By the autumn of 1951 – about the time 'Poem on his Birthday' was completed – he had written half the play. He told Marguerite Caetani that he was writing it 'simply and warmly & comically with lots of movement and varieties of moods, so that ... you come to know the town as an inhabitant of it'. Eight months later, when he was back from his American tour with Caitlin, the play had made little progress. Douglas Cleverdon, waiting patiently at Broadcasting House, tried to prod him into activity. The BBC was still refusing to pay for any work by Thomas until it arrived. So he found it easier to write straightforward scripts, like his introduction to 'Spoon River Anthology', introducing poems by Edgar Lee Masters, which he wrote for Cleverdon in the summer of 1952.* In the end, thanks to Cleverdon's intervention, approval was given for a scheme suggested by Thomas whereby he would be paid five guineas every time he delivered a thousand words of 'Llareggub'. This was charitable but of little practical value, given the extent of Thomas's money troubles. The fee for the finished play was to be only ninety guineas. Cleverdon went down to the Boat House for a weekend in October to talk about the script. On the Monday Thomas wrote in his engagements book: 'SOLID WEEK ON LLAREGGUB, TO FINISH IT.' Then he had a realistic afterthought and changed 'WEEK' to 'SIXTEEN DAYS'. The play was not finished in that time, and by early November he was off again to give readings in London and Gloucester.

Collected Poems 1934–1952 was published on 10 November, dedicated to Caitlin. It contained all but one poem† from his three previous books of verse in Britain, with the addition of the six poems written since 1946, to make a total of ninety. In a 'Note' that preceded the verse 'Prologue' Thomas said the book 'contains most of the poems I have written, and all, up to the present year, that I wish to preserve. Some of them I have revised a little, but if I went on revising everything that I now do not like in this book I should be so busy that I would have no time to try to write new poems.' Thomas is said to have been depressed when he was working on the proofs. W. R. Rodgers, a poet and BBC writer, heard him say gloomily, 'I'm only a stabbed grampus,' though he 'took a sort of valedictory pride' in the poems. But the book was greeted as a major event. Philip Toynbee wrote in the *Observer* that the language Thomas had evolved was often mannered and occasionally that of a charlatan, but concluded that he was 'the greatest living poet' in English. Cyril

* It was to write this script, according to Cleverdon, that Thomas was 'locked in the BBC reference library all night'. This memory of a distant episode is contradicted by Thomas's letter to Cleverdon, sending the script from Laugharne on 19 August 1952: 'I am sorry I couldn't arrange the poems better ... but I had only that one afternoon in the library with the book.'

† The missing poem was 'Paper and sticks', from *Deaths and Entrances*; Thomas decided it was 'awful'. It was deleted at the page-proof stage, and 'Do not go gentle', which was to have been the last-but-two poem, moved back to take its place. Perhaps Thomas, with his father in mind, felt also that 'Do not go gentle' would be less conspicuous in the middle of the book. A 1940 poem not previously published in book form, 'Once below a time', was also included.

Connolly said in the *Sunday Times* that 'at his best he is unique, for he distils an exquisite moving quality which defies analysis as supreme lyrical poetry always has'. Most reviewers quoted a phrase from the 'Note', about the poems being 'written for the love of man and in praise of God'; Thomas was one of the few poets who could make such a statement and, on the whole, get away with it.

Not all the praise was uncritical, and not all the critics saw the later poems as an improvement. G. S. Fraser in the *New States-man* said that 'one's question about some of the later poems ("In Country Sleep", "Over Sir John's hill") is whether he is a little too deliberately suppressing the desperately sad and forcing the joyously assertive note'. William Empson wrote after Thomas's death that 'I was disinclined to review the *Collected Poems* when it came out during his lifetime, because I would have had to say I liked the early obscure ones best, and I was afraid this would distress him'. The review that most pleased Thomas – he said he found it 'the clearest, most considered and sympathetic' – was by Spender. Thomas wrote to him to say that no other critic had ever attempted 'to set out, plainly, the difference between the writing of poetry towards words and the writing of poetry from words – though that's, of course, oversimplification'.*

A local reporter who interviewed Thomas early in December in Llanelli, where he had gone to read poems to the theatre club, asked him about Toynbee's phrase, 'greatest living poet'. Thomas said modestly that he must have meant somebody else. It may have been more than modesty. His confidence seemed more fragmented than ever. In one of his long, purple-prose letters to Marguerite Caetani, sent in November, he talked about giving up writing altogether.

> My need – as I imagine it – to write, may be all conceit. The bellows that fan the little flicker is nothing but wind, after all ... Ach, my

---

* Spender had said that 'the romantic characteristic of Dylan Thomas is that his poems contain the minimum material which can be translated into prose. [Words] are related to one another within the poem, like the colours of a painting, by the exercise of that sensuous word-choosing faculty of his imagination, which cares more for the feel of words than for their intellectual meanings ... In this poetry the reader feels very close to what Keats yearned for – a "life of sensations" without opinions and thoughts.'

endless bleating of private woes because I am not 'allowed' to write, as though the trees would grow inward, like toenails, if I renounced this passion for self-glorification. 'Peace, let me write. Gag the tradesmen, I must write. Alms, for the love of writing.' Perhaps I should be better off pulling teeth. But even this momentary disgust I blame upon the weather. And even this disgust is 'material for writing' just as trees, and toenails, and glorification, and teeth.

As always, when he chose, Thomas summed up Thomas accurately, the writer whose reality was somehow the words on the page, not the things the words represented.

He muddled through the same old difficulties. Like a film being run again, he appealed to Spender to appeal for money. But this time the literary establishment declined to help. Marged Howard-Stepney was his best hope that winter. He had persuaded her to buy the Boat House for him, which would remove the danger that Margaret Taylor could no longer afford to let them live there for little or no rent. Marged's mother, Lady Howard-Stepney, had died earlier in the year. Marged inherited the Welsh estates, but there were difficulties in the way of her laying hands on the capital. She visited the Boat House with her advisers. Her agent did his best to curb her unwholesome obsession with wasting money on an improvident poet. The wheels turned slowly.

Family problems continued to trouble Thomas. Caitlin was steadfastly opposed to his new life as a public performer. Writing to Oscar Williams and his wife early the following year, she said that he had virtually given up writing for acting; adding that anything he sold now was either a rehash of his adolescence* or a promise of things to come, never to be fulfilled. No doubt she continued to be suspicious about other women. A couple of letters survive from Thomas to Ellen Kay, a woman he had met in America, who was now in London, written in November and

---

* 'The Followers', a story published in *World Review* in October 1952, and probably written shortly before, reads like another of his attempts, not very successful, to return to the *Portrait of the Artist* material. The Swansea trams hiss as they do elsewhere, the pub with notices on the wall is the one in 'Old Garbo', the barmaid is familiar, the adolescent boys recall childhood visits to the cinema. Thomas either remembered or took the trouble to look up the names of six or seven American actors of the silent movies – Milton Sills, Hoot Gibson, Noah Beery...

December. Writing from Laugharne on 9 December, after they had failed to meet in London shortly before, Thomas said that 'I was very sorry to miss you, and moped and snarled ... and was melancholy, tragic, and a bit sick – like an old, round adolescent. But, even if my note had reached you, it would have given you very little time. As soon as I know I'm going to London next, I'll give you plenty of warning, and if you don't come I'll cut my throat on a rusty poem.' The day before was Caitlin's thirty-ninth birthday and he wrote her some affectionate doggerel:

> For Caitlin Thomas on Her Birthday
> 8th December 1952, from her Husband
>
> Caitlin I love you
> And I always will.
> I love you in Brown's Hotel,
> The Cross House, Sir John's Hill,
> London, New York, bed.
> In any place, at any time,
> Now, then, live, dead –
>
> This is all that I
> Have to say
> On your birthday,
> My Caitlin:
> As sure as death is sure,
> So is my love for you everlasting

In the summer he had seen his sister Nancy, visiting from India, where she lived with her second husband. Nancy, now forty-six years old, was unwell. Cancer was diagnosed, and she had an operation in London before returning to India in September. Dylan was more concerned about his father's health. D.J.'s illness became critical at the start of December, and it was clear that he was dying. Aneirin Talfan Davies met Thomas in Swansea. They walked to an Italian café and sat with cups of coffee. 'There he is, dying,' said Thomas, 'cursing the only thing he's ever believed in.' Davies took this to be another sign of religious faith. Thomas was morose and unhappy. He had never ceased to regard his father with understanding and respect, and the pattern of his life was in some measure a response to D. J. Thomas and his wishes. For the early books that Dylan Thomas read, the rhythms he absorbed, and probably for his obsession with the magic of the poet's function, he was indebted to D.J. There was something about his father, the man of letters, to which he aspired.

Writing to Alfred Janes, Thomas said that 'he was in awful pain at the end and nearly blind.* The day before he died, he wanted to get out of bed & go into the kitchen where [he thought] his mother was making onion soup for him. Then, a few hours afterwards, he suddenly remembered everything, & where he was, & he said, "It's full circle now".' He died on 16 December. On 29 December, Thomas wrote to Watkins to thank him for a letter of condolence. 'I miss him a great deal,' he said. 'This is only a little – after, years? – to say Happy New Year to you & Gwen & the children.'

On 5 January 1953, he wrote to Oscar Williams, looking for more dollars, to say that 'Christmas here has been so confused that I'm still $\frac{1}{2}$ daft with it'. Besides his father's death, 'The children have been ill. Caitlin's pregnant again. The water pipes have burst & the house is flooded, etc. etc. And the etceteras are almost worse than the rest.' In London, David Higham had a feeling that events were edging towards real disaster. 'If there is a crisis in your general affairs that you would like to talk over with me, I'd be more than ready to do so,' he wrote. Later the same month, Thomas's affairs suffered another setback. Marged Howard-Stepney was found dead in her London house, where she lived with a woman companion. She had taken a sleeping drug; not long before, she had been under treatment in a nursing home. She was found kneeling with her head in a cushion, suffocated. The verdict at the inquest was misadventure. For the Thomases, her death came at an awkward moment, since she had not bought the Boat House in time. Later in the year he

---

* Thomas seemed anxious to emphasise D.J.'s blindness. On 3 December he had written to a correspondent about a function he couldn't attend, saying that his father 'has been blind and very ill for a long time'. David Hughes, the doctor who attended D.J., said that his sight failed only at the very end. Perhaps the image of the father raging at 'the dying of the light' in 'Do not go gentle into that good night' – which was written nearly two years before D.J.'s death – was too potent for Thomas to resist, and anticipated the actual blindness. See Note to pp. 319–20, about Marjorie Adix of Salt Lake City, who swore that Thomas said in April 1952 that his father had already gone blind and died.

was heard in New York complaining about the 'bastards' who prevented him owning the house and the 'bloody woman' who had died.

In February, writing a kindly letter to the poet Idris Davies, who was ill, he said they were soon to move from Laugharne. 'We're losing our love for the place, which is just as well for we're losing the house we live in too.' He hoped they would go to Rhossili, 'where an old & ratty rectory owned by a batty farmer is empty at the moment'. Rhossili was the village at the end of the Gower peninsula, where Extraordinary Little Cough ran the length of the sands. The Old Rectory was half a mile down a steep path from the village, which lacked a pub. Margaret Taylor saved them from this fate by letting them remain at the Boat House.

On the surface it still seemed that his difficulties could be overcome. *Collected Poems* won the Foyle's Poetry Prize, worth two hundred and fifty pounds, which, so Thomas told Brinnin, 'put paid to baby', implying another expensive termination (though Caitlin said this was a lie, and the abortion, her second in little over a year, was done cheaply by a backstreet doctor). Nancy's husband in India was helping to pay Mrs Thomas's rent at the Pelican. David Higham worked to rationalise Thomas's money affairs, setting aside funds for tax and bills, from an income that was now rising steadily. The BBC was broadcasting more of his poems, which brought in copyright fees. *Collected Poems* was selling briskly in Britain, and, from 31 March, in America, generating royalties. Dent were planning a new collection of stories (and worrying, still, that the early ones about burning babies and lecherous clergymen were 'too raw' for publication). Thomas had signed a contract with Oxford University Press to edit a collection of Welsh fairy tales and legends. Even the Caedmon record was bringing in a little money.

In the first few months of the year Thomas earned more than a thousand pounds in income that passed through his agents, and in other sums that came direct from Oscar Williams. These included a payment for additional paperback rights in *Adventures in the Skin Trade* and, probably, money for worksheets. On 3 March Thomas was sending Williams the 'Prologue' drafts to see what he could raise on them; a few months earlier, a hundred and forty-three worksheets of 'Poem on his Birthday' had fetched two hundred and fifty dollars from an American collector (which was fifty dollars more than *Atlantic* paid to publish it). It is true that half of all the money that went through Higham's hands was now being deducted, with Thomas's agreement, to service debts and taxes. But this was merely a sign that his affairs were in the hands of competent advisers. There is no evidence to sustain a view of him in 1953 as the penniless poet being harassed towards the tomb. It would be more accurate to see him as the feckless poet in the process of being rescued by events – late in the day, but not too late.

But that view in turn is unsatisfactory. If Thomas felt desperate, he must have had his reasons. The legend of how he was cornered by debts at the end of his life was created by Thomas himself. He undoubtedly felt harassed and trapped. 'Money' was the obvious scapegoat (as 'drink' was for Caitlin); it had caused enough trouble in the past. But whatever it may have been when he was younger and poorer, his financial muddle now was more of a symptom than a cause. What the real cause may have been is buried deep in his nature. It has been tentatively explored already; it is a matter about which it is impossible to be more than tentative.

Ever since the early poems where he wonders if he 'dares', and the letters to Pamela with their reiteration of 'littleness', there are hints of an uncertainty about himself. The decision to make poetry his career was momentous, a bold attempt to succeed on his own difficult terms. Poetry was the reality he lived by, an end in itself, an excuse for everything. To beg, borrow, steal, dodge, pretend and prevaricate was included in the poet's licence. It was a self-indulgence that worked for years and might have worked for longer if he had gone on producing the poetry that justified it. Instead, youth receded, and it became more difficult – as it must for any poet – to write the lyrical, egotistical verse that had intoxicated him when he was twenty. It is useless to suggest, as some commentators have done, that Thomas's alienation from his childhood – from Fernhill and Cwmdonkin and 'the listening summertime of the dead' – could have provided a new source of energy for the poems of middle age. What has been possible for luckier or steelier poets was not possible for him. After the backward glances of 'Fern Hill' he failed to find a lasting theme in his regrets for what had gone; and as the gap widened between past and present, so his energies waned. The fear of being unable to write was nearer the root of his troubles than the fear of not being able to pay the grocer. John Davenport said that in the last eighteen months of his life, he was in 'a great state of terror' – about his health, his nature, and his ability to write poetry.

James A. Davies has suggested that either the life he lived sapped his 'creative determination', or a decline in his powers led him to live as he did. But cause and effect are hard to separate. His way of living was to depend on others, the 'soft, white silly ravens' who would feed the poet. Did that dependency have its roots in the same savagely childish, inward-looking nature that produced the poetry in the first place? Was it life he lost confidence in or his poetry, or were they the same thing?

Some of his despair was surely driven by Caitlin, who led him towards his last spiral of hopelessness. He was the most dependent of men: she was the least dependent of women. Three months after his death she was writing to a lover that what she missed about Dylan was his need of her, not her need of him. In letter after letter to her, Thomas dwelt on this dependence, which at times seems pathological, on his 'beautiful Cat', his 'Cattle-anchor'. Having swallowed her infidelity for years, he saw it grow into open promiscuity, and did nothing, or very little. His letters to friends are silent on the subject; nor is there evidence that he spoke to them about it. No doubt Caitlin had lost patience with him. He had always been feckless and weak, enough to try a saint. Now he was ceasing to be a poet as well; Caitlin, telling Oscar Williams that all he did was rehash his adolescence, perceived the decline. And by being unfaithful to her, breaking her one-sided code, he rendered himself less lovable, less worthy of her understanding; so she grew angrier and drunker and crueller. When she had her backstreet abortion early in 1953, she didn't know if the child was Dylan's or some other man's. What was in her heart by that time? What was in his?

Thomas's difficulty in writing extended to all manner of work. 'Llareggub' was making little or no progress. A book about America that he was supposed to be producing for the publishing firm of Allen Wingate was not being written. Money had been advanced, and the head of the firm, Charles Fry, was growing impatient. Thomas wrote to him on 16 February 1953. He spelt out his troubles: his father's death ('of cancer'), shortage of money, the fact that 'early this year, my best friend in the world, a woman of my own age, died of drink and drugs' (this was Marged Howard-Stepney; she was not his best friend). Then he moved on to the real trouble. It is hard to decide how much of his letter to believe. But – allowing for the exaggerations, the laying-on of excuses, the artful efforts to keep a publisher happy – one can see it as some indication of what was wrong. Thomas referred to 'the real reason' why the book was still unwritten –

that is what you want explained. And how can I write that reason down? *That* is the thing itself: for a whole year I have been able to write nothing, nothing, nothing at all but one tangled, sentimental poem as preface to a collection of poems written years ago.

Perhaps it doesn't sound and seem – that phrase, 'I have been able to write nothing' – the throttling bloody hell it's been to me for this whole waste of a twisted year. And this letter is sure to be silly and pretentious enough without my griping on about words being the light and reason of my life etcetera. I went to America, as you know, about this time last year, and kept a jungle of a diary which I felt quite certain that I could, on my return to this wet idyllic tomb on the coast, shape and order into a book neither you nor I would be ashamed of; and I was excited, as I still am, at the thought of wheedling and hacking a proper work out of the chaos of places and people I'd scrawled in planes and trains and bedrooms-like-boilers. I went on all over the States, ranting poems to enthusiastic audiences that, the week before, had been equally enthusiastic about lectures on Railway Development or the Modern Turkish Essay; and gradually I began to feel nervous about the job in front of me, the job of writing, making things in words, by myself, again. The more I used words, the more frightened I became of using them in my own work once more. Endless booming of poems didn't sour or stale words for me, but made me more conscious of my obsessive interest in them and my horror that I would never again be innocent enough to touch and use them. I came home fearful and jangled. There was my hut on a cliff, full of pencil and paper, things to stare at, room to breathe and feel and think. But I couldn't write a word. I tried then to write a poem, dreading it beforehand, a few obscure lines every dumb day, and the printed result shook and battered me in any faith in myself and workman's pride left to me.* I couldn't write a word after that. These are the most words I have written for a year...

Now I can understand that one ordinary, I suppose, reaction would be to this endless jumbled dull confession: Here's somebody who read aloud and lectured too much too often and too long in a too-hospitable place and who became sated with public words and with his own exhibitionism. On his return, he couldn't get down to work; he missed the willing audience, the easy, but killing, money; as time went on, he became frightened of his failure to meet his literary commitments and now, groaning as though all disinterested heaven were lurching on to his head, conjures up, to a squeal of Welsh bagpipes, some vague psychological hoo ha to account for his timidity and sloth.

I know it goes deeper than that. I've lived with it a long time, or so it seems, and know it horridly well, and can't explain it. I haven't been able to write a word, of anything. Behind me, all the time, I heard, And you'll never be able to write a word again. I thought it would break me up into little self-pitying bits.

But an odd thing's happened, and only now. Or perhaps it isn't odd, and time alone has done it. Whatever the reason, since the disasters, big and midget, I mentioned some time ago, on page 93 of this letter, I've got unknotted. Now for God's sake I can't explain that; but there it is. And Higham is going to get lots of other difficulties straightened out, so that I can get down to those ogre words again without nightmares of doubt and debt, and my dear diabolic family shall be protected for a time. And I'll write that American book, or die.

Higham did, indeed, help to straighten out his affairs. But the book remained unwritten. Thomas remained as before. At the end of February he was vowing not to go ahead with a plan for a third visit to America in the spring. By the middle of March he was making the arrangements. Any escape was better than none. The knot, 'the thing itself', stayed tight.

---

* Presumably this was 'Prologue'.

Chapter Fourteen

RUNNING FASTER

Thomas's health in the last year of his life was not satisfactory. But as usual, it is difficult to put a finger on the trouble. The most persistent ailments were to do with his chest. His letters refer to flu and bronchitis. A morning cough heralded the day. Margaret Taylor said he suffered from 'breathlessness' and talked of going to live in East Anglia, where the air was drier. After Thomas's death his mother told an interviewer that he had been suffering so badly with chest trouble that 'I don't wish him back'. If he walked from Boat House to Pelican, he was 'so exhausted that he couldn't speak'. As the post-mortem on Thomas was to show, his lungs were emphysematous – they had lost some of their elasticity, and so performed less efficiently. A tendency to be asthmatic, coupled with heavy smoking all his life, could have produced this condition. Another of his ailments was gout. 'I've got gout today,' he wrote to Oscar Williams on 3 March 1953. 'God, that reads like GOAT. I mean, the one in the toe. Every time a bird flies by, I yell, thinking it might land on my toe. All I can think about is TOE.'

The possibility that Thomas had some form of diabetic condition – even an improbable scenario in which he had been diabetic all his life – was proposed in 1997 by Nashold and Tremlett. A phrase that Thomas used when he was eighteen in a letter to Pamela Hansford Johnson, 'that twice-damned, diabetic doctor', is interpreted to mean that his GP in Swansea gave him two pieces of bad news: one, that he had diabetes and two, that he might develop tuberculosis, the 'romantic' disease that Thomas liked to dwell on and his mother feared. Diabetes in some form has been hinted at for years. FitzGibbon mentioned it in the official biography. David Higham told at least one person, the writer John Prichard, that he believed Thomas was diabetic. If true, one would expect it to have been evident to Thomas himself, who was medically examined from time to time.

In 1940 he had more than one examination to prove himself unfit for the Army; in 1946 he was an in-patient at St Stephen's Hospital in London, and he may have been treated for alcoholism in 1950. On some if not all of these occasions his diabetes should have been recognised. Conceivably it was, and he chose to ignore the diagnosis, as he ignored so much else. But the theory of adolescent diabetes is far-fetched, and it is likely that if Thomas was affected by the disease, it was confined to his later years and was present in the less severe form not uncommon among overweight, middle-aged men and women who drink too much and have a poor diet.

There are stories that he was having blackouts by 1953 – it is said that he 'fell like a stone as he stood by the mantelpiece of the bar in Brown's Hotel', and was unconscious for two minutes, after which he 'ordered another drink as if nothing unusual had happened'. The blackouts, as well as the impotence that has also been rumoured, can be fitted into the diabetic scenario; but they fit equally well into others. His lifetime history of heavy drinking underlies any medical assessment. Whatever his degree of ill-health, he didn't consult the family doctor at St Clears, David Hughes, who looked after Caitlin and the children; nor, as far as Hughes could tell, did Thomas go to any of his colleagues in the county. Hughes said he thought he would have been too frightened to consult a doctor.

No question of health appears to have been raised when Thomas was planning his new trip to America. The only reason for not going, once he had made up his mind, was Caitlin. She was promised 'mythical dollars', as she called them; there was talk of a winter holiday in Portugal. But she could hardly be expected to believe him any more. As he told Brinnin on 18 March, she accused him of wanting to go for 'flattery, idleness and infidelity'. (The right words, added Thomas, making a lame joke of it, were 'appreciation, dramatic work and friends'.) Presumably to appease her, he asked Brinnin to arrange a tour lasting no longer than six weeks. A month later, after furious quarrels, he was on his way to New York, in a 'hell-ship', in rough seas, writing another of his pleas of forgiveness for 'all my nastiness, mad-dog tempers, of the last days & weeks ... To think that *I* was angry because *you* did not want me to go away. I was angry, really, only with myself, because I did not want to go away and yet was going. But I shall bring money back & we will go [to] the sun very soon.' Meanwhile the sea rocked, the engines screamed, the wind howled and despair was in 'everything except in our love'.

Thomas arrived on 21 April. His programme in America included the usual campus readings. But this time the centrepiece, when he had finished it, was to be 'Llareggub' on the stage. Brinnin hoped he would be bringing the complete manuscript. Thomas disappointed him, but said there would be no difficulty in having it ready for its first performance in mid-May, when he was back in New York. Before leaving for his first engagement, in Boston, Thomas met Brinnin's assistant at the Poetry Center, appointed since he was last in America, a self-possessed young woman called Elizabeth Reitell. Neither took to the other. It was her responsibility to arrange the stage production, and to begin with, her only interest in the visiting poet with the reputation was in laying hands on a text so that she could begin rehearsing the actors. Thomas was evasive about the unfinished manuscript, frivolous about its content. As Reitell remembered it, '*He* thought, she's one of those cold American girls. *I* thought, why all the fuss over this fool?'

Thomas's engagements, which also sent him south to Washington DC and Philadelphia, were mainly in New England. In between, he worked on the play. At some point in previous months it had acquired its title of *Under Milk Wood*. According to Brinnin, Thomas suggested it to him in a taxi, when they met briefly in London the previous autumn.* In Cambridge, Mass., on a Sunday evening, 3 May, an American audience heard *Milk Wood* for the first time when Thomas read a still unfinished version of it. Overnight he lost the manuscript; it was found next day, on top of a piano at a house where he had been to a party.†

* The title has never been satisfactorily explained. The wood, identified as 'Milk Wood' only briefly in the play, is of no special significance. One ingenious critic has suggested a connection with the milkwood tree, which secretes latex. The implication – since the wood is a haunt of 'courting couples' – is that Thomas was making a private joke about condoms; the 'milk' could also be semen. Given his sense of humour and fondness for word-play, this is not impossible.

† Mislaying the manuscript of *Under Milk Wood* became a habit. In March Thomas had left it at the Park Hotel in Cardiff, in a battered briefcase tied together with string, after reading extracts to the English society of the university college. Later in the year he famously lost it in London.

At another party, or perhaps the same one, Thomas was seen to be ill at ease, talking to Dr I. A. Richards, a literary critic. Mrs Gardner Cox, the society hostess who was giving the party, thought he was tongue-tied. Richards embarked on a complicated question about the new play, which involved references to T. S. Eliot's *Murder in the Cathedral*. The question lasted a long time, 'and at the end of it,' said Mrs Cox, 'Dylan Thomas shuffled his feet and said, "I s'pose so." And then the silence descended for ever.' The real party came later, when the intellectuals had departed, and Thomas and a few cronies stayed on with Mrs Cox and her husband. He drank moderately but was there till dawn. She remembered only one thing he said, that giraffes had been known to copulate at eighty miles an hour.

Thomas had until 14 May to have the play ready for its first performance with a cast. Between more readings he found time in Boston to see Pearl for the last time. A few days later he was back in New York, where *Under Milk Wood* was finally put together, with some makeshift passages, with less than an hour to go before the curtain went up. 'Liz' Reitell and Brinnin were at hand with two typists to turn Thomas's last-minute scribbles into typescripts for the cast – three men and two women, besides himself. Because *Milk Wood* had been conceived as a radio play (although the BBC was still waiting for it), there were many small parts involving only a few lines. The cast shared fifty characters between them, while Thomas himself took the weight of the narrative, as 'First Voice', and played three other parts as well. There were no stage directions because it was 'a play for voices', not primarily intended for the theatre. But the only incentive to finish the play for the BBC was the remainder of a ninety guinea fee. The Americans paid better, and so they had the première.

Thomas and actors sat in a row on stools, at reading desks. It was customary to tape poetry readings, and a microphone was set up, to provide the only record of Thomas performing in his own play. His opening speech – 'To begin at the beginning ...' – fell on a silent audience. The silence extended through the first jokes; perhaps no one was expecting to be made to laugh. Al Collins as Mr Mog Edwards, the draper mad with love, struck the first spark with the speech, four or five minutes into the play, where he tells his unattainable beloved, Miss Myfanwy Price who keeps the sweetshop, 'I will warm the sheets like an electric toaster.' Soon the audience realised that they were hearing a romantic comedy, and responded accordingly. Thomas was exporting a caricature, the sad and comical Welsh in their potty little village; many of the real Welsh bridled when they heard it later from the BBC, taking special offence at the bawdy passages. But *Milk Wood* created a world of its own. The play ends at nightfall; darkness lies ahead. The first performance received a long ovation. Brinnin said the cast took fourteen curtain calls before Thomas, 'squat and boyish in his happily flustered modesty', stepped out alone.

A second performance followed two weeks later, during which time Thomas went on revising and adding to the play, working closely with Reitell. The mutual dislike was forgotten and they began an affair; may have begun it even before the first *Under Milk Wood*. Reitell, a handsome dark-haired woman with high cheekbones, was thirty-three and had been through two marriages. She had been a painter, a dancer, a lieutenant in the Women's Army Corps. Thomas, anxious as always to be looked after, slipped easily into a relationship that Caitlin needn't know about. Everyone at the Poetry Center knew about the affair. The house manager, Molly Brodney,* remembered her as 'a flap-sandal-clad, artsy-craftsy type', very possessive of Thomas: the 'nurse, guard, secretary, tiger mother' who pops up when famous men need looking after. 'The few times I saw them together, Dylan was hostile to Liz and made personal, hurtful remarks I would not have accepted from God but she, of course, "understood".'

Protective for his sake and jealous for her own, Reitell joined the throng of those who were never the same again. Afterwards she confessed sadly that his vulnerability had exposed hers. At the time she found 'complete ecstasy' in his company, but failed to realise the nature and extent of his problems.

It was not the best time to fall in love with Thomas. All his solutions were temporary. His affairs grew still more complicated.

---

* Seven years later Ms Brodney married a British landowner, Mark Murray Threipland. By an odd coincidence, he was the son of Marged Howard-Stepney, Thomas's Welsh benefactor, the 'bloody woman' who disappointed him by dying before she could buy the Boat House.

At the end of April his solicitor in Swansea (Stuart Thomas, a friend from Grammar School days) had issued a writ against Time-Life International, alleging libel in an article in *Time* of 6 April. The phrases objected to concerned his drinking and general unreliability.* Stuart Thomas told friends that the motive for suing was outrage, not avarice. Time-Life meant to defend their remarks by saying they were true. Later, a private detective was hired to obtain evidence of Thomas's goings-on in New York.

His wife remained as indispensable as ever. On 23 May – while staying with Brinnin in his house at Cambridge before returning to New York for the second *Milk Wood* and more dallying with Reitell – he wrote another love letter to her.

Cat sweetheart, Caitlin my love three thousand miles away darling Cat you are so near. And your beautiful letter tore all the time and distance away and I was with you again, again in our bed with the beating seaweather, as I read the words of the letter over & over and as I saw your hand writing it and as I could see your face & hair and eyes my darling darling. You are with me always, Cat, as God is with the devout; other people around me are lousy with their personal interests, are unhappy & lost, but I am certain in my body & my heart & that makes all the miraculous difference. I'm certain that we are together; I am sure that I love you; I know that you are Caitlin; and I am smug about it. But always through the smugness comes the terrible fear: Caitlin may always be distant, perhaps she or I will die, my true incredibly-lovely Cat doesn't, can't, love me any more. I love you, Caitlin Macnamara, I love & love you. People here know that, although I would never say it. They can see the love for you around me; they can know I'm blessed. I'm damned if I'm blessed, but all the eyes of the strangers can see that I am in love with you. I love you. I'm writing this again in Brinnin's Memorial Drive; Brinnin is away; his mother is shopping, I suppose. And I love you.

As in 1950, he said he was returning to Britain later than planned.

* '... When he settles down to guzzle beer, which is most of the time, his incredible yarns tumble over each other in a wild Welsh dithyramb in which truth and fact become hopelessly smothered in boozy invention. He borrows with no thought of returning what is lent, seldom shows up on time, is a trial to his friends, and a worry to his family...'

The plane (he now seemed resigned to air travel) that he meant to catch on 26 May had been removed from the schedules because the new Queen, Elizabeth II, was being crowned on 2 June – 'rich bitches' had taken all the seats, so he would not be in London until the day of the coronation. As if to compensate, he offered a revised version of the dream of happiness.

> ... can you – this is important – make plans well-beforehand to be away with me the whole of July. Alone, without Colm or Aeron. You & me. I know that at the end of July, Llewelyn comes out of school, but somehow it must be arranged. You and me must, at the beginning of July, go together to Hollywood. We can get a boat from London, direct but slow, to San Francisco, & then fly to Los Angeles in an hour or so. Outside Hollywood, in a huge easy house in the hills, we're to stay for the month with Stravinsky. I've seen him, just now, in Boston, and we've thought of an opera and it is – for me – so simple that the libretto can be written in the time we're there. That's not just optimistic: it *can*, & will be. In advance, I'll be given 500 pounds & our passage, firstclass, & then another £500 – & then royalties until we die. We'll go back from Hollywood to Laugharne, &, in the winter, we'll go to Majorca. There'll be plenty of money. This time it's working. Majorca seems to be the cheapest place in the sun there is: I've got lots of information about it. We can stay at a pension, & then get a house & two servants. It sounds mad but I think it's true & can be done. I love you.

Near the end of the letter he asked if his sister was dead. Unknown to him, Nancy had died in India on 16 April, just as he left for America.

Perhaps he was lingering in New York for as much 'flattery, idleness and infidelity' as possible, using the news about Stravinsky to mollify Caitlin. More likely he convinced himself that the prospects were as good as they appeared. The proposal came from the Opera Workshop of Boston University, who cabled Thomas on 21 May to ask if he would be willing in principle to write a libretto for Stravinsky. Assuming that poet and composer agreed, the Workshop could offer an advance of $1500 and a similar amount on completion. This was a substantial sum. But Thomas was earning still more substantial sums by reading poetry, and they all dribbled away. In addition, he would have to produce an exacting piece of work; and he was finding it difficult to produce anything at all. For the moment he was enthusiastic. Thomas had visited Stravinsky at his hotel. The idea they discussed was a 're-creation of the world', perhaps by denizens of outer space who arrive on a devastated Earth and begin again with a new Eden. Brinnin saw him shortly afterwards, exhilarated, inventing absurd plots for operas. But no firm commission had yet been offered.

He had nine or ten days in New York before flying to London. Much of his leisure time was spent with Reitell. He liked to walk around Greenwich Village with her. She became worried by his drinking. Years later she decided that he was 'terribly, clinically alcoholic. I didn't know about those things then. There was no great muse that made Dylan drink. He drank because he was an alcoholic. He had all the devils, and some of the angels, too.' He was having attacks of gout and gastritis. He fractured his arm again, falling down a flight of stairs when drunk, while on his way to the theatre with her and another friend. At first he didn't realise he had broken a bone. At the theatre he complained loudly that his arm hurt. The play was Arthur Miller's *The Crucible*. Thomas and the friend began swearing and jeering, and were asked to leave. The evening ended in confusion. Later, writing to his son Llewelyn about the broken arm, Thomas said it happened in his hotel bedroom when he tripped over a suitcase in the dark. 'I screamed and screamed,' he explained, 'but nobody came so I had to go back to bed.' Liz Reitell took him to her doctor, Milton Feltenstein. His arm was put in plaster, and Feltenstein treated him for his gout and gastritis. It is not known what drugs he used. He also tried to persuade his patient to drink less, and to consult a doctor when he returned home. Thomas took to Feltenstein, who seems to have given injections freely; he used to talk about the doctor's 'winking needle'.

Barbara Holdridge and Marianne Mantell were alarmed at his appearance when they saw him for a second recording session. They collected him from the Chelsea in the evening. He was leaving for London next day. His features were bloated. Besides the arm in a sling, there was a cut over his eye, and his suit was smeared with what looked like vomit. He explained the broken arm with a garbled story about an incident involving a drunken sailor. In the studio he was morose, staring into space. Holdridge and Mantell felt he was under more strain than formerly, though the recording shows no sign of this; 'And death shall have no dominion' and 'Lament' were given the usual treatment. Mrs Holdridge said he had difficulty reading 'If I were tickled by the rub of love'. One version sounded like 'the rubber's love'. Thomas swore violently at the microphone. Later Mrs Holdridge 'took the tape and passed it over the eraser head, so that it couldn't become a party piece'. 'Poem on his Birthday' also caused him trouble. He failed to read the last line, 'As I sail out to die', in a way that satisfied him. With several versions on the tape, he told them to choose whichever one they liked. 'I can't,' he said. 'I'm finished.'*

Next day he flew home. In London it was the Coronation – 'miles of cock-deep orange-peel, nibbled sandwiches, broken bottles, discarded vests, vomit and condoms, lollipops, senile fish, blood lips, old towels, teeth, turds, soiled blowing newspapers by the unread mountain'. He found himself at a party. 'Oh, my immortal soul,' he wrote to Oscar Williams, 'and, oh, my tissues!' A letter to Elizabeth Reitell survives, written two weeks after his return, giving her the address of the Savage Club in London to reply to. It begins 'Liz love, I miss you terribly much,' and throws in an 'Oh, I miss you Liz' before the end, but is colourless by his standards.

In Laugharne, one of his first engagements was a visit from a journalist, Mimi Josephson. Thomas came to the door of the Boat House 'dressed in an old tweed jacket, open-necked shirt, grey flannels and a pair of plimsolls'. He talked to her about the opera, about *Milk Wood* ('prose with blood-pressure'), and about a new play he wanted to write. She was told that he was finishing a humorous novel, *Adventures in the Skin Trade*. A photographer accompanied her, and when the article appeared in *John O'London's* later in the summer, a picture showed Thomas in his hut, his plaster-cased arm resting on manuscripts, a cigarette stuck aggressively in the corner of his mouth; the affectation had not changed in twenty years. He wrote to Mimi Josephson to thank her for making 'such a splendid rumbustious figure of this melancholy bad-natured slob mouldering away in his mud-hole by

---

* The other poems recorded at this session were 'Should lanterns shine'. 'There was a saviour', 'A Refusal to Mourn the Death' and 'A Winter's Tale'.

the wish washy water'. A draft of the letter shows that he began by writing, 'this melancholy bad-natured slob who finds it as hard to write as to squeeze blood from an old pudding'.

He was back in the rut. A few things got done. Revisions were made to *Milk Wood*. One of the new sections added after America was about an undertaker. In the original version he was 'Thomas the Death' – 'To him, the eyes of all the inhabitants are full of fear. "Not me, not me," eyes scream at him.' But he was made less forbidding and renamed Evans. The *Milk Wood* revisions dragged on through the summer. In July, Thomas went to North Wales to write about the International Eisteddfod at Llangollen for the BBC. Aneirin Talfan Davies, the producer, said he was in a 'bewildered haze' most of the time. He took Caitlin and Aeron with him. It was the month he was supposed to be taking Caitlin to California. Llangollen was a poor substitute, but the opera plans were receding. Boston University was still looking for the money. In the meantime Stravinsky had written to say he would be delighted to have Thomas as a house-guest later in the year, if he didn't mind sleeping on a sofa in the living room. The date slipped back to the autumn.

Also in July, Vernon Watkins was at the Boat House. Watkins had made his own name as a poet (though he still worked for the bank) but the friendship had grown tenuous. His widow Gwen has said that the relationship between the two was never intimate. Each had something the other needed. Watkins helped with money and could offer technical advice about poems, in as much as Thomas ever wanted it. Thomas, in her view, offered an example of life without inhibitions that might have lessons for the other. 'Dylan,' she wrote, 'was [Vernon's] *alter ego*; when he supported, protected, admired Dylan it was because of the life he had never lived himself.' She saw them both as immature – 'each had turned from life, which he could not control, to words, which he could'. Only the masks they wore made them different.

At the Boat House in July 1953, Watkins saw how near the surface the violence of the Thomases came. After drinks at Brown's and lunch at the Boat House, they were sitting on the verandah when Thomas read one of Caitlin's poems, perhaps (said Gwen Watkins) to conciliate her. Vernon asked him to read 'Over Sir John's hill'. When he reached the phrase, 'Fishing in the tear of the Towy', he pronounced the word 'tare', as in tearing a fabric. Caitlin corrected him, saying 'tier', to mean weeping. Soon they were screaming 'tare' and 'tier' at one another. 'But for Christ's sake,' shouted Thomas, 'the bloody word is *there* – I wrote it!' He looked as if he was going to hit her. The children, Aeronwy and Colm, ran away screaming.

Most of the summer he was at Laugharne, with occasional trips to broadcast or read poems. In August he made his first solo appearance on television, reading a comic piece about a charabanc outing in a series called 'Speaking Personally'.* The script was not completed until after he had arrived for the broadcast. Caitlin watched him on a set at Brown's Hotel, making sardonic remarks.

Thomas is known to have worked on one poem that summer, 'Elegy'. It was not finished. The subject was his father's death:

> Too proud to die, broken and blind he died
> The darkest way, and did not turn away,
> A cold, kind man brave in his burning pride
> On the darkest day...†

Some bleak manuscript notes survive from this period. One page of a notebook has

> The magnificence of suffering.
> Live, Damn you, again.
> Dying in agony.
>
> His body burned until he died
> And then she [*sic*] slid into the fire.
>
> What were his eyes saying? My son, I am burning.

* Broadcast from the Dean's Library at St Asaph Cathedral in North Wales, because the Welsh BBC was short of studio facilities. The Controller of TV Programmes in London sent a memo to Cardiff complaining that 'Thomas did not know his story and I thought the programme was appalling.' Cardiff rejected his criticism and quoted reviews in national newspapers calling the programme 'a joy' and 'almost a tour de force'. The story, with the title of 'A Story', was later bought by the American *Harper's Bazaar*. It is now known as 'The Outing'.

† Vernon Watkins assembled the fragments and published them in tentative form. The lines quoted here are taken from the worksheets.

Other sheets have scraps of doggerel:

> Cask Bass
> Oh to bask in cask
> Bass with
> Tast.

In a letter to Daniel Jones on 24 August Thomas said:

> ... I have to see T.V. [producer] D. J. Thomas in Swansea, *and* Aneirin [Talfan Davies], but will get that over quickly and then – oh, to bask unasked in a Bass cask, etc!
>   Isn't life awful? Last week I hit Caitlin with a plate of beetroot, and I'm still bleeding. I can't finish a poem, or begin a story, I chew my nails down to my shoulders, pick three-legged horses with beautiful names, take my feet for grey walks, moulder in Brown's, go to bed as though to an office, read with envy of old lonely women who swig disinfectant by the pint, think about money, dismiss it as dirt, think about dirt...

There are some maudlin verses about his parents, perhaps written when Thomas had been drinking; perhaps scribbled for relief as the children played on the sands beyond the house, artillery thumped on the Pendine range, and poems remained inaccessible. In the notebook:

> Come back, come back, Mother
> Oh Mother, Oh Mother, Oh Mother
> Come back to your only son
> And sorry for what he done.

On a scrap of paper:

> I am blind, too, my son.
> And father, dear mother, & father?
> Is he the only one
> Who can see the green trees blow
> And the sunshine & the snow.
> No, my son, no
> Your Father is blind as well.

On a sheet drilled through with a cigarette burn:

> A little child stood at the doorway
> With wonder in its eyes
> It cd not see the fields of may
> Or the clouds in the blue skies.

Underneath is a sentence from 'A Story' – 'And over the bridge &
up the hill and under the singing wood and along the dusty road
we wove, slow cows & ducks flashing by . . .'

Drafts of a letter to Marguerite Caetani, written on or around
26 August, make disturbing reading. Thomas was concocting
another tale of woe, but the process was out of hand. Texas has
at least eight attempts, none of them completed. Each begins,
'What can I say?' He was writing, not about his financial problems, but about the problem of why he wrote her such contorted
letters. His method was to write a letter that was even more
contorted than usual:

> What can I say?
>   Why do I coil myself always into these imbecile grief-knots, sew
> myself blindfold & handcuffed in a sad sack, weight it with guilt
> and pigiron, & then pitch me to sea, so that time & time again I
> must scrabble out & unravel in a panic, babbling & blowing bubbles
> like a puny wheezy Houdini tangled with polyps . . .

Thomas was using his *Thesaurus* to help find the right word: one
of the pages has class numbers associated with the word 'knot'.
The 'Houdini' idea led to a search for the right phrase – he tried
'like a halfpenny Houdini', 'a teeny wheezy Houdini', 'a sea-
slimed Houdini', 'a sea-slugged windy Houdini'. The thought
that he is trapped is paramount. He must escape the 'man-
trapping sea', or the 'pitfall sea', or the 'sea-clutch', or the 'claws
and bars and breasts of the man-trapping seabed'. The 'freak
user of words' – his self-description to Pamela in 1934 – has lost
touch with outside reality. He is not so much writing a letter to
a woman in Rome who will send him money, as playing uneasily
with words, the things themselves, to give shapeless expression
to old fears of helplessness and death:

... time and time again I cry to myself as I kick clear of the cling of my stuntman's sacking, 'Oh, one time the last time will come and I'll never struggle, I'll sway down here forever, handcuffed and blindfold, sliding my wound-around music, my sack trailed in the slime, with all the rest of the self-destroyed escapologists in their cages, drowned in the sorrows they drown and in my piercing own, alone and one with the coarse and cosy damned seahorsey dead, weeping my tons.' What can I tell you? ... Why must I parable my senseless silence? my one long trick? my last dumb flourish? It is not enough that, by the wish I abominate, I savagely contrive to sink lashed and bandaged in a blind bag to those lewd affectionate raucous stinking cellars: no, I must blare my engulfment in pomp and fog, spout a nuisance of fountains like a bedwetting whale in a blanket...

Whatever levels of meaning can be read into Thomas's scribblings in the summer of 1953, they suggest he was in serious trouble. Brinnin, in Europe at the end of the summer, revisited Laugharne in September, and found him uneasy, apprehensive, anxious to placate Caitlin, equally anxious to run off to America again – 'almost any means of escape seemed attractive'. Stravinsky had written to say that Boston was still finding it difficult to raise the money, and that he and Thomas should make a start on their own. Brinnin tried to persuade his friend to stay in the one place, the Boat House, where he was likely to work well. When he saw this was useless, he agreed to help arrange more performances at the Poetry Center. Caitlin listened and said little.

Before Brinnin left, they went on a tour of south Carmarthenshire by car. Rollie McKenna was there to take photographs for the magazine *Mademoiselle*, which had bought the publication rights of *Milk Wood*. Dylan's mother went with them. They called at Fernhill; the owner let Dylan tour the rooms, the orchard and the barn. They went up the lane to Llwyn Gwyn and called at the Blaen Cwm cottages. In the evening they stopped at Llanybri to look at the family graves. Brinnin noted that Thomas had drunk only one glass of beer all day.

Another visitor to the Boat House was a young film cameraman at the BBC – a stranger, who saw the Thomases without preconceptions. David Gardner was with the Outside Broadcasts unit that filmed 'A Story' in the makeshift studio. Afterwards he had a drink with Thomas, who asked him to call if he was ever in Laugharne. In September he drove there and was invited to stay the night. The only eccentricity he observed was during a conversation about poetry on television, when Thomas said that it would have to be *bad* poetry, and began to parody John Masefield:

> I must go down to the fucking sea again,
> To the fucking sea and the fucking sky,
> And all I ask is a tall fucking ship
> And a fucking star to steer her by.

Young Gardner was shocked to hear such language in front of a woman. There was something uncontrolled about it. As for Caitlin, the visitor found her courteous and dignified. He remembered a 'lovely lunch', and the way she sat sewing name-tapes on Aeron's school clothes.*

Among the odd jobs with which Thomas occupied himself, while he marked time before he left for New York again, was to record a radio talk, 'A Visit to America'. He filled it with material he had used on his tours. A joke about the Elgin Marbles (in which somebody, perhaps a man from the BBC, or a Welsh hairdresser showing off in London, speaks 'like a man with the Elgin Marbles in his mouth') had been used from Llanelli to San Francisco. On the same day, 5 October, Thomas recorded a brief contribution to a radio programme about Laugharne that was to be broadcast on 5 November: 'Off and on, up and down, high and dry, man and boy, I've been living now for fifteen years, or centuries, in this timeless, beautiful, barmy (both spellings) town...'

Caitlin was not going to America, though she was to travel as far as London, where she and Dylan would spend a little time together. The evening before they left, they went to the cinema in Carmarthen. According to Florence Thomas, Dylan fainted

---

* Gardner, telling the story in 1992, was speaking as an ex-lover. After Thomas's death, Caitlin sought him out, and he was involved with her for two or three years. He believed she had always been in love with Dylan. When he stayed at the Boat House, they never used the double bed where she had slept with her husband.

during the film. Dr David Hughes, who was at the cinema that evening, disputed this. He and his wife were sitting immediately in front of the Thomases. Before the film started, Caitlin 'asked me if I would see Dylan because he had been having severe headaches and was off to America in the morning'. He said he would take them back to his house in St Clears after the film and examine him there. But when the lights came on, Dylan had vanished, probably to the Boar's Head. The doctor went home without seeing him. His mother believed he had a premonition of death; when he left next day, he came back three times to kiss her. Mrs Dark had cut his hair for the journey. Mr Dark, Caitlin's lover, had supplied him with a new pair of trousers at cost price. It sounds like *Under Milk Wood*.

In London the Thomases stayed at Hammersmith with Harry and Cordelia Locke. They were there longer than expected because the plane ticket was sent to Laugharne instead of London, and Thomas missed the original booking. Caitlin was still opposed to the trip; the atmosphere was strained. A few people were to recall meeting Thomas during the week or ten days he was in the city. Most of the time he seems to have been melancholy rather than drunk. Constantine FitzGibbon met him by chance outside Broadcasting House, and they drank together in a deserted bar; his future biographer found him 'subdued, even sad'. FitzGibbon wrote: 'He certainly did not seem to me to be at all suicidal in his attitude, though others who saw him during these days have told me that he talked, almost willingly, of his impending death – but then he had been doing that, in one way and another, for thirty years.' This time the circumstances were different. Thomas felt threatened as never before. Nevertheless, the picture of Thomas in London during those last days is utterly different from the scenes that were to follow in New York. There was an evening with Philip Burton, when Thomas talked energetically about a new play he hoped to write. The tentative title was 'Two Streets'.* In a South Wales town that might have been Swansea, two children, a boy and a girl, are born in

---

* Thomas telephoned Richard Burton from Philip Burton's apartment, hoping to borrow two hundred pounds 'for the education of my children'. Failing that, he offered to sell the rights to his new play, 'the story of a love affair between two streets', for the same amount. Richard Burton refused.

neighbouring streets. Strangers, their lives slowly come together. Thomas was vague about the details. He wanted a midwife who would attend both births. Philip Burton, as a drama producer, argued about the opening scene. 'Please,' said Thomas, 'please let me have two prodigiously pregnant women.' Burton found him equally vague about the opera. Now that the time to visit Stravinsky in California was approaching, he may have wondered if he would be able to write the libretto. FitzGibbon, to whom he spoke about the project, thought it frightened him. Margaret Taylor believed it would have overwhelmed him, like the *Peer Gynt* fiasco on a larger scale.

To Douglas Cleverdon's relief, the script of *Milk Wood* was delivered, after more last-minute delays, on Thursday, 15 October. Cleverdon had it typed for duplicating, and returned the original to Thomas on the Saturday. Thomas lost it over the weekend; before he left for America, he told Cleverdon he could keep it if he found it. A day or two later Cleverdon tracked it down to a Soho pub, with interesting legal consequences. In the meantime, Thomas had been given duplicated copies of the play to take with him to America.

A mixed party saw him off at the Victoria Air Terminal on 19 October. Cleverdon was there. So were Mrs Taylor and the Lockes. Thomas was sober and unhappy. Caitlin is said to have had premonitions of disaster. But it was the kind of occasion that memory distorts as people silently rearrange events, making significance out of nothing. Cordelia Locke's last glimpse of him was through the window of the coach; he was giving a thumbs-down sign.

Chapter Fifteen

ALCOHOL AND MORPHIA

Dylan Thomas's troubles had begun long before, and what happened in New York is best seen as the end of an inevitable process. It is true that there was one major element of chance in the final events that led to his collapse and death. But Thomas put himself, or let himself be put, in a position where accidents were likely to happen. A psychiatrist offers an analogy: 'A depressed, desperate middle-aged man whose marriage is in ruins, and who has failed to realise his aims, may take to driving a car in a reckless way because he does not value himself and his life. He is not actually suicidal. He doesn't care.' Margaret Taylor said that her friend died of being Dylan Thomas. Caitlin, who could say one minute that he might have lived to be a grand old man of letters, could say the next that he wanted to be dead before he was forty; no doubt she was influenced by her own physical decline, which she felt keenly.

Thomas arrived in New York on Monday, 19 October, and went to stay at the Chelsea. He had been expected there several days earlier, so his reservation had lapsed, and he had to make do with a small back room. He complained that it was dingy. 'The cockroaches have teeth,' he remarked to Liz Reitell, who was his close companion from the moment he arrived. He spoke of having 'escaped' from London, and upset her by referring to Caitlin as 'my widow'. When they were walking near Greenwich Village the day after his arrival, he saw a poster advertising a film about Houdini, and said that to be hopelessly trapped was the worst horror in the world; later he gave her the manuscript of his 'Houdini' letter to Marguerite Caetani. For two or three days he seems to have been abstemious. To Reitell they were 'the loveliest days I had with him. He wanted to take walks. He wanted to eat. But he was also frightened.' Then he made himself ill with a heavy bout of drinking. He was nauseated and vomiting at a rehearsal of *Milk Wood*, which was to have two performances at the weekend, and told Herb Hannum, a friend of Reitell, that he was too tired to sleep. In Brinnin's account,* he said to Hannum, 'I've seen the gates of hell tonight. Oh, but I do want to go on – for another ten years anyway. But not as a bloody invalid.'

Reitell later insisted that there was no question of Thomas wanting to die: 'His instinct for life was very strong. He was killed physiologically, by alcohol, not psychologically. During his last two conscious weeks he made strenuous efforts to get better.' But another conversation with Hannum the following day, as Reitell reported it back to Brinnin for his book, had sinister undertones. Thomas said he would have to 'give up something'. Hannum asked if he meant life. Thomas's reply, with the original ellipses, is given as: 'No. I don't know ... I want to go on ... but I don't know. I don't know if I can. I don't feel able any more. Without my health I'm frightened. I can't explain it ...'

Towards the end of the week (probably on Friday, 23 October) Liz Reitell took him to Milton Feltenstein for a consultation. The doctor warned him about his way of living and gave him an injection of ACTH, a cortisone analogue. Steroids were a novelty in 1953. Presumably Feltenstein was using them to control Thomas's general symptoms of malaise, and possibly for his gout. For a while Thomas seemed better, though Brinnin was shocked to find him looking so unwell when he arrived from Boston during the final rehearsal for the Saturday *Milk Wood*. ('His face was lime-white, his lips loose and twisted, his eyes dulled, gelid, and sunk in his head.') At the Poetry Center they noticed that he

---

* For events between 19 October, when Thomas reached New York, and 4 November, when he collapsed, Brinnin's chief source of information was Elizabeth Reitell; he was in New England except for the weekend of 24–5 October. She said that she wrote 'enormously long notes' for him, and that they spent days going through her narrative. Neither she nor Brinnin had the notes in later years, or knew what became of them. Brinnin even suggested they may never have existed. This chapter is based on the account in Brinnin's book; on conversations with Reitell, Jack Heliker, David Lougée, Rose Slivka and others; on mss by Ruthven Todd at Texas; on certain medical and other papers, and on conversations with a diabetologist, Dr Ken Paterson. Reitell is a key witness in any account of Thomas's last days; her testimony to Brinnin included verbatim reports of things that Thomas said, to her and to others, of as much as several hundred words at a time. For obvious reasons her narrative has to be viewed with caution. In 1953 she was emotionally involved and deeply upset; later she found it difficult to rake over her past.

was sweating, and had blotchy skin and unpleasant breath. Some of his remarks to Reitell were hurtful. At a party given by Rollie McKenna that evening, Thomas was seen to be avoiding alcohol. Asked why, he said, 'It's just that I've seen the gates of hell, that's all.' The real experience, assuming it had been real, was already turned into words, into 'material'.

Over the weekend both Reitell and Brinnin felt that Thomas was drawing apart from them. On Sunday there was a matinée performance of *Milk Wood*, reportedly the best of the four given in New York. At a party afterwards Thomas gulped whisky and disappeared upstairs with a woman. At a second party, he, Reitell and Brinnin were reconciled in a tearful scene. ('Standing behind me as he held me very firmly, Dylan spoke the last words I was ever to hear him say directly to me: "John, you know, don't you? – this is for ever." ') By now Reitell was aware of the dangers of entanglement with someone as demanding and destructive as Thomas, who would 'never let you go but never let you help him'. When they were returning to Greenwich Village in a taxi later that night, she stopped it near her own apartment and hurried away, leaving him to his own devices. This seems to have been as far as her attempt at self-preservation went. Next day, Monday, 26 October, he summoned her by telephone to the Algonquin Hotel, where she found him at the bar in mid-afternoon, drinking whisky and raving about war, blood and mutilation. He implied he had taken part in wartime combat himself, that his family had been in danger, that Turkey or the Middle East had been involved. It seems likely that the Commando captain, bursting into the bungalow at New Quay with his machine-gun, was in his mind.

Outside, Thomas made faces at passers-by. He was swearing and staggering. Reitell took him to a cinema and then to a bar, and although he became calmer, he continued to behave irrationally. He said repeatedly that he feared he was going mad and that 'sex' was involved in his mental state. When he saw a boy and girl with their heads together, he said, 'How filthy!' Soon he was telling his companion that he was a puritan. He recovered during the evening, but it seems likely that he had been temporarily deranged. Reitell was shaken by the episode. Perhaps Thomas was additionally upset because the next day was his thirty-ninth birthday. A stranger approached him as they left the bar, after midnight, and asked if he was Dylan Thomas. Thomas said he was only posing as the poet. Next evening he had to leave a birthday party at the Slivkas because he was unwell. Reitell took him back to the Chelsea, where he flung himself on the bed and talked of what a 'filthy, undignified creature' he was. He wept and spoke of his 'agony'.

Yet on the next two days, 28 and 29 October, he carried out two engagements without mishap. On 28 October he spoke at a symposium on 'Poetry and the Film' organised by a group called Cinema 16, playing his usual game of needling the intellectuals. A transcript of the session exists. Maya Deren, who made experimental films, was another member of the panel. When she spoke about the 'vertical' nature of poetry and contrasted it with the 'horizontal' nature of drama, Thomas was baffled, or pretended to be. He made some unfunny jokes about up-and-down movements and said that for him, poetry in the cinema 'might have been in the UFA films or something that I saw as a child. Or somebody coming down some murderous dark, dark silent street, apart from the piano playing. Or it might have been a little moment when Laurel and Hardy were failing to get a piano up or down a flight of stairs. That always seemed to me the poetry.' Pressed by the chairman, he fell back on his old statement of method: 'Well, just as a poem comes out ... one image makes another in the ordinary dialectic process (somebody left out the word "dialectic", well, I may as well bring it in, you know). So, as in a poem one image breeds another, I think, in a film, it's really the visual image that breeds another – breeds and breathes it. If it's possible to combine a verbal image to a visual image in this sort of horizontal way, I'd rather see horizontal films, myself. I like stories. You know, I like to see something going on.' (Laughter and applause.)

On 29 October, a Thursday, Thomas gave a public reading of poems at lunchtime at the City College of New York (the 'proletarian Harvard'), travelling by subway to uptown Manhattan because, he told Reitell, he was conserving money so that he would have something to take back to Laugharne. After the reading he moved on to a near-by restaurant with a small party from the college; he drank beer and appeared normal. His next engagements were not until the following week. There was still no decision about Stravinsky and the opera, but he was to read in New England and Chicago. For the moment he was free to enjoy himself, if that is what he was doing, in New York. On Thursday and Friday he spent his time with Liz Reitell and at least one other woman, and attended parties. On Saturday night, 31 October, he was drinking heavily, according to the detective hired by *Time*.* At nine p.m. he arrived, drunk, at the White Horse with two friends, Dave Slivka, and David Lougée; he was observed to drink lager, beer and whisky, and was said (erroneously) to have been drinking non-stop for ten days. At Toppers bar and grill on 7th Avenue he spoke of sexual impotence and said how much he loved his wife; other women were only substitutes for Caitlin. He described his first sexual relations (at the age of fifteen), and said that when he had gonorrhoea as a teenager, it took a month to cure, and had to be concealed from his family. All he wanted, he said, was to be regarded as an average human being. At two thirty a.m. he was 'seen taking Benzedrine'. It must have been a tiring night for the detective.

On Sunday morning, 1 November, Thomas spoke to Reitell on the phone, and told her that he had a faint memory, from the night just passed, of taking a dislike to a woman who was with him in a taxi, and of throwing her into the street. Nothing further about the incident came to light; Reitell wondered later if it was a confused version of what had happened a week earlier, when she left the taxi to go home by herself. It was probably during this weekend that Thomas said he saw a mouse at Howard Moss's apartment. On Sunday night, at the same apartment, he is unreliably reported to have scratched his eyeball on a rose-thorn.

At the Chelsea on Monday morning, Ruthven Todd found him in bed, unwell but making lugubriously comic remarks about his condition. Todd noted that he was drinking beer, and that an unopened bottle of Old Grandad, his favourite American whisky, was on the dressing table. During the day he was out and about with Reitell. They were invited to dinner at the Colony

---

* A small notebook used by FitzGibbon when he was preparing his biography of Thomas is among FitzGibbon's research material deposited at Texas. A page headed 'TIME DETECTIVE' contains notes made by FitzGibbon, presumably from the *Time* material, though not used by him in his book. It mentions events on four days: 28 and 31 October and 2 and 4 November.

Restaurant. Thomas behaved normally except that he was not wearing socks.

On Tuesday, 3 November, Thomas was again in bed at the Chelsea, alternately drinking with friends who looked in, and sleeping. Todd was there when Thomas offered a drink to the maid who arrived to clean the room. She accepted a whisky from the bottle of Old Grandad, which was opened for the purpose. Brinnin says that one of the callers was a lecture agent, and that Thomas signed a contract guaranteeing him a thousand dollars a week. Later in the day, complaining that he was exhausted, he went out with Reitell to keep two appointments for drinks, but returned to the Chelsea in mid-evening. In the bedroom he seemed to break down entirely, weeping, telling her that he wanted to die and 'go to the garden of Eden', that he couldn't bear the thought that he would never see Colm again, that there was 'an illumination' about Caitlin. At two o'clock in the morning he got out of bed, declaring that he must have a drink. Reitell failed to dissuade him. He was absent for an hour or an hour and a half. When he returned, he spoke the words that were quickly embedded in the legend: 'I've had eighteen straight whiskies. I think that's the record.' Then he told Reitell, 'I love you, but I'm alone,' and fell asleep.

It is not a satisfactory story. In the first place, why did he go out at all when there was whisky in the room? Ruthven Todd and other friends tried to establish how much whisky he had drunk that night. The bottle of Old Grandad was found to have only the one drink missing. The friends went to the White Horse, where Thomas had apparently been seen. The proprietor concluded, on the evidence of his stocks, that he could not have drunk more than six whiskies, or eight if two regulars who usually took Old Grandad as a nightcap had changed their brand. No one had noticed anything excessive about Thomas's drinking. Reitell, on the other hand, thought that he used a bar closer to the Chelsea. But Todd was convinced that Thomas had been exaggerating. This was only to be expected. In a manuscript of *Adventures in the Skin Trade*, a character was made to say, 'I remember once I drank twenty-nine Guinnesses straight off.' Then Thomas had second thoughts and altered it to read 'forty-nine Guinnesses'. In Cornwall in 1937 he boasted that he had drunk forty pints of beer, an unlikely feat.

If Thomas did, in fact, drink eighteen US measures of whisky (equivalent to at least twice that number of British 'singles'), he had taken a dangerous amount of alcohol. Death could result from direct brain damage; or a lack of oxygen if breathing was depressed by the effect on the brain of alcohol. Even a dozen double whiskies, British measure, drunk over a short period, may be fatal. The phrase that came to be used of Thomas's collapse was that he had suffered 'a severe insult to the brain'.*

But in that case, events should have followed a different course. In all probability he would have collapsed within a few hours. Instead, he slept until the middle of the morning – it was now 4 November – when he woke saying that he was suffocating and must have some air. Reitell walked with him to the White Horse, at least half a mile away, where he had 'two glasses of beer' before returning, unwell, to the Chelsea. Feltenstein was sent for. Brinnin said he gave Thomas 'medications that would relieve his sufferings, temporarily at least', after which Thomas slept fitfully through the afternoon. By this time most of his blood-alcohol would have been eliminated; although if his nocturnal drinking had been heavy, he could still have been drunk to some degree, with the lunchtime beers adding marginally to the effect. But he was suffering severe discomfort. Gastritis, which had troubled him for years, was causing him pain and making him vomit; the attack could have been brought on by drinking spirits on an empty stomach. Liz Reitell remembered 'ghastly racking spasms'. He also had pain from his gout. Feltenstein was summoned again, and injected more ACTH. When he had left, Thomas promised her that he would begin a new regime, as the doctor insisted. During the evening he slept for 'a couple of hours', vomited again, and presently told her that he was seeing things – 'not animals ... abstractions'. She thought she recognised delirium tremens, and for the third time Feltenstein came to the hotel.

What happened then was debated for years, although the

---

* Brinnin quoted an unnamed doctor – 'we learned that it was now established that Dylan had sustained "a severe insult to the brain" and that this was due to direct alcoholic poisoning of brain cells and brain tissue'. But as the post-mortem made clear, 'direct alcoholic poisoning' was never established. FitzGibbon went further and said the post-mortem gave the cause of death as 'insult to the brain'. No such phrase appears in the report. The unnamed doctor was probably William Gutierrez-Mahoney.

answer was on record all along in the office of the Chief Medical Examiner for New York City. Brinnin wrote, 'As Dylan, raving now, begged to be put out, the doctor gave him a sedative.' At the time it was rumoured that this sedative was morphine. Howard Moss, who was friendly with Feltenstein, asked him if it was true. Feltenstein replied, 'He was in pain.' But to assert publicly and positively that a doctor gave morphine to a patient in Thomas's condition was more than any third party cared to do. Feltenstein refused to answer letters on the subject, a wise course. What he had done was to inject Thomas with half a grain of morphine sulphate, the form in which the drug is commonly given. Even without any special reason for avoiding morphine, it is too powerful and addictive to be administered merely for discomfort and malaise. The medical consensus is that under no circumstances would it be given for gout or gastritis. Reitell described Feltenstein as 'rather a wild doctor who thought injections would cure anything'. Whatever his logic, his motives were still unexplained when he died in 1974.

He not only gave Thomas morphine, he gave him what is, in medical terms, a large amount. A normal dose to relieve acute pain is one-sixth of a grain. Thomas received three times as much. In the absence of other factors it is well below a lethal dose. But other factors were present. The 'breathlessness' from which Thomas had suffered in Wales was probably the result of asthma and smoking, which impaired the function of his lungs. Conceivably there was still sufficient alcohol in his blood to depress his breathing. It is possible that the pneumonia which soon developed had begun already; it could have been caused by inhaling a particle of vomit. If Thomas was suffering from any difficulty in breathing, the effect of half a grain of morphine could be catastrophic.

In any event, the injection was given, and once more Reitell was left alone with him. According to Brinnin, Feltenstein suggested that someone should stay with her, in case 'delirium tremens might make Dylan uncontrollable'. She telephoned a painter, Jack Heliker, who arrived within a few minutes.*

---

* Perhaps there were other visitors that night. The detective was prowling; a bare entry in FitzGibbon's 'TIME DETECTIVE' notebook refers to a 'get-together' at the Chelsea, then says: 'Reitell. Friends left.'

Between dozes, Thomas said that he still had 'the horrors', and spoke of 'abstractions, triangles and squares and circles', echoing his words to Pamela long ago, when, neurotic and sleepless, he told her how he lay in the dark and thought of 'God and Death and Triangles'. Thomas's life was marked with these ghostly echoes. Reitell and Heliker sat, talked and waited. Making conversation, she mentioned that a friend of hers with DTs saw white mice and roses. Thomas, playing with words, said, 'Roses plural or Rose's roses with an apostrophe?' She was lying on the bed beside him, fully dressed. Heliker was in the room. His recollection is that Reitell telephoned him at about 11 p.m. When he arrived at the hotel, he 'understood that Dylan had been given a sedative shortly before. When I came into the room, Liz said, "This is Jack," and Dylan sat up in bed and said, "Hello, Jack." He wanted a drink very badly, but she wouldn't give him one.' Heliker thinks he sat in the bedroom for about an hour. On a desk or table near the bed were some of Thomas's papers, and Heliker remembers reading a line that 'went something like, "He cried for death in his mother's breast"'. This must have been from the unfinished 'Elegy', which has the line, 'Above all he longed for his mother's breast'. According to Heliker, Thomas's last words were: 'After thirty-nine years, this is all I've done.'

Reitell said she thought he was falling asleep. Then she heard him breathing with 'a terrible sound'. He was unconscious. Feltenstein was telephoned and arranged for an ambulance, although it's not clear if he returned to the hotel at any stage. The hospital he contacted was St Vincent's, the oldest charity hospital in the city, which was staffed by Roman Catholic nuns. The call requesting an ambulance is thought to have been made about 1 a.m. on 5 November. The time of Thomas's admission is in the official record at almost an hour later, a long time for an emergency. His breathing was severely impaired, and it is said that as late as 2.30 am., doctors were still having problems with his respiration.

The medical notes, as later summarised by the hospital for the New York Medical Examiner's Office, said, 'Patient brought into hospital in coma at 1.58 a.m. Remained in coma during hospital stay. History of heavy alcoholic intake. Received $\frac{1}{2}$ grain of M.S. shortly before admission ... Impression on admission was acute alcoholic encephalopathy, for which patient was treated without response.'

News of this 'alcoholic encephalopathy', which simply means damage to the brain by alcohol, was released at the time, and passed into popular myth as the 'insult to the brain', thus confirming what everyone thought they knew, that the poet died of drink. But the true 'insult' was almost certainly the half-grain of morphine, which caused the breathing difficulties, deprived the brain of oxygen and set in train the fatal process. This was Feltenstein's fault, and he and the hospital kept quiet about it. I came across the evidence more than twenty years later – shortly after Feltenstein died with his lips still sealed – and read Thomas's death in that context. A later investigation, suggesting that Thomas was an undiagnosed diabetic, and putting forward an extravagant theory in which the disease is seen as the crucial factor in his death, has little to commend it.*

---

* Nashold and Tremlett, *The Death of Dylan Thomas* (1997), gave a detailed narrative of events at St Vincent's, here summarised: Two young doctors, McVeigh and 'Turnball' (a pseudonym), who saw Thomas on admission on 5 November, concluded within twenty-four hours that he was suffering from 'diabetic shock'. Feltenstein, although he had no authority at the hospital, refused to accept this, despite evidence of raised sugar levels, and threatened to ruin their careers if they interfered. On 6 November, the Friday, they appealed successfully to the head of neurology, William Gutierrez-Mahoney, who barred Feltenstein from the case. Mahoney is said to have told him, 'Alcohol may have been a factor in this case, but the primary cause of the patient's condition was your overdose of morphine and his incipient diabetes.' Mahoney, McVeigh and Feltenstein are dead. When Nashold researched the medical history in 1996, 'Turnball' was alive but unwilling to be identified; two other doctors who had been at St Vincent's were also interviewed. There is too much hearsay and reconstruction in the narrative to prove anything. It appears to ignore the best clinical explanation consistent with modern diabetology, but not available in 1953, that the patient's raised sugar levels in blood, urine and spinal fluid were the *result* of brain damage – brought about by the morphine injection, given to a man with a background of heavy drinking and bronchial problems, which resulted in hypoxia, i.e. oxygen starvation – and not the *cause* of it. Whether or not he was diabetic is immaterial to his death. What killed Dylan Thomas was the hypoxia, which led to coma and oedema – swelling of the brain tissue. The damage was irreversible. *The Death of Dylan Thomas* has a wider agenda. George Tremlett believes that Thomas, far from being at the end of his tether in 1953, was on the brink of artistic triumphs and material prosperity which would have changed his life. His death was thus an accident caused by an undiagnosed illness, rather than the product of his history and character. I believe that Thomas put himself in situations where he was at the mercy of drink, ill-health and a bad doctor like Feltenstein. By fastening

On the evening of his first day in hospital, Thursday 5 November, Thomas's radio talk about Laugharne, recorded before he left, had been included in the live broadcast from Laugharne's Memorial Hall. It was cut to make it fit. Caitlin was in the audience. As the programme was going out, a telegram arrived from David Higham in London to tell her that Dylan had been 'hospitalised'. Her first reaction was to go to a dance and get drunk. Next day she prepared to fly to America.

For the remainder of the week, and through the weekend, Thomas lay in a coma. The incompetent Feltenstein, of whom he once wrote, 'I haven't found a doctor like Milton, nor will I ever', had been superseded. But by this time, it made little difference what anyone did. A tracheotomy to relieve his breathing was performed and he was inside an oxygen tent, the coma as deep as ever. A shifting group of friends, acquaintances and hangers-on stood in a corridor outside the ward, and looked in at him through a window. Factions developed; sinister accusations were whispered. It was rumoured that he had been given barbiturates as well as morphine in those last hours at the hotel; that the doctors at St Vincent's had found it difficult to obtain a proper medical history; that Caitlin was being discouraged from coming to New York. Immediately after Thomas's death, Edith Sitwell, who was visiting America, found herself bombarded with telephone calls from strangers, denouncing one another to her. (She concluded loftily that 'he did know the most awful people'.) These antagonisms were to last a lifetime. Dylan the clown and good companion was regarded as common property by too many people for comfort when they all crowded to the deathbed.

Caitlin arrived at Idlewild airport at eight o'clock on Sunday morning, fortified by drink. She knew what no one else did, that at the beginning of the week, two days before Thomas collapsed, she had written him a letter to say they were finished. Angry and unhappy, she berated him for his weakness, his lies, his drunkenness, his infidelity and, worst of all, for having left her without money. Her threats to kill herself or go whoring, she

on diabetes, and extending it back to Thomas's adolescence, Tremlett produces a spectre at the poet's side, rattling its chains and slowly debilitating him, until it finally embraced him in 1953. I think this a gross misreading of what Thomas was, and in what direction he was travelling.

said, were not a joke. It is the only one of her letters to Dylan that seems to have survived, so there is no way of knowing how typical or untypical it is. She addressed it care of Brinnin in Boston. By the time it arrived, Thomas was in hospital. Brinnin opened it and kept it for the rest of his life.

From the airport Caitlin was driven into Manhattan with an escort of police motor-cycles. She arrived at St Vincent's with Rose Slivka and is said to have asked, 'Is the bloody man dead yet?' She made violent scenes, while Brinnin's party tried to make sure that she didn't catch sight of Reitell (according to Rose Slivka, she did). Perhaps by arriving with a flourish and storming angrily to the bedside, she hoped that somehow she would generate the power to awaken him; this was how the faithful Slivka interpreted Caitlin's mixture of grief and rage. Caitlin wrote of the demons that possessed her and the madness of a broken heart. She smashed a crucifix and a figure of the Virgin, and attacked various people, including Brinnin, while Slivka screamed, 'Go for the jugular, baby!' Both Caitlin and Rose were put in straitjackets, and Caitlin was taken to a private clinic on Long Island. She was still there when her husband died.

In Wales, Vernon Watkins had been telephoned by the London *Times* and asked to provide an obituary at short notice. It took him most of Sunday at Pennard. 'Innocence is always a paradox,' he wrote, 'and Dylan Thomas presents, in retrospect, the greatest paradox of our time.' Thomas lived through one more night. He died when a nurse was washing him at lunchtime on Monday, 9 November. The post-mortem found the primary cause of death to be pneumonia, with 'pial oedema', the pressure on the brain, as the 'immediate cause', and a fatty liver, the sign of a heavy drinker, as an 'antecedent'. There were other signs associated with alcoholism, and the death was classified under two headings, 'Acute and chronic ethylism', which means the same as alcoholism, and 'Hypostatic bronchopneumonia'. As far as the pathologist was concerned, Thomas died of drink. There was no mention of morphine.

Among the effects that came back to Wales were fragments of Thomas's last poem to his father, 'Elegy', and a copy of his radio script, 'Return Journey'; letters from the Savage Club, Stravinsky, Philip Burton, Caitlin, 'Jean', Stephen Spender and his bank manager; the *Sunday Pictorial* Diet Sheet; an inhaler, a tube of pills and a prescription from Dr Milton D. Feltenstein; a fountain pen, a box of cigars, four suits, four shirts, two vests, two hot-water bottles, an empty chequebook with blank stubs, and a few pounds in cash. He died intestate, as befitted a poet, and a nominal value of a hundred pounds was put on his possessions. It was a little time before the income from his books, records and play began to flood in, the public's homage to a poet who thoughtfully died young, or young enough for tears, in bizarre circumstances, having kept up his performance or caricature to the last.

In Laugharne, years after his death, they were still selling scraps of cloth to visitors and pretending they were true relics from the Boat House. His younger son, visiting Wales in 1975 from the other side of the world, where he had made his home, wrote in the visitors' book, 'It used to be a good house to live in,' and signed it with his full name, Colm Garan Dylan Thomas. The herons still ruled the estuary. The Boat House became a tourist location, attracting the curious and now and then the pilgrim. In Swansea, occasional Americans and Japanese call at 5 Cwmdonkin Drive and ask to see the bedroom by the boiler. Or they walk down the steep side of Cwmdonkin Park to examine the stone memorial that bears the last three lines of 'Fern Hill', incised in letters slowly succumbing to the Welsh weather.

POSTSCRIPT: THE THOMAS BUSINESS

After Dylan Thomas's death there was no shortage of events to nourish the legend. Literary New York buzzed with rumours about how he had died. He was said to have fallen at a party and banged his head. The morphine episode was referred to in whispers. Diabetes was mentioned. Some people, among them Edith Sitwell, pretended to believe the story that he had scratched his eyeball on a rose-thorn shortly before he collapsed, and that this was mysteriously connected with his death. Rayner Heppenstall had seen Thomas with a bloodshot eye in London years earlier, and was told then that a rose-thorn was to blame. As Heppenstall wrote sarcastically, 'A very suitable misadventure for a poet.'

While Thomas's body was being embalmed and prepared for its return to Britain, friends and hangers-on squabbled about whether he had been properly looked after. Brinnin was quick to record his version of events, which was essentially the version that he gave in *Dylan Thomas in America* two years later. Writing to John Davenport on 15 November 1953 he said that Thomas had spoken of suicide in his last days, and that his final collapse followed a drinking bout; delirium tremens, said Brinnin, led to 'a comatose condition'. Drugs were not mentioned. Davenport heard a different version from George Reavey, who said that morphine was involved and that the facts of Thomas's death were not emerging. Caitlin, who remained in New York until she came back to Britain in the ship that brought the coffin, was looked after by Rose Slivka, who took her on shopping expeditions. At Lord & Taylor's she meant to buy a black dress to take home. Instead she found one she liked better in pink velvet.

Thomas was buried at Laugharne on 24 November, fifteen days after he died. Of the children, only Colm, aged four, was at the Boat House. Aeron, who had been told of her father's death by her Aunt Nicolette, was at boarding school in Hertfordshire.

Llewelyn was at Magdalen College school in Oxford; he heard the news from the headmaster. Before the funeral the coffin was at the Pelican, where old Mrs Thomas lived, the Boat House being inaccessible. Neighbours who called to pay their respects were allowed to raise the lid and view the body, dressed in a new suit supplied by the Manhattan funeral parlour. Adverse comments were made about the clothes and especially the gloves they gave him, things, as the joke went, that he wouldn't have been seen dead in.

Caitlin had no time for the gloomy trappings of a Welsh funeral and afterwards was contemptuous about provincials wearing their best suits. David Gardner, there as a mourner, not a cameraman, saw her touch the lid of the coffin as it passed down the aisle of St Martin's Church. He thought it 'a nice gesture, I think rehearsed'. John Davenport said that as the coffin went through the lych gate, 'a cock began crowing redly'. Louis MacNeice, passing the grave with a bunch of flowers, was said to have dropped a packet of sandwiches by mistake. Nicolette Devas said it was 'a passionate day of sorrow and drinking ... a time of dignity and farce'. The pubs were open till all hours. Caitlin drank whisky and did some brawling and dancing about, almost restrained by her standards. While the drinking went on, the literary robbers were already at work. At least two signed copies of books by Thomas were stolen before the day was out.

In 1953 Caitlin was left with three children, a house that didn't belong to her, and a backlog of debts against her husband's apparently non-existent estate, although funds in Britain and America brought in substantial sums. On the day of the funeral, one friend and two acquaintances agreed to seek Caitlin's approval for a trust to administer the small income that Thomas's work was expected to generate. The friend was Dan Jones, who initiated the scheme. He and Stuart Thomas, the solicitor, discussed it and brought in David Higham, the literary agent. They moved quickly, no doubt anxious to protect the three children, since Caitlin, given unrestricted access to the money, would have made it disappear as fast as it came in. Dan Jones regarded her as unhinged. A trust deed was drawn up, dated 28 December; Caitlin probably signed it early in December, in Stuart Thomas's office on her way to London for the first of many escapades.

At first, in 1954, the trustees spent much of their time finding people who had been owed money by Dylan, and paying them off. Cheques that had bounced were re-presented by creditors who had given up hope of seeing their money again. Debts in Laugharne had to be met. The milkman, owed for nine months' milk, asked that five pounds be deducted from his bill and given to the family. Months after Thomas's death, the trustees were still calculating prudently that over the next six or seven years his writings and recordings might with luck earn a total of three thousand pounds. In the event, by 1955 far more than this was being earned in a single year.

Collected Poems was a best-seller. So was the text of *Under Milk Wood*, the British edition of which sold twenty-five thousand copies within six months of Thomas's death. A year later, in May 1955, the book was in its seventh British impression. Earnings from America were still more surprising to those conditioned to equate Thomas with poverty. The copyrights of the Caedmon records and tapes became the most lucrative of all the properties. Material from Thomas's two formal sessions in 1952 and 1953 was supplemented by poems and prose recorded at the Poetry Center and elsewhere, the first stage production of *Milk Wood*, and a number of BBC recordings. Thomas made rich women of Barbara Holdridge and Marianne Mantell.

No modern poet has generated so much criticism, gossip, reminiscence and biography. Books dealing entirely or mainly with the life began with John Malcolm Brinnin's *Dylan Thomas in America* (1955), which dealt narrowly but vigorously with its subject; the passages where Brinnin quotes Thomas's accounts of his own past are more fiction than fact. A play by Sidney Michaels, *Dylan*, which had a successful run in New York in 1964, was based partly on Brinnin's book, partly on Caitlin's powerful if disjointed elegy for the dead Dylan, *Leftover Life to Kill* (1957). John Ackerman's admirable *Dylan Thomas. His Life and Works* (1964) was written without access to the papers. *The Days of Dylan Thomas* (1964) by Bill Read, who was John Brinnin's partner, was a short illustrated book (many of its photographs by Rollie McKenna) which failed to do justice to Read's research; he, too, was not allowed to quote from letters and other material. This ban was in anticipation of the official biography, Constantine FitzGibbon's *The Life of Dylan Thomas* (1965), the only full account until Ferris's *Dylan Thomas* (1977).

The Growth of 'Milk Wood' (1969) by Douglas Cleverdon was a scholarly account by the BBC producer who persuaded Thomas to keep writing the play. Andrew Sinclair's *Dylan Thomas. Poet of His People* (1975) was an unexceptional text, handsomely illustrated. *My Friend Dylan Thomas* (1977) by Daniel Jones was a slim volume of reminiscence, sensitive but guarded. Gwen Watkins, drawing on accounts she heard from her husband Vernon (d. 1967), published the invaluable *Portrait of a Friend* (1983). Rob Gittins' *The Last Days of Dylan Thomas* (1986) was a disappointing account. Ackerman's *Welsh Dylan* (1979) drew on material in his 1964 book; he also published *A Dylan Thomas Companion* (1991). The pre-eminent work of this kind, though unrealistically priced, is by James A. Davies, *A Reference Companion to Dylan Thomas* (1998), which includes a succinct biography in a hundred pages. Davies has also written *Dylan Thomas's Places. A Biographical and Literary Guide* (1987). George Tremlett's *Dylan Thomas. In the Mercy of His Means* (1991) presented Thomas as an artist killed in his prime by fame. *Dylan. The Nine Lives of Dylan Thomas* (1993) was a straightforward account by Jonathan Fryer. *The Death of Dylan Thomas* (1997) by James Nashold and George Tremlett tried hard to show that diabetes did for him.

Fiction or faction about Thomas includes (besides the Sidney Michaels play) *Dylan*, a novel of 1970 by John Summers. A spoof Thomas poem, 'How should my wellspring cat', was used to good effect in Christopher Hood's novel *Banana Cat* (1985). Richard Lewis made a TV biopic in 1978, *Dylan. The Life and Death of a Poet*, written by Ferris.

Books by Thomas have continued to appear, and most of his work was in print at the end of the twentieth century. The standard edition of the poetry is *Dylan Thomas. Collected Poems 1934-53* (1988), edited by Walford Davies and Ralph Maud. The same editors presented a 'definitive' *Under Milk Wood* in 1995, which combines the First and Second Voices into a single narration, on the grounds that the roles are indistinguishable. Daniel Jones edited *Dylan Thomas. The Poems* in 1971; this included everything in the original Collected edition and added more than a hundred other poems, most of them taken from the early notebooks. It was thus a mixture of poems that Thomas wanted to keep in print and poems in which, presumably, he had no lasting interest. Most of the accessible verse by Thomas that has escaped publication in one form or another is in manuscript collections, mainly American. Much of it is doggerel, but there is a manuscript of an unfinished poem of about 1936, 'For as long as forever is', which is mentioned by Watkins; this (together with one of the juvenile poems, several of which are in manuscripts at Texas) is printed here as an Appendix.

The Collected Stories (1983) was edited by Walford Davies, with a foreword by Leslie Norris; *The Broadcasts* (1991) was edited by Ralph Maud. Earlier collections of stories and broadcasts include *Quite Early One Morning* (1954) and *A Prospect of the Sea* (1955). Some of Thomas's critical articles, esoteric stories and juvenilia were collected in *Dylan Thomas. Early Prose Writings* (1971), edited by Walford Davies. A number of film scripts have been published, among them *The Beach of Falesá*, *20 Years A-Growing* (both 1964), *Me and My Bike*, *Rebecca's Daughters* (both 1965), *The Doctor and the Devils, and Other Scripts* (1966). John Ackerman edited *The Filmscripts* (1995). The limp satire written jointly with John Davenport, *The Death of the King's Canary*, appeared in 1976.

The important *Poet in the Making. The Notebooks of Dylan Thomas* (1967) has the contents of the four poetry notebooks at Buffalo, transcribed and edited by Ralph Maud. A shorter version with fewer annotations was published in 1989 as *Dylan Thomas. The Notebook Poems 1930–1934*. A *Collected Letters* edited by Ferris appeared in 1985 and a revised edition is in preparation. Previously FitzGibbon had edited an unreliable *Selected Letters* (1966). *Letters to Vernon Watkins* was meticulously edited by Watkins in 1957. Jeff Towns has published, in a collectors' edition, *Letter to Loren*, a previously unknown verse letter rich in puns that Thomas wrote to the painter Loren MacIver, one of his hosts in America in 1950 (Salubrious Press, Swansea, 1993).

Caitlin Thomas published *Not Quite Posthumous Letter to My Daughter* (1963), which failed to match its predecessor, *Leftover Life to Kill*. One of her unpublished manuscripts, *Double Drink Story. My Life with Dylan Thomas*, edited by her son Francesco, appeared in 1997. Her letters, a truer guide to her remarkable nature, remain unpublished apart from those that were used in Ferris's biography, *Caitlin. The Life of Caitlin Thomas* (1993).

Dylan Thomas's letters and other papers have found a ready market. Bert Trick sold his important five Thomas letters to an American dealer for $1500 in 1965. Douglas Cleverdon sold his manuscript of *Under Milk Wood* to the Times Book Co. for £2000 in 1961; it is said to have changed hands later for five times as much. Among the prices paid in London for papers in the first twenty years after Thomas's death, a short letter thanking T. S. Eliot for his cheque made £110 (1966); two sheets of drafts for 'A Story', £150 (1966); three pages of drafts for 'Elegy', £150 (1966); a one-page letter to Nigel Henderson, £220 (1970); a one-page letter to Cordelia Locke (about renting her cottage at South Leigh), £100 (1972); three letters to Robert Byron, author, and one to Edith Sitwell, £300 (1972); a notebook with eighteen pages of notes about the Llangollen Eisteddfod and a press ticket, £550 (1973). Any scrap of paper with Thomas's handwriting on it – a copied-out poem by someone else, a galley-proof with a couple of corrections – has found a market. The Texas collection includes a betting slip, a tax-exemption certificate and a restaurant bill. A duplicated copy of the script of a radio documentary about Thomas (dozens of which would have been run off by the BBC), inscribed by a friend of Thomas, was catalogued in London at £80.

By the 1990s, a good Thomas letter was worth £1000 or £2000. An early letter to Caitlin went for £4000. The eleven letters to Percy Smart made £9500 (1992), the group of letters to Desmond Hawkins £21,275. The four letters that Caitlin kept in her handbag till her death fetched £12,650. Jeff Towns paid nearly $10,000 in 1986 for the verse letter to Loren MacIver, probably the largest sum ever made by a single Thomas letter. Two worksheets of 'Do not go gentle' were auctioned in New York for $30,000.

The principal collection of Thomas material is at Texas. Buffalo has the poetry notebooks and much other material, including letters to Trevor Hughes and Pamela Hansford Johnson. Other material is at Harvard, Indiana and Ohio universities, the Berg Collection of the New York Public Library and the University of Victoria in Canada. In London the British Library has the letters to Vernon Watkins and a few other items. The National Library of Wales in Aberystwyth, after a slow start, has built up a major collection.

Over the years earnings from Thomas's copyrights rose steadily until, decades after his death, the trustees were administering an annual income in the region of a hundred thousand pounds. Half went to Caitlin, one-sixth each to her three children by her husband. After her death in 1994 the trust income was divided between these three.

The Boat House remained her home until October 1954, when she returned to Elba and the man she had fancied in 1947. In the spring of 1955 she went back to Laugharne, and conceived a plan to have her husband's remains brought from the graveyard and re-interred in the garden of the Boat House, facing the estuary. The Home Office gave provisional approval, but the matter was not pursued. For another year or two Caitlin moved between Britain and Italy, spending much of 1956 on the island of Procida, living with a fisherman of twenty-something, whom her children (then aged seventeen, thirteen and seven) were expected to take in their stride when they came from England for the summer holidays. In 1957 she settled in Rome, met Giuseppe Fazio and began a new life that was never free of echoes from the old.

Her life had been one of endless confusion. In the 1960s she gave up drink, more or less, at the insistence of her partner, Giuseppe; who had more success in that respect than anyone else. But she and Dylan were too complicated to have themselves explained by alcohol addiction.

Marriage had subdued but never removed her conviction that she had some destiny to achieve. Everything was a drama with her at the centre. Thus her frustration with being Mrs Dylan Thomas arose from his failure to be a satisfactory part of her story (in which he was *her* poet, her private treasure), while at the same time she was dragged into playing a walk-on part in his. She was probably too honest to consider that his poetic gifts owed anything to her, which of course they didn't.

Now he was dead, she could be herself again, the leading player. She had a powerful streak of self-indulgence; at the same time she had a harsher side that believed in punishment and 'just deserts', for herself as well as for others. It was this Caitlin, rigorous and anxious to create in her own right, who despised her father for having dissipated his talents and regretted her husband's weaknesses in the same department. Her own talent for dancing, if she ever had one, had long since vanished in drunken ecstasies. If she were to achieve any artistic individuality, it would have to be as a writer. By and large this attempt failed, unless there is anything of consequence (rather than rehashed autobiography) to be mined from her unpublished manuscripts. In later life she adopted some feminist values and made a case for herself as a woman who suffered from men in general and Dylan in particular. She remained enraged by her inability to bend the world to her will. Her single-minded projection of a 'hidden self' that she believed in was tragic but in an odd way heroic as well. Through the bitchiness and bloody-mindedness she was always struggling for the light.

Her vain attempts to overturn the Thomas trust or re-interpret its provisions cost her a fortune. For years she complained that she was penniless in Italy, abandoned by the wicked trustees. This was nonsense. If intermittent hardship was involved, it was largely because her domestic finances were out of control. Money had to be set aside for the children's education and coming-of-age, whereas Caitlin saw the trust as a treasure-chest to which she wanted, or, as she would have put it, needed the key. At the same time, Stuart Thomas, though convivial, was not always the easiest man to get on with. If he had treated her with more understanding over the years, she might not have been so hostile.

In Caitlin's declining years, she spent more time and money on attempts to have Francesco, her son (b. 1963) by Fazio, admitted as a beneficiary. This would have needed the unanimous approval of her three children by Dylan, and, unsurprisingly, given the personal undercurrents, it was not to be had. After her death the war of attrition was carried on by Francesco Fazio. It is as if the unquiet ghosts of the Thomases, Dylan and Caitlin, will never be at peace.

Appendix

TWO UNPUBLISHED POEMS BY DYLAN THOMAS

La Danseuse
(written as a child; see Note to p. 36)

She moved like silence swathed in light,
Like mist in moonshine clear;
A music that enamoured sight
Yet did elude the ear.

A rapture and a spirit clad
In motion soft as sleep;
The epitome of all things glad,
The sum of all that weep.

Her form was like a poet's mind,
By all sensations sought.
She seemed the substance of the wind,
One shape of lyric thought;

A being 'mid terrestrial things
Transcendently forlorn;
Through time bound far on gleaming wings
For some diviner bourn.

The rhythms of the swooning heart
Swayed to her sweet control;
Life in her keeping all was art,
And all of body soul.

Faint-shimmering in the roseate air
She seemed to ebb and flow
Like memories perilously fair,
And pale from long ago.

She stooped to grief's remembered tears,
Yearned to undawned delight.
Ah, beauty – passionate from the years!
Oh, body – wise and white!

She vanished like an evening cloud,
A sunset's radiant gleam.
She vanished. Life awhile endowed
The darkness with a dream.

For as long as forever is

(unfinished, circa 1936 – see *Letters to Vernon Watkins*, pp. 47–8). Thomas abandoned the poem because the opening line was 'completely out of place'. Later he used it as the last line of the poem 'Twenty-four years'. (See also Note to p. 148.)

For as long as forever is
And the fast sky quakes in the web, as the fox in the wave,
With heels of birds & the plumed eyes,
Shakes in its stride the partridge fence and the sea-duck rows,
And a flame in a wheel jumps the nave,
As a dozen winds drop the dark by the one moonrise,
And a stag through a trap grave,
Forever the hunted world at a snail's gallop goes.

Over the packed nests now, the snare & the she-bear's floes,
Through the cats' mountain & the cave
By the market & feather street near the townspires,
Narrowly time's slow riders shave ...

NOTES

Where an informant is named but no context given for the information, it can be assumed it was in an interview with the author. Similarly, unless otherwise stated, 'in a letter' means in a letter to the author.

The following abbreviations are used:

Papers:

Texas mss	Harry Ransom Humanities Research Center, the University of Texas at Austin.
Buffalo mss	Lockwood Memorial Library, State University of New York at Buffalo.
Harvard mss	The Houghton Library, Harvard University.
Berg mss	The Berg Collection, New York Public Library.
Indiana mss	The Lilly Library, the Universities Libraries, Indiana University.
Wales mss	National Library of Wales.
B.L. mss	British Library.
D.H.A.	Papers seen at David Higham Associates. Texas has since acquired D.H.A. files of the period.
BBC Archives	BBC Written Archives, Caversham, Berkshire.

Books and magazines (book page-references to English hardcover edition unless stated):

The Poems	*Dylan Thomas: The Poems* (ed. Daniel Jones).
T.F.F.	*Two Flamboyant Fathers* (Nicolette Devas).
A.W.R.	*Anglo-Welsh Review.*
C.P.	*Dylan Thomas. Collected Poems 1934–1953.*

E.P.W.	*Dylan Thomas: Early Prose Writings* (ed. Walford Davies).
Q.E.O.M.	*Quite Early One Morning* (ed. Aneirin Talfan Davies).
Tedlock	*Dylan Thomas: the Legend and the Poet* (ed. E. W. Tedlock).
L.V.W.	*Dylan Thomas: Letters to Vernon Watkins* (ed. Watkins).
Leftover	*Leftover Life to Kill* (Caitlin Thomas).
Prospect	*A Prospect of the Sea* (ed. Daniel Jones).
Brinnin (with page-reference)	*Dylan Thomas in America* (John Malcolm Brinnin), Ace Books (paperback), 1957.
FitzGibbon (with page-reference)	*The Life of Dylan Thomas* (Constantine FitzGibbon).
Skin Trade	*Adventures in the Skin Trade.*

Introduction

p. xv 'My busy heart ...': 'Especially when the October wind', stanza 1.

p. xv To Percy Smart: [Dec 1932]

p. xvii FitzGibbon to Higham: Trust archives.

pp. xxii–xxiii Michael Hulse: in Alan Bold (ed.) *Dylan Thomas. Craft or Sullen Art* (1990), pp 119, 123.

p. xxiii The private collector: Andrew MacAdie.

1. Names from the Past

p. 1 'Silly ravens': Thomas to Vernon Watkins, 20 December 1938.

p. 2 Six poems at Laugharne: 'Over Sir John's hill', 'In the White Giant's Thigh', 'Lament', 'Do not go gentle', 'Poem on his Birthday', 'Prologue'.

p. 2 Rehashing his adolescence: Caitlin to Oscar Williams and Gene Derwood, 9 February 1952, error for 1953. Harvard mss.

pp. 7–10 Information about the Thomas family in the nineteenth century: (a) *Dictionary of Welsh Biography;* (b) W. Greville-Griffiths, whose grandmother was one of D. J. Thomas's sisters; (c) Mrs Rachael Evans (a cousin of D. J. Thomas), Miss Mary Davies (with whom Florence Thomas lived temporarily towards the end of her life) and A. E. Savage (who knew D. J. Thomas in his youth), all three interviewed in Carmarthen in December 1963 by Kent Thompson. Thompson, an American post-graduate student at Swansea University College, later wrote his Ph.D. thesis on 'Dylan Thomas in Swansea' (1965). He interviewed many local people.

p. 9 'Elegy' notes: photocopy in Texas mss.

pp. 11–16 The Williams family, and Florence's marriage to D. J. Thomas: (a) interviews, including (in Carmarthenshire) Mrs Mary Ann Williams, Llwyn Gwyn; Mrs Annie Lewis, Lletyrneadd; Alderman J. Davies, Llanybri. 'Dr Dan' was recalled at both Llwyn Gwyn and Lletyrneadd. (In Swansea) Mrs Addie Elliott, Miss Ethel Ross and Mrs Irene Howell, whose grandmother was a sister of Anna Williams; (in Cardiff) Mrs Theodosia Legg, daughter of Florence's brother, John. (b) Kent Thompson's ms. The gravestones at Capel Newydd, Llanybri, were also useful.

p. 11 'Undeniably mad peasantry': Thomas to Oscar Williams, 30 July 1945.

pp. 14 'I hate you': Gwen Watkins. She heard the line from Vernon Watkins, who remembered Thomas reading it to him.

pp. 15–16 Florence and D.J.: Ethel Ross kept a diary in which she noted these and other statements by Mrs Thomas.

p. 16 The midwife was Mrs Gillian Williams, quoted by Ethel Ross, 'We Had Evidence and No Doubt', *Gower*, No. 16, 1964. Ross, with Mrs Williams as her source, says that Florence 'lost her first child'. (FitzGibbon (p. 22) says it was her *second* child that died.)

p. 17 D.J. at Blaen Cwm: Mrs Hettie Owen (see Note to p. 32).

p. 17 etc. D.J. as schoolmaster, etc.: interviews with Wynford Vaughan-Thomas, Stuart Thomas, Charles McKelvie, John Prichard, Waldo Clarke (who were all more or less contemporary with Dylan Thomas at the Grammar School); Gwevril Dawkins, Nancy's friend; J. Morgan Williams, former master at the school. Letter from E. G. Lewis, former master. Charles Fisher, *Herald of Wales*, 12 March 1938. *Swansea Grammar School Magazine*, March 1937, article on D. J. Thomas's retirement.

p. 17 The journalist was C. Gordon Glover. See pp. 251–2.

p. 18 Caitlin on D.J.: copy of a fragment in Caitlin's hand. Texas mss.

p. 18 D.J. teaching Welsh: interview with Florence Thomas, 24 May 1955. I interviewed Mrs Thomas for an article that I wrote for *Everybody's*, 'Go and Write, Boy', 21 April 1956. Much of her information was not used, but the original notes survived.

p. 18 etc. Paying the tradesmen, and other household information: Mrs Elliott, who as 'Addie' was the maid at 5 Cwmdonkin Drive.

p. 21 Born at 11 p.m.: Thomas gave this information in a letter of 27 November 1939 to a friend, Rayner Heppenstall, who was interested in astrology.

pp. 21–2 Difficulties over name: Florence Thomas, 1955 interview. FitzGibbon suggests that 'D.J. cannot fail to have been reminded of the name Dylan in the year of his son's birth. In July of 1914 an opera was staged at Covent Garden with the title *Dylan, Son of the Wave*. The music was by Josef Holbrook, the libretto by T. E. Ellis, which was the pseudonym of Lord Howard de Walden. This opera, of which D.J. must have heard from Dr Vaughan Thomas, the composer, whom he was seeing at the time, was part of an attempted "Welsh Revival"...'

p. 21 'Dillan' or 'Dullan': Dr Daniel Jones, Thomas's friend, argued in *The Poems*, p. 259, that even in Welsh, the pronunciation should be 'Dillan', on the ground that in the *Mabinogion* 'the name occurs with a circumflex over the "y"'. When Thomas became a regular broadcaster, he asked the BBC to stop using the orthodox Welsh pronunciation of 'Dullan'. The Cardiff *Western Mail* of 4 March 1954 quoted a letter written by a BBC official which said, 'We originally used the Welsh pronunciation of the name Dylan, but changed this in May 1946 to the anglicised form of Dill-an at the request of Mr Dylan Thomas himself.'

2. *His Father's Son*

p. 24 Pocock: in a BBC radio documentary about Dylan Thomas that was hurriedly put together by Marguerite Scott, following his death in November 1953. Home Service, 11 December.

p. 24 Ruthven Todd: BBC radio talk, reprinted in the *Listener*, 17 December 1959.

p. 24 Locked in in Hampshire: Thomas to Charles Fisher, 11 February 1938.

p. 25 Feather bed: Nicolette Devas, *T.F.F.*, p. 207.

p. 25fn 1. Lord Marley: in an interview.

p. 25fn 2. Murphy: *Br. J. med. psychol.* (1968), 41, 149.

pp. 25–6 The *Struwwelpeter* theory: Michael Neill's 'Dylan Thomas's "Tailor Age"', *Notes and Queries*, February 1970, p. 59. *Dylan and the Scissor-men*, Christopher Page, *A.W.R.*, Summer 1974, and Murphy, op. cit. Thomas mentions the book in his radio feature, 'Return Journey': 'In the afternoons, when the children were good, they read aloud from *Struwwelpeter*.'

pp. 26–7 Thomas to Treece: 31 December 1938.

p. 27 'A broader-minded man': Thomas to Hansford Johnson [early November 1933].

p. 27 Ruthven Todd: unpublished ms, Texas mss.

p. 28 Answers to a student: the replies, to five questions, were reprinted in *Texas Quarterly*, Winter 1961, and in *E.P.W.*, as 'Poetic Manifesto'; they were given in 1951 to a research student in Wales who was writing a thesis. The original consists of nine ms pages.

p. 28 Dylan in church: Mrs Gwen Nobbs.

p. 29 'Cwmdonkin' means 'Donkin's Valley'. The Thomases' street was on the lower slopes of the Town Hill, long since covered with houses. Not far away is a cleft in the hillside, formerly known as Cwmdonkin or Cwmdawkin. Dawkin has been a Swansea name at least since the 18th century. Information from James A. Davies.

p. 30 Jim Jones borrowing money: Mary Ann Williams, Llwyn Gwyn.

p. 30 The ms notes about Fernhill also say: 'I made that story "The Peaches" out of a number of tiny incidents that occurred that happened [*sic*] one summer holiday when I was a child; "The Peaches" was based on a true incident; but what made the story were many other tiny incidents, and memories, of many other holidays. I worked them in all together to make one story.' Texas mss.

pp. 30–1 Idris Jones died in 1959.

p. 31 The hangman, who was to appear in early poems, is recalled in local gossip as a real person, and Fernhill as 'the hangman's house'. A local resident said it had the reputation of being an unlucky house. The owner of Fernhill in 1975, Ken Davies, said he had researched the hangman story and established that the man was Robert Ricketts

Evans, assistant to the Carmarthen hangman. Evans's daughter, who had money of her own that Evans wanted to get hold of, is supposed to have run off with a German. One story goes that her father locked her up in Fernhill to keep her away from her lover – the windows were said to have been barred – but that she escaped and walked to Carmarthen in her nightgown. Ken Davies, who claimed to have seen a woman's ghost at Fernhill, gave the year of Evans's death as 1901. Dylan Thomas's ms notes about Fernhill include the following: 'Very lonely. The hangman used to live there, though not in my time. I remember the bars he'd put across the window: I suppose to keep out the incensed relations of his involuntary customers, or even the customers themselves. He committed suicide: of course with his rope. It was a lovely farm.' The former Carmarthenshire County Archivist, Major Francis Jones, said that Fernhill was a nineteenth-century house of no historical significance, adding that he had seen 'no documentary proof or other evidence' to support the hangman story and its romantic embellishments.

p. 32 The acquaintance who met Mrs Bassett was Gwevril Dawkins.

p. 32 D.J. Thomas's brothers: Mrs Hettie Owen, who (with her husband, Ken) lived at Blaen Cwm during the war and knew the Thomas family well. Mrs Owen came from Port Talbot, on Swansea Bay, and in the 1930s Arthur Thomas moved from nearby Aberavon and lodged with her family. Mrs Owen remembered Arthur as 'a kind-hearted man who liked his pint, an ordinary sort of man, not educated'.

p. 33 etc. Dylan, school and health: Florence Thomas, 1955 interview.

p. 33 Mrs Hole's school: Evelyn Burman Jones; Kent Thompson, interviewing Mrs Dorothy de Mattos, Mrs Hole's daughter, in 1963.

pp. 33–4 Jerseys, etc.: Evelyn Jones.

p. 34 Dylan as the colonel: Mrs de Mattos.

p. 34 'Reminiscences of Childhood' was written in two versions. The extract is from the second.

p. 36 Thomas to Watkins: [summer 1940]. The originals of this correspondence are in B.L. mss. Watkins's version in *L.V.W.* is scrupulous, but he made deletions to avoid offending people.

p. 36 Walking in August: the radio talk was 'The Crumbs of One Man's Year', 27 December 1946, BBC Home Service, reprinted in *Q.E.O.M.*

p. 36 Juvenilia: Hettie Owen was helping Florence Thomas clear out cupboards at Blaen Cwm after her son's death, when Mrs Thomas found the poems and asked her friend to burn them. Mrs Owen got her permission to keep the poems. They are now in Texas mss. There were seven: 'The Maniac', 'Inspirations', 'Decision', 'The Mishap', 'My Party', 'Little Dreams' and 'La Danseuse'.

p. 36 Mrs Thomas on juvenilia: 1955 interview.

3. A Sort of Schoolboy

p. 38 D.J. and the chair of English: this persistent local story was doubted by Professor Cecil Price of Swansea University College. But E. Glyn Lewis, former senior English master at the Grammar School (where his career briefly overlapped that of D. J. Thomas) was 'convinced from all that I have heard and from my own inferences that the university chair story is true'. Glyn Lewis adds (in a letter): 'The Grammar School of my time had only two fine teachers – D. J. Thomas and W. S. Davies – both of a kind and both close friends so far as they could be friends with anybody.'

p. 38 D.J. and T.J. Rees: Gwevril Dawkins.

p. 38 etc. D.J. as schoolteacher: much of the information was from J. Morgan Williams.

p. 39 'His Requiem': The *Sunday Telegraph* printed it on 30 May 1971. Its follow-up story a week later reported the observant reader, Mr Richard Parker of London. Thomas's changes included dropping two words to give two of the lines an iambic beat, and replacing 'the cortège grim' with 'the coffin grim'.

p. 40 School magazine: Thomas contributed to the issues of December 1925, December 1926, March 1927, July 1927; to all three of each year's issues for 1928, 1929 and 1930; to those of April 1931 and July 1931, his last term at school. After he left he had a signed poem in the July 1933 issue. December 1933 and July 1934 each carries a story signed 'Old Boy', probably Thomas. *Dylan Thomas in Print*, pp. 45–7.

p. 41 '... self-deprecating writers': 10pp. of undated ms notes, beginning 'I'm going to read some modern poems tonight'. Most of the passage quoted has been lightly crossed through. Probably in Texas mss; I saw a copy elsewhere. In the last few years of his life, Thomas's lecture notes, and some of his radio talks and other pieces, cannibalise one another for phrases and sometimes long passages. The 10pp of lecture notes echo or are echoed by the 1951 'Poetic Manifesto' (see note to p. 28).

p. 43 'A bad boy': P.E.S., i.e. Percy Smart, 'Under Milk Wood and a reminiscence of school-days' in *Spread Eagle*, published by Barclays Bank, April 1954.

p. 43 Bad language: Guido Heller, a contemporary, quoted by Kent Thompson.

p. 43 Florence's Welsh: 1955 interview.

p. 43 'Old Smalley': Raymond Mitchell.

pp. 43–4 School sports: the photograph was in the *Cambria Daily Leader*, 23 June 1926; the caption said he was aged twelve, but he was eleven. This may have been the 'yellowed newspaper clipping' of a photograph that Thomas kept in his wallet and showed John Brinnin in New York in 1950.

p. 44 Childhood accidents: Florence Thomas, 1955; Kent Thompson; Gwevril Dawkins; Professor Armel Diverres, then a neighbour; Raymond Mitchell.

p. 44 Running at Rhossili: John Bennett said in a letter, 'I remember [Dylan] saying to me, "Can't understand why you people pick your feet up so much" – his running style was most unorthodox – he seemed to raise his feet a little and glide over the ground.'

p. 45 I had a nodding acquaintance with Daniel Jones. But he had been at work on his own reminiscences for years, and decided not to talk to me.

p. 45 Joint plays: an exercise book has a draft of 'Bismuth'. The characters include Arnold, an impotent architect; Patricia, his wife; Derek, a homosexual; Phoebe, also homosexual, and Arthur, 'of doubtful parentage, sex and inclination'. Texas mss.

p. 45 'Bram': this is a rather formal way of saying 'fart' in Welsh. Perhaps Thomas and Jones were also thinking of Bram Stoker, author of *Dracula*.

pp. 45–6 Jones on joint poems: Tedlock, pp. 16–17.

p. 47 Warmley Broadcasting ms: Texas mss.

pp. 48ff Thomas to Jones: from 'Glen Lough Meenacross nr. Glencolumkille Lifford Co Donegal Irish Free State. Tuesday August 14

1935. Addressed, unavoidably, to Fred [Janes]. And to be read either late at night or when at least *half* tipsy.'

p. 51 Letter to 'another correspondent': A. E. (Bert) Trick [summer 1935].

p. 52 McInerny: to Kent Thompson, and in letters.

p. 52 Obscurity: McInerny, who heard Thomas defend an obscure line in another poem in discussion with a master, remembered the line (apparently never published) as 'They toil, powdered with a white music'. Thomas said it had 'come into his head', and was the best thing he had written. A poem by McInerny, 'The Sun', published anonymously in the school magazine, was later unearthed by a German researcher and attributed to Thomas.

p. 52 'The Elm': *The Poems*, p. 226.

p. 54 Models for writing: 'Poetic Manifesto'.

p. 55 Survey of modern verse: *Swansea Grammar School Magazine*, December 1929; reprinted in *E.P.W.*, p. 86.

p. 55 Disastrous results: Armel Diverres.

p. 56 Haemorrhage: the Colin Edwards interview (see p. 22fn).

p. 56 Breakdown: 1955 interview with Florence Thomas.

p. 56 Charles Fisher: in a letter.

p. 56 'Little Dogs' ms: Texas mss.

p. 57 Thomas to Smart: undated, annotated (by Smart?) 'Dec 6'. Attributable to December 1930.

p. 58 Dates and notebook poems: no doubt most of the dates appended to poems are close to the date of composition. But none of the original drafts of these notebook poems survives, and time may have elapsed between draft and fair copy. For example: a notebook poem dated July 1931, beginning 'Sever from what I trust', appears in a slightly different form as a pencilled draft, itself probably a copy, at the back of a book of Osbert Sitwell's poems, *Argonaut and Juggernaut* (published 1927) and dated 29 April 1931, which is in Texas mss.

p. 59 Borrowing from the headmaster: Thomas to Smart, 25 June [1931].

4. *Reporter, Actor, Poet*

p. 62 'A good opening': 1955 interview with Florence Thomas.

p. 62 The printers' reader: Trevor Ogborn, in the 1953 radio documentary.

p. 62fn Nellie Wallace interview: Thomas presumably went to see her while he was still a copy-holder; or even before he left school. The article was unsigned and headed: 'Nellie Wallace's Mimicry – Marie Dressler Her Favourite Star – Harder Work'. It described how 'Last night, in her dressing-room, Miss Wallace gave a *Daily Post* reporter just one example of her art of mimicry – with a perfect impersonation of Marie Dressler, whose latest films are the only ones that she has found interesting, for she is very interested in films as a whole. On the subject of talkies, however, she said that she felt that they were not gaining ground . . .' Wynford Vaughan-Thomas's account: the *Listener*, 16 January 1958, reprinting an Overseas Service talk.

p. 63 Older colleague: Eric Hughes, another Grammar School boy who went to the *Post*.

p. 63 Thomas to Treece: 31 December 1938.

p. 63 The matron: Florence Thomas, 1955.

p. 64 J.D. Williams on Dylan: in his review of *Twenty-five Poems* ('Some of His Joyous Adventures in a Newspaper Office'), *Herald of Wales*, 19 September 1936. Reprinted in *Dylan Thomas in Print*, pp. 58–60.

p. 64 American newshound: Charles Fisher, in a letter.

p. 65 'The Three Lamps': Thomas wrote in 'Old Garbo' that his father was 'visiting Uncle A. in Aberavon', the nearest he ever came to writing about D.J.'s brothers.

p. 68 Landore and Killay are suburbs of Swansea. 'The boxer' is probably the reporter Freddie Farr. An 'Edith' ran the newspaper's teleprinter room in the late 1940s, and is probably the woman Thomas admired.

p. 69 'After note' to Smart: in the original (Wales mss) it follows the letter about the drunken outburst. But this is the result of intelligent guesswork by the cataloguer; it doesn't prove that the items are related.

p. 71 D.J.'s appearance: Hettie Owen.

p. 72 Affluent Taylor: local gossip remembered him as improbably affluent, earning '£2000 a year as a quantity surveyor'. He was based in Swansea, selling asbestos bricks. In later life he was a prosperous businessman.

p. 72 *Evening Post* paragraph: 9 September 1932, identified by Haydn Taylor.

p. 73 Nancy's letters were in the possession of Haydn Taylor, who made the extracts.

p. 76 'End of a Great Ministry': 5 November 1932. It is just possible that Thomas's dutiful response to the retirement of this unfavourite uncle was the starting point for a poem about (among other things) hypocrisy, 'I have longed to move away'. In the notebook this is dated 1 March 1933. The published version has 'the old lie burning on the ground'. The longer notebook version makes it clear that Thomas was thinking of fireworks ('like some sulphurous reminder of November'). 5 November is fireworks night, when, conceivably, the poem or the mood that led to it was germinating.

pp. 76–7 Thomas to Smart: undated, probably December 1932.

p. 77 Jones and the hunchback: *The Poems*, p. 271.

p. 78 Trevor Hughes: biographical details in 'A Friend who Lives on in a Dylan Thomas Story', by Bernard Lloyd, *A. W. R.*, Autumn 1971. 'Trevor Tregaskis Hughes of Harrow, who had been on the British Railways staff at Euston for ten years, died in November 1966 at the age of sixty-two ... Hughes had been taught by Dylan's father at the Grammar School. "I first met Dylan," Hughes wrote later, "when he was sixteen and about to leave school. I called at his home in Cwmdonkin Drive. His sister and he were listening to a gramophone record of a Negro spiritual ... On those first evenings which we spent together, he would sit on the settee and read aloud. He was pushing out his immature poems, watching his listener's face" ... Hughes [whose family moved to London] also helped Dylan to accustom himself to London on his first visits there. About the end of 1931 he accompanied Dylan to the British Museum, where Dylan is said to have mistaken a meteorite for a piece of abstract sculpture ... Sometime in 1935, however, the close friendship cooled – perhaps because Dylan thought an article Hughes wrote about his *18 Poems* was "exaggerated praise". Also Dylan did not like Hughes's story "A Cobbler's Vane" – in which Hughes portrayed Dylan as an eighteenth-century cobbler – "he told his tales until the variety of drinks confused him and Caleb's rhymes lost their reason".' Possibly Hughes knew from Thomas that his great-uncle Gwilym Marles had been a cobbler.

pp. 78–9 February letter: Thomas says in it that his mother has gone to Carmarthen to be at Aunt Ann's deathbed. Ann Jones died 7 February.

p. 79 'Out of the sighs': the lines quoted are from the notebook, and differ slightly from the published version.

p. 80 'Was there a time': the notebook version, which begins 'Hold on whatever slips beyond the edge/To hope', is more than twice as long. Maggots on 'my' track had become a single maggot on 'their', i.e. children's, track, by the time the poem was revised for publication.

p. 81 Bert Trick: his ms account of 'The Young Dylan Thomas' is in Texas mss. Also Kent Thompson interviewed him.

p. 82 James A. Davies: see *A Reference Companion to Dylan Thomas*, e.g. pp. 25ff, 108ff, 117–18, 127ff.

p. 82 Informal group: among the names Trick recalled for Kent Thompson were Tom Warner, Leonard Morris (later a musician), Fred Janes and 'sometimes, although rarely, Dan Jones'. Their cosy private gatherings are reflected in the *Portrait* story, 'Where Tawe Flows', in which 'young Mr Thomas' and three older friends meet to plan a novel.

p. 83 'What colour is glory': Thomas first used it in the notebook version of 'Why east wind chills' ('What colour is glory? the children ask'), 1 July 1933; the phrase disappeared when the poem was revised.

p. 83 Naming the child: Nell Trick.

p. 83 Bert Trick told Kent Thompson the story of 'And death shall have no dominion'.

p. 84 Sleeping badly: 'Last night I slept for the first time this month ... Minute by minute through the eight hours of the dark I lay and looked up into the empty corners of this room ... soon my lips would speak sentences aloud, and I listen to them ...' Thomas to Pamela, n.d., written in the week of 11 November, 1933.

p. 86 Poems to the end of August 1933: The twelve already written that were close to or strongly suggestive of their final form were: 'The spire cranes', 'The hunchback in the park', 'Out of the sighs', 'Was there a time', 'I have longed to move away', 'And death shall have no dominion', 'Why east wind chills', 'Here in this spring', 'Find meat on bones', 'Ears in the turrets hear', 'Shall gods be said', 'The hand that signed the paper'. The eleven poems that were more substantially revised (in some cases losing all but a few phrases) became 'How shall my animal', 'Today, this insect', 'After the funeral', 'On no work of words', 'On the marriage of a virgin', 'O make me a mask', 'Not from this anger', 'We lying by seasand', 'Incarnate devil', 'The tombstone told when she died', 'Grief thief of time'. It is likely that missing notebooks contained early versions of other published poems.

p. 86 *18 Poems* written later: Ralph Maud was probably the first to draw attention to the order in which Thomas wrote his poems, in 'Dylan Thomas' *Collected Poems: Chronology of Composition*', *Publications of the Modern Language Association of America*, June 1961.

5. A Case of Cancer

p. 88 First London visit: FitzGibbon cites Hughes and Reavey, but thinks they were wrong. Florence Thomas said Dylan first went to London 'the year Nancy got married', i.e. 1933, according to a recording she made at Carmarthen in 1957 for Ethel Ross. The recording has much family detail. Transcript published in the *Arts Festival Magazine* of the Swansea College of Education, 1966.

p. 89 Connolly: reviewing *New Verse: An Anthology*, *New Statesman*, 16 September 1939.

p. 89 Thomas to Grigson: [summer 1933].

p. 90 Jones at Steyning: he mentions his visit in *The Poems*, p. 258, but doesn't say why he was there.

p. 90 'That sanity be kept': Stephen Spender thought it was this poem which led him to write to Thomas. But a letter from Thomas to Spender in March 1934 suggests that their first contact followed 'Light breaks' in the *Listener*. See p. 103.

p. 90 D.J.'s cancer: it was possible to trace details of this distant episode because Gwevril Dawkins remembered that when D.J. was admitted to hospital in London, a junior doctor called Thurgar, a former pupil at the Grammar School, examined him. John Thurgar, FRCS, turned out to be a surgeon living in Scotland. He remembered the case and was able to produce the clinical notes.

p. 91 Thomas to Hughes: [early January 1934].

p. 92 Thomas upset: Eric Hughes.

p. 92 '... green fuse': William Empson in the *New Statesman*, 15 May 1954, said that 'what hit the town of London was the child Dylan publishing "The force that through the green fuse" as a prize poem in the *Sunday Referee*, and from that day he was a famous poet; I think the incident does some credit to the town, making it look less clumsy than you would think.' There are small variations between the *Referee* version and the version of *18 Poems* and later. The notebook version is inscribed 'To E.P.', possibly Evelyn Phillips, an attractive girl in the group that included Thomas. She said there was no special reason why the poem should have been dedicated to her.

p. 92 'Beat-pounding rhythms': 'On Reading One's Own Poems', BBC Third Programme, 24 September 1949; reprinted in *Q.E.O.M.* A Texas ms, probably written for a Third Programme broadcast in 1947, 'The Poet and His Critic', has more to say about early poems:

> A house where you once lived and where you were happy and sad, in love, in peace or at war ... may, when you visit in again, raise only doubt and ghostly curiosity. Why did I live there? and did I really, at all? Then suddenly, on a stone of the house, you see a little meaningless mark scraped with a nail. And you remember the nail itself, and the day you scraped with it on the stone, and the time of the day, and the weather, and exactly how you felt when you did it, and why. That alone of the house makes memories move in you. For the rest: the house is for other people. Re-reading an early poem, the poet may see, perhaps in one rearing line or one clumsy word, the nail-mark of the past, all that is left to him alone of the original reason for the poem ...

p. 93 Three poems in November: the other two were 'When once the twilight locks no longer' and 'I fellowed sleep'.

p. 93 Thomas to Fisher: [early 1935].

p. 94 Sex at fifteen: the fact that Thomas talked about it is reported in FitzGibbon's 'Time detective' notebook. Texas mss. See p. 355fn.

p. 94 Thomas's lecture: ms fragment, probably written for an American audience, beginning 'Looking back, from an eminence which I have little hope, or ambition, of ever achieving ...' Texas mss.

pp. 94–5 Girls: Kent Thompson says that 'On one occasion [Thomas] and his friends were chased away from the Strand ... because they were too well dressed. One of them [Raymond Mitchell] recalls their horror when an aged prostitute addressed them with "I only want a pint, boys, and I ain't got disease." But Dylan went back, dressed for the occasion, and presumably made a habit of this.' Perhaps he only *said* he went back.

p. 96 Letters to Pamela: at one time Lady Snow thought she had about a hundred letters from Thomas; but she was positive that the twenty-five or so that she deposited at Buffalo were all that then existed. Following her death, her daughter, Lindsay Avebury, found two further letters, both written after the relationship had cooled. Many of the letters are undated. Some are only fragments. Kent Thompson commented that they are 'more like a journal – written, like a personal memoir, to impress and elucidate – than they are like a personal correspondence'.

When the correspondence began is not certain. Lady Snow always said that she first wrote after she read 'That sanity be kept' on 3 September. But in an early letter to her, probably 15 October 1933, Thomas wrote: 'I, too, should like to meet you. This possibly can be arranged, but not before the beginning of September when I am going to see my sister near Chertsey.' This suggests they were already corresponding in August. Some of the early letters have certainly disappeared. Lady Snow told the author that 'I met Dan Jones at Steyning before I met Dylan. Dylan wrote, "I have met a man who has met you and doesn't seem to like you!"' This remark doesn't seem to be in an existing Thomas letter.

p. 96 The little vest: 15 April [1934]; 'no health at all': 25 December 1933; height and weight: [about 21 December 1933].

p. 97 'Four years, my sweet': [week of 11 November 1933].

p. 99 'Like a dead man exulting': [about 21 December 1933].

p. 99 'my solid and fluid world': [early November 1933].

p. 100 'a literary oddity': [week of 11 November 1933].

p. 101 Lady Snow's diaries of the period are in Buffalo mss. There are photocopies of some sections in Texas mss.

p. 101 etc. Lady Snow on Thomas: from an interview and correspondence with her; Dylan Thomas Memorial Number of *Adam*, 1953; *Important to Me* (1974), where she devotes a chapter to 'the story of Dylan, as much as I care to say'.

p. 103 The *Listener* row: Janet Adam Smith, then on the staff of the magazine.

p. 103 Letters from Eliot, etc.: mentioned in a letter to Pamela, 'Round about March 21 '34.'

pp. 103–4 Sitwell's comments were in *Aspects of Modern Poetry*. She quoted at length but didn't name Dylan Thomas. In an undated letter to Glyn Jones, December 1934, he refers to 'Edith Sitwell's latest piece of virgin dung' and calls her 'a poisonous thing of a woman, lying, concealing, flipping, plagiarising, misquoting...'

p. 104 'The hole in space': see p. 257, where a dream about falling inside a hill (related by Thomas in 1949) echoes a passage about 'holes in hills' in a draft of his unfinished novel, *Adventures in the Skin Trade*. This occurs in a fragment in the Texas mss (the published version is different): 'Joseph Bennet in common striped pyjamas too short for him with his dog-brown hair disturbed from the dented, womanly pillow, and his eyes still heavy from a dream of untouchable city women and falling down the holes in hills, opened the living-room door and peered uneasily around him.' In 'The Fight', 'The school had vanished, leaving on Mount Pleasant hill a deep hole that smelt of cloakrooms and locker mice ...' In a notebook poem (15 September 1933), 'A hole in space shall keep the shape of thought.' In a letter to Oscar Williams, 30 July 1945, 'Over the hiss, the hoarse noise of a train carrying holes to Hugh's Castle.'

p. 105 'There is no necessity': [15 October 1933].

p. 105 Caitlin: Elisabeth Lutyens in *A Goldfish Bowl* (p. 154) recalls Caitlin at the Lutyens' house in London, knocking on bedroom doors at night 'to borrow some matches with which to burn Dylan's handkerchiefs, saying they were so bourgeois'.

p. 106 Thomas to Treece: 16 May 1938.

p. 106 Glyn Jones: *The Dragon Has Two Tongues*, p. 199.

p. 108 'Evil oozing': Glyn Jones, ibid., p. 193.

p. 109 The critic: Raymond Stephens, *Dylan Thomas: New Critical Essays*, p. 42.

p. 109 'Huddled': Glyn Jones, op. cit., p. 194.

p. 109 Mescaline experiment: Peter McKellar, *Imagination and Thinking*, p. 106.

p. 109 Clare review: *Adelphi*, June 1935; reprinted in *E.P.W.*

p. 110 Dried eyes: Gwen Watkins.

p. 110 Oswell Blakeston: in an interview and a typescript headed 'Dylan at Wimbledon and after'.

p. 110 Grigson and Glyn Jones on the drawings: in interviews.

p. 111 'This horrifying skin': R. B. Marriott, *Adam* Memorial Number.

p. 111 'That creature ...': the 10pp. of ms cited in the note to p. 41.

p. 111 Confession: the 'friend of mine' may have been a former reporter on the *Evening Post*, two or three years older than Thomas, the 'Ted Williams' (a pseudonym) of 'Old Garbo' who 'dreamed of Fleet Street'. He died in 1975.

p. 113 Thomas to *Swansea Guardian*: 9 June 1934.

p. 113 Trick on the Mosley meeting: ms draft of a letter from Trick to 'My dear Bill Read'.

p. 114 Thomas to Grigson: [27 August 1934].

p. 114 'I've always wondered': [October 1934].

p. 114 *New Verse* poems: 'Our eunuch dreams', 'When once the twilight locks no longer', 'I see the boys of summer in their ruin', 'If I were tickled by the rub of love'.

p. 114 The answers to *New Verse* were reprinted in *E.P.W.* as 'Answers to an enquiry'.

p. 115 Glyn Jones on Thomas: *The Dragon Has Two Tongues* and an interview.

p. 115 Caradoc Evans: writing to Pamela (probably October 1934), Thomas described how he and Evans 'made a tour of the pubs in the evening, drinking to the eternal damnation of the Almighty & the soon-to-be-hoped-for destruction of the tin Bethels', with no mention of Glyn Jones. Jones thought he might have been describing a second visit to Aberystwyth.

p. 115 Thomas to Treece: 1 June 1938.

pp. 115–16 Thomas to Spender: 9 December 1952.

pp. 115–16 Spender's review: *Spectator*, 5 December 1952.

p. 116 What Watkins failed to notice: his Introduction to *L.V.W.*, p. 15.

p. 116 Thomas to his publisher: to E. F. Bozman at Dent, 10 September 1952.

p. 117 Letter to an editor: to 'Dear Mr Miles', perhaps Hamish Miles of Cape, the publishers, and drafted in a 'Walter Bram' exercise book where joint Thomas–Jones poems are entered. On adjoining pages are draft lines and working notes for the opening of 'I dreamed my genesis', which show that it was altered from its original form to make it a 'syllable-count' poem. In the notebook it has straightforward iambic stresses, like most of Thomas's poems at the time. The first four lines read:

> I dreamed your genesis in sweat of sleep
> Breaking the dark and the rotating shell,
> From limbs that had the worm upon the shuffle
> Let off the creaking flesh. Since first I sucked...

But in the published version (and presumably in the version sent to Miles) the poem had an extra word tacked on to three out of four iambic lines:

> I dreamed my genesis in sweat of sleep, breaking
> Through the rotating shell, strong
> As motor muscle on the drill, driving
> Through vision and the girdered nerve...

This pattern of 12, 7, 10 and 8 syllables is then repeated, with minor divergences, through six stanzas.

p. 117 Telling Pamela: [October 1934].

p. 118 Trick's account: 'The Young Dylan Thomas'. Texas mss. Thomas's letter: [?February 1935].

6. *London*

p. 119 Thomas to Trick: [?February 1935].

p. 119 Collapsing bed, etc.: Florence Thomas, tape-recorded by Ethel Ross.

p. 119 'Apples carved in oil': 'Swansea and the Arts', a scripted radio discussion in which Thomas took part, BBC Welsh Home Service, 24 October 1949. Extract in *Q.E.O.M.*

p. 121 Publication of *18 Poems*: in a letter to Pamela, 2 August 1934, Thomas wrote: 'I'm glad, too, that he [Neuburg] hasn't been able as yet to get my book published, for I want to cut some of the poems out & substitute some of the later ones.' Other details: Runia Sheila Macleod, Neuburg's assistant, in 'The Dylan I Knew', *Adam* Memorial Number; Miss Macleod wrote that 'for history's sake, one should add that the initial thirty pounds for the printing were supplied by Mr Mark Goulden, on behalf of the *Sunday Referee*, and that David Archer contributed the rest – twenty pounds'. Mark Goulden said it was 'not true' that he paid only part: 'I defrayed the costs, whatever they were.'

p. 122 Eliot's secretary: Erica Wright, to whom Thomas wrote on 4 November 1934.

p. 122 Only £4 or £5: Thomas to George Reavey, 16 June 1938.

p. 122 At the Kardomah: Mervyn Levy.

pp. 122–3 Henry Treece: *Dylan Thomas: 'Dog among the Fairies'*, pp. 96–7.

p. 123 *Referee* interview: 30 December 1934, 'Our Literary "Gangsters" – Young Poet Attacks Modern Writers.'

p. 123 *Swansea Guardian* review: 11 January 1935.

pp. 123–4 *Time & Tide* review: 9 February 1935.

p. 124 *Listener* review: 27 February 1935.

p. 124 Anthony Powell was reviewing FitzGibbon in the *Daily Telegraph*, 14 October 1965.

pp. 124–5 Thomas to Trick: [?February 1935].

p. 126 *Herald of Wales* poem: the notebook version, which is longer, says 'Poem completed March 31 '33'. Its title for publication on 8 June 1935 was 'Poet, 1935'. In the first version of his radio talk 'Reminiscences of Childhood' (*Q.E.O.M.*) Thomas quoted eight lines of it, disparagingly; he said it was 'a poem never to be published'.

pp. 126–8 Vernon Watkins and Thomas: Watkins wrote about their relationship in *L.V.W.* and a 19-page typescript, 'Notes on Dylan Thomas', owned by Gwen Watkins. Watkins's mental illness was first noted in a monograph about him by Roland Mathias in the *Writers of Wales* series (1974). Other details from Gwen Watkins.

p. 127 What a bore: Caitlin, interviewed for BBC Wales, 1977.

p. 127 Barking at Antonia White: Ian Henderson.

p. 128 A religious poet: Watkins told Jane McCormick shortly before his death, 'Yes, I still believe Dylan to be a religious poet, but he was not a religious man, and certainly not a Christian. I mean, if you're a Christian, it changes your life, doesn't it? Dylan certainly never changed. If he had had half the respect for his life that he had for his poetry, he would have been a good man – and alive today.' 'Sorry, Old Christian', *A.W.R.*, February 1970.

p. 128 Taylor's autobiography: *A Personal History*, pp. 168–9.

p. 129 Cameron on Thomas: Geoffrey Grigson.

p. 129 Cutting a poor figure: in Texas mss, attached to an undated letter [November 1934], Thomas to Grigson, is a typewritten poem, on the back of which Grigson has written 'DYLAN, MY GOD'. Grigson said (letter to the author) that the poem was a version by Thomas of some verses by Wilhelm Busch, the 'German Edward Lear'. Grigson and Cameron were fond of his poems. Thomas saw them in one or the other's flat, and 'said he would make some English versions if we gave him a literal crib (he knew no German). I gave him such a crib of Busch's elephant poem & that's what he did with it, my God. He should have known better & we should have known better; though there was something in common between Busch's verbal extravaganza & Dylan's (conversational) verbal form.' The poem consists of twelve couplets, beginning

> The Elephant one sees afar
> Goes for a walk in Africa
>
> He goes with nosey airs and graces
> To drink a lot at the oasis
>
> A Blackamoor for spite and fun
> Pops at the Jumbo with his gun
>
> Then round turns Jumbo bumpeting
> And follows Nigger trumpeting
>
> The bad Moor sprints! no use! he's here!
> The Elephant nabs him by the ear...

p. 129 Caitlin on Thomas's father: *Leftover*.

p. 130fn Burton's review: *New York Herald Tribune* (European edition) 26 October 1965.

p. 131 Todd's annotation: Jeff Towns, in his notes to *Dylan Thomas. Letter to Loren*, p. 56.

pp. 131–2 Connolly: in a recording, transcript in Indiana mss.

p. 132 Stories and poems: a notebook revision of 'Grief thief of time' has the note: 'Written and copied in later, August 1935. Glen Lough. Donegal.'

p. 133 Long letter to Trick: undated, from 'Glen Lough Co. Donegal Meenacross Lifford'.

p. 134 Estrangement: Grigson said (in a letter), 'After Ireland I saw less and less of him. No "break", but a slide away. Both Norman Cameron and I found him less engaging, and more interested in arse-licking the eminent; and there was the business of welshing ... in Donegal.'

p. 134fn2. 'Should lanterns shine' is not in a notebook, so can't be dated.

p. 135 Sending poems to Church: Thomas's letter is dated 8 October 1935 – 'Here, anyway, are most of the manuscripts. I haven't titled any of them ...'

p. 135 Church and Thomas: Church gave some details when he reviewed Prospect in Country Life, 18 August 1955; and L.V.W. in Truth, 15 November 1957.

p. 135 Church's reply: 26 November 1935. Copy typescript at Dent.

p. 136 Poems to choose from: between 1933 and 1936, Thomas published in journals eight poems that were not re-published in book form: 'Green Play in a Garden' (Herald of Wales, 15 July 1933); 'That sanity be kept' (S. Referee, 3 September 1933); 'No man believes' (Adelphi, September 1933); 'Love me, not as the dreaming nurses' (S. Referee, 7 January 1934); 'Out of the pit' (New English Weekly, 25 January 1934); 'The Woman Speaks' (Adelphi, March 1934); 'Poet, 1935' (Herald of Wales, 8 June 1935); 'Before we mothernaked fall' (New English Weekly, 30 July 1936).

p. 137 Thomas to Grigson: Grigson, however, was 'almost sure' it was written in June 1935, 'certainly before we went to Donegal'. If so, and if the letter is about gonorrhoea, this may be the reason Thomas's friends packed him off to Ireland for the summer. But he was ill later in the year. His letter to Church of 6 October says that 'this wretched illness of mine keeps me indoors'.

p. 139 Telling her cronies: Kent Thompson, interview with Mrs Gwilym Morgan, family friend.

p. 139 Thomas to Sitwell: He was nineteen, not eighteen, when he wrote the poem.

p. 140 Sitwell's advice: another Thomas letter, 24 January 1936, says, 'You must have listened to a great deal of the woes of young poets. And to take a regular job is the most sensible suggestion in the world. I would willingly and gladly, but have, apart from the little writing, reviewing, hack journalism, and odd-jobbery I've done, hardly any qualifications.'

p. 140 Heppenstall: *Four Absentees*, p. 95.

p. 140 Limericks: Rayner Heppenstall said there was a sequence of three. 'The second of the cycle was not composed. The third, which is not so good as the first, went:

> Now, Joe was the kind of a bloke
> Who looked for his bit of a poke
> And when he found Mary
> 'd been fucked by a fairy
> He didn't think much of the joke.

Wynford Vaughan-Thomas remembered walking with Dylan one night on Townhill, overlooking Swansea, when he produced the following:

> I wish I was a baby
> I'd look up Mummy's clothes
> And see the Cockett Tunnel
> Where Daddy's engine goes.

(Cockett, a suburb of Swansea, has a railway tunnel.)

p. 142 Playing at dogs: Tillyard, letter to *Times Literary Supplement*, 27 April 1962. He said that Thomas, 'the new adolescent prodigy', was aged sixteen or seventeen. The event may have been early in 1937 (Gwen Watkins, *Portrait of a Friend*, p. 42, thinks it was February; Thomas to Emily Holmes Coleman, 28/29 January 1937, suggests it was March). In either case, that makes him twenty-two.

p. 142fn The undergraduate: Wyn Lewis, in Gwen Watkins, op. cit., p. 42ff.

p. 143 Howard Moss: *New Yorker*, 7 October 1967.

p. 143 Glyn Jones: *The Dragon Has Two Tongues*, p. 185.

p. 143 Cordelia Locke: in an interview.

p. 143 G. S. Fraser: Tedlock, p. 82.

p. 144 Glyn Jones: op. cit., p. 197.

p. 145 Thomas to Wyn Henderson: 9 March 1936.

p. 146 Thomas to Church: 17 March 1936.

p. 146 Thomas to Watkins: [postmarked 20 April 1936].

p. 147 Church's letter: 28 April, copy typescript at Dent.

p. 147 Thomas to Church: 1 July. Thomas's letter sending the final batch of poems, on 22 June, said: 'Do forgive me for being so long in sending them. I haven't, actually, been at all well...'

p. 148 To Desmond Hawkins: [March 1936].

p. 148 Thomas to Watkins: [postmarked 20 April 1936].

p. 148 Poems in 1936: 'We lying by seasand' was revised from a notebook version and published in *Poetry* (Chicago), January 1937 (later in *Map of Love*. In the US, the poem is included in the 1957 New Directions edition of *Collected Poems*). 'It is the sinners' dust-tongued bell' appeared in *Twentieth Century Verse*, January 1937 (later in *Map of Love*). In 'Notes on Dylan Thomas', Watkins wrote of this poem: 'I remember [Dylan] coming to my house one day in a state of excitement. He had been given his next poem by a particularly dull thriller in which his eye had suddenly fallen on the sentence: "The shadow is dark directly under the candle." The poem he projected from this statement is the poem about churches ...' An unpublished poem, written about this time, is 'For as long as forever is'; see Appendix. In Texas mss, this poem is written on the reverse of a sheet which has part of 'It is the sinners' dust-tongued bell', with small variants from the published form.

p. 149 Book earnings: D.H.A.

7. *Caitlin*

p. 150ff The Macnamaras: *T.F.F.* Nicolette Devas and other family members. Yvonne Macnamara's written answers to questions from Bill Read: Texas mss.

p. 153 Dancing by herself: *Leftover*, p. 52.

p. 153 T. S. Eliot in the audience: Rupert Shephard.

pp. 155–6 Caitlin's gonorrhoea: Caitlin Thomas with George Tremlett, *Caitlin. A Warring Absence*, p. 35.

p. 157ff Caitlin and Rupert Shephard: his unpublished memoirs, owned by his estate. A painter, Shephard later married Caitlin's sister, Nicolette, after her husband – another painter, Anthony Devas – died.

p. 158 Writing for *Janus*: Royston Morley.

p. 158 Thomas as reviewer: over the years he dealt with poems, novels and thrillers. A book that impressed him deeply when he reviewed it for *Light and Dark* (March 1937) was the fantastical *Nightwood* by Djuna Barnes. Distant echoes can be heard in the *Portrait* stories.

p. 158 Welsh travelogue: letters to Richard Church, 1 May 1936; David Higham, 9 February 1937; Mervyn Peake [?March 1938].

p. 159 etc. Thomas to Coleman: the correspondence is at the University of Delaware, Special Collections.

p. 160 Trick and Holyhead in 'The Young Dylan Thomas', unpublished ms, Texas.

p. 161 Gascoyne's journal: David Gascoyne, *Collected Journals* (Skoob Books Publishing, 1991).

p. 161 BBC contract: 'Cardiff Registry' file, BBC Archives. Previously one or two Thomas poems had been broadcast, read by others: 'The Romantic Isle', of which there is no trace in BBC Archives; and 'Especially when the October wind' – a BBC letter to Thomas, 21 January 1937, says that 'it is possible we may wish to include' the poem in a reading on 6 February, and offers a fee of fifteen shillings. George Barker presented a selection of poems in the Regional Programme on 6 February, and Thomas's may have been among them.

p. 161fn To Bert Trick: [?February 1935].

p. 162 Plaintive requests: BBC Archives.

p. 163 D.J. retires: J. Morgan Williams; Trick, 'The Young Dylan Thomas', op. cit.; Thomas to Coleman [29 March 1937].

p. 164 Dylan Thomas to his parents: Haydn Taylor was sent it by D.J. Thomas as part of his campaign to stop the marriage.

p. 165 The £20: Ethel Ross, quoting Florence.

p. 168 'I am lost in love': [1937, ?September].

8. *Marriage*

p. 169 Augustus John to Caitlin: Wales mss.

p. 169 'Somebody's boring me': Heppenstall: *Four Absentees*, p. 139.

pp. 169–70 To Johnson: 6 August 1937.

p. 170 To Sitwell: 20 August 1937.

p. 170 Thomas to Watkins: Nicolette Devas said that 'Bluebell Wood' and 'Cuckoo Hill' were names invented by the Macnamara children.

p. 171 'A warring absence': Thomas's explanations were to Hermann Peschmann, 1 February 1938, and Desmond Hawkins, 14 August 1939.

p. 173 Four notebook poems: the other three were 'O make me a mask', 'Not from this anger' and 'How shall my animal'. All can be dated by references in letters to Watkins, to whom they were sent.

p. 173 Warm slippers: Caitlin interviewed for BBC Wales television in Rome, 1977.

pp. 173–4 Empson: *New Statesman*, 29 October 1965.

p. 174 Thomas to Fisher: 16 March 1938.

p. 174 Money in advance: Thomas wrote to the BBC, 'My fare, I am afraid, will have to be paid from Laugharne to Manchester, & not from Swansea. Also, owing to my circumstances, I find it necessary to have to be given the rail fare & subsistence allowance *before* I travel.'

p. 174 'four rooms . . .': Thomas to Treece, 16 June 1938.

p. 175 Thomas to Treece: ibid.

p. 175 Cockles underfoot: John Davenport, *Vogue*, August 1955.

p. 175 The plums: Gwen Watkins, *Portrait of a Friend*, p. 64.

p. 176 Davenport at Laugharne: ibid.

p. 176 Thomas to Rhys: 10 March [1938].

p. 177 Thomas to Rhys about *Wales*: incomplete and undated, ?1937.

p. 177fn *Western Mail* letter: quoted in J. A. Davies, *A Reference Companion to Dylan Thomas*, p. 266.

p. 178 Dent's objections: Thomas to Watkins, n.d., about 20 March 1939.

p. 178 T. S. Eliot backwards: Alan Brien, *Sunday Times*, 25 March 1973.

p. 178 Llanmadog backwards: Sybil Walters.

p. 178 Church's proposal: letter to Thomas, 28 April 1936. Copy typescript at Dent.

p. 178 'A Visit to Grandpa's': published in *New English Weekly*, 10 March 1938.

p. 179 'Illuminated reporting': Watkins, 'Notes on Dylan Thomas'.

p. 179 'Mostly pot-boilers': Thomas to Trick, 27 October 1939.

p. 179 'Patricia ...' ms.: Buffalo mss.

p. 179 'Dead youth ...': 'Old Garbo', p. 195.

p. 179 Thomas to Treece, on Church: February or March 1938.

p. 179fn 'Flippant title': Thomas to Watkins, about 30 January 1940.

p. 180 'Brawling hypocrite': Thomas to Tambimuttu, 9 June 1941.

p. 180 Thomas to Treece, on poverty with dignity: 23 March 1938.

p. 180 Thomas to Treece, on cruel Laugharne: 16 June 1938.

p. 180 'Straight poems' written first: Thomas to Treece, 6 or 7 July 1938. Treece seems either to have forgotten or to have ignored this information, which no one else had at the time, when he published his critical study of Thomas, '*Dog among the Fairies*', in 1949.

p. 180 Thomas to Treece, on writing poetry: 23 March 1938.

p. 180 Thomas to Treece, on taking poems literally: 16 May 1938.

p. 180 Thomas to Treece, on Sitwell: 1 June 1938. Thomas is concerned with her 'interesting misreadings, or, rather, half-readings' of lines in 'A grief ago' and the first of the 'Altarwise by owl-light' sonnets, in the *Sunday Times*.

p. 180 Thomas on beast and angel: 16 May 1938.

pp. 180–1 Thomas to Treece, 'cut out that remark': probably May 1939.

p. 181 Thomas to Treece, on poets: 23 March 1938.

p. 181 to Keidrych Rhys: 28 October 1937.

p. 182 Society for Welsh authors: Thomas to W. T. (Pennar) Davies, July 1939.

p. 182 Five poems: the other three were 'On no work of words', a notebook revision dated 'Laugharne. September 1938'; 'The tombstone told when she died', another revision, similarly dated; and the four-line 'I, the first named', published only in the magazine *Seven*, October 1938, in Thomas's lifetime.

p. 182 Thomas to Watkins: postmarked 14 October 1938. 'A saint about to fall' was provisionally titled 'In September'.

p. 182 'Boom boom boom': Thomas to Davenport, 23 June 1939.

p. 182 radio anthology: Thomas to T. Rowland Hughes, BBC Cardiff, 2(?) October 1938 (second numeral illegible).

p. 183 'shouting under the sea': Thomas to T. Rowland Hughes, 1 November 1938.

p. 183 'In a rush': Watkins quoting Thomas, annotation to *L.V.W.*, p. 57.

p. 183 Thomas to Laughlin: 28 March 1938.

p. 184 A few pounds: Thomas to Davenport, 24 August 1938: '[Laughlin] gave me, when I was broke and hungry, eight pounds, which I regarded foolishly as a present. Later, he sent me a contract to sign that said the eight pounds was an advance on royalties ...' Laughlin said (letter to the author) that small payments would have been for material in a *New Directions in Poetry and Prose* anthology, where a number of Thomas poems and stories appeared in 1938 and 1939. Laughlin thought it was Edith Sitwell who told him about Thomas.

p. 184 Book earnings: D.H.A.

p. 185 Thomas to Higham: 24 November 1938.

p. 185 Thomas to Watkins: 20 December 1938.

p. 185 New poems at Blashford: others were: (a) 'Once it was the colour of saying', sent to Watkins about 8 January 1939. In 'Notes on Dylan Thomas' Watkins said it was 'about the room in the house in Cwmdonkin Drive where he wrote many poems. Its wide windows looked across the road to a sloping field where girls used to play hockey.' (In fact, the room was the best bedroom.) Watkins saw it as a key poem, anticipating a change of style by Thomas to a more straightforward manner, 'in the direction of the living voice' (*L.V.W.*, pp. 20–21). But it sounds as if it may have originated much earlier in a notebook, now missing.

(b) 'If my head hurt a hair's foot', sent to Watkins with letter of 3

March 1939 – 'I've got to do the proofs of my new book of poems [*The Map of Love*] this week, & I'm thinking of putting in this poem just finished.'

p. 186 Poem from a dream: Watkins, 'Notes on Dylan Thomas'.

p. 186 Explaining the poem: to Desmond Hawkins, 14 August 1939.

p. 186 Miller, Durrell, 'nightmare London': Thomas to Watkins, about 8 January 1939.

p. 186 Thomas to Trick: probably March 1939.

p. 186 Money from Dent: Thomas to Higham, probably July 1939.

p. 186 Five-shilling plan: Thomas to Davenport, 11 May 1939, 23 June 1939 and [?May 1939].

p. 187 'Surely there must': to Davenport, ?July 1939.

p. 187 Thomas to Watkins: about 25 August 1939.

p. 187 Thomas to his father: 29 August 1939.

p. 187 Thomas to Treece: 6 or 7 July 1938, and n.d., July 1939.

p. 187 Thomas to Trick: 29 September 1939.

p. 188 Thomas to D. S. Savage: 27 October 1939.

p. 188 Thomas to Patchen: 27 November 1939.

p. 189fn BBC memo: BBC Archives.

p. 190 Connolly on *Map of Love*: 16 September 1939.

p. 190 *Map of Love* earnings etc.: D.H.A.

p. 190 The tribunal: Keidrych Rhys, in an interview; Vernon Watkins 'Notes on D.T.'.

p. 191 Gwynfor Evans: letter from Evans (later a Welsh Nationalist Member of Parliament).

p. 191 'Punctured lungs': Ethel Ross, quoting Florence Thomas.

p. 191 'Scarred lungs': Vernon Watkins, quoted at second hand in Bill Read's papers. Texas mss.

p. 191fn Thomas to Spender: 13 May 1940.

p. 192 The bed: Thomas to Watkins, 6 March 1940.

p. 192 'TA for the pound': n.d., pres. 1940.

p. 192 Appeal to Spender: 13 May 1940.

p. 192 'Life's quite different': to Spender, 4 June 1940.

pp. 192–4 At Marshfield: interviews with Antonia White, Ian Henderson and William Glock.

p. 193 *Canary* in 1938: to Charles Fisher, 16 March 1938.

p. 193 *Canary* and *Horizon*: a galley-proof of 'The Parachutist' is in Texas mss, with a note signed by Cyril Connolly to say it was 'set up by *Horizon* ... but not published owing to lack of space'. 'Request to Leda' appeared in the July 1942 issue.

p. 193 Air-raid dreams: Thomas to Watkins, summer 1940.

p. 194 'Talked itself away': Thomas to Davenport, 8 January 1941.

p. 194 Caitlin's little fling: she first told me the story in 1978. Glock confirmed it in 1992.

p. 194 'Muddled and unhappy': 8 January 1941.

pp. 194–5 In London briefly: BBC internal memo, 12 December 1940, asking that Thomas be sent a cheque immediately 'if humanly possible ... He came in to see me today, in an exceedingly nervous state, having been bombed. He is terribly anxious to leave London and is unable to do so as he has no money till this cheque reaches him.' BBC Archives.

p. 195 Train to Wales: Thomas to Davenport, 8 January 1941.

p. 195 Alec Waugh: Thomas to Davenport, 27 January 1941.

p. 195 'Long-legged Bait': a letter to Davenport, probably 25 April 1941, says: 'I've just finished my ballad. Too late, unfortunately, for the May Horizon. It's about 220 lines long, a tremendous effort for me ...' Watkins wrote in 'Notes on D.T.':

> I saw Dylan a great deal when he was writing the 'Ballad of the Long-legged Bait', and I saw this poem grow from its first fifteen lines through all the stages of its composition. He wrote the four-lined verses in pairs. The poem is full of visual imagery. It was so much a visual poem that he made a coloured picture for it which he pinned on the wall of his room, a picture of a woman lying at the bottom of the sea. She was a new Loreley revealing the pitfalls of destruction awaiting those who attempted to put off the flesh.

p. 195 Connolly and 'Ballad': 'Dylan Thomas', BBC radio documentary, 9 November 1963.

p. 195 BBC scripts: The undated letter to the producer (Royston

Morley) says, 'Is this kind of propoganda [*sic*] too sticky?' In a letter to another official, 6 May 1941, Thomas thanks him for sending on documents about the Czech Legation to be used in a script, but adds:

> I'm afraid I found them pretty useless: just dry accounts, with no personal detail to speak of, of the taking of towns and military positions. 'Then we took Omsk and Tomsk and Bomsk. We lost 40 wagons and 3 men. This was in April' ... The Czech officers who so very kindly wrote their reminiscences have apparently so little dramatic feeling that they could make their reminiscences of Dunkirk as uneventful as a meeting of the Coke Board. I hope the script is not too unsatisfactory ...

pp. 195–6 Thomas to Clement Davenport: 2 April 1941.

p. 196 Meeting Trick: 'The Young Dylan Thomas'.

p. 196 D.J. on Polly, and other Blaen Cwm details: Hettie Owen.

pp. 196–7 Bus conductor: Haydn Taylor.

p. 197 Thomas to Watkins: 22 May 1941.

p. 197 Same age as Keats: FitzGibbon, p. 281.

p. 197 'happy while it lasted': dated 1 July 1932; later it was part of the poem published as 'Out of the sighs'.

p. 197 Sale to Buffalo: *Poet in the Making*, pp. 273–4.

p. 198 Thomas to Fisher: 15 July 1941.

p. 198 'Squeeze another drop': Thomas to Watkins, May 1941.

p. 198 Pollinger to Thomas: D.H.A.

p. 198 *Skin Trade* first mentioned: n.d., summer 1940. Watkins wrote in his Foreword to *L.V.W.* that 'in Dylan's first plan, as far as I can remember it, there were to be seven skins. At the end of the story the character would be naked at last. It would be in one way a journey through the Inferno of London, but it would also be a comedy.' Perhaps the recollection of a 'journey through the Inferno' owed more to Watkins's imagination than to Thomas's.

p. 198 'My prosebook': Thomas to Watkins, 22 May 1941.

p. 198 'My novel blathers on': 28 May 1941.

p. 198 'the Rimbaud of Cwmdonkin Drive': in a 1950 radio discussion which included Roy Campbell, Thomas said, 'I won't forgive you for the Swansea's Rimbaud, because you called me that first, Roy, I remember'. 'Poetic Licence', BBC Home Service, 13 December 1950. BBC Archives.

p. 198. Dent's £25: reported by Laurence Pollinger to Thomas, 3 June 1941. D.H.A.

pp. 198–9 Hadfield to Pollinger: 10 July 1941. Texas mss.

p. 199 Watkins staying with Thomas: reported by Watkins in his Foreword to *Skin Trade*, op. cit, p. 9.

p. 199 Profitable *Skin Trade*: a magazine, John Lehmann's *Folios of New Writings* V, published the first part as 'A Fine Beginning' in autumn 1941. Later the ms passed through the hands of other London publishers. Graham Greene read it in 1947 for Eyre & Spottiswoode and was interested (Thomas to David Higham, 8 October and 12 November 1947. Higham to Thomas, 24 November 1947, D.H.A.). So were Dent again, briefly. Everyone thought Thomas was sure to finish it sooner or later. In the USA the New American Library paid a $397 advance for the first two chapters in 1952 and published them in a *New World Writing* selection (New American Library to Thomas, 9 May 1952. Indiana mss). NAL later published the third chapter as 'Four Lost Souls'. Since Thomas's death the unfinished book has been published in several editions in Britain and the USA.

p. 199 'Dawn Raid': sent to Watkins with undated letter. First published in *Life and Letters Today*, August 1941.

p. 199 'friendless London': Thomas to Watkins, 28 August 1941.

p. 199 In London, August 1941: the date is disputed. Donald Taylor told Bill Read he hired Thomas on a fine summer's evening in 1940 (letter of 15 November 1963, Texas mss). FitzGibbon, presumably using the same source, also says 1940 (pp. 277–8). But until the end of August 1941, Thomas was based in Laugharne, writing poverty-stricken letters. His first letter on Strand Films writing paper is dated 6 January 1942; his first film credit was in May 1942, 'This is Colour' (*Dylan Thomas in Print*, p. 135). Ivan Moffat says (in a letter) that the 'summer of '41 sounds reasonable', although he may have introduced Thomas and Taylor the previous year.

p. 200 £10 a week: Taylor to Read, 15 November 1963. Texas mss.

9. *War and 'Fern Hill'*

p. 201 Ten films: *Dylan Thomas in Print* (pp. 135–41) identifies eight; FitzGibbon (p. 401) the other two.

p. 201 Taylor on Thomas: letter to Read, op.cit.

p. 201 etc. Moffat quoted: in letters to the author, unless otherwise indicated.

pp. 201ff Maclaren-Ross: *Memoirs of the Forties*. 'The Pole Star Neighbour'.

pp. 202–3 'These Are the Men' extract: John Ackerman, *Dylan Thomas. The Filmscripts*, p. 41.

p. 203 'Green Mountain . . .': ibid., pp. 28, 31–2.

p. 203 'Green Mountain, Black Mountain': the film runs for about twelve minutes. It uses two narrators and has the inevitable Welsh chorus in the background.

p. 204 MOI's Welsh office: Arthur Calder-Marshall.

p. 204 'Our Country': Ackerman, *The Filmscripts*, p. 70.

pp. 204–5. Corruption: Lindsay, *Meetings with Poets*, pp. 6–7.

p. 205 The Thomases at the Herberts': FitzGibbon, p. 288.

p. 205fn Ripping up mss: Elisabeth Lutyens, *A Goldfish Bowl*, pp. 205–6.

p. 206 Manresa Road: *T.F.F.*, pp. 199–200; FitzGibbon, pp. 289–90.

p. 206 To Caitlin, from Manresa Road: undated, 1943.

p. 207 To Caitlin, from King's Arms: undated, probably 1943.

p. 208 Maclaren-Ross: op. cit., p. 132.

p. 208 Lindsay's story: Lindsay, *Meetings with Poets*, p. 11.

p. 209 Ruth Wynn Owen: in an interview.

p. 209 Thomas to Wynn Owen from Strand: n.d., perhaps May 1942.

p. 209 Thomas to Wynn Owen from Talsarn: 28 August 1942.

p. 210 Ms of a poem: Thomas seems to have written this out for her benefit, heading it 'For Ruth'. Perhaps it was conceived with her in mind. But as Ruth Wynn Owen observed, 'Most young poets carry some half- or even completely-formed piece that they can dash off

spontaneously and give to someone.' The poem was published in
Poetry (London), April 1944, as 'Last night I dived my beggar arm';
it is one of the few poems known to have been written after the 1930s
that does not appear in *C.P.* The version in Ruth Wynn Owen's
possession had variants throughout, and two pairs of alternative
words:

> Last night he ⎱ dived my beggar arm
>   I ⎰
>
> Into her breast that wore no heart
> For me ⎱ alone only the deep drum
>   her ⎰
> Telling her hurt heart
>
> That her luminous, tumbled limbs
> Will plunge his betrayal through the sky
> So the betrayed will read in the sunbeams
> Of a death in another country.

The *Poetry (London)* version is in *The Poems*, p. 175.

p. 210 One further letter: Thomas to Wynn Owen, 19 September
1943. '... I've been in Wales for some weeks now, and have had time
and a rinsed head enough to be able to write what I want. In London,
I mean to write you every day, but the laziness, the horror and selfpity,
that London drizzles down on me, stop everything but the ghost of a
hope that perhaps you will ring...'

p. 210 Ties; the dachshund: Donald Taylor, letters to Bill Read. Texas
mss.

p. 210 Stealing the silver: Rupert Shephard's memoirs.

p. 210 Thomas's devious letter: to Lorna Wilmott (Mrs Shephard), 28
February 1940.

p. 210 Elisabeth Lutyens: in an interview.

p. 211 Ivan Moffat: in 'Dylan Thomas', the 1963 radio documentary.

p. 211 Davenport on Thomas: ibid., and in unused BBC recordings.

p. 211 Hugh Porteus: *Spectator*, 2 September 1950. 'Nights Out in the
Thirties'.

p. 211 William Saroyan: *Books and Bookmen*, July 1964, 'The Wild
Boy'. One of the other writers was Ivan Moffat. Moffat's account (in

a letter) is not at all like Saroyan's. 'Dylan would sometimes start the morning off with a couple of double Pimms, but this would usually be when travelling, or before some non-working occasion on a weekend (as on the morning I brought him and William Saroyan together at the Café Royal early in '44, during which Saroyan uttered a thousand sentences and Dylan one, though he poked his face about pretty expressively – a face much stretched and flushed with Pimms)...'

pp. 211–12 Gwen Watkins: *A.W.R.*, Winter 1972. 'A Newly-Discovered Letter: Dylan Thomas to Vernon Watkins'.

p. 212 At the Devases: *T.F.F.*, pp. 238–9.

p. 212 'To correct the imbalance': Ivan Moffat, in a letter.

p. 213 Jack Lindsay: *Meetings with Poets*, pp. 20–25.

p. 213 Margaret Taylor: in an interview.

p. 213 Caitlin on TV: 'Tonight', BBC 1, 3 December 1975. She was in Rome, interviewed from London, shortly before her husband's letters to her were put up for auction in London. Bidding failed to rise above £2100, perhaps because of fears that she would make difficulties about allowing the letters to be published, and they were withdrawn. Eventually she sold them to Maurice Neville in California.

p. 213fn Thomas to Taylor and Tennant: 28 October 1944; 28 August 1945.

p. 214 Thomas to Watkins: 27 July 1944, from the Blaen Cwm cottage.

p. 214. The bungalow: Mrs Evans, Lampeter, widow of the doctor who owned it.

p. 214 'Ceremony After a Fire Raid': first published in *Our Time*, May 1944.

p. 215 'Holy Spring': sent to Watkins 15 November 1944, from Majoda – 'a poem ... which I started a long time ago but finished very recently, after a lot of work'.

p. 215 'Vision and Prayer': sent to Watkins 28 October 1944, from Majoda.

p. 215 Christian position: Aneirin Talfan Davies, the most persistent advocate of Thomas as religious poet (and crypto-Roman Catholic), believed that 'the turning point in his poetic career came in the patterned poem, "Vision and Prayer", in the style of George Herbert, one of Dylan's favourites ... It is a poem about birth and re-birth, and twice in crucial sections of the poem, he speaks of being "found".' Lecture to Dylan Thomas Summer School, Swansea University College, 1974.

p. 215 Sending 'Poem in October': Thomas to Watkins, 30 August 1944.

p. 215 Watkins on 'Poem in October': 'Notes on Dylan Thomas'.

pp. 215–16 Grigson's view: *New Statesman*, 8 December 1964, 'Dylan and the Dragon'.

p. 216 Watkins: foreword to *Skin Trade*, pp. 15–16.

p. 216 'Catllewdylaer': Thomas to Watkins, 30 August 1944.

p. 216 Verse letter to Earp: postmarked 21 September 1944.

p. 217 Punning letter to Earp: 1 July 1943.

p. 217 To Smart: December 1932.

p. 217 At Majoda: Mrs Evans.

p. 217 The cousin: Mrs Theodosia Legg, of Cardiff.

p. 217 Thomas to Taylor: 28 October 1944.

p. 217 *Twenty Years A-Growing*: Bill Read, *The Days of Dylan Thomas*, p. 106.

p. 218 Burke and Hare: Thomas to Taylor, 19 September 1944. 'I hope you're not quite so penniless, & in debt, as I am, but, anyway, the dough from B & H will be, I'm sure, welcome. And oh the difference to me!'

p. 218 'A Book of Streets': Wales mss, which has the synopsis and a file of publisher's correspondence.

p. 219 'ON NOT TURNING UP': sent with letter to Watkins, 28 October 1944.

p. 219 Gwen Watkins on 'fake letter': *A.W.R.*, Winter 1972.

p. 219 At the Café Royal: Gwen Watkins, ibid.

pp. 219–20 The real apology: 26 February 1945. Misspellings include 'occassion', 'expells', 'dissapations' and 'acheived'.

p. 221 'Book of Streets': the second letter was written 6 February 1945.

pp. 221–3 The shooting incident: interviews with the former Captain Killick and his wife; *Welsh Gazette*, 12 April 1945 (reprinted *Dylan Thomas in Print*, p. 72) and 28 June 1945; *News of the World*, 24 June 1945. Donald Taylor wrote an account in a letter to Bill Read, in Texas mss. The incident is often recalled in garbled form. One version, which I heard in a long and detailed account in 1976 from an acquaintance of Thomas, was set in the west of England. Thomas was supposed to have been pursued by a vengeful American army officer. The officer had a machine-gun, and chased the poet down lanes and through fields. Trouble over a woman was given as the reason. No doubt Thomas invented this stirring tale.

p. 222 Brawl with Caitlin's brother: *T.F.F.*, p. 242.

p. 223 Thomas to Watkins: 28 March 1945.

p. 223 *Deaths and Entrances*: Laurence Pollinger to Thomas, 15 November 1944, said Dent would like to publish in 1945, and were offering an advance of £50. D.H.A.

p. 224 Thomas to Patchen: 27 November 1939.

p. 224 Thomas to Laughlin: 10 February 1945.

p. 224 'A little ladleful': 28 March 1945.

p. 224 'Revelations': Glyn Jones said that Thomas never used the correct form, 'Revelation'.

pp. 224–5 Thomas to Williams: 30 July 1945.

pp. 226–7 Thomas to Caitlin: 1945, ? mid-August.

p. 227 London not impressed: memo from G. R. Barnes, Director of Talks in London, to Aneirin Talfan Davies, 6 January 1945: 'I should have thought the wit would have been much better appreciated if it had been read caustically, or, at least, dryly ...' BBC Archives.

p. 228 Worksheets: Brinnin, p. 95.

10. *A Voice on the Radio*

p. 230 Moving to London: a letter from Thomas at Blaen Cwm to 'Dear Francis' [Butterfield] is headed 'Friday 21, 45'. 21 September 1945 was a Friday. The letter concerns arrangements for a return to London: 'Caitlin and I are sending up some things to London – a trunk or two and a single bed among them – which we want temporarily put among our other things in the studio ... we might be in London before then [Wednesday the 26th] staying temporarily with Toni...'

p. 230 Visa: Thomas to Oscar Williams, 5 December 1945, from 39 Markham Square, Chelsea, where the Thomases were staying with Caitlin's sister, Nicolette Devas.

p. 230 Thomas in hospital: FitzGibbon, p. 313.

p. 231 Jack Lindsay: *Meetings with Poets*, pp. 21-2.

p. 232 *Deaths and Entrances*: 3000 copies, *Dylan Thomas in Print*. Other printing details: Thomas to Higham, 25 March 1946.

p. 232 Titles for stories: Thomas to Higham, ibid.

p. 232 Officially a freelance: Leslie Andrews (accountant) to David Higham, 7 April 1948. D.H.A.

p. 232 John Arlott: 'Dylan Thomas and Radio', *Adelphi*, February 1954.

p. 232 With James Stephens: 18 June 1946, in a series called 'Books and Writers'. Extracts are in *Q.E.O.M.*, titled 'On Poetry.' Fuller text, *Encounter*, November 1954.

pp. 232-3 With Edward Shanks: 'What Has Happened to English Poetry', in a series called 'Freedom Forum', recorded 11 October 1946, for transmission later that month. The BBC Archives transcript doesn't indicate who is speaking, and not all the remarks can be safely ascribed. But it must have been Thomas who described the Georgian revival as 'a revival of rather tepid poets, sitting in deck chairs outside public houses in the country: or inns, I'm sorry. Sitting outside inns and writing poems about how lovely it was to see a cow or a bull or even an obscure bird for perhaps the third time.'

p. 233 'The Londoner': recorded 15 July 1946, for transmission later that month to Africa and North America.

p. 233 Gilliam: letter to Thomas, 18 July 1946, praising 'a most sensitive and successful piece of radio'. BBC Archives.

p. 233 Margate programme: 'Margate – Past and Present' recorded 22 September 1946.

p. 233 Elisabeth Lutyens: in an interview.

p. 233 Oxford by car: FitzGibbon, p. 317.

p. 234 Campbell: 'Memories of Dylan Thomas at the BBC', *Poetry* (Chicago), November 1955.

p. 234fn Richard Burton: *Book Week*, 24 October 1965.

p. 235 Third Programme memo: 10 December 1951, from the Controller, Third Programme to the Head of Copyright. BBC Archives.

p. 235 Margaret Taylor sees a crony: in an interview.

p. 235 The perfect contract: Elisabeth Lutyens, *A Goldfish Bowl*, p. 155.

p. 235 Seeking employment: memo from Controller, Third Programme, to Controller, Talks, 18 August 1950. BBC Archives.

p. 235 Trip to Ireland: FitzGibbon, p. 324. A letter to John Ormond (Thomas), then on the staff of *Picture Post*, 6 March 1948, promises 'no repetition of the disastrous PUCK FAIR VISIT!'

p. 235 Thomas to Taylor: 29 August 1946.

pp. 235–6 Thomas to Laughlin: 24 November 1946.

p. 236 Edith Sitwell to John Lehmann: *Edith Sitwell. Selected Letters*.

p. 236 Sitwell pulls strings: ibid., letters to Lehmann, 11 December 1946, and Ronald Bottrall, 25 February 1947.

p. 236 The scholarship: The Society of Authors has a 'Travelling Scholarship Fund', set up in 1943 by an anonymous donor to 'help British creative writers to keep in touch with their colleagues abroad'. The donor was apparently the writer known as 'Bryher', born Annie Ellerman (1894–1983), daughter of the wealthy shipowner Sir John Ellerman. In her time she also helped James Joyce and Edith Sitwell. Bryher owned the magazine *Life and Letters Today*, which in the 1930s and 1940s published work by many Welsh writers, among them Dylan Thomas. Its editor, Robert Herring, and his place among the Bryher connections, is examined in Meic Stephens' 'The Third Man: Robert Herring and *Life and Letters To-day*', in *Welsh Writing in English: A Yearbook of Critical Essays*, Vol. 3, 1997.

p. 236 Thomas to Durrell: ? December 1937.

p. 236 'Return Journey': after some internal politicking by the Welsh Region of the BBC, the programme was presently handed over to them, and made in Cardiff; the producer was P. H. Burton, Richard Burton's unofficial guardian and mentor. The notebook, in Texas mss, also contains notes on Oxford eccentrics, headed 'Eccentric figures'. 'Return Journey' was first broadcast 14 June 1947, Home Service.

p. 237 Swansea friend: Cecil Price, *Adam* Memorial Number.

p. 237 Mrs Ferguson and Mrs Hole: Thomas to Margaret Taylor, 11 July 1947.

p. 237 Who went to Italy: Thomas to Charles Fisher, 1 March 1947.

p. 237 Lost luggage: Thomas to parents, 11 April 1947; Thomas to Taylor, 12 April 1947.

pp. 237–8 'No escape': Thomas to Taylor, 12 April 1947.

p. 238 Eating without children: Aeronwy Thomas-Ellis, *Christmas and Other Memories. A daughter remembers Dylan*, booklet published by Amwy Press.

p. 238 To parents, about Rome etc: 5 May 1947.

p. 240 'The slowest in the world': Thomas to Margaret Taylor, 4 June 1947.

p. 240 Thomas to Davenport: 29 May 1947.

p. 240 Thomas to Earp: 11 July 1947.

p. 241 Gazing into space: Mario Luizi, *Adam* Memorial Number. 'Entering the *Giubbe Rosse* late of an evening, he was to be found entrenched behind a small forest of bottles, a full glass in his hand, and one wondered whether those large pale blue eyes [they were brown] were gazing upon something ineffable or merely into vacancy.'

p. 241 In the wardrobe: Gwen Watkins.

p. 241 Thomas to Taylor: 12 April 1947.

p. 241 Manor House details: Thomas to parents, 5 June 1947.

p. 241 Thomas to Taylor (thanking her): 4 June 1947.

p. 242 William York Tindall: *A Reader's Guide to Dylan Thomas*, p. 285.

p. 242 Woman admirer: Helen Bevington, who described the conversation in *When Found, Make a Verse Of*. She met Thomas at Duke University, May 1953.

p. 242 The reporter: Mary Ellin Barrett, *The Reporter*, 27 April 1954. She met Thomas in New York, 21 February 1952.

p. 242 The American student: Alastair Reid, then at Sarah Lawrence College, New York.

p. 243 'Windmill arms': 3 August 1947.

p. 243 Broken arm: FitzGibbon, p. 333.

pp. 243ff Thomases at South Leigh: Cordelia Locke in an interview, and in letters to Bill Read and a manuscript about the period in Texas mss.

p. 245 Taylor to Higham: D.H.A.

p. 245 Payments to Thomas: Higham to Thomas, 10 October 1947; D.H.A.

p. 245 Thomas and British National: Sydney Box, letters to Bill Read, Texas mss; Cordelia Locke; memo, 11 September 1947, D.H.A.

pp. 245–6 Thomas at Gainsborough: letters from Box to Bill Read, Texas mss; Jan Read, former script editor at Gainsborough.

p. 246 Thomas's earnings: D.H.A.

p. 248 Italian creditor: letter to Thomas from 'J.T.', 10 March 1950, with Oscar Williams papers. Indiana mss.

p. 248 'Grand opera': Thomas to parents, 12 January 1947.

pp. 248–9 Michael Ayrton: BBC Radio 3, 18 October 1975, 'Man of Action'.

p. 249 Thomas to BBC producer: to Ursula Keeble, 11 January 1947.

p. 249 Irritable memorandum: Keeble to Director of Schools Broadcasting, 13 May 1947. BBC Archives.

p. 249 'Poems, 1934–1947': Thomas to Higham, 7 October 1947.

p. 249 *Skin Trade*: Thomas to Higham, 12 November 1947. See Notes to p. 199.

p. 250 Thomas to Caitlin: ?January or February 1948.

p. 250 'Saucepans and operations': ?summer 1948.

pp. 252–3 Thomas to Frances Hughes: 10 October 1948.

p. 253 Radio talk: 'Living in Wales', Scottish Home Service, 23 June 1949. FitzGibbon prints it (pp. 338–42). A BBC memo from London (where the talk was recorded) to the Scottish Region said: 'Dylan Thomas's piece for you is first-class rococo. He makes an exuberant attack on British Railways buffet cars, and Oxford residents, and paints a pretty dreary picture of Wales; the only country not attacked is fortunately Scotland. We shall record at three o'clock today, but wish to warn you that a solemn railway official might take treble umbrage. Please return discs here: I shall recommend it to Third.' BBC Archives.

p. 253 Speaking at Edinburgh: the talk went on, 'Caradoc Evans, by the way, had his portrait painted some years ago by Evan Walters of Swansea, who offered it, free, to Swansea Art Gallery. I was a newspaper reporter at the time, devoting myself to critical reviews of performances, in Ystradgynlais, by girls' schools' dramatic societies of the *Mikado*, and inquests on drinkers of methylated spirits ... And as a reporter I attended, sucking a glove, the Art Gallery meeting in which the offer of the portrait of Caradoc Evans was discussed.

'The chairman of the Art Gallery Committee was Sir Dai Davies, the proprietor of the newspaper for which I doodled. "About this picture of Caradoc Evans, now," he said. "Caradoc Evans is a liar. He says that Welshmen are narrow-minded hypocrites. I throw that lie in his teeth. We are not hypocrites. We are not narrow-minded. We'll show him. I refuse to have his portrait hung in our gallery ..." ' *Voice of Scotland*, December 1948. A dialect poem, possibly by Thomas, is appended.

p. 253 *Picture Post*: Thomas to John Ormond [Thomas], 6 March 1948.

p. 253 Mrs Taylor and Gosport: from interviews in Laugharne.

p. 253 Richard Hughes's house: Thomas to Frances Hughes, 10 October 1948.

p. 254 Bicycle accident: Thomas to Higham, 21 December 1948.

p. 254 Thomas in Prague: Jack Lindsay, *Meetings with Poets*, pp. 36–7; FitzGibbon, pp. 343–7.

p. 254 Thomas to Margaret Taylor: postmarked May 11.

11. *Laugharne and America*

p. 255 Shed and house are described in 'Poet in the Boat House', Mimi Josephson, *John O'London's*, 7 August 1953; *T.F.F.*, pp. 204–5 etc.; Glyn Jones, *The Dragon Has Two Tongues*, p. 197.

p. 256 Mains water: this, and converting the garage into the work-shed, cost about £150.

p. 256 Elisabeth Lutyens: in an interview.

p. 256 Thomas at work: *Leftover*, p. 36.

p. 256 Bottles of ale: Margaret Taylor.

p. 256 'In Country Heaven' design: radio talk and reading, BBC Third Programme, 25 September 1950; reprinted as 'Three Poems' in *Q.E.O.M.* (Dent edition only).

p. 257 Bread for the birds: Florence Thomas, tape-recorded interview with Colin Edwards.

p. 257 'most perfect poem': Watkins in a recording made for the BBC radio documentary, 'Dylan Thomas', 1963.

p. 257 Leo Abse: in an interview.

p. 257 Brinnin's invitation: he was appointed director of the Poetry Center on 4 April 1949, and wrote to Thomas on 14 April (letter to the author).

p. 257fn Dannie Abse: in a BBC television programme about Thomas, 9 April 1976. 'Once just after the war Dylan Thomas told my elder brother Leo of a dream he'd had recently. Of how in his dream he had floated into a large unlit cavern and there saw Job smitten by boils sitting with his three false comforters. That cavern led into another, and that one into yet another, and back and back in time Dylan wandered in his dream, seeing one Biblical scene after another ... Until he wandered right back to the darkest cave of all, the very first one, and there saw a man and a woman hand in hand. I doubt if this was a real dream but it does illustrate the direction of Dylan Thomas's imagination. A journey back to Paradise ...'

p. 258 Thomas to Laughlin: 24 October 1949.

p. 258 *The Plain Dealer*: a letter from David Higham Associates to Thomas, 10 February 1945, says the BBC will not pay more than seventy-five guineas for the script. But he was offered a further twenty-five guineas for acting in it. BBC Archives.

p. 258 'perfectly bloody': to Wilfred Grantham, 28 May 1949.

p. 258 *The Trojan Women*: BBC memo from Royston Morley, 29 September 1947: 'Special acting version of Euripides' *The Trojan Women* by Dylan Thomas. I have been in touch with Dylan Thomas about the above, and he is interested.' BBC Archives.

p. 258 Auden approached: Royston Morley.

p. 258 'a favourite play': Thomas to Robert McDermott, head of television drama, 6 January 1949. McDermott had written on 20 December, 'How allergic are you to Peer Gynt? I ask because we want to do a full-scale television production of it ...' BBC Archives.

p. 259 Thomas to his agent: 9 July 1949.

p. 259 'Awful', 'wretched', script: Thomas to Davenport, 11 October 1949; to Margaret Taylor, 28 November 1949.

p. 260 and fn Thomas the clubman: letter from Mervyn Levy to Bill Read says Thomas was elected to the Savage on 10 March 1949; and was a member of the National Liberal Club from January 1947 to February 1949. Texas mss. Thomas to Davenport, 26 August 1948: 'And thank you very much for putting me up, with Parry as seconder, for the Savage. In a year, then, unless I am blackballed ... I can give up the National Lavatory and be bad in worse company.'

p. 260 Swansea broadcast: 'Swansea and the Arts'. BBC Welsh Home Service, 24 October 1949. 'We speak from the Grove of Swansea. But if anyone in the deep damp caverns of the rustic dead, in some Welsh tenebrous regional, should have seen this programme announced in the Radio Tombs, turned on his badger's set, tuned in on a long-forgotten gravelength and caught that opening statement, let me hasten to tell him that he, alas, would hardly recognise the Grove at all ...' BBC Archives. A brief extract is in Q.E.O.M. as 'Wales and the Artist'. The Grove (where Kingsley Amis lived once), is a side-street in the Uplands, a few hundred yards from the house where Thomas was born.

p. 260 Thomas to Laughlin: 23 November 1949.

p. 260 'White Giant's Thigh' worksheet: Indiana mss. In the 'Three Poems' broadcast, 25 September 1950, Thomas said the poem was 'just written'.

pp. 260–1 The opening line: Watkins, 'Notes on Dylan Thomas'.

p. 261 Caetani: the London meeting and £100 advance are mentioned in Thomas's letter to her, 2 November 1949.

p. 261 The finished letter: Thomas to Caetani, 24 November 1949.

p. 261 Thanking a correspondent: to Brinnin, 23 November 1949. Draft with alterations, Indiana mss.

p. 262 BMA letter: Thomas to C. J. Cellan-Jones, 10 January 1950.

pp. 262–3 The car journey: Mervyn Levy and Bernard Gutteridge; Dan Davin, *Closing Times*, pp. 135–8.

p. 263 Brinnin as agent: Brinnin (p. 52) says: 'As agent for Dylan's first tour, I retained ten per cent of his payments. Actually, this amounted only to a token payment' (because of his outgoings on Thomas's behalf). Writing to David Higham on 1 December 1949, Thomas said:

> John Malcolm Brinnin has written to me at length, suggesting that he, as a wellknown lecturer, literary journalist, etc., in the States, and as Director of the Poetry Center ... should become my secretary and agent for my stay there ... He said that the Lecture Agencies, which prefer novelists anyway, have nowhere near his own acquaintanceship with the institutions etc. which like poets, and would take, for their services, anything up to 40%. He, although he would do it for friendship, as a fellow poet (dear God!), cannot afford to do so, & would have to ask 15% of what I make on my appearances as a reader and lecturer. I cabled back & agreed ... believing that Brinnin will really do a good job for me. (I hear extremely well of him from Laughlin) ...

p. 263 Thomas to Brinnin: 23 November 1949.

p. 263 Thomas to Laughlin: 23 November 1949.

pp. 263–4 Glyn Jones visit: *The Dragon Has Two Tongues*, p. 197.

p. 264 The telegram: BBC Archives.

p. 264 Thomas to Davenport: 30 January 1949 (error for 30 December 1949).

p. 264 Posh dentist: in an undated (probably February 1950) letter from the Savage Club, Thomas told Caitlin that his visa and the bank were taken care of; said he was to visit a 'posh dentist'; and asked her to collect and send him his suit from the cleaners so that he could be in a Picasso play. The play was *Desire Caught by the Tail*. Thomas appeared in it at the Rudolf Steiner Hall, Baker Street, in a 'theatrical evening' organised by the Institute of Contemporary Arts. Reviewed by Alan Dent, *News Chronicle*, 18 February 1950.

p. 264 Radio talk: 'A Visit to America', recorded in Swansea, 5 October 1953, broadcast posthumously (BBC Welsh Home Service) 30 March 1954. Printed in *Q.E.O.M.* A duplicated BBC typescript, privately owned, has variants, in the form of corrections and additions in Thomas's hand; e.g. the sentence, 'And there shiver and teeter also, meek and driven, those British authors' etc. (*Q.E.O.M.*, p. 65) inserts between 'driven' and 'those' the words 'their little eyes lost and rabbit-scared behind bi-focal glasses steamed over by the smoke of countless cocktail parties'.

pp. 264ff Thomas in New York: unless otherwise stated, the chronology is Brinnin's.

p. 265 'Gigantic fuck': William York Tindall, *A Reader's Guide to Dylan Thomas*. Presumably what Thomas said was 'fuck', but Tindall used a dash instead, and now cannot remember what it signified. Tindall wrote (p. 302) that Thomas 'looked like, and acted the part of, an amorous Volkswagen, driven by Harpo Marx. Chasing the girls round the room, he blew down their dickies. Everyone, wives and husbands alike, took this in good part, except John Malcolm Brinnin, who sat frowning in a corner. Thomas was a poet, after all, and we were academic bourgeoisie, except John Malcolm Brinnin. It was plain, moreover, that the harmless poet, doing his best, was doing what he thought expected of him or else was hiding shyness under what he thought its opposite.'

p. 265 'Out of the mists': Reel 12 of Dylan Thomas tapes at the Poetry Center. These tapes consisted of fragments apparently arbitrarily linked, and with no index or check-list. Some items, including this one, could be dated by internal evidence.

p. 265fn Thomas at Llanelli: *Llanelly Star*, 13 December 1952: 'Wales, by Dylan Thomas. In an address to Llanelly Little Theatre at the British Legion buildings, Vauxhall, last week'. The newspaper printed a verbatim report of Thomas's opening remarks, presumably taken down in shorthand. 'Llanelly' was the spelling in Thomas's day.

p. 266 Thomas to parents: 26 February 1950.

p. 266 Thomas to Caitlin: 25 February 1950.

p. 267 *Reuben, Reuben*: de Vries's Thomas-figure was Gowan Glamorgan McGland, with Irish and Scots blood, but mainly Welsh. 'How' (speculates a character) 'could a man who mumbled so in conversation read with such ethereal magic on the public platform and into phonograph mikes?' And, 'He was a rogue and we both knew that.'

p. 267 At the Hymans': Brinnin, pp. 30–31.

p. 267 Gill's account: *Here at the New Yorker*, p. 248. Gill defends it (in a letter): 'My account came directly from Stanley Hyman, very soon after the event. Stanley was amused that it was the floor-plan of the old house they were living in at the time that made the pursuit of Shirley possible – a circular steeplechase. Three less Grecian-urn-like people it would be hard to imagine.'

p. 268 Brinnin on Yale: pp. 32–3.

p. 268 Norman Pearson: in an interview.

p. 268 Diary: about five inches by seven, bound in tartan cloth. Texas mss. It was presumably provided by Brinnin; the only entries in Thomas's hand are phone numbers, addresses and occasional reminders of appointments.

p. 268 Telegram: Mt Holyoke files.

pp. 268ff Thomas at Mt Holyoke: Joseph McG. Bottkol, Ben Reid, Marianne Brock, Peter Viereck.

p. 269 University of California recording: issued by Caedmon Records as part of 'An Evening with Dylan Thomas', CDL 51157. Apart from Thomas's two formal recording sessions for Caedmon, in 1952 and 1953, Caedmon's material is drawn from local recordings of Thomas talking and reading, and from the BBC.

pp. 269–70 Brinnin on Mt Holyoke: pp. 34–5.

p. 270 Holyoke story challenged: 'A Poet's Corpse: or, Me and Dylan', by Dorothy Van Ghent, *Centaur*, Spring 1956.

p. 270 Gray Burr: in an interview.

pp. 271–2 Thomas at Amherst: Armour Craig.

p. 272 What Thomas wouldn't talk about: *Leftover*, p. 53.

p. 272 Brinnin's cable: Mt Holyoke files.

p. 273 Thomas to Margaret Taylor: 18 June 1950.

p. 273fn List of poets: Thomas to Margaret Taylor: 18 June 1950.

pp. 273–4 Introducing Hardy: Caedmon CDL 51157, op. cit.

p. 274 At the Poetry Center: Reel 10 of Center's tapes.

p. 274 'No tepid don': Caedmon CDL 53006 (2c), part of the 'Complete recorded stories and humorous essays' series, 'A Few Words of a Kind', recorded at MIT, Cambridge, Mass., by a local radio station, WGBH.

p. 274 'Don't ask me any questions', etc.: ibid.

p. 274 Thomas to Margaret Taylor: 18 June 1950.

p. 275 Dartmouth College magazine: *The Dartmouth*, 14 May 1952.

p. 275 Bryn Mawr fee: college files.

pp. 276–7 At Cornell: David Daiches, in the *Adam* Memorial Number, and an interview.

p. 277 Thomas to Caitlin: 15 and 16 March 1950.

p. 278 Thomas's itinerary: Louise Baughan Murdy's thesis (later a book), *Sound and Sense in Dylan Thomas's Poetry*, contains a detailed itinerary of Thomas's four visits to the USA; it has a few omissions and minor errors. FitzGibbon printed it as an Appendix.

pp. 278ff Ray West: 'Dylan Thomas in Iowa 1951' (error for 1950), *San Francisco Fault*, October 1972.

p. 278 Teeth: Thomas knew they were unsightly; Glyn Jones (see p. 263) saw him cover his mouth. In Peter de Vries's *Reuben, Reuben*, his Thomas-figure, McGland, suffers 'the agonies of hell' worrying about his teeth, and commits suicide when he hears he must have them all out. This is an odd fancy to get from nowhere. De Vries said (in a letter): 'An interview with Dylan Thomas, I think in the [New York] *Sunday Times Book Review*, in which he said something like, "Say I'm balding and toothlessing", put me on the track of his probably acute dental problems. He was ostensibly satirising American journalese which makes verbs of nouns and adjectives, but publicly betraying an actual private obsession – so I surmise. It was only a step, or leap, of the imagination to make me suspect what a horror terminal tooth loss might be to a chronic womaniser, something tantamount to emasculation ... We've all suffered enough in a dentist's chair to know that dental can become mental, and hindsight makes me seriously suspect clairvoyance in my divination of Dylan's teeth woes and anxieties vis-a-vis McGland's.'

p. 279 Howard Moss: in an interview.

p. 279 Letter to radio producer: Thomas to E. J. King Bull, 26 December 1946.

p. 280 Davin: *Closing Times*, p. 133.

p. 281 Thomas to Caitlin, on the train: about 5 April 1950.

pp. 283–4 Moffat's story: in letters to the author.

pp. 283–4 Shelley Winters: her autobiography, *Best of Times, Worst of Times*, p. 31ff.

p. 284 Thomas to Witt-Diamant: 10 October 1951.

p. 285 Thomas at Pomona College: Ernest A. Strathmann of the college, in a letter.

p. 285 Thomas at Berkeley: Mrs B. J. Connors, in a letter.

p. 285 The Berkeley appointment: Professor Garff B. Wilson, who was a member of the committee, in a letter.

p. 285 Thomas at Vassar: interview with the secretary of Vassar, May 1975; *Vassar Chronicle*, 13 May 1950.

pp. 285–6 Vernon Venable: in an interview.

p. 286fn *Picture Post* essay: a Swansea friend who worked for the magazine, John Ormond (Thomas), asked Thomas to write something about Christmas; they had met by chance at Waterloo Station, and caught the same train. Thomas refused at first, saying he had written too much about Christmas, but accepted before the journey was over, for a fee of £50.

pp. 286–7 At the party: John Gruen: *The Party's Over Now*, pp. 27–30.

pp. 287 'Liquid, libidinous': Thomas to John F. and Mrs Nims, 17 July 1950.

p. 287 Spouting verse: Thomas to Taylor, 18 June 1950.

p. 287 In love with Pearl, etc.: quoted by Brinnin, p. 71.

12. *No Money, Few Poems*

p. 289 Florence Thomas: in the 1963 radio documentary, 'Dylan Thomas'.

p. 289 Earnings in America: D.H.A. In a letter to Higham (21 July 1952) Thomas mentions a figure of £1907 earned in the US in 1950. This was presumably after business expenses had been agreed; the file suggests these were about £1000. Brinnin implied (p. 53) that tax was paid in the US, but later said (in a letter) that he didn't think this happened. D.H.A. files suggest that only UK tax was paid.

p. 289 $800 for Caitlin: Brinnin, p. 64.

p. 290 Unwritten script: a BBC memo, 28 August 1950, refers to a thirty-minute feature, 'Letter to America', for which Thomas would have received fifty guineas. BBC Archives.

p. 290 Seeking BBC post: memo from Grisewood to the Head of Features, 18 August 1950. It is marked, 'After discussion with H.F. decided not to proceed'. BBC Archives.

p. 290 Thomas to Caitlin: (1) 18 April 1950 (2) 7 May 1950.

p. 290 TV interview: BBC TV, 3 December 1975, op. cit.

p. 291 'This arsehole': Thomas to the Nims, 17 July 1950.

p. 291 Caitlin on Laugharne: *Leftover*, p. 15; *Am I the Perfect Fool?* (unpublished manuscript).

p. 291 Margaret Taylor: in an interview.

p. 291 Dressing for market: *Leftover*, p. 57.

p. 291 Davenport: 'Patterns of Friendship', BBC radio, Home Service, 12 December 1961. BBC Archives.

p. 291 Fighting: Caitlin, BBC television, 3 December 1975.

p. 292 'Dylan kicked me': Dr David Hughes.

p. 293 Brinnin on Thomas, and Pearl's visit: Brinnin, pp. 65–71.

pp. 293–4 Heppenstall: *Four Absentees*, p. 180.

p. 294 Letters intercepted: Brinnin, pp. 72–3.

p. 294 Reading Pearl's 'sugar': Caitlin opened her heart to Helen McAlpine, in letters now with Texas mss.

p. 294 Thomas makes excuses for Pearl: Caitlin's BBC TV interview in Rome, 19 February 1977.

p. 294 Thomas to Davenport: written from '*You know where*', signed, '*You know who*'.

p. 294 Thomas to Brinnin: 12 April 1951.

p. 295 'In Country Heaven': a version based on material in Texas mss was assembled by Vernon Watkins, and published in the *Weekend Telegraph* magazine, 16 December 1968, with an article by Douglas Cleverdon. Daniel Jones prints a slightly different version in *The Poems*. By Thomas's 25 September 1950 broadcast (reprinted in *Q.E.O.M.*), certain phrases from the draft poem had already been written (e.g. 'Bushes and owls blow out like candles'). One of the worksheets has a draft letter to 'Dear Sir' (probably a bank manager) dated 8 December 1950, on the other side. Caedmon CDL 51281, ' "In Country Heaven". The Evolution of a Poem', includes a reminiscence by Humphrey Searle – 'He told me he had two long poems in mind, one of which was about the shepherds on the moon watching the earth after it had been destroyed in an atomic war. And I asked him when he hoped to be able to finish the poem, but he said he didn't think he could finish it, which was very sad. He was feeling at this time rather depressed about his work.'

p. 295 Third Programme agreed: Cleverdon to Thomas, 20 October 1950. BBC Archives.

p. 295 The original *Milk Wood* plot: Douglas Cleverdon, *The Growth of Milk Wood*, pp. 4–6; some of Cleverdon's information came from Gwen Watkins. The book gives a detailed history of the play, and includes much information about Thomas's relationship with the BBC.

p. 295 Cleverdon to Thomas, 5 December: '... Sorry to keep on pestering you, but I am frightfully anxious to get the programme on the air. Moreover, I can get the whole thing paid for immediately the script is approved ...' BBC Archives.

pp. 295–6 Savage Club note: The 39-page ms is assumed to be lost.

p. 296 The Iranian film: Ronald Tritton, formerly head of BP information. The BP file has disappeared.

p. 296 'These strange, lost days': Thomas to Caitlin, n.d., from Isfahan, Iran.

p. 297 Thomas to Pearl; a typescript of the letter, which is apparently an extract only, is with FitzGibbon's copies of letters, Texas mss.

p. 297 'water on troubled oil'. Thomas to Oscar Williams, 25 March 1951.

p. 297 'Persian Oil': Home Service, 17 April 1951, in a series called 'Report to the People'. BBC Archives.

p. 297fn1. Callard's theory: *New Welsh Review*, No. 43, winter 1998–99. 'Dylan Thomas in Iran: an Adventure in the Spy Trade?'

p. 297fn2. Memo about proposed script: Douglas Cleverdon to Maurice Brown, 13 March 1951. BBC Archives.

p. 298 David Wright: in a letter.

p. 298 'The Miner's Lament': Texas mss.

p. 298 Thomas to Caetani: 'Lament' was first published in November 1951, in her *Botteghe Oscure*.

p. 298 One critic: Michael Neill in *Notes and Queries*, February 1970. Another critic, David Holbrook, sees 'lament' as 'mad with abandon to the joys of hate'. However interpreted, it has a streak of desperation.

p. 299 Swansea acquaintance: Cecil Price, in the *Adam* Memorial Number.

pp. 299–300 Amis's account: 'An evening with Dylan Thomas', *Spectator*, 29 November 1957; Geoffrey Nicholson, *Sunday Times* Magazine, 29 January 1967. A draft of a talk (probably this one, because it refers to 'Ralph's', a Swansea second-hand bookshop), is in Texas mss. It begins: 'If only I hadn't scribbled this, with invisible ink, on pieces of wet wallpaper, & then left them in the sun, maybe I could understand them better.' See Thomas's letter to Michael Forty, chairman of the English Society, 7 April 1951.

p. 301 Anxious letters: for example, an undated draft, probably 1950:
  Dear Sir, I am applying for a Grant because I most urgently need financial help so that I can go on working and be able to make enough money to keep myself and my family.
  I am extremely badly in debt; these debts are pressing, and daily and horribly becoming more so; and it seems that I cannot think of anything else at all.
  Surrounded by these debts, hurt and worried to despair in the very middle of them, and seeing and hearing my home crumble because of them, I cannot write, they come between me and everything else I do. And, as I can't write, I can't make any money, and so new day-by-day debts arise; and I can't see any good end to this, and I would be insane if I could.
  Less and less do I seem able to concentrate on anything except these worries and despairs – (the writing of this letter is a kind of torture, my mind keeps jerking painfully away to the thoughts of writs and tradesmen's bills) – and more and more important grow these beastly little griefs to me ... [the fragment ends].

p. 301 Thomas to Brinnin: 12 April 1951.

p. 301 Billy Williams: his account of the outing is in Min Lewis, *Laugharne and Dylan Thomas*, pp. 93–4. *Cf.* Brinnin's account, pp. 80–84.

p. 302 Lacking discipline: BBC TV interview in Rome, 19 February 1977.

p. 302 Thomas to Williams: 28 May 1951.

p. 303 'Happy' poems: Brinnin, pp. 96–7.

p. 303 Synopsis of 'Poem on his Birthday': Bill Read printed it, thinly disguised as a paraphrase, in *The Days of Dylan Thomas* (p. 149). It was also copied at second hand by Patricia Leong for her thesis written at Mt Holyoke, 'Dylan Thomas: the Creative Process'.

p. 303fn Dating 'Poem on his Birthday': Thomas sent it to Oscar Williams in New York with an undated letter (October or November 1951). He described the enclosure as 'a long new poem'. But if the poem was begun in 1949, when he was aged thirty-five, as in the synopsis, this would explain a remark in a letter to Margaret Taylor of 28 November 1949 that 'my poem is now eighty lines long'. The only poem of this length written in his last years was 'Poem on his Birthday', with 108 lines. Further evidence in this direction is in a letter from Daniel Jones to a collector, now in Texas mss, which refers to rough workings of the poem in Jones's possession. According to Jones's letter, Thomas stayed with him in Swansea in the autumn of 1949, when he was writing 'Poem on his Birthday', and completed it during the visit, taking away a fair copy and leaving the worksheets with Jones. From this, one might conclude that the poem was written before the end of 1949; put aside because Thomas was dissatisfied with it; and rewritten in 1951. But in editing *The Poems*, Jones said unequivocally that a reference in the poem to a thirty-fifth birthday was 'misleading', and that it was 'written after Thomas's return from Persia, when he spent the summer [1951] in Laugharne'; he cited FitzGibbon as his authority. In his lifetime Jones was unhelpful over the discrepancy between his accounts, as he was over most things.

p. 304 'Poem on his Birthday' worksheets: Texas mss.

p. 304fn Holbrook: 'The Code of Night', in *Dylan Thomas: New Critical Essays*, pp. 283–9.

p. 305 The notebook: Texas mss.

p. 306 Marged Howard-Stepney's son: Mark S. Murray Threipland, who says (in a letter) that 'I only met Dylan Thomas on one occasion when, aged seventeen and having just passed my driving test, I drove my mother from Cilymaenllwyd [the family house at Llanelli] to Laugharne, where we met Thomas in the pub. I can remember being very disapproving about the evening, as Thomas had had a lot to drink, and my mother was not far behind him. I sat at a table sipping orange squash while they sat at the bar, and my mother borrowed money from me to pay for the drinks. I know that on another occasion Thomas came to Cilymaenllwyd and read poetry to all the members of the staff, and everyone else my mother could gather ... My mother was extremely generous to a number of people, one of them being Dylan Thomas. I suspect that she gave him quite a lot of money and that this would have been in cash and therefore unrecorded.'

pp. 307–8 Income details: D.H.A.

p. 308 Williams's sales: Indiana mss.

p. 308 Weeks to Williams: Indiana mss.

p. 308 Thomas to Witt-Diamant: This is the letter already quoted from in Ch. 11.

p. 309 Thomas to Taylor: n.d., but there are references to Elisabeth Lutyens's visit and Delancey Street.

pp. 309–10 Elisabeth Lutyens at Laugharne: in an interview, and *A Goldfish Bowl*, pp. 202–6.

p. 310 Vera Killick: in an interview. Gwen Watkins: *Portrait of a Friend*.

p. 312 'Say the Word': a D.H.A. memo, 13 November 1951, says Thomas would like to do more quiz programmes.

p. 312 'Floe's Tusks': the title, and perhaps the idea for a story, seem to have originated in an obsessive play on two words that occur in a number of 'Poems on his Birthday' worksheets, 'floes' (presumably ice floes) and 'tusks', e.g. the published line, 'On skull and scar where his loves lie wrecked', read at one stage, 'On scars and floes where his loves lie wrecked'. On another sheet are 'Flo's tusks' and 'floes' tusks'; the published poem has: 'And the tusked, ramshackling sea exults'. In the notebook, a second version of the notes for the story emphasises the connection with Thomas's past life – Samuel Bennet, in a bed-sitting room 'near the Fulham Road, brushed off the Woodbine ash from the first scrawled page of "Love and the Sea, A Sonnet Sequence", and wrote down firmly, in violet ink, Flo's Tusks'.

p. 312 'Such Things Do Happen': Texas mss.

13. *The Knot*

p. 314 Thomas to Brinnin: 3 December 1951.

p. 314 Student at Sarah Lawrence: in an interview.

p. 314 Resenting the enterprise: *Leftover*, pp. 59, 62–3.

pp. 314–15 'all dirt' and 'stuffed shirts': Brinnin, pp. 109, 107.

p. 315 Nelson Algren to Ellen Borden Stevenson: Texas mss. A later account of the evening by Algren, when he reviewed Brinnin in the *Chicago Sun-Times* ('An Intimate Look at Dylan Thomas', 1 January 1956), gave a different emphasis:

> 'Anyhow,' I told him, 'I once knew a man named Champaign who drank nothing but beer.'
>
> 'I knew a man named Beers who drank nothing but champagne,' Thomas assured me.
>
> I decided I liked him whatever his trade, and we went forth in search of either beer or champagne. We found both.
>
> I never saw Thomas after that night. But I began listening to his recordings that I had not till then heard. Before he died it was at last borne in upon me that I had been greatly privileged. I had been with a great man, the only great man I had ever known.
>
> I had also been with a babyish self-indulgent fellow carrying too much weight for his size . . .

p. 315 Professor Alfred: in an interview.

p. 315 Oscar Williams and Caitlin's poems: there are references in correspondence between them. Harvard mss.

p. 315 Rose Slivka: in an interview.

p. 316 'a feebler Soho': Thomas to Caitlin, 25 February 1950.

pp. 316–17 The *Time* interview: Barrett, later a novelist, was Irving Berlin's daughter. She said (in an interview) that Thomas told her to put away her notebook, so she had to rely on memory and frequent trips to the cloakroom where she could make hurried notes. Her account was published in the *Reporter*, 27 April 1954.

pp. 318–19 Holdridge and Mantell: in interviews; Barbara Holdridge 'Dylan as He Was', *New York*, the Sunday *Herald Tribune* magazine, 12 January 1966.

p. 319 Caedmon recording: CDL 51002.

p. 319 University of Vermont: Samuel N. Bogorad, 'I Remember Dylan

Thomas', *Centaur* (University of Vermont), Spring 1956.

p. 319 Skidmore College: from an interview.

p. 319 University of California: *Occident*, student magazine, Spring 1952.

pp. 319–20 University of Utah: a student who was present, Marjorie Adix, reported the session from memory without notes, and her account has been widely reprinted (including Tedlock, pp. 60–6). It has an odd discrepancy. Thomas is made to declare that his father 'went blind and was very ill before he died'. But in April 1952, D. J. Thomas was still alive. Marjorie Adix said (letter to the author) she was 'astonished to find his father had not died by then. I can only suggest that maybe, for Thomas, he had.' Olive Ghiselin: her article, 'Dylan', *Alumnus* magazine, University of Utah, Fall 1967.

p. 320 Engagements book: this is a 'year book' in a red binding, supplied with dates but not the days of the week. Like the 1950 diary, it seems to have been used only for engagements and addresses. Thomas continued to use it, intermittently, for brief entries when he returned to Britain. Texas mss.

p. 320 Penniless in Arizona: Brinnin, p. 123.

p. 320 Llewelyn's fees: Thomas to Brinnin from San Francisco, 4 April 1952. At the back of the engagements book Thomas has written: '£100 unpaid for two previous terms. £50 for present term. And I must pay another term (£50) *at least* before Ll. will be taken back after this holiday *which is coming very soon*. Minimum = £200. But £250 wd. be better.'

p. 321 Rose Slivka, Alastair Reid: in interviews.

p. 321 'Farewell performance': Poetry Center tape, Reel 7. No date is shown, but it can only have been 1952. On the 1950 trip, the last Poetry Center reading was more than two weeks before he left America. On the April–June 1953 trip, Thomas read at the Center ten days before he left, by air.

p. 322 'Poems 1934–1950': D.H.A. memo, September 1951.

p. 322 £100 for Preface: D.H.A.

p. 322 Dent 'howling': Higham to Thomas, 2 May 1952. D.H.A.

p. 322 Party at Margaret Taylor's: the engagements book. Texas mss.

p. 322 Thomas to Higham: 28 June 1952.

p. 322 How *Prologue* began: Brinnin's account, pp. 94–5, places the conversation at Laugharne in the summer of 1951. This seems more than a year too soon. They met in London in September 1952. But Brinnin dismissed this date. He said (in a letter) that 'I may have been shown an early version of the poem, because I definitely did not discuss it anywhere else with Dylan but in the confines of his little shack. It's possible that my account may be coloured by thoughts on later readings of the poem, but my memory of the poem itself – on long, legal-sized pages held together by a straight pin – remains clear.'

pp. 322–3 Thomas to Williams: 3 March 1953.

p. 323 Cat and mouse: B.L. mss.

p. 323 Thomas to Fry: 16 February 1953.

p. 323 Davenport: *Vogue*, August 1955.

p. 323 'Llareggub': Thomas to Caetani, October 1951.

p. 323 'Spoon River Anthology': correspondence in BBC Archives.

p. 324 The five-guinea scheme: BBC memo from Head of Copyright, 2 September 1952. Thomas proposed a somewhat different scheme in a letter to Cleverdon, 23 August 1952: '... If the BBC could pay me a weekly sum (not less than £10 a week) for the period of 6 weeks [which he said he needed to complete the play], I could shove all other small jobs aside & work on "Llareggub" only ... I could devote my time, with the greatest enjoyment, to writing imaginative full-length things for the radio if I could be paid a weekly wage. Otherwise, it's bits & pieces for me all the time ... ' Cleverdon told the BBC management that 'I have sufficient confidence in [Thomas] to guarantee the Corporation (by deduction from my salary) against any loss that may be incurred'. BBC Archives. BBC memos show Thomas in a weak position when it came to negotiating fees. The BBC already had the first half of the play. They decided they could use this even if no more script was forthcoming, and pay him forty-five guineas. But all they would pay him on account of this first half was fifteen guineas.

p. 324 W. R. Rodgers: reviewing FitzGibbon in the *Sunday Times*, 17 October 1965.

p. 324 Toynbee: 'A Great Poet', 11 November 1952.

p. 324fn2. 'Paper and sticks': Thomas to E. F. Bozman, 20 September 1952. 'Proofreading the Collected Poems, I have the horrors of "Paper & Sticks" on page 116.' Corrected proofs of *C.P.*: Texas mss.

pp. 324–5 Connolly: 'The Boyhood of Merlin', 11 November 1952.

p. 325 G. S. Fraser: 'Craft and Sullen Art', 29 November 1952.

p. 325 Empson: 'Books in General', *New Statesman*, 15 May 1954.

p. 325 Thomas to Spender: 9 December 1952.

p. 325 Llanelli interview: 'Poet likes Llanelly', *Llanelly Star*, 13 December 1952. 'Mr Thomas is a friendly man, with the pride and humility of a real poet.'

pp. 325–6 Thomas to Caetani: 6 November 1952.

p. 326 Appeal to Spender: letter from Thomas, 22 November 1952.

p. 326 Marged's difficulties: interview with her former solicitor.

p. 326 Caitlin to Oscar Williams: 9 February 1952, error for 1953. Harvard mss.

p. 327 Nancy's illness: Gwevril Dawkins.

p. 327 Aneirin Talfan Davies: Dylan Thomas Summer School, Swansea University College, 1974.

p. 328 Thomas to Fred Janes: 5 January 1953.

p. 328 Higham to Thomas: 8 January 1953. D.H.A.

p. 328 Marged's death: reports in *Llanelly Star*, 24 January, 31 January and 7 February 1953; interview with Margaret Taylor.

p. 328fn The correspondent: an unidentified 'Mr Evans'.

pp. 328–9 Boat House purchase: Margaret Taylor said that contracts for Marged's purchase of the Boat House were ready to be exchanged when she died, and that the deal might have already gone through had it not been for delays in Laugharne.

Under the borough's ancient charter, all property in the town must be offered to the Corporation. It is only a formality, but Laugharne is fond of its formalities. Mrs Taylor believed that the Boat House was not offered, and that this held up the transaction. If so, Thomas was the victim of an episode worthy of *Milk Wood*. But Marged's former solicitor insisted there was 'hardly any negotiation'.

p. 329 To Idris Davies: 16 February 1953.

p. 329 'put paid to baby': Thomas to Brinnin, 18 March 1953.

p. 329 The backstreet abortion: Caitlin Thomas and George Tremlett, *Caitlin. Life with Dylan Thomas*, pp. 172–3.

p. 329 Nancy's husband: Thomas to Brinnin, 18 March 1953.

p. 329 Rationalising Thomas's affairs: a D.H.A. memo of 23 February 1953 says, '... D.H. intends to try to put his affairs on an even keel. [Dylan] is to let us have a list of his debts – he says that his local debts amount to about £200 now. Outside of local debts he says he has only one, of £100 he borrowed ... He is anxious that some provision should be made ahead for the schooling of his two elder children. The eldest's fees are £150 a year and the other one's will be the same probably. His other large debt is the income tax one, and some provision would have to be made to pay this off and keep enough to pay regularly in future. When Dylan sends the information, we'll see what can be devised...'

p. 329 Collected stories: Thomas to Bozman, 31 March 1953.

p. 329 'Too raw': Thomas to Higham, 6 April 1953.

p. 329 Fairy tales: a contract, with £50 on signature, was signed in February 1953. D.H.A.

pp. 329–30 Thomas's earnings: D.H.A.

p. 329 *Skin Trade* payment: New American Library to Thomas, 9 May 1952. Indiana mss.

p. 329 'Prologue' worksheets: Thomas to Williams, 27 February 1953 and 3 March 1953.

pp. 329–30 'Poem on his Birthday' worksheets: receipt in Indiana mss.

p. 331 Davenport: the 1963 radio documentary, 'Dylan Thomas'.

p. 331 James A. Davies: *A Reference Companion to Dylan Thomas*, p. 79.

p. 333 Going to America: D.H.A. memo, 23 February: 'He isn't going to America.'

p. 333 Making arrangements: Thomas to Brinnin, 18 March 1953.

14. *Running Faster*

p. 334 Chest trouble: Florence Thomas, talking to Colin Edwards.

p. 334 'diabetic doctor': week of 11 November 1933.

p. 334 Prichard: in an interview.

p. 335 'Fell like a stone': Min Lewis, *Laugharne and Dylan Thomas*, p. 94.

pp. 335–6 Thomas to Caitlin: 20 April 1953.

p. 336 etc. Reitell on Thomas: in telephone conversations and letters.

p. 336 Losing the typescript: Joe Everingham of MIT.

p. 336 fn1. The ingenious critic was J. S. Dugdale, in Brodie's *Notes on Under Milk Wood*, p. 52.

p. 336 fn2. Cardiff incident: Thomas's letter to Charles Elliott, 17 March 1953, refers.

p. 337 Mrs Gardner Cox: in an interview.

p. 337 Recording *Milk Wood*: the Caedmon tapes are CDL 52005 (1c and 2c). Caedmon's programme note says that the recording 'owes its existence to the chance thought someone had just before curtain time of setting up the little tape recorder that was at hand and laying a microphone on the floor at the centre of the stage'. Brinnin says (in a letter) it was definitely not an afterthought.

p. 338 *Milk Wood* and the BBC: the play was first broadcast on 25 January 1954, on the Third Programme. Behind the scenes there was much agonising over whether parts of it were fit to be heard. Cleverdon fought fiercely against censorship, arguing that the play 'should be acceptable in uncut form to any reasonable Third Programme listener. The humour is broad but never dirty; and the whole work is on a plane of poetic imagination which would entitle it to disregard the pettifogging hypocrisies of those who never listen to the Third, but whose hostility would be encouraged rather than placated by timidity on our part ... To leave Dylan's script untouched, as the work of a major poet of our time, is a defensible position; but to cut half a dozen sentences leaves us open to attack for not cutting two dozen or more.' Among the phrases that were threatened but which survived were 'Parlez-vous jig-jig' and 'let me shipwreck in your thighs'. Apparently the only cuts that were finally made were 'wriggle her roly poly bum' (Davies and Maud edition, p. 34); 'strip her to the nipples and the bees' (p. 46), and 'draws circles of lipstick round her nipples' (p. 57). These were referred to at Broadcasting House as the 'two tits and a bum'. Third Programme reception in Wales was poor at that time, and the programme was barely audible in Laugharne. A senior BBC official in Wales wrote to London that it was 'not a programme for the Welsh

Home Service', or indeed for any 'family or home listening'. But the Controller of the Third told Cleverdon it was 'the best radio production I have ever heard'. BBC Archives.

p. 338fn Molly Murray Threipland: in letters and telephone conversations.

p. 340 Opera proposal: telegram from Sara Caldwell, director of the Opera Workshop, to Thomas. Texas mss.

p. 341 Thomas to Llewelyn: 23 June 1953.

p. 341 Recording session: issued by Caedmon, CDL 51018.

p. 342 'Miles of orange peel': Thomas to Oscar Williams, 22 June 1953.

p. 342 Thomas to Reitell: 16 June 1953.

p. 342 *John O'London's* article: 'Poet in the Boat House', 7 August 1953.

pp. 342–3 Thomas to Mimi Josephson: 25 August 1953.

p. 343 Draft of letter to Josephson: Texas mss.

p. 343 *Milk Wood* revisions: Texas mss, which have many worksheets.

p. 343 Llangollen: the radio talk was broadcast 5 June 1951, Welsh Home Service; reprinted *Q.E.O.M.* Some of Thomas's notes are in Texas mss, mixed up with *Milk Wood* worksheets.

p. 343 Stravinsky to Thomas: 22 June 1953. Texas mss.

p. 343 Watkins's *alter ego*: Gwen Watkins, *Portrait of a Friend*, p. 215.

pp. 343–4 Watkins at the Boat House: ibid, pp. 138–9.

p. 344 and fn1 'Speaking Personally': later reprinted as 'A Story' in *Prospect* (in the US: 'The True Story' in *Skin Trade*). A few worksheets are in Texas mss; more in Wales mss. The producer, D. J. Thomas, was previously a master at Swansea Grammar School, and a colleague of D. J. Thomas, Thomas's father. The memos: BBC Archives.

p. 344 Caitlin at Brown's: Rollie McKenna, who was staying at Laugharne.

pp. 344–5 'Elegy' worksheets and other notes: Texas mss.

p. 347 Stravinsky to Thomas: 26 August 1953. Texas mss.

pp. 347–8 David Gardner: in interviews.

p. 348 'A Visit to America': this, and the Laugharne talk, are in *Q.E.O.M.*

pp. 348–9 At the cinema: Florence Thomas, the 1955 interview; Dr David Hughes.

p. 349 Leaving Laugharne: Mrs Thomas, quoted by Ethel Ross, *Gower*, No. 16, 1964.

p. 349 Haircut and trousers: Jane Dark.

p. 349 Plane ticket: Brinnin, pp. 184–5.

p. 349 FitzGibbon: pp. 390–1.

p. 349 Philip Burton: *Adam* Memorial Number.

p. 349fn Richard Burton: Paul Ferris, *Richard Burton* pp. 74–5.

p. 350 Taylor on Stravinsky: in an interview.

p. 350 The lost script: Cleverdon's *The Growth of Milk Wood*, p. 35; *Bookseller*, 12 and 19 March 1966. Caitlin contended in the High Court that the script (which Cleverdon sold to the Times Book Company in 1961) belonged to her husband's estate. The action failed.

p. 350 At the air terminal: Cordelia Locke.

15. *Alcohol and Morphia*

p. 351 Dead before he was forty: BBC TV, 3 December 1975.

p. 354 'Poetry and the Film': part of the transcript was published by Gotham Book Mart, 1972. Arthur Miller was on the panel. The account in Brinnin (p. 198) flatters Thomas, if the transcript is a fair guide.

p. 354 At City College: Professor Samuel Middlebrook.

p. 356 *Skin Trade* ms: Harvard mss.

p. 356 In Cornwall: Wyn Henderson.

p. 359 'Death and Triangles': Thomas to Pamela, 9 May 1934.

p. 361 Sitwell: letter to Sir Maurice Bowra, 25 November 1953. *Edith Sitwell. Selected Letters.*

pp. 361–2 Caitlin's last letter: University of Delaware, Special Collections.

p. 362 Caitlin's demons: *Leftover*, pp. 79, 80.

p. 362 Obituary: *The Times*, 10 November 1953.

pp. 362–3 Thomas's effects: papers at D.H.A.

Postscript: The Thomas Business

p. 364 Edith Sitwell: quoted in *Time*, 30 May 1955.

p. 364 Heppenstall: *Four Absentees*, p. 170.

p. 364 Brinnin to Davenport: copy typescript from Arthur Calder-Marshall.

p. 364 Reavey to Davenport: ibid.

p. 365 Davenport: *Vogue*, August 1955.

BIBLIOGRAPHY

Most of the books listed are those I have read and used.

The standard bibliographies are J. Alexander Rolph, *Dylan Thomas. A Bibliography* (Dent, 1956) and Ralph Maud, *Dylan Thomas in Print. A Bibliographical History* (Dent, 1970).

Works by Dylan Thomas

18 Poems (*Sunday Referee* and Parton Bookshop, 1934)
Twenty-five Poems (Dent, 1936)
The Map of Love (Dent, 1939)
Portrait of the Artist as a Young Dog (Dent, 1940)
Deaths and Entrances (Dent, 1946)
The Doctor and the Devils (Dent, 1953)
Quite Early One Morning (Dent, 1954)
A Prospect of the Sea (Dent, 1955)
Letters to Vernon Watkins (ed. Vernon Watkins) (Dent and Faber, 1957)
The Beach at Falesá (Cape, 1964)
Twenty Years A-Growing (Dent, 1964)
Rebecca's Daughters (Triton, 1965)
Poet in the Making. The Notebooks of Dylan Thomas (ed. Ralph Maud) (Dent, 1968)
Dylan Thomas. The Notebook Poems 1930–1934 (ed. Ralph Maud) (Dent, 1990)
Adventures in the Skin Trade (Aldine Paperback, Dent, 1969)
Dylan Thomas: The Poems (ed. Daniel Jones) (Dent, 1971)
Dylan Thomas: Early Prose Writings (ed. Walford Davies) (Dent, 1971)
Dylan Thomas, The Collected Stories (ed. Walford Davies) (Dent, 1983)
The Death of the King's Canary (with John Davenport) (Hutchinson, 1976)

Collected Letters (ed. Paul Ferris) (Dent 1985; Paladin 1987). Out
   of print at the time of writing; revised edition in preparation.
Dylan Thomas. Collected Poems 1934–1953 (ed. Walford Davies
   and Ralph Maud) (Dent, 1988)
Dylan Thomas, The Broadcasts (ed. Ralph Maud) (Dent, 1991)
Dylan Thomas. Under Milk Wood (ed. Walford Davies and Ralph
   Maud) (Dent, 1995)
Dylan Thomas. The Filmscripts (ed. John Ackerman) (Dent, 1995)

Critical Books, Biographies, etc

The editions cited are not always the first and not necessarily the
latest. Place of publication is London unless otherwise stated.

Ackerman, John, *Dylan Thomas: His Life and Work* (OUP, 1964)
– *Welsh Dylan* (Granada, 1980)
– *A Dylan Thomas Companion* (Macmillan, 1991)
Bevington, Helen, *When Found, Make a Verse of* (Simon and Schus-
   ter, New York, 1961)
Bold, Alan (ed.), *Dylan Thomas: Craft or Sullen Art* (Vision Press,
   1990)
Brinnin, John Malcolm, *Dylan Thomas in America* (Ace Books,
   Harborough Publishing Co., 1957)
Cleverdon, Douglas, *The Growth of Milk Wood* (Dent, 1969)
Coleman, Emily Holmes, *The Shutter of Snow* (Virago, 1981)
Davies, Aneirin Talfan, *Dylan. Druid of the Broken Body* (Dent,
   1964)
Davies, James A., *Dylan Thomas's Places. A Biographical and Lit-
   erary Guide* (Christopher Davies, Swansea, 1987)
– *A Reference Companion to Dylan Thomas* (Greenwood Press,
   Westport, Conn. and London, 1998)
Davies, Walford (ed.), *Dylan Thomas: New Critical Essays* (Dent,
   1972)
– *Dylan Thomas* (Open University Press, Milton Keynes, 1986)
Davin, Dan, *Closing Times* (OUP, 1975)
Devas, Nicolette, *Two Flamboyant Fathers* (Hamish Hamilton,
   1985)
Dugdale, J. S., *Dylan Thomas. Under Milk Wood* (Notes on chosen
   English texts) (James Brodie, 1964)
Emery, Clark, *The World of Dylan Thomas* (Dent, 1971)

Ferris, Paul, *Caitlin. The Life of Caitlin Thomas* (Hutchinson, 1993; Pimlico, 1995)

FitzGibbon, Constantine, *The Life of Dylan Thomas* (Dent, 1965)

Fryer, Jonathan, *Dylan. The Nine Lives of Dylan Thomas* (Kyle Cathie, 1993)

Fuller, Jean Overton, *The Magical Dilemma of Victor Neuburg* (W. H. Allen, 1965)

Gill, Brendan, *Here at the New Yorker* (Random House, New York, 1976)

Gittins, Rob, *The Last Days of Dylan Thomas* (Macdonald, 1986)

Grigson, Geoffrey, *The Crest on the Silver* (Cresset Press, 1950)

Grindea, Miron (ed.), *Adam International Review* 238 (1953). Dylan Thomas Memorial Number.

Gruen, John, *The Party's Over Now. Reminiscences of the Fifties* (Viking Press, New York)

Heppenstall, Rayner, *Four Absentees* (Barrie & Rockliff, 1960)

Holbrook, David, *Llareggub Revisited. Dylan Thomas and the State of Modern Poetry* (Bowes & Bowes, 1962)

Holroyd, Michael, *Augustus John* Vol. II, *The Years of Experience* (Heinemann, 1975)

Hood, Christopher, *Banana Cat* (Secker & Warburg, 1985)

Johnson, Pamela Hansford, *Important to me. Personalia* (Macmillan, 1974)

Jones, Daniel, *My Friend Dylan Thomas* (Dent, 1977)

Jones, Glyn, *The Dragon Has Two Tongues* (Dent, 1968)

Lewis, Min, *Laugharne and Dylan Thomas* (Dennis Dobson, 1967)

Lindsay, Jack, *Meetings with Poets* (Muller, 1968)

Lutyens, Elisabeth, *A Goldfish Bowl* (Cassell, 1972)

McKellar, Peter, *Imagination and Thinking. A Psychological Analysis* (Cohen & West, 1957)

Maclaren-Ross, Julian, *Memoirs of the Forties* (Penguin, 1984).

Marland, Michael, *Dylan Thomas* (The Times Authors No. 3) (Times Newspapers, 1970)

Mathias, Roland, *Vernon Watkins* (University of Wales Press, 1974)

Maud, Ralph, *Entrances to Dylan Thomas' Poetry* (Scorpion Press, Lowestoft, 1963)

Nashold, James, and George Tremlett, *The Death of Dylan Thomas* (Mainstream Publishing, Edinburgh, 1997)

Ray, Paul C., *The Surrealist Movement in England* (Cornell University Press, 1971)

Read, Bill, *The Days of Dylan Thomas* (Weidenfeld, 1964)

Sitwell, Edith, *Selected Letters* (Macmillan, 1970)

Swansea City Council, *Dylan Thomas. Word and Image*, introduction to an exhibition based on the Jeff Towns/Dylans Bookstore Collection; text by Towns

Symons, Julian, *The Thirties. A Dream Revolved* (Cresset Press, 1960)

Taylor, A. J. P., *A Personal History* (Coronet Books, 1984)

Tedlock, E. W. (ed.), *Dylan Thomas: The Legend and the Poet* (Heinemann, 1960)

Thomas, Caitlin, *Leftover Life to Kill* (Putnam, 1957)

– *Not Quite Posthumous Letter to My Daughter* (Putnam, 1963)

– *Double Drink Story. My Life With Dylan Thomas* (Viking, Toronto, 1997)

Thomas, Caitlin, with George Tremlett, *Caitlin. A Warring Absence* (Secker & Warburg, 1986)

Tindall, William York, *A Reader's Guide to Dylan Thomas* (Thames & Hudson, 1962)

Todd, Ruthven, *Fitzrovia & The Road to the York Minster* (Michael Parkin Fine Art, 1973)

Treece, Henry, *Dylan Thomas: 'Dog among the Fairies'* (Lindsay Drummond, 1949)

Tremlett, George, *Dylan Thomas. In the mercy of his means* (Constable, 1991)

Watkins, Gwen, *Portrait of a Friend* (Gomer Press, Llandysul, 1983)

Welsh Arts Council, *Welsh Dylan*, 'Catalogue of an exhibition to mark the twentieth anniversary of the poet's death' (1973)

INDEX

Note: (P) = Poem; (S) = Story

Abercrombie, Lascelles, 134

Abertawe (Welsh name for Swansea), 12fn

Aberystwyth, 115; University College, D. J. Thomas at, 10, 38

Abse, Dannie, on a Thomas dream, 257fn and Note

Abse, Leo, on a Thomas dream, 257

Ackerman, John, 366, 368

Adelphi, publishes 'No Man Believes', 88; editor solicits poems, 99; publishes 'The Woman Speaks', 102; Thomas reviews for, 114

Adix, Marjorie, Note to 319–20, 328fn

Adventures in the Skin Trade (unfinished novel), plot summarised, 121; Thomas first mentions, 198; talk of filming, 202; Vernon Watkins on, 216; shows to Graham Greene, 249; echoed in later notes, 312; in New York conversation, 318; paperback rights sold, 329; 'humorous novel', 342; 'forty-nine Guinnesses', 356; printing history, Note to 199

Advocate (Harvard), party for Thomases, 315

Aeron, River, Thomas's daughter named after, 206

'After the Funeral' (P), Thomas's aunt as subject, 13, 32; early version, 80–1; Vernon Watkins supplies phrase, 127; rewritten, 173; 'came in a rush', 183; in *Map of Love*, 189

Agate, James, on Thomas's 'nonsense verse', 185

'The Album' (story title), 312

Alfred, William (Harvard), 315

Algonquin Hotel, 353

Algren, Nelson, 315 and Note

Allen Wingate (publisher), 331

'Altarwise by owl-light' (P), 135, 147

Alwyn, William, 204

Aman, Leigh, *see* Marley, Lord

America, Thomas's hopes of visiting, 224, 230, 235–6; explains poems there, 242; invited to read there, 257–8; first visit to (1950), 264–88 *passim*; earnings there, 289; Caitlin's unhappiness over, 290; Thomas claims to take drugs there, 293; Thomas plans further visit, 301–2; second visit (with Caitlin, 1952), 314–21 *passim*; plans for third visit, 335; third visit (April–June 1953), 336–42; further visit mooted, 347; Thomas's departure for, 348–9; last days in New York (October–November 1953), 351–62

American audiences, 5, 264ff, 319–20, 336–8

American publishers, Thomas's. *See* Laughlin, James; New Directions

Amherst College, 270–1

Amis, Kingsley, 299–300

'Among those Killed in the Dawn Raid' (P), 199

'And death shall have no dominion' (P), 273; philosophy behind, 83; genesis and publication, 84–5; Thomas unhappy with, 136; possible intention of, 193; Thomas records, 342

Archer, David, helps publish *18 Poems*, 122; literary connections, 134

Arlott, John, on Thomas as broadcaster, 232; cricket commentator, 241

Arthur's Stone (Gower), 114

Atlantic, buys 'Poem on his Birthday', 308, 330; publishes 'In the White Giant's Thigh', 318

Auden, W. H., 258, 285, 308; in broadcast with Thomas, 174fn; Thomas film script echoes his style, 203; BBC treats as 'celebrity', 235; Thomas reads his poems, 265, 273fn

Autobiography of a Super-Tramp (W. H. Davies), Thomas reads for radio, 244

Ayrton, Michael, 248–9

Bacon, Francis, 142

'Ballad of the Long-legged Bait' (P), Thomas's longest poem, 195; Vernon Watkins on its imagery, Note to 195; worksheets sold, 197; Thomas explains, 265 and Note; records, 319

'Balloon Site 568' (film), Thomas works on, 202

Banana Cat (Christopher Hood), has spoof Thomas poem, 367

Band Wagon (magazine), features Thomas, 251

Barker, George, 181

Barnes, George (BBC), Note to 227, 234

Barrett, Mary Ellin, 316–17 and Note, 319

Bassett, Jack (childhood friend of Thomas), 31, 33, 35

Bassett, Mrs, of Swansea, 31–2

Battle of Britain, 193

The Beach of Falesá, film proposed, 246; Thomas's script published, 368

BBC (British Broadcasting Corporation) and Thomas: pronouncing 'Dylan', 21; 'The Romantic Isle' (P) as competition entry, 83, broadcast, 85; his first broadcast, 161–2 and Note to 161; Thomas demands rail fare in advance, 174; seeks openings, suggests Welsh anthology, 182–3; Welsh discussion cancelled (September 1939), 189; hack scripts for Latin America, 195; its help sought in avoiding war work, 195; Thomas writes reminiscent talks, 227; busy with radio work, 230–54 *passim*; Third Programme, 233–5, 242, 244, 258, 290, 294, 295, 312, Note to 338; Thomas seeks

BBC – *contd*
    regular employment, 235,
    290; irritates Schools
    producer, 249; 'Living in
    Wales' talk, Note to 253; *The
    Trojan Women* project, 258;
    The Plain Dealer script
    unwritten, *Peer Gynt* TV
    script fiasco, 258–9; Thomas
    doesn't take part in 'How I
    write', 144, 263–4; his
    reading and acting style, 232,
    234, 244; Swansea
    discussion, 260; 'In Country
    Sleep' broadcast, 242, 294–5
    and Note to 295; 'Persian Oil'
    talk, 297; pleads for advance
    payment, 301; hopes to work
    with Ted Kavanagh, 302; in
    quiz show, 312; writes 'Spoon
    River Anthology' script, 323–
    4; more Thomas poems
    broadcast, 329; Llangollen
    eisteddfod talk, 343; 'A Story'
    on TV, 344; 'A Visit to
    America', 348; records item
    for Laugharne programme,
    348; Laugharne broadcast,
    361. *See also* titles of
    programmes; *Under Milk
    Wood*; *Listener*; Thomas
    letters to
Beddoes, Thomas Lovell, 102
Beekman Tower Hotel, 265
'Before I knocked' (P), 91
Bennett, John (childhood
    friend), 44–5, 46, 47
Berkeley, Lennox, 192
Bertorelli's (restaurant), 158,
    259
Bishopston (Swansea), 163,
    191, 195, 196, 247
Blackburn, Tom, 142

Blaen Cwm (family cottages),
    11; Thomas writes poems
    there, 4; 'Uncle Bob' lives
    there, 15; D.J. there in
    retirement, 17; Thomas stays
    there, 98; haven from air-
    raids, 196, 214; 'Poem in
    October' completed there,
    215; Dylan and Caitlin there,
    224; more poems written
    there, 227–8; breaks journey
    at, 235; domestic crisis there,
    249–50; Thomas revisits, 347
Blake, William, 128, 233
Blakeston, Oswell, 144; on
    Thomas fantasies, 110;
    'sexual play' with Thomas,
    130–1; in Cornwall, 169. *See
    also* Thomas letter to
Blashford (Hampshire), 155fn,
    172, 173, 174, 176, 178, 180,
    182, 186, 192, 199; Caitlin
    brought up there, 151;
    Thomas writes poems there,
    185; Thomas dislikes it, 207
Blasket Islands, 217, 235
Boar's Head public house
    (Carmarthen), 349
Boat House (Laugharne), a
    poet's property, 1–3; Florence
    Thomas interviewed there,
    22fn; Margaret Taylor buys,
    254; Thomas and family settle
    there, 255ff; Marged
    Howard-Stepney's plans to
    buy, 326, thwarted, 328–9; its
    relics and visitor's book, 363;
    proposal to reinter Thomas
    there, xxi, 370; visited by:
    John Malcolm Brinnin, 301,
    347; Glyn Jones, 144, 263;
    Elisabeth Lutyens, 256, 309,
    310; a journalist, 342; Vernon

Watkins, 343; David Gardner, 347–8. *See also* Laugharne

'A Book of Streets', or 'Twelve Hours in The Streets' (synopsis), 218, 221

'Book of Verse' (radio programme), 232

Boston (Mass.), 268, 315, 336, 352

Boston University, proposes opera commission, 340; difficulty in raising money, 343

Botteghe Oscure (magazine), 261, 298, 321. *See also* Caetani, Marguerite

Bottkol, Joseph McG. (Mt Holyoke), 268ff

Box, Sydney, 245

Boy's Own Paper, source of plagiarised poem, 6, 39; publishes Thomas poem, 'The second best', 40

Bozman, E. F., 323. *See also* Thomas letters to

Brechfa (Carmarthenshire), 7

Brighton, 293

Brinnin, John Malcolm, 268, 272, 275, 276, 278, 303; invites Thomas to America, 257–8; offers services as agent, 263; with Thomas in New York, 264ff; in New England, 266–8; his Mt Holyoke account challenged, 269–70; his Shelley Winters anecdote contradicted, 283–4; Thomas's sexual confidant, 287; smuggles money to Caitlin, 289; meets Thomas in London, 293; visits Laugharne (1951), 301; and 1952 visit to America, 314–17

passim; on genesis of 'Prologue', 322 and Note; and title of *Under Milk Wood*, 336, and stage productions, 336ff; visits Laugharne (1953), 347; on Thomas's last days, 352ff; Reitell as his source, 352fn; hoards Caitlin letter, 362; his *Dylan Thomas in America*, 267, fictions therein, 366. *See also* Thomas letters to

Bristol, Thomas stays at, 263

British Medical Association, Swansea branch, waits in vain for Thomas, 262–3

British National (Films), Thomas writes for, 245, 249

Broadcasting, *see* BBC

Brock, Marianne (Mt Holyoke), 269, 271

Brown's Hotel (Laugharne), 174, 192, 256; Thomas visits in 1934, 108; Caitlin watches TV there, 344

Bryn Mawr College, Thomas visits, 274–5

Burke and Hare, film about, Thomas writes script, 202, 218, 245. *See also The Doctor and the Devils*

'The Burning Baby' (S), suggested by the story of Dr William Price, 115

Burr, Gray (New England), 268, 270

Burton, Philip, 362; hears Thomas describe a play, 349–50; produces 'Return Journey', Note to 236

Burton, Richard, reports Thomas anecdote, 130fn; acts with Thomas, 234; refuses to lend money, 349fn

Caedmon (Records), 366, Note to 337; Thomas records for (1952), 319; (1953), 341–2

Caetani, Marguerite, 297; wealthy American, 261, a patron, 300; Thomas phones her for money, 310; receives 'Do not go gentle', 298; Thomas drafts letter to her, 346–7. *See also* Thomas letters to; *Botteghe Oscure*

Café Royal (London), 202, 210, 219, 294

California, University of (at Los Angeles), Thomas reads at, drunk, 269; (at Berkeley), fails to get appointment, 284–5; interviewed by magazine, 319

Callard, David, chimera of 'Thomas the Spy', 297fn

Cambridge University, Thomas visits, 142

Cameron, Elfriede, 145, 150. *See also* Thomas letter to

Cameron, Norman, 125, 132, 134 and Note, 144, 159, 186–7; befriends Thomas, 129; 'Norman the Nagger', 129, 138

Campbell, Roy, 279; directs Thomas radio readings, 234; coins 'Swansea's Rimbaud', Note to 198

Canada, Thomas visits, 281–2

Cardiff, 127, 194, 248, 264; Thomas loses *Under Milk Wood* there, 336fn

Carmarthen/shire, 98, 154, 197, 249, 310; Thomas's family connections with, 7–16 *passim*; two *Portrait* stories located there, 179; Thomas sees wartime tribunal there,

190; Caitlin at C. market, 291; 'fainting' incident there, 348–9; C. hangman, 31 and Note. *See also* Johnstown

'Ceremony After a Fire Raid' (P), 'religious' content of, 214–15; Thomas records, 318fn

Chaplin, Charlie, Thomas visits, 283–4

Chapman, Max, 168, 169; 'sexual' episode with Thomas, 130–1

Chelsea (London), 101, 119, 120, 131

Chelsea Hotel (New York), 356; Dylan and Caitlin stay there, 316ff; 'the cockroaches have teeth', 351; Thomas distraught there, 354, 355, 356; collapses there, 357–8

Chicago, 278, 280, 315

Chicago, University of, Thomas visits, 278

'A Child's Christmas in Wales' (recorded for Caedmon), 228, 319

'A Child's Memories of Christmas in Wales' (*Harper's Bazaar* title of 'A Child's Christmas in Wales'), concocted from BBC talk and *Picture Post* essay, 286

Church, Richard (Thomas's publisher at Dent), 139; Thomas poems worry him, 134–6; Thomas ultimatum to, 146; takes the plunge, 147; shrinks from 'sensual' stories, 178; Thomas castigates, 179, parodies, 262fn. *See also* Dent; Thomas letters to

Circus (magazine), publishes

Thomas, 262fn

City College of New York, Thomas visits, 354

Clare, John, 109, 134fn

Cleverdon, Douglas, midwife to *Under Milk Wood*, 295, 323–4, Note to 324, 367; on 'locked in library' episode, 324fn; receives *Under Milk Wood* ms, 350; sells it, Note to 350, 369; writes about 'In Country Heaven', Note to 295; his book about *Under Milk Wood*, Note to 295, 367; memo about Thomas and Persia, 297fn and Note; fights cuts to *Under Milk Wood*, Note to 338. *See also* BBC and Thomas; *Under Milk Wood*

Coleman, Emily Holmes, xxiii; affair with Thomas, 158ff. *See also* Thomas letters to

Collected Poems 1934–1952 (Thomas), 5, 93, 323; many composed in early years, 86, 147; Spender praises, 115–16, 325; publication and reviews, 324–5; wins Foyle's Poetry Prize, 329; sells briskly, 329, best-seller, 366

Comus (Milton), Thomas acts in, 233

Connolly, Cyril, on Geoffrey Grigson, 89; entertains Thomas, 131–2; damns *The Map of Love*, 190; publishes (in *Horizon*) Thomas's 'Request to Leda', 193, 'Deaths and Entrances', 194, 'Ballad of the Long-legged Bait', 195

'Conversation about Christmas', Thomas essay in *Picture Post*, 286fn. *See also* 'A Child's Memories of Christmas in Wales'

'The conversation of prayers', (P), written at New Quay, 4; sent to Vernon Watkins, 223

Cornell University, Thomas reads at, 276

Cornwall, 153, 161fn; Thomas visits with Wyn Henderson, 145ff; there with Caitlin, 164–70 *passim*; married there, 168

'Country Magazine' (radio programme), Thomas in, 244

Cox, Mrs Gardner, Boston hostess, 337

Craig, Armour (Amherst College), 271–2

Creation and Destruction: Notes on Dylan Thomas (B. W. Murphy), 25fn

Criterion (magazine), 103; publishes Thomas, 148

Crowley, Aleister, 90

Cwmdonkin Drive, 6, 14, 24, 30, 55, 67, 88, 102, 121, 159, 363; newly built house, 20; Thomas born there, 21; Uncle Arthur stays there, 32; home life, 20–1, 43, 73–6; Dan Jones visits, 45; Thomas writes in, 59; Thomas returns for Christmas 1934, 122; recuperates there, 137–8; parents leave, 163; Thomas's model, 173; subject of 'Once it was the colour of saying', Note to 185

Cwmdonkin Park, 20; a secret place, 29; origin of 'Cwmdonkin', Note to 29;

Cwmdonkin Park – *contd*
setting of 'Patricia, Edith and
Arnold', 29; Thomas's
playground, 43; in 'Old
Garbo', 65; its hunchback,
77, recalled in poem, 77, 198;
Thomas memorial there, 363
Czechoslovakia, 182; Thomas's
radio script about, 195;
Thomas visits, 254, and
recalls in fantasy, 280

Daiches, David, Thomas's host
at Cornell, 276–7
'La Danseuse' (P), ms corrected
by D. J. Thomas, 36; text,
372–3
'Dare I?' (P) (later 'Ears in the
turrets hear'), 87
Dark, Howard, Caitlin's lover,
292, 349
Dark, Jane, 292, 349
Davenport, Clement, 192, 194.
See also Thomas letter to
Davenport, John, 240, 323, 364;
drinking buddy, 176; raises
money for Thomas, 186–7;
host at Marshfield, 192ff;
writes book with Thomas,
193; notes Thomas's misery,
211; asks Thomas for money,
250; proposes Thomas for
club membership, 260fn; on
'henpecked' Thomas, 291; on
Thomas's 'state of terror',
331; at Thomas's funeral,
365. *See also* Thomas letters
to
Davies, Aneirin Talfan (radio
producer), 227, 327, 343; on
Thomas the Bard, 117fn; on
Thomas as 'religious' poet,
Note to 215

Davies, James A., 82, 232, 331
Davies, Lorraine, commissions
'Memories of Christmas' for
radio, 227
Davies, W. H., 244
Davies, W. S. ('Soapy'), 85;
schoolmaster friend of D. J.
Thomas, 18
Davies, Walford, 368
Davies, W. T. (Pennar Davies),
177fn, 182. *See also* Thomas
letter to
Davin, Dan, on Thomas's
Welshness, 262; on his
morning cough, 280
Dawkins, Gwevril, a friend of
Nancy Thomas, xviii, 19–20;
babysits at Cwmdonkin
Drive, 32; sees how the
Thomases live, 42; on Nancy,
72, 88–9; and D. J. Thomas's
cancer, Note to 90
The Death of Dylan Thomas
(Nashold and Tremlett),
360fn
The Death of the King's Canary
(novel), with John
Davenport, 193, 368
Deaths and Entrances (book),
planned for 1945, 223;
Thomas adds 'Fern Hill', 228;
published 1946, 232
'Deaths and Entrances' (P),
about invasion, 194
de la Mare, Walter, judges poetry
competition, 85; Thomas
discusses, 233
Delancey Street (London),
Margaret Taylor acquires
house there, 302, 308;
Thomases arrive, 311, depart,
322
Dent (J. M. Dent, publishers),

168, 185; consider Thomas, 134–5, publish *Twenty-five Poems*, 146–7; not amused by 'Llareggub', 178, dismayed by *Adventures in the Skin Trade*, 198–9; loyal to Thomas, 184; seek value for money, 198; plan collected poems (1947), 249, 250, (1950), 322, collected stories, 329; publish *Collected Poems* (1952), 324. *See also* Bozman, E. F.; Church, Richard; Thomas letter to

Deren, Maya, 354

Derwood, Gene, 286, 316

Devas, Nicolette (née Macnamara, later Shephard), xxiv, 154fn, 166, 191, 212, 364; Thomas's sister-in-law, 24; on Thomas's fantasies, 110; her childhood with Caitlin, 151–2; on Dylan and Caitlin as newly-weds, 170–1

de Vries, Peter, entertains Thomas, caricatures him in *Reuben, Reuben*, 266–7, Note to 267; on Thomas's teeth, Note to 278

The Doctor and the Devils, as film script, 202, 245; as book, 202. *See also* Burke and Hare

Donegal, Thomas visits, 132–4

Dietrich, Marlene, 284

'Do not go gentle into that good night' (P), xxii, 303, 321fn; expresses Thomas's grief, 9; sends to Marguerite Caetani, 298; couldn't show to his father, 298; Thomas records, 319fn; repositioned in *Collected Poems*, 324fn; and his father's blindness, 328fn

Durrell, Lawrence, 186, 236. *See also* Thomas letter to

Dylan, mythical origin of name, 20

Dylan (novel, John Summers), 367

Dylan (play, Sidney Michaels), 366

Dylan (biopic, Lewis and Ferris), 367

Dylan Thomas: 'Dog Among the Fairies' (Henry Treece), 321–2

Dylan Thomas in America (J. M. Brinnin), 267, 287, 366. *See also* Brinnin, John Malcolm

'Dylan Thomas in Swansea' (thesis, Kent Thompson), 35

Dylan Thomas: The Poems (ed. Daniel Jones), 39, 46fn, 367–8

Dylan Thomas Trust, xvii, xx, 365, 371

Earp, T. W. *See* Thomas letters to

'Ears in the turrets hear' (P), expresses self-doubt, 86, 87; appeals to Richard Church, 135

Edinburgh, Thomas visits, 253 and Note

Edwards, Colin, 22fn

18 Poems, 48, 131, 134, 148, 179, 180, 183; intensely written, 186; assembling the poems, 105; finding a publisher, 121–2; published and reviewed, 122–4; Vernon Watkins reads, 126; Edith Sitwell reviews, 138

Elba, Thomases visit, 243

Eldridge, John (film director), 204, 221, 222

'Elegy' (unfinished poem), 302,
    362; Thomas's notes on, 9;
    for his father, 344
Eliot, T. S., 285, 308, 337;
    notices Thomas, 103; dithers
    over *18 Poems*, 122; Thomas
    meets, 147–8; publishes 'The
    Orchards', 147–8, 178;
    watches Caitlin dance, 153;
    sends Thomas money, 300–1.
    See also Thomas letter to
Elliott, Addie (maidservant),
    xviii, 28; on marriage of
    Dylan's parents, 10; joins
    household, 20; cuddles
    Dylan, 25; in D. J. Thomas's
    poem, 27; takes Dylan to
    park, 29
'The Elm' (P), 52
Empson, William, 193; on
    Thomas's self-pity, 173–4;
    won't review *Collected
    Poems*, 325; on 'The force
    that through the green fuse',
    Note to 92
Ennistymon (Ireland), 157, 235;
    home of the Macnamaras,
    150. *See also* Falls Hotel
Ernst, Max, 320
'Especially when the October
    wind' (P), 108; published by
    Listener, 103
Evans, Caradoc, 158; Thomas
    visits, 115; Thomas mentions
    in lecture, 253 and Note
Evans, Gwynfor, 191
Evans, Will (painter), 120–1
*Evening Post, see South Wales
    Evening Post*
'Extraordinary Little Cough'
    (S), true to life, 44

Falls Hotel (Ireland), Caitlin

Macnamara at, 157–8, 160
Farr, Freddie, 94; drawn from
    life in 'Old Garbo', 65
Fazio, Francesco, Caitlin's
    natural son, xix, 368, 371
Fazio, Giuseppe, Caitlin's
    partner, xix, 370, 371
Feltenstein, Dr Milton D., Liz
    Reitell's doctor, treats
    Thomas, 341; gives him
    steroids, 352, 357; morphine,
    358, 360; admits Thomas to
    hospital, 359; barred from
    case, 360fn; incompetent,
    361; his pills and
    prescription, 362–3
'Fern Hill' (P), xxii, 69, 183,
    229, 257, 273, 363; about
    lost childhoods, 5; a poem
    without people, 32; added to
    Deaths and Entrances, 228;
    Thomas records, 319fn
Fernhill (farm), 4, 15, 80, 107,
    144, 174; run by Ann and Jim
    Jones, 13; described, 29–30;
    in 'The Peaches', 30ff, 179;
    Thomas revisits, 347;
    'hangman's house', 31 and
    Note
Festival of Britain, 290, 301
'The Fight' (S), 6, 53, 251fn;
    describes meeting Dan Jones,
    45; lost poems quoted in, 59
Fisher, Charles, 109; fellow
    pupil, 56; fellow reporter, 70;
    and *King's Canary*, 193. *See
    also* Thomas letters to
FitzGibbon, Constantine,
    130fn, 197, 206, 287, 349,
    350, 354fn, 357fn; writes
    authorised life of Thomas,
    xvii; and 'diabetes' story, 334
Fitzroy public house, 76, 124,
    159

'Floe's Tusks' (story title), 312
and Note, 313
Florence, Thomases visit, 238
'The Flying Bum' (William
Plomer), 274
'The Followers' (S), 326fn
'For as long as forever is' (P),
Note to 148, 368; text, 373
'The force that through the
green fuse drives the flower'
(P), 98, 272; composition and
publication, 92; dedicated to
E(velyn) P(hillips)?, Note to
92
Forster, E. M., 235
Fraser, G. S., 143, 325
'From love's first fever to her
plague' (P), 93; reference to
father's cancer, 91
Frost, Robert, 308
Fry, Charles (publisher), 331.
See also Thomas letter to
Fuller, Jean Overton, 22fn

Gainsborough (Films), Thomas
writes for, 245–6, 250
Garbo, Greta, 284
Gard, Lillian, 39, 42fn
Gardner, David, 347–8, 365
Gargoyle Club, 213fn
Gascoyne, David, 160–1
Ghiselin, Brewster, 320
Gill, Brendan, on an evening
with Thomas, 267 and Note
Gilliam, Laurence (BBC Head of
Features), 234, 290, 301;
encourages Thomas, 233;
won't hire him, 235
Glendower, Pamela, 208
Glock, Sir William, 192; liaison
with Caitlin Thomas, 194
Gosport, Laugharne, 253
Goulden, Mark, 90, 104fn

Gower (peninsula), 2, 6, 100,
114, 127; Thomas camps
there, 44–5; an 'orgy' there,
111; two Portrait stories set
there, 179
Graham, Malcolm, in Little
Theatre with Thomas, 71, 101
Graham, Ruby, 114
'Greek Play in a Garden' (P), 85–
6
'Green Mountain, Black
Mountain' (film), Thomas
writes script, 203
Greene, Graham, 249, Note to
199
Greenwich Village (New York),
316, 341, 351, 353
Gribben, Vera, 152–3
'A grief ago' (P), Edith Sitwell
approves of, 138–9
Grigson, Geoffrey, 115, 123,
125, 129, 182; influential
editor, 89; accepts poem by
Thomas, 103; recalls Thomas
drawings, 110; distaste for
Thomas, 129; on Thomas
version of Wilhelm Busch
poem, Note to 129; with
Thomas in Ireland, 132;
disenchanted with him, 134
and Note, 138; turns against
Thomas's poetry, 134, 215–
16. See also Thomas letters to
Grisewood, Harman (BBC), 290
Group Theatre, 153
Gruen, John, 286, 287
Guggenheim, Peggy, 187
Gutierrez-Mahoney, Dr
William, 357fn, 360fn

Hadfield, John, 198–9
Hamnett, Nina, 76, 124; in
Death of the King's Canary,
193

'The hand that signed the paper' (P), 134fn, 135; perhaps about Hitler, 82

Hansford Johnson, Pamela, *see* Johnson, Pamela Hansford

Happy Mag, 42fn

Hardy, Thomas, 262, 265, 273–4

Harper's Bazaar, 286, 319, 344fn

Harvard University, 226, 315; Thomas reads there, 268

Hawkins, Desmond, xxiv–xxv, 123–4, 148, 171, 186. *See also* Thomas letters to

Hay Fever (Noël Coward), Thomas acts in, 71

Heliker, Jack, 352fn

Henderson, Nigel, 145; on Thomas the joker, 141; meets Caitlin Thomas, 171

Henderson, Wyn, 159, 162fn, 169; meets Thomas, 144–5, sleeps with him, 145–6; pays for his marriage licence, 168. *See also* Thomas letter to

Heppenstall, Rayner, 97, 364; Thomas's drinking companion, 124; recalls Thomas limericks, 140–1, Note to 140; in Cornwall, 169; meets Pearl, 293–4

Herald of Wales, Thomas contributes to, 63–4, 76, 85–6, 126; reviews *18 Poems*, 148

A High Wind in Jamaica (Richard Hughes), 153

Higham, David, Dylan Thomas trustee, xvii, xx, 365; Thomas's literary agent, 158, 168, 184, 185, 186, 190, 198, 246, 247, 249, 322, 328, 329–30, 333, 334; advises Thomas on army medical, 191. *See also* Thomas letters to

'His Requiem' (P), 39–40, 42fn, 46fn; in *Western Mail*, 6

Hitler, Adolf, may have inspired 'The hand that signed the paper', 82; satirised in Thomas film commentary, 202–3

Holbrook, David, notes Thomas's use of Roget, 304fn; on 'Lament', Note to 298

Holdridge, Barbara, 318–19, 341–2, 366. *See also* Caedmon

Hole, Mrs (school proprietor), 33, 237

Hollywood, Thomas visits, 283–4

Holyoke (Mass.), 271. *See also* Mount Holyoke

'The Holy Six' (S), gives offence, 178

'Holy Spring' (P), 215

Holywell Ford (Oxford), 231

Hood, Christopher (*Banana Cat*), 367

Hopkins, Gerard Manley, 116, 234, 321

Horizon, 190, 193, 194, 195, 224fn. *See also* Connolly, Cyril

'The Horse's Ha' (S), 158

Howard, Sir Stafford, 306

Howard-Stepney, Lady, 306, 326

Howard-Stepney, Marged, Thomas's patron, 300; biography, 306; intends to buy Boat House, 326; her death, 328–9, 332. *See also* Thomas letters to

'How shall my animal' (P), 58

'How soon the servant sun' (P), Vernon Watkins finds meaningless, 136; *Times Literary Supplement* finds obscure, 148

'How To Be a Poet' (article), 262fn, 308

Hughes, David (Thomases' doctor), 175, 291–2, 328fn, 335, 349

Hughes, Frances, 206, 306. *See also* Thomas letter to

Hughes, Richard, 153, 154, 158, 182, 197, 253

Hughes, Trevor, 59, 67, 88, 91, 112; early friend, 78 and Note; in 'Who Do You Wish Was With Us?', 78, 179. *See also* Thomas letters to

Hulse, Michael, xxii–xxiii

'The hunchback in the park' (P), 199; about Cwmdonkin, 43, and a real hunchback, 77; quarried from notebook, 198

Hyman, Stanley Edgar, 267 and Note

'I dreamed my genesis' (P), 'based on Welsh rhythms', 117; ms version, Note to 117

'Idylls of Unforgetfulness' (P), 51–2

'If I were tickled by the rub of love' (P), 105; Thomas has difficulty in recording, 342

'If the Gods had but given' (P), published in *Western Mail*, 40

'I have longed to move away' (P), 134fn; and Uncle David Rees, Note to 76

'I, in my intricate image' (P), technical virtuosity of, 116

Illinois, University of, 278

'I make this in a warring absence' (P), earlier 'Poem (for Caitlin)', about sexual jealousy, 171–2

'In Country Heaven' (unfinished poem; also title of larger work), 242, 256, 295 and Note

'In Country Sleep' (P), 316, 325; written in Italy, 241–2; variously explained by Thomas, 242; broadcast, 295

'In my craft or sullen art' (P), 273; Thomas adds to *Deaths and Entrances*, 228

In Parenthesis (David Jones), Thomas acts in, 233, 295

'Inspirations' (P), 37

'In the White Giant's Thigh' (P), 242; Thomas writes it with difficulty, 260–1; completed, 294; sold via Oscar Williams, 308; projected sequel, 312; upsets *Atlantic* subscribers, 318

Iowa, State University of, Thomas visits, 278

Iowa City, Thomas visits, 278–81

Ireland, 48, 49, 135; Thomas visits with Grigson, 132–4; and Caitlin Macnamara, 150–3, 157–8, 160; Dylan and Caitlin visit, 235 and Note

Isherwood, Christopher, 283

'Is Your Ernie Really Necessary?' (film), 203

Italy, 236, 249; Thomas visits with his family, 3, 237–43; Caitlin lives there as widow, xix, xxiv, 370

'ITMA' (radio programme), 302

Jackson, Shirley, 267 and Note
Janes, Alfred ('Fred'), 66, 149,
    153, 293, 328; Swansea
    friend, 70; shares room with
    Thomas, 117, 119, 138; in
    radio programme, 260. See
    also Thomas letter to
'January 1939' (P) (later called
    'Because the pleasure-bird
    whistles'), 185–6
John, Augustus, 158, 187; friend
    of the Macnamaras, 150; the
    'Caitlin's father' story, 150,
    her 'uncle', 166; shelters
    Macnamaras, 151; paints
    Caitlin, 152, 169; scuffles
    with Thomas, 153–4; in
    Cornwall, 169; stays at
    Laugharne, 175; parodied in
    Death of the King's Canary,
    193
John, Caspar, and Caitlin
    Macnamara, 152
John, Vivien, 152
John O'London's (magazine),
    342
Johnson, Pamela Hansford, 59,
    66, 90, 97, 119, 154, 330,
    334, 346; important
    correspondence with
    Thomas, 23, 96ff, Note to 96;
    meets Thomas, 101; their
    relationship and letters, 101ff;
    forgives erring Thomas, 112;
    their relationship falters, 114;
    'Comrade Bottle' intervenes,
    124; she writes him off, 126;
    missing letters from Thomas,
    Note to 96. See also Thomas
    letters to
Johnstown (Carmarthen), 7, 12,
    15, 178fn
Jones, Ann (maternal aunt), of

Fernhill, 13, 15, 144;
    Thomas's memories of, 30–2;
    her death inspires 'After the
    funeral', 79–80
Jones, Dr Daniel Jenkyn, 42, 52,
    66, 70, 75, 77, 85, 293, 295;
    edits Thomas's poems, 39,
    46fn, 367–8; Thomas's best
    friend, 45ff; poetry
    collaborations, 45–6;
    Warmley days, 47ff; a difficult
    man, 51; meets Pamela
    Hansford Johnson, 90, 96 and
    Note; in radio programme,
    260; former copyright trustee,
    365. See also Thomas letters
    to
Jones, Evelyn Burman, 95–6,
    114; childhood friend, 33, 34
Jones, Glyn, 126, 144, 263–4;
    friend and admirer, 102–3,
    141; on Thomas as poet, 103,
    106, 109, 115, 118; in
    Laugharne with Thomas,
    107–9. See also Thomas letters
    to
Jones, Jim (uncle by marriage),
    13, 30
Jones, Thomas S., 52
Jones, Watkin (BBC), 189fn
Josephson, Mimi, 342. See also
    Thomas letter to
'Just Like Little Dogs' (S),
    ending changed, 56

Kavanagh, Ted, 302
Keats, John, 197
Keene, Ralph ('Bunny'), 296
Kent, Rockwell, 132
Kenyon College, Ohio, 277
Killick, Vera, 34, 173, 205, 208,
    210, 217, 221–2, 310. See
    also Machine-gunning
    incident

Killick, William, 205, 210, 221–3

'Lament' (P), 2, 299, 303;
  reflects his frustrations, 298;
  Thomas records, 342
Laugharne, xviii, 1, 2, 5, 6, 24,
  107–9, 111, 144, 153, 154,
  182, 186, 192, 194, 205fn,
  214, 249, 253, 284, 288, 289,
  290–2, 298, 301, 302, 303,
  304, 310, 311, 344, 347, 348,
  361, 363, 364, 370;
  Thomases live there, 174, at
  Sea View, 174–5; Under Milk
  Wood set there, 227, 253;
  Thomases return there, to
  Boat House, 253ff; Caitlin
  deplores, 291. See also Boat
  House
Laugharne-Allen, Misses, 253
Laugharne Castle, 197, 198,
  253
Laughlin, James, 190fn, 224,
  235; Thomas's American
  publisher, 183–4, Note to
  184. See also Thomas letters
  to
Leavis, F. R., 181
Leftover Life to Kill (Caitlin
  Thomas), xix, 368
Lehmann, John, 125, 236
Letters to Vernon Watkins, Note
  to 36
Levy, Mervyn, Swansea friend,
  70, 93–4, 120, 248, 263
Lewis, C. Day, 181, 235
Lewis, E. Glyn, Note to 38
Lewis, Saunders, 181
Lewis, Wyndham, 124
Life and Letters Today,
  publishes Thomas, 178fn, 199
'Life and the Modern Poet'
  (radio talk), 161

The Life of Dylan Thomas
  (Constantine FitzGibbon),
  xvii, 366
'Light breaks where no sun
  shines' (P), published in
  Listener, 93, 103
Lilliput (magazine), 218
Lindsay, Jack, 204–5, 208, 230;
  on Thomas's drinking, 213;
  at Holywell Ford, 231
The Listener, 93, 103, 124;
  Thomas poem offends
  readers, 103
Little Theatre (Swansea), 72,
  95–6; Thomas joins, 71;
  ejected from play, 100–1
Llanelli, 191fn, 265fn, 306, 325
Llangain, 11, 197, 214
Llangollen, 343
Llanmadog (Gower), 178
Llanstephan, 11, 197, 214
Llanybri, 11, 12, 80, 107, 347
Llareggub, as a joke-name, 178;
  used for Under Milk Wood,
  203, 323, 324, 331, 336.
'Llaberos & Muberab', 179fn
Llwyn Gwyn (farm), 15, 347
Locke, Cordelia and Harry, 143,
  244–5, 250, 349, 350
London, not good for Thomas's
  poetry, 5, or prose, 121;
  Thomas's first visit to, 88;
  walks there with Spender,
  113; goes there to live, 117,
  119–20, 124–5, 138; escapes
  its 'trials', 125; his visits hard
  to chronicle, 140; Thomas
  less agreeable there, 132, 142;
  'money breeds there', 172–3;
  'insane city', 185; 'nightmare
  L.', 186; 'stinking, friendless
  L.', 199; in wartime, 201–14
  passim; still the pleasure city,

London – *contd*
210; seeks dwelling place
there, 226; in hospital there,
230; reluctant return to L.,
302, 311–12; L. interlude
over, 322; Thomas's last visit,
348–50. *See also* Chelsea;
Soho

London Mercury (magazine),
138, 149

'The Londoner' (radio script),
233

Long, Dolly, 311–12

Lougée, David, 352fn, 355

Lowell, Robert, 279

Lutyens, Elisabeth, 176, 205fn,
210, 233, 256, 309–11

Lye, Len, 316

McAlpine, Helen and Bill, 235,
288, 294, 297, 298

MacCarthy, Desmond, 132

McInerny, E. F., 52 and Note, 53

McKenna, Rollie, 315, 347,
353, 366

Mackenzie, Compton, 90

Maclaren-Ross, Julian, 201,
202, 203, 208

Macnamara, Brigit (sister-in-
law), 151, 152, 237, 238

Macnamara, Caitlin, *see*
Thomas, Caitlin

Macnamara, Francis (father-in-
law), 150, 151, 157, 176

Macnamara, John (brother-in-
law), 222

Macnamara, Nicolette, *see*
Devas, Nicolette

Macnamara, Mary (Yvonne)
(mother-in-law), 170;
Augustus John's lover, 150;
deserted by husband, 150–1;
her lesbian affair, 151

MacNeice, Louis, 116, 181,
259; broadcasts with Thomas,
174fn; Thomas acts in his
play, 233; at Thomas's
funeral, 365

Mabinogion, The, as source of
'Dylan', 21

Machine-gunning incident
(New Quay), 4, 34, 221–3,
228, 353

Mademoiselle (magazine), 347

Magdalen College, 231

Magdalen College School, 241

Majoda (New Quay bungalow),
216, 217, 221, 222, 224, 227

Malting House (Marshfield),
192–4

Mantell, Marianne, 318–19,
341–2, 366. *See also* Caedmon

The Map of Love (stories and
poems), 178, 194, 232;
published, reviewed, 189–90

Marionettes (Francis
Macnamara), 150

Marlais, River, 9, 21

Marley, Lord, 25fn

Marnier, Brigit, *see* Macnamara,
Brigit

Marsh, Edward, 85

Marshfield, 192–4, 195, 198

Marx Brothers, 293

Masters, Edgar Lee, 323

Maud, Ralph, 92, 367, 368

Me and My Bike (film), 246

'Memories of Christmas' (radio
talk), 227–8, 286fn. *See also*
'A Child's Memories of
Christmas in Wales'

Mermaid Hotel (Mumbles), 114

Michaels, Sidney, 366, 367

Milan, 237

Miles, Hamish, Note to 117

Miller, Arthur, 341

Miller, Henry, 186, 282

Milton, John, 233

'The Miner's Lament' (P) (early version of 'Lament'), 298

Ministry of Information, 203, 204

Mirador Crescent School (Swansea), 33

Mitchell, Raymond, 42fn

'The Modern Muse' (BBC poetry readings), 174fn

'Modern Welsh Poets' (BBC), 189

Moffatt, Ivan, friend in films, Note to 199, 201, 202fn, 211 and Note, 212, 283–4

Monroe, Marilyn, 284

Montpellier Street (Swansea), 16

Moore, George, 83

Moore, Henry, 124, 192

Morgan, John, 69

Morgans, J. Grey, 59

Morley, Royston, 158, Note to 195, 259

Morning Post, 123, 129, 137–8

Mosley, Sir Oswald, 113

Moss, Howard, 143, 279, 355; hears morphine story, 358

Mount Holyoke (Mass.), 268–71 passim

'The Mouse and the Woman' (S), 26, 127

Mousehole, 145, 146, 169

Mumbles (Swansea), 14, 44, 70, 72, 114

Mumbles Railway, 35

Muir, Edwin, 158

Murder in the Cathedral (T. S. Eliot), 337

Murphy, Dr B. W., 25fn

'My hero bares his nerves' (P), 92; written at Blaen Cwm, 4

'My world is pyramid' (P), 83

Nashold, James, 334, 360fn

National Liberal Club, 260fn

Neuburg, Victor, 104fn, 107, 161; runs 'Poets' Corner', 90; prints 'The force that through the green fuse', 92; 'the Vicky Bird', 100

New American Library, Note to 199

'New Apocalyptic' movement, 179

New Directions, Thomas's American publishers, 183, 184, 190fn, 232, 316. See also Laughlin, James

New English Weekly (first London magazine to publish Thomas), 83, 84–5, 88

New Haven, 267, 268

Newlyn, 169, 170

New Quay (Cardiganshire), 34, 216, 217, 228; poems written there, 4–5; Thomases move to, 214; machine-gun incident, 221–3; Under Milk Wood connection, 227

New Republic, 224fn

New Statesman, 148, 190, 325

'New Towns for Old' (film), 202

New Verse, Geoffrey Grigson founds, 89; publishes Thomas, 103–4, 114, 129, 134; reviews 18 Poems, 124

New York (city and state), 2, 94, 236, 242, 257, 272, 275, 276, 282, 285–7, 314, 315–19, 335–42 passim, 351–62 passim; Thomas's first visit to, 264–6

New York State University (Buffalo), 53, 197

New Yorker, 143, 267, 312
Nicholson, Geoffrey, 300
'No Man Believes' (P), 88
No Room at the Inn (film), 245
Notre Dame University (Indiana), 278
'Now' (P), 136, 148

Observer, 90, 324
O'Casey, Sean, 101, 321
Ohio, 264, 277
'Old Garbo' (S), about Thomas's newspaper days, 63, 65, 70, 94, 312, 326fn
Old Grandad whisky, 355, 356
Old Rectory (Rhossili), 329
'On a Wedding Anniversary' (P), 194
'Once below a time' (P), 324fn
'One Warm Saturday' (S), 94-5, 312; date written, 178-9
Opera Workshop (Boston), 340
Orage, A. R., 84-5, 88
'The Orchards' (S), 69; T. S. Eliot accepts, 147-8; source of 'Llareggub', 178
'Osiris, Come to Isis' (P), 53
O'Sullivan, Maurice, 217
'Our eunuch dreams' (P), Edith Sitwell dislikes, 103-4; Thomas disparages, 139
'Our Country' (film), 204
'Out of the sighs' (P), 79-80
'Over Sir John's hill' (P), 242, 259, 294-5; theme and content, 256-7; G. S. Fraser on, 325
Owen, Hettie and Ken, Note to 32, 36 and Note, 196
Owen, Ruth Wynn, 209-10, Note to 210. *See also* Thomas letter to
Owen, Trevor, 41

Oxford, Thomas lives in, 3, 231, 233, 235, 236; visits, 262
Oxford University, 10, 17, 27
Oxford University Press, 329

'Paper and sticks' (P), Thomas dislikes, 324fn
Paraclete church (Swansea), 14, 28, 76, 126
'The Parachutist' (parody of Spender), 193
Paradise Lost (Milton), 244, 295
Parton Bookshop, 122, 134
'Patricia, Edith and Arnold' (S), about Cwmdonkin Park, 29; ms of, 179
'The Peaches' (S), xvii, 35-6, 42, 94fn; about Fernhill, 13, 30-1, Note to 30; date written, 179
Pearl, a Thomas girlfriend, 287; Thomas 'in love' with, 287; in London, 293-4; gone away, 294; last meeting, 337
Pearson, Norman Holmes, 267-8
Peer Gynt (Ibsen), 350; Thomas fails to adapt for TV, 258-9
Pelican (parents' house in Laugharne), 255, 256, 311, 329, 365
Penguin New Writing, xvii
Pennard (Gower), 127, 149
Pentowin (farm), 13, 144, 255
Pen-y-coed (farm), 11
Persia, Thomas in, 296-8
Peter Lunn (publishers), 218, 221
Philadelphia, 272
Phillips, Vera, *see* Killick, Vera
Picture Post, 235, 253, 286fn
The Plain Dealer (Wycherley),

Thomas fails to adapt for
radio, 258, 259
'A Plea for Intellectual
Revolution' (letter), 113
Plomer, William, 113fn, 274
Pocock, Robert, 24
'Poem (for Caitlin)' (P) (later 'I
make this in a warring
absence'), 171-2
'Poem in October' (P), 4, 257,
273; completed at Blaen
Cwm, 215; first publication,
224fn; 'birthday' poem, 303
'Poem on his Birthday' (P), 2,
303, 306, 312, 316, 323;
forced optimism, 303-4;
worksheets, 304-5;
uncertainty over dating,
303fn and Note; sold to
Atlantic, 308; worksheets
sold, 329-30; Thomas
records, 342
'Poem to Caitlin' (title), 312
'Poem to Colm' (title), 312
The Poems (ed. Daniel Jones),
see Dylan Thomas: The
Poems
Poetry (Chicago), 134fn
Poetry (London), Note to 210
'Poetry and the Film', Thomas
at symposium, 354
Poetry Center (New York), 352;
Thomas invited to, 257-8;
readings at, 265, 266, 274,
286, 318, 321, 347, 366;
Under Milk Wood performed
at, 337-8, Note to 337
'The Poets' Corner' (newspaper
feature), 80-1, 92
'The Poets of Swansea'
(newspaper articles), 63-4, 77
Pollinger, Laurence, 198. See
also Thomas letter to

Pomona College (Claremont),
285
Poplar Cottage (Johnstown), 15,
178fn
Porter, Katherine Anne, 265
Porteus, Hugh, 211
Porthcurno (Cornwall), 145,
150
Portrait of the Artist as a Young
Dog, 32, 45, 59, 94, 110,
121, 198, 232, 237, 251fn,
326fn; autobiographical, 29-
32; written 1938-1939, 178-
9; unwritten stories, 179;
published, reviewed, 190;
'flippant' title, 179fn
Powell, Anthony, 124
Prague, Thomas in, 254, 257
Price, Dr William, 115
Prichard, John, 260, 334
Prichard, Llewelyn, 63-4, 65
Priestley, J. B., 158, 207
'A process in the weather of the
heart' (P), 102
'Prologue' (P), 303; complex
rhyme-scheme, 116-17;
genesis, 322-3, Note to 322;
worksheets for sale, 329
'Prologue to An Adventure' (S),
obscenity fears, 177
'Prose and Verse' (proposed
magazine), 59, 78
'A Prospect of the Sea' (S), 26,
178
A Prospect of the Sea (book),
178fn
Puck Fair, 235
Pudney, John, London friend,
125, 140, 141-2, 161-2, 173,
205; on Thomas's 'unreality',
143

Quadrangle Club (Chicago),
278

'Quite Early One Morning' (radio reminiscence), 227

Rank Organisation, 245
Ransom, John Crowe, 279
Rapallo, 237, 238
Read, Bill, 301, 303, 366
Read, Herbert, 192
Reavey, George, 88, 177; on Thomas's death, 364. *See also* Thomas letter to
Rebecca's Daughters (film), 245–6
Redcliffe Street (London), 119
Rees, Rev. David (uncle by marriage), 14, 28, 126; Thomas's dislike of, 14, 'the Reverend Crap', 76fn; retires, 76; may be connected with poem, Note to 76; death, 196
Rees, Sir Richard, 88, 99
Rees, Theodosia ('Dosie', maternal aunt), 13–14, 15, 196
Rees, T. J., 38
'A Refusal to Mourn' (P), 273; written at New Quay, 4; its equivocal message, 223; first published, 224fn; Thomas records, 342fn
Reid, Alastair, 109, 321
Reid, Ben, 269
Reifenstahl, Leni, 202
Reitell, Elizabeth, Thomas meets at Poetry Center, 336, 337; his lover, 338ff; 'nurse, guard, secretary', 338; on Thomas's drinking, 341; happy days with Thomas, 351; Thomas's companion and confidante, 351–9 *passim*; witness of Thomas's last days, 352fn; on Dr

Feltenstein, 358; at the hospital, 362. *See also* Thomas letter to
'Religio Laici' (Dryden), 234
'Reminiscences of Childhood' (radio), 34, 227
Repton school, 127, 128
'Request to Leda' (parody), 193
'Return Journey' (radio feature), 43, 63, 71, 179, 362; Thomas researches in Swansea, 236–7, Note to 236
Reuben, Reuben (Peter de Vries), satirises Thomas, 267 and Note, Note to 278
Rhossili, 44, 329
Rhys, Keidrych (William Ronald Rees Jones), 176, 189, 190, 208; founds *Wales* magazine, publishes Thomas, 177. *See also* Thomas letters to
Richards, Dr I. A., 337
Rodgers, W. R., 324
Roget's *Thesaurus*, Thomas searches, 304fn, 346
'The Romantic Isle' (P), Thomas sends to BBC, 83; broadcast, 85
Rome, 238
Romola (George Eliot), 238
Ross, Ethel, confidante of Florence Thomas, 15, 19, 42; in Little Theatre, 100–1
Rota, Bertram, 197
Royal family, in Thomas anecdotes, 143–4, 268
Royal Literary Fund, 184–5

'A saint about to fall' (P), about Thomas's unborn child, 182
St Mary Abbott's Hospital (London), 208

St Mary's Hospital (London), 230

St Stephen's Hospital (London), 230, 231

St Thomas (Swansea), 10, 12–13, 14, 15, 18, 32, 196

St Vincent's Hospital (New York), 359–62 *passim*

Salisbury (public house), 294

San Francisco, 264, 282–3, 320; 'the best city on earth', 281

Sarah Lawrence College (New York State), 314, 321

Saroyan, William, 211

Savage, D. S., 188

Savage Club, 260, 294, 295, 362

Scofield, Paul, 244

Scott, William, 120

Sea View (Laugharne), 174–5, 186, 192

'The second best' (P), 40

Second World War, Thomas's attitude to, 187, 188ff; air-raids, 193–4, 196, 214–15

Selected Writings, 232

Shanks, Edward, 232–3

Shaw, George Bernard, 90

Shephard, Lorna, 210

Shephard, Nicolette, *see* Devas, Nicolette

Shephard, Rupert, 157, 160, 210

Shepherd's Bush Hotel, London, 246

'Should lanterns shine' (P), 134fn; Thomas records, 342fn

The Shutter of Snow (Emily Coleman), 158–9

Sibthorp, Veronica, a girlfriend, 162fn

Singleton, Mr Justice, 223fn

Sir John's hill, 255

Sitwell, Edith, 170, 180, 184, 186, 190, 233, 265, 361, 364; dislikes Thomas poem, 103–4, changes her mind, 138–40; hails *Twenty-five Poems*, 149; opposes American visit, 236. *See also* Thomas letters to

Sitwell, Sacheverell, 104

Sketty (Swansea), 16, 18, 19, 38, 45, 51, 78; Sketty Avenue, 16; Sketty Green, 85

Skidmore College (New York State), 319

Slivka, Dave, 355

Slivka, Rose, 321, 354, 362, 364; Caitlin's friend, 315–16

Smart, P. E., boyhood correspondent, xv, xxiii, 57, 59, 67, 76, 217. *See also* Thomas letters to

Smith, R. D. (BBC), 236

Snow, Lady, *see* Johnson, Pamela Hansford

Snow, Lord (C. P.), 96

Society of Authors, 236

Soho (London), 124, 144, 202, 208, 316, 350

'Sometimes' (P), 52

'A Song for St Cecilia's Day' (Dryden), 234

South Leigh, Thomas lives in, 3, 241, 243–53 *passim*

South Wales Daily Post, 62, 69. *See also South Wales Evening Post*

South Wales Evening Post, Thomas employed by, 62–74 *passim*; Thomas leaves, 76–7; and threatened libel action, 76

'Speaking Personally' (TV series), 344

Spectator, reviews Thomas, 124, 148

Spender, Stephen, 127, 129,
     181, 322; approaches
     Thomas, 103; with Thomas in
     London, 113; on Thomas's
     'Welsh influences', 116fn;
     broadcasts with Thomas,
     174fn; raises money for
     Thomas, 192; Thomas
     parodies, 193; reviews
     Collected Poems, 325. *See also*
     Thomas letters to
'The spire cranes' (P), notebook
     version, 58
'Spoon River Anthology' (radio
     script), 323–4
Squire, Sir John, 252
The Stag (public house), 293–4
Stearns, Marshall W., 265
Stephens, James, 232
Stephenson, Adlai and Ellen
     Borden, 315
Stevenson, Robert Louis, 246
Steyning (Sussex), 90, 96 and
     Note
'A Story' (TV broadcast), 344fn,
     347
Strand (Swansea), 94
Strand Films, Thomas works for,
     Note to 199, 200ff, 209, 217
Stravinsky, Igor, 350; Thomas
     invited to collaborate with,
     340–1; writes to Thomas,
     343, 347, 362
Struwwelpeter, 26
'Such Things Do Happen' (story
     synopsis), 312, 313
Summers, Nora, photographs
     Caitlin, 151
Summersby, Gordon (Nancy
     Thomas's second husband),
     249, 327
Summersby, Nancy, *see*
     Thomas, Nancy

Sunday Referee, 105, 107;
     announces 'Poets' Corner',
     89–90; prints Thomas poems,
     90, 92, 96, 100, 102; as co-
     publisher of *18 Poems*, 104,
     121–2
Sunday Telegraph, 39
Sunday Times, 90, 149, 325
Surrealism, 46, 61, 146, 148,
     160–1; Thomas decries, 50,
     135–6; Thomas at S.
     Exhibition, 137, 147
Swansea, Thomas's critical years
     there, 5–6, 51; anglicised S.,
     7; mother's family there, 12–
     15; town described, 12–13; its
     suburbs, 18–19; foreshore
     and seascapes, 34–5; 'the
     queer, Swansea world', 48–
     51; Thomas's 'S. network',
     70; unemployment in, 81–2;
     Thomas leaves, 117; always a
     bolthole, 126; prepares
     Twenty-five Poems there,
     136; six *Portrait* stories set
     there, 179; air-raids and
     damage, 193–4, 196, 236–7;
     in 'Return Journey', 236–7;
     Thomas broadcasts from,
     260, and lectures in, 299–
     300; recalled in New York,
     316
Swansea Empire, 62fn, 312
Swansea Grammar School, 62,
     85; D.J. at, 16, 17–18, 19, 27,
     104; Thomas at, 38–61
     passim; fails exams, 40, 55–
     6; Thomas writes for
     magazine, 38–9, 51–2, 55, 59,
     61; edits magazine, 57, 60, 61
Swansea High School, 71
Swansea University College, 38,
     299

Swansea and West Wales Guardian, 113, 123. *See also* Thomas letter to

'Swiss pub' (London), 208

Taf, River (Laugharne), 108, 255

'Take the needles and the knives' (P), 91

Talsarn (Cardiganshire), 205, 209

Tanning, Dorothea, 320

Tawe, River (Swansea), 12fn

Taylor, A. J. P., 3, 231; his dislike of Thomas, 128

Taylor, Donald, 204, 214, 221, 232, 245, 302; employs Thomas in films, Note to 199, 200ff. *See also* Thomas letters to

Taylor, Haydn (brother-in-law), xviii, 89, 101, 121, 163; observes Nancy's family, 72–3; engaged to Nancy, 73; and D.J.'s illness, 90–1; and Thomas's marriage, 166–7. *See also* Thomas, Nancy; Thomas letters to

Taylor, Margaret, 35, 140, 173, 191fn, 235, 242, 243, 247, 250, 252, 274, 300, 329, 334, 350, 351; Thomas's benefactor, 1, 3, 231–2; on Thomas's drinking, 213; accommodates Thomases at Oxford, 231ff; buys them a house at South Leigh, 241; buys the Boat House, 253–4, which Thomas rents, 326; installs mains water, 256; Thomas's 'almost national debt' to her, 260; her cottage in Laugharne, 291; informs on Thomas, 294; provides flat in London, 302, 312; mocked by Thomases, 312. *See also* Thomas letters to

Taylor, Nancy, *see* Thomas, Nancy

Tennant, David, 213fn. *See also* Thomas letter to

'That sanity be kept' (P), *Sunday Referee* publishes, 90; Pamela Hansford Johnson notices, 96; Stephen Spender and, Note to 90

'There was a saviour' (P), Thomas records, 342fn

'These Are the Men' (film), 202–3

This Bed Thy Centre (Pamela Hansford Johnson), 101

'This side of the truth' (P), 223, 273

Thomas, Aeron(wy) (daughter), xix, 231, 238, 283, 311, 343, 364; birth, 205–6; and 'In Country Sleep', 242

Thomas, Ann (grandmother), 7, 9, 28

Thomas, Ann (great-grandmother), 7

Thomas, Arthur (uncle), 32 and Note

Thomas, Caitlin (née Macnamara, wife), and biographers, xix–xx, xxiii–xxiv; her sharp tongue, 2; on Dylan's father, 18, 129; family and upbringing, 150–3; rumoured daughter of Augustus John, 150, his mistress, 152, his 'niece', 166; meets Dylan, 150, 153; in Ireland, 153, 157–8, 160; in hospital, 155–6; together

Thomas, Caitlin – *contd*
  again, 160–1; marriage plans,
  164ff, married, 168; like
  children, 170; 'a corn
  goddess', 171; early infidelity,
  171–2; married life in
  Laugharne, 174–6; her son
  Llewelyn born, 186; sexual
  escapade, 194; in London,
  199ff; daughter, Aeron(wy)
  born, 205–6; her views on
  adultery, 208; at her sister's,
  212; on Dylan's drinking,
  213; at Holywell Ford, 231;
  enjoys Italy, 238; getting her
  own back, 239–40, 243;
  slaving at South Leigh, 243–4,
  looking after parents-in-law,
  250; pregnant in Laugharne,
  255; second son, Colm, born,
  256; men and other
  weaknesses, 288; the
  discontented wife, 290, 291–
  3; contempt for Laugharne,
  291; casual sex, 292; hears
  about Pearl, 294, is
  embittered, 294; eyes another
  poet, 298; opposes second
  American visit, 301–2;
  pregnancy terminated, 302fn;
  Caitlin's side of the story, 309–
  10, 315–16; in America with
  Dylan, 314–21 *passim*; 'Irish
  fighting drunk', 316; 'I am the
  problem', 316; another
  abortion, 329, 331; her anger
  with Dylan, 331; opposes
  third American trip, 335, 349;
  consults doctor about Dylan,
  349; premonitions of disaster,
  350; flies to America, 361; her
  valedictory letter, 361–2; at
  Dylan's deathbed, 362;
  returns with his coffin, 364; at
  his funeral, 365; approves
  copyright trust, 365; her
  writings, xix, 368–9; her later
  life in Italy, xix, 370; her
  nature and tragedy, 370–1;
  her war with the Thomas
  trust, xx–xxi, 371
  the stronger partner, xxiv,
    238–9, 288, 291–2, 301–2,
    331
  on Dylan's appearance,
    character, behaviour, 35,
    44, 71, 171, 204–5, 225,
    272, 292–3, 326
  mothering Dylan, 24, 171,
    193, 244
  fights and quarrels, 250, 291–
    2, 301, 309, 310, 311, 314,
    335, 343–4
  dancer, 46, 152–3, 197, 208,
    293, 309, 371
  writer, xix, 157, 290, 293,
    309, 315, 368–9, 371
  drinker, 153, 157–8, 170,
    192, 213, 292, 293, 331,
    370
  appearance, 151–2, 153, 168,
    171, 174, 245
  character and opinions, 173,
    199, 208, 288, 291, 292,
    331
  housewife, 170, 175–6, 195,
    226, 231, 243–4, 256
  See also Thomas letters to
Thomas, Colm Garan (son), xix,
  283, 294, 309, 311, 312, 356,
  364; birth, 256; revisits Boat
  House, 363
Thomas, David John ('D.J.')
  (father), xviii, 25, 41, 62, 72,
  104, 119, 137, 139, 155, 167,
  168, 187, 255, 331;

background and character,
7ff; the disappointed man, 9–
10, 38, 129; forced marriage,
10–11, 15, 16; not religious,
15, 28; his appearance, 15–
16, 71; his fastidiousness, 17;
his diction, 17; teaches Welsh
part-time, 18; and drink, 18,
74; chooses name 'Dylan', 20;
ambitious for son, 27; recites
poetry to infant Dylan, 27; his
brothers, 32; corrects Dylan's
poems, 36–7; derides wife's
diction, 43; told of Dylan's
plagiarism, 53; castigates
Dylan over exam, 56;
described in Nancy's letters,
73–6 *passim*; his cancer, 90–
2, 100; Dylan's respect and
feelings for, 9, 27, 40–1, 98,
132, 196, 256, 327–8; retires,
163; hears of Dylan's
marriage plans, 164–5;
opposes them, 165–6; in old
age, 196–7, 249–50; chronic
ill health, 223, 241, 260, 298;
death, 327–8.
   subject of 'Elegy', 9, 303,
   344; subject of 'Do not
   go gentle', 9, 298–9, 303
   See also Thomas letters
   to
Thomas, Dylan Marlais, his
   background, legend, nature,
   1–7; birth, 21; his name, 9,
   21–2; early notebooks, 23;
   indulgent mother, 23ff, 138;
   sexual undercurrents, 25–7;
   father as catalyst, 27ff, as
   model, 39; power of words,
   28; taken to church, 28; in
   Cwmdonkin Park, 29; at
   Fernhill, 29–32; attends

private school, 33–4;
significance of the sea, 34–5;
happy childhood, 35–6;
introspection, 35–7; first
poems, 36–7; schoolboy poet,
38ff; plagiarist, 6–7, 39–40,
52–3; no scholar, 40–1;
thieving, 42—3, 73, 75;
charming, 43; games and
accidents, 43–4; camping, 44–
5; enter Daniel Jones, 45, their
poetry and fantasies, 45–51;
lying, 53; begins the poetry
notebooks, 53; fails school-
leaving exam, 55–6;
schoolboy cynic, 57;
'anatomical' poems, 58–9;
self-exploration, 60–1; leaves
school, 61
1931–1934: newspaper
reporter, 62ff; learns to
drink, 64–7, 69; the
Kardomah gang, 70;
amateur actor, 71; his sister,
74–5; the Thomases at
home, 73–6; leaves
newspaper, 76; themes of
his poetry, 77ff; 'I am
always ill', 78; meets Bert
Trick and politics, 81–3;
submits poems, 83; seeks a
'philosophy', 83; poem
published in London, 84–5;
August 1933 a turning
point, 86; first visit to
London, 88; apocryphal
story of theft, 88–9; *Sunday
Referee* publishes him, 90;
father's cancer, 90–1,
affects his poetry, 91–2;
distinctive style emerges,
92–3; sex and
masturbation, 93–4;

Thomas, Dylan Marlais – *contd*
  1931–1934 – *contd*
    encounters with girls, 94–6;
    Pamela Hansford Johnson
    writes to him, 96; their
    correspondence, 96ff;
    'consumptive', 96–8; meets
    Pamela, 100; his writing
    prospers, 102; literary
    London takes notice, 103–
    4; bourgeois doubts, 105;
    growing obscurity, 106;
    'torture in words', 108–9;
    horror fantasies, 110–11;
    describes 'orgy', 111–12;
    dabbles in politics, 112–13;
    visits Caradoc Evans, 115;
    as a 'Welsh' poet, 115–16;
    moves to London, 117
  1934–1939: in bedsitter-land,
    119ff; *18 Poems* published,
    121–2, well reviewed, 123–
    4; in Soho and Fitzrovia,
    124; recuperates in
    Swansea, 126; meets
    Vernon Watkins, 126–8;
    fascinated by madness,
    127; meets A. J. P. and
    Margaret Taylor, 128;
    reviews thrillers, 129;
    homosexual encounters,
    130–1; at Cyril Connolly's,
    131–2; in Ireland with
    Grigson, 132–4; sends
    poems to J. M. Dent, 134–
    6; 'gonorrhoea' episode,
    137–8; embraced by Edith
    Sitwell, 138–40; his chaotic
    movements, 140; rude
    limericks, 140–1, Note to
    140; horseplay, 141–2; the
    fantasist, 142–4; in
    Cornwall, 145–7; at

    Surrealist Exhibition, 147;
    Twenty-five Poems
    published, 148, reviewed,
    148–9; poetry earnings,
    149; meets Caitlin
    Macnamara, 153; first love-
    letter, 154; affair develops,
    154ff; plans for stories,
    158; interlude with Emily
    Coleman, 158ff; back with
    Caitlin, 160–1; first radio
    broadcast, 161–2;
    childhood home vacated,
    163–4; tells parents of
    marriage plans, 164–5;
    marriage, 168; sexual
    jealousy, 169, 171–2;
    respectable poverty, 170;
    not a bohemian, 173; life at
    Laugharne, 174ff; male
    chauvinist, 176; helps
    found *Wales* magazine, 177;
    short stories as fantasy,
    177, as autobiography,
    178–9; on writing poems,
    180–1; on fellow-poets,
    181–2; his output, 182–3;
    finds American publisher,
    183–4; seeks patronage,
    184–5; son Llewelyn born,
    186; his 'five-shilling fund',
    186–7
  1939–1949: indignant
    pacifist, 187–8, escapist,
    189; publishes *Map of
    Love*, 189–90, and *Portrait
    of the Artist as a Young
    Dog*, 190; avoids military
    service, 190–1; flees
    creditors, 192; stays with
    the Davenports, 192–4;
    discovers Caitlin's infidelity,
    194; hack work for radio,

195; returns to Laugharne, sells his notebooks, 197; begins *Adventures in the Skin Trade*, disappoints publishers, 198–9; moves to London, 199–200; writes propaganda films, 200ff; wartime separations, 205; daughter, Aeron(wy), born, 205–6; his infidelities, 208ff; meets Ruth Wynn Owen, 209; the good companion, 210–11; the darker side, 211–12; destructive drinking, 212–13; back in Wales, 214; poems flow, 214–15; winter at New Quay, 216ff; 'A Book of Streets', 218; misses Vernon Watkins's wedding, 218–20; machine-gunned, 221–3; dreaming of America, 224, 226; his 'vegetable background', 225; writes radio 'talks', 227; writes 'Fern Hill', 228–9; in postwar London, 230; guest of A. J. P. Taylor at Oxford, 231; *Deaths and Entrances* published, 232; performs on radio, 232ff; uneasy relationship with BBC, 235; remembering Swansea, 236–7; in Italy, 237–43, hates it, 238, 240–1; lives at South Leigh (Oxfordshire), 243ff; earnings improve, 245; writes for cinema, 245–6; financial muddles, 246–8; domestic problems, 249–51; hankers for Wales, 252–3; visits Czechoslovakia, 254; moves to the Boat House, Laugharne, 254, 255

1949–1952: life at Laugharne, 255–7; writes 'Over Sir John's hill', 256–7; second son, Colm, born, 256; invited to America, 257–8; fails to write BBC scripts, 258–9; work stagnates, 260ff; flies to America, 264; shock tactics in New York, 265; first poetry reading, 265–6; in Connecticut, 266–7; Yale, 267–8; Harvard, 268; 'an old ham' at Mt Holyoke, 268–9; a legend in the making, 269–71; self-parody, 272–3; his poetic repertoire, 273–4; interviewed at Bryn Mawr, 274–5; begins nationwide tour, 276; 'westward into the night', 277; in Chicago, 278; relaxes in Iowa City, 278–81; on West Coast, 281–5; misbehaves at Charlie Chaplin's, 283–4; fails to get teaching post, 284–5; in New York, 285ff; his unhappiness, 285–6; affairs with women, 287; sails for Britain, 287–8; his American earnings, 289; refused employment by BBC, 290; ailing relationship with Caitlin, 291ff; escorts American girlfriend in London, 293; marital troubles, 293–4; works on radio play (later

Thomas, Dylan Marlais – *contd*
  1949–1952 – *contd*
    Under Milk Wood), 295–6;
    in Persia as film writer,
    296–7; guerrilla warfare at
    home, 298; writes 'Do not
    go gentle', 298–9; addresses
    Swansea students, 299–
    300; man in a dream, 300;
    writes 'Poem on his
    Birthday', 303, with forced
    optimism, 304; Marged
    Howard-Stepney as his
    patron, 306ff; sells poems
    in America, 307–8; runs
    away to Swansea, 310–11;
    London interlude, 311–12;
    unwritten stories, 312–13;
    to America with Caitlin,
    314; at the Chelsea Hotel,
    316–19; lunch with *Time*
    reporter, 316–18; records
    for Caedmon, 318–19; his
    reading tour, 319–21; 'a fat
    little fool', 320; sails home,
    321
  1952–1953: *Collected Poems*
    delayed, 322, writes verse
    Prologue, 322–3; tries to
    finish radio play, 323–4;
    Collected Poems published
    and reviewed, 324–5;
    muddling through, 326; his
    father's death, 327–8;
    Marged Howard-Stepney
    dies, 328–9; he wins Foyle's
    Poetry Prize, 329;
    brightening prospects,
    lengthening shadows, 329–
    30; his dependence on
    Caitlin, 331; poor health,
    334–5; to America (April
    1953), 335; first
    performance of *Under Milk
    Wood*, 336–8; new woman
    friend, Liz Reitell, 338; sues
    Time, 339; his sister dies,
    340; invited to write
    libretto for Stravinsky,
    340–1; heavy drinking in
    New York, 341–2; flies
    home, 342; Boat House
    blues, 342–3; reads 'A
    Story' on television, 344;
    disquieting ms notes, 344–
    7; leaves Laugharne, 348–
    9; discusses new play, 349–
    50; flies to America
    (October 1953), 350;
    unhappy, unwell, 351–4; at
    film symposium and City
    College, 354; 'eighteen
    straight whiskies', 356–7;
    half a grain of morphine,
    358; reported last words,
    359; in hospital, 359–62;
    death and post-mortem,
    362, 365; his personal
    effects, 362–3; his
    memorial, 363; his funeral,
    364–5; his commentators,
    366–8; his papers, 369–70
  appearance, 33, 34, 43, 44,
    64, 71, 96–7, 101, 102,
    114, 120–1, 132, 171, 174,
    175, 201–2, 263–4, 275,
    299, 341, 342
  dreams, 31, 34, 84, Note to
    104, 186, 193–4, 257,
    257fn and Note
  drinking, 2, 65ff, 83, 100–1,
    112, 120, 124, 131, 132,
    140ff, 192, 202, 210–11,
    Note to 211, 230, 234, 235,
    236, 256, 267, 268ff, 280,
    284, 285, 286–7, 310, 341,
    351–62 *passim*

health, accidents, 16–17, 33,
41–2, 44, 56, 96–8, 105,
129–30, 137–8, Note to
137, 140, 147, 156, 161,
162–3, 191, 230, 254, 258,
260, 263, 264, 276, 279–
80, 308, 309, 348–9, 351–
62 *passim*; the diabetes
story, 334–5, 360fn; his
teeth, 263, 278 and Note
morbid tastes and fears, 11,
26–7, 31, 57, 61, 67–9, 77–
8, 80–1, 83–4, 86, 91–2,
98, 107, 108, 110–11, 127,
132–3, 145, 220, 252, 346–
7, 353, 359
sex, real or imagined, 25, 26,
31, 53, 66, 77, 93ff, Note
to 94–5, 103, 110–12, 117–
18, 129, 137–8, 144, 145–
6, 155, 159, 162–3, 170–1,
208, 267, 270, 279, 286–8,
293–4, 353; 'homoerotic',
130–1
vocation, sense of, xvi, 39, 54,
55, 59–60, 78–9, 93, 114–
15, 327–8
Wales and the Welsh, attitudes
towards, 3, 4, 5, 89, 98,
115–17, Note to 117, 176–
7, 182, 224–5, 252–3,
Notes to 253, 265fn, 290–
1
words and word-play, xv–xvi,
28, 39, 45ff, 67–9, 82–3,
108–10, 122, 178, 216–17,
Note to 312, 325, 359
writing, habits and methods,
59, 99, 100, 135–6, 180,
183, Note to 195, 256,
304fn, 346, 354;
plagiarism, 6, 39–40, 52–3
uncollected verse (chiefly

juvenilia and doggerel)
quoted, 3, 36, 37, 39, 40,
46, 67–8, 96, Note to 129,
Note to 140, 141, 201,
Note to 209, 216, 240, 249,
305, 306, 307, 344, 345,
346; film commentary, 202–
3, 204, 297–8. *See also*
Appendix
Letters *quoted* to:
BBC (various producers),
Note to 174, 182–3, 195
and Note, 249, 258, 279,
296, 301, Note to 324,
324fn
Blakeston, Oswell, 131
Bozman, E. F., 323, Note to
324fn2
Brinnin, John Malcolm, 261,
263, 294, 301, 311, 314,
329, 335
Butterfield, Francis, Note to
230
Caetani, Marguerite, 261,
298, 323, 325–6, 346–7
Cameron, Elfriede, 145–6
Church, Richard, 135–6, 147
and Note
Coleman, Emily, 159–60,
160, 161
Davenport, Clement, 195–6,
197
Davenport, John, 177–8, 182
(*see* Note), Note to 184,
184–5, 186, 187, 194, 195,
240, 250–1, 259–60, Note
to 260fn, 261, 264, 294
Davies, Idris, 329
Davies, W. T., 182
Dent, J. M. & Co., 228
Durrell, Lawrence, 236
Earp, T. W., 205, 216, 217,
240

Thomas, Dylan Marlais – *contd*
Eliot, T. S., 300–1
Fisher, Charles, 93, 193, 198, 237
Fry, Charles, 323, 331–3
Glover, C. Gordon, 17 (*see* Note), 251–2
Grigson, Geoffrey, 89, 114, Note to 129, 137–8
Hawkins, Desmond, 148, 155, 168, 171–2
Henderson, Wyn, 145
Higham, David, 185, 247, 249, Note to 263
Howard-Stepney, Marged, 3, 306–7
Hughes, Frances, 252–3
Hughes, Trevor, 78, 79, 80, 91, 112
Janes, Alfred, 328
Johnson, John, 153
Johnson, Pamela Hansford, 4, 27, 96–114 *passim*, 117, 118, Note to 121, 121–2, 126, 130, 169–70, 334
Jones, Daniel, 48–51, 133, 320, 345
Jones, Glyn, Note to 103–4, 104, 126
Josephson, Mimi, 342–3
Kay, Ellen, 326–7
Laughlin, James, 224, 235–6, 258, 260, 263
Nims, John F. and Mrs, 287, 291
Ormond (Thomas), John, Note to 235, 253 (*see* Note)
Owen, Ruth Wynn, 209, 210
Patchen, Kenneth, 188–9, 224
Peter Lunn (Publisher), 221
Pollinger, Laurence, 191
Reavey, George, 122 (*see* Note), 177

Reitell, Elizabeth, 342
Rhys, Keidrych, 176, 177, 181–2, 189fn
Sitwell, Edith, 139–40, Note to 140, 170
Smart, Percy, xv–xvi, 57, 67–9, 69–70, 76–7, 217
Spender, Stephen, 115–16, 191, 192, 325
Swansea and West Wales Guardian, 113
Taylor, Donald, 213fn, 217, Note to 218
Taylor, Margaret, 235, 237–8, 240, 240–1, 242, 243, 254, 260, 263, 273, 287, 289–90, Note to 303, 309, 311
Taylor, Nancy and Haydn, 136–7, 167–8
Tennant, David, 213fn
Thomas, Caitlin, 154, 155, 156–7, 162–3, 206, 207–8, 226–7, 238–9, 249–50, 264 and Note, 266, 277, 278, 281, 282–3, 287–8, 290, 296–7, 316, 327, 335–6, 339–40
Thomas, D. J. and Florence, 164–5, 187, 237, 238, 248, 266
Thomas, Llewelyn, 341
Treece, Henry, 26–7, 63, 106, 115, 174 (*see* Note), 175, 179, 180, 181, 187
Trick, A. E. (Bert), 51 (*see* Note), 118, 119, 124–6, 132, 133–4, 161fn, 186, 187
Watkins, Vernon, 36, 127, 146–7, 148, 170, 172–3, 179fn, 182, 183, 185 and Note, 187, 192, 193–4,

197, 198, 200, 214, Note
to 215, 215, 217, 219, 219–
20, 223, 230, 231, 254, 328
Williams, Oscar, 11 (*see*
Note), Note to 104, 224,
225, 226, 297, 302, 308,
322–3, 328, 334, 342
Witt-Diamant, Ruth, 284,
308–9
See also America; BBC and
Thomas; titles of works
Thomas, Evan ('Thomas the
Guard', grandfather), 7ff, 12,
15, 16, 178fn
Thomas, Florence (mother),
xviii–xix, 10, 31, 38, 62, 63,
65, 76, Note to 78–9, Note to
88, 90, 139, 196, 214, 247,
289, 329, 348, 365;
background, 11ff; marriage,
10, 15–16; Dylan's birth, 21;
worries about his well-being,
15–16, 33, 41–2, 44, 56, 119,
121, 138, 191, 334, 349;
'romancer', 19–20; as
housewife, 18ff; as mother,
19, 23–8, 32, 334; chooses
private school, 33; and
Thomas's juvenilia, 36 and
Note; diction derided by D.J.,
43; rows with her daughter,
73–6; son perceives as 'vulgar
humbug', 98; keeps an eye on
Caitlin, 194; breaks leg, 249;
Caitlin cares for, 250; living in
Laugharne, 255. *See also*
Thomas letters to
Thomas, Llewelyn Edouard
(son), xix, xx, 207, 220, 241,
250, 283, 311, 341, 365;
subject of pre-natal poem,
182; birth, 186; left at
Blashford, 199; school fees

unpaid, 290, 320 and Note,
Note to 329. *See also* Thomas
letter to
Thomas, Nancy Marles (sister),
xviii, 9, 18, 19, 20, 21, 32,
42, 43, 88–9, 90, 101, 166,
327; birth, 16; 'amazing
imagination', 20; character
and interests, 71–2; observes
home life, 73–6; first marriage
(to Haydn Taylor), 73, 88,
249; looks after parents at
Blaen Cwm, 249, 250; second
marriage (to Gordon
Summersby), 249; death, 17,
340. *See also* Thomas letters
to
Thomas, Stuart, Dylan Thomas
trustee, xvii, xx, xxi, xxii,
xxiv, 365, 371; Thomas's
solicitor, 339
Thomas, William (great-
grandfather), 7; in 'A Visit to
Grandpa's', 178fn
Thomas, William ('Gwilym
Marles', great-uncle), 7–9,
11, Note to 78
Thomas, Wynford Vaughan *see*
Vaughan-Thomas, Wynford
Thompson, Kent, 35, 82, 94
Three Lamps public house
(Swansea), 65
Three Weird Sisters (film), 25fn,
245
Threipland, Mark Murray,
338fn
Threipland, Molly Murray
(Brodney), 338
Tillyard, E. M. W., 142
Time magazine, 94, 226, 316,
339, 355, 358fn
Time and Tide, 123, 190
Times, The, 196, 362

Times Literary Supplement, 124, 148, 190

Tindall, William York, 242 and Note

'Today, this insect' (P), 58

Todd, Ruthven, 10, 24, 27, 316, 352fn; didn't write Thomas's biography, xvii

'Top Hat and Gasworks' (story title), 232

'The Town that Was Mad' (precursor of *Under Milk Wood*), 295–6

Towns, Jeff (Dylans Book Store), xxv, 368, 369

Toynbee, Philip, 324

Tredegar, Lord, 187

Treece, Henry, 106, 122–3; as commentator on Thomas, 179–81, 321–2. *See also* Thomas letters to

Tremlett, George, 334, 360fn, 367

Trick, A. E. ('Bert'), Note to 82, 85, 118, 119, 124, 126, 129, 133, 161fn, 186, 187, 197; befriends Thomas, 81–3; introduces him to politics, 81–2, 112–13; influences Thomas's poetry, 84; last sees Thomas, 196; sells Thomas letters, 369. *See also* Thomas letters to

Trick, Nell, 83, 95

Trick, Pamela, provides phrase for poem, 83

'Triumph of the Will' (film), 202

Twenty-five Poems, 134fn, 136, 190, 232; written before *18 Poems*, 86, 180; published, reviewed, 148–9; printing history, 149

'Twenty-four years' (P), 182, 189, 303, 373

Twenty Years A-Growing (Maurice O'Sullivan), 217; Thomas film script, 368

Two Flamboyant Fathers (Nicolette Devas), insured against Caitlin, xxiv

'Two images' (P), 59

'Two Streets' (play title), 349

Under Milk Wood (play), 2, 160, 203, 221, 246, 259, 339, 347, 349; about Laugharne, 227; earlier script hints at, 233; original version of, 295–6; working title 'Llareggub', 323; fees for, Note to 324, 337; its title, 336; in America, 336–9, 351, 352, 353; first performance of, 337; losing the ms, 336, 350 and Note; 'prose with blood pressure', 342; revising it at Laugharne, 343; best-seller as book, 366; ms sold, 369; recordings of, 337–8, Note to 337, 366; 'censorship' issue at BBC, Note to 338. *See also* Cleverdon, Douglas

'Unluckily for a death' (P), 228

Uplands (Swansea), xxi, 5, 18–19, 20, 32, 42, 51, 81, 82, 90, 98fn, 133, 205, 299; Cinema, 43, 260; Hotel, 100, 300

Utah, University of, 319–20

Vancouver, 281, 282

Vanity Fair (film), 246

Vassar College, 285

Vaughan-Thomas, Wynford, 62fn, 70, 124; Dylan Thomas trustee, xvii; on Thomas fantasy, xx; Dylan mistaken for, 244

Venable, Vernon, 285–6

Vermont, University of, 270, 319

Viereck, Peter, 271

'The Village that Was Mad' (later *Under Milk Wood*), 295

'Vision and Prayer' (P), 215 and Note

'A Visit to America' (radio talk), 348

'A Visit to Grandpa's' (S), 178, 197

Vogue, 290

Wales (magazine), 177. *See also* Rhys, Keidrych

Wallace, Nellie, 62fn and Note

Walton, William, Thomas doesn't write libretto for, 248–9

Warmley (Dan Jones's house), 45ff, 82

Warner, Tom (Swansea friend), 47

'Was there a time' (P), written after Ann Jones's death, 80–1

Watkins, Gwen, 128, 173, 175fn, 211–12, 218–19, 220, 293; on the Thomas–Watkins relationship, 343

Watkins, Vernon, 36, 149, 175fn, 179fn, 186, 190–1, 199, 200, 223, 344fn; their correspondence, Note to 36; important friendship with Thomas, 70; meets Thomas, 126–7; mental breakdown, 127–8; sees Thomas as religious poet, 128 and Note; and Thomas's writing, 116, 136, 148, 180, Note to 185, Note to 195, Note to 198, 215, 216, 257; brings gifts, 175, lends money, 192, 198;

Thomas misses his wedding, 218–20; broadcasts with Thomas, 260; remains loyal to Thomas, 293; last visit to Boat House, 343; writes Thomas's obituary, 362. *See also* Thomas letters to

Waugh, Alec, 195

Waugh, Evelyn, 132, 195

Waunfwlchan (farm), 11

The Way of the World (Congreve), Thomas acts in, 95

Welsh fairy tales, Thomas to edit, 324

Welsh nationalism and character, 7, 8, 116, 176–7

'Welsh travelogue' (projected book), 158, 160, 164, 198

West, Ray B. (Iowa City), 278–81

Western Mail, 177fn; publishes Thomas juvenilia, 6, 39, 40, 53

'The Western man has lost one lung' (P), 82

Westport (Conn.), 268; Thomas at, 266, 267

Wheatsheaf public house (London), 144, 153, 159

'When, like a running grave' (P), hints at infantile fears, 26

'Where Have the Old Words Got Me' (unwritten work), 312

'Where once the waters of your face' (P), 102

'Where Tawe flows' (S), Note to 82, 312

White, Antonia, 127, 159, 192, 193

White Horse Tavern (New York), 316, 321, 355, 356

'Who Do You Wish Was With Us?' (S), 78, 179

'Why east wind chills' (P), 86

Williams, Ann, *see* Jones, Ann

Williams, Anna (maternal grandmother), 11–12, 13, 15

Williams, Bob (maternal uncle), 12, 14, 15, 30, 196; 'Bob's My Uncle' (unwritten story), 232

Williams, Daniel ('Dr Dan'), 12

Williams, David George, 12

Williams family (of Laugharne), 1, 108, 174, 191fn, 301

Williams, Florence, *see* Thomas, Florence

Williams, George (maternal grandfather), 11–12, 13, 15

Williams, J. D. (Swansea editor), 62, 64, 148

Williams, J. Morgan (schoolmaster), 38, 41

Williams, John (maternal uncle), 14, 217

Williams, Dr Oscar (Llanelli), 191fn

Williams, Oscar (American anthologist), 224, 286, 287, 315, 316, 326, 331; sells poems for Thomas, 224, 286, 307–8, 329; 'old crazy friend', 308. *See also* Thomas letters to

Williams, Polly (maternal aunt), 13, 14, 15, 73; the chatterbox, 196

Williams, Theodosia, *see* Rees, Theodosia

Williams, Thomas (maternal uncle), 13

Winters, Shelley, touched by Thomas, 283, 284

'A Winter's Tale' (P), 183, 223, 224fn; written at New Quay, 4; Thomas records, 342fn

Witt-Diamant, Ruth (San Francisco), 284. *See also* Thomas letters to

'The Woman Speaks' (P), 102

The World I Breathe (poems and stories), 184fn

World Review, 326fn

'Written for a personal epitaph' (P), 79

Wright, David, 298

Wycherley, William, 258

Yale University, 267, 268

Yeats, W. B., 126, 128; Thomas reads, 265, 321